THE
OXFORD GUIDE TO
ARTHURIAN
LITERATURE
AND
LEGEND

THE
OXFORD GUIDE TO
ARTHURIAN
LITERATURE
AND
LEGEND

Alan Lupack

OXFORD
UNIVERSITY PRESS

OXFORD
UNIVERSITY PRESS

Great Clarendon Street, Oxford OX2 6DP

Oxford University Press is a department of the University of Oxford.
It furthers the University's objective of excellence in research, scholarship,
and education by publishing worldwide in

Oxford New York

Auckland Cape Town Dar es Salaam Hong Kong Karachi
Kuala Lumpur Madrid Melbourne Mexico City Nairobi
New Delhi Shanghai Taipei Toronto

With offices in

Argentina Austria Brazil Chile Czech Republic France Greece
Guatemala Hungary Italy Japan South Korea Poland Portugal
Singapore Switzerland Thailand Turkey Ukraine Vietnam

Oxford is a registered trade mark of Oxford University Press
in the UK and in certain other countries

Published in the United States
by Oxford University Press Inc., New York

© Oxford University Press 2005

Database right Oxford University Press (maker)

First published 2004

British Library Cataloguing in Publication Data

Data available

Library of Congress Cataloging in Publication Data

Data available

Typeset by Kolam Information Services Pvt. Ltd, Pondicherry, India
Printed in Great Britain
by Biddles Ltd., King's Lynn, Norfolk

ISBN 0–19–280287–9
ISBN 978–0–19–280287–3

3 5 7 9 10 8 6 4 2

Acknowledgements

❖

I am especially grateful to several of my colleagues at the University of Rochester: to Phyllis Andrews, who made it possible for me to complete this project; to Rosemary Paprocki, who took on extra work with her usual efficiency, professionalism, and good humour during the course of this project; to Ryan Harper, my research assistant; to the graduate students who staff the Robbins Library; and to Ron Dow, Dean of the River Campus Libraries, for allowing me the time to write this book.

Other colleagues in Rush Rhees Library who have contributed greatly to my work on this project include the staff of the Inter-Library Loan unit who, with great skill and efficiency, tracked down many books and articles; Tom Hickman and the staff of the Microtext unit, who made available works accessible only on microfilm; and all those who enquired about the project and gave moral support.

I am grateful to a number of people at Oxford University Press: to Michael Cox, for initiating the project; to Pam Coote, who helped to shape it in its early stages; and to Joanna Harris, who has worked with me as the book developed and has seen it through to completion.

Any study of this sort can be done only by standing on the shoulders of giants, past and present, Arthurian criticism like Arthurian literature being a continuing tradition in which later writers build upon earlier ones and depend on their ideas even when altering them. While generations of scholars have influenced the ideas in this book, I wish to give special thanks to a few. Norris Lacy, whose contributions to Arthurian Studies are too numerous to list here and too well known to need listing, has been generous in sharing his vast knowledge of Arthurian literature. Dan Nastali and Phil Boardman, co-authors of the *Arthurian Annals*, have been generous in allowing me to use information from their invaluable database, which is the result of years of studying Arthurian literature; Dan also read the manuscript of this book and offered numerous helpful suggestions for revision. I am similarly grateful to Kevin Harty, whose publications on and knowledge of Arthurian film have been important resources. I am indebted to Russell Peck of the Department of English at the University of Rochester for his advice, for his enthusiastic support of this project, and for ideas generated during conversations with him about Arthurian literature and film. To all of these scholars, I am grateful for the information and ideas they have shared, for the encouragement they have offered, but even more for their friendship.

My greatest debt is to my wife Barbara, to whom I dedicate this book. She is not only a creative and insightful scholar, whose ideas contributed immensely to this study, and the best editor I have ever known, but also the inspiration of this book and of all my work.

A.L.

Contents

Introduction

A legend with its origins in the Middle Ages and its focus on a king and the nobles of his court might seem to have little relevance to the modern world, especially to western Europe and North America where democratic values and ideals prevail. Yet just the opposite is true. The stories surrounding King Arthur and the knights and ladies of Camelot enjoy a tremendous vitality and are retold with increasing frequency and variety. Almost universally recognized, the major characters and symbols of the legend appear in novels, plays, poems, films, music, art, and popular forms, including comic books, toys and games, and advertisements.

One reason the legend has remained such a staple of culture, both high and popular, lies in the nature of the Arthurian matter itself. Although Arthur, as king or military leader, historical figure or legendary hero, is the focal point of the tales, the Arthurian legends are in fact a complex of narratives with a wide array of stories and a large cast of characters. Those stories and characters, moreover, are often adapted to the values and concerns of the ages or audiences for which they are reinterpreted.

For example, within that complex of stories is the familiar tale of the young Arthur's drawing of the sword from the stone, a tale often adapted for children because it depicts a young boy seemingly destined to the secondary position of serving his elder brother. But by accomplishing a feat that no one else can, Arthur proves his innate ability and his superiority and demonstrates that he deserves—in fact, is destined for—kingship. In another tale of a youngster proving his worth, Gareth serves a year in Arthur's kitchen and endures the abuse of Sir Kay before undertaking a dangerous quest during which he must fight far more seasoned knights. By these acts, Gareth reveals that he is one of the noblest knights and wins the beautiful lady Lynette as his wife.

Among the Arthurian legends, there are also tales of magic and prophecy, the most fascinating of which is the account of Merlin, adviser to Arthur. Yet neither his wisdom nor his ability to foresee the future can prevent Merlin from being enchanted, figuratively and then literally, by the lady he loves. Vivien is, as poet Richard Wilbur called her, a creature to bewitch a sorcerer. Under her spell, the wisest man in the world becomes a fool for love. There is also the magic of Morgan le Fay, who over the years changes from a benign healer to a wicked enemy of Arthur and then to a woman whose own values and concerns become central in some retellings of the Arthurian story.

The Arthurian legends also include many tales of love, the greatest of which is the tragic love of Lancelot and Guinevere. Lancelot's love for the queen is so true that he can never forsake it, even when he tries to perfect himself in the quest for the Holy Grail and even though it causes him, a knight whose word is his bond, to live a lie that harms the king to whom he is devoted. Lancelot's love is so great, in fact, that after Guinevere renounces the world to lead a holy life, he follows suit. But it is Lancelot's struggle to balance different and conflicting ideals such as love and duty that makes him so real, and his dilemmas and desires so recognizable, even to a reader in the twenty-first century.

The tragic love of Tristan and Isolt has also inspired numerous retellings in literature, music, art, and film. Their love, often caused or symbolized by a love potion, is irresistible; and so, even though it is adulterous, it seems beyond blame. Yet it has—and must have—a tragic end. As with the love of Lancelot and Guinevere, the relationship between Tristan and Isolt defies traditional values; thus their enemies can use traditional concepts of power and morality against them.

There are also tales of unrequited love, such as that of Elaine of Astolat, a young maiden who is enamoured of Arthur's best knight. But since that knight is Lancelot, who loves no one but the queen, he is unable to return her affection. When Elaine realizes her plight, she chooses to die and have her body placed in a barge to float down to Camelot, with a letter clutched in her hand proclaiming her unwillingness to live without the man she loves. The image of the poor dead beautiful woman in her barge, an icon both of unwavering devotion and of foolish waste of potential, captured the imagination of the Victorians and became one of the most frequently depicted scenes in the art of the age as well as a tale often retold in other ages.

The legends also contain tales of the highest spirituality. The quest for the Holy Grail, undertaken by Perceval in some versions of the story and by Galahad in others, is a task that requires dedication, perseverance, and purity. The virtuous Galahad is able to achieve the quest because of his single-minded pursuit: he is not distracted by love, licit or illicit, or even by allegiances to king or other knights; and he is divinely protected, even before he wins the shield that is destined for him. Once he achieves his quest, he prays to leave the earthly world, since his trust and his interest are completely in the heavenly sphere.

But most of the knights do have worldly ties, even when, like Lancelot, they strive for perfection in the spiritual realm. Gawain, for example, is sometimes concerned with the honour of his family even more than with the honour of his king or of himself. Thus he obsessively pursues Lancelot, who has accidentally slain his brother Gareth during the rescue of the queen, even as Arthur's Round Table and his reign collapse. In other tales, Gawain is the model of courtesy but is nonetheless torn, as he is in the masterly *Sir Gawain and the Green Knight*, between conflicting values: the desire to save his own life and the perfect truth and loyalty for which he strives.

Within the legends, there are also tales of great courage and adventure. Questing knights must prove their bravery against powerful villains, dragons and wild beasts, physical hardships, and moral temptations. To further justice or to protect a lady, to defend the weak or to demonstrate their love, knights often take on great challenges. Yet even as the legends offer numerous examples of friendship, virtue, and nobility, they do not ignore tales of treachery, betrayal, and evil, such as the duplicity and ultimate treason of Mordred, Arthur's illegitimate son.

And there are tales of return—the return of Arthur who, according to some versions of his legend, was taken after the last battle to the isle of Avalon to be healed of his wounds and who remains there until his people have need of him again. Merlin, too, sealed in a tree or a cave by Vivien, can return, released from her spell, sometimes to assist Arthur, sometimes to work magic of his own. And of course, thanks to the genius of Mark Twain, the pattern can be reversed so that a contemporary character travels to the time of Arthur and interacts with him and his knights and ladies.

To be sure, the cast of Arthurian characters is broad and the adventures that writers, artists, musicians, and film-makers have, over the centuries, conceived for them even broader. The legends themselves, suited to a wide variety of creative purposes and temperaments, afford opportunities for exploring all manner of human striving and foible. As William Caxton observed in his preface to Malory's *Morte d'Arthur*, the story contains examples of chivalry, courtesy, kindness, friendship, courage, love, and affection, as well as cowardice, murder, and hatred, examples of virtue as well as sin. His observation suggests the range of human emotions, the values, the engagement with reality, and the universal appeal that the Arthurian legends offer.

A fundamental question concerning the legends (and one that is particularly relevant to this guide) is what exactly constitutes an 'Arthurian' work. Defining the term may seem simple, but in fact it evokes disagreement, especially when one moves beyond canonical medieval texts. For the purposes of this guide, I make several assumptions, the first of which is that there is an Arthurian tradition that begins in, but is not limited to, the Middle Ages. The richness and variety of the post-medieval tradition can easily be demonstrated in works by Spenser, Wagner, Tennyson, T. H. White, and many others. Trends in recent criticism make it clear that much is gained not only by studying the many medieval versions of Arthur's story, which often have fascinating intertextual connections, but also by exploring the post-medieval development of the legends. While Arthurian Studies will always be grounded in the medieval versions of the legend, the field is richer and deeper when the influence of the medieval stories on later literature, culture, and history is considered.

The development of the tradition includes modern works that recast one or more of the medieval stories in a modern setting, a pattern common with the Tristan story, the Grail quest, and a number of other tales, even when those works take liberties with their sources by incorporating non-traditional characters or settings—for example, the homeless Grail seeker Parry in the film *The Fisher King*. Modern adaptations of the legend sometimes use a major Arthurian symbol—Excalibur, Avalon, the Grail—as a controlling device. Also part of the tradition are works, both medieval and modern, that contain allusions to the legend that rise to such a level that they control the plot, define the characters, or are essential to the meaning—works such as John Updike's novel *Brazil*, for example.

Excluded from this guide are those tales of knights or quests, medieval or modern, or of errant heroes in the modern world that are influenced generally by medieval romance but not explicitly by the Arthurian tradition. Their number is so vast and their link to Arthurian legend so tangential that it would be impossible to discuss them here. Of course, that still leaves a very large number of texts and other cultural artefacts. The purpose of this guide is not to attempt to treat every Arthurian work that exists but rather to document, discuss, and classify many of them as a way of exemplifying the depth and breadth of the tradition and the interesting and occasionally surprising course that it has taken over the years. To that end, I consider most of the major Arthurian texts but also many of the minor ones, since they are influenced by the more prominent and canonical texts at the same time that they put those texts in cultural and aesthetic perspective.

Another important question, and perhaps the most commonly asked question about the legends (and one that influences the consideration of many Arthurian texts and artefacts), is whether or not a real, historical Arthur ever existed. This is, in effect, a question of origins. It asks whether, like the tales surrounding Charlemagne, the material that comprises the Arthurian tradition has its origin in a person whose deeds, exaggerated and dehistoricized though they may be, have their foundation in fact or are simply based on fabrications by medieval storytellers.

The answer to this question requires some discussion of the historical context into which the figure of Arthur must be placed by those who would argue for his historicity. As the Roman Empire began to collapse, the native British population, having lost the protection of the Roman legions, sought the aid of mercenary Germanic tribes from the continent. The British ruler Vortiger is remembered, and generally vilified, for inviting into Britain those Germanic tribes (traditionally said to be the Angles, Saxons, and Jutes). Some of the chroniclers assign a date of 449 to the beginning of the Germanic invasion, but the conquest of Britain, a fact demonstrated by the English language (a member of the Germanic branch of the Indo-European languages), surely was not complete in one year or even one generation.

Arthurian prehistory, the story of Britain from the beginning of the invasion until the birth of Arthur, becomes an essential part of the legend. In many medieval chronicles, Arthur appears during this time of crisis first as a military leader rallying the British and opposing the Saxons, and eventually, as the story grows, as an emperor who conquers not only all of the British isles but most of Europe as well. Some modern scholars and historians have defended the historicity of a figure upon whom these stories have been based; others have categorically denied it. If indeed an Arthur or an Arthur-like figure actually lived, he would have been a sixth-century warrior and not a late medieval king and knight with medieval castles and armour. While incontrovertible proof of such a historical figure neither exists nor is likely to be discovered, it is also unlikely that the negative will ever be absolutely proven. Thus the most reasonable position, though one that will surely be criticized by those on both sides of the debate, is to be an agnostic about the question of Arthur's historicity.

While the question of Arthur's historicity is critical to the historian and intriguing to anyone interested in the legends, there is a sense in which it does not matter. Real or not, Arthur has inspired a vast cultural tradition, which is manifested in poetry, fiction, drama, music, art, film, and popular culture, and has been adapted to the concerns of each succeeding age that reinterprets the tradition. From the loftiest works of literature to sentimental romances, from pornography to the postmodern novel, from opera to heavy metal music, from fine paintings and sculptures to comic books and Barbie dolls, one finds the indisputable influence and the true reality of the legends.

Citations

In general for foreign works, the citations in the text refer to English translations except when otherwise indicated or when no translation exists. In the bibliographies, however, I have generally included editions in the original language as well as translations.

Names

When referring to names which are spelled in different ways in different texts, I have used the form that appears in the edition or translation cited for the text under discussion. When referring to a character in a general sense and not as he or she appears in a given text, I have adopted a standard form (e.g. Guinevere, Lancelot) and have used that consistently throughout the volume. In the list of 'Arthurian People, Places, and Things' that concludes this volume, I have not attempted to include every variant of a name that appears in every medieval or modern text, but rather I give representative examples.

In each of the seven major chapters of this book, the first occurrence of a name which appears in the list at the end of the volume is marked with an asterisk. (If the name appears first within a quotation, the asterisk is added without placing it in brackets.) Cross-references within the list of 'Arthurian People, Places, and Things' are also indicated by an asterisk.

The Structure and Use of This Volume

There are many ways to arrange and discuss the various traditions and works that are part of the Arthurian legend. Because the material is intensely intertextual, one way to approach it is to follow certain threads throughout the centuries. Since, however, those threads intersect and diverge frequently, and connections between the elements of the tradition typically transcend genre, time, and place, a volume treating Arthurian literature and legend in all its forms and throughout the ages must be hypertextual; that is, there will necessarily be references back and forth. And while within certain sections there is an advantage to treating texts chronologically, it is also important to follow some themes from the Middle Ages to the present, and then to return to another thread at its origin.

This guide is designed so that the book as a whole may serve as a critical history of the Arthurian legend. By selecting one chapter, a reader may follow some of the main traditions from their origins to the present. Within chapters, material is divided into topics, which are listed in the contents of the volume so that one may focus on a particular theme or major work relating, for example, to the Grail or the romance tradition. There is also a complete index which provides another means of access and allows the book to serve as a quick reference to any of the numerous topics, authors, and works treated.

BIBLIOGRAPHY OF BASIC RESOURCES FOR THE STUDY
OF THE ARTHURIAN LEGENDS

General Sources

Guerreau-Jalabert, Anita. *Index des motifs narratifs dans les romans Arthuriens Français en vers (XIIe–XIIIe siècles) [Motif-Index of French Arthurian Verse Romances (XIIth–XIIIth Cent.)]*. Geneva: Droz, 1992.

Lacy, Norris J. (ed.). *Medieval Arthurian Literature: A Guide to Recent Research*. New York: Garland Publishing, 1996.

—— and Ashe, Geoffrey, with Mancoff, Debra N. *The Arthurian Handbook*, 2nd edn. New York: Garland, 1997.

—— et al. (eds.). *The New Arthurian Encyclopedia*. New York: Garland, 1991.

Ruck, E. H. *An Index of Themes and Motifs in Twelfth-Century French Arthurian Poetry*. Cambridge: D. S. Brewer, 1991.

Journals

Arthuriana. (NOTE: An earlier Arthurian newsletter—*Quondam et Futurus*—was combined with the journal *Arthurian Interpretations* to become *Quondam et Futurus: A Journal of Arthurian Interpretations*. *Arthuriana* has replaced these earlier publications and is now the official journal of the North American Branch of the International Arthurian Society.)

Arthurian Literature. (Published annually by Boydell and Brewer.)

Arthurian Yearbook. (Published annually by Garland from 1991 to 1993, now discontinued.)

Avalon to Camelot. (Only vols. 1–2 were published.)

Tristania. (A journal devoted to the study of all aspects of the Tristan legend.)

Arthurian Names

Ackerman, Robert W. *An Index of the Arthurian Names in Middle English*. Stanford, Calif.: Stanford University Press, 1952.

Bruce, Christopher W. *The Arthurian Name Dictionary.* New York: Garland, 1999.

English, Mark. 'Place-Names and "The Matter of Britain"', appendix 3 in Jeffrey Spittal and John Field (eds.), *A Reader's Guide to the Place-Names of the United Kingdom: A Bibliography of Publications (1920–1989) on the Place-Names of Great Britain and Northern Ireland, the Isle of Man, and the Channel Islands.* Stamford: Paul Watkins, 1990.

Moorman, Charles, and Moorman, Ruth. *An Arthurian Dictionary.* Jackson: University Press of Mississippi, 1978.

West, G. D. *An Index of Proper Names in French Arthurian Prose Romances.* Toronto: University of Toronto Press, 1978.

—— *An Index of Proper Names in French Arthurian Verse Romances.* Toronto: University of Toronto Press, 1969.

(NOTE: Important names can also be found in *The New Arthurian Encyclopedia* and in the 'Arthurian Glossary' section of *The Arthurian Handbook*.)

Bibliographies

On-line Bibliographies of Arthurian Literature

The Arthuriana/Camelot Project Bibliographies: www.lib.rochester.edu/camelot/acpbibs/bibhome.stm.

Medieval Arthurian Literature

Barber, Elaine (comp.). *The Arthurian Bibliography*: iv: *1993–1998*. Cambridge: D. S. Brewer, 2002. (NOTE: Vols. iii and iv of *The Arthurian Bibliography* also contain numerous references to discussions of modern Arthurian literature.)

Bibliographical Bulletin of the International Arthurian Society. (Published annually.)

Gaines, Barry. *Sir Thomas Malory: An Anecdotal Bibliography of Editions 1485–1985.* New York: AMS Press, 1990.

Jost, Jean E. *Ten Middle English Arthurian Romances: A Reference Guide.* Boston: G. K. Hall, 1986.

Kelly, Douglas. *Chrétien de Troyes: An Analytic Bibliography.* London: Grant & Cutler, 1976.

—— et al. *Chrétien de Troyes: An Analytic Bibliography, Supplement 1.* London: Tamesis, 2002.

Life, Page West. *Sir Thomas Malory and the Morte Darthur: A Survey of Scholarship and Annotated Bibliography.* Charlottesville: University of Virginia Press for the Bibliographic Society of the University of Virginia, 1980. (Lists editions and critical studies.)

Palmer, Caroline (comp.). *The Arthurian Bibliography*: iii: *1978–1992*. Cambridge: D. S. Brewer, 1998.

Parry, John J. *A Bibliography of Critical Arthurian Literature for the Years 1922–1929.* New York: The Modern Language Association, 1931.

—— and Schlauch, Margaret. *A Bibliography of Critical Arthurian Literature for the Years 1930–1935.* New York: The Modern Language Association, 1936.

Pickford, C. E., Last, R. W., and Barker, C. R. (eds.). *The Arthurian Bibliography* (vol. i: *Author Listing*; vol. ii: *Subject Index*). Cambridge: D. S. Brewer, 1981, 1983.

Reiss, Edmund, Reiss, Louis Horner, and Taylor, Beverly. *Arthurian Legend and Literature: An Annotated Bibliography*, i: *The Middle Ages.* New York: Garland, 1984. (NOTE: only vol. i has been published.)

Rice, Joanne A. *Middle English Romance: An Annotated Bibliography, 1955–1985.* New York: Garland Publishing, 1987. (Contains a section on Arthurian literature as well as entries for individual romances.)

Sharrer, Harvey L. *A Critical Bibliography of Hispanic Arthurian Material*, i: *Texts: The Prose Romance Cycles*. London: Grant & Cutler, 1977.

Shirt, David J. *The Old French Tristan Poems: A Bibliographic Guide*. London: Grant & Cutler, 1980.

Modern Arthurian Literature

Novels

Mediavilla, Cindy. *Arthurian Fiction: An Annotated Bibliography.* Lanham, Md.: The Scarecrow Press, 1999.

See also the bibliography in Raymond Thompson's book in the 'Overviews' section below.

Plays

See the 'Checklist of Printed Arthurian Drama' in *Arthurian Drama: An Anthology*, listed in the 'Anthology' section below.

All Genres

See the bibliography in Beverly Taylor and Elisabeth Brewer's book listed in the 'Overviews' section below, and the bibliography in Alan Lupack (ed.), *Modern Arthurian Literature*, in the 'Anthologies' section below, for critical articles on modern Arthurian literature.

Nastali, Daniel P., and Boardman, Phillip C. *The Arthurian Annals: The Tradition in English from 1250 to 2000*. Oxford: Oxford University Press, 2004.

Wildman, Mary. 'Twentieth Century Arthurian Literature: An Annotated Bibliography', *Arthurian Literature*, 2. (NOTE: In vol. 3 of *Arthurian Literature*, there is 'A Supplementary Bibliography of Twentieth Century Arthurian Literature'. A further update by A. H. W. Smith appears in vol. 10.)

Films

Harty, Kevin J. 'Cinema Arthuriana: A Comprehensive Filmography and Bibliography', in Kevin J. Harty (ed.), *Cinema Arthuriana: Twenty Essays*. Jefferson, NC: McFarland, 2002: 252–301.

Overviews and Studies of Particular Countries, Periods, or Genres

Barron, W. R. (ed.). *The Arthur of the English: The Arthurian Legend in Medieval English Life and Literature*. Cardiff: University of Wales Press, 1999.

Brinkley, Roberta Florence. *Arthurian Legend in the Seventeenth Century.* 1932; repr. New York: Octagon Books, 1970.

Bromwich, Rachel, Jarman, A. O. H., and Roberts, Brynley F. (eds.). *The Arthur of the Welsh: The Arthurian Legend in Medieval Welsh Literature*. Cardiff: University of Wales Press, 1991.

Claassens, Geert H. M., and Johnson, David F. (eds.). *King Arthur in the Medieval Low Countries*. Leuven: Leuven University Press, 2000.

Echard, Siân. *Arthurian Narrative in Latin*. Cambridge: Cambridge University Press, 1998.

Entwistle, William J. *The Arthurian Legend in the Literatures of the Spanish Peninsula*. 1925; repr. New York: Phaeton Press, 1975.

Fletcher, Robert Huntington. *The Arthurian Material in the Chronicles: Especially Those of Great Britain and France*, 2nd edn., expanded by a bibliography and critical essay for the period 1905–65 by Roger Sherman Loomis. 1906; 2nd edn. New York: Burt Franklin, 1966.

Fries, Maureen, and Watson, Jeanie (eds.). *Approaches to Teaching the Arthurian Tradition*. New York: The Modern Language Association of America, 1992.

Gardner, Edmund G. *The Arthurian Legend in Italian Literature*. 1930; repr. New York: Octagon Books, 1971.

Jackson, W. H., and Ranawake, S. A. (eds.). *The Arthur of the Germans: The Arthurian Legend in Medieval German and Dutch Literature*. Cardiff: University of Wales Press, 2000.

Kalinke, Marianne E. *King Arthur North-by-Northwest: The Matière de Bretagne in Old Norse-Icelandic Romances*. Copenhagen: C. A. Reitzels, 1981.

Lagorio, Valerie M., and Day, Mildred Leake (eds.). *King Arthur through the Ages*. 2 vols. New York: Garland Publishing, 1990. (Contains essays on Arthurian literature from the Middle Ages to the present.)

Loomis, Roger Sherman (ed.). *Arthurian Literature in the Middle Ages: A Collaborative History*. Oxford: Clarendon Press, 1959.

—— *The Development of Arthurian Romance*. London: Hutchinson University Library, 1963.

Lupack, Alan, and Lupack, Barbara Tepa. *King Arthur in America*. Cambridge: D. S. Brewer, 1999.

Lupack, Barbara Tepa (ed.). *Adapting the Arthurian Legends for Children: Essays on Arthurian Juvenilia*. New York: Palgrave Macmillan, 2004.

Mancoff, Debra N. (ed.). *The Arthurian Revival: Essays on Form, Tradition, and Transformation*. New York: Garland, 1992.

Merriman, James Douglas. *The Flower of Kings: A Study of the Arthurian Legend in England between 1485 and 1835*. Lawrence: University of Kansas Press, 1973.

Michelsson, Elisabeth. *Adapting King Arthur: The Arthurian Legend in English Drama and Entertainments 1485–1625*. Uppsala: Uppsala University Library, 1999.

Millican, Charles Bowie. *Spenser and the Table Round: A Study in the Contemporaneous Background for Spenser's Use of the Arthurian Legend*. 1932; repr. New York: Octagon Books, 1967.

Pearsall, Derek. *Arthurian Romance: A Short Introduction*. Malden, Mass.: Blackwell Publishers, 2003.

Simpson, Roger. *Camelot Regained: The Arthurian Revival and Tennyson 1800–1849*. Cambridge: D. S. Brewer, 1990.

Slocum, Sally K. (ed.). *Popular Arthurian Traditions*. Bowling Green, Oh.: Bowling Green State University Popular Press, 1992.

Starr, Nathan Comfort. *King Arthur Today: The Arthurian Legend in English and American Literature 1901–1953*. Gainesville: University of Florida Press, 1954.

Summers, David A. *Spenser's Arthur: The British Arthurian Tradition and the Faerie Queene*. Lanham, Md.: University Press of America, 1997.

Taylor, Beverly, and Brewer, Elisabeth. *The Return of King Arthur: British and American Arthurian Literature since 1800* [title page erroneously reads '1900']. Cambridge: D. S. Brewer, 1983.

Thompson, Raymond H. *The Return from Avalon: A Study of the Arthurian Legend in Modern Fiction*. Westport, Conn.: Greenwood Press, 1985.

Guides to Major Arthurian Texts

Archibald, Elizabeth, and Edwards, A. S. G. (eds.). *A Companion to Malory*. Arthurian Studies 37. Cambridge: D. S. Brewer, 1996.

Brewer, Derek, and Gibson, Jonathan (eds.). *A Companion to the Gawain-Poet*. Cambridge: D. S. Brewer, 1997.

Brewer, Elisabeth. *T. H. White's The Once and Future King*. Cambridge: D. S. Brewer, 1993.

Dover, Carol (ed.). *A Companion to the Lancelot–Grail Cycle*. Cambridge: D. S. Brewer, 2003.

Eggers, J. Phillip. *King Arthur's Laureate: A Study of Tennyson's Idylls of the King*. New York: New York University Press, 1971.

Hasty, Will (ed.). *A Companion to Gottfried von Strassburg's 'Tristan'*. Columbia, SC: Camden House, 2003.

—— (ed.). *A Companion to Wolfram's 'Parzival'*. Columbia, SC: Camden House, 1999.

Arthurian Characters and Symbols

Aurner, Nellie Slayton. *Hengest: A Study in Early English Hero Legend*. Iowa City: The University of Iowa, n.d.

Barber, Richard. *The Holy Grail: Imagination and Belief*. London: Allen Lane, 2004.

Biddle, Martin, et al. *King Arthur's Round Table: An Archaeological Investigation*. Woodbridge: The Boydell Press, 2000. (A comprehensive study of the Winchester Round Table.)

Cross, Tom Peete, and Nitze, William A. *Lancelot and Guenevere: A Study in the Origins of Courtly Love*. New York: Phaeton Press, 1970.

Goodrich, Peter, and Thompson, Raymond H. (eds.). *Merlin: A Casebook*. New York: Routledge, 2003.

Gowans, Linda M. *Cei and the Arthurian Legends*. Arthurian Studies XVIII. Cambridge: D. S. Brewer, 1988.

Grimbert, Joan Tasker (ed.). *Tristan and Isolde: A Casebook*. New York: Garland, 1995.

Groos, Arthur, and Lacy, Norris J. (eds.). *Perceval/Parzival: A Casebook*. New York: Routledge, 2002.

Harward, Vernon L., Jr. *The Dwarfs of Arthurian Romance and Celtic Tradition*. Leiden: E. J. Brill, 1958.

Kennedy, Edward Donald (ed.). *King Arthur: A Casebook*. New York: Garland, 1996.

Mahoney, Dhira B. (ed.). *The Grail: A Casebook*. New York: Garland, 2000.

Newstead, Helaine. *Bran the Blessed in Arthurian Romance*. New York: Columbia University Press, 1939.

Reno, Frank D. *Historic Figures of the Arthurian Era: Authenticating the Enemies and Allies of Britain's Post-Roman King*. Jefferson, NC: McFarland, 2000.

Walters, Lori J. (ed.). *Lancelot and Guinevere: A Casebook*. New York: Garland, 1996.

Watson, Jeanie, and Fries, Maureen (eds.). *The Figure of Merlin in the Nineteenth and Twentieth Centuries*. Lewiston, NY: The Edwin Mellen Press, 1988.

Weiss, Adelaide Marie. *Merlin in German Literature: A Study of the Merlin Legend in German Literature from Medieval Beginnings to the End of Romanticism*. 1933; repr. New York: AMS Press, 1970.

Arthurian Art

Loomis, Roger Sherman. *Arthurian Legend in Medieval Art*. London: Oxford University Press, 1938.

Mancoff, Debra N. *The Arthurian Revival in Victorian Art*. New York: Garland, 1990.

—— *The Return of King Arthur: The Legend through Victorian Eyes*. New York: Harry N. Abrams, 1995.

Poulson, Christine. 'Arthurian Legend in Fine and Applied Art of the Nineteenth and Early Twentieth Centuries: A Catalogue of Artists', *Arthurian Literature*, 9 (1989), 81–142. (The 'Subject Index' appears in vol. 10 (1990), 111–34.)

—— *The Quest for the Grail: Arthurian Legend in British Art 1840–1920*. Manchester: Manchester University Press, 1999.

Rushing, James A., Jr. *Images of Adventure: Ywain in the Visual Arts*. Philadelphia: University of Pennsylvania Press, 1995.

Scherer, Margaret R. *About the Round Table: King Arthur in Art and Literature*. 1945; repr. New York: Arno Press, 1974.

Simpson, Roger. 'Update II: Arthurian Legend in Fine and Applied Art of the Nineteenth and Early Twentieth Centuries', *Arthurian Literature*, 11 (1992), 81–96.

Whitaker, Muriel. *The Legends of King Arthur in Art*. Cambridge: D. S. Brewer, 1990.

Arthurian Music

Barber, Richard (ed.). *King Arthur in Music*. Cambridge: D. S. Brewer, 2002.

Nastali, Dan. 'Arthurian Pop: The Tradition in Twentieth-Century Popular Music', in Elizabeth S. Sklar and Donald L. Hoffman (eds.), *King Arthur in Popular Culture*. Jefferson, NC: McFarland, 2002: 138–67.

Nevins, John P. 'Musical Arthuriana: A Partial and Informal Listing', *Quondam et Futurus*, 10.4 (Summer 1990), 6–12.

Reel, Jerome V., Jr. 'Arthurian Musical Theatre: A Listing', an *Arthuriana/Camelot Project Bibliography* (www.lib.rochester.edu/camelot/acpbibs/reel.htm).

Arthurian Sites

Alcock, Leslie. *Was This Camelot?: Excavations at Cadbury Castle, 1966–1970*. New York: Stein and Day, 1972.

Ashe, Geoffrey. *A Guidebook to Arthurian Britain*. London: Longman, 1980.

—— *The Landscape of King Arthur*, with photographs by Simon McBride. New York: Henry Holt, 1987.

—— Alcock, Leslie C. A., Radford, Ralegh, and Rahtz, Philip. *The Quest for Arthur's Britain*. 1968; repr. St Albans: Paladin, 1976.

Anthologies

Barber, Richard (ed.). *The Arthurian Legends: An Illustrated Anthology*. Totowa, NJ: Littlefield and Adams, 1979.

Goodrich, Peter (ed.). *The Romance of Merlin: An Anthology*. New York: Garland, 1990. (Contains literature about Merlin from the Middle Ages to the twentieth century.)

Lupack, Alan (ed.). 'Arthur, the Greatest King': An Anthology of Modern Arthurian Poetry. New York: Garland, 1988.

—— (ed.). *Arthurian Drama: An Anthology*. New York: Garland, 1991.

—— (ed.). *Modern Arthurian Literature: An Anthology of English and American Arthuriana from the Renaissance to the Present*. New York: Garland, 1992.

—— and Lupack, Barbara Tepa (eds.). *Arthurian Literature by Women*. New York: Garland, 1999.

White, Richard (ed.). *King Arthur in Legend and History*. London: J. M. Dent, 1997.

Wilhelm, James J. (ed.). *The Romance of Arthur: An Anthology of Medieval Texts in Translation*. New York: Garland, 1994. (Contains major medieval Arthurian works.)

Early Accounts of Arthur, Chronicles, and Historical Literature

The *Gododdin*

Perhaps the earliest text to mention *Arthur is the poem known as the *Gododdin*, an elegy for warriors from a tribe known as the Gododdin, who inhabited a region in the south-east of Scotland. The heroes commemorated were slain at the battle of Catraeth in about 600. Two lines in the poem, which appears in the late thirteenth-century manuscript known as the Book of Aneirin, are of particular interest: a warrior named Gwawrddur is praised for his prowess and is said to have 'fed black ravens [i.e. he slaughtered the enemy and left their bodies for ravens to eat] on the rampart of a fortress | Though he was no Arthur' (Aneirin pp. xxiv and 64). The poem is preceded by the line 'This is *Y Gododdin*; Aneirin sang it'; and if the poem were written by Aneirin, a poet of the late sixth century, and if he were responsible for the reference to Arthur, these facts would be compelling evidence for his historicity, coming shortly after the real Arthur would have lived and fought. As with all 'evidence' for the historical Arthur, however, this early reference is fraught with problems. Though Aneirin may have been the author of the elegy for the Gododdin, the text that survives—in a thirteenth-century manuscript of a poem first written down in perhaps the ninth century—may have gone through many changes. In addition, of the two versions of the poem preserved (usually called A and B), the reference to Arthur appears in just one, and 'it is only when a passage occurs in both the A and the B Versions that there can be any confidence that it goes back before the ninth or tenth century' (Charles-Edwards 15).

As with many medieval Arthurian works, the *Gododdin* has been reinterpreted in modern literary texts, in this case two novels. *The Shining Company* (1990) by Rosemary Sutcliff tells of the battle at Catraeth, where the shining company, a band of warriors much like Arthur's knights of the *Round Table, lose their lives because their king is no Arthur but because of whose sacrifice 'the Saxon flood is stayed... as it was for Artos after *Badon' (261). The battle of Catraeth is also elaborately described in the novel *Men Went to Cattraeth* (1969) by John James, which is narrated by Aneirin and gives a prominent role to Owain. Such interplay between early and modern works is an essential part of the Arthurian tradition, as will be seen in each of the chapters in this volume.

Gildas

In the mid-sixth century, a cleric named Gildas wrote a treatise called *De excidio et conquestu Britanniae* (*On the Destruction and Conquest of Britain*). Though not intended as history, Gildas's work is one of the key documents for information about the Saxon invasions and the condition of Britain at the time. Gildas considers the ravages of the Saxons a result of the sins of the British; nevertheless, he offers an account of the withdrawal of the Romans, the pillaging by the Scots and Picts, and the crucial event of the decision by a 'proud tyrant', identified as *Vortigern in other sources, that the 'Saxons (name not to be spoken!) hated by man and God, should be let into the island like wolves into the fold, to beat back the peoples of the north', an act, in Gildas's opinion, of utter blindness and desperate stupidity (26).

Gildas also tells of the resistance by the British people under the leadership of *Ambrosius Aurelianus, a Roman-British nobleman. This resistance culminates in the 'siege of Badon Hill', which was the 'last' major defeat of the Saxons and 'certainly not the least' (28). That Gildas does not ascribe the victory at Badon to Arthur, as Nennius and later chroniclers do, has been used by some as evidence against the historicity of Arthur. O. J. Padel even suggests that if the manuscript is read without the paragraph divisions added by modern editors, the mention of Ambrosius Aurelianus is not separated from the account of Badon; thus, he concludes, 'Mount Badon reads naturally as the victory which crowned the career of Ambrosius Aurelianus himself' (17). Others have theorized that Arthur is deliberately omitted because of his offences against the Church, as recounted in some early saints' lives (discussed below), or that his name is left out, as was Vortigern's, either because it was not important to Gildas's moral purpose or because it would have been common knowledge that Arthur was the victor and therefore went without saying.

Whatever the reason for the omission of Arthur's name, Gildas describes and defines for future writers the basic pattern of a foolish invitation to the Saxons, an eventual resistance by the British people under an effective leader (or leaders), and a crucial victory at Mount Badon followed by a period of peace.

Bede

In 731, the British monk Bede (673–735), known as the Venerable Bede, completed his *History of the English Church and People* (*Historia ecclesiastica gentis Anglorum*), which conforms in its general outline to Gildas's account of the coming of the Germanic tribes to Britain as mercenaries and his explanation of the ravages of the Saxons as God's punishment for the wicked ways of the British people. Bede also names Ambrosius Aurelianus as the leader of the resistance against the Saxons and writes of the 'considerable slaughter of the invaders' at the battle of Mount Badon (57–8); but he does not refer to Arthur in conjunction with this battle or anywhere else. However, Bede adds some details not in Gildas's account. He sets the initial invitation to the Saxons in 449, and he names Vortigern as the king who invited them and *Hengist and *Horsa as the Saxon leaders. Bede's chronicle is more interested in the religious than in the political and military history of Britain. Nevertheless, it is an important source for later writers.

Nennius

Around 800, a chronicle known as the *Historia Brittonum* (*History of the Britons*) was written by an author named in the text as Nennius, who claims to have made 'a heap' from all the chronicles available to him (9). Like Bede, he recounts the coming of the Saxons under the leadership of Hengest and Horsa and the complicity of Vortigern in their obtaining a foothold in Britain, and he tells for the first time (in surviving chronicles) the story of Vortigern's attempt to build a fortification. When the tower Vortigern is building collapses each night, he is advised by his wizards to sprinkle on the site the blood of a child with no father. His envoys search for and find such a child—here Ambrosius, son of a Roman consul, and not *Merlin, as in the accounts of Geoffrey of Monmouth and others—who reveals that two dragons reside in a lake beneath the foundation.

*Vortimer, Vortigern's son, opposes his father's Saxon allies and defeats them in four battles; but upon Vortimer's death the invaders return and ask for a meeting to discuss peace, at which they treacherously slay the assembled British lords. In time, when Hengest is dead and his son Octha is ravaging Britain, Arthur, as the 'leader in battle' (or 'dux ... bellorum') of the British (35), defeats them in *twelve battles, the last of which is at Mount Badon, where Arthur alone kills 960 of the enemy.

While Nennius is surely drawing on earlier sources for this list of battles and for most of what he records, details like Arthur's superhuman deeds at Badon make his account of little value as a historical document. Nennius also appends to his chronicle a report of the wonders of Britain that include a stone with the footprint of Arthur's dog *Cafal that always returns to the pile of stones on which it rests even if someone takes it more than a day's journey away, and a description of the tomb of *Amr, son of Arthur, which is a different length each time it is measured. And, Nennius adds, 'I have tried it [measuring the stone] myself' (42). Thus his credibility as a historian, even for things of which he claims to have first-hand knowledge, is suspect. He does, however, influence later chroniclers like Geoffrey of Monmouth; and his account of Arthur's twelve victories is a classic passage in Arthurian literature, a passage that is echoed in as late a work as Tennyson's *Idylls of the King* and that has inspired many historical novels as well as numerous studies by historians.

Annales Cambriae

The *Annales Cambriae* (*Welsh Annals*), which briefly lists significant events for 533 years beginning in 447, survives in several manuscripts, the earliest dating from about 970; but it may reflect a tradition that is somewhat older. These annals contain two entries of particular significance to the Arthurian tradition. One agrees with Nennius in associating Arthur with the victory at Badon. It records the 'Battle of Badon in which Arthur carried the Cross of our Lord Jesus Christ for three days and three nights on his shoulders [which may be a misreading for "shield"] and the Britons were the victors'. The other records 'the battle of *Camlann, in which Arthur and Medraut [*Mordred] fell' (45), though it does not indicate whether Arthur and Medraut were fighting against each other or as allies.

ARTHUR IN WELSH LITERATURE

In the surviving medieval Welsh literature about Arthur, there is a wealth of allusions to characters and narrative material that suggests a rich tradition even before Geoffrey of Monmouth and Chrétien de Troyes shaped the Matter of Britain into the form that is most recognizable to modern readers. Welsh prose and verse texts present a world of folklore and legend that sometimes intersects with history. Some of these works depict a heroic world of warriors and battles, some 'a world of magic and monsters, rapid-fire adventures and the outwitting or overpowering of supernatural opponents' (Padel 32).

The surviving Arthurian Welsh prose tales are part of a collection of stories first edited and translated (1838–49) by Lady Charlotte Guest (Charlotte Elizabeth Schreiber, 1812–95) and called by her the *Mabinogion*, a work of great importance because it introduced these stories to the English-speaking world. The term 'mabinogion' was long thought to correspond to 'the French *enfance*, the story of a hero's youth from conception and birth to early manhood' but 'broadened to include episodes in which the hero is no longer young' (Foster 31), though now some believe that the term refers to tales about the British god Maponos (cf. Ford 3). Under either of these definitions, the term does not fit very well the Arthurian tales; and some scholars choose not to use it (though others still use the term to refer to the entire group assembled by Guest).

Culhwch and Olwen
The earliest surviving Welsh prose tale is *Culhwch and Olwen* (*Culhwch ac Olwen*, c.1100), the *Mabinogion* story of Arthur's assistance to his cousin Culhwch in winning the hand of Olwen, daughter of the giant Ysbadadden. Culhwch requests his boon in the name of all of those who serve Arthur, which allows for an extensive list of names that includes some familiar characters from other stories, such as Cei (*Kay) and Bedwyr (*Bedivere) and *Taliesin, and allusions to well-known events, such as the battle of Camlan. But also embedded in the list are numerous unfamiliar names and suggestions of many tales that have not survived. Those listed include Osla Big-Knife, whose knife laid across a river formed a bridge that the hosts of Britain could cross; Gwrhyr Interpreter of Tongues, who knows all languages; Clust who, 'were he to be buried seven fathom in the earth, would hear an ant fifty miles off when it stirred from its couch of a morning'; and others with similarly exceptional qualities or abilities (trans. Jones and Jones 104, 106).

Arthur is thus depicted as the leader of a band of superheroes. And only with the help of such extraordinary warriors can Culhwch expect to win the hand of his beloved because her father, who will die when she leaves with a husband, demands that a series of tasks be accomplished before he will give his daughter in marriage. Ysbadadden rattles off the seemingly impossible quests, such as obtaining the cauldron of Diwrnach the Irishman so he can boil meat for the wedding, the blood of the Black Witch that he needs to prepare his beard for cutting, and the 'comb and shears that are between the two ears of *Twrch Trwyth', the giant boar, which he needs for grooming his hair (trans. Jones and Jones 116, 117). To each of these demands, Culhwch responds with the refrain, 'It is easy for me to get that, though thou think it is not easy', his confidence inspired by the support of Arthur and his warriors.

Some of the required tasks are glossed over or omitted from the subsequent narrative; others are described in detail. The hunting of the giant boar Twrch Trwyth, for example, by Arthur and his dog Cafal, an incident referred to in Nennius' *Historia Brittonum*, is an elaborate narrative inset. In the end, the tasks are completed. Culhwch and some of Arthur's men return to shave the giant, cutting off his beard, his skin, his flesh down to the bone, and his two ears, after which he gives Olwen to Culhwch but says that Culhwch should 'thank Arthur who secured her for thee' (trans. Jones and Jones 136). Ysbadadden is then beheaded, and the lovers marry.

Culhwch and Olwen presents a picture of the Arthurian court before it is transformed by Geoffrey and Chrétien. It also demonstrates that some of the material that these and later authors use has an earlier source. The picture of Cei, for example, as someone less than welcoming to strangers, as someone who is stubborn and yet valiant, is perfectly consistent with his later characterization. At the same time, Cei is a fairy-tale superhero like others described in the tale: 'nine nights and nine days his breath lasted under water' and 'when it pleased him he would be as tall as the tallest tree in the forest' (trans. Jones and Jones 107). He is part of a world earlier than and different from that of Arthurian romance.

The Dream of Rhonabwy

The Dream of Rhonabwy (*Breuddwyd Rhonabwy*) is a somewhat later tale, perhaps dating from the thirteenth century, from the *Mabinogion* that tells of a man named Rhonabwy who is sent by Madawg, son of Maredudd, to seek his brother Iorwerth. One night on his quest, Rhonabwy is given poor hospitality in a dirty house. Unable to sleep on a flea-infested blanket, Rhonabwy goes to a dais and lies on a yellow ox skin, sleeps, and has a dream in which he meets Iddawg the Embroiler of Britain, who, before the battle of Camlan, was sent by Arthur with a message of peace to Medrawd; but he spoke those words 'the ugliest way' he could (trans. Jones and Jones 140) and thus caused the battle instead of averting it, an act for which Iddawg later did penance.

Iddawg brings Rhonabwy to Arthur's camp. The fact that Camlan is Arthur's last battle is ignored or irrelevant in the dream world where the battle of Badon is about to take place. Rhonabwy sees Arthur engage in the board game gwyddbwyll with *Owain, son of *Urien. As they play, they hear first that Arthur's troops are harassing Owain's ravens and then that the ravens are harassing Arthur's troops. Owain asks that Arthur call off his troops, and Arthur makes a similar plea that Owain call off his ravens; but neither complies and they continue playing until Arthur crushes the golden pieces on the board and the fighting stops. Cei instructs those who would follow Arthur to join him in Cornwall, thus causing a commotion in the dream, which wakes Rhonabwy.

The Dream of Rhonabwy is a curious but fascinating example of a dream vision in which Iddawg serves as an instructor for the dreamer Rhonabwy. Within the tale there is an assertion that no bard or storyteller can know this tale without a book because of the number of colours on the arms and trappings of the horses and on the mantles and magic stones described. A conscious literary work, *The Dream of Rhonabwy* has been read as 'satirizing the whole fabric of Arthurian literary conventions' partly because of Arthur's inactivity in the tale (Lloyd-Morgan 192). But the allusions to Badon and Camlan also allow it to be read as a reminder of the glory of the Celtic Arthurian past, a past undone as much by strife and betrayal among the Celtic people as by the threats of invaders.

The Birth of Arthur

The Birth of Arthur, a Welsh tale about Arthur that is not included in the *Mabinogion*, survives in a fifteenth-century manuscript. The narrative describes the pulling of the sword from the stone and the crowning of Arthur as king. The details of the story are generally similar to those known from Malory and French romances. In this tale, after Kai breaks his sword in play, Arthur takes the sword, named Kaletvwlch, from the stone to replace it. That sword bears an inscription identifying it as 'a sign' from God and asserting that only one person, with divine aid, can withdraw it. At his coronation, Arthur is instructed by Archbishop Dyfric that he must protect the Church, the weak, and the poor and that he must make good laws and punish evildoers.

Taliesin

A tale about Taliesin, *Taliesin*, appears in Lady Charlotte Guest's collection but is omitted from many later translations of the *Mabinogion*. Surviving only in manuscripts from the sixteenth to the eighteenth centuries, it tells how the witch Ceridwen boils a cauldron of Inspiration and Science for her son, who is so ugly that she fears he will not prosper among noble men without some special knowledge. Three drops from the cauldron fall upon the fingers of her servant Gwion Bach, who was charged with stirring the cauldron. When he puts his burning fingers to his lips, 'he foresaw everything that was to come' (trans. Guest 472). To punish him for spoiling her labour and obtaining the power she intended for her son, Ceridwen pursues Gwion Bach. In the chase, both of them turn into various animals, until finally he transforms himself into a grain of wheat and she becomes a hen and eats him (an episode that almost certainly inspired the contest between Madam Mim and Merlin in T. H. White's *The Sword in the Stone*). In nine months, he is reborn from her as Taliesin. She then wraps him in a leather bag and casts him into the sea.

Elphin, son of Gwyddno, finds the baby in a weir and raises him, calling him Taliesin, meaning 'radiant brow', because the weir-ward who first opened the leather bag and saw the child said, 'Behold a radiant brow!' When Elphin laments that he has had so little from the weir, Taliesin, though only a baby, speaks and tells him in 'the first poem that Taliesin ever sang' (trans. Guest 473–4) that he will serve Elphin more than a large catch of salmon.

Some years later, when Elphin boasts of the virtue of his wife and the skill of his bard, King Maelgwn puts him in prison until the truth of his claims can be tested. After helping to thwart an attempt by Maelgwn's son Rhun to undermine the virtue of Elphin's wife, Taliesin goes to Maelgwn's court and proves himself the greatest of bards, much of the tale at this point being taken up with songs sung by him. Taliesin not only frees Elphin but also reveals the spot where a cauldron filled with gold is buried and gives the gold to Elphin as a reward for having rescued him from the weir and raised him.

Welsh Verse

One of the great collections of Welsh verse is found in the early fourteenth-century manuscript known as the Book of Taliesin (National Library of Wales, Peniarth MS 2). This manuscript contains a number of poems dedicated to Urien of Rheged and his son Owain, which are often accepted as having been originally composed by the historical sixth-century bard named Taliesin. There are also, however, many legendary rather than historical or heroic poems in the manuscript that are no longer accepted as Taliesin's work. At some point, the historical figure apparently metamorphosed into or merged with the legendary bard of Elphin. As Sir Ifor Williams has noted, 'it is unlikely that the scribe drew a distinction between the work of the legendary Taliesin, Elphin's bard, and the work of the historic Taliesin, Urien's bard' (Williams p. xix). The picture is complicated even further because the legendary Chief Bard of Britain is naturally attracted into the sphere of Arthur, the chief warrior of Britain, and becomes identified in literature as Arthur's bard.

Arthur is alluded to in several poems in the Book of Taliesin, such as 'The Battle of the Trees' and 'The Poem of the Horses', but receives more extended treatment in one of the most intriguing poems in the manuscript, 'The Spoils of Annwn' ('Preiddeu Annwn'), which places Arthur in a mythological context. Presumably spoken by Taliesin, the poem recounts Arthur's leading of a raid on Annwn, the Celtic otherworld, to free Gwair (identified in Triad 52 as one of the 'Three Exalted Prisoners of the Island of Britain') and to make off with the magical cauldron of the Chief of Annwn, which is 'kindled up' by 'the breath of nine maidens' and which 'boils not a coward's food'. Arthur, sailing to Annwn in his ship *Prydwen, leads a force of three boatloads of warriors. The poem's refrain tells of the cost of the mission: 'but for seven, none returned' (Coe and Young 137). The 'highly allusive' poem, which 'no one could characterize ... as coherent narrative', offers little in the way of explanation or resolution though it does provide 'one of the most informative depictions of Arthur' in the context of 'a larger Celtic heroic tradition' that survives (Budgey 392, 399).

Arthur and Arthurian characters are also found in a number of poems in the thirteenth-century manuscript known as the Black Book of Carmarthen (National Library of Wales, Peniarth MS 1). The 'Stanzas of the Graves' ('Englynion y Beddau') speaks of the graves of Gwalchmai (*Gawain), of Owain son of Urien, of Bedwyr, of March, and of Arthur, whose grave is said to be a 'wonder' ('anoeth', a word which might also mean 'difficult to find'). This designation is sometimes interpreted as referring to the belief that Arthur is not truly dead.

Two other poems in the Black Book of Carmarthen mention *Llachau, Arthur's son. In 'I Have Been' ('Mi a wum'), the narrator says, 'I have been where Llachau was slain, | the son of Arthur, awful in songs, | when ravens croaked over blood' (Coe and Young 125). In the allusive style of much Welsh poetry, the poet gives no explanation of how Llachau died. The poem 'What Man' ('Pa Gur') begins with Arthur asking what man is the porter of a house he has come to and then vouching for his men, whom he lists and whose abilities he enumerates. In his account of Cai, Arthur notes his superhuman achievements in battle, where 'he would slay like a hundred', his ability to drink from a horn 'like four', and his killing of witches and a giant cat. The poem observes that unless God brought it about, 'Cai's death would be impossible', and then says that Cai and Llachau 'fulfilled battles' (Coe and Young 131–3). This line is usually taken to mean that the two warriors fought on the same side, 'but the two could be opponents fighting to the death', a possibility heightened by the fact that 'the Welsh translator of *Perlesvaus*, translating the story of Cai's treacherous murder of Arthur's son *Loholt, replaced the name *Loholt* with *Llacheu*' (Sims-Williams 44).

Also contained in the Black Book of Carmarthen is 'Gereint Son of Erbin', written sometime from the ninth to the eleventh century. This poem in praise of *Gereint speaks of his prowess, especially in a battle at Llongborth. Though a sixth-century figure, Gereint is seen as fighting alongside Arthur's warriors; and, significantly, the poem refers to Arthur as both 'emperor' and a military commander: 'leader in toil' (Coe and Young 119). We have here an Arthur of the historical struggle against the Saxons, even if chronology is distorted by having him fight with Gereint, the same Gereint who is part of the Arthurian world in a tale from the *Mabinogion*, in a romance by Chrétien, and, because of them, in a number of later works.

Arthur appears elsewhere in Welsh poetry. In 'The Dialogue of Arthur and the Eagle' ('Ymddiddan Arthur a'r Eryr', probably written in the twelfth century), the eagle is Arthur's deceased nephew Eliwlod. From this instructor, Arthur, as 'a typical member of the secular aristocracy, as in the Welsh saints' lives', receives 'basic Christian instruction' (Sims-Williams 57–8). Another poem, 'The Dialogue of

Gwenhwyfar and Arthur' ('Ymddiddan Gwenhwyfar ac Arthur'), sometimes and probably more accurately called 'The Dialogue of Gwenhwyfar and Melwas', is a confrontational dialogue between *Gwenhwyfar and Melwas, known from the *Life of St Gildas* (and, as *Meleagant, in later texts from Chrétien's *Lancelot* on) as the abductor of Arthur's queen. Her abduction is certainly the story behind this dialogue. Melwas makes reference to his ability to defeat Cai, which may suggest an attempt by him, as in Chrétien's romance, to defend Gwenhwyfar.

Another source of Arthurian material is the *Triads* (*Trioedd*), bardic lore organized thematically into groups of three, perhaps as a mnemonic device or as a hint of longer stories a bard might tell. Whatever their function, the *Triads* contain allusions to a wealth of lost narrative material. In Triad 12, for example, Arthur is said to be one of the three frivolous bards of the Island of Britain; and in Triad 20, he is called one of the three red ravagers of the Island of Britain. In Triad 47b, he is listed as one of the *Nine Worthies. Among the three harmful blows given in the Island of Britain, the second is the one 'Gwenhwyfach struck upon Gwenhwyfar: and for that cause there took place afterwards the action of the Battle of Camlan' (Triad 53). Triad 54 lists the three unrestrained ravagings of the Island of Britain, one of which was when Medrawd came to Arthur's court and another was when Arthur came to Medrawd's court. Triad 56 records Arthur's three great queens, and Triad 57 names his three mistresses. In these, as in Triad 65, which tells of the three unrestricted guests of Arthur's court, and in a number of other triads, there are suggestions of what must have been a rich body of narrative. Unfortunately, many of these stories have not survived.

Characters referred to in early Welsh poems and tales remain a source of allusion in Welsh poetry of the fourteenth and fifteenth centuries. Fourteenth-century poet Dafydd ap Gwilym refers to Indeg, one of Arthur's three mistresses in Triad 57, as a great beauty. And in several poems Dafydd uses *Enid and Tegau, two of the three splendid maidens of Arthur's court (Triad 88), as symbols of beauty. Tegau has a similar function in the poem 'A Cloak from Elen of Llŷn' by fifteenth-century poet Guto'r Glyn, as does Enid in the poem 'Request for a Bed' by Lewys Glyn Clothi, who also writes in the fifteenth century.

Welsh Arthurian lore, while not reinterpreted as often in modern works as are the Arthurian romances of the later Middle Ages, enjoyed a revival in the nineteenth century. Thomas Love Peacock (1785–1866) drew on early sources for his novel *The Misfortunes of Elphin* (1829). Lady Charlotte Guest's translation of the *Mabinogion* made an important body of Welsh material accessible and was a source for one of Tennyson's idylls. And late in the century, Ernest Rhys (1859–1946) included Welsh themes and some poems that reworked Welsh texts in his volume *Welsh Ballads and Other Poems* (1898).

David Jones

In the twentieth century, one of the major figures to incorporate motifs from and allusions to early Celtic literature as well as other medieval Arthurian literature in his writing and his art was David Jones (1895–1974). Jones referred to his fragmentary poem 'The Hunt', published in 1974 in the volume *The Sleeping Lord*, as 'an incomplete attempt based on the native Welsh early medieval prose-tale, Culhwch ac Olwen' (69). Arthur 'is envisaged as a kind of Harrower of Hell in pursuit of the monstrous Boar Trwyth' (Blamires 78). In 'The Sleeping Lord', the title poem of the volume, allusions to the great boar (89–90) and other Arthurian literature as well as to British history identify the sleeping lord both as Arthur in the role of archetypal king and as the land itself.

David Jones, of Welsh and English ancestry, saw his own background paralleled in both the First World War and Arthurian legend. In the preface to his masterpiece *In Parenthesis* (1937), a book that is part novel, part poem, part autobiography, he writes of the way in which the war brought together Englishmen and Welshmen (p. x); and in his essay on 'The Myth of Arthur' (first published in 1942), he observes that the Arthurian legend is 'important to the Welsh' because 'there is no other tradition at all equally the common property of all the inhabitants of Britain' (216). *In Parenthesis* reflects this shared heritage by combining allusions from Celtic literature, including *Culhwch and Olwen* and the *Gododdin*, quotations from which introduce the parts of the poem, with references to Malory and the *Grail quest, in order to provide a picture of the devastated *wasteland and emotional trauma caused by the trench warfare of the First World War. Writing of the death of the soldier Aneirin Lewis, for example, Jones says that 'Properly organised chemists can let make more riving power than ever Twrch Trwyth' and that the dead soldier is 'unwholer, limb from limb', than any who fell at Catraeth (the battle memorialized in the *Gododdin*) or at Camlan (155).

Similar allusions are found in Jones's poem *The Anathemata* (1952), in the preface to which he says that Nennius' apology that he made a 'heap' of all he found might serve as an apology for his own work (9). Indeed, Jones piles together allusions to many works in this elaborately footnoted poem. Among the central images are those of the wasteland and the Grail quest, including references to '*Pellam's land' and the life-restoring question that must be asked by the questing knight (50, 226).

SAINTS' LIVES

In a number of saints' lives, a picture of Arthur emerges that is sometimes at odds with the heroic image found in many of the chronicles and romances. Perhaps the earliest depiction of Arthur in a saint's life is found in the *Legend of St Goeznovius* (*Legenda sancti Goeznovii*), said in the manuscript to have been written in 1019, though the date has been disputed. The small Arthurian portion of this text is noteworthy because it mentions Vortigern's inviting of the Saxons into Britain and Arthur's victories in Britain and, interestingly, in Gaul ('in Britannicis et Gallicis partibus' (Chambers 242)). It also contains a reference to Arthur's being called from human activity at the end of his life, a phrase which is ambiguous, perhaps referring only to his death but perhaps suggesting that he survives outside the normal sphere of human activity (cf. White 13).

The Life of St Illtud (Vita Illtuti, twelfth century) identifies the saint as a cousin of Arthur. Illtud is a soldier until an angelic visitor tells him to give up his worldly life and serve God. Arthur has no adventures here, but the young Illtud hears of Arthur's reputation and desires 'to visit the court of so great a conqueror' (Wade-Evans 197).

Though such references to Arthur hardly seem out of the ordinary, episodes in other saints' lives are much less conventional and sometimes portray Arthur as in opposition to the saint or the Church or as a foil to reveal the power of God working through the saint. In the twelfth-century Life of St Carannog (Vita sancti Carantoci), for example, Arthur meets Carannog as he searches for a dragon that has been ravishing the land. (As Peter Korrel (44) observes, a similar 'monster-slaying hero protecting his country' appears in La Vie de saint Efflam (The Life of St Efflam), a Breton saint's life in which Arthur is again aided by a saint in subduing a destructive dragon.) Carannog, who has cast into the sea a wondrous altar sent to him by God to discover which way God wanted him to go, asks Arthur if he has seen the altar. Arthur replies that he will answer if Carannog will bring forth the dragon, a deed the saint accomplishes through his prayers. Using his stole as a leash, he 'led it like a lamb' (Wade-Evans 145) and then frees the dragon with the instruction to do no more harm. Arthur, who had earlier appropriated the altar and had intended to use it as a table, was frustrated in this plan because anything placed on it was thrown far from it; and so he returns it to Carannog.

In the Life of St Padarn (Vita Paterni), another twelfth-century text, Arthur sees the saint's tunic and is 'pierced with the zeal of avarice'. When Padarn tells him the tunic is fit only for a cleric, Arthur leaves in a rage but returns. Padarn prays for the earth to swallow him, whereupon 'the earth opens the hollow of its depth, and swallows Arthur up to his chin', forcing him to beg forgiveness. After the earth delivers him, Arthur takes Padarn 'as his continual patron' (Wade-Evans 261).

The prologue to The Life of St Cadoc (Vita Cadoci, late eleventh century) by Lifris of Llancarfan depicts Arthur playing dice with Cai and Bedwyr when they see a king named Gwynllyw leading Gwladus, the woman he loves, and being pursued by her father Brychan. Although Arthur's first instinct is to lust after her, he is reminded by his companions, in a statement that foreshadows later ideals of the Arthurian court, that 'we are wont to help the needy and distressed' (Wade-Evans 27). Arthur and his companions then help to defeat Brychan's troops; and the lovers marry and become the parents of Cadoc. This somewhat traditional role for Arthur as helper of those in need is combined with that seen in other saints' lives when, years later, Arthur pursues a warrior known as Long Hand, who had killed three of his soldiers. Cadoc gives Long Hand sanctuary for seven years. After learning of Long Hand's whereabouts, Arthur arrives with his warriors but is unwilling to violate sanctuary. Cadoc suggests submitting the dispute to a group of holy men, clerics, and elders as judges, who decide that Arthur should be paid in cattle for the lost men. Although Arthur will accept only cows that are red in front and white behind, Cadoc instructs that ordinary cows be brought, and they are 'changed by divine power, in accordance with Arthur's perverse desire, into the aforesaid colours' (Wade-Evans 71). When Arthur, Cai, and Bedwyr take possession of them, the animals turn into bundles of fern. After Arthur asks Cadoc for forgiveness for the wrong he did to him by making an unreasonable demand, the cows are found safely back in their stalls.

Arthur appears again in the *Life of Gildas* (*Vita Gildae*, c.1130) by Caradoc of Llancarfan (d. 1147?), where he is said to be a contemporary of Gildas and the slayer of Hueil, one of the saint's brothers, an act for which Gildas forgives him and for which Arthur does penance. Caradoc also tells of Gildas's role in the return of Arthur's queen Gwenhwyfar, who had been abducted by Melvas, king of the summer country, which includes *Glastonbury. Melvas secures her in his castle at Glastonbury 'owing to the asylum afforded by the invulnerable position due to the fortifications of thickets of reed, river, and marsh' (Caradoc 99). Gildas advises Melvas to restore the queen to her husband, which he does. In gratitude, Arthur and Melvas give lands to the abbot of Glastonbury and agree to obey the abbot and 'never to violate the most sacred place' (Caradoc 101).

GEOFFREY OF MONMOUTH AND HIS INFLUENCE

Geoffrey of Monmouth

While Welsh literature and saints' lives offer fascinating early views of Arthur, the character and his legend became central to medieval literature and literary tradition when Geoffrey of Monmouth (c.1100–1154 or 1155) told his story. The account of Arthur's reign told by Geoffrey in his *Historia regum Britanniae* (*History of the Kings of Britain*, completed in 1138, though revisions were made until about 1147) is one of the most significant and influential developments in the history of Arthurian literature. Geoffrey was a teacher, a cleric, and ultimately a bishop of St Asaph in Wales; but it was as a writer that he left a permanent legacy. His history became one of the most popular books of the Middle Ages: it survives in some 215 manuscripts, a remarkable number.

The popularity of Geoffrey's work is due in part to its political usefulness, since it demonstrates precedents for rulers of Britain to claim authority in and allegiance from continental nations, as Arthur does when the Roman procurator *Lucius demands tribute from him. Even more important are Geoffrey's additions to the story of Arthur, perhaps the most significant of which is to give Arthur a place in the line of British kings and to describe the glories of his court and the conquests that make him emperor of the civilized world. It is likely that Geoffrey created much of the Arthurian matter himself, though he also had popular material on which to draw. Part of Geoffrey's significance lies in his elaboration upon this earlier material, a process that paved the way for the development of a romance tradition at the same time that it added vitality, though not historical accuracy, to the chronicle tradition. When later writers like Wace and Layamon adapted Geoffrey's story and added their own elaborations, they not only bring the Arthurian matter into the vernacular but also produce works that can be called romances rather than chronicles, even though they are clearly in the chronicle tradition. The romance tradition, as defined in the next chapter, is thus different from romance as a genre.

Geoffrey claims that Walter, Archdeacon of Oxford, gave him 'a certain most ancient book in the British language' that recounted the deeds of all the kings of Britain, and that Walter asked him to translate it into Latin (3). Surely Geoffrey had available written as well as oral sources, but whether or not there was one ancient book that provided much of his material is impossible to say. No such source survives, and it is not unheard of for medieval authors to invent sources to give their works authority. Whatever the truth about the text that Geoffrey claims as a source, much of the Arthurian portion of his history is almost certainly the product of his fertile imagination.

After a dedication and a description of the island of Britain, Geoffrey begins his history of its kings with the founding of Britain by *Brutus, the great-grandson of Aeneas, who is instructed by a vision of the goddess Diana to lead a band of exiles from Troy to the island of Albion, which he calls Britain, 'after his own name' (26), and to build there a new Troy. As Michael Curley has observed, 'The foundation legend thus assimilates the British people into the dignified civilization of the ancient Mediterranean, and at the same time, draws them into the legendary past of the French and the Normans' (15).

Geoffrey recounts much of the legendary history of Britain, including the tale of Lear and his three daughters, and the reign of Belinus, who with his brother Brennius conquers Gaul and receives tribute from the Romans, an event to which Arthur later refers when Rome asks for tribute from him. Much of the early material in Geoffrey's *History*, like the story of Belinus and Brennius, sets the stage for the history of King Arthur, which makes up more than a third of the book, considerably more than is devoted to any other king. This section must therefore be seen as the narrative focal point.

An essential part of Geoffrey's chronicle is the account of Arthurian prehistory beginning with the three sons of King *Constantine: *Constans, Aurelius Ambrosius, and *Uther Pendragon. Geoffrey tells how Vortigern, himself eager to rule, convinces Constans, who has become a monk, to accept the crown so that he (Vortigern) can be the power behind the throne. Geoffrey develops the picture of Vortigern as a wicked ruler whose ambition and treachery wreak havoc on Britain, a picture that remains fairly standard in later chronicles. Not only does Vortigern arrange for his Pictish allies to kill Constans, after which he has them put to death, but he has himself crowned and invites the Saxons, led by Hengist and Horsus, into Britain. It is also through Vortigern that Merlin is introduced into the story. When Vortigern tries to build a tower, it falls each night; his wizards advise him that the solution to this problem is to seek a child who had no father and to sprinkle his blood on the site. When Vortigern's messengers hear a child being taunted for being fatherless, they bring him to the king. The youth tells Vortigern the true reason his tower will not stand, that under its foundation is a pool of water in which two dragons live.

Geoffrey combines the figure of the youth Ambrosius Aurelianus from Nennius and the Celtic figure of Myrddin in his character Ambrosius Merlinus; and in so doing he virtually creates the figure of Merlin as we know him from almost all later Arthurian literature, another of Geoffrey's seminal contributions to the Arthurian tradition. His Merlin interprets the struggle between the red and white dragons as emblematic of the ultimate defeat of the British (the red) by the Saxons (the white). He predicts the glory of Arthur, the Boar of Cornwall in the prophecy, and then launches into a long series of prophecies which occupy all of book 7 of the *History.* Originally written as a separate book in 1130, the *Prophetiae Merlini* was later included in the longer work. Many of the prophecies contain the obscure language and symbolic animal imagery familiar from later prophecies attributed to Merlin, and the book ends in an even more obscure apocalyptic prediction. (Geoffrey also wrote a poem called the *Vita Merlini* (*Life of Merlin*), discussed in Chapter 6.)

When Aurelius returns to Britain, he defeats Hengist and orders a memorial to be built to the British nobles treacherously killed by the Saxons at what was supposed to be a meeting to discuss peace. Merlin advises that the stone circle called the Dance of the Giants be obtained from Ireland, a feat which only he can engineer; he reassembles the stones, thus creating the monument known as *Stonehenge. Aurelius himself is buried there after he is poisoned by the Saxon Eopa, who poses as a monk familiar with the healing arts. Later, Uther, similarly poisoned by the Saxons, is buried alongside Aurelius.

The death of Aurelius and the succession of Uther is signalled by a comet 'stretching forth one ray whereon was a ball of fire spreading forth in the likeness of a dragon, and from the mouth of the dragon issued forth two rays', one of which reached beyond Gaul and the other of which ended 'in seven lesser rays'. Merlin interprets this portent, from which Uther takes the title Pendragon, as representing Uther and his two children, a son who shall have dominion over all the lands that lie beneath the long ray and a daughter whose sons and grandsons shall rule Britain (Geoffrey 169–70).

The brief description of Uther's reign recounts some of his victories over the Saxons and then focuses on his infatuation with Igerna (*Igraine), the wife of *Gorlois, Duke of Cornwall, who supported Uther, and Aurelius before him, in the wars against the Saxons. Perceiving Uther's attraction to his wife, Gorlois leaves court without permission and puts her in the impregnable castle of *Tintagel. Merlin uses his magic to change Uther's form so he resembles Gorlois and can enter the castle and satisfy his lust. Arthur is conceived on this night; and after the death of Gorlois and the marriage of Uther and Igerna, they have another child, a daughter named *Anna, who marries Loth (or *Lot) of Lothian and bears him two sons, Gawain and Modred. The introduction of the story of Arthur's marvellous birth, which has remained a part of the Arthurian tradition even into modern films and novels, is yet another of Geoffrey's innovations.

In describing the coronation of Arthur, Geoffrey begins to transform the *dux bellorum* of Nennius into the once and future king. And when Geoffrey writes that Arthur 'invited unto him all soever of most prowess from far-off kingdoms and began to multiply his household retinue' (194), he takes a step towards the order later referred to as the Knights of the Round Table. Arthur's reign is the supreme example of what Siân Echard has called the central theme of Geoffrey's book, 'the need for strong and legitimate central rule'; and since Arthur is 'a ruler who is strong, shrewd, and just, . . . the text continues to dwell on the golden results [of his reign] for some time' (Echard 38, 47). Those results include not only victories over the Saxons but also conquests on the continent.

After conquering Gaul, Arthur receives a letter from the Roman procurator Lucius demanding that he return the conquered lands to the Roman Empire and that he pay the tribute which Britain has owed to Rome for some time. Arthur's counter-demand for tribute from Rome sets the stage for an epic battle. His allies promise large numbers of knights to fight in his cause, so that he is able to raise an army of 183,200 knights as well as foot soldiers so numerous that they 'were not so easy to reckon' (208–9). Despite the scope of this struggle, Arthur's exploits begin with a personal triumph over the *Giant of St Michael's Mount, who has terrorized the territory of Arthur's ally *Hoel and kidnapped, attempted to ravish, and killed Hoel's niece. Arthur's victory over the giant, foreshadowed by his dream of a dragon (representing himself) defeating a horrendous bear (representing the giant), is followed by deeds of great valour by Arthur and other of his knights, especially Gawain, against the forces assembled by Rome. Ultimately, Arthur is victorious; but the joy of victory is short-lived because word comes to Arthur that his nephew Modred, who had been left in charge of the realm in the king's absence, has taken both Arthur's throne and his queen. The betrayal by Modred and the infidelity of Guinevere are still other of Geoffrey's innovations.

Upon Arthur's return to Britain, Gawain is killed in the battle against Modred; Guinevere flees to Caerleon to become a nun; and, finally, in a battle at the River Camel, Modred is killed. But Arthur too receives a fatal wound and is carried to 'the Isle of Avallon for the healing of his wounds' after yielding the crown to *Constantine, son of *Cador, Duke of Cornwall (236). The text seems contradictory in its assertion that Arthur goes to *Avalon to have his wound, which is said to be fatal, healed—though Geoffrey makes no claim that Arthur will return.

For many in the Middle Ages, Geoffrey provided authority for a historical king who conquered widely and who ruled gloriously. He also provided a wealth of material for writers both medieval and modern to build upon and reinterpret. Making Arthur into a medieval king and conqueror, the marvels surrounding whose birth marked him as special and who brought together the best of the chivalry of the world; the depiction of Merlin as a prophet and adviser to kings; the treachery of Modred and the infidelity of Guinevere—these are elements that now seem essential to the Arthurian tradition but that were popularized by Geoffrey.

Translations and Adaptations of Geoffrey's *Historia*

In addition to the many copies of Geoffrey's history that circulated in the Middle Ages, there were numerous translations and adaptations of the work. A translation into French verse, for example, survives in fragments containing 3361 lines from books 5–10 of Geoffrey's *Historia* (Blakey 45) in a manuscript known as the Harley *Brut* in the British Library's Harley collection. The Old Norse *Breta sögur* (*Sagas of the British*) is a loose translation of Geoffrey's book. A Latin verse version known as the *Gesta regum Britanniae* (sometimes attributed to William of Rennes) was written in the thirteenth century. There were also several translations 'often known as *Brut y Brenhinedd*, "the Brut of the Kings" ', into Welsh, three in the thirteenth century, two in the fourteenth, and 'amalgams of versions or combinations of texts were made up to the eighteenth century' (Roberts 111). And in the late fifteenth century Ponticus Virunnius, an Italian humanist, wrote a greatly abridged version in Latin prose. Although Geoffrey's history was not translated into English until 1718 when Aaron Thompson undertook the project, it nonetheless influenced English and French poems in the Middle Ages.

Gaimar and Wace

In the twelfth century, Geffrei Gaimar wrote a French version of Geoffrey's *Historia* and, in a work known as the *Estoire des Engleis*, continued the account of the history of Britain beyond where Geoffrey's ends. In all of the manuscripts in which this later history survives, Gaimar's adaptation of Geoffrey has been replaced by the more popular history written by Wace (cf. Tatlock 452).

The Norman poet Wace (b. *c*.1110, d. after 1174) wrote lives of St Marguerite and St Nicholas and a piece on the conception of Our Lady as well as the *Roman de Rou*, a chronicle of the dukes of Normandy. In 1155, he adapted Geoffrey's history in his *Roman de Brut*, written in French verse. Thus, though not the first to adapt Geoffrey into French, he was of great significance in popularizing the history of Britain, including the story of Arthur's reign, in a vernacular language. Working from what has been called the 'variant version' of Geoffrey's *Historia*, a 'redaction' of Geoffrey's text 'by an unknown contemporary of Geoffrey' sometime between 1138 and the early 1150s (Wright p. lxx), Wace sometimes condenses and sometimes adds descriptive passages (as in the account of the embarkation of Arthur's forces for the continent) but generally follows the narrative as set out in his source. He recounts, for example, most of the Arthurian prehistory in Geoffrey but declines to translate the prophecies of Merlin because he does not know how to interpret them, though he does record Merlin's predictions of Vortigern's death and of Arthur's glory.

In the *Roman de Brut*, upon the death of Uther, Arthur, as his son, is made king without contention or controversy. Arthur's courtly virtues are recognized, and he acquits himself well in battle. In one contest, he himself kills 400 Saxons, more than were killed by all his forces (cf. Wace 235). Since Arthur's nobility and courtesy make his court the most renowned in the world, it attracts the most noble knights. Because each of the 'noble barons' who comes to Arthur's court 'felt he was superior' and 'considered himself the best', Arthur orders the Round Table constructed so that all of them 'were placed equally round the table and equally served' and no one of the barons 'could boast he sat higher than his peer' (245). Wace's introduction here of the Round Table as a gathering of the greatest nobles of the world meeting as equals establishes a symbol that becomes a vital part of the Arthurian tradition.

Arthur's victories create a period of peace for twelve years, during which, writes Wace, 'the wondrous events appeared and the adventures were sought out which . . . are so often told about Arthur that they have become the stuff of fiction. . . . The raconteurs have told so many yarns, the story-tellers so many stories, to embellish their tales that they have made it all appear fiction' (247). As this passage confirms, even at this early date there existed a rich body of oral stories about the adventures of Arthur and his court, some of which may have provided material for Wace, who seems influenced by the courtly values that led to the flowering of the romance tradition in the works of Chrétien de Troyes and others. Wace's Uther, for example, acts like a courtly lover: 'even before seeing her [Ygerne], he had loved and desired her' (217).

When Arthur marries *Guinevere, Wace emphasizes her lineage and her courtly virtues: she was from 'a noble Roman family' and was beautiful, courteous, and well spoken with perfect manners and behaviour. But in addition to recounting her courtly qualities, Wace notes that she and Arthur 'produced no heir nor could they have any children' (243).

During a magnificent Pentecost feast at Caerleon, envoys from the Roman emperor demand tribute; and Arthur begins preparations for his continental war. Entrusting the kingdom to Modret and Guinevere, Arthur journeys to the continent, where he kills the Giant of St Michael's Mount and then advances to engage the Roman forces. In the war, Walwein distinguishes himself, but Kay and Bedivere are slain. Arthur is victorious, but his triumph is disturbed by news that Modret has usurped the throne and taken his wife; and so, realizing that 'All of his conquests would be of little value to him if he lost Britain, his own domain' (327), he returns to punish the traitor. In the landing back in his own realm, Walwein is killed. Guinevere goes to a convent, becomes a nun, and is never heard from again. In a final battle, at a place that Wace calls Camble, Modret is slain, and Arthur receives a mortal wound (though Wace does not indicate that they wounded each other). Wace acknowledges the belief of the Britons that Arthur was taken to Avalon and will return again, but he himself will say only what Merlin said: that Arthur's death would be doubtful. Thus, Wace is a witness to the belief in Arthur's survival, just as he is to oral tales about Arthur.

Layamon

Toward the end of the twelfth century or early in the thirteenth, an English clerk named Layamon (or Laȝamon) adapted Wace's chronicle into alliterative verse.

Layamon's verse form, which seems well suited to certain types of narrative, particularly accounts of battle, is midway between the strict Old English line and the looser line of the *Alliterative Revival. His half-lines are frequently linked by rhyme as well as by alliteration. In vocabulary as well as in verse form, Layamon is typically English—though the later Otho manuscript of the *Brut*, as opposed to the earlier Caligula manuscript, updates some of the language, sometimes using French forms where the earlier manuscript used native ones. Layamon also employs more dialogue than Wace and more extended similes.

Layamon follows the narrative structure of Wace's *Roman*, beginning with Brut and proceeding to Cadwalader, the last of the kings of Britain. And as in Wace, the Arthurian story is central to his book. Layamon does, however, abbreviate some parts of Wace's narrative and expand upon others, such as the story of the Round Table. Elaborating on the brief mention in Wace, Layamon describes a riot that breaks out when all those who have come to Arthur's famous court vie for a place at his table. It begins with loaves of bread and bowls of wine being thrown and escalates to fisticuffs and then to the use of weapons. Arthur needs a hundred armed men to bring order; and he punishes the man who started the riot by having him thrust into a bog, having his nearest kinsmen beheaded, and having the noses cut off his near kinswomen so their looks are ruined. A craftsman who has heard of the riot offers to make for the king a round table that will seat more than 1,600 people and that will ensure by its shape that the high will be on a par with the low so no one can claim precedence. Layamon adds that the British boast of this table and create many fables about Arthur.

The *Brut* also includes a number of supernatural elements, some of them traditional but some not. When Arthur is born, fairies take charge of him and enchant him so that he will live long, be the best of knights, and become a powerful and generous king (494). Merlin of course figures prominently in Arthur's birth and in the moving of the giant stones from Ireland to construct Stonehenge. Though, like Wace, Layamon does not include the extended prophecies of Merlin recounted by Geoffrey, he does make repeated mention of Merlin's predictions of Arthur's glory and of the mage's reliability as a prophet. Arthur's return from Avalon is mentioned not only at the end of the text but also earlier, in the context of Merlin's prediction that Arthur would journey to Avalon and be healed by a woman named *Argante, who is said to be 'fairest alre aluen' (the fairest of all fairies) (cf. Laȝamon 592 and 732). Given that Layamon comments on the veracity of Merlin's prophecies several times, including in the second of the references to Arthur's return, he is clearly endorsing the belief in the return, which the Britons still await.

Layamon's account of the events surrounding the end of Arthur's reign is distinctive not only in the naming of Argante (which may or may not be a variant of *Morgan, who is Arthur's healer in the *Vita Merlini*). His *Brut* introduces a premonitory dream in which Arthur is bestriding a high hall which becomes unstable when Modred cuts through the posts supporting it and Guinevere pulls down the roof with her bare hands. After Arthur falls and breaks his arm, he cuts off

Modred's head, hacks Guinevere to pieces, and thrusts her into a dark pit (718). A lion carries Arthur to the sea, where a fish brings him back to land. The dream obviously predicts the end of Arthur's realm because of the treachery of Modred and Guinevere and Arthur's slaying of Modred—though in actuality Guinevere is not hacked to pieces, as in the dream, but goes to Caerleon and becomes a nun. Layamon adds a cryptic statement about her, saying that it was not known whether she was dead when she herself was drowned in the water ('isunken in þe watere', Laȝamon 728). This phrase is sometimes interpreted as meaning 'when she disappeared', but only because otherwise it would refer to an unprecedented end for the queen. It is possible, however, that Layamon had in mind some story not elsewhere recorded.

Layamon's poem is of great significance because it is often a lively, sometimes dramatic, and wonderfully descriptive version of the Arthurian story. But perhaps more important is the fact that by adapting Wace's version of Geoffrey of Monmouth's history, Layamon made the story of Arthur as king and emperor available for the first time in (surviving) English verse.

Perceforest

As late as the fourteenth century, the direct influence of Geoffrey on romance can be seen in the long French prose tale *Perceforest* (written *c.*1337–44). Opening with an account, based on Geoffrey's *Historia*, of Britain's history from its founding by Brutus 'to the rather insignificant King Pir, whose death leaves the kingdoms of England and Scotland in a state of political and chivalric abjection' (Taylor, 'The Sense' 100), the romance tells of the coming of Alexander the Great to Britain with his companions Gadifer and Bétis, who later takes the name Perceforest. Alexander and his companions create an order of chivalry, the Franc Palais, which prefigures Arthur's Round Table, and restore order to the island until Caesar destroys the courtly culture they have established. Although chivalry is revived, it suffers again with the Danish invasions. Arthur, who is descended from Perceforest, restores chivalry once again. The romance concludes with the coming of *Joseph of Arimathea and the Grail, perhaps as the culmination of the development of chivalry and religion in Britain.

Romances Focusing on Arthur

The Middle English romance known as the *Alliterative Morte Arthure*, written in alliterative verse in the late fourteenth century, is among the greatest Arthurian romances of the Middle Ages and one of the few firmly in the chronicle tradition. There is disagreement as to the exact source used by the author—Geoffrey of Monmouth, Wace, Layamon, and various chronicles influenced by Geoffrey have been suggested—and it is generally acknowledged that he drew on various French romances, including an Alexander romance, as the source of some episodes. The author was also familiar with the history of Arthur in some form that derives from Geoffrey's *Historia* but used his own talents for portraying epic scope and significant detail, for producing artistic parallels that are not boringly symmetrical, and for depicting heroic valour and heroic humour.

The *Alliterative Morte Arthure* recounts the Roman wars and the end of Arthur's reign. It begins, after some preliminaries which tell of Arthur's conquests, when the Roman Emperor Lucius sends envoys to demand tribute from Britain and Arthur assembles his allies for an expedition to the continent to meet and defeat his adversary. There are two movements in the poem, the first detailing the war between the two emperors and the second depicting Arthur's return to Britain to take vengeance on his traitorous nephew Mordred, who has usurped the king's throne and taken his wife. Each of the movements is foreshadowed by a dream.

Arthur's first dream is of a fierce bear fighting with and ultimately being killed by a dragon. The struggle between these two beasts is told in lively verse and with descriptive brilliance. It is, of course, only one of many different kinds of conflicts skilfully described in the poem, which is among the greatest battle poems in English literary history and second only to *Sir Gawain and the Green Knight* as a masterpiece of the Alliterative Revival. In addition to the battle between the beasts, there are epic conflicts between armies, single combats, skirmishes and pitched battles on land, and sea battles—all described with alliterative enthusiasm.

As in Geoffrey's *Historia*, the first dream foreshadows Arthur's fight with the Giant of St Michael's Mount, a scene that exemplifies the author's skill at using tradition and yet artistically shaping details. Arthur, accompanied as usual by only Kay and Bedivere, encounters the governess of the Duchess of Brittany, who in this account is said to be Arthur's wife's cousin (158) and who has been abducted, raped, and killed by the giant. The giant, who lives outside the law, also dines on children seasoned with 'pickle and powder of precious spices'; and when Arthur first sees him, he is chomping on a human thigh, as maidens forced into his service tend a pot full of animal and human meat and turn a spit on which christened children are being roasted (162–4). The poet then gives a grisly description of the giant that extends for thirty alliterative lines. In his fight with the giant and before he gives him his fatal wound, Arthur cuts asunder the giant's genitals, an appropriate punishment for this ravisher of Christian maidens. As the injured giant tries to squeeze the life out of the king and breaks three of his ribs, Arthur stabs him to death with his dagger.

In the dream that begins the second major movement of the poem, Arthur sees Fortuna spinning her wheel and bringing low the Worthies, the greatest conquerors and most powerful kings who have ever lived. Arthur is, of course, the first of the Christian Worthies and thus one of those who will have a fall, which begins when Sir Craddok brings word from Caerleon that Mordred has taken the king's throne and his wife (called Waynor or Gaynor rather than Guinevere in the poem). In interpreting Arthur's second dream, his philosophers accuse him of excessive pride and warn him to repent. As Thorlac Turville-Petre has observed, some modern critics see these lines and a few other references to sin 'as the key to the poem' which, in this reading, becomes a condemnation of Arthur's excesses. But Turville-Petre is undoubtedly correct when he writes that this 'explanation suggested for the hero's fall by his philosophers, and taken up at various points in the poem, simply does not accord with the tone of the poem as a whole' (103). Nor does it accord with the final scenes of the poem in which the narrator, Gawain, Arthur, and Mordred himself blame Mordred for the tragic events surrounding Arthur's fall. This is not to say that the poem does not describe a Boethian tragedy of fortune, as some critics have suggested, but that such a tragedy occurs not as a punishment for sin and not because Arthur has become evil, which he has not, but because it is the nature of worldly fame and fortune to pass. This meaning seems clear from Arthur's dream, in which all the Worthies who preceded him have had their falls, including David, who is remembered in the poem for having slain Goliath and composed the Psalms and not for any wicked deeds.

In the first movement of the poem, Gawain begins the fighting between the two armies when, as Arthur's envoy to the Romans, he is offended by the insults of Sir Gayous, Lucius' uncle, and beheads him in the Roman camp. Similarly, in the second movement of the poem, Gawain begins the fighting by leading the landing back onto British soil. But in both movements, it is Arthur himself who has the climactic victory. Arthur ends the war by slaying Lucius, thus framing his continental expedition with victories over a giant and an emperor. This significant detail is not found in other versions. In Geoffrey's *Historia*, for example, Lucius is killed by a spear-thrust from an unknown hand. While the anonymous slaying may suggest the realities and confusion of a pitched battle, it does not give the decisive victory to the hero of the work, which is what the author of the *Alliterative Morte* does. In the second movement of the poem, Arthur himself slays Mordred in a battle made all the more poignant because Mordred fights with Arthur's sword *Clarent, the location of which in Arthur's wardrobe only Waynor knew (257). Thus, the very presence of the sword is a reminder of the depth of Mordred's crimes and sins.

A masterful romance in the chronicle tradition, the *Alliterative Morte Arthure* is distinctive in that it has Arthur as its hero. There are only a few other romances in which Arthur is the central figure, the knight errant fulfilling quests himself, and not merely the symbolic force and moral centre who sends other knights to right wrongs and have adventures. The fourteenth-century Latin prose romance *Arthur and Gorlagon*, for example, describes Arthur's search for an understanding of women, which his queen has told him he lacks. He vows not to eat until he has achieved that understanding and visits three brothers, each of whom urges him to dismount and eat and promises to give him the knowledge he seeks the next day. Arthur complies with the requests of the first two but finds that they cannot enlighten him. He refuses to dine with the third brother, Gorlagon, until he has his answer. Gorlagon tells him a tale of a man turned into a werewolf by his wife. Gorlagon himself was the werewolf and, after being helped by his brothers and turned back to a man, he punished his former wife by making her keep the bloody head of her lover before her and kiss it whenever he kissed his new wife. Arthur then eats, presumably having learned something about the nature of women; but there is no mention of whether the queen thinks he now understands them.

In *Le Chevalier du Papegau* (*The Knight of the Parrot*), a French prose romance of the early fifteenth century, Arthur himself sets off just after his coronation on what Jane Taylor has called a 'year-long chivalrous sabbatical' ('The Parrot' 532). His journey is prompted by a damsel requesting aid for her lady, who is plagued by a knight who destroys her knights and her realm. Early in his quest, Arthur wins a parrot which sings and talks, thus providing entertainment and advice as well as the name by which Arthur is known throughout the tale. As the Knight of the Parrot, Arthur has many stock romance adventures, including assisting several damsels in distress, jousting with knights thought to have no peer in battle, encountering unicorns, dwarfs, and giants, and crossing a perilous bridge.

Arthur is again prominent in a late prose account of *The Famous History of That Most Renowned Christian Worthy Arthur King of the Britaines, and his Famous Knights of the Round Table*. Written by Martin Parker (d. 1656?), known as a writer of ballads, and published posthumously in 1660, *The Famous History* briefly recounts Arthur's birth, Merlin's tutoring, Arthur's ascension to the throne, his defeat of the Saxons, his foreign victories, and his founding of the Round Table. Parker names all 150 knights who sat at the table, some of whom are traditional but many of whom are not. In the final movement of the tale, Arthur leads his knights to Palestine and achieves 'the total rout of the whole Pagan host' (Parker 18). Hearing of Mordred's treachery, Arthur must return to Britain, where both he and Mordred are slain in the final battle.

But aside from these romances and portions of larger ones like Malory's *Morte d'Arthur* that have been influenced by the chronicle tradition, there are few medieval works in which the deeds of Arthur, as opposed to his symbolic presence, are crucial.

OTHER LATIN CHRONICLES

A number of Latin chronicles reveal interesting details about Arthur and the legend of his survival. They also demonstrate knowledge of various sources, including Nennius and at times Geoffrey, but sometimes reflect other traditions not found in the standard histories.

William of Malmesbury (*c.*1095–*c.*1143), for example, in his *History of the Kings of England* (*Gesta regum Anglorum*, 1125), speaks briefly of Arthur's role in the wars against the Saxons, observing that he 'was long the mainstay of his falling country, rousing to battle the broken spirit of his countrymen' and winning a great victory at Mount Badon (27). William also describes the finding of Gawain's grave on the seashore, where he was killed either in battle or 'by his fellow-citizens at a public feast'. William adds that Arthur's grave has not been found.

Henry of Huntingdon (*c.*1088–*c.*1157) tells in some detail of the ravages of the Saxons in Britain in his *History of the English People* (*Historia Anglorum*), which was finished about 1129 and then updated to about 1154. Henry says of Arthur, whom he describes as the 'commander of the soldiers and kings of Britain': 'Twelve times he led in battle. Twelve times was he victorious' (99); Henry then recounts the twelve battles as in Nennius. About 1139, in a 'Letter to Warin the Breton', Henry explains why he began his history with Julius Caesar and not with Brutus by saying that he had no authority for the earlier events until he discovered a book (Geoffrey's *Historia*), which he summarizes. In this letter, which includes not only the early material from Geoffrey but also other information not found in his own history, he mentions Arthur's continental wars and the treachery of Mordred, who usurps the throne and marries Arthur's wife. Arthur returns to behead Mordred but dies from the wounds he receives in the battle. Henry adds that the Bretons think he lives on and they await his return.

The *Vera historia de morte Arthuri* (*True History of the Death of Arthur*) (c.1200) is a short Latin prose account of the death of Arthur notable for its variations from traditional versions of the story. Arthur, wounded at the last battle, is attacked by a handsome youth who hurls a 'shaft of elm' that has been sharpened and tempered and 'daubed with adders' venom' (85) into the king. Though Arthur slays the fleeing youth, he dies after being taken to Avalon, which is said to be in Gwynedd. As his body lies outside the chapel of the Virgin Mary, whose entrance is too narrow to allow the bier inside, a terrible storm arises, followed by a mist so dense that people can see nothing. When the mist passes, the body is gone. As a result, some believe Arthur is still alive; others believe that he is in his tomb, which was found sealed when the mist dispersed.

The *Draco Normannicus* (*The Norman Dragon*, 1169), written in Latin verse by Etienne de Rouen, sees in certain events of twelfth-century history the fulfilment of prophecies by Merlin. It includes an account of the deeds of Rollo, the Viking who founded the Norman duchy; of the dukes of Normandy, including William's conquest of England; of French political history, including Charlemagne's reign; and of the accession of Henry II to the British throne and his problems in Brittany and elsewhere. Etienne then inserts into his 'primarily factual' chronicle the 'Breton hope' of Arthur's return (Day 154) in the form of letters between Henry and King Arthur, in which Arthur recounts his battle with Emperor Lucius, the betrayal of Mordred, and his being healed in Avalon by Morgan, who makes him immortal ('perpetuumque facit') (Etienne de Rouen 703); and Arthur threatens to return if Henry does not relent in his attacks on Brittany. In his response, Henry asserts his claim to Brittany but agrees to hold it as Arthur's vassal. (This is followed by an account of the death and burial of Empress Matilda, the cause of Henry's concluding his campaign in Brittany and an event foreseen by Arthur, and other historical events with no Arthurian connection.) But the 'true impact' of Henry's arrangement with Arthur is that he will not be a fairy king like Arthur but will 'hold Brittany under the law of Christ' (Day 157).

While Merlin's prophecies are accepted by the *Draco Normannicus*, they are ridiculed by William of Newburgh (1136?–c.1198?) in the preface to his *History*

(*Historia rerum Anglicarum*, 1198). In fact, William chastises Geoffrey for trying to 'dignify' the fictions about Arthur 'with the name of authentic history' (William of Newburgh 398).

THE CONTINUING CHRONICLE TRADITION IN ENGLAND AND SCOTLAND

English Metrical and Prose Chronicles
Robert of Gloucester

Robert of Gloucester (*fl.* 1260–1300) is the author of part, though probably not all, of *The Metrical Chronicle*, an English verse history in rhyming couplets beginning typically with the fall of Troy and progressing, in the longer of the two versions of the chronicle, up to the year 1272. The chronicle tells in detail the pre-Arthurian history of the arrival of the Saxons and their gaining a foothold in Britain thanks to Vortiger's folly, of the treachery of the Saxons, of Vortiger's attempt to build a castle that will not stand and the finding of the boy with no father, Merlin, who predicts Vortiger's death. Merlin also foresees the birth and the victories of King Arthur, but his other prophecies are said to be omitted because they are 'so derc to simplemen', that is, incomprehensible to common men (1. 201). 'Robert' depicts well Arthur's conquests and the betrayal of Modred and Gwenwar (Guinevere), who advised Modred to have himself crowned. After slaying Modred, Arthur is taken to 'an yle' to have his wounds healed; but 'Robert' is sure of Arthur's death since his bones have been found at Glastonbury (1. 317, 324), a reference to the discovery of a grave purported to be Arthur's at Glastonbury in 1190 or 1191.

Though the verse of *The Metrical Chronicle* is often maligned, it is as workmanlike as that of much Middle English narrative poetry for a popular audience. Occasionally it can be quite lively, as in the story of the Giant of St Michael's Mount. And at times the author uses some interesting, if not unique, images, as when he says that he could not recount all the grandeur of Arthur's Whitsuntide feast even if his tongue were made of steel (1. 292–8, 277).

Short Metrical Chronicle

The anonymous *Short Metrical Chronicle* (completed *c.*1307), also in rhymed couplets, which gives an abbreviated version of the history of Britain, exists in several different versions in various manuscripts. In one manuscript, Arthur is hardly mentioned. Others give more details about him, but the details vary. He is said in one to have been betrayed by Mordred, who seized England and committed adultery with the queen. In this account, Arthur returns to Britain, reclaims it, and, contrary to tradition, lives ten more years (69–70). But in another version, more influenced by the romance than the chronicle tradition, Arthur fights a war against *Lancelot over the queen; Lancelot returns her to the king but promises further war if Arthur reproaches her.

Robert Mannyng of Brunne

English poet Robert Mannyng of Brunne (Bourne in Lincolnshire) (*fl.* 1288–1338) was the author of the religious instructional poem *Handlyng Synne*, which was translated early in the fourteenth century from the Anglo-Norman *Manuel des péchés*. He also composed a *Chronicle* (sometimes called *The Story of England*) (1338) based largely on the *Roman de Brut* by Wace and the *Chronicle* of Pierre de Langtoft (*fl.* 1271–1307) but also borrowing from Geoffrey of Monmouth and other sources to tell the history of Britain from its origins to the death of Edward I (1307).

Mannyng's verse *Chronicle* gives a fairly standard account of Arthurian prehistory, including Vortigern's folly and treachery and his struggles with the three sons of Constantine, Merlin's revelation of the reason why his tower will not stand and his prediction of Vortigern's death, the treachery of the Saxons and the death of the three brothers, as well as Uther's love for Igerne. But Mannyng admits that he does not recount Merlin's prophecies because they are too obscure: 'I haf no witte | to open þe knottis þat Merlyn knytte' (I am not learned enough to untie the knots that Merlin has tied) (285). He does, however, include a delightful account of Merlin's building a monument at Stonehenge by using cunning and wisdom to move the megaliths that giants had brought to Ireland when the stones could not be moved with ropes and pulleys and the brute force of the men who had been sent to fetch them.

Yet Merlin's greatest feat remains the engineering not of Stonehenge but of the birth of Arthur, whose reign is a high point of British history. The feast at Arthur's coronation, at which Bedivere and a thousand men clad in ermine serve the wine and the guests enjoy games and minstrelsy of all sorts, is described with as much grand detail as Arthur's conquests on the continent and his war with Emperor Lucius. Arthur's glory is brought to an end, however, when Mordred, his sister's son, betrays him by taking possession of the king's land and by taking Arthur's queen as his 'hore' (422). Upon his return to Britain, Arthur kills Mordred and is himself mortally wounded. Mannyng recognizes the belief that Arthur still lives and will return; but he mocks the notion, saying 'if he life [live], his life is long', and then asserts unequivocally that the king was mortally wounded (428).

Thomas Castleford's *Chronicle*

The verse *Chronicle* (c.1330) ascribed to Thomas Castleford, whose name appears on the manuscript but for whose authorship of the text there is no evidence (cf. Eckhardt in Castleford p. xi), contains an extended account of Arthurian prehistory and of Arthur's reign. Perhaps the most notable feature of the events preceding Arthur's birth is the inclusion of Merlin's prophecies for the first time in an English text (cf. Eckhardt in Castleford p. xiii). Also prominent is the role of Gorlois, who demonstrates his importance as a military ally in Aurelius' campaign against Hengist and as an adviser when Uther's forces are almost defeated by Occas and Eose. In an extended speech, Gorlois advises an attack that leads to the capture of the Saxon commanders and the defeat of their forces. The prominence given to

Gorlois and the emphasis on his service to the crown make Uther's betrayal of him seem much more disturbing than in those accounts in which Gorlois is hardly mentioned before Uther lusts after Igraine.

Arthur's reign, however, is presented as glorious and triumphant. He restores destroyed churches and ushers in twelve years of peace before conquering Norway, Denmark, and France. His coronation feast is as magnificent as the one described by Mannyng. And he defeats the Roman Emperor Lucius before being betrayed by Modred and Gainor (Guinevere). Although Castleford earlier included Merlin's prophecy that Arthur's death would be in doubt, he says twice that Arthur lived only a short time after being taken to Avalon.

John Hardyng

Another English metrical chronicle, this one in rhyme royal stanzas, was written by John Hardyng (1378–c.1465) and survives in two versions, a longer one completed by 1457 and a shorter one completed by 1464 In the shorter version, Hardyng reduces the story of Merlin's birth and his prophecies (even eliminating the prophecies of the downfall of Vortiger and the coming of Arthur) because he is unable 'to write of such affirmably' (Hardyng, ed. Ellis 115), but he does recount the coming of the Saxons, led by Hengist and Horsus, and their treachery in killing Vortimer, Aurelius, and Uther.

According to Hardyng, Arthur's reign begins in 516. After subduing the Saxons and conquering France, he returns to England, where at a great Whitsuntide feast, *Galahad arrives. Hardyng is of particular interest among chroniclers for including an account of the quest for the Holy Grail. He notes that Uther constructed the Round Table and the *Siege Perilous in memory of Joseph of Arimathea's Grail table. As is traditional, Galahad is able to sit in the Siege Perilous as a sign that he is the chosen Grail knight; but contrary to tradition, Galahad is born to Launcelot and King *Pelles' daughter 'in very clene spousage' (Hardyng, ed. Ellis 131). The same phrase is used in the long version of the chronicle to exonerate Igraine from any blame when she sleeps with Uther 'Trustyng it was so done in clene spousage' (Hardyng, ed. Harker 78); the implication is that Launcelot and Pelles' daughter are married when Galahad is born.

After Galahad achieves the Grail, Arthur receives the demand from Lucius for 'truage', which leads to the war in which Arthur slays Lucius and sends his head to Rome in payment of the tribute and his body for the 'arerage' or back payments (Hardyng, ed. Ellis 144). Arthur is crowned emperor and spends the winter in Rome; but his triumph is interrupted by news that Mordred has claimed the crown and wed Gwaynour (Guinevere). Arthur and Mordred wound each other mortally, and the king goes to Avalon to have his wounds healed. Hardyng, however, leaves no doubt about his death; he observes that Arthur is buried at Glastonbury. Gwaynour becomes a nun; and Launcelot joins Geryn, another of the king's knights, in contemplation as 'preastes' who were 'about his [Arthur's] toumbe alwaye' saying prayers, wearing hair shirts, fasting, and doing penance (Hardyng, ed.

Ellis 147). This account of Lancelot is unusual in the chronicle tradition and, like Hardyng's inclusion of the Grail quest, demonstrates the fluidity of the boundaries between romance and chronicle.

Arthur

In the fifteenth-century manuscript known as the Red Book of Bath (Longleat MS 55), there is a short chronicle in Latin prose beginning with the coming of Brutus to Albion. Inserted into the Latin of the chronicle is the story of Arthur in English rhyming couplets. After Arthur's reign, the Latin resumes with the reign of Constantine. The manuscript is also distinguished by a crude drawing of Arthur's sword (called *Caliburnus in a Latin gloss but 'Brounstell' in the text) at the point at which he uses it to slay Frollo. The account of Arthur's reign is much abbreviated. It does, however, include the fight with the Giant of St Michael's Mount, said to be a giant from Spain, and Arthur's conquests on the continent, including his defeat of Lucius, whose forces, despite numerical superiority, have no more chance than twenty sheep against five large wolves (15). The short poem (just over 640 lines) is punctuated with six injunctions to recite the Paternoster or the Pater and the Ave Maria, almost as if the prayers are in gratitude for or in support of Arthur's activities. The poem ends with the death of Arthur and the report that the Bretons and Cornish believe he will come again.

English Prose Chronicles

In 1387, John of Trevisa (1340s–1402) translated Ranulf Higden's *Polychronicon* into English prose. The section on Arthur is brief, alluding to rather than recounting the conquests on the continent. Arthur's battles in Britain, leading up to Badon, are listed; and his death at the hands of Mordred, his burial, and the discovery of his body are recorded. Though Trevisa spends little time on Arthur's reign, he defends Arthur's historicity against the charges that he is not referred to in continental chronicles by arguing that each nation emphasizes its own heroes and pointing out that John recounts incidents in his Gospel that are not treated by the other evangelists. Trevisa does, however, admit that there are far-fetched ('magel') tales about Arthur, including the legend that he will return to rule Britain (339).

Versions of the chronicle known as the *Prose Brut* written in French and Latin as well as in English survive in more than 240 manuscripts, and there were numerous early printings, including two by Caxton (cf. Matheson 1–8). Such dissemination suggests that the *Prose Brut* was a standard popular account of British history—and also that the text was dynamic, with variations and additions in different manuscripts. The English rendition of the *Prose Brut*, written late in the fourteenth century, seems like a condensed version of Arthurian history as it appears in Geoffrey's *Historia* and other chronicles. Often just the bare bones of the narrative are given. For example, in Arthur's fight with the giant of the Mount of St Bernard (as it is called here, instead of the typical St Michael's Mount), there is none of the delight in the details of the struggle that is found in some versions of this tale; the narrative says only that Arthur fought with the giant and killed him (85). Other conflicts, including the world war of Arthur's forces against the Roman emperor's and the civil war of Arthur's forces against Mordred's, are handled with similar abbreviation. Without the elaborations of battles or the magnificent description of an account like Robert Mannyng's, this chronicle sometimes reads like a primer of British history.

The story of Arthurian Britain is condensed almost to nothingness in the *Abbreuiation of Cronicles* (1462–3) by John Capgrave (1393–1464), which makes only a brief mention of Arthur as a conqueror and of his dying at Avalon. Capgrave also records the finding of the bones of Arthur and his second wife 'Veneraca' at Glastonbury (69, 110).

Scottish Chronicles (in Latin and Scottish)

A number of Scottish chroniclers offer a fairly traditional view of Arthur. Andrew of Wyntoun (1350?–1420?), for example, writes in his Scottish verse history, the *Original Chronicle* (c.1420), of Arthur's valour and his conquests and of how he and his Round Table were undone by the 'tressoune till him done' by Mordred (24). Similarly John Leslie (1527–96), in his *Historie of Scotland* (written in Latin prose as *De origine, moribus, et rebus gentis Scotorum* in 1578 and translated by James Dalrymple in 1596), speaks of Arthur's courage, honour, and nobility, and tells of the Round Table that Arthur created to prevent any of his twenty-four knights from feeling slighted because he was set lower at table. Leslie doubts the veracity of accounts of Arthur's conquests on the continent as well as in places like Scotland and the Orkneys. He also claims that ultimately Arthur was slain by the Scots and Picts and that his wife Guanora was kept in custody by the Picts after his death.

Other Scottish histories are more chauvinistic in their chronicling of events. Some of these chronicles enhance the role of the Scots in resisting the Saxon invaders. Several go so far as to question the right of Arthur to rule and suggest that Mordred was justified in his rebellion because Arthur had violated a pledge he had made concerning succession.

John of Fordun and Walter Bower

In his long Latin history of the Scots, *Chronica gentis Scotorum* (c.1385), Scottish chronicler John of Fordun (d. 1384?) tells briefly the events of Arthurian prehistory, drawing largely on Geoffrey of Monmouth for accounts of Vortigern's inviting the Saxons to protect the British from the attacks of the Scots and Picts, of his son Vortimer's attempt to drive the Saxons from Britain, and of Aurelius Ambrosius' resistance of the Saxons. Fordun even makes reference to Merlin's prophecies but records only a few of them. In Fordun's account, though the Picts ally themselves with the Saxons, the Scots fight with the Britons against the foreign invaders. Aurelius is poisoned by the Saxons and succeeded by his brother Uther, 'a man excessively given to stirring up civil war among his subjects' (Fordun i. 98). When Uther is also poisoned by the Saxons, his son Arthur, in Fordun's words, 'by the contrivance of certain men, succeeded to the kingdom; which, nevertheless, was not lawfully his due, but rather his sister Anna's or her children's. For she was begotten in lawful wedlock and married to Loth, a Scottish consul and lord of Laudonia (Lothian),... and of her he begat two sons—the noble Galwanus and Modred—whom, on the other hand, some relate, though without foundation, to have had another origin' (Fordun i. 101). Thus Fordun implies that Arthur's birth was illegitimate and that Gawain and Modred had a right to the throne; he claims that Arthur was chosen king because of expediency, the need to have someone old enough to lead men in battle against the Saxons—Gawain being only 12 at the time. Fordun argues that necessity 'has no law, both with gods and men' (Fordun i. 102), and suggests that it was this unlawful crowning of Arthur that led Modred to rebel against him.

In the *Scotichronicon*, his continuation of Fordun's chronicle written in Latin in the 1440s, Walter Bower notes the same contradiction in Geoffrey's account that John of Fordun did, that is, that at one point Geoffrey suggests that Anna is the sister of Aurelius (Bower ii. 67). Though both authors think it more probable that she is Arthur's sister, as Geoffrey also writes, the mention of this discrepancy raises the possibility that, as the son of Aurelius' sister, Mordred would have an even stronger claim to the throne.

Hector Boece and his Translators

Hector Boece (c.1465–1536) published his Latin prose chronicle *Scotorum historiae* in 1527, and it was translated into Scottish prose by John Bellenden (*fl.* 1533–87) at the command of James V. In Bellenden's account, completed in 1533, the Scots and sometimes the Picts fight with the British against the invading Saxons. And Anna is said to be the daughter of Ambrose (Ambrosius Aurelianus)—'Ambrose, King of Britonis, had twa dochteris [surely a mistranslation or misprint for "sisters", the reading of the verse translation of Boece's chronicle discussed below], of quhilkis þeldest, namyt Anna, was marijt on Lothus, King of Pichtis' (Bellenden i. 352)—and not the sister of Arthur; and thus her children Modred and Waluanus (Gawain) have a better claim to the throne than Arthur. Lothus (Lot), here said to be king of the Picts, fights with the Saxons against the British only because they 'intendit to defraude his sonnys of þe crovne of Britain' (Bellenden i. 362). Uther is presented as degenerate and shameful in his lust. Since he sires Arthur before the death of Gothlois (Gorlois), there is no question but that Arthur is 'gottin in adultery' (Bellenden i. 360). Even so, Modred's rebellion comes only after Arthur names Constantine as his successor, in violation of his agreement that no one should succeed to the throne of Britain after his death except the sons of Lot and Anna and their heirs. Nor is Mordred's legal and moral position tainted by stealing Arthur's wife, as it is in some accounts. His cause is presented as just since he claims only what has been promised by the king.

Boece's chronicle was translated into Scottish verse, also at the command of James V, by William Stewart (c.1480–c.1550) as *The Buik of the Chroniclis of Scotland* (1535). Stewart is even stronger than Bellenden in his justification of Modred's rebellion. Anna is clearly the elder of Aurelius' two 'sisteris' (Stewart 189). And

Stewart describes at some length the promise Arthur makes that Lot's heirs should rule after Arthur's death. But Arthur is persuaded by the British nobles, who have been led astray by their prosperity, to break the oath. Stewart says repeatedly that Arthur and the nobles act contrary to their 'aith' (oath) and 'oblissing' (a word suggesting moral and/or legal obligation) or, in the verbal form, what they had 'obleist' (Stewart 250, 251, and 252). Modred acts reasonably at first, petitioning Arthur to keep his word. It is only when Arthur resorts to sophistry and asserts that since the oath was made to Lot, it is not binding after his death, that Modred mounts a rebellion to claim what is rightfully his. In the end, Stewart's judgement is that Arthur was 'faithles and wntrew | To king Modred' (Stewart 262), thus according Lot's son the title that Arthur denied him. Stewart, who like Bellenden does not depict Arthur as the conqueror of Europe or an emperor, suggests that Arthur is like Finn MacCool and Robin Hood, in that many lies are told about him and that anyone who claims more for Arthur than he has recorded is deceived or deceiving (Stewart 261–2).

John Major

In his *Historia Majoris Britanniae* (*History of Greater Britain*, 1521), John Major (b. 1469 or 1470) gives a fairly conventional account of Arthurian prehistory, including Vortiger's folly, his love for Hengist's daughter Ronovem, and Hengist's treachery. The stories of Merlin's strange birth and his being taken before Vortiger and revealing the water and the two dragons beneath the tower Vortiger is trying to build and of the poisoning of Aurelius are told much as they are in Geoffrey of Monmouth. But unlike Geoffrey, Major offers three explanations for Merlin's birth: that his mother lied about knowing a man because he was a religious or was related or was of low birth, that his mother was impregnated by a 'sucubus demon', or that a demon opened her chamber door and let a man in. Major rejects the second explanation and denies that Merlin had no father (75–6). Major also denies to Merlin great powers of prophecy. He says that 'the demon' revealed to Merlin such things as the water and dragons beneath the tower because he could 'read the signs of the times and forecast the future more clearly than is possible to man'; but the demon is unable to foretell 'things future and contingent'; and later Major criticizes the murky nature of the prophecies ascribed to Merlin, because of which their meaning is not recognized until after an event happens (77, 81). Major also blames Merlin for sinning when he assisted Uther in fulfilling his lust by sleeping with another man's wife.

Major agrees with other Scottish chroniclers that Arthur was chosen king over the sons of Anna, whom he identifies as 'the sister of Aurelius'. While he recognizes 'the rights of the people to transfer from one race to another the kingly power', he believes such transfer should be done only after careful deliberation (82). He is thus, though a self-professed native of Lothian, less critical of Arthur's reign than some Scottish chroniclers and even admits that Arthur was noble, chivalrous, and valiant; but he rejects the idea that Arthur will return and dismisses many of the stories about Arthur and Gawain, 'unless indeed they were brought about by craft of demons' (85).

George Buchanan

Scottish historian George Buchanan (1506–82) wrote his history of the Scots, *Rerum Scoticarum historia*, in 1582. Like Major, Buchanan is critical of Merlin who, he asserts, was an 'egregious impostor and cunning pretender, rather than a prophet' because his 'vaticinations are . . . obscure, and contain nothing certain, on which, before the event happens, any rational anticipation can be founded. . . . Besides, they are composed in such a manner, that the same oracle may be twisted and accommodated to a great number of events' (238). Buchanan also considers Merlin to be Uter's 'procurer' because he assisted Uter as he 'overcame her [Igerne's] modesty' and then helped concoct 'a fable' about the transformation of Uter into the shape of Gorlois in order to 'dignify the misconduct of his wife'. Nevertheless, it is clear that Arthur was conceived in 'adulterous intercourse' (241).

Like earlier Scottish chroniclers, Buchanan considers Anna, the mother of Modred and Gawain, to be the sister of Uter and Aurelius and not Uter's daughter. He explains the confusion by suggesting that Uter 'had a daughter, another Anna, by a concubine' (240). Thus when Arthur names Constantine, son of Cadore, as his successor in contradiction to the treaty he had made guaranteeing that Lot's sons would succeed him, Modred rebels and claims the throne for 'the preservation of his dignity' (247). Despite the indignities to the Scottish line, Buchanan has much that is good to say about Arthur, who was brave, loved his country, and restored the true religion to Britain. Buchanan rejects, however, Geoffrey's tales of Arthur's conquests on the continent and claims that the 'fabulous accounts' of his exploits bring into doubt even those deeds that are true.

The Historical Arthur after the Middle Ages

Renaissance England, concerned as it was with questions of kingship and succession, turned primarily to chronicles for its Arthurian subject matter and sometimes used this material for political purposes. Henry VII, the first of the Tudor monarchs, traced his lineage and his claim to the throne back to Arthur and reinterpreted the legend so that not Arthur himself but his descendant, in the person of Henry VII, was said to have returned at a time of need (the Wars of the Roses) to restore stability to Britain. This Tudor myth was fostered initially by Henry VII, who named his first son Arthur, and then by Henry's successors.

Thus it is not surprising that an Englishman like John Leland (1503?–1552) would feel compelled to respond to the attacks on the historicity of Arthur written by the Italian Polydore Vergil. As King's Antiquary during the reign of Henry VIII, Leland had travelled throughout Britain gathering information on its past, a pursuit that gave him the evidence he needed to refute Vergil's charges. Leland's *Assertio inclytissimi Arturii regis Britanniae* (*Assertion of the Moste Renowned King Arthur of Britain*), published in 1544 and translated in 1582 (during the reign of Elizabeth I) by Richard Robinson, is the equivalent of a modern scholarly article based on both a reading and interpretation of earlier authors and his personal observations. From his travels, Leland offered as proof of historicity a detailed description of Arthur's seal, a transcription of the legend on the cross found at Arthur's grave site, and reports of local lore associating Cadbury with *Camelot.

Leland also provided more objective evidence. He cites numerous historians, complete with the Renaissance equivalent of footnotes. He presents an impressive number of sources, from Gildas and Nennius to writers of his own day. Astute enough both as historian and as rhetorician to recognize that some of the marvels referred to in the medieval chronicles are beyond belief, Leland draws a distinction between the fantastic and the factual and concludes that while the excesses of some earlier writers are regrettable, the weight of the evidence supports the historicity of Arthur.

This is an opinion that one might accept even today. As James Carley has said, 'In the final analysis, modern scholarship has not moved far beyond Leland in its approach to the question of Arthur's historical existence.... The conclusions reached by most historians in the twentieth century may be closer to Vergil's ... but the methodology resembles Leland's' (Carley 192). In fact, many of the issues Leland raises are still being debated by scholars: why does Gildas not mention Arthur as the victor at Badon? How reliable are historians who accept accounts of marvels that could not possibly be true? Is Cadbury Camelot? How accurate are the accounts of the finding of Arthur's grave and of the cross marking it at Glastonbury?

In *The History of Britain*, written over a period of many years and first published in 1670, John Milton (1608–74) drew on Gildas, Bede, Geoffrey of Monmouth, and other medieval historians for his account of early Britain. Milton, who had considered writing an Arthurian epic but rejected the idea in favour of a more religious theme, often cites the sources for his information and notes discrepancies, as when Nennius calls 'that Child without Father that propheci'd to *Vortigern* ... not *Merlin* but *Ambrose*' (Milton 155); and he uses his careful reading of sources to question Arthur's reputation and even to cast doubt on his very existence. He sees a contradiction between the figure of Arthur the great warrior and victor described by Nennius and the Arthur of Caradoc's *Life of St Gildas*, in which Melvas holds Arthur's queen for a year and Arthur must recover her by 'entreaty of *Gildas*, rather then for any enforcement' that he and his 'Chivalry could make against a small Town defended only by a moory situation' (Milton 167). He is similarly sceptical about Arthur's continental conquests, asserting that Arthur could not have undertaken such a campaign until after the twelve battles mentioned by Nennius, but that at that time, as Gildas says, civil war broke out among the British and so the urgency of the situation in Britain would have prevented foreign expeditions. Milton also challenges the tales on military grounds, since Arthur 'much better had made War in old *Saxony*, to repress thir flowing hither, then to have won Kingdoms as far as *Russia*' (170).

Even after the seventeenth century, the question of Arthur's historicity continued to be debated. Joseph Ritson (1752–1803) acknowledged that some have considered Arthur greater than Julius Caesar or Alexander the Great but that 'his very existence has, by others, been, positively and absolutely, denied' (Ritson p. i). His study, published posthumously in 1825, was called *The Life of King Arthur*, the very title suggesting acceptance of historicity, whatever scepticism Ritson may express about details contained in early chronicles.

Even in the twentieth century, as influential a chronicler as Winston Churchill (1874–1965) comments on the reserve of modern historians who 'timidly but resolutely' accept the historicity of Arthur. Churchill himself prefers to believe that the story Geoffrey of Monmouth told 'is not all fancy'. But Arthur has more the reality of symbol than historical fact, for, Churchill writes, 'King Arthur and his noble knights, guarding the Sacred Flame of Christianity and the theme of a world order, sustained by valour, physical strength, and good horses and armour, slaughtered innumerable hosts of foul barbarians and set decent folk an example for all time' (59–60). Churchill views Arthur as the model Christian ruler resisting the forces of heathen barbarism. As such, his struggle is an archetype of the resistance to the Nazis in the Second World War and to the Communists whom Churchill saw as a threat to Christian civilization.

ARTHUR'S DEATH AND SURVIVAL

The chronicle tradition persists in drama, poetry, and fiction after the Middle Ages. Some elements of that tradition have particular resonance. There are, for example, works that respond to accounts of the finding of Arthur's grave and that are influenced by the belief, recorded in a number of chronicles, that Arthur survives and will come again. Arthur's twelve battles, the general account of the Saxon invasions, the naming of Arthur as a 'dux bellorum', the withdrawal of the Roman army, and the survival of Roman traditions and families in Britain—all are motifs taken up in the post-medieval historical literature.

Arthur's Grave

The chronicles and the chronicle tradition have influenced literary history in a number of ways. Sometimes characters or events from the chronicles are the basis for later works, as is the case with the finding of Arthur's grave at Glastonbury. Described in a number of the chronicles discussed above, it is also recounted by Giraldus Cambrensis (1146?–1223?) in his *De principis instructione* (1193) and in his *Speculum ecclesiae* (1215). Giraldus records the inscription on the cross discovered in the grave, which names the site as the Isle of Avalon and the occupants of the grave as Arthur and his second wife Guinevere. And in both the *De principis* and the *Speculum ecclesiae*, Giraldus tells the story of the greedy monk who grabbed the lock of Guinevere's hair only to have it crumble to dust in his hands.

In 1777, Thomas Warton (1728–90) wrote a poem called 'The Grave of King Arthur' in which he described the songs of two bards to Henry II. The first tells a fabulous tale of Arthur's survival but the second, with a greater regard for historical fact, tells of Arthur's burial at Glastonbury and instils in Henry the desire to find and honour the tomb. The pre-Romantic enthusiasm for the subject exhibited in Warton's poem is apparent also in a painting (which survives only in sketches and an engraving) by John Hamilton Mortimer (1740–99) entitled *The Discovery of Prince Arthur's Tomb by the Inscription on the Leaden Cross* (c.1767). Aubrey De Vere (1814–1902) also treated the subject in 'King Henry the Second at the Tomb of King Arthur' (1892), in which the crumbling of the lock of Guinevere's hair found in the tomb makes Henry realize that 'all mortal pagentries' are but 'idle show' (102). John Masefield's poem 'Dust to Dust' (1928) makes a similar point. In 'The Grave of Arthur' (1930), another poem about Arthur's tomb, G. K. Chesterton (1874–1936) recognizes the distinction between fact and fiction not only about Arthur's death but about the very myth of Arthur. Chesterton observes both that 'Dead is a King that never was born' and that 'Dead is the King who shall not die' (3 (unnumbered)).

A novel by Diana Norman (b. 1948), *King of the Last Days* (1981), also revolves around the discovery of Arthur's grave. Norman postulates that Giraldus Cambrensis, who gives the date of the discovery as 1190, the year after Henry II's death, was unreliable and that the discovery actually took place in 1189. Her account suggests that *Excalibur was found in the tomb and that a prioress, a knight, and a monk attempt to deliver it to the ailing and beleaguered king.

Arthur's Survival and Return

The myth of Arthur's survival (usually on the Isle of Avalon but occasionally in Sicily or inside a mountain or cave in Britain) and his return at a time of need for his people has been adapted in numerous works in various genres. The motif has sometimes been reinterpreted to suggest, as it was by the Tudors, that the line of Arthur would regain power, or, as it has been by some artists, that the return is through an Arthur-like figure.

Even in the Middle Ages, the motif of Arthur's survival appears. Gervase of Tilbury (1140–1220) records in his *Otia imperialia* (*Recreations for an Emperor*) how a groom followed a bishop's runaway horse along a path into Mount Etna, where he found Arthur reclining on a couch and heard from the king 'that he had been living there for a long time, suffering from some old wounds received when he had joined battle long ago with his nephew Mordred and Chelric, duke of the Saxons; these wounds broke open afresh every year' (337). The motif of Arthur in Etna reappears in a late thirteenth-century Tuscan poem, *Il detto* [*The Saying*] *del Gatto Lupesco* (cf. Gardner 14–15), in which the narrator meets two knights seeking Arthur in Mount Etna. It recurs in the fourteenth-century text *La Faula* (*The Tale*) by Guillem de Torroella (1348–75). Written in 'a Provençal that struggles with Catalan varied by speeches in a Majorcan French', *La Faula* describes the poet's dream, in which he is taken by a whale to an island where Morgan le Fey, appearing to be 16, leads him to Arthur, who is fortified each year by the Grail until it is time for him to return (Entwistle 81–4).

The motifs of Arthur's survival and return can also be found in a number of works of the nineteenth and twentieth centuries, where they are sometimes used for purposes of humour, satire, or social commentary. Thomas Love Peacock's 'The Round Table; or King Arthur's Feast' (1817) is a mildly didactic piece designed to offer instruction in British history. It depicts a bored Arthur on an island awaiting the time of his return. To amuse him, Merlin has Pluto deliver up all the kings who have reigned since Arthur's time.

Another work (in prose with verse interludes), *The Marvellous History of King Arthur in Avalon and of the Lifting of Lyonnesse: A Chronicle of the Round Table Communicated by Geoffrey of Monmouth* (1904) by William John Courthope (1842–1917), writing under the pseudonym of Geoffrey Junior, purports to be an account of Arthur's sleep in Avalon. He is kept there under a spell by Morgan le Faye, who also deludes many of his knights into thinking they are in Britain. When Merlin is freed from imprisonment, he wakes Arthur and then raises Lyonnesse and establishes him as king. The work is a mild satire of British political and economic institutions. Arthur allows these institutions to exist but insists that his subjects put aside a tithe for charity and another for defence. Arthur's new reign in Lyonnesse will let 'all the knightly virtues rise again' (108).

Two nineteenth-century American poets create interesting versions of the return of Arthur. Sallie Bridges, who is virtually unknown today, wrote a sequence of poems called 'Legends of the Round Table', which appears in her collection *Marble Isle, Legends of the Round Table, and Other Poems* (1864). The sequence contains fourteen poems that tell Arthur's story from the pulling of the sword from the stone to his resting in Avalon ('Avilion' in Bridges's poem). While most of the poems are merely versified versions of tales from Malory, 'Avilion', the final poem, is strikingly original; its narrator, regretting that her work will soon be forgotten, wishes she could go to rest in the Happy Isle, as Arthur did. As she weeps, her tears become a lake on which a barge comes to bear her to Avilion, where she meets Arthur. The king asks if men still hope for his return 'to win for them the right' and is touched by the narrator's response. She gives him 'a picture of the times, | And how the nations groan'd because was found | No strong, true leader pure in life and aim' (230). So Arthur decides he should return 'To lead the way to truth through seas of blood!' (231). Though no specific allusion is made to contemporary events, the poem is certainly a comment on the events surrounding the American Civil War: Arthur is for Bridges a figure needed to preserve the unity of the United States. Another American, Frank O. Ticknor (1822–74), a physician and poet from Georgia, addresses his poem 'Arthur, the Great King' to Jefferson Davis, president of the Confederacy, and suggests that Davis is an Arthur figure.

'The Return of Arthur' (1922) by American poet Irvine Graff compares another historical figure, Lord Kitchener, British Secretary of War at the beginning of the First World War, to Arthur come again at a time of need. The great achievement of Kitchener, who died at sea in 1916 when the boat he travelled in struck a mine, was encouraging millions, known as 'Kitchener's Mob', to join the armed forces. These troops are said to be the 'modern counterparts' of the knights of the Round Table (11).

In his poem 'The Queen's Crags' (1912), Georgian poet Wilfrid Wilson Gibson (1878–1962) adapts the legend that on Midsummer Eve Arthur and his knights ride forth from the hill in which they sleep. In Gibson's poem, a modern man claims to have seen Guenevere on that night twice in the past. On a third occasion and accompanied by a witness, he claims the queen is coming, but it is in fact only a local woman. Similarly, the play *Potter Thompson* (1919) by F. W. Moorman is based on the legend that 'King Arthur and his Knights are lying asleep beneath the castle rock' at Richmond, in the North Riding of Yorkshire, until 'England shall have need of them' (47). In the play, a potter who discovers Arthur and some of his knights sleeping informs the king that the country needs him. Arthur says he will not come again to 'battle for the right' but that he now dreams of peace (63), and he sends Potter Thompson back to spread this message. Another discovery of Arthur and his sleeping knights is described in 'King Arthur's Sleep' (1898) by Ernest Rhys (1859–1946). A young boy who has seen the sleepers in a cave spends the rest of his life trying to rediscover them. Although he fails, the story is passed on for generations; and the expectation that Arthur will return persists.

The series of seven radio plays collectively titled *The Saviours* (1942) by British playwright and novelist Clemence Dane (pseudonym of Winifred Ashton, 1888–1965) presents another version of Arthur's return. In the first of the plays, Merlin, who appears as a character and narrator throughout the sequence, predicts to Vortigern the coming of Uther and Arthur. The second play dramatizes the story of Arthur from his coming to his passing, including his resistance to the invading 'Germans' (26), a name carefully chosen in this play written during the Second World War, and ends with Merlin's prediction that 'An Arthur will yet come to help his people' (59). The remaining plays tell of how 'at need saviours arose—kings, priests, rebels, poets and fighting-men' (244)—to help keep Britain free from foreign invaders and domestic oppressors. These plays focus on King Alfred, Robin Hood, Elizabeth and Essex, Lord Nelson, and the Unknown Soldier of the First World War.

Arthur returns in modern literature not just because of the danger posed by war but also because of other threats to society. Irish-born novelist Leonard Wibberley (1915–83) recounts Arthur's return to an England overly controlled by bureaucracy in his novel *The Quest of Excalibur* (1959). Aided by an English princess and a California graduate student, a modern Lancelot and Guinevere who put duty before their love, Arthur helps to ease the government restrictions on individual freedom.

Similarly, British poet Martyn Skinner has Merlin bring Arthur back from Avalon on the verge of the new millennium in 2000 to a world suffering from 'a disease called progress' caused by 'technical indulgence' (13) which, in epic fashion, Satanic forces have introduced. The 'satiric epic' (written in the rhyme royal stanzas that Byron used in his satiric poem *Don Juan*) began in *Merlin* (1951) and continued in *The Return of Arthur* (originally published in two parts in 1955 and 1959). The three books were gathered together, completed, and published in final form in 1966 as *The Return of Arthur*, in which Skinner describes a world that has become a technological hell: people are spied upon by 'tele-allrecorders' (112) that transmit sounds, sights, and even smells. The ruling totalitarian forces have a 'psycho-scopic ray' that reveals whatever is in a person's mind. The fear of a takeover of men's minds and of the earth itself has obvious anti-Communist overtones. One of the leading government officials is named Karl Kremlin Hengist; the devils who unleash these technological horrors on mankind form a 'politburo'; and Satan addresses them as 'Comrades' (47, 52).

In Skinner's trilogy, earth's leaders have revised the historical past by eliminating accounts of heroic deeds. Without these examples, people are not even aware of their plight. Merlin brings Arthur back so he and his values can restore social, political, and moral health. To correct people's lack of vision, Arthur recounts the story of his reign and of the knights of the Round Table. Through this device, Skinner asserts the relevance of heroic legends, particularly the Arthurian legends, for the modern world.

Popular novels too take up the theme of Arthur's return. In Peter David's comic novel *Knight Life* (1987), Arthur, wielding both Excalibur and an American Express card, returns to twentieth-century New York City to run for mayor. He is assisted by Merlin, who is living backwards in time (a concept taken from T. H. White) and is now an 8-year-old boy who calls Arthur 'Wart' (32). Other Arthurian characters—Morgan and Modred, as well as Lancelot and Gwen de Vere (Guinevere)— have also returned. In the end, Modred, inhabited by the spirit of Morgan, kills Arthur; but he is dead only a minute before paramedics revive him. He and Gwen decide to rest in 'Avalon, a small resort community near Atlantic City' (191), until he assumes his duties as mayor. Stephen Lawhead's *Avalon* (1999), a sequel to his Pendragon Cycle, tells of Arthur's return as James Arthur Moray, who inherits the throne after the death of King Edward IX. With the help of Merlin, Arthur proves, at a time when England is about to dissolve the monarchy, that a king can be relevant as a symbol and an embodiment of the values for which the British nation should stand. His own courage and integrity lead to the defeat of a referendum to abolish the monarchy. And in Molly Cochran and Warren Murphy's novels *The Forever King* (1992), *The Broken Sword* (1997), and *The Third Magic* (2003, by Cochran alone), Arthur is reincarnated as a twentieth-century boy, Arthur Blessing, who is aided by Merlin and Hal Woczniak, an alcoholic former FBI agent. Guinevere, Merlin, many of Arthur's knights—riding motorcycles—and Excalibur and the Grail join Arthur in the future.

Juvenile fiction also draws on the theme of Arthur's survival. In Jane Curry's *The Sleepers* (1968) and Nancy Faulkner's *Sword of the Winds* (1957), children—in the former, in the twentieth century; and in the latter, in the sixteenth when England is threatened by the Spanish Armada—discover the sleeping Arthur.

Even in one of the most ambitious Arthurian comic book series, Arthur's return is a central theme. In Mike Barr and Brian Bolland's twelve-part *Camelot 3000* (1982-5),

Arthur, a group of his knights, and Merlin return in the year 3000 to save Britain from an invasion from outer space, engineered by Morgan. Some of the knights are reincarnated in new forms: *Tristan is a woman, Gawain is African, Galahad Japanese, and *Percival a mutant. The emphasis is on achieving a diverse Round Table to combat the enemy.

HISTORICAL VERSE

Renaissance interest in the historical Arthur and the Arthurian associations of numerous places in Britain as noted by Leland and in other works such as William Camden's *Britannia* (first published in Latin in 1586 and first translated into English in 1610) led to the writing of verse that commemorated British sites associated with Arthur. Thomas Churchyard (1520?–1604) dedicated his largely topographical poem *The Worthines of Wales* (1587) to Queen Elizabeth who, according to Churchyard, was descended from Arthur. He defends the historicity of Arthur against the attacks of writers like Polydore Vergil and argues that Caerleon, as the site of Arthur's court, should be as famous as Troy and Athens. Michael Drayton (1563–1631) similarly highlights Arthurian topography in his *Poly-Olbion* (1612), which, like Churchyard's *Worthines*, is a long poem with explanatory prose passages. Drayton writes of such places as Glastonbury, famed for being the site of Arthur's tomb and of the thorn trees that bloom in the winter, and Carmarden, known as the place where Merlin was born (56, 101). In both the prose and the verse, Drayton gives bits of Arthurian lore, including references to Merlin's building of Stonehenge and his being deceived by 'his loving of an Elfe', Arthur's twelve battles, his victory at Badon, his conquests on the continent, Mordred's treachery, and Arthur's death (cf. Drayton 76–8).

Sir Richard Blackmore

In the later seventeenth century, the concept of an Arthurian epic, considered but rejected by John Milton, was taken up by Sir Richard Blackmore (d. 1729). In two long poems, *Prince Arthur* (1695) and *King Arthur* (1697), Blackmore blends content and formal elements from Geoffrey of Monmouth, Virgil, and Milton to create an allegory of contemporary events. His first epic depicts Arthur's coming to power as an allegory of the triumph of William of Orange. In *King Arthur*, Arthur's conquest in Gaul is an allegory for the defeat of Louis XIV by William. The poems thus exemplify the ways in which the Arthurian material is used to comment on historical events; artistically, however, they are inept and are perhaps best remembered for Pope's reference in *The Dunciad* to 'Blackmore's endless line'.

Richard Hole

Richard Hole (1746–1803) wrote a 'Poetical Romance' called *Arthur or the Northern Enchantment* (1789). Typically pre-Romantic, it contains long passages of natural description, depictions of peasants leading an idyllic rustic life, conflicts in which emotion overcomes reason, images borrowed from Ossian, and references to Celtic and Germanic mythology and antiquities. Although *Arthur or the Northern Enchantment* is a poem and not a play, its plot, not to mention its melodrama, seems closer to Dryden's *King Arthur* than to any of the earlier Arthurian tales. The poem has Miltonic overtones reminiscent of, but not as overbearing as, those in Blackmore's poems. Arthur fights Germanic invaders and loves a woman, in this case Merlin's daughter Inogen, who is also loved by his Saxon rival Hengist. Hengist is assisted in his designs by the three Weird Sisters or Fates, Urda, Valdandi, and Skulda, who are ultimately and uncharacteristically bested in their attempt to control fate by Merlin, who is assisted by the Genius of the Isle of Britain.

When Hengist wishes for Arthur's fame and for Inogen's love, the Fates change his form so he appears to be Arthur. This transformation allows Hengist to entice Inogen to leave the magically protected bower that Merlin has provided for her. But when he, in the form of Arthur, kills Arthur's ally Cador, who had slain Hengist's brother, she runs from him, only to be captured by another Germanic invader, Hacon of Norway. Rescued by one of Arthur's knights as she is about to be put to death, Inogen still believes Arthur to be cruel and treacherous. Arthur, in turn, assumes that she has been faithless because she left her bower with another knight. Merlin reconciles them by explaining the deception perpetrated by the Weird Sisters and then warns Arthur of the dangers of ambition and advises that he should only 'Fight to protect, and conquer but to bless' (253). The suggestion is that Arthur, an instrument of heaven's will and not of the perverted, ambitious, and destructive plan of the Fates, must use his reign for 'nobler thoughts' and 'acts humane' since by 'blessing, man is blest' (136).

H. H. Milman

H. H. Milman's (1791–1868) poem *Samor, Lord of the Bright City* appeared in 1818. Like Blackmore and other poets such as Milton and Dryden, Milman thought the story of Britain's struggle with the Saxons worthy of epic treatment. The twelve books of his epic do not, however, focus on Arthur but rather on the character who 'appears in most of the Chronicles, as Edol, or *Eldol*'. Eldol, Milman explains, has the title of Earl of Gloucester and is described in one chronicle as 'Eldulph de Samor' (p. vii). This is the character whom Geoffrey of Monmouth identifies as Eldol, Count of Gloucester (called by the Britons 'Caer Gloew' or 'the Bright City'), one of the noblemen invited to a meeting to discuss peace with Hengist and his Saxon lords. At this meeting, the Saxons betray their hosts by concealing weapons and, on Hengist's command, slaughtering the assembled British noblemen. Eldol defends himself with a wooden stake and slays many Saxons before being forced to flee. He then fights bravely against the Saxons in battle, captures Hengist, and is allowed to behead him. Geoffrey's Eldol becomes Milman's Samor, who throughout the poem is called 'the Avenger' since he tries to avenge the slaughter at the peace council and other Saxon treacheries.

Samor fights for British freedom, a recurring theme in the poem. He assists Aurelius and Uther in regaining control of Britain. Arthur appears as the child of Uther and Igerna, Uther's legal wife who is kidnapped by Gorlois and freed by Samor, and later as a young warrior fighting in a climactic battle against the Saxons, but not as the leader or even as the greatest warrior in the battle. Milman says that he is writing about the ancestors 'of that fam'd chivalric race' celebrated 'in old song', such as 'White-handed *Iseult, Launcelot of the Lake, | Chaste Perceval, that won the Sangreal quest' (317). The poem is aware of the future in another way: Milman has Merlin utter a lengthy prophecy which foresees Arthur's glory but also that of future British rulers and events, such as Alfred, Elizabeth, the Wars of the Roses, and William and Mary.

Set in the context of Vortigern's foolish invitation to the Saxons and his infatuation for *Rowena, the poem chronicles the struggle with the invaders, often led by Samor. After their victory over Hengist, Aurelius and Uther appoint Samor judge of the captured Saxons. While he shows mercy to one of their lords, he condemns Hengist, despite Rowena's plea for mercy for her father. Thus he becomes the Avenger of the 'nobles foully slain | At the Peace Banquet' (351).

John Lesslie Hall

American poet John Lesslie Hall (1856–1928), an Anglo-Saxon scholar, sees the Saxon invasions quite differently from Milman and most of the English poets who deal with the subject. In his *Old English Idyls* (1899), Hall assumes 'the rôle of an English gleeman of about A.D. 1000' and therefore writes in 'the spirit' and 'the metre' of Old English verse. More important than his use of alliterative verse, kennings, compound nouns and adjectives, and motifs adapted from Anglo-Saxon poetry—such as gift-giving, descriptions of mead halls and sea journeys, named swords, boar images on helmets, the beasts-of-battle theme, and barrows for dead heroes—is his adopting of the Saxon perspective to tell the history of the establishment of the Germanic tribes in Britain.

The first poem in the volume, 'The Calling of Hengist and Horsa', focuses on the embassy Vortigern sends to seek help protecting Britain from invaders. Though Hengist feels it would be better for Vortigern to fight for himself, he nevertheless agrees to make the journey, which is described in the next poem, 'The Landing of Hengist and Horsa'. As soon as they land, Hengist asks to be given the Isle of Thanet before he will fight in Vortigern's cause, a request the British king readily grants. The story of Vortigern and Hengist continues in the poem 'The Lady Rowena', which opens with a rebellion against the British king by his own people. When the 'Woe-begone king, the womanish, white-livered | Liegelord of Albion' (20), learns of the rebellion, he once again calls on Hengist, who enlists even more Germanic warriors from the continent. But the central theme of the poem, which suggests its Anglo-Saxon perspective, is Vortigern's lust for Rowena. When Hengist uses Rowena to elicit a rash promise from Vortigern that Kent will pass to him in return for her hand, he is described as 'most artful of athelings' (30). The picture of Rowena herself is unusual. In the chronicles, Rowena is described as a treacherous poisoner; but in Hall's poem she is 'the peerless, precious princess Rowena' (31). She and Vortigern live together happily for six years, and then, as told in the poem on 'The Death of Horsa', 'hot-hearted Kentmen . . . cruelly vexed her' by saying that she robbed Vortigern of his 'metal and valor' (34).

'Cerdic and Arthur', the final poem dealing with material from the Arthurian legends, tells of the time after Hengist's death when a new Saxon leader, *Cerdic, comes to Britain. Though Arthur's name is said to be 'far-reaching' (50) and, like Beowulf, Arthur is 'eager for glory' (51), he is only temporarily favoured by Wyrd (Fate) and ultimately dies, in a manner not explained in the poem—though there is an allusion to the involvement of a foul 'traitor, hated of heroes' (52). But the focus is on the heroic deeds of Cerdic, who is praised both as the 'Father of England' (54) and as the 'founder of freedom' (52). The rewriting of Arthurian history and prehistory from a Saxon perspective is, finally, a means of glorifying the heritage of laws and the defence of freedom that Hall sees as descending from the Anglo-Saxon rulers of England.

John Masefield

The Victorians looked primarily to Malory and the romance tradition for their Arthurian material, but a number of twentieth-century works were influenced by the chronicle tradition. Some of the poems in *Midsummer Night and Other Tales in Verse* (1928) by John Masefield (1878–1967) borrow from the Celtic tradition, folklore, and romance, while others try to create a historical setting for Arthur. Particularly interesting is Masefield's 'The Sailing of Hell Race', an adaptation of 'The Spoils of Annwn'. After achieving peace, Arthur wishes to test himself by undertaking an adventure never before achieved. He sails beyond the furthest point to which anyone has journeyed before until he comes to Hell Race, the channel of swift water running into the underworld. Many of his men are lost to temptation or despair; but with the assistance of his divine Helper, Arthur returns with seven men. The folklore theme (discussed above) of Arthur's survival is treated in the title poem 'Midsummer Night', in which the narrator comes upon an entrance into a hill in which Arthur and his companions are found on Midsummer Eve. Arthur, Modred, Gwenivere, and others recount their parts in the 'tragic plot'; but most poignant is Arthur's desire to return 'when the trumpet summons' to 'build the lasting beauty left unbuilt | Because of all our follies and our guilt' (85).

In the historical poems in the volume, Masefield attempts to treat conventional parts of the story from a new and usually more realistic perspective. In 'The Begetting of Arthur', for example, Uther disguises himself as Merchyon, Ygerna's father, to enter his castle and carry off his beloved. They are married by a hermit and spend one night together before they are caught by her father and Breuse, his wicked follower, who kill Uther and bring Ygerna back to Tintagel.

In 'Badon Hill', Masefield describes the Saxons' desire to raid a rich region of Britain. After Arthur has burnt their ships, he and his men slaughter the Saxons in the ensuing battle, a victory that initiates a period of peace because other raiders fear a similar fate.

Masefield tells two tales of the final events of Arthur's reign. In one, Arthur refuses to condemn Gwenivere and Lancelot, helps them escape, and then declares them banished. In 'The Old Tale of the Breaking of the Links', as opposed to the newer tale he has written, Masefield retells the version of the 'French poets', which is the more common tale, as told by Malory. Thus he emphasizes the distinction between the romantic approach to the Arthurian material and the historical one that he adopts in many of the poems in *Midsummer Night*.

Some of the best poetry in the volume occurs in poems like 'Gwenivere Tells' and 'The Death of Lancelot', which blur the boundaries between historical and romantic verse. These two poems, which attempt to give Gwenivere her own voice, describe the persistence of her love and provide a perspective that seems truer than her typical rejection of Lancelot, though not as morally correct. In the former, Gwenivere tells of her love, symbolized by a rose, which contrasts with the withered, grey olive spray that Lancelot sends her after his pilgrimage to the Holy Land. The sense of a love that outlasts tragedy and repentance also appears in 'The Death of Lancelot', in which Gwenivere leaves the convent when she hears that Lancelot is dying. In this reversal of the typical pattern, it is she who arrives too late to see him before his death. The sorrow of the situation is conveyed nicely in the image of Lancelot's lifeless sword-hand not being able to hold the crucifix placed in it as he is fitted out for burial. An equally powerful image is that of Gwenivere, having left the convent to see him, gathering flowers, a visual reiteration of her statement that 'April will out', that is, that love will endure because it is a natural force stronger than even the 'nun's and marriage-vows' (150) that she has broken because of it.

John Heath-Stubbs

Like a number of the historical poems about Arthur, *Artorius* (1973) by John Heath-Stubbs adopts epic scope and form. Its twelve parts are related to the signs of the zodiac and the labours of Hercules; each part adopts a new form. With perhaps an overemphasis on the classical, some of these forms seem at odds with the material and with each other. One section imitates Sophoclean tragedy, another comedy in the style of Aristophanes. Some sections are in alliterative verse, which is sometimes handled quite skilfully; but the native English and the classical forms clash. The classical forms, however, as well as the emphasis on Arthur's Roman background, may suggest a need for order; and the faith and courage symbolized by the king and his rule are presented as an answer to the problems of disorder and chaos in the Arthurian and the modern world. In one of the best passages in the poem, the goddess Ceridwen gives Arthur a vision of Britain's future, which includes wars and destruction and culminates in the bombing of London during the Second

World War. In spite of this, Arthur accepts from her a 'crystal cup, clearer than moonlight' and 'a burnished blade', Caliburn (44), and thus takes upon himself the moral and political leadership that these treasures represent.

HISTORICAL DRAMA

The Misfortunes of Arthur by Thomas Hughes

In 1587, Elizabethan playwright Thomas Hughes wrote a tragedy called The Misfortunes of Arthur. Hughes, a member of Gray's Inn, was assisted in the preparation of the dumb shows that precede each act by other members, including Francis Bacon. Drawing on the chronicle tradition descending ultimately from Geoffrey of Monmouth to dramatize Arthur's downfall, Hughes recounts Gueneuora's betrayal of Arthur with Mordred, Mordred's usurpation, Arthur's return from his wars on the continent, and the final battle against Mordred. On the one hand, the Misfortunes is in the tradition of the medieval tragedy of fortune. Arthur complains about Fortune's fickleness, and the chorus proclaims that Fortune overturns the lofty. Arthur's ally Cador sums up the inevitable turning of the wheel of Fortune: 'thus Fortune gibes: | She hoyseth vp to hurle the deeper downe' (Hughes 284); and the messenger who reports events of the battle observes that: 'There Fortune laid the prime of Brytaines pride, | There laide her pompe, all topsie turuie turnde' (Hughes 279).

Despite the play's medieval roots, it has been thoroughly adapted to the conventions of its time. Besides using numerous classical allusions, it adopts many of the conventions of the revenge tragedy popularized by Renaissance interest in Senecan drama. The action of the Misfortunes begins, as does Shakespeare's Hamlet, with a ghost calling for revenge—in this case, the ghost of Gorlois, first husband of Igerna, seeking revenge on the house of Uther Pendragon. The play makes abundant use of stichomythia, the line-for-line exchanges typical of Senecan style; and the major gory action of the play, including the events of the final battle up to the killing of Mordred and the fatal wounding of Arthur, is reported by a messenger and not depicted on the stage.

King Arthur by John Dryden

John Dryden (1631–1700), who, like Milton, considered and rejected the idea of writing an Arthurian epic, did write a 'dramatic opera' called King Arthur, the music for which was composed by Henry Purcell (1659–95). Originally written in 1684 during the reign of Charles II (ruled 1660–85), the play was, according to Dryden's preface, revised radically for its publication in 1691 and first performance in January of 1692 to reflect a new political situation, the reign of William and Mary (1689–1702). Dryden's original intention in writing the play was to honour King Charles as a modern incarnation of Arthur, a position that would have been less politic when it was finally published and performed.

The action of the play seems strange to a modern audience. Of the familiar characters of the legend, only Arthur and Merlin appear in the play, which is set in the context of the Saxon invasions. Guinevere is replaced as the object of Arthur's love by Emmeline, the blind daughter of Arthur's ally Conon, Duke of Cornwall. She is loved, in turn, by both the Saxon leader Oswald and his magician Osmond. The play builds on the chronicle tradition of Arthur's battles with the Saxons but, unlike *The Misfortunes of Arthur* and other Renaissance plays dealing with the chronicle material, Dryden's work is a heroic Restoration play that is more interested in amorous than dynastic conflict. The military struggle between Arthur and Oswald, who, as James Merriman has observed, are 'nothing but a pair of Restoration beaux' (63), is subordinated to their struggle for Emmeline; Arthur even offers to share his kingdom with Oswald if he will surrender Emmeline. Both conflicts culminate in a single combat in which Arthur is the victor. But before this resolution is possible, Merlin must overcome the magic of the heathen sorcerer Osmond, who binds Emmeline with a charm that can be overcome only when the spell he has placed on the forest is broken. As this description suggests, the play employs a good deal of the spectacle typical of heroic drama. Osmond changes the scene 'to a Prospect of Winter in Frozen Countries' (Dryden 46). Sirens arise from the water beneath a bridge to tempt Arthur. A tree bleeds when Arthur strikes it with a sword; a figure who seems to be Emmeline emerges from the tree; a beneficial spirit strikes the figure with Merlin's wand and turns it into the wicked spirit Grimbald. And the play ends with a masque performed by mythological and allegorical characters.

In contrast to the wicked, deceptive heathen Osmond, who even betrays Oswald because of his own lust for Emmeline, Merlin uses his magic to enlighten Arthur and others, a function that is depicted symbolically by his curing Emmeline of her blindness. In the end, Merlin restores order in such a way that even the enemy is accommodated. He predicts not only Arthur's fame as the first of the three Christian Worthies but also the eventual union of the British and the Saxons, who will be bound together 'in perpetual Peace' by 'One Common tongue, one Common Faith' (60). Yet, despite the harmonious resolution, the play, not one of the high points of Arthurian literature, remains 'a commercial product whose direct modern heir is the Broadway musical' (Merriman 64). The commercial viability of the play is evident in the fact that it was adapted by David Garrick in 1770 with not only Purcell's music but also additional music by Thomas Arne.

Arthur, Monarch of the Britons by William Hilton

In 1759, British poet William Hilton completed his verse play *Arthur, Monarch of the Britons* (first published in 1776). The play takes place after Modred has usurped the throne while Arthur was fighting on the continent 'to set th' oppressed free' in Armorica (173). Modred dotes on the queen, who has run off in guilt, and is more concerned with regaining her than with the war he is waging, to the chagrin of his Pictish allies. In a plot built around awkward encounters and events improbable in terms of the drama and of Arthurian tradition, Arthur slays Modred, forgives Guinever, and, since Galvan (Gawain) is also mortally wounded, names Constantine as his successor with the injunction that he remember 'that Britons must be free' (246), a notion that is the underlying theme of the play.

Vortigern by William Ireland

William Ireland (1777–1835) adapts material from the *Chronicles of England, Scotland, and Ireland* by Raphael Holinshed (d. 1598) to create his forgery, the historical play *Vortigern* (written in 1795 and performed in 1796), which he initially claimed was written by Shakespeare. The play tells of Vortigern's ambition and his folly in inviting the Saxons into Britain, a folly compounded by his lust for Rowena, Hengist's daughter, because of whom he divorces his wife, thus driving her into a Lear-like madness. Vortigern's own children desert him and join forces with Aurelius and Uter. In the end, as in Holinshed, Vortigern is captured by Aurelius. Vortigern's daughter Flavia pleads for her father's life, and since she and Aurelius are in love, the request is granted. Vortigern recognizes Aurelius as king and gives him Flavia in marriage. The play has certain Shakespearian touches: lines that echo those in some of Shakespeare's plays; a female character, Flavia, who makes an escape by dressing as a man; a wise fool. But it lacks dramatic, poetic, and thematic distinction.

The Dragon King by J. F. Pennie

The Dragon King (1832) by J. F. Pennie (1782–1848) is a strange Romantic creation, full of Celtic and Germanic lore that is often documented in endnotes, and dramatic deaths which at times make the play seem more Gothic than historical. Arthur is betrayed, as in many of the chronicles, by his wife Gwenyfar and Mouric Medrawd (Mordred) while Arthur struggles against the Saxons, led by Cerdic and his son Kenrick. Upon learning of Gwenyfar's infidelity, Arthur calls her an 'adulterous pest' (450), and when she is captured, he turns her out of the city gates to be at the mercy of the heathens and robbers. Instead, she meets Cissa, a Saxon chieftain, who wants to make her one of his many wives. Another love affair, between Kenrick and Arthur's sister Imogenia, interweaves with that of Gwenyfar and Mouric. Cerdic will not allow the match and wants to use Imogenia as a sacrifice to the gods for victory in battle. When Kenrick says he will kill himself if she does not convert to his religion, an act which he believes will save her, she forsakes her faith and burns incense to Thor and Odin. Cerdic is not mollified and intends to sacrifice her anyway after he defeats Arthur. At the last moment, Imogenia renounces all pagan gods and dies a Christian.

Gwenyfar is treated with similarly murderous hospitality by the Saxons. When Cissa dies, she is forced to mount his pyre and burn with him because he had claimed her as a wife. After severely wounding Arthur, Mouric too meets his end, not in battle but by a stone thrown by a British woman in a burning tower. Arthur goes to 'Avalonia's isle' in the hopes of having his wound healed but orders that if he dies, there should be 'the veil | Of dim uncertainty' flung over his fate so that his name will 'keep the patriot fire' burning 'for ever bright' (497).

Twentieth-Century Historical Drama

Although Arthurian drama written in the late nineteenth and early twentieth centuries favoured romantic themes, there was renewed interest in historical drama later in the twentieth century. American dramatist A. Fleming MacLiesh used Arthurian material to comment on contemporary conditions. His play *The Destroyers* (1942) depicts Arthur in the midst of war trying to determine who his real enemies are. So full of suspicion that he puts to death a loyal general, Arthur fails to detect the scheming of Medrawt and Loth. When Medrawt learns from his mother Anna that Arthur is his father and that he is the product of an incestuous relationship, his hatred increases to the point that even his lover Ginevra leaves him and returns to the king. As the play, set in 'the period circa 500 A.D.' (7), introduces flares, sidearms, trucks, planes, and artillery in addition to swords, lances, and shields, it becomes clear that Arthur's war is every war, including the one being waged as the play was being written. That point is emphasized when Ginevra speaks of the deaths 'beyond all sense' and Merlin refers to the cyclical nature of such human suffering (126–8).

Three British plays are noteworthy examples of modern historical drama. By focusing on one Romano-British family, *The Long Sunset* (1955) by R. C. Sherriff creates a sense of the effects of the withdrawal of the Roman forces from Britain. After hearing that the last legions have left the country, wealthy land-owners Julian and Serena unite with two of their neighbours to invite Arthur to protect them and to lead the resistance that they believe will preserve some of the values and ideals they cherish. Arthur trains their servants to fight the invaders; their son joins Arthur's warriors; and their daughter marries Gawain. Nevertheless, ultimately they are left alone and undefended. Just before they leave their home and the way of life they have established, Julian adopts his wife's Christian religion in the hope that they will be together after the almost certain death that awaits them.

The title of the play has a double meaning. It refers to 'the sunset of an Island that once belonged to Rome'; but it also refers literally to the sunsets in Britain, which are long by comparison to those in Italy. Julian tells Arthur that 'it's in the nature of men to do their best and deepest thinking when the sun's going down' (62) and encourages him to use that time to ponder the ideals that the Roman Empire represented and to make them the basis of his defence of Britain.

The Island of the Mighty by John Arden and Margaretta D'Arcy was published in 1974 but completed some years earlier. (A version of the play was written in 1953, but the final version was not completed until 1972.) In the play, various regions of Britain are represented by the three poets Taliesin (Chief Poet of Strathclyde), Aneurin (Chief Poet of Gododdin), and Merlin (Chief Poet of Arthur's realm). The play depicts some of the factionalism plaguing Britain and the dissolution of order in the chaotic time of fallen empire, invasion, and internal strife. The undisciplined violence of *Balin and the rejection of Arthur by *Balan in the first part, the struggle between Celtic and Roman values and the rebellion of Medraut in the second, and the madness of Merlin in the third reflect the political and social chaos of Britain. In his preface to the play, John Arden has commented on its political implications, noting that 'British Imperialism in decline had much in common with its Roman precursor'. His remarks demonstrate that in his revisions of his original text, he was also concerned about American involvement in Vietnam and elsewhere and about 'the cultural confusion prevalent in the late sixties' (12–14).

In Howard Brenton's *The Romans in Britain* (1980), another Arthurian play that is historical in setting and political in theme, the invasions of Britain by Caesar and the brutality of Roman soldiers towards the native Celtic population are juxtaposed with the Saxon invasions and the problems in modern Ireland. In one of the scenes set in the twentieth century, a British officer equates 'a Roman spear' and a 'Saxon axe' with a 'British Army machine-gun' and calls them all the 'weapons of Rome, invaders, Empire' (89). In the final scene, one of the characters speaks of a king whose 'Government was the people of Britain'. The last lines of the play name this king Arthur, thereby making him a symbol of native rule and popular opposition to invading forces.

HISTORICAL NOVELS

In his 'Author's Note' to *The Winter King*, Bernard Cornwell writes: 'When I began the book I was determined to exclude every anachronism, including the embellishments of Chrétien de Troyes, but such purity would have excluded Lancelot, Galahad, Excalibur and Camelot, let alone such figures as Merlin, Morgan and *Nimue.' It was a wise decision not to leave out such 'anachronisms' and 'embellishments', for without these characters and the romantic vision of Arthur and Camelot, much of the timeless quality of the Arthurian legends is lost. Many authors of historical Arthurian novels try to balance the legendary elements which make up the bulk of the Arthurian tradition and the scant historical facts at the base of that tradition. The few facts mentioned in the early chronicles figure prominently in many of the novels: the general account of the Germanic invasions of Britain as listed in *The Anglo-Saxon Chronicle*; the story of Vortigern's inviting the Saxons into Britain and the struggle against them by Aurelius and Uther and ultimately by Arthur, as told by Geoffrey of Monmouth; Arthur's twelve battles as listed by Nennius, particularly the battle at Mount Badon; and the fact that Arthur is called a *dux bellorum* rather than a king. Sometimes the novelists try to explain rationally or realistically the fantastic elements of the story; sometimes they try to locate in a historical context characters and events that are fictional; but always they must find a balance between the desire to create a credible depiction of real people in a historical period and the need to work within a tradition that, whatever historical background it may have, has been built largely on non-historical characters and motifs.

Alfred J. Church

The collapse of Roman Britain is a theme in a number of historical novels. In *The Count of the Saxon Shore* (1887), Alfred J. Church (1829–1912) writes what is the earliest historical novel with an Arthurian connection, though that connection comes only at the very end of the book. The count of the title is a Roman named Ælius who protects the coast of Britain with a small fleet of ships. He has a daughter and an adopted daughter, named Carna, who becomes a central figure. When two Saxons are captured, one on the verge of death, her kindness to them wins the lasting affection of the other, the brother of the fatally wounded prisoner. This brother, named Cedric, escapes and, after the fall of Rome, returns with a band of Saxons. Because of Carna's kindness, however, he refuses to shed British blood. In the final chapter, he is present at the battle of Mount Badon but only protects his lord as best he can without killing any of the British. When his lord is dead and he is fatally wounded, he enquires about Carna, who is now a nun ministering to those on the battlefield. She is brought to him and he asks to be baptized, a service performed by Arthur himself.

William H. Babcock

American novelist William H. Babcock's (1849–1922) *Cian of the Chariots* (1898), a book that is subtitled *A Romance of the Days of Arthur Emperor of Britain and his Knights of the Round Table, How They Delivered London and Overthrew the Saxons after the Downfall of Roman Britain*, attempts to capture the chaos and the intrigues that resulted from the Roman withdrawal from Britain, the subsequent Anglo-Saxon invasions, and the conflicts between Christian and pagan religions as well as among Romano-British, Celtic, and Saxon cultures. Babcock takes the name of his title character, a poet and a warrior, from Nennius, who included Cian along with 'Neirin' and Taliessin as poets who recounted British bravery against the invaders. Unlike many later historical novelists, who draw heavily on Geoffrey of Monmouth for their material, Babcock depends primarily on the few details about the Arthurian age that Nennius and Gildas provide and on the scholarship of his day.

The setting for much of the action of Babcock's novel is the time between the sixth and seventh of Arthur's battles as listed by Nennius, that is, between the battle on the River Bassas and the battle in Celydon Forest. Babcock proceeds to chronicle the subsequent battles, leading up to a climactic battle at Camelot. In addition to the battles, Babcock focuses on the conflicts between the native Celtic religion, represented by the title character Cian, and the Christian religion that Arthur adopts and to which he gives preference. When a priest presents Arthur with a cameo depicting the Virgin Mary, Arthur has it set into his shield as a boss, and when he wins his next battle, he decides that 'It was Mary, Queen of Heaven, ... who had saved him, and won the victory.' Cian finds Arthur's interpretation 'well-nigh insufferable' (326) since it was Cian's timely arrival with his charioteers that assured the victory. The religious rift between the two increases when Cian absents his forces from the battle 'on the strand of Trath Tribuit' (341) because Arthur insists that those fighting with him renounce any non-Christian beliefs. But in the battle at Camelot Cian swallows his pride and rides to the rescue. The fight is going badly for Arthur, but Cian and his charioteers break through the Saxon ranks. This time there is no question about credit for the victory: it belongs to Cian. As a result, the goodwill between Arthur and Cian is restored 'with no compulsion of faith' (388); and the friendship and tolerance last until the end of Arthur's reign. Cian, we are told, fought with Arthur at 'Mount Baden' and was with his emperor at 'the utter disaster of Camlan' (395). Aside from its significance as the first American historical novel to depict Arthur, *Cian of the Chariots* is noteworthy because it turns the historical account of Arthur's battles into an argument for freedom of religion.

Warwick Deeping

While Arthur is frequently presented as a military leader in historical novels, Uther does not often figure in them. He appears in Henry Treece's *The Great Captains* (discussed below) as a Celtic tribesman who lacks any of the sophistication of Romano-British culture. But a very different Uther appears in *Uther and Igraine* (1903), a novel by Warwick Deeping (1877–1950), in which Uther is so ruled by conscience that he almost loses his beloved Igraine. Nor is this the Uther of romance, though there are romance elements in the story. Uther had left Igraine, thinking she was a nun, though she was only a noviciate who had no intention of taking vows. In fact, it is Gorlois who enlists Merlin's aid to have him (Gorlois) appear to be Uther so he can deceive Igraine into thinking she is marrying the man she loves. Not until Uther learns that Gorlois is abusing Igraine does he challenge him to combat and kill him.

But even more important to the novel than Uther is Igraine, whose courage and defiance make her far from the typical damsel of medieval story. She is willing to defy powerful men like Gorlois and to resist his attempts to break her spirit and force her to be a dutiful wife. After being tricked into marriage, she tells her husband that she hates him; and as he goes off to battle, she says she will pray for his death. When she escapes from Tintagel, for a time she wears the armour of a knight killed in battle, and she herself saves a damsel in distress. In elevating 'a female character to a role of great prominence' and in portraying her as a decisive, courageous, independent woman, Deeping anticipates 'later developments in Arthurian fiction that we tend to associate with the second half of the twentieth century and the works of such writers as Mary Stewart, Marion Zimmer Bradley, and Parke Godwin' (Conlee 94).

Deeping's last and posthumously published work was a novel of Arthurian Britain, *The Sword and the Cross* (1957), which recounts the adventures of its narrator Gerontius and the woman he loves, Igerna, as they are displaced from their homes and wander through a Britain overrun by Saxon invaders. Ultimately Gerontius meets Artorius and assists him in defeating the invaders and in promoting the cross of Christianity by using the sword to combat its enemies. An earlier novel, *The Man Who Went Back* (1940), features a modern man who travels back in time, much like

Twain's Connecticut Yankee, to Roman Britain, where he helps in resisting Germanic invaders. He is conscious of the legendary Arthur, but Arthur is not a character in the novel, which equates British resolve in Roman Britain with the resolve in the modern war 'for freedom, for the beauty and mystery and loveliness of things'. He determines to fight in that 'crusade' in his own time by becoming part of 'the winged chivalry', the air force that will fight for those values (382, 376).

T. H. Crosfield

A Love in Ancient Days (1908) by T. H. Crosfield, who in her preface suggests that the story she is about to tell is made from visions that 'seem to show her fragments of previous existences' (p. x), presents an unusual depiction of a Saxon lord. When the protagonist of the novel, Avanwy, who is a cousin to Ambrosius, and her sister Patra are captured by the Saxons, Cerdic, the son of old King Cerdic, is courteous and considerate and shows them kindness. The sisters escape the Saxons with some regret because Avanwy has come to love Cerdic, who returns her affection.

At the battle of Badon—in which Ambrosius' forces participate with those of Arthur, who is referred to only occasionally and, except in the case of Badon, is said to be fighting Picts in the north—the sisters find a badly wounded Cerdic and nurse him back to health. Avanwy and Cerdic marry; and as they are about to set off together to live in peace, his father says that the Saxons will prevail though the younger Cerdic will not be there to help them. Avanwy responds, 'may we not help too, though perhaps not by war? Cerdic and I are types of two races in the same isle—not at war, but united in peace' (396). Thus she predicts a pattern for the triumph not of one race over another but of both as they join to create a new nation.

Farnham Bishop and Arthur Gilchrist Brodeur

The American historical novel *The Altar of the Legion* (1926) was written by Farnham Bishop (1886–1930) and Arthur Gilchrist Brodeur (1888–1971). Brodeur was himself a medieval scholar who later wrote a piece on the historical Arthur called *Arthur: Dux Bellorum* (1939) as well as studies devoted to Old English and Old Norse topics. Bishop and Brodeur's novel is actually set in the time just after Arthur's death. The only one of his warriors left alive is an ageing Owain, who still leads a band of horsemen known as the Ravens. And even though Owain is killed in battle with the Saxons halfway through the novel, his memory, like the memory of Arthur, continues to inspire the people of Britain. As Nathan Comfort Starr observed in *King Arthur Today*, 'Bishop and Brodeur's novel . . . emphasizes sixth-century rather than medieval chivalric warfare and the resounding fame of Arthur as a leader. It comes closer than any previous work to suggesting the presence of the *dux bellorum*' (90).

A good portion of the action of *The Altar of the Legion* is set in the fabled land of *Lyonesse, whose 'soft-sounding name', 'the time-worn remnant of a bit of soldiers' Latin: Legionis Asa, the Altar of the Legion' (p. ix), explains the title. The authors conclude that 'it may well be that Lyonesse the Fair was once the farthest outpost of Roman power and Roman grandeur' (p. viii). Despite the legendary setting, Bishop and Brodeur describe well the struggle for independence of the last outposts of free Celtic people in Britain. The novel chronicles the constant warring with the Saxon invaders, the shifting fortunes of both sides of the conflict, and the political intrigues among Saxons and Celts that contribute to victory or defeat.

At the end of the novel, as Saxon and Celt battle for the crucial region, a force more powerful than either intervenes: an earthquake and the resultant tidal wave devastate the city. Legionis Asa, with all its Roman splendour, sinks into the sea to be remembered as the legendary land of Lyonesse. A handful of survivors head to North Wales, the land of Owain, to continue the struggle against the Saxons. The heroic Romanized soldier Drusus, who carries on the struggle after the deaths of Arthur and Owain, declares himself no longer a Roman but a Celt committed to the protection of his motherland.

W. Barnard Faraday

In *Pendragon* (1930) by W. Barnard Faraday, a female character, Gwendaello (Guinevere), plays a crucial role in the battle of Mount Badon. The novel depicts the political struggles among British chieftains while the country is being attacked by the Irish, Picts, and Saxons. When Gwendaello claims her hereditary right to the title of Pendragon of Britain, Arthur does not initially support her, espousing instead the leadership of Aurelian, son of Ambrosius, who, like Arthur, is of Roman heritage. Nevertheless, Arthur saves Gwendaello from an assassination plot—with the help of Gildas, who appears as a ranting preacher but also as someone with a great deal of knowledge about events throughout Britain. At Mount Badon, even though Arthur and his troops fight valiantly, they are on the verge of defeat until Gwendaello arrives with her forces and turns the tide of the battle. The novel ends with Gwendaello kissing Arthur, thus introducing an element of romance, in two senses, into a novel that otherwise has little of the traditional romance motifs.

Edward Frankland

Edward Frankland's historical novel *Arthur, the Bear of Britain*, originally published in 1944, reflects some of the bleakness and brutality of the age in which it was written. Frankland captures very well the confusion and the intrigues of Britain at a time when local leaders mistrust each other as much as they do the Saxon and Pictish invaders. Like many writers of historical Arthurian fiction, Frankland borrows from early Celtic and Latin sources the details and characters that underlie his story.

Frankland builds much of the first half of his book around Arthur's twelve battles as described by Nennius. The climactic victory at Badon is, however, not the end but rather the midpoint of Frankland's story. When Arthur, who wishes only to be a military leader (a *dux bellorum*—although Frankland does not use that term), would build on the success of that famous victory, the other rulers of Britain fear his growing power and refuse to assist in his dream of clearing the island of invaders.

Arthur must contend not only with the suspicions of these rulers but also with the ambitions of Medraut, his nephew and his ally in the early campaigns. Medraut believes, however, that the future of power in Britain lies in alliance with the invaders rather than in trying to eliminate them from the island. Borrowing from earlier works in the chronicle tradition, Frankland makes Gwenhyvar complicitous in Arthur's downfall; but his novel attempts to explain how and why she is. Her attraction is to a seemingly more romantic, bolder, harp-playing Medraut, whereas Arthur is 'god-like' (58) like the old Roman emperors. In the end, though, Medraut betrays Gwenhyvar as much as he does Arthur because, having won her, he is interested in her only so far as she may help him to power. As Frankland develops the characters of Gwenhyvar and Medraut, so too does he try to understand Arthur, a man driven by a vision of a Britain free of invaders but also tormented by the accusations of Gildas and other clerics that the leaders of Britain are being punished by God for their sins.

John Masefield

Some novelists posit an interest in the province of Britain by the empire established in Constantinople after the collapse of Rome. One such novel is *Badon Parchments* (1947) by John Masefield, which, like Frankland's novel, is greatly influenced by the events of the Second World War. The novel takes the form of a letter sent by one John of Cos to Emperor Justinian and Empress Theodora. John has accompanied Arthur back to Britain from Byzantium, where he was trained. Much of the novel recounts the indecisiveness of British politicians when faced with the Saxon threat. Self-interest, petty rivalries, lack of vision, appeasement, commitment to out-moded tactics and notions about war—all contribute to British defeats. In the climactic battle at Mount Badon, the description of which contains the liveliest writing in the novel, Arthur arrives with a mounted force and overcomes the Saxons just as they are on the verge of victory. Because of what he has seen of British character and despite the flaws he has witnessed, John of Cos recommends that the emperor try to keep Britain a province of the empire. He believes that the British 'only really live, only truly show themselves, in religion, or in some high cause that can be died for like religion' and that if the empire 'could restore a faith and hope to them, they would have charity enough in them to move the world' (151).

Alfred Duggan

Conscience of a King (1951) by Alfred Duggan (1903–64) is narrated by a member of a Romano-British family, and its narrative culminates in the climactic battle of Badon. Conventional as these devices may be, Duggan introduces a clever twist into his story. The narrator Coroticus, a third son with no hope of inheriting, plots to advance himself, even if it means doing away with his elder brother. In a battle against the Saxons, he takes from one of them a rich chalice. Rather than surrender the chalice to his brother, he kills him; seen in the act, he is forced to flee. Since he has been taught the German language, he offers his service to Hengist's son Oisc, who renames him Cerdic Elesing. Soon he gets Oisc's sister pregnant and must seek a new master. He then serves another Saxon, Aella, whom he helps to raid his (Cerdic's) father's lands and his former home. When Aella learns from a dying Roman of Cerdic's true identity and his shameful deeds, Cerdic must flee yet again. He kills his wife who is plotting against him; and with his son, he establishes a settlement and finally leads his own warband on raids, on one of which he is defeated by Arthur's troops at Mount Badon. The novel is a fascinating character study of an unscrupulous man driven by self-interest and redeemed only by the love of his son and his ultimate concern as the founder of Wessex for 'the fortunes of my remote descendants' (242).

Meriol Trevor

Post-Roman Britain of 576 and 577 is the setting for Meriol Trevor's *The Last of Britain* (1956). The novel focuses on the family of Lucius Candidian and other Roman and British nobles holding out against the Saxons. Gildas appears in the novel as an adviser and a helper of the dispossessed. His dying words, conveyed to a group of noblemen, help to inspire them in a final valiant but futile battle against the invaders. In particular, Farinmail, 'the son of the accursed race of Vortigern' (388), becomes a general worthy of the heritage of the Dragon of Britain and bravely directs the battle in which the soldiers cry 'Badon' in memory of Arthur's great victory and pray to the 'Virgin of Badon' (420). Despite Farinmail's heroics, the battle seems nearly the last gasp of British and Roman glory.

Henry Treece

British author Henry Treece (1911–66)—who wrote a juvenile novel about Arthur's Britain, *The Eagles Have Flown* (1954), and the novel *The Green Man* (1966), which brings together Amleth (Hamlet) and Arthur—also wrote a brutally realistic novel centring on Arthur. In *The Great Captains* (1956), Treece, like many of his counterparts, uses the chronicle accounts of Arthur's twelve battles to depict Arthur as a *dux bellorum*. But his picture of Arthur is far different from the Romano-British leader of some novels. Treece's Arthur is a brutish, often cruel leader of a British tribe who becomes Count of Britain and battle leader when an aged Ambrosius, accompanied by Medrodus (Mordred), comes to Uther's village. Half in jest, Arthur takes the sword of authority from Ambrosius; and when Medrodus protests that it has been promised to him after Ambrosius' passing, Arthur thrusts it into an oak log and says that it is Medrodus' if he can pull it out—but he cannot, whereas Arthur can. Nevertheless, Medrodus, who kills Ambrosius in anger, becomes a valued adviser and warrior of Arthur's and assists him in several battles against the Saxons. But when Arthur finds him in the bed of his wife, a woman named Lystra, he sends her to dance before a wild bull. After the creature gores her to death, Medrodus causes a riot by accusing Arthur of excessive cruelty. Having alienated many of the British leaders, Arthur ultimately loses their support and any real claim to being a *dux bellorum* for Britain. Medrodus, wounded by Arthur and later captured and castrated by the Saxons, becomes delusional and, thinking Arthur to be Ambrosius and reliving his former vengeance, stabs him to death in a final mad act—just before the citizens of Londinium, Saxon and British, rush in and kill Bedwyr, the last of Arthur's loyal followers.

Edison Marshall

In 1959, popular novelist Edison Marshall (1894–1967) wrote a historical novel called *The Pagan King*, which both borrows and deviates from traditional sources such as Geoffrey of Monmouth. Perhaps the most radical deviation is that Arthur (who is given various names throughout the novel) is said to be the son begotten in an incestuous relationship between Vortigern and his daughter Anna. The fact that Vortigern tried to have Arthur killed as a baby creates hostility between the two men. Vortigern's other son Modred is Arthur's second nemesis in his struggle to gain the throne and battle the Saxons who support Vortigern.

As in most historical novels, elements of romance inevitably become part of the plot and receive a rational explanation. Marshall's Vivain (Vivian) is the daughter of Vortigern's first wife, whom Arthur degrades, and so Vivain seeks Arthur's downfall. She sets a trap that causes a tree to fall on Merlin, break his back, thighs, and loins, and ultimately kill him. Merlin's wish that he not be moved from the spot, either in life or in death, inspires the 'legend' that 'Merlin was not dead' but 'lay in enchanted sleep where the witch Vivain had cast him, and that an invisible wall had been built around him by the same spell' (330).

Rosemary Sutcliff

One of the finest of the historical novels is *Sword at Sunset* (1963) by Rosemary Sutcliff (1920–92). To tell the story of the rise to power and ultimately the death of Artos, Sutcliff draws on Nennius' account of Arthur's battles and the tradition of Arthur's appropriating wealth from the Church to support his wars against the Saxons. Among Artos's inner circle are Cei, Bedwyr, and Gwalchmai, who, as in certain medieval traditions surrounding Gawain, is portrayed as a healer.

The novel, told from Artos's point of view, gives a realistic depiction of the relationship between Artos and his wife Guenhumara, whom he marries not because he loves her but because she brings a dowry of one hundred men and horses. Their marriage is strained by the death of a child, and as Guenhumara nurses the wounded Bedwyr, Artos's most faithful friend and warrior, the two fall in love. The lovers are banished; and Artos's band of elite warriors, the Companions, begins to fragment when the relationship is revealed by the illegitimate and ambitious Medraut.

In a final battle, Artos kills Medraut but also receives a fatal wound from him. So that his British followers will fight more bravely in expectation of his return, Artos gives orders that his death should not be reported; but he has his sword thrown into a lake as a sign to Constantine, his designated successor, that he may begin wielding power. Artos dies with the realization that his resistance to the invaders has lasted long enough so that 'something will remain' (480) of the dream for which he has fought.

Walter O'Meara

The battle of Badon is the climactic event in *The Duke of War* (1966) by Walter O'Meara. The narrator of the novel is a young Romano-British woman named Flavia, whose grandfather Marius has asked her to document the events at their villa, which Arthur uses as his headquarters as he plans 'to force a great battle that will settle, for a long time at least, the issue of this Island's fate' (54–5). That battle is Mount Badon, which lasts for two days and takes a great toll in British and Saxon lives. Ultimately, Arthur is victorious and a period of peace settles on Britain. O'Meara also weaves into his historical account quite a few romance elements, including references to Enid and Geraint, Lancelot and *Elaine, Merlin and Vivian (here called Vivlian), and the quest for the Grail. These elements are, however, treated superficially, and it is the events surrounding the battle of Badon, including the planning of the battle and the tactics used, that are the real interest and the strength of the novel.

George Finkel

In some historical novels, Bedwyr or Bedivere takes on the role of narrator. Such is the case in George Finkel's *Twilight Province* (1967), published in the United States as *Watch Fires to the North* (1968). Bedwyr, a Romano-British prince from a northern settlement called Turris Alba, is among those who defeat a band of Saxons and free their prisoners, one of whom is Artyr (Arthur). Together Bedwyr and Artyr travel to New Rome, the capital of the Byzantine Empire, to get training in military tactics and to buy swift, strong horses. Upon their return to Britain, they create a cavalry unit that allows them crushing victories over the Saxons, including one at Mount Badon (here, contrary to almost all other accounts, placed in the north of Britain). Artyr's skill as a general leads to his being named *dux bellorum*. Artyr marries Bedwyr's cousin and foster-sister Gwenyfer, who remains a good and faithful wife and who plays no part in the rebellion which leads to Artyr's death. When a Thracian recruit tries to use Bedwyr's half-brother Mordredd to take power, a final battle is fought in which Artyr is severely wounded. Put into a ship to be brought to a hermitage for treatment, Artyr never reaches the other shore, perhaps because the boat is swept out to sea; nevertheless, stories arise about Artyr's 'sleeping on a magical island, awaiting the hour of need to come again' (311).

Godfrey Turton

Godfrey Turton allows stories from romance to dominate his historical novel *The Emperor Arthur* (1967). The narrator is not Bedivere but *Pelleas, who joins Arthur's cavalry and is part of the major events of his reign, including the battles at Badon and Camlan. In a strange departure from tradition, Merlin plots against Arthur, as do Gildas, Illtyd, and the Christian monks influenced by them. Merlin wishes to gain power for the Druids, the others for Christianity.

Pelleas's affair with *Ettard is brief. He soon learns that she is looking for status more than love, so it is easy for him to forgive Gawain for sleeping with her. Pelleas turns to his true love Vivian, whose mother Nimuë has been murdered by those plotting against Arthur and who in turn arranges for Merlin to be taken back to the continent by the Saxons to be killed. Merlin survives, though, and returns as a leader of a Saxon band that allies itself with Mordred. The abduction of Guinevere by Melwas and the quest for the Grail are events engineered by the monks conspiring against Arthur, the former to bring Lancelot and Guinevere together and the latter to have Galahad proclaimed emperor over Arthur. In the final battle, Mordred treacherously strikes Arthur, and Pelleas slays Mordred. Arthur is healed by Vivian but then disappears in a retreat where they are hiding from Merlin and the forces that wish them dead; but 'his spirit lives on, waits till the times are ready for his return' (322). That spirit is kept alive in part by the account Pelleas is writing, which will rival Gildas's own history, which is referred to at the end of the novel.

Adam Fergusson

While a number of Arthurian novels focus on religious struggles within Britain, Adam Fergusson's Roman Go Home (1969) has a political rather than a religious agenda. It depicts the withdrawal of Roman troops from Britain in terms that reflect modern views of colonialism. Vortigern, a scheming politician, uses Celtic nationalist movements and rhetoric about Roman imperialism (and, after the departure of the legions, about neo-colonialism) to attain power in Britain. After installing Constans, his half-brother, as a puppet king and then having him killed by Druids, who represent an extreme form of Celticism rejected by most of the leaders of the tribes of Britain, Vortigern enters into an alliance with Hengist and Horsa that is ultimately more damaging to the freedom and self-rule of the British people than was Roman rule. Vortigern soon becomes 'a Saxon puppet' (278) and is forced to give them more and more land and power. When Vortigern's niece Imogen expresses concern for the people of Britain, Hengist decides that she has lived too long under the influence of imperialism and is in need of corrective training, and he sends her Roman lover back to the empire. Thus the two who could have overcome the prejudices that existed on both sides are prevented from marrying and from providing an example of happiness found through human emotions rather than political dogma.

Roy Turner

As in Finkel's novel, Bedivere is the narrator in British novelist Roy Turner's King of the Lordless Country (1971), which tells the story of Arthur 'from the point of view of a Brythonic Celt' (Turner 7). Bedwyr's skill as an archer is instrumental in his gaining renown as a warrior and military leader. Along with Arthur, he is enlisted into the Circle, the elite warriors headed by Gwenhwyfar. The novel culminates in the victory at Badon, where Arthur and his followers win for their people peace and a place for their values as well as 'a story to hand from generation to generation' (205).

Jayne Viney

Like Treece and others, British author Jayne Viney makes Arthur a Celtic leader in *The Bright-Helmed One* (1975). Viney divides her novel into three parts, creating a triptych; though the seams show as she shifts from a first-person narrative by Anwas, one of Arthur's followers, to a more objective narrative in the second and third parts, which continue the story of Arthur but focus on his half-Jutish, half-Celtic wife Winifrith and on Cai. In the first two parts, Viney describes some of the battles from Nennius' list, culminating in Arthur's great victory at Badon. In the third part, Cai rapes Arthur's bride Winifrith days before her wedding—in order to have something that Arthur never will—and kills Arthur's son Llachau; but his loyalty triumphs over his jealousy and he returns to aid Arthur in his final battle.

Arthur's relationship with Cai is developed throughout the novel. As boys, they have divergent styles and ideas of battle. Cai is jealous of Arthur but at some level loves him. Also weaving together the parts of the novel is the character of Arthur, who has 'a code of honour' and 'high ideals of justice and peaceful living' (65). Right to the end of the book, Arthur maintains a nobility that explains his leadership. When he learned that Winifrith had slept with Cai, Arthur had her, despite her innocence of any wrongdoing, sent to the convent at Ambresbury. She and Cai forgive Arthur and ask for his forgiveness because 'the example of his own behaviour had been the instigator of theirs' (250).

Victor Canning

British novelist Victor Canning's three Arthurian novels—*The Crimson Chalice* (1976), *The Circle of the Gods* (1977), and *The Immortal Wound* (1978)—were combined as *The Crimson Chalice* (1978) to tell the story of Arturo (Arthur) from his youth to his death. The title derives from a small chalice once owned by the uncle of Arturo's mother and passed on to her and then to Arturo himself, a chalice that at one point has a crimson glow and seems to have healing properties (cf. 315). In the first half of the 1978 *The Crimson Chalice*, Canning provides an *enfance* for Arthur. As he notes in his foreword, he feels no need to conform to the traditional story of Arthur 'largely because I do not think it bears much relation to the truth. What the truth was, nobody knows.' He gives an account of Arturo's parents, here not Uther and Igraine but Baradoc, the son of a Celtic chieftain, and Gratia, called Tia, the daughter of Romano-British parents. Canning recounts Arturo's birth and the assistance given to his parents by Merlin, the separation of the parents when Baradoc is captured and forced into service by a plunderer, and their eventual reunion. Arturo gathers a band of followers and wins a series of battles, which bring him the title of *dux bellorum*. In his victory at Badon, Arturo's father dies, as does Gawain; and Arturo himself is wounded but recovers. Later Mordreth, banished 'for trying to lay hands in drunken lust on the lady Gwennifer' (468), returns with ten followers and, in a fight with Arturo and six of his warriors, reopens the wound Arturo received at Badon. Arturo dies without any enmity between him and his wife.

Douglas Carmichael

Pendragon (1977) by Douglas Carmichael (b. 1923) draws on early chronicles, saints' lives, Celtic poetry, and romance. He demythologizes the raid described in 'The Spoils of Annwn', and he tells the story of Arthur's demand for cattle from *The Life of St Cadoc*, but when the cattle are turned to ferns, it is a futile and somewhat foolish trick, not a miracle. Carmichael uses Arthur's twelve battles as listed by Nennius as a controlling device for much of the novel, which culminates in Arthur's great victory at the battle of Mount Badon. Elements from romance, primarily from Malory, such as the refusal of Lot and other kings to accept Arthur as their leader, Arthur's siring of Medraut on *Morgause, the story of Balin (here called Bali), and the love of Lancelatus and Vinavera, are also introduced. Yet Carmichael tries to give logical explanations for some of romance's magical elements. For instance, Nimu traps Myrddin in the cave by dislodging a boulder to block the entrance, using not a charm but 'the principles of leverage' of Archimedes that Myrddin taught her. The blend of chronicle and romance material in this and many of the historical novels is not always smooth; but it demonstrates the weight of the two traditions with which authors of any Arthurian novel have to contend.

John Gloag

Artorius Rex (1977) by British novelist John Gloag is similar in concept to Masefield's *Badon Parchments*. It is presented as a report to the emperor by Caius Geladius (Cai or Kay). When Artorius was sent by his uncle Ambrosius Aurelianus to Constantinople to complete his education and learn military arts, Caius was appointed as his tutor and thus became his close companion for forty years. Caius' report chronicles Artorius' wars with the Picts and Saxons. It also speaks of Merlin's prophetic utterances, King *Marc's role in the defence of Britain, and Artorius' troubles with his promiscuous Saxon wife Gwinfreda. Said to be 'everyman's secret appetite' (187), Gwinfreda ultimately betrays Artorius with another Saxon ally, Wencla, whom she subsequently marries. In the end, Caius remembers Merlin's judgement that 'Artorius will be remembered for all the wrong things. For deeds of bravery in battle; for a whim about a woman; for misfortunes of his own making...not for his competence as an imperial general but for his personal prowess as a fighting king' (183).

Peter Vansittart

Arthur's reputation is also an issue in one of the bleakest of the historical novels, Peter Vansittart's *Lancelot* (1978), which is narrated by Ker Maxim, the Romano-British name of the figure more commonly known as Lancelot. Vansittart depicts a group of characters who have none of the qualities of their counterparts in romance and virtually none of the heroism of their counterparts in other historical novels. Artorius and Lancelot are not even friends. Lancelot complains that he and Medraut are 'obviously more gifted than Artorius yet posterity will deem us negligible'; he says too that Artorius is 'grossly unimaginative' (139–40). Just before the battle at Badon, Artorius is nowhere to be found. His followers prepare for the conflict without his help, and during the battle Artorius makes tactical errors— though he does lead one crushing charge. Gwenhever is not a queen but a whore who is shared by Artorius, Lancelot, and many others and who finally 'surrendered to disease or neglect' (165). Gawayne fawns on Arthur and childishly seeks his attention. Lancelot describes himself as lacking 'magnetism and real compassion' (173). Thus Vansittart tries to capture the historical reality of the characters by deromanticizing all of them to the point that there is little nobility left in the story.

Catherine Christian

Catherine Christian's *The Sword and the Flame* (1978), published in the United States as *The Pendragon*, is, like Finkel's novel, narrated by Bedivere, Arthur's childhood friend who becomes 'the Pendragon's Bard and Arthur's chief Companion' (500). Arthur's twelve battles culminating in his victory at Badon form the frame for much of the story, but the battles are not described in as much detail as in some other historical novels. Christian also interweaves elements from romance and makes the love of Lancelot and Guinevere and the hatred of Mordred the driving forces in the latter part of her novel. The Grail quest is told with heavy Tennysonian overtones, except that Lancelot's son *Peredur takes the role traditionally assigned to Galahad.

The novel owes a debt to Malory, as its subtitle, 'Variations on a Theme of Sir Thomas Malory', indicates. This subtitle and the musical terms used as titles of sections of the book also suggest something of Christian's approach, as she combines motifs reworked from Malory with historical themes and elements from her own imagination to create a new work but one that pays homage to its predecessors.

Parke Godwin

Perhaps the only female character in a historical novel who is more independent and courageous than Deeping's Igraine is Parke Godwin's Guenevere, who appears in two of his novels and even becomes the central character in the second. Told in the words of Arthur himself, *Firelord* (1980), the first novel in Godwin's Arthurian 'triptych', portrays the king as a visionary who strives to restore life and purpose to a mighty nation. Arthur spends time with the Prydn, the Faerie-folk; fathers Modred on their ruler Morgana; and achieves his military successes by uniting the people of Britain. Though often idealistic, he can be cruel in his dealings with the Saxons, whom he defeats decisively at Mount Badon. His falling out with Guenevere comes when she, who has lost one child and is unable to have another, discovers that Arthur has fathered a son. Guenevere has Morgana and some of her followers killed, a move she claims is for political reasons (although in the sequel to *Firelord* she admits it was motivated by jealousy as well). After Arthur imprisons Guenevere, she is rescued and leads a force against him. They make peace when Arthur offers to restore her to the throne and apologizes for imprisoning her. Wishing to avenge his mother, Modred has Arthur shot with a poisoned Prydn arrow but is himself killed in the ambush. As Arthur lies dying in Avalon, he dictates his tale, the story told in the novel.

Godwin's *Beloved Exile* (1984) continues the story. Told by Guenevere, it shows how she attempts to retain control of the kingdom. After several betrayals, she is captured by Saxons and sold into slavery. Her experiences there teach her to respect some of the values of the people she considered enemies; she is particularly impressed that they have 'a machinery whereby men can pass judgment on the very laws that bind them' (213). When she returns to her former associates and is banished by Constantine who now rules, her final words reflect some of the democratic notions she has learned from the Saxons. She suggests that kings pass but the people remain, and so the people are paramount. Thus Godwin, who 'made Arthur a universal type, a spiritual Everyman so that his joy and sorrow echoed eternal truths about the human condition' (Letter) in *Firelord*, makes Guenevere not only a powerful woman to parallel Arthur's strength in the earlier novel but a prophet of the democratic values that the Saxons introduce into Britain.

The Last Rainbow (1985) purportedly completes Godwin's trilogy but is only tangentially related to the first two novels and to the Arthurian story. It goes back in time, to the life of St Patrick before he became a saint. Living among British pagans, he meets Dorelei, the Prydn ruler who teaches him the powers of the earth and the pleasures of love; in turn, he offers her and her people a new god and saviour. The slight Arthurian element occurs later, when Patrick meets Ambrosius Aurelianus, who has begun his struggle for British autonomy.

Well written and original in their approach to the Arthurian tradition, Godwin's novels are also noteworthy for their attention to the role of Guenevere and other women within their respective societies.

Bernard Cornwell

British novelist Bernard Cornwell is the author of The Warlord Chronicles, a trilogy that takes place in the latter part of the fifth century when the Romans have withdrawn from Britain as their empire is collapsing. Cornwell, like many historical novelists, depicts Arthur as a *dux bellorum* rather than a late medieval king, but what he does better than any of his predecessors is to show the political conflicts in Britain and to define Arthur's role in those conflicts. The first novel of his trilogy, *The Winter King* (1995), focuses on the internal discord among the British chieftains, and, while the Saxon invaders are a presence and a factor in the political intrigue, it is clear that the war against them will not be central until the second volume. Cornwell's tale is narrated by a former warrior named Derfel, who is now a Christian monk writing the story of Arthur for a British queen named Igraine. Derfel tells of an Arthur trying to keep in check the civil strife in Britain. In addition, there is conflict between Christianity and the British religion, promulgated by Druids like Merlin and his followers, including Morgan and Nimue. In a twist on the approach taken by authors like Godwin and Bradley, Cornwell presents Guinevere as an opponent of Christianity as well. Cornwell's complex

Guinevere, who is strong enough not to be intimidated by Arthur, promotes her own religious beliefs despite opposition from the Christian hierarchy. In a telling comment, when the woman for whom Derfel writes his story says that she does not like Guinevere, Derfel says, 'Then I have failed' (190).

Cornwell also challenges some of the conventional views of other Arthurian characters. His Galahad is neither the son of Lancelot nor the Grail knight. Rather, he is a skilled warrior and the half-brother of Lancelot, son of King *Ban. Cornwell's Lancelot would rather leave the fighting to others, although he is a master at taking credit for victories in which he played little part. By having the poets whom his father supported create exaggerated songs of his deeds, he has acquired a reputation far in excess of his accomplishments.

Cornwell's Arthur, who is central to the novel, can be brutally practical; but he is also an idealist. He believes that soldiers should use their power to protect the weak. And it is in Arthur that the 'historical' and the legendary best blend, as can be seen in an exchange between Derfel and Igraine, who has heard embellished tales about Arthur and his realm not long after his death. When Derfel tells Igraine that Arthur had a vision of a world in which he offered help to the weak, she says, 'he wanted Camelot'. Derfel replies, 'We called it Dumnonia' (190). But Igraine wants it 'to be the poet's Camelot: green grass and high towers and ladies in gowns and warriors strewing their paths with flowers'. Derfel rejects this vision but says that Arthur's Camelot 'was special ... because Arthur gave the land justice' (190).

The trilogy continues in *Enemy of God* (1996), which is not as well crafted as *The Winter King*. The second instalment treats Merlin's attempt to find the last of the *Thirteen Treasures of Britain, the Cauldron of Clyddno Eiddyn, which he believes to be the key to power in Britain. As Cornwell explains in his author's note, he considers the Grail story 'a Christianized re-working of the much older cauldron myths' of the Celts (395) since the Cauldron, like the Grail, has the power to restore life. Against the background of the quest for the cauldron and the struggle for possession of it, Cornwell tells the story of Lancelot's attempt to become king of Britain and of Guinevere's betrayal of Arthur. The narrator Derfel remains the truest companion of Arthur and continues to revere him as someone who tried 'to change the world and his instrument was love' (210).

Excalibur (1997), the concluding novel in the trilogy, tells of Arthur's consolidation of power in Britain by overcoming first the rebellious Lancelot and then the Saxons. As in many of the historical novels, the battle at Mount Badon is crucial. The battle begins when a small force led by Derfel, and including Guinevere, must use the mount as a strategic position from which to escape and defend themselves from a band of Saxons. After the main body of invaders surrounds the mount, believing Arthur is there, a strategy devised by Guinevere prolongs the battle long enough for Arthur and his allies to arrive and defeat the Saxons. The novel concludes with a battle at Camlan, in which Arthur must fight and kill Mordred, a prince of Britain who is the son not of Arthur but of another Mordred, son of Uther Pendragon (Arthur being presented in the novel as Uther's illegitimate son).

Though Arthur supported him as king, Mordred has become cruel and dangerous. Arthur finally kills him and instructs Derfel to throw Excalibur, one of the treasures of Britain sought by a wicked Nimue, into the water. Arthur is then taken off in the ship Pridwen, which has been prepared by Merlin for the voyage, and is not heard from again.

Jack Whyte

Another sequence of novels, Canadian author Jack Whyte's multi-volume saga (called A Dream of Eagles in Canada and The Camulod Chronicles in the United States) begins in Roman Britain. Narrated by Gaius Publius Varrus, a Roman soldier, ironsmith, and weaponmaker, the first two volumes, *The Skystone* (1996) and *The Singing Sword* (1996), tell of Varrus' friendship with the Roman general Caius Cornelius Britannicus, his commanding officer and his lifelong friend, and of their establishment of a colony in Britain called Camulod in anticipation of the withdrawal of the Empire's troops. Varrus uses an innovative technique and design to fashion a powerful sword for use by cavalry. After obtaining a special metal from a meteor, a skystone, that lay at the bottom of a lake and creating from it a statue of Coventina, the Celtic goddess of water, he calls the statue the *Lady of the Lake. Later, he melts down the statue and uses some of the metal to form a sword of his new design, which he calls Excalibur.

The third volume of the sequence, *The Eagles' Brood* (1997), tells of the maturing of Uther, the grandson to whom Varrus entrusted Excalibur, and of Merlyn, grandson of Britannicus. The novel is narrated by Merlyn, who recounts a conflict between Camulod and Lot. When Uther and Igraine, Lot's wife and Uther's lover, die at the end of the novel, their son Arthur is entrusted to Merlyn. Uther's story is retold in *Uther* (2001) in what Whyte calls a 'parallel novel' to *The Eagle's Brood*, sharing common elements with it but 'unfolding independently' of the tale of Merlyn's upbringing told in it (*Uther* 9). Merlyn's tale continues in *The Saxon Shore* (1998) and *The Fort at River's Bend* (1999), in which Merlin cares for the young Arthur and the sword Excalibur as invasions threaten his grandfather's dream of Camulod. As Merlyn says, 'My goals were simple, their realization complex: I had to bring a boy to manhood, teaching him to perform a task the like of which had never been set for any man before. I had to breed a kingdom from a single colony. I had to lead a people into a new age of hope and wonder' (*Fort* 14).

In *The Sorcerer: Metamorphosis* (1999), Merlyn decides it is time to return from the Fort at River's Bend, where he was taken for safekeeping after an attempt on his life. In the course of the novel, Merlyn metamorphoses from a warrior and a protector of the young Arthur into a sorcerer, as his reputation for magic spreads when he uses disguises and poison to slay Britain's enemies. But there is also a metamorphosis of Arthur from a child in need of instruction to a warrior and, at the end of the novel, into the High King of Britain, the man destined to receive Excalibur.

BIBLIOGRAPHY

Early References to Arthur

Aneirin. *Y Gododdin: Britain's Oldest Heroic Poem*, ed. and trans. A. O. H. Jarman. Llandysul: Gomer Press, 1990.

Annales Cambriae, in *British History and the Welsh Annals*, ed. and trans. John Morris. Arthurian Period Sources 8. London: Phillimore, 1980: 85–91.

Bede. *A History of the English Church and People*, trans. Leo Sherley-Price. Baltimore: Penguin Books, 1965.

Charles-Edwards, Thomas. 'The Arthur of History', in Rachel Bromwich, A. O. H. Jarman, and Brynley F. Roberts (eds.), *The Arthur of the Welsh*. Cardiff: University of Wales Press, 1991: 15–32.

Gildas. *The Ruin of Britain and Other Works*, ed. and trans. Michael Winterbottom. London: Phillimore, 1978.

James, John. *Men Went to Cattraeth*. London: Cassell, 1969.

Nennius. *Historia Britonnum*, in John Morris (ed. and trans.), *British History and the Welsh Annals*. Arthurian Period Sources 8. London: Phillimore, 1980: 50–84.

Padel, O. J. 'The Nature of Arthur', *Cambrian Medieval Celtic Studies*, 27 (Summer 1994), 1–31.

Sutcliff, Rosemary. *The Shining Company*. New York: Farrar, Straus, Giroux, 1990.

Arthur in Welsh Literature

[*The Birth of Arthur*.] J. H. Davies, 'A Welsh Version of the Birth of Arthur', *Y Cymmrodor*, 24 (1913), 247–64.

Blamires, David. 'The Medieval Inspiration of David Jones', in Roland Mathias (ed.), *David Jones: Eight Essays on his Work as Writer and Artist*. Llandysul: Gomer Press, 1976: 73–87.

Budgey, Andrea. ' "Preiddeu Annwn" and the Welsh Tradition of Arthur', in Cyril J. Byrne, Margaret Harry, and Pádraig Ó Siadhail (eds.), *Celtic Languages and Celtic Peoples*. Halifax: D'Arcy McGee Chair of Irish Studies, St Mary's University, 1992: 391–404.

Coe, Jon B., and Young, Simon (eds. and trans.). *The Celtic Sources for the Arthurian Legend*. Felinfach: Llanerch, 1995.

Foster, Idris Llewelyn. '*Culhwch and Olwen* and *Rhonabwy's Dream*', in Roger Sherman Loomis (ed.), *Arthurian Literature in the Middle Ages: A Collaborative History*. Oxford: Clarendon Press, 1959: 31–43.

Jones, David. *The Anathemata: Fragments of an Attempted Writing*. 1952; repr. London: Faber and Faber, 1979.

—— *In Parenthesis: Seinnyessit e gledyf ym penn mameu*. 1937; repr. New York: Chilmark Press, 1961.

—— 'The Myth of Arthur'. 1942; repr. in Harman Grisewood (ed.), *Epoch and Artist: Selected Writings*. London: Faber and Faber, 1959: 212–59.

—— *The Sleeping Lord and Other Fragments*. London: Faber and Faber, 1974.

Lloyd-Morgan, Ceridwen. '*Breuddwyd Rhonabwy* and Later Arthurian Literature', in Rachel Bromwich, A. O. H. Jarman, and Brynley F. Roberts (eds.), *The Arthur of the Welsh: The Arthurian Legend in Medieval Welsh Literature*. Cardiff: University of Wales Press, 1991: 183–208.

Loomis, Richard, and Johnston, Dafydd (eds.). *Medieval Welsh Poems: An Anthology*. Binghamton, NY: Pegasus Books, 1992.

The Mabinogi and Other Medieval Welsh Tales, trans. Patrick K. Ford. Berkeley and Los Angeles: University of California Press, 1977.

The Mabinogion, trans. Gwyn Jones and Thomas Jones, rev. edn. London: J. M. Dent, 1989.

The Mabinogion from the Welsh of the Llyrf Coch o Hergest (The Red Book of Hergest), trans. Lady Charlotte Guest. London: Bernard Quaritch, 1877.

Padel, O. J. *Arthur in Medieval Welsh Literature*. Cardiff: University of Wales Press, 2000.

Sims-Williams, Patrick. 'The Early Welsh Arthurian Poems', in Rachel Bromwich, A. O. H. Jarman, and Brynley F. Roberts (eds.), *The Arthur of the Welsh: The Arthurian Legend in Medieval Welsh Literature*. Cardiff: University of Wales Press, 1991: 33–71.

Trioedd ynys Prydein: The Welsh Triads, ed. Rachel Bromwich. Cardiff: University of Wales Press, 1978.

Williams, Sir Ifor (ed.). *The Poems of Taliesin*. Dublin: Dublin Institute for Advanced Studies, 1987.

Saints' Lives

Caradoc of Llancarfan. *Vita Gildae*, in *Two Lives of Gildas by a Monk of Ruys and Caradoc of Llancarfan*, trans. Hugh Williams. Felinfach: Llanerch, 1990.

Chambers, E. K. *Arthur of Britain*. 1927; repr. Cambridge: Speculum Historiale, 1964.

Korrel, Peter. *An Arthurian Triangle: A Study of the Development and Characterization of Arthur, Guinevere and Modred*. Leiden: E. J. Brill, 1984.

La Vie de S. Efflam, in Albert Le Grand (ed.), *Les Vies des saints de la Bretagne armorique*, 5th edn. Quimper: J. Salaun, 1901: 582–90.

Wade-Evans, A. W. (ed. and trans.). *Vitae sanctorum Britanniae et genealogiae*. Cardiff: University of Wales Press Board, 1944.

White, Richard (ed.). *King Arthur in Legend and History*. New York: Routledge, 1997.

Geoffrey of Monmouth and his Influence

Alliterative Morte Arthure, in Larry D. Benson (ed.), *King Arthur's Death*, rev. Edward E. Foster. Kalamazoo, Mich.: Medieval Institute Publications for TEAMS, 1994: 129–284.

Arthur and Gorlagon, ed. G. L. Kittredge. 1903; repr. New York: Haskell House, 1966.

Blakey, Brian. 'The Harley *Brut*: An Early French Translation of Geoffrey of Monmouth's *Historia regum Britanniae*', *Romania*, 82 (1961), 44–70.

Breta sögur, in E. Jónsson and F. Jónsson (eds.), *Hauksbók udgiven efter de Arnamagnæanske Håndskrifter no. 371, 544 og 675, 4°* . . . . Copenhagen: Thieles Bogtrykkeri, 1892: 231–302.

Le Chevalier du Papegau, ed. Ferdinand Heuckenkamp. Halle: Max Niemeyer, 1896.

Curley, Michael. *Geoffrey of Monmouth*. New York: Twayne, 1994.

Echard, Siân. *Arthurian Narrative in the Latin Tradition*. Cambridge: Cambridge University Press, 1998.

Geoffrey of Monmouth. *History of the Kings of Britain*, trans. Sebastian Evans, rev. Charles W. Dunn. New York: E. P. Dutton, 1958.

Gesta regum Britanniae, ed. Francisque Michel. Bordeaux: Printed by G. Gounouilhou for the Cambrian Archaeological Association, 1862.

The Knight of the Parrot (Le Chevalier du Papegau), trans. Thomas E. Vesce. New York: Garland, 1986.

Laȝamon. *Brut or Hystoria Brutonum*, ed. and trans. S. C. Weinberg. Harlow: Longman, 1995.

P[arker], M[artin]. *The Famous History of That Most Renowned Christian Worthy Arthur King of the Britaines, and his Famous Knights of the Round Table*. London: Francis Coles, 1660.

Perceforest, 4 parts in 7 vols., part 1, ed. Jane H. M. Taylor, parts 2–4, ed. Gilles Roussineau. Geneva: Droz, 1979–99. (Part 1 has the title *Roman de Perceforest*; parts 2–4 have the title *Perceforest*.)

Roberts, Brynley F. 'Geoffrey of Monmouth, *Historia regum Britanniae* and *Brut y Brenhinedd*', in Rachel Bromwich, A. O. H. Jarman, and Brynley F. Roberts (eds.), *The Arthur of the Welsh*. Cardiff: University of Wales Press, 1991: 97–116.

Taylor, Jane. 'The Parrot, the Knight and the Decline of Chivalry', in Keith Busby and Norris Lacy (eds.), *Conjunctures: Medieval Studies in Honor of Douglas Kelly*. Amsterdam: Rodopi, 1994: 529–44.

—— 'The Sense of Beginning: Genealogy and Plenitude in Late Medieval Narrative Cycles', in Sara Sturm-Maddox and Donald Maddox (eds.), *Transtextualities: Of Cycles and Cyclicity in Medieval French Literature*. Binghamton, NY: Medieval & Renaissance Texts and Studies, 1996: 93–123.

Thompson, Aaron (trans.), *The British History, Translated into English from the Latin of Jeffrey of Monmouth*. London: J. Bowyer, 1718.

Turville-Petre, Thorlac. *The Alliterative Revival*. Cambridge: D. S. Brewer, 1977.

Virunnius, Ponticus. *Viri doctissimi Britannicae, historiae libri sex*. London: Apud Edmundum Bollifantum, 1585.

Wace. *Roman de Brut/A History of the British: Text and Translation*, ed. and trans. Judith Weiss. Exeter: University of Exeter Press, 1999.

Wright, Neil (ed.), *The 'Historia regum Britannie' of Geoffrey of Monmouth II. The First Variant Version: A Critical Edition*. Cambridge: D. S. Brewer, 1988.

Other Latin Chronicles

Day, Mildred Leake. 'The Letter from King Arthur to Henry II: Political Use of the Arthurian Legend in *Draco Normannicus*', in Glyn S. Burgess and Robert A. Taylor (eds.), *The Spirit of the Court*. Cambridge: D. S. Brewer, 1985: 153–7.

Etienne de Rouen. *Draco Normannicus*, in Richard Howlett (ed.), *Chronicles of the Reigns of Stephen, Henry II, and Richard I*. Rolls Series 82/2. London: Longman and Trübner, 1885.

Henry, Archdeacon of Huntingdon. *Historia Anglorum: The History of the English People*, ed. and trans. Diana Greenway. Oxford: Clarendon Press, 1996.

[*Vera historia de morte Arthuri*.] 'An Edition of the *Vera historia de morte Arthuri*', ed. Michael Lapidge, *Arthurian Literature*, 1 (1981), 79–93.

William of Malmesbury. *Gesta regum Anglorum: The History of the English Kings*, ed. and trans. R. A. B. Mynors, completed by R. M. Thomson and M. Winterbottom. 2 vols. Oxford: Clarendon Press, 1998.

William of Newburgh. *The History of William of Newburgh*, trans. Joseph Stevenson. 1856; repr. in facsimile Felinfach: Llanerch, 1996.

The Continuing Chronicle Tradition in England and Scotland

Andrew of Wyntoun. *The Original Chronicle*, vol. iv, ed. F. J. Amours. STS 54. Edinburgh: For the STS by William Blackwood and Sons, 1906.

Bellenden, John (trans.). *The Chronicles of Scotland Compiled by Hector Boece*, ed. R. W. Chambers and Edith C. Batho. 2 vols. STS 3rd series 10, 15. Edinburgh: William Blackwood, 1938, 1941.

Bower, Walter. *Scotichronicon*, vol. ii (of 9 vols.), ed. and trans. John and Winifred MacQueen. Aberdeen: Aberdeen University Press, 1989.

Buchanan, George. *The History of Scotland from the Earliest Period to the Present Time*, vol. i, division 2. Glasgow: Blackie and Son, 1852.

Capgrave, John. *John Capgrave's Abbreuiacion of Cronicles*, ed. Peter J. Lucas. EETS os 285. Oxford: Oxford University Press, 1983.

Carley, James. 'Polydore Vergil and John Leland on King Arthur: The Battle of the Books', in Edward Donald Kennedy (ed.), *King Arthur: A Casebook*. New York: Garland, 1996: 185–204.

Castleford, Thomas. *Castleford's Chronicle or The Boke of Brut*, ed. Caroline D. Eckhardt. 2 vols. EETS os 305, 306. Oxford: Oxford University Press for the EETS, 1996.

Churchill, Winston S. *A History of the English-Speaking Peoples*, i: *The Birth of Britain*. New York: Dodd, Mead, 1956.

Fordun, John of. *John of Fordun's Chronicle of the Scottish Nation*, trans. Felix J. H. Skene, ed. William F. Skene. 2 vols. 1872; repr. Lampeter: Llanerch, 1993.

Furnivall, Frederick J. (ed.). *Arthur: A Short Sketch of his Life and History in English Verse*. EETS os 2, 2nd edn. 1869; repr. London: Oxford University Press for the EETS, 1965.

Göller, Karl Heinz. 'King Arthur in the Scottish Chronicles', in Edward Donald Kennedy (ed.), *King Arthur: A Casebook*. New York: Garland, 1996: 173–84. (Repr. from *Anglia*, 80 (1962), 390–404.)

Hardyng, John. *The Chronicle of Iohn Hardyng: Containing an Account of Publick Transactions from the Earliest Period of English History to the Beginning of the Reign of King Edward the Fourth. Together with the Continuation by Richard Grafton, the Thirty Fourth Year of King Henry the Eighth*, ed. Henry Ellis. London: Printed for F. C. and J. Rivington, etc., 1812.

—— 'John Hardyng's Arthur: A Critical Edition', ed. Christine Marie Harker. Diss. University of California, Riverside, 1996.

Langtoft, Pierre de. *The Chronicle of Pierre de Langtoft, in French Verse, from the Earliest Period to the Death of King Edward I*, ed. Thomas Wright. 2 vols. Rolls Series 47. London: Longmans, Green, Reader, and Dyer, 1866, 1868.

Leland, John. *Assertio inclytissimi Arturii*, trans. Richard Robinson as *The Assertion of King Arthur*, in *The Famous Historie of Chinon of England Together with The Assertion of King Arthure*. EETS os 165. London: Humphrey Milford for the Early English Text Society, 1925. (Leland's Latin text was originally published in 1544 and Robinson's translation in 1582.)

Leslie, Jhone. *The Historie of Scotland*, trans. Father James Dalrymple, ed. Father E. G. Cody, vol. i. STS 5, 14. Edinburgh: For the STS by William Blackwood and Sons, 1888.

Major, John. *A History of Greater Britain as well England as Scotland*, trans. Archibald Constable. Publications of the Scottish History Society 10. Edinburgh: T. and A. Constable for the Scottish History Society, 1892.

Mannyng, Robert, of Brunne. *The Chronicle*, ed. Idelle Sullens. Binghamton, NY: MRTS, Binghamton University, 1996.

Matheson, Lister M. *The Prose Brut: The Development of a Middle English Chronicle*. Tempe, Ariz.: Medieval & Renaissance Texts and Studies, 1998.

Milton, John. *Complete Prose Works of John Milton*, vol. v, part 1, ed. French Fogle. New Haven: Yale University Press, 1971.

[*Prose Brut.*] *The Brut or The Chronicles of England*, ed. Friedrich W. D. Brie. 2 vols. EETS os 131, 136. London: Kegan Paul, Trench, Trübner, 1906, 1908.

Ritson, Joseph. *The Life of King Arthur: From Ancient Historians and Authentic Documents*. London: Payne and Foss, 1825.

Robert of Gloucester. *The Metrical Chronicle of Robert of Gloucester*, ed. William Aldis Wright. Rolls Series 86, part 1 and part 2. London: Her Majesty's Stationery Office, 1887.

[*Short Metrical Chronicle*.] *An Anonymous Short English Metrical Chronicle*, ed. Edward Zettl. EETS os 196. London: Humphrey Millford for the EETS, 1935.

Stewart, William (trans.). *The Buik of the Croniclis of Scotland or A Metrical Version of the History of Hector Boece*, ed. William B. Turnbull. Rolls Series 6, part 2 (of 3). London: Longman, Brown, Green, Longmans, and Roberts, 1858.

Summerfield, Thea. *The Matter of Kings' Lives: The Design of Past and Present in the Early Fourteenth-Century Verse Chronicles of Pierre de Langtoft and Robert Mannyng*. Amsterdam: Rodopi, 1998.

Trevisa, John (trans.). *Polychronicon Ranulphi Higden monachi Cestrensis: Together with the English Translations of John Trevisa and of an Unknown Writer of the Fifteenth Century*, ed. Joseph Rawson Lumby. Rolls Series 41, part 5. London: Longman, 1874.

Arthur's Death and Survival

Barr, Mike W., and Bolland, Brian. *Camelot 3000*. 12-part series, 1982–5, by DC Comics. Repr. in one volume: New York: DC Comics, 1988.

Bridges, Sallie. *Marble Isle, Legends of the Round Table, and Other Poems*. Philadelphia: J. B. Lippincott, 1864.

Chesterton, G. K. *The Grave of Arthur*. Ariel Poems 25. London: Faber and Faber, 1930.

Cochran, Molly. *The Third Magic*. New York: Forge, 2003.

—— and Murphy, Warren. *The Broken Sword*. New York: TOR, 1997.

—— —— *The Forever King*. New York: TOR, 1992.

Curry, Jane Louise. *The Sleepers*. New York: Harcourt, Brace & World, 1968.

Dane, Clemence. *The Saviours: Seven Plays on One Theme*. London: William Heinemann, 1942.

David, Peter. *Knight Life*. New York: Ace Fantasy, 1987.

[*Il Detto del Gatto Lupesco. (The Saying of Gatto Lupesco)*] *Il Gatto Lupesco e il mare amoroso*, ed. Annamaria Carrega. Turin: Edizioni dell'Orso, 2000.

De Vere, Aubrey. 'King Henry the Second at the Tomb of King Arthur', in *The Search after Proserpine and Other Poems Classical and Meditative*. London: Macmillan, 1892: 97–103.

Entwistle, William J. *The Arthurian Legend in the Literatures of the Spanish Peninsula*. 1925; repr. New York: Phaeton Press, 1975.

Faulkner, Nancy. *Sword of the Winds*. Garden City, NY: Doubleday, 1957.

Gardner, Edmund G. *The Arthurian Legend in Italian Literature*. 1930; repr. New York: Octagon Books, 1971.

Geoffrey Junior [pseudonym of William John Courthope]. *The Marvellous History of King Arthur in Avalon and of the Lifting of Lyonnesse: A Chronicle of the Round Table Communicated by Geoffrey of Monmouth*. London: John Murray, 1904.

Gervase of Tilbury. *Otia imperialia: Recreation for an Emperor*, ed. and trans. S. E. Banks and J. W. Binns. Oxford: Clarendon Press, 2002.

Gibson, Wilfrid Wilson. 'The Queen's Crags', in *Borderlands*. London: Elkin Mathews, 1914: 9–28.

Giraldus Cambrensis. *De principis instructione*, ed. George F. Warner. Rolls Series 21/8. London: Her Majesty's Printing Office, 1891.

—— *Speculum ecclesiae*, ed. J. S. Brewer. Rolls Series 21/4. London: Her Majesty's Printing Office, 1873.

Graff, Irvine. 'The Return of Arthur', in *The Return of Arthur*. Boston: The Stratford Co., 1922: 1–19.

Lawhead, Stephen R. *Avalon: The Return of King Arthur*. New York: Avon Books, 1999.

Masefield, John. 'Dust to Dust', in *Midsummer Night and Other Tales in Verse*. London: William Heinemann, 1928: 152.

Moorman, F. W. *Potter Thompson*, in *Plays of the Ridings*. London: Elkin Mathews, 1919: 47–70.

Norman, Diana. *King of the Last Days*. London: Hodder and Stoughton, 1981.

Peacock, Thomas Love. *The Round Table; or King Arthur's Feast*. London: John Arliss, 1817. (Repr. in *The Works of Thomas Love Peacock*, vi: *Poems*. London: Constable, 1927: 315–34.)

Rhys, Ernest. 'King Arthur's Sleep', in *Welsh Ballads and Other Poems*. London: David Nutt, n.d. [1898]: 20–6.

Skinner, Martyn. *The Return of Arthur: A Poem of the Future*. London: Chapman and Hall, 1966.

Ticknor, Frank O. *The Poems of Frank O. Ticknor, M.D.*, ed. K. M. R., with an Introductory Notice of the Author by Paul H. Hayne. Philadelphia: J. B. Lippincott, 1879.

Torroella, Guillem de. *La Faula*. Tarragona: Edicions Tàrraco, 1984.

Warton, Thomas. 'The Grave of King Arthur', in *Poems: A New Edition*. London: T. Becket, 1777: 63–72.

Wibberley, Leonard. *The Quest of Excalibur*. New York: Putnam, 1959.

Historical Verse

Blackmore, Richard. *King Arthur: An Heroick Poem in Twelve Books*. London: Awnsham and John Churchil, 1697.

—— *Prince Arthur: An Heroick Poem in Ten Books*. London: Awnsham and John Churchil, 1695.

Camden, William. *Britannia*. 1587; repr. London: Georg Bishop, 1594.

Churchyard, Thomas. *The Worthines of Wales*. London: G. Robinson, 1587; repr. New York: Franklin, 1967.

Drayton, Michael, *Poly-Olbion*, vol. iv of *Works*, ed. J. William Hebel. Oxford: At the Shakespeare Head Press by Basil Blackwell, 1933.

Hall, John Lesslie. *Old English Idyls*. Boston: Ginn & Co., 1899.

Heath-Stubbs, John. *Artorius: A Heroic Poem in Four Books and Eight Episodes*. London: Enitharmon Press, 1974.

Hole, Richard. *Arthur or the Northern Enchantment: A Poetical Romance in Seven Books*. London: G. G. J. and J. Robinson, 1789.

Masefield, John. *Midsummer Night and Other Tales in Verse*. London: William Heinemann, 1928.

Milman, H. H. *Samor, Lord of the Bright City*. London: John Murray, 1818.

Historical Drama

Arden, John, and D'Arcy, Margaretta. *The Island of the Mighty: A Play on a Traditional British Theme in Three Parts*. London: Eyre Methuen, 1974.

Brenton, Howard. *The Romans in Britain*, in *Plays: Two*. London: Methuen Drama, 1989: 1–95.

Dryden, John. *King Arthur or The British Worthy*, in *The Works of John Dryden*, vol. xvi, ed. Vinton A. Dearing. Berkeley and Los Angeles: University of California Press: 1–69.

Garrick, David. *King Arthur or The British Worthy.* London: W. Strahan, 1770.

Hilton, William. *Arthur, Monarch of the Britons: A Tragedy*, in *Poetical Works*, vol. ii. Newcastle upon Tyne: T. Saint, 1776: 169–251.

Hughes, Thomas. *The Misfortunes of Arthur*, in *Early English Classical Tragedies*. Oxford: Clarendon Press, 1912: 217–96. (The play was written in 1587.)

Ireland, W. H. *Vortigern: An Historical Drama.* London: Joseph Thomas, 1832.

MacLiesh, A. Fleming. *The Destroyers.* New York: John Day, 1942.

Merriman, James. *The Flower of Kings: A Study of the Arthurian Legend in England between 1485 and 1835.* Lawrence: University Press of Kansas, 1973.

Pennie, J. F. *The Dragon King*, in *Britain's Historical Drama: A Series of National Tragedies.* London: Samuel Maunder, 1832: 413–547.

Sherriff, R. C. *The Long Sunset.* London: Elek Books, 1955.

Historical Novels

Babcock, William H. *Cian of the Chariots: A Romance of the Days of Arthur Emperor of Britain and his Knights of the Round Table, How They Delivered London and Overthrew the Saxons after the Downfall of Roman Britain*, ill. George Foster Barnes. Boston: Lothrop Publishing Co., 1898.

Bishop, Farnham, and Brodeur, Arthur Gilchrist. *The Altar of the Legion*, ill. Henry Pitz. Boston: Little, Brown, and Co., 1926.

Canning, Victor. *The Crimson Chalice.* New York: William Morrow, 1978.

Carmichael, Douglas. *Pendragon: An Historical Novel.* Hicksville, NY: Blackwater Press, 1977.

Christian, Catherine. *The Sword and the Flame: Variations on a Theme of Sir Thomas Malory.* London: Macmillan, 1978.

Church, A. J., with Putnam, Ruth. *The Count of the Saxon Shore or The Villa in Vectis.* London: Seeley & Co., 1887.

Conlee, John. 'Warwick Deeping's *Uther and Igraine*', *Arthuriana*, 11.4 (Winter 2001), 88–95.

Cornwell, Bernard. *Enemy of God: A Novel of Arthur.* New York: St Martin's, 1996.

—— *Excalibur: A Novel of Arthur.* New York: St Martin's, 1997.

—— *The Winter King: A Novel of Arthur.* New York: St Martin's, 1996.

Crosfield, T. H. *A Love in Ancient Days.* London: Elkin Mathews, 1908.

Deeping, Warwick. *The Man Who Went Back.* New York: Alfred A. Knopf, 1940.

—— *The Sword and the Cross.* London: Cassell, 1957.

—— *Uther and Igraine.* 1903; repr. New York: Alfred A. Knopf, 1928.

Duggan, Alfred. *Conscience of a King.* New York: Coward-McCann, 1951.

Faraday, W. Barnard. *Pendragon.* London: Methuen, 1930.

Fergusson, Adam. *Roman Go Home.* London: Collins, 1969.

Finkel, George. *Watch Fires to the North.* New York: Viking, 1968.

Frankland, Edward. *Arthur, the Bear of Britain.* 1944; repr. Oakland, Calif.: Green Knight, 1998.

Gloag, John. *Artorius Rex.* London: Cassell, 1977.

Godwin, Parke. *Beloved Exile.* New York: Bantam, 1984.

—— *Firelord.* Garden City, NY: Doubleday, 1980.

—— *The Last Rainbow.* New York: Bantam, 1985.

—— Letter to Alan Lupack. 19 Jan. 1981.

Marshall, Edison. *The Pagan King.* Garden City, NY: Doubleday, 1959.

Masefield, John. *Badon Parchments.* London: William Heinemann, 1947.

O'Meara, Walter. *The Duke of War.* New York: Harcourt, Brace & World, 1966.

Starr, Nathan Comfort. *King Arthur Today: The Arthurian Legend in English and American Literature 1901–1953.* Gainesville: University of Florida Press, 1954.

Sutcliff, Rosemary. *Sword at Sunset.* London: Hodder & Stoughton, 1963.

Treece, Henry. *The Eagles Have Flown.* London: Allen and Unwin, 1954.

—— *The Great Captains.* New York: Random House, 1956.

—— *The Green Man.* London: The Bodley Head, 1966.

Trevor, Meriol. *The Last of Britain.* London: Macmillan, 1956.

Turner, Roy. *King of the Lordless Country.* London: Dennis Dobson, 1971.

Turton, Godfrey. *The Emperor Arthur.* Garden City, NY: Doubleday, 1967.

Vansittart, Peter. *Lancelot.* London: Peter Owen, 1978.

Viney, Jayne. *The Bright-Helmed One.* London: Robert Hale, 1975.

Whyte, Jack. *The Eagles' Brood.* New York: Forge, 1997.

—— *The Fort at River's Bend.* New York: Forge, 1999.

—— *The Saxon Shore.* New York: Forge, 1998.

—— *The Singing Sword.* New York: Forge, 1996.

—— *The Skystone.* New York: Forge, 1996.

—— *The Sorcerer: Metamorphosis.* New York: Forge, 1999.

—— *Uther.* New York: Forge, 2001.

The Romance Tradition

In the twelfth century, as Geoffrey of Monmouth was reshaping literary history by laying the foundation for a long tradition of chronicle and historical literature about *Arthur, another significant tradition was developing. That tradition, the romance tradition, created a new type of literature by combining elements of what came to be known as 'courtly love' with concepts of chivalric conduct.

Though romances often contain strikingly realistic descriptions, they are essentially not realistic in their approach. Not only do they present wonders not found in the real world, but they also depict a world of superlatives: of the most beautiful ladies, the bravest knights, the fiercest opponents, the ugliest ogres, even, as in Chrétien de Troyes's *Lancelot*, 'the most beautiful tombs' and 'a sycamore tree of unequaled beauty' (193, 255). Among the superlatives is often the truest love. The term 'romance' itself, from *roman*, originally referred to the French language, which was descended from Latin or the Roman language (the term romance language now applies to any language derived from Latin). The term came to mean a story or a tale told in French, without the modern associations with love. Ultimately it was applied to the types of tales told by the French; and since many of the early French *romans* or romances told of knightly deeds and great loves, the word *roman* or 'romance' eventually came to be associated with such tales.

'Courtly love' is a problematic term. As some scholars have pointed out, the designation itself (or rather its French equivalent 'amour courtois') was coined by French critic Gaston Paris in 1883 and is generally not used in medieval texts. There are, however, in some of these texts comparable terms, such as 'fin amour', that refer to the love element. The code of courtly love (a term I will use for convenience) is outlined in a work called *De amore* (translated under the title *The Art of Courtly Love*), usually dated *c*.1180. This book is attributed to an author named Andreas Capellanus, who is thought to be a contemporary of Chrétien de Troyes and Countess Marie de Champagne, who, along with other noblewomen, is presented as rendering decisions on questions of love. Whether such judgements were ever actually offered by noble ladies is not known; if they were, it was surely as a kind of courtly play and not as a way of redefining the role of love in society. Critics have, however, raised many questions about courtly love and the *De amore* in which it is codified, including the identity of Andreas and the date of his book. Peter Dronke has suggested that there may not have been a clerk of Marie's court named Andreas, that the name itself may be a pseudonym alluding to a lost romance about Andreas of Paris and the Queen of France, and that a date of composition in the 1230s is 'far more probable' than one in the 1180s, the allusion to Marie of Champagne thus being 'part of an elaborate game' (55–6).

Whatever one thinks of Dronke's theory, it is clear that a new attitude towards and emphasis on love pervades romance literature beginning in the twelfth century. Andreas presents true love as something existing outside marriage and subject to a series of rules, including the following: 'When made public love rarely endures'; 'Every lover regularly turns pale in the presence of his beloved'; 'He whom the thought of love vexes, eats and sleeps very little'; 'A true lover considers nothing good except what he thinks will please his beloved'; and 'A true lover is constantly and without intermission possessed by the thought of his beloved' (42–3). While Chrétien de Troyes and others writing about love in the new manner sometimes depict true love within the framework of marriage, it often does exist outside marriage—*Tristan and *Isolt, and *Lancelot and *Guinevere are two obvious examples. And all of the other rules quoted above, as extreme as they may appear, can be demonstrated in the works of Chrétien.

Nor was Andreas the only author to present an extreme view of love and the obligations it places on a lover. The German minnesinger Ulrich von Liechtenstein (*c.*1200–1275) wrote an account of his love for a woman who was reluctant to return his affection in *Frauendienst* (*Service of Ladies*, 1255). Ulrich describes a tournament in which he was struck in such a way that his finger was cut and 'hung by a single cord' (84). He sends to the lady he loves word of the injury he sustained while fighting to honour her. Though unmoved by this sacrifice, she is nevertheless offended when she learns that he has not actually lost his finger, which doctors were able to reattach. Ulrich is so disturbed at having vexed his lady that he has a friend cut off the offending finger, which he sends to her. She does not reject the offering but assures him that she will continue to scorn his affection. Ulrich is pleased, however, that she will keep the finger and therefore be reminded of how well he serves her.

Whatever its relationship to everyday life and social practices, courtly love was unquestionably a concept that had a tremendous influence on the literature of western Europe. As F. X. Newman observed in the preface to a collection of essays that he edited, 'courtly love is a doctrine of paradoxes, a love at once illicit and morally elevating, passionate and disciplined, humiliating and exalting, human and transcendent. Perhaps the ultimate paradox of courtly love is that a doctrine in many ways so unmedieval should be considered the unique contribution of the Middle Ages to the lore of love' (p. vii).

The codification of rules about courtly love or examples of the ideal in practice provide a code of behaviour, implicit in most works, by which to judge the actions of the hero. A good deal of the complexity of early romances comes from putting the code of love in conflict with another code, that of chivalry. In his classic study, Maurice Keen comments on the complexity of the concept of chivalry but observes that 'as it is described in the treatises', it is 'a way of life' that has 'three essential facets, the military, the noble, and the religious' (16). One such treatise, *The Book of the Ordre of Chyvalry*, a Middle English version of Ramón Lull's *Le Libre del Orde de Cauayleria* published by William Caxton, notes that it is the duty of the knight to defend the Church and to support his lord and his land. In order to do this, the knight needs physical skills, which are to be maintained by jousting, participating in tournaments, and hunting (27). But physical skills alone are not sufficient. A knight must also have a range of virtues; and his 'inner courage' is as important as his physical prowess because it cannot be 'overcome by any mere man' (32). He should also defend women and the weak and show mercy and pity but punish the wicked (34–7).

The codes of love and chivalry are interrelated. As Keen observes, 'the conception that chivalry forged of a link between the winning of approbation by honourable acts and the winning of the heart of a beloved woman . . . proved to be both powerful and enduring' (Keen 249–50). They are certainly related in the literature of the Middle Ages. Yet paradoxically the very act of winning a woman's love sometimes puts the knight at odds with the political and social or even the religious demands of chivalry; or the very act of honour can sometimes put him at odds with the woman for whom he is winning it.

Chrétien de Troyes

Just as there was one dominant figure, Geoffrey of Monmouth, in the development of the chronicle tradition, so is there one author whose work and influence played a major role in shaping this parallel and eventually intersecting tradition, largely by combining and placing in conflict the demands of love and chivalry. Chrétien de Troyes, writing in the latter part of the twelfth century, explored love and chivalry and their relationship to one another in four great verse romances. (Chrétien's fifth Arthurian romance, *Perceval*, will be discussed in Chapter 4.) At the beginning of *Cligés*, Chrétien lists his previous work, including a romance about King *Mark and Iseult (*Complete Romances* 87), but this work has not survived. In his extant romances, Chrétien shows himself to be a conscious literary artist. He uses a critical vocabulary that suggests he was thinking about such concepts as subject matter, theme, structure, and coherence within a narrative. He comments at the beginning of his *Lancelot* that his patron Marie of Champagne gave to him the 'matter and the meaning' (*Complete Romances* 170; 'matiere et san' in the French—cf. Kibler's edition, p. 2). In the beginning of *Erec et Enide*, he talks of creating in his tale of adventure a 'bele conjointure' (cf. the edition of Mario Roques, p. 1; translated by Staines as a 'pleasing pattern'), a term that has elicited much comment, but which, in this context, is clearly a literary-critical term that embodies notions of structure and coherence. As part of his excellent, extended analysis of the term, Douglas Kelly notes that 'Chretien's use of *conjointure* permits two applications, the one material and the other formal. It denotes, first, a combination of elements drawn from a *conte d'aventure*—his *matiere*—and, second, his own arrangement of those elements, which is *bele*. *Conjointure* brings out and enhances the quality of the source *matiere*, like the sower's seed in good ground' (20; cf. pp. 15–31 for a more complete discussion of the term).

Erec et Enide (c.1165) is Chrétien's earliest surviving Arthurian romance and the earliest surviving Arthurian romance by any author, although it draws on other, earlier tales, either oral or written. The romance is justly famous both for its primacy and for its aesthetic qualities. It opens with a hunt for a white stag. The knight who captures it will be allowed to kiss the most beautiful maiden. Arthur wins the contest and must bestow the kiss. This situation is, however, fraught with problems since each knight considers his beloved to be the most beautiful. Although the granting of the kiss, as well as the tension it causes, is delayed, a new problem arises. As she observes the hunt, the queen is insulted when her handmaiden and then Sir *Erec, who watches with her, are struck by a malicious dwarf who serves *Yder, a haughty knight. Erec vows to avenge the insult and bring the knight back to the queen. As he follows Yder, he is given lodging by an elderly vavasour who has been reduced to poverty but who has a beautiful daughter, *Enide.

Erec learns that Yder is holding a tournament, the prize for the winner being a sparrowhawk and the right to declare his lady the most beautiful, an honour that Erec bestows on Enide after defeating Yder. When Erec brings Enide back to court to marry her, all agree that she is the woman who deserves the kiss that has been delayed from the hunt for the white stag. Having Enide's unanimously accepted beauty be the solution to the potential discord from the earlier episode is an effective way of joining two tales and bringing a harmonious resolution to them. That harmony seems to be reflected in Erec's personal life. His total happiness with his wife and with married life seems ideal, but it creates a problem for the social and chivalric order since he no longer engages in knightly pursuits. When he overhears his wife grieving because she has 'brought shame on him' by causing him to abandon 'all deeds of chivalry' (32), he decides to set off on a quest that will re-establish his reputation and prove her loyalty to him.

Enide accompanies him faithfully, but she is not a patient Griselda yielding to her husband's every whim, no matter how foolish. Erec instructs her not to speak to him during their journey; but when he is threatened, she warns him. Later, a count professes his love for her and says he will kill Erec. Enide decides that it is 'better that she lie to him [the count] than that her lord be slaughtered' (43). She suggests that Erec not be slain in open court but that she be abducted in the morning, an act that will force Erec to fight to defend her and allow him to be captured and killed. Because of this deception, she can wake Erec before the plot comes to fruition and they escape. Her love for Erec and her character are demonstrated again when Erec seems to be dead from combat with giants. The

Count of Limors intends to force her to marry him, but she refuses to eat or drink unless she sees Erec do so first (60). Even when the count beats her, she still refuses to comply. Erec awakes and kills the count, and, realizing Enide's loyalty, forgives her for any offence she may have committed against him. Erec 'had tested her well', the narrator says, 'and discovered her deep love for him' (64).

The romance does not end with this resolution of the problem in their personal relationship. Yet another feat marks Erec as a great knight. As if his victories against giants, formidable opponents, and great odds were not enough, he undertakes an adventure known as the Joy of the Court. Erec must fight a knight, the nephew of King Evrain, who had promised his lover, without even knowing what she would ask because 'a lover does all the will of his beloved if he possibly can' (75), that he would remain in an enchanted garden until he was defeated by another knight. The adventure is called the Joy of the Court because releasing the knight from the promise brings 'great joy to the court' of his uncle and his friends (76). Although this episode may seem merely extraneous, a multiplication of adventures and knightly deeds, it is, on the contrary, part of Chrétien's *bele conjointure* because it provides a picture of a woman who reacts very differently from Enide by trying to keep her knight to herself, away from the court and the larger world, instead of encouraging him to fulfil his social and chivalric obligations.

Chrétien's next romance, *Cligés* (c.1176), has been called an 'anti-*Tristan*' and a 'hyper-*Tristan*' but is best seen, according to Jean Frappier, 'as a revised and corrected version, a "neo-*Tristan*" ' (80). Like Thomas's *Tristran* (discussed in Chapter 7), *Cligés* begins with an account of the parents of the hero. Alexander, the son of the Emperor and Empress of Greece and Constantinople, goes to Arthur's court to prove himself and later accompanies Arthur and Guinevere when they travel to Brittany, as does Soredamors, *Gawain's sister. On the voyage, Alexander and Soredamors fall in love. Because of their love, they change colour and turn pale (93), a condition which the queen mistakes for seasickness and which, as Karl D. Uitti observes, recalls the punning in Thomas's *Tristran* on *mal de mer* and *mal d'amer*, seasickness and love sickness (55).

In Britain, Count Angres, who has been entrusted with keeping order while Arthur is away, rebels—in a scene reminiscent of *Mordred's rebellion in Wace's *Roman de Brut* (Frappier 83). When Arthur and those who accompanied him to Brittany return, Alexander is valiant in the fight to put down the rebellion; and he himself captures Angres, for which he is richly rewarded by Arthur. Guinevere recognizes the love between Alexander and Soredamors and is instrumental in getting them to confess their affection and to marry. They soon have a son, *Cligés.

Just as Angres has betrayed his trust in Britain, so in Alexander's native land his younger brother Alis treacherously assumes control of the realm when their father dies. In order to keep the peace, Alexander agrees to let Alis rule so long as he vows never to marry or have children and to let Cligés rule after him. But Alexander dies before his brother, and Soredamors dies of grief soon after. Alis then accepts the advice of his counsellors and performs another treacherous act: he breaks his word and takes a wife, Fenice.

Cligés grows to be a handsome and courtly young man. He knows 'more about hawks and hunting dogs than Tristan' and is wise, generous, and strong (121); and, as with Tristan and Iseult, Fenice loves the nephew more than the uncle. Yet she does not want to be like those lovers of romance, whose story she knows. 'I would rather be torn limb from limb than have the two of us be reminiscent of the love of Tristan and Iseult', she laments. Fortunately, her nurse Thessala knows more about magic than Medea did (124); using her craft, she prepares a potion that makes Alis think he is enjoying Fenice on her wedding night while he is actually only dreaming that he is doing so.

Cligés goes to Arthur's court, which he considers the touchstone for proving valour. There, in four days of tournament, he defeats *Sagremor, Lancelot, and *Perceval, and proves himself equal to Gawain. Having demonstrated his knightly abilities, he can return to Fenice and profess his love. Though she reciprocates his feelings and, thanks to Thessala's magic, is still a virgin, she does not want him to be called Tristan or herself to be called Iseult, 'for then the love would not be honorable but base and subject to reproach' (151). Nor will she run off to Britain with him because 'then the entire world would talk of us the way people do of the blonde Iseult and Tristan' (151–2). Instead, Fenice decides to feign death with the help of Thessala's potions. The ruse is elaborately planned: Cligés has a master craftsman construct a tower for her that is so skilfully made that no one can find an entrance; and Thessala prepares for the fake death by presenting to Fenice's physicians the urine of a seriously ill woman as if it were from Fenice. When Fenice drinks the potion and seems to be dead, three doctors from Salerno arrive and assert that there is still life in her body. To prove their point, they torture her, lashing her and pouring melted lead on her hands—in effect, making her a martyr for love. Fortunately for the lovers, as the doctors prepare to grill her until she is completely burned, more than a thousand ladies, having learned what the phys-icians are doing, throw them out of the window. Clearly the 'martyrdom' has elements of humour, a fact emphasized by the narrator's comment that 'No ladies had ever done better' than those who hurled the doctors to their destruction (160). Fenice and Cligés are happy in their tower and avoid the world's scorn until a knight climbs the wall surrounding its garden and sees the lovers together, forcing them to flee. Cligés goes to Arthur's court and complains of the wrong done him by Alis, whereupon Arthur raises an army and prepares to restore the young knight to the throne that is rightfully his. But word comes that Alis has died 'from his distress at being unable to find' Cligés (168); so the army is disbanded, Cligés returns home, and he is accepted as rightful ruler without a fight.

Chrétien has joined together more than the narratives of parents and child, and the courts of Greece and Britain. He has told a tale that comments on the story of Tristan and Iseult. Though there is much humour in Chrétien's handling of the Tristan story and the courtly love motifs—Uitti calls the romance 'a work of high comedy' (58)—the tale also makes a serious point: Fenice is right to reject the model of Tristan and Iseult because it creates a conflict between the lovers and their lord; Cligés is more justified in his actions than Tristan because he is the rightful ruler and Alis has broken his vow (something particularly blameworthy in a ruler) by marrying.

Unlike his other romances, Chrétien's *Lancelot* or *Le Chevalier de la charrete* (*The Knight of the Cart*) (1179–80) tells of lovers who do not become husband and wife, though they are happy in their love. Chrétien asserts that since the 'matter and meaning' of the romance were given to him by his patron Marie de Champagne, he undertook only 'to shape the work, adding little to it except his effort and his careful attention' (*Complete Romances* 170). Though Chrétien left the completion of the romance ('from the time Lancelot was imprisoned in the tower' to the end) to Godefroi de Leigni, *Lancelot* is significant for introducing and bringing into prominence the adulterous love of Lancelot and Guinevere, a motif from which much of the Arthurian tradition derives. It also depicts courtly love in such an extreme form that critics debate whether it is the supreme example or an ironic parody of the concept.

The romance begins with a challenge to Arthur's court by the wicked knight *Meleagant, who announces that he holds captive knights and ladies from Arthur's kingdom and will free them only if the king will send out the queen with one knight to defend her. Through his petulance and a threat to leave the court, *Kay obtains a rash promise from Arthur to grant him whatever he wishes; and he asks to be allowed to fight for the queen. As is typical, Kay has a higher regard for himself than he can support with deeds of arms. He is easily defeated, and Meleagant rides off with the queen. A knight whose name is not given until well into the tale, but who is ultimately revealed to be Lancelot, sets out with Gawain in pursuit of Meleagant. After his horse is killed by Meleagant's men, Lancelot encounters a dwarf, who agrees to reveal where the queen is if Lancelot will ride in his cart, a shameful act since carts were used for criminals. As Reason and Love have a brief debate in his mind, Lancelot hesitates 'for just two steps' before jumping in (174). As a result of riding in the cart, Lancelot is insulted and belittled throughout his quest.

Yet riding in the cart is hardly the most extreme example of the triumph of Love over Reason in the romance. At one point, when Lancelot is lodging in a castle, he sees Guinevere and leans so far out the window that he might have fallen to his doom had not Gawain pulled him back in (177). At another point on his journey, he is so preoccupied with thoughts of Guinevere that he does not hear the challenge issued by another knight and is toppled from his horse. Later, finding a comb with strands of Guinevere's hairs in it, 'he began to adore them. To his eyes, his mouth, his forehead, his cheeks, he touched them a hundred thousand times'; and he believes they will protect him from illness and injury more than medicines, antidotes to poison, or even prayers (188). When he is told that there are only two ways into Meleagant's kingdom, he chooses the quicker but more treacherous

*Sword Bridge even though it is 'sharper than a scythe' and cuts his hands and feet as he crosses (208). When he finally reaches the castle where the queen is being held and fights with Meleagant—without giving his injuries from the bridge time to heal—he cannot take his eyes from Guinevere even though it means defending himself behind his back, until a maiden instructs him to manoeuvre Meleagant so that he can fight face to face and still see the queen.

Despite all of his trials in reaching Guinevere, when Lancelot obtains her release, she will not speak to him. He accepts this treatment since a lover should not question the will of his beloved. Though he fears that she rejects him because he disgraced himself by riding in a cart, her reason is that he hesitated the two steps before leaping in and thus was not unquestioningly committed to her service. Later Lancelot is captured and there are rumours of his death, which cause Guinevere to contemplate suicide. Lancelot, hearing rumours of her death, actually attempts suicide by tying his belt as a noose around his neck and slipping from his horse so that it drags him and chokes him. He is, however, saved from death by his captors.

Once the lovers are reconciled, Guinevere invites Lancelot to come to her room. To do so, he must bend iron bars, on which he cuts himself. He bleeds on her sheets, and the next morning, Meleagant sees the blood and accuses the queen of infidelity with Sir Kay, who slept in the same room. Guinevere's accuser does not accept her excuse of having had a nosebleed, and Lancelot must fight to defend her. At the request of Meleagant's father *Bademagu, the fight is postponed when it seems clear that Meleagant will be defeated and killed, the combatants swearing to meet in a year at Arthur's court. Meleagant treacherously imprisons Lancelot, but he is freed by Bademagu's daughter, whose enemy Lancelot had killed earlier in the romance. Thus he is able to return just in time to fight and to slay Meleagant.

For Lancelot, undertaking to rescue the queen is both a chivalric and a personal quest: he responds to a challenge and a threat to Arthur's kingdom as well as to an affront to the woman he loves. By releasing the queen from captivity in Meleagant's kingdom of *Gorre, he frees all of Arthur's subjects held there because of the custom of the country that 'when one captive was liberated, all the others were free to leave' (217). It is because he is so extreme in his love for the queen that he is able to defend Arthur's subjects. Lancelot as lover is inseparable from Lancelot as knight in service to king and country. The complexity of the joining of love and chivalry in Chrétien's romances does not imply, however, that readers should not see a certain absurdity in the extreme nature of courtly love as depicted in the romance. Surely Norris Lacy is correct in saying that Chrétien 'seems to have had considerable fun at the expense of his hero, of his genre, of the tradition he was treating. And certainly this fact and his particular use of narrative point of view offer ample evidence that he did not mindlessly endorse his theme or his hero. But I think they also prevent our simply identifying him with the opposite view.... thus he lends the weight of his narrative authority neither to the advocacy of fin' amors nor to its denunciation' (59–60).

Lancelot is a fascinating text in part because of its ambiguous attitude towards courtly love. It is also significant for popularizing certain traditions about Lancelot that influence almost all later accounts of his life and deeds. It speaks of Lancelot as being raised by a fairy (199). It depicts Lancelot as the greatest knight, a role that much early literature, including other of Chrétien's romances, assigns to Gawain or Perceval. And it portrays Lancelot as the lover of Guinevere, thus introducing the triangle that is often at the heart of later Arthurian literature.

Chrétien's *Yvain* (1179–80) is a return to a tale of married lovers that explores the balance between social and chivalric duties and personal relationships, much as *Erec et Enide* did. But it shifts the emphasis from a knight who is too devoted to his wife and therefore neglects his reputation and chivalric obligations to one who is so involved with his chivalric pursuits that he is forgetful of his duties and promises to his wife.

Yvain begins with a tale told by Sir Calogrenant about an adventure he had at a spring: when he poured water from the spring onto a stone, a fierce storm arose, after which a knight challenged and unhorsed him. *Yvain decides to avenge his cousin Calogrenant's disgrace. Performing the same ritual, he causes the storm and fights with the knight, Esclados le Ros, defeating him and chasing him back to his castle. As Yvain pursues the mortally wounded knight, he is trapped by a portcullis, which cuts his horse in half as it falls, and is saved by a resourceful young woman named Lunete, to whom he had once shown courtesy, perhaps a comment on the unexpected benefits of courtly behaviour. Lunete gives Yvain a ring that makes him invisible (and that recalls the magic ring given to Lancelot by the fairy who raised him to protect him from enchantments (198–9)) and allows him to hide from Esclados's followers, who seek to kill him.

Lunete conceals Yvain in her room until she persuades her lady Laudine, the wife of Esclados, that a better knight than her dead husband is needed to defend the magic spring. In a virtuoso display of logic and rhetoric, Lunete, who is called by Karl Uitti 'the most interesting character' in the romance and whose 'achievements are due to her natural command of rhetoric' (84), convinces Laudine that the man who killed her husband must be a superior knight by the very fact that he defeated Esclados and therefore that Laudine should wed him.

But in Chrétien's complex world, the story does not end with the happy marriage of two people who have reason not to love each other. Gawain reminds Yvain of the need for a knight to be conscious of his reputation and his accomplishments. 'Will you be like those men who are less worthy because of their wives?' Gawain asks. One cannot help thinking of Erec, and it may be that Chrétien expected his audience to know the romance that explored Erec's failure in chivalry because he did not, in Gawain's words, '[b]reak loose from the bridle and halter' (286–7). An audience familiar with *Erec* would see *Yvain* as exploring another side of the same problem. Such intertextual reading is supported by the fact that Chrétien interweaves the events of this romance with those of *Lancelot*. Characters in *Yvain* who would have appealed to Gawain for help are unable to do so because Kay lost the queen to a knight and Gawain went in search of her (301 and 303); and there is another reference to Lancelot's having been imprisoned in a tower by Meleagant (313).

Laudine is not opposed to Yvain's undertaking knightly deeds and even gives him a ring that will protect a true lover from imprisonment and loss of blood; but she elicits a promise from him that he will return to her in one year. When he breaks that vow, Laudine sends a lady to retrieve the ring and to tell Yvain never to return. After a period of madness caused by the loss of his beloved, Yvain regains his senses. He then acquires a new name, the Knight of the Lion, when he kills a serpent that attacked a lion, and the lion becomes his faithful and submissive companion, to the extent that the beast wants to commit suicide when it thinks Yvain is dead.

With the lion's help, Yvain accomplishes great deeds. Eventually he comes upon a lady imprisoned in a chapel and sentenced to die the next day for treason. The lady is Lunete who, not knowing the identity of the knight she addresses, says that only Gawain or Yvain, 'for whose sake I shall be unjustly delivered tomorrow to the agony of death' (300), could save her by fighting her three accusers. Yvain does fight the three. Despite his instruction to the lion not to help him, the beast comes to his aid, and the three are defeated and then burned on the pyre they had prepared for Lunete.

After Yvain undergoes a series of adventures, he returns to the spring where he causes a storm. Since Laudine is now without a champion, Lunete suggests to her that the Knight of the Lion might help if he could overcome the sorrow he suffers over losing his lady's favour. Laudine promises to do all she can to help him. The Knight of the Lion is revealed to be Yvain; thus once again Lunete has put her mistress in a position where she must accept the man towards whom she feels great enmity. Laudine says to Lunete, 'you have now trapped me neatly' (337); but she is true to her word and so she forgives her husband and happiness is restored, a happiness that results from the understanding that both characters have achieved of the balance that is necessary between love and chivalric pursuits.

The significance of Chrétien de Troyes would be hard to overstate. He introduced a pattern for chivalric romances in which various adventures are conjoined. He explored in his romances a tension between love and chivalry, between private concerns and public responsibility, that many subsequent medieval authors would investigate. He was able to use humour even as he treated serious themes. He often entered into the minds of his characters, sometimes recording a character's lengthy internal debate. And he 'enriched considerably' the Matter of Britain 'when he took it beyond the stage of simple "adventure tales" ' (Frappier 25). In addition, his romances were reworked and retold by authors in various countries and influenced many romances in France and elsewhere.

THE INFLUENCE OF CHRÉTIEN DE TROYES

Chrétien's romances were translated and adapted and even occasionally parodied. Their influence can be seen throughout the Middle Ages. In medieval France, a work known as the *Prose Yvain*, found in one fourteenth-century manuscript, describes the adventures of a number of knights besides Yvain; but the first part of the romance recounts Yvain's rescue of the lion and some of the battles in which the lion assists him (cf. Muir 355–6). In the fifteenth century, prose adaptations of *Cligés* and *Erec et Enide* were written for the Burgundian court. Early in the sixteenth century (*c*.1520), Pierre Sala (*c*.1457–1529) modernized *Yvain* in his verse romance *Le Chevalier au lion*.

Other romances make use of Chrétien's narratives and themes, sometimes accepting them but sometimes reacting against them, without directly adapting his romances. The thirteenth-century *Durmart le Galois*, for example, describes characters in terms of attributes familiar from Chrétien's romances and has several parallels to Chrétien's *Erec*; it includes 'explicit didactic passages extolling the virtues of equality in marriage which represent a clear rejection of *Erec et Enide*, and criticizes Chrétien's works on a structural' as well as on this thematic level (Blumenfield-Kosinski 87, 91–2).

Fergus and the Dutch *Ferguut*
One of the most interesting of such reactions to Chrétien's works in medieval French literature is the verse romance *Fergus* (*c*.1225) by Guillaume le Clerc, who adapts characters, incidents, and motifs from a number of Chrétien's romances (and from a number of other romances as well) to produce a work that is paradoxically both a parody of some of the excesses of the genre and a tribute to it. In many of his adventures, the Scottish knight Fergus—a naive youth who lives away from the world, seeks knighthood from Arthur, and is mocked by the acerbic Kay—is like Perceval. (Chrétien's *Perceval* will be discussed in Chapter 4.) Early in the tale, as in *Erec et Enide*, there is a hunt for a white stag, but Guillaume differs from Chrétien in that he gives an elaborate description of the hunt itself and the horrendous death of the animal. Like Erec, Fergus encounters and defeats robber knights, outdoing Erec by defeating fifteen at one time. Like Yvain, Fergus nearly goes mad and lives in the wild because he has lost his beloved Galiene, a grief he says he brought on himself (Guillaume le Clerc, *Fergus of Galloway* 44), not by being false to her but by being more interested in the quest he was pursuing than in accepting her love when she came to his bed. As in a number of Chrétien's works, the internal debate of a character, in this case Galiene, pondering questions of love, is presented at some length. But in a manner typical of this text, she is so troubled by her thoughts that 'she turns her bed upside down, so violent are the joustings of love' (31). And like Yvain, Fergus takes on another identity, one that comes from the shield he has acquired by slaying both a dragon and a giant hag with a scythe. As the Knight of the Shining Shield, he protects Galiene's lands by fighting two of her

persecutors in a single battle and is ultimately reunited with her. After their marriage, Gawain begs Fergus 'not to abandon knightly deeds for his wife' (112). This final echo of *Yvain* makes it clear that Guillaume is playing a literary game with the romances he knew, particularly those of Chrétien. Coming at the end of the romance, it does not become thematic or raise a problem of love as in *Yvain*. It seems rather to be a comment on and tribute to the excellence of Chrétien, who raises questions of love and chivalry so skilfully in his romances.

Some twenty-five years after Guillaume wrote *Fergus*, a Dutch translation, *Ferguut*, was composed, perhaps by two authors. The beginning of the poem (up to line 2592) follows its French source closely 'in an abridging fashion', but from that point on 'it would seem that the Middle Dutch adaptor is continuing the narrative from memory, instead of referring to a written source' (Claassens and Johnson 26). The Dutch adaptors add some names and details not found in the French and use fewer 'intentional intertextual references to the work of Chrétien de Troyes' (Claassens and Johnson 27), though the progression of the narrative, ending with the marriage of Ferguut and Galiene, is similar.

Hartmann von Aue

Medieval Germany produced a version of Chrétien's *Cligés* that was either written or completed by Ulrich von Türheim (cf. Meyer 107) and that survives only in fragments. More important were the adaptations of two of Chrétien's romances by Hartmann von Aue, who lived from the middle of the twelfth century into the second decade of the thirteenth and whose verse romances are among the great achievements of medieval German literature. In reworking Chrétien's *Erec* (c.1180), Hartmann followed the basic outline of his French sources; but he added details, descriptions, and metaphors that are not contained therein. These additions are often designed to emphasize some of the basic premises of the story: Enite's beauty and loyalty, Erec's valour, or courtly or chivalric conduct. When Erec first comes to the home of Enite's father Koralus and Enite tends his horse, Hartmann comments that 'if God himself were riding about here on earth, he would be glad to have a groom like this one'; even Erec's horse is 'pleased to get its fodder from such a stable boy' (35). Having contended for the sparrowhawk and defeated Iders, Erec says that he will have the hand of the dwarf who struck him and the queen's maiden cut off. He does not intend to inflict such a severe punishment 'but only wanted to warn the dwarf against any more such acts' that do not show the proper respect to ladies and knights; he quickly relents and has the dwarf beaten instead (43). When Erec and Enite arrive at Arthur's court, Hartmann gives a long list of the knights in attendance there. And the account of the tournament following the wedding of Erec and Enite is four times longer than the corresponding passage in Chrétien, just as the final duel with Mabonagrin is three times as long (cf. Hasty 38). Thus there is great attention paid to the scenes in which Erec demonstrates his valour—though in the latter contest which ends the adventure of the Joy of the Court, Hartmann adds a humorous touch when, after a long and fierce fight, the swords of both combatants break; since Erec had 'learned as a boy... to wrestle very well' (137), he is able to overthrow his opponent and pummel him until he yields. A similar touch of wit is found in Erec's fight with Iders, which is described in an extended metaphor comparing the contest to a dice game.

In these combats and elsewhere, Hartmann seems to be having fun with some of the excesses of chivalric and courtly descriptions. Perhaps he is making a similar game of courtly description and romance superlatives as he elaborates more than tenfold on Chrétien's depiction of the saddle and trappings of Enite's horse. He says, for example, 'It was indeed a splendid cloth that bore Jupiter and the goddess Juno when they sat on the bridal throne in their lofty realm, but it could compare with this saddle cover—I assure you—only as the moon with the sun' (117–18).

It may be that the game Hartmann makes of such romance excesses comments on the story he tells. Erec is initially excessive in his love for Enite. He becomes excessive in his testing of her as he demands that she not speak to him and then criticizes her when she warns him and saves his life. Similarly, the Joy of the Court episode suggests the excesses of the courtly world, as a knight slays other good knights in a game devised by his lady merely to avoid losing his company. Erec must learn to balance his obligations as knight and lover without tending to the extreme in either sphere.

Hartmann's other adaptation from Chrétien, Iwein (c.1200), which follows Yvain fairly closely, is usually considered to be the best and the last of his romances. Iwein explores the nature of honour and truth in the context of chivalric duty and Arthurian romance. At Arthur's court, Keii (Kay) is said to be concerned with 'comfort, not honor' (trans. Thomas 56). As is often the case, Keii is a foil for the hero; he is the epitome of a superficial concern with reputation and is known as one who mocks and insults good knights. Keii is not able to match his deeds to his words; nevertheless, he affects the actions of his fellow knights. For instance, Iwein, 'forgetting his courtly manners', pursues the dying Ascalon whom he has defeated at the spring because he realizes that if he does not have proof of his victory, 'Keii would deprive him of any fame' (67). Iwein's fear of Keii's mockery is mentioned twice more (73 and 75), even after he sees and loves Laudine.

After Lunete has made peace and Iwein marries Laudine, Gawein advises him not to abandon knightly pursuits. In a passage expanded considerably from the comparable one in Chrétien, Gawein warns Iwein to 'take care that your wife's beauty does not bring you shame' and not to 'turn wholly to a life of ease, as Sir Erec did' (89). The reference to Erec makes it clear that in Iwein Hartmann is exploring another side of the problem of the balance between love and courtly and social responsibility. The need for this balance is seen even in the character and actions of Laudine. Her insistence that Iwein return within a year is not due to an obsessive need to have her lover with her, like that of Mabonagrin's lady in the Joy of the Court episode in Erec. It is prompted in part by her responsibility to her land, whose safety depends on having a knight valiant enough to defend the spring. Thus when Iwein fails to return in a year, he proves untrue as a lover and fails in the

responsibility he accepted by marrying Laudine. Significantly, Lunete is the messenger whom Laudine sends to retrieve the ring she had given Iwein and to berate
him for his infidelity. Lunete reminds him that she vouched for him and persuaded
the woman whose husband he had killed to marry him. He has betrayed both of
them for when he became a 'traitor', he made her 'unfaithful and a liar' (93). The
ramifications of his breaking his word are apparent later when Lunete, accused of
treason herself for arranging the match with Iwein, is condemned to die unless she
can find someone to fight three opponents at once. In the end, Iwein, assisted by the
lion he saved from a dragon, defeats the three and rights the wrong done to Lunete.

The lion itself is instrumental in Iwein's learning about the nature of loyalty and
honour. Not only does the beast become his constant companion and risk its life
whenever Iwein is threatened; but when the lion, believing that Iwein has died after
falling from his horse and wounding himself with his own sword, is about to
commit suicide, it teaches Iwein 'that true loyalty is no small thing' (102). Subsequently, Iwein endures a series of trials in which he fights not for personal fame or
to avoid the scorn of Keii and his ilk but rather for a just cause. Similarly, when he
fights the three accusers of Lunete and comments that God and Truth are with him
and so the odds are three to three, not three to one, he demonstrates true honour
and loyalty.

Lunete, having been saved, is instrumental in the reconciliation between Iwein
and Laudine. As she did earlier, she convinces her mistress that she needs someone
to defend the spring. Lunete suggests that the Knight with the Lion, whose identity
Laudine does not know, might take on the obligation if only he could win back his
lady. Laudine traps herself by vowing to do all she can to reconcile the lovers. Since
she knows all too well the dangers of breaking an oath, she serves both her
personal and public interests by forgiving Iwein. And Iwein, having learned a
lesson, apologizes and vows never to offend her again. In the course of the
romance, Iwein becomes worthy of being a knight of Arthur's court, the narrative
and moral setting in which Hartmann places his story from the very beginning of
the romance: 'He who turns his heart to true kindness will have God's favor and
man's esteem. One sees this with the noble King Arthur, who knew how to strive
for fame with a knightly spirit. He lived in such a manner that he wore the crown of
honor in his time, and his name does even now.' It is because of such qualities that
Arthur's countrymen are correct to believe him still alive, Hartmann adds, because
'although he is dead, his name lives on' and he provides an example to those who
would live without shame (55).

Hartmann's *Iwein* was the main source for the *Iban*, a late fifteenth-century
adaptation by Ulrich Fuetrer (b. *c.*1420), which was part of his compilation of
Arthurian texts known as the *Buch der Abenteuer*. In the *Iban*, Fuetrer has been said
to have 'no interest in interpretation or psychology, contenting himself with a one-
dimensional treatment which sacrifices all to narrative concision' (Hunt 208).
Another German work, *Gauriel von Muntabel* (written in the late thirteenth century) by Konrad von Stoffeln (*c.*1250–sometime after 1300), which tells of Gauriel,

the Knight with the Goat, 'can be read as a correction of *Iwein*, especially with regard to Laudine's role'. *Gauriel* has been seen as 'closely following the structure of Chrétien/Hartmann romances' (Meyer 103). While the plot varies considerably from that of *Iwein*, the hero is absent from his new bride for a year as he pursues adventure.

Erex saga and *Ívens saga*

Even in Scandinavian countries, the influence of Chrétien was strong. King Hákon Hákonarson of Norway, who ruled from 1217 to 1263, commissioned a series of translations of Anglo-Norman and French poems. Chrétien's *Erec* and *Yvain* were among the French romances adapted to Old Norse prose, the *explicit* (i.e. statement at the end of the manuscript) of the latter adaptation, *Ívens saga*, noting that it was one of those works that 'King Hákon the Old had translated from French to Norse' (83). It is probable that *Erex saga* was also the result of Hákon's initiative, though there is no specific evidence for this. And neither mentions the name of the translator, although a Brother Robert is said to have translated many of the texts produced for Hákon.

In spite of the fact that it adds two episodes not found in the French original, *Erex saga* severely reduces Chrétien's romance. The surviving version is probably not a faithful reflection of 'the style, substance, and structure of the original Norwegian translation' but a revision by an Icelandic copyist (Kalinke 193–4). While maintaining the basic story of Erex and his beautiful wife Evida from the stag hunt to the contest for the sparrowhawk to the journey of Erex and Evida and the culminating episode of the Joy of the Court, the Icelandic version combines the fairly redundant attacks by three and then five robbers into one episode with eight robbers. It also adds a scene in which Erex saves a knight from the jaws of a flying dragon and slays the beast. On the other hand, the Icelandic adaptation eliminates some of the elaborate description and the soul-searching found in Chrétien's text.

Ívens saga is closer to the French original, though it too survives only in Icelandic manuscripts and shows 'evidence that Icelandic copyists were also interpreters who revised the texts they were copying' (Kalinke 187). While generally following the narrative sequence of the events in *Yvain*, the saga, like *Erex saga*, reduces description and accounts of the characters' thought processes. But it also occasionally adds details. For example, when Luneta is accused by the steward and condemned to be burned to death, it is in part because the 'steward had been continually stealing' from her lady and 'he hated me [Luneta] with all his heart because I knew of his misconduct' (66).

Herr Ivan Lejonriddaren (1303), a Swedish version of *Yvain*, 'was translated in Norway at the instigation of Eufemia [d. 1312], the German wife of King Hákon Magnússon'. It seems likely that the author of *Herr Ivan*, a fairly close adaptation of Chrétien's romance, had available a copy of *Ívens saga* (Kalinke 14–15). But the Swedish version, unlike the saga, is written in rhymed couplets, the verse form of Chrétien's text.

Gereint Son of Erbin and *Owain* (*The Lady of the Fountain*)

Two Welsh prose romances, probably written in the thirteenth century, are analogous to Chrétien's *Erec* and *Yvain*. *Gereint Son of Erbin* and *Owain* are found in the *Mabinogion*, the collection of Welsh tales first translated into English in the nineteenth century by Lady Charlotte Guest. (A third Welsh romance, *Peredur*, an analogue of Chrétien's *Perceval*, will be discussed below in Chapter 4.) The exact relationship of these two texts to Chrétien's has not been determined. It is possible that both Chrétien's romances and the Welsh texts are based on some other Celtic tales or that Chrétien's were a direct source for the Welsh romances.

*Gereint corresponds to Chrétien's Erec, and his story as given in the Welsh tale corresponds to the French 'episode by episode, and it is not unusual to find close resemblances or even phrases that would serve as exact translations'; nevertheless, 'the story-telling is unmistakably Welsh' (Middleton 148, 150). Some interesting details distinguish *Gereint* from *Erec*. For example, the reward for killing the stag is giving its head and not a kiss to the lady of the successful hunter's choice. And during the hunt, it is 'Arthur's favorite dog' *Cafall who causes the stag to turn towards his master. But perhaps the most significant change is the explanation given for Gereint's journey and his treatment of Enid, who is told to travel in her worst dress (not her best one, as in other versions). When Enid laments that 'it is through me that these arms and this breast are losing fame and prowess', Gereint believes that 'it was not out of care for him that she had spoken those words, but because she was meditating love for another man in his stead' (251).

Similarly, a key point that is perhaps implied but not made explicit in the source is explained in *Owain*. As Cynon recounts the visit to the fountain at which he was defeated and shamed, he says that the knight who comes to defend the fountain asked, 'Didst not know that to-day's shower has left alive in my dominions neither man nor beast of those it found out of doors?' (161). This question explains why those who pour water from the fountain pose a threat to the realm.

In *Owain*, Arthur and his entourage arrive at the fountain not two weeks but three years after *Owain, when Arthur has a longing to see Owain; 'and if I be the fourth year without the sight of him my life will not stay in my body', he laments to *Gwalchmai. In a tale that has a penchant for things in threes, Arthur asks the Lady of the Fountain, whom Owain has married, if her husband can come to his court for three months; but he stays three years before his wife sends a messenger to berate him for being a 'false treacherous deceiver' (173).

After Owain goes mad and is cured by a precious ointment, he comes upon the lion and serpent fighting and assists the nobler creature. Perhaps to emphasize the beast's fantastic nature or its symbolism, it is described as 'a pure white lion' (177). In his battle against the giant who has captured two of Owain's host's sons, intending to kill them unless he is given the lord's daughter, the lion assists Owain and disembowels the giant. He then aids in slaying Luned's two accusers. Owain brings his wife to Arthur's court, with no explanation of their reconciliation, and they are together as long as she lives. After what seems a natural conclusion, the tale adds the story of Owain's freeing of twenty-four ladies from the 'court of the Black Oppressor' (181), following which Owain remains in Arthur's court as the captain of his warband until the unspecified time when he returns to his own possessions, 'the three hundred swords of the descendants of Cynfarch (Owain's grandfather), and the flight of ravens (which appears also in *Breuddwyd Rhonabwy* and plays an active role there)', which 'may well belong to genuine tradition but . . . have no part in this tale' (Thomson 161).

Ywain and Gawain

The only Middle English adaptation of a work by Chrétien is the early fourteenth-century metrical romance *Ywain and Gawain*. The English poet, who abridges his source largely by cutting out the thoughts of the characters, otherwise follows Chrétien's story fairly closely. This makes for a more direct narrative and one that, typical of English adaptations from the French, focuses more on action than on soul-searching or courtly description. But the romance does have a thematic focus, established at the outset. It is concerned with 'trewth' (truth) in the wide range of the meanings that word can have in Middle English, which include honour, loyalty, friendship, love, honesty, adherence to one's word, diligence, and conscientiousness.

The romance begins with a statement about King Arthur who was 'trew . . . in alkyn thing' (true in every respect). Arthur's court is held up as an example because there was more 'trewth' among its members than is seen in the present when 'trowth and luf es al bylaft' (truth and love have been completely abandoned) (84–5). But, as the romance demonstrates, even knights of the *Round Table have to learn that being true is no simple matter. Ywain, one of the great knights, is true to his word, despite Kay's suggestions to the contrary, when he promises to avenge Colgrevance's shame at the well. But he is less conscientious in keeping his word to his wife Alundyne. When Ywain has overstayed his term at court, Alundyne's messenger publicly accuses him of being a false and wicked deceiver of ladies ('losenjoure') and of having practised 'gilry' (guile or deceit). She addresses him as an untrue traitor and one who is 'trowthles' (125). The repeated emphasis on his falseness and betrayal (in lines 1600–27) leaves no doubt as to the nature of the offence he has committed. He has pursued truth in the sense of knightly honour but has lost his honour by being untrue to his wife and his word.

Ywain must undergo a series of trials through which he learns the nature and extent of truth and 'he shows a new understanding of duty and fidelity in a sequence of adventures which demand increasing self-sacrifice and devotion to the service of others' (Barron 162). Perhaps more importantly, he fights on the right side in these contests. He helps the lion, a noble beast, against the dragon, a symbol of evil. His rescue of Lunet, falsely accused of treason because she has been true to Ywain and to Alundyne, establishes the truth of her character and leads to the punishing of her false accusers.

Even though he must fight against the three accusers at once, Ywain believes that with God, right, and the lion on his side, the odds are four against three, and he thus has the advantage (148). In his battle against Gawain, which establishes him as a knight equal to the greatest knight, he fights for the rights of the younger sister whose land has been wrongly taken from her by her elder sister, for whom Gawain fights. And when Lunet, described as 'trew Lunet' in the closing lines of the poem, convinces her mistress to pledge to help the Knight with the Lion reconcile with his lady, Alundyne must accept Ywain back into her good graces because she must be true to her word: 'That I have said, I sal fulfill' (186). Ywain apologizes, promises never to trespass again, and asks for forgiveness. The fact that Ywain, Alundyne, Lunet, and even the lion live in joy and bliss until their death is the result of the 'truth' that all of them have shown.

The Continuing Tradition

A number of modern authors have reinterpreted Chrétien's romances. American poet Marion Lee Reynolds reworked the story of Enid and Geraint in *Geraint of Devon* (1916), a book-length poem written in blank verse. Reynolds was influenced by Chrétien, the Welsh *Owain*, and Tennyson (whose version of the tale of Enid and Geraint will be discussed in the next chapter). *Geraint of Devon* also contains much original material, including the introduction of a character named Honolan, a villain who suggests to Geraint that Enid's sadness is caused by her longing for an absent lover. Thus when Geraint overhears her say at the end of her complaint that she is 'false indeed' (97), he assumes that she loves another rather than that she is berating herself for not telling him that people are saying that he has become cowardly, a rumour started by Honolan. Reynolds adds passages of extended description, of the activity surrounding the tournament and of nature, for example. A depiction of a desolate landscape when Geraint sets out on his journey to test Enid parallels an earlier journey through a beautiful forest in the joyous days of their new love (cf. 101, 67–8). Reynolds tells of the adventures with the robbers and the earl who desires Enid, the fight with Guivret the Little, and the beheading of Earl Limours but does not include the Joy of the Court episode. Instead, the poem ends with the reconciliation of the lovers and a frank discussion between them of the misunderstanding that caused Geraint's jealousy.

British poet and playwright Ernest Rhys (1859–1946) wrote a short play called *Enid* (1908), which is based on the version of the tale in the *Mabinogion*. Rather than expanding the medieval material as Reynolds did, Rhys condenses the events and the characters so that 'Geraint's several antagonists are all resolved into one—Earl Dwrm . . . and the struggle for Enid, the Sparrow-Hawk, and the town and castle, is all cast into a romantic duel between the two chief male characters', Geraint and Dwrm (7).

British playwright Donald R. Rawe, in *Geraint: Last of the Arthurians* (1972), takes a more historical approach to Geraint and Enid. For Rawe, Geraint is the historical figure, the warrior and ruler whose exploits are described in Celtic verse and other sources. The play tells of an aged Geraint on the verge of death who, though married to Enid, has a last affair with and impregnates a young woman named

Jowanet. Geraint's friend Bishop Teilo, who has come to be with the dying king in his last days, works to have Jowanet's child named as his successor, something that is possible because Geraint's elder son Jestyn wants to lead a holy life and never marry, and his younger son Selyf is wounded and maimed in battle and will never father children. The Enid depicted in the play has become unbalanced, and there is no love left between her and her husband. With the passing of Geraint, the only surviving warrior to have fought with Arthur, 'the days of Arthur are truly over' (30); but there is hope that Jestyn, who wishes to fight the Saxons with the word of God, and Geraint's son by Jowanet, Kenwyn (whose name means 'splendid chief'), will continue the defence of Cornwall in the spirit of Geraint, the last of the Arthurians.

Like Geraint and Enid, Yvain continues to be a subject of interest for modern authors. British novelist Kathleen Herbert uses a historical setting for her tale of Owain, *Bride of the Spear* (1988), a revision of her earlier novel *The Lady of the Fountain* (1982). Herbert's Owain is a warrior who falls in love with Taniu the daughter of Loth (*Lot), with whom he has a brief affair; but believing her not to be a virgin, he feels deceived and leaves her to the shame of bearing a child out of wedlock. That their son is St Kentigern is based on 'an ecclesiastical legend of the birth of Saint Kentigern, whose reputed father is Owain' (Herbert in Thompson, 'Interview'). But like the historical novels dealing with Arthur, *Bride of the Spear* draws on the romance tradition as represented by Chrétien's *Yvain* and the Welsh *Owain*. Herbert has said that, among other romance elements, 'I wanted to develop the motif of the Magic Fountain and this moment of beauty that you discover through very great peril. The fountain persists in ecclesiastical, as well as romance, versions of the story, even though the narrative does not require it. It seems to be one of those places, like the well at the world's end, where worlds meet. This meeting of worlds takes place in history also, as the foundation legends of England, Scotland, and Wales are being made' (Herbert in Thompson, 'Interview'). The second of two fountain scenes in the novel occurs in a vision beheld by the wounded Owain. As Taniu, who entered a convent and became a renowned healer, gives him a curing potion, he sees her coming from a spring as 'the Goddess herself, the Lady of the enchanted springs' (291). When Owain is cured, he and Taniu are reunited and return together to rule Cumbria.

The story of Yvain and the Lady of the Fountain is also told by American poet Jack Hart in *The Lady of the Fountain* (1986), a poem in rhyme royal stanzas that draws on and refers to *Yvain*, *Owain*, and Tennyson. In the course of retelling the traditional story, Hart's self-conscious narrator comments on the writing of poetry, inspiration, and legendary stories. He complains that writing poetry is neither popular nor profitable. And he launches into Marxist, Freudian, and archetypal interpretations of the story he is telling, perhaps as an ironic explanation of why poetry is no longer popular.

While Chrétien's story of the Knight of the Cart is not the beginning of the tradition of recounting the abduction of Guinevere, it is certainly the most influential work in that tradition. 'The Dialogue of Gwenhwyfar and Melwas' and the *Life of St Gildas* (both discussed in Chapter 1) refer to Guinevere's abduction by Melwas. And an early twelfth-century carving on an archivolt on the north portal of the cathedral of Modena, Italy, depicts Arthur and a group of his knights, including 'Galvagin' (Gawain) and 'Che' (Kay), attacking a castle wherein 'Winlogee' is held by 'Mardoc'. This scene is significant because it represents the earliest surviving Arthurian sculpture and because it suggests that a version of the abduction of Guinevere recorded in later romance existed at a very early date.

The abduction motif is perhaps the basis for the medieval Spanish ballad 'Nunca fuero caballero', which 'Cervantes delighted to quote'. The ballad is sometimes thought to represent 'the impertinences of Meleagance and his death at Lancelot's hand' (Entwistle 199), though the text speaks only generally of a knight's boast that he would come to the queen in bed 'in spite of' Sir Lancelot, who ultimately beheads the knight (385–6).

Of course, Chrétien transforms the story by making the rescue a symbol of Lancelot's total and unquestioning love for the queen. The story of Guinevere's abduction as told by Chrétien influences a Knight of the Cart episode in the *Vulgate Cycle, through which it comes to Malory and from him on to T. H. White and other twentieth-century writers, such as British poet James Ormerod, whose brief play 'Meliagrance and Guenevere' (1913, published 1928) begins with Guenevere already a prisoner in Meliagrance's castle. After Lancelot visits the queen in her chamber, Meliagrance accuses her of infidelity, and Lancelot ultimately kills the treacherous knight. A more recent version of the abduction story appears in the film *First Knight* (Columbia, 1995; dir. Jerry Zucker), in which Lancelot (Richard Gere) rescues Guinevere (Julia Ormond) from the wicked knight Malagant (Ben Cross). Though *First Knight* rides roughshod over the ultimate tragedy of Arthurian tradition by providing a Hollywood ending in which Arthur passes his kingdom on to Lancelot and Guinevere, who can then live happily ever after, the film is interesting as an Americanization of the abduction story. It is the only place in the tradition where Lancelot is not of noble birth. He is, however, of noble character, which in much of the American Arthurian tradition is more important. Lancelot survives by fighting for money in town squares, a criticism that one of the other knights is quick to raise when Arthur proposes making Lancelot a member of the Round Table as a reward for his bravery in rescuing the queen a second time. But Arthur recognizes Lancelot's innate virtues: while Lancelot has 'no wealth, no home, no gold', he possesses 'the passionate spirit that drives [him] on.' That spirit, moreover, is what Arthur increasingly values, as he confirms by his dying wish that Lancelot serve as 'First Knight' of *Camelot and that he take care of Guinevere. In the democratic tradition of other American Arthurian films, Lancelot thus rises from low-born outsider to a position of privilege—in this case, to control of Arthur's kingdom—by earning his rank through deeds of moral courage and bravery.

LANCELOT AND GUINEVERE

Ulrich von Zatzikhoven

Ulrich von Zatzikhoven wrote *Lanzelet*, the first German tale about Lancelot, in rhyming couplets around 1200–4 (McClelland 27), not long after Chrétien told the story of the Knight of the Cart but apparently without knowledge of the French work. Ulrich says that he is translating a French book that came to his attention when Richard the Lionheart was captured on his return from the Third Crusade by Duke Leopold of Austria and gave hostages as warrant for fulfilment of the terms of his ransom. One of those hostages, generally thought to be the Hugh de Morville involved in the murder of Thomas Becket, brought with him the book that Ulrich ultimately translated. The very existence of an earlier book about Lancelot suggests that written and, no doubt, oral tales about him were circulating even before Chrétien made him the best of knights.

Ulrich's *Lanzelet*, an episodic tale that presents a biography of Lanzelet from his birth to his death, provides an account of how he came to be raised by a mermaid or water-fey, which explains why he is called 'du Lac' or 'of the Lake'. Lanzelet is taken to her realm when the vassals of his father King Pant (*Ban) rebel against him because he is a cruel and greedy overlord—one of the many variations from what became the accepted story of Lancelot. The realm to which Lanzelet is taken is idyllic: it is in bloom all year round; no anger or envy exists there; and whoever dwells there for even a day always feels joy (28)—though Lanzelet does experience sadness at points in the story. The realm is inhabited by 10,000 women and no men, so that when Lanzelet wants to learn to use a sword and shield and to hunt and hawk, he must request that mermen be brought in to teach him. It is not until he leaves this land at the age of 15 that he learns to ride and to joust; some humorous scenes describe Lanzelet letting his horse take him where it will because he does not know how to use the reins. However, after he has some basic training in riding and knightly combat, he soon becomes invincible.

Lanzelet is also a great lover. But unlike the Lancelot of the French and English tradition, he has a series of lovers, won by his prowess. Yet he loves one woman, Yblis the daughter of Iweret, better than all others. He wins her by killing Iweret in battle; and since Iweret had wronged Mabuz the Cowardly, the son of the mermaid who raised Lanzelet, he is additionally rewarded for his victory by being told his name and heritage. Later, when Lanzelet observes the custom of the Castle Pluris and jousts with and defeats 100 knights, he wins another lady, that castle's queen, who has him watched so that he will not ride off and escape her. When some of Arthur's knights come to the castle looking for him, they joust with the hundred: Karyet (*Gareth) unhorses sixty-four, Erec seventy-three, before Walwein unhorses ninety-nine but not the hundredth. Lanzelet then asks to be let out to joust with them and promises that he will return immediately afterwards. He avoids breaking his word by not jousting with any of them but instead returning with them to his beloved Yblis.

An important episode in the romance involves the abduction of Ginover. Earlier, a King Valerin claimed that he was betrothed to Ginover before Arthur and thus had a right to her. Lanzelet fought as Arthur's champion and defeated Valerin. Returning from his captivity at Pluris, Lanzelet learns that, while Arthur and his knights were unarmed because they hunted a white stag, Valerin abducted the queen and took her to his impregnable castle. Tristrant suggests enlisting the help of Malduc, the wizard of the Misty Lake. But Malduc, who has a grudge against Walwein and Erec, will help only if they are handed over to him, a condition to which Arthur must agree if he is to rescue his queen. Malduc works a spell to put to sleep the serpents surrounding Valerin's castle and all the people who inhabit it. Then Arthur and his men can enter, slay Valerin and his followers, and free Ginover.

It is interesting that Lanzelet plays only a minor role in the rescue. He is, however, the leader of an expedition to free Walwein and Erec from the wizard's castle, where they are being starved to death. There is not a hint of an affair between Lanzelet and Ginover; and Lanzelet's true love is Yblis, with whom he has four children (one daughter and three sons), who inherit the four kingdoms Lanzelet and Yblis rule—Genewis, which Lanzelet's father lost and he reclaims, and the three won from Iweret. Lanzelet and Yblis 'grew old in great honor and died' without enduring tragedy or the downfall of Arthur's kingdom.

The hero of Ulrich's poem is both a courtly, chivalric champion and a fairy-tale hero who enlists the aid of a giant to help him cross a river and rescue his fellow knights and who undertakes the adventure of kissing a dragon and thereby restoring it to its original form as a beautiful woman. He loses his inheritance, is raised by a mermaid, becomes the greatest knight in the world serving the greatest king, and then regains his inheritance and lives happily ever after. While there are a number of events in Ulrich's tale that are analogous to those found in the better-known French and English traditions, there is also much that is different—material that is perhaps reflective of narratives that have not survived.

The Vulgate Cycle or Lancelot–Grail Cycle

Among the most significant developments in the Arthurian tradition is the sequence of prose romances written in France between about 1215 and 1235. Known as the Vulgate Cycle or the Lancelot–Grail Cycle, it contains five romances: *Estoire del Saint Graal* (*The History of the Holy Grail*), *Estoire de Merlin* (*The Story of Merlin*), *Lancelot*, *Queste del Saint Graal* (*The Quest for the Holy Grail*), and *Mort Artu* (*The Death of Arthur*). The Cycle is the culmination of a process that began when Chrétien de Troyes left his *Perceval* unfinished and various authors attempted to continue and complete the romance. Drawing on the original and the continuations, Robert de Boron wrote three verse romances outlining the history of the *Grail, *Merlin's role in the story of the Grail, and the Grail quest. These tales were then adapted into prose romances. The Vulgate or Lancelot–Grail Cycle was the next step in creating a complete history of the Grail and of the role of Arthur's court in the quest. (*Perceval*, its continuations, Robert de Boron, and the cyclic romances about *The History of the Holy Grail* and *The Quest for the Holy Grail* will be discussed at greater length in Chapter 4; and *The Story of Merlin* will be discussed in Chapter 6.) Neither Robert de Boron nor his prose adaptors include a tale about Lancelot. (There is, however, an early thirteenth-century romance called *Lancelot do Lac*, which 'names Perceval as the Grail hero and does not seem to anticipate Galaad' (Kelly 36) and which ends with the death of *Galehaut, but this is a non-cyclic text.)

The authors of the great Lancelot–Grail Cycle of romances are not known. The statement in the *Queste* and the *Mort Artu* that these romances were composed by Walter Map (c.1140–c.1210), a clerk at the court of Henry II, has long been recognized as false (since Map died before the works attributed to him were written), and so the cycle has been called by some the Pseudo-Map Cycle. E. Jane Burns considers the attribution to Walter Map as part of an elaborate 'fiction of authority' in which 'Merlin and the other author-heroes of King Arthur's court, the bogus author-translator Walter Map, the vernacular *scriptor* *Blaise, and the richly ambiguous voice of *li contes*' and even a book given by Christ are all said, at different points, to be the source of the story (41, 18). Yet, while the sequence of romances seems not to have a single author, neither are those romances a collection of unrelated texts. There are links among them that make it likely that a controlling hand, what Jean Frappier has called an architect, designed the whole (cf. Frappier 144: 'Si le *Lancelot–Graal* est l'œuvre de plusieurs auteurs, je crois qu'une image pareille au labyrinthe de la cathédrale de Reims symboliserait au mieux la nature de leur collaboration; il faudrait figurer au centre, et plus grand que les autres, celui qui a conçu le plan d'ensemble dans son unité, celui qui mérite d'être appelé le premier maître de l'œuvre ou, d'un seul mot, l'Architecte').

After recounting the history of the Grail and the story of Merlin, the cycle takes up the tale of Lancelot. The *Lancelot* (sometimes called the *Lancelot Proper*), by far the longest romance in the sequence, was the first written—between c.1220 and 1225. It begins, like Ulrich von Zatzikhoven's *Lanzelet*, with an account of Lancelot's parents and youth and his upbringing by the *Lady of the Lake, here identified with the *Ninianne who learned magic from Merlin before confining him forever. But whereas Ulrich, whose work did not influence the *Lancelot*, suggests that Lanzelet's father's barons rebel against him because he was a cruel overlord, here King Ban of Benoic, Lancelot's father, loses his realm and his life because of the treachery of *Claudas, who seizes his lands. Just as the Lady of the Lake takes Lancelot into her realm to protect him and to raise him, so too does she protect his cousins *Lionel and *Bors, who are also threatened by Claudas. Lancelot remains with the Lady until he is 18, at which time, in preparation for his entrance into the world, she instructs him about knighthood. In a passage that reads like a manual of chivalry, she describes the virtues necessary for a knight, explains the obligation a knight has to defend the Church, explicates the symbolism of the knight's arms, and provides examples of knights who possess all the virtues she enumerated. Lancelot then goes to Arthur's court to be knighted by the king, who dubs him but does not complete the ceremony by girding on a sword. On his first quest, Lancelot sends a message to Guinevere requesting that she provide him with a sword 'if she wishes to win me forever' (ii. 71).

A good part of the *Lancelot* describes the quests and exploits of Lancelot and other knights, frequently alternating stories within the larger framework of the romance, that is by beginning one tale, leaving it unfinished to turn to another, and then returning later to the former in an interlacing pattern. (This interlacing, 'entrelacement' in French, is typical of the narrative structure of much of the cycle.) But Lancelot's relationship with Guinevere is central to the romance. In an important addition to the story of their love, a knight named Galehaut invades Arthur's lands. So impressed with Lancelot's valour and chivalry is Galehaut that, at the point at which he is triumphant over Arthur's forces, he yields to Lancelot's request that he surrender to the king. Galehaut and Lancelot become fast friends. (So great is their friendship that, later in the romance, Galehaut himself, believing Lancelot to be dead, dies out of grief.) Learning of Lancelot's love for the queen, Galehaut arranges the first private meeting between them. After Galehaut's intercession, Lancelot becomes, throughout the romance, the queen's champion, rescuer, and protector as well as her lover.

When a messenger brings a charge that Guinevere is not in fact the rightful queen but that she has supplanted the true Guinevere, Lancelot must come to the queen's aid. The charge is made by a *False Guinevere, the daughter of King *Leodagan by his seneschal's wife. Arthur falls in love with the False Guinevere, who looks exactly like the true one, and proclaims her queen; and Lancelot must fight to win the true Guinevere's freedom. Arthur's unjust actions cause a breach between him and Lancelot, which foreshadows the breach that will occur in the final section of the cycle because of the love between Lancelot and Guinevere. It is only when the False Guinevere and her champion, an ageing knight named Bertelay, contract an illness that causes their flesh to rot that they realize that they are being punished for their sins and confess their deception. Ultimately, the king and the queen are reconciled, as, through Guinevere's intercession, are Arthur and Lancelot.

Lancelot must rescue the queen again when she is abducted by Meleagant. While the cyclic romance makes specific mention of Chrétien's *Knight of the Cart* and follows his basic pattern in retelling the story, there are some crucial differences. For example, Guinevere's refusal to see Lancelot does not hinge on his having delayed before leaping into the cart. He leapt 'immediately' into the cart (iii. 6), perhaps as a sign of the perfection of his love. But she is angry because earlier he had gone from the court without taking leave of her and because he no longer has the ring she gave him, since *Morgan took it and substituted a counterfeit. After the rescue of the queen, a dwarf arrives at court driving a cart in which a knight is riding. The knight can be freed only if someone else will ride in the cart; but no one is willing to do that. Consequently, the knight is reviled and then, when he attempts to sit with the other knights, is rejected by all of them except Gawain. Later, the cart returns carrying the Lady of the Lake. When Gawain enters the cart to free her, she scolds Arthur for not jumping in and says that 'all cart riders should be praised forever more' in honour of Lancelot (iii. 28). As a result, the queen and the king enter the cart; and finally all of Arthur's knights ride in it, thus ending forever the cart's stigma.

Lancelot's love for Guinevere leads to his imprisonment by Morgan, who hates the queen for coming between her and her lover, Guinevere's nephew *Guyomar of Carmelide. While in prison, Lancelot is inspired by love to paint murals depicting all his exploits, including his love of Guinevere. Morgan later (in *The Death of Arthur*) shows these murals to the king, and they reinforce the suspicions that *Agravain has planted in his mind.

Some of the events in the *Lancelot* prepare for the Grail quest that is to follow. Perceval is brought to Arthur's court by his brother *Agloval. The virginity of Bors is discussed; and the one time he slept with a woman, the daughter of King Brandegorre, is explained to be the result of a magic ring which made him love her. The love passed quickly when the ring fell from his finger, and he remained celibate ever after. Most importantly, the new Grail knight *Galahad is introduced. After Lancelot removes the daughter of King *Pelles from a tub of burning water, a feat that Gawain was unable to accomplish, she tricks him, with the help of her tutor *Brisane, into sleeping with her. Lancelot is disturbed by this affair and is driven to madness by Guinevere's anger over his relationship with the maiden. Yet, just as in Bors's encounter with King Brandegorre's daughter, in which God's 'grace and divine will' worked in such a way that she conceived a great knight, *Helaine the White, there is a fortunate aspect to Lancelot's transgression in that Galahad, who is destined to achieve the quest of the Grail, is conceived. The romance ends with the curing of Lancelot's madness by the Grail and the announcement of the coming of Galahad, the knight who will sit in the *Siege Perilous. Thus the structural blocks are in place for the building of the next section of the cycle, the quest for the Grail.

Following the Grail quest, the cycle returns to the love of Lancelot and Guinevere in the *Mort Artu* (*The Death of Arthur*). Less than a month after his return from the quest, on which thirty-two of the knights of the Round Table have died, Lancelot 'lapsed into sin with the queen'. No longer as discreet and prudent as before, they behave 'so foolishly that it became apparent to Sir Gawain's brother Agravain' (iv. 91). They therefore violate one of the tenets of courtly love, that is, that it should be kept secret. From the beginning of the *Mort*, there is a process of dissolution of the Round Table and of the happiness that lovers can achieve, an inevitable hurtling towards the end of Arthurian glory. Norris Lacy has observed that the romance abandons the interlace pattern typical of earlier parts of the cycle in favour of 'a fundamentally linear structure' which 'marks a surrender to inevitability' and is reflected in the emphasis on the role of Fortune (95).

The Wheel of Fortune, about which Arthur dreams, crushes in its turnings the innocent and the guilty alike. The *Maiden of Escalot, whose sleeve Lancelot wears in a tournament as a favour, learns that the great knight does not requite her love and dies as a result. Arriving at Camelot in a barge draped in rich silk, the Maiden's body is a reminder of the dangers of love, a reminder underscored by the letter she has written, which is found in a purse hanging from her belt. The letter proclaims that she died because she loved faithfully 'the most valiant and yet the vilest man in the world' (iv. 114).

Bors also comments on the dangers of love. In reaction to Guinevere's rejection of Lancelot because he wore the token of another lady, he observes that he has never known 'a noble man who stayed in love for a long while without finally being ruined by it', and he mentions some of the standard exempla of medieval misogynist literature: David, Samson, Hector, and Achilles, and thousands of others who died because of Helen of Troy. He also adds a contemporary to the list: Tristan, whose death because of Iseult is not even five years in the past (iv. 109). Though Bors's words are too one-sided, they are nevertheless prophetic. Lancelot, visiting the queen while Arthur is off hunting, is trapped in her room by Agravain and his followers. Fortunately for Lancelot, Bors had advised him to take a sword, and he is able to kill the first knight through the door and frighten off the others. Lancelot escapes, but when he must return to rescue the queen, he kills not only Agravain but also Gaheriet (Gareth), who does not share the scheming nature of his brother and whose death so troubles Arthur and especially Gawain that they wage war against Lancelot, pursuing him even after the pope forces Arthur to accept the return of Guinevere and Lancelot leaves *Logres.

Even in the war, Lancelot demonstrates his nobility by refusing to slay Arthur when he has him at his mercy and refusing to kill Gawain, who has insisted on single combat (although the wound that Lancelot gives Gawain ultimately kills him). While besieging Lancelot, Arthur learns that the Romans have invaded France and destroyed Burgundy, so Arthur's forces fight and defeat them and Arthur himself kills the emperor. But this war seems an afterthought, almost an interruption of the main action rather than the height of Arthur's glory that it is in some of the texts in the chronicle tradition.

Although Gawain has been severely wounded by Lancelot, after the treachery of Mordred he advises Arthur to ask Lancelot for assistance. Arriving too late to assist Arthur in his battle against Mordred, wherein father and son kill each other, Lancelot and Bors and their forces nevertheless pursue and kill Mordred's two sons. After this battle, Lancelot becomes a hermit until his death and then is buried, as he requested, at *Joyous Guard in the tomb where Galehaut lies.

Though *Excalibur is returned to the lake by *Girflet and a barge carries Arthur away, there is no question of his survival or his return. He is buried alongside *Lucan in the Black Chapel. The details emphasize that his death is unambiguous and support the message of the dream of the Wheel of Fortune, that all earthly glory passes.

Shortly after the Lancelot–Grail Cycle was completed, there followed a Post-Vulgate Cycle, which includes a history of the Grail, a story of Merlin, an account of the quest for the Grail, and a shorter *Death of Arthur* and which omits the *Lancelot*. The Post-Vulgate Cycle is not preserved as a complete cycle; but fragments of it are found in French, and translations of parts of it appear in Portuguese and Spanish.

The *Lancelot* was nonetheless internationally influential in transmitting the story of Lancelot and Guinevere. Around 1250, a German translation of the *Lancelot*, *Queste*, and *Mort* known as the *Prosa-Lancelot* was undertaken. The same three romances were also translated into Dutch (c.1280) in the great Dutch Arthurian manuscript known as the *Lancelot Compilation or Lancelot-Compilatie*, a manuscript that contains seven other Arthurian romances as well and that was apparently the second of two manuscripts of Arthurian texts. A good portion of the beginning of the *Lancelot* does not appear in this second volume and was presumably found in the first, which is no longer extant but which might also have contained some version of a history of the Grail and a *Merlin* (cf. Claassens and Johnson 5–7). An even earlier Dutch adaptation of the *Lancelot* (c.1260), known as *Lantsloot vander Haghedochte* (*Lancelot of the Cave*), is closer to the original in time but further from it in style: the *Lantsloot* translates the Old French prose in rhyming couplets and returns 'to the Arthurian world à la Chrétien'. And there is evidence of at least one and perhaps two other Dutch translations of the French *Lancelot* (Claassens and Johnson 23–6).

An Italian romance *Lancillotto dal Lago* (1558–9), 'a translation of the French printed *Lancelot du Lac* published in Paris in 1533', contains versions of the Vulgate *Lancelot*, the *Queste*, and *Mort* (Gardner 307). Even earlier, Dante must have known some version of the story of Lancelot and Guinevere similar to that found in the Vulgate Cycle since in canto V of the *Inferno* he has Francesca tell how she and Paolo read 'Of Lancelot, and how Love held him in thrall'. The story leads to a kiss, and so the book 'Was a Galahalt to us, and he beside | That wrote the book' (30). In the late 1440s, the noted Italian Renaissance painter Pisanello (Antonio Pisano) (1395–1455) also designed a series of frescos for the ducal palace of Lodovico Gonzaga. The frescos depict scenes and characters from the tournament won by Bors (Bohort) at King Brangoire's castle, as recounted in the Vulgate *Lancelot*; and, though never completed, they represent 'the only Renaissance painting on an Arthurian theme to survive in Italy proper' (Woods-Marsden p. xxii).

There is also a Hebrew romance, *Melech Artus* (*King Artus*) (1279), which translates from the Vulgate a small portion of the *Merlin* that recounts the birth of Arthur and a portion of the beginning of *Mort*, apparently (although the Hebrew text breaks off early in the story, before the end of the Winchester tournament) with the intention of translating all of the latter.

The influence of the Vulgate text extends even to south-western Poland, where a remarkable group of murals, found in a castle in Siedlecin near Jelenia Góra, includes scenes from the Vulgate *Lancelot* along with a number of religious themes. Though some restoration of these paintings was done in the 1930s, the Arthurian subject matter was not recognized until the 1990s. Among them are depictions of Lancelot and Lionel, Lancelot asleep under the apple tree, Lancelot fighting *Tarquyn, and the abduction of Guinevere by Meleagant (cf. Witkowski). These paintings, along with the numerous translations of the text, attest to the popularity and influence of the Vulgate Cycle.

Lancelot of the Laik

The fifteenth-century Scottish poem *Lancelot of the Laik*, which adapts a portion of the Vulgate *Lancelot* into rhyming couplets, has generally been considered of little literary value. Critics focused on the long expansion of a portion of the French text in which a wise man advises Arthur (found in the French *Lancelot* ii. 120–4); the corresponding advice by Amytans to Arthur on the nature of kingship and the duties of a king (in *Lancelot of the Laik*, lines 1294–2144, pp. 49–73) has sometimes been seen as inspired by 'the degraded state of government in Scotland under James III' (Vogel 5). The Amytans section dominates the second book of the poem and resonates in the unfinished third book. But to say that it is important is different from considering it the *raison d'être* of the poem.

Perhaps the reason for the emphasis on this passage as well as for the disparaging comments on the poem as a whole is that *Lancelot of the Laik* is incomplete. As a result, the passage of advice occupies a large percentage of the surviving lines—even though it would not loom so large if the poem had been completed as projected. Imagining the completed work makes it clear that *Lancelot of the Laik* is not a courtesy book but a romance in which the advice plays a significant but subsidiary role. Such projection requires a reader to consider the poet's own summary of the contents and the changes made by the English author in adapting the French romance. In lines 299–313, the author says he will tell of the wars between Arthur and Galiot, of how Lancelot 'berith the renownn' in these wars—this is the subject of the surviving books and would have continued at least to the end of book III. Then, in a bridging section, he will relate how Lancelot brings about peace between the two rulers. Finally he will tell—probably in a section at least comparable in length to the first three books—how Venus rewards Lancelot for bringing about 'concorde' by allowing him to have his lady's (i.e. Guinevere's) favour.

In the process of creating a verse romance from the prose of the French, the Scottish poet has translated some passages fairly closely, changed details in others, and sometimes expanded, sometimes abbreviated the text. But the most obvious change he makes is to select and focus on a portion of the much longer source. That the poet knew the longer romance and is not working from an incomplete manuscript is demonstrated by the fact that he lists in his prologue many of the events that he will not treat. His sense of various parts of the French romance as stories in themselves is made apparent when he says that one of the many incidents he has referred to in his *occupatio* would provide material for a 'gret [i.e. long] story' (20). In fact, the author of *Lancelot of the Laik* adapts his source in a manner that has been described by Larry Benson as typical of Middle English romancers: with 'concentration on action...and...preference for simple, brief, relatively straightforward narrative lines in contrast to the structural complexities of French works' (43).

The prologue is essential to the understanding that *Lancelot of the Laik* is a romance and not a poem of political advice. This section, which has no parallel in the French source, contains the poet's love complaint and a dream vision in which a messenger from the god of love instructs him either to tell his lady of his love for her or to write a 'trety' (narrative) of love or arms—something joyful, not sorrowful—which will let his lady know that he is in her service. After a disclaimer about his lack of literary talent, he decides to write for his beloved the story of Lancelot. However conventional such an opening might be, it puts the poem in a particular context, that of romance and not of the courtesy book or political treatise. In fact, the poet explains in the prologue that Arthur's war with Galiot is important because Lancelot was the reason for Arthur's victory and because he won the most honour in those wars. And the love of Guinevere was his reward for his achievements (20–1). The changes that the Scottish author made in his source indicate that he is deliberately enhancing Lancelot's position and reputation. The cumulative effect of such changes is to make the poem a self-contained romance about Lancelot as the exemplar of love and valour.

The *Stanzaic Morte Arthur*

The same emphasis on action and straightforward narrative found in *Lancelot of the Laik* is seen in the fourteenth-century English *Stanzaic Morte Arthur* as well. The *Stanzaic Morte* has its ultimate source in the Vulgate *Mort Artu*, though it is much changed from the French work and is possibly, as some have suggested, based on an intermediary source that has not survived. The poem offers an interesting contrast to the other English verse account of Arthur's death, the *Alliterative Morte Arthure*. Whereas the latter is composed in alliterative verse, the former is written in a lively eight-line stanza; and, while the poet makes much use of alliteration, there is a fairly regular abababab rhyme scheme. The alliterative poem reflects the chronicle tradition in which Mordred's treachery is the prime cause of the downfall of Arthur's kingdom, whereas the stanzaic poem is in the romance tradition in which the love of Lancelot and Guinevere gives Mordred the opportunity to betray Arthur.

The *Stanzaic Morte Arthur* begins shortly after the Grail quest when Lancelot and Guinevere have resumed their affair. The tragic nature of love is exemplified early in the poem by the fate of the daughter of the Lord of Ascalot, who is enamoured of Lancelot and who believes he returns her affection when he wears her token in a tournament. When Gaynor (Guinevere) hears from Gawain that Lancelot has a lover, she tells him that there is no love left between them. After serving to a Scottish knight an apple poisoned by a squire who intended to kill Gawain, she is without a champion when the knight's brother *Mador accuses her of murder, for the king 'might not be again the right' (38) and so cannot fight for her. The knights who might have defended her attended the dinner, saw what happened, and, suspecting her guilt, will not champion her. Only Bors agrees, reluctantly, to fight for her if no one else will.

Just as Gaynor learns that Arthur will not defend her, a boat bearing the body of the Maiden of Ascalot arrives with a letter from her explaining that she died because Lancelot would not love her. Gaynor realizes that she has driven away her champion because of her own jealousy. Lancelot, however, hears of the queen's plight and arrives in time to fight for her and clear her name. This danger avoided, a new one arises when Agravaine, who very early in the poem is said to spy on the lovers 'both night and day' (12) to catch them together, betrays them to the king and plans to trap them while Arthur is away hunting. Fortunately, Bors has advised Lancelot to take his sword when he visits the queen; thus, when the lovers are confronted, Lancelot is able to kill a knight, take his armour, and put the others to flight. He escapes but must return to rescue Gaynor, who has been condemned to be burned. Gawain's three brothers Agravaine, *Gahereis, and Gaheriet are killed during the rescue, driving Gawain, who wanted no part in the accusation against the lovers, to turn on Lancelot and demand that he be punished. Threat of an interdict by the pope persuades Arthur to reconcile with his queen, but Gawain's desire for revenge against Lancelot prompts a continuing war against Lancelot in France. When Mordred, who was not the prime mover in the attempt to trap the lovers, is left behind as regent, he sees an opportunity to seize the throne and so forges a letter saying that Arthur is dead and has himself declared king. To frustrate his intention to marry her, the queen must take refuge in the Tower of London.

Learning of the treachery, Arthur returns to England. Gawain, struck with an oar where he had received a head wound from Lancelot, dies in the landing but returns as a ghost to advise the king, shortly after his ominous dream of the Wheel of Fortune, not to fight Mordred the next day. While Arthur is meeting with Mordred to arrange a truce, an adder stings a knight, who draws his sword to slay it and inadvertently starts a great battle in which both armies are destroyed, including the leaders. Arthur slays Mordred with a spear, but not before he himself receives a fatal wound. Shortly after *Bedivere returns the king's sword to the water, a barge arrives to take Arthur to *Avalon for his wounds to be healed. Not long afterwards, however, Bedivere sees the king's tomb.

Lancelot, arriving in England to help Arthur, finds the king and the traitor Mordred dead. He then goes to the convent at Aumsbury, where the queen has taken the veil. She tells him to return to his realm and take a wife; but he says he would never be so untrue and adopts a holy life as a hermit in order to share the 'same destiny' (115) as Gaynor. This final meeting between the lovers is a dramatic and moving addition to the tale as well as a testament to the depth of Lancelot's love, since he will not entertain the thought of loving and marrying any other woman. Thus, though his deep love causes a tragedy, it also leads him to a holy life and ultimately to salvation. Upon his death, the bishop, who has been among those who shared the hermit's life with Lancelot, dreams that 37,000 angels bear him to heaven. Shortly after, Gaynor dies and is buried with Arthur at *Glastonbury.

The *Stanzaic Morte Arthur* as well as the Vulgate Cycle influenced Thomas Malory's *Morte d'Arthur*, and his book in turn influenced a vast body of literature. (Malory's *Morte* and the works influenced by it will be discussed at length in the next chapter.) These great works have established the love of Lancelot and Guinevere as an essential part—and for some, the central event—of the Arthurian tradition.

ROMANCES WITH NON-TRADITIONAL HEROES

In addition to the romances that focus on the love of Lancelot and Guinevere, there are numerous romances about the Grail and its heroes, and about Gawain, Merlin, and Tristan and Isolt (all of whom will be discussed in separate chapters). Some romances imitate the patterns of the great narratives that preceded them but tell of the loves and battles, the quests and conquests of knights other than the traditional superheroes. These romances often exceed their predecessors in the use of supernatural or unnatural characters, beasts, and events which the hero encounters as he proves himself the best of knights.

Several French romances recount the adventures of such knights. The lengthy *Claris et Laris* (begun in 1268), which runs to more than 30,000 lines, tells of the loves of the two heroes for whom the tale is named—of Claris for Lidoine, wife of the King of Gascony, whom he marries after her husband dies, and of Laris for Marine, the sister of Yvain. Their chivalric adventures, along with those of the many knights searching for Laris, who is twice abducted, are woven together in what has been called the most elaborate and 'the most striking example of systematic interlace' (Kelly 63).

Floriant et Florete (written between 1250 and 1275) relates in verse the life and adventures of the son of the King of Sicily, Floriant, who is born after his father's death and carried off by Morgan le Fay to be educated and then sent to Arthur's court. Like many of these later independent romances, *Floriant* borrows motifs from earlier tales. For example, after the hero's marriage to Florete, daughter of the Emperor of Constantinople, the criticism of his lack of knightly activity causes him to set out a second time for Arthur's Britain. He takes Florete on the journey with him, a motif inspired by Chrétien's *Erec*.

One of the most interesting of the French romances about a non-traditional hero is the anonymous lai *Melion* (c.1200), which tells of Melion, a knight of Arthur's court who vows never to love any maiden who has loved another man. Because of this, women hate him; but one day he encounters a lady he can love and marry, the daughter of the King of Ireland, who says she never has and never would love another. While hunting, Melion shows a great stag to his wife, who declares she will not eat until she can taste that animal's meat. Telling her of a ring he possesses that can change him into a wolf and then back again to a man, Melion has her touch him with the ring. As a wolf, he kills the stag and returns, only to find that his wife and his squire have run off together to Ireland. Still in lupine form, he follows; and ultimately, when Arthur and some of his knights come to make peace with the King of Ireland, Melion attaches himself to Arthur. After Melion attacks the squire at the King of Ireland's castle, Arthur questions him, learns the truth, and forces Melion's wife to give him the ring so he can restore her husband to his natural form. Melion wants to change her into a wolf in punishment but is persuaded by Arthur not to do so for the sake of their children; he does, however, leave her behind in Ireland. The lai ends with Melion offering a misogynistic moral, which matches the tone of the poem: 'Whoso believeth his wife in all things cannot help but come into mischance at the end, for it is not meet to set your trust in all her sayings' (92).

The French verse romance *Yder*, believed to have been written during the reign of King John (1199–1216) (cf. *Yder* 12–13), is noteworthy not only for its recounting of the exploits of Yder, son of Nuc, but also for its depiction of Arthur and Kei (Kay). Yder, upset with Arthur for forgetting in only one day his service in saving the king's life, sets out to assist a lord whose castle Arthur is going to besiege. On the way, he encounters Ivenant, who agrees to knight Yder if he can resist the temptations of Ivenant's wife. He does resist, even though it requires him to kick the wife in the belly when she draws too close (39). At the siege, Yder unhorses Kei three times and then, with just three others, defeats the thirty knights Kei has sent against him—thus earning Kei's enmity.

Not only is Kei mean-spirited and ill-spoken, as he often is, but in this romance he is so wicked and jealous that he attempts to kill Yder treacherously. After Kei has been shamed at the siege, he rides up and wounds Yder from the side, prompting even the narrator to curse him. Later in the romance, Arthur forces Genievre (Guinevere) to name the person she would choose to love if he were killed. Though she first says her grief would be so great that she would probably die, Arthur presses her for an answer. When she chooses Yder, who has rescued her from a bear in addition to performing numerous other acts of valour, Arthur becomes jealous and wishes for his death. His jealousy is, however, baseless because Yder is devoted to Guenloie, the woman for whom he does his deeds of great prowess.

When Guenloie says she will marry whoever brings her a certain knife owned by two giants, the king takes Yder, Kei, Gawain, and Yvain with him to the giants' home. Kei enters first and is gone so long that his companions think he has been killed. Yder enters next and finds Kei hiding from the giants. He then kills both giants and obtains the knife. But that evening Kei draws water from a spring he knows to be poisoned and gives it to the thirsty Yder, who swells up and becomes so disfigured that he looks barely human. His companions leave him for dead; fortunately, however, two Irish knights arrive and have a curative root. Returning with the knife, Yder wins the right to marry Guenloie. The romance ends happily with the reunion of Yder with his father, the marriage of his father to his mother (Yder having been born out of wedlock), and the marriage of the hero to his beloved. Nevertheless, *Yder* is striking in characterizing Arthur as a husband so jealous that he wishes his imagined rival dead and Kei as a knight so wicked that he will resort to base murder.

The Occitan romance *Jaufre* (probably written in the first third of the thirteenth century), recounts its hero's seeking of knighthood at the court of Arthur, where he is insulted by Kay, who typically misjudges the young man's potential when Jaufre vows to avenge the murder of one of the king's knights by the haughty Taulat de Rogimon. On his quest to find and punish Taulat, Jaufre has adventures with other knights, with a demon who fights as a knight, and with a leprous giant who kills babies so he can bathe in their blood to cure his illness.

Jaufre is clearly influenced by earlier romances, especially Chrétien's *Yvain*, which has been called 'the *prétexte* of the Occitan work' in which the author 'reslants motifs and themes and situations' from the earlier work, even 'concluding his romance with a fountain adventure' (Hunt ii. 127, 141). There also seems to be a humorous response to Chrétien's *Perceval* in which the hero is greatly at fault for not asking a question about the suffering of the lord of the Grail castle. Jaufre comes to the castle of Brunissen the Beautiful, the woman with whom he falls in love, and finds her and all the people of her land grieving terribly. In a reversal of the pattern in *Perceval*, Jaufre asks repeatedly about the grief; but each time he is attacked, even by his father's old friend. Ultimately, he learns that the grief is for the lord of the land who has been captured and tormented for seven years; but he gets this information only after his question has earned him beatings and rebuke.

Jaufre finally encounters and defeats Taulat and makes him a friend and an ally of Arthur's. All ends happily with the wedding of Jaufre and Brunissen, who are rewarded by Fada de Gibel, the lady whose lands and person he saved in the fountain adventure, with magic powers that will protect Jaufre from any beast and make Brunissen pleasing to everyone who sees her.

A number of romances written in German also aggrandize new heroes. The thirteenth-century author known as Der Stricker, whose name means the Weaver or the Spinner of Tales, wrote, in addition to a version of *The Song of Roland* and *mären* or popular and amusing tales, a romance called *Daniel of the Blossoming Valley* (*Daniel von dem blühenden Tal*) (between 1210 and 1225). The romance is full of monsters, marvels, and exotic creatures. A dwarf with an invincible sword, a giant who rides on a camel, a creature without a stomach ('bellyless demon', 38), an old artisan who sires giants and can run faster than horses, a head that kills, a magic net, an ointment that gives night vision, elephants that carry castles on their backs, a strange bird called a babian which hovers to provide shade by day and gives off light at night—all these and more are part of the fabulous romance world created by Der Stricker.

Daniel, the hero of the tale, proves himself in traditional knightly ways, but his 'most striking quality' is his 'cunning, *list*, perhaps better translated as "astuteness" or "cleverness" ' because of its positive connotations (Wallbank 90). Upon arrival at Arthur's court, Daniel demonstrates his valour by the conventional means of unhorsing all of Arthur's knights except Gawein, Iwein, and Parzival. In these jousts, neither knight is thrown to the ground. He also wreaks havoc on the enemy in the king's battles in the land of Cluse. Still, Daniel's wit is as important as his valour. He kills a dwarf by tricking him not to use a sword that can pierce any armour. With the dwarf's sword, he kills giants whose skin is so hard that no conventional weapon can harm them. To slay a monstrous creature who carries a head that kills anyone who looks on it, Daniel uses a mirror so he does not have to gaze directly at the fatal head and then uses the head to kill the creature and his army. He again depends on his wits to kill an ogre who stuns anyone who hears his voice and who bathes in the blood of knights to cure a disease.

Though Arthur is held up as an exemplar of courtly behaviour, it is the cleverness of Daniel that time and again saves the day and indeed saves Arthur and his reputation. For example, when the king (and not the queen, as is traditional) is abducted, Daniel thinks of the magic net as a way to capture the abductor who is too smart to approach an armed knight and too quick to be caught. The poem praises cleverness and seems to summarize its own theme when it proclaims that 'one man alone can accomplish with cunning that which a thousand men, however strong they might be, could never do together' (140).

Another author writing in German is the Austrian poet known as Der Pleier (the Glass Blower, probably 'one of the many fanciful pen-names used by professional poets to indicate their calling' (Wallbank 92)). Der Pleier is the author of three Arthurian romances written between 1240 and 1280, the earliest of which, *Garel von dem blühenden Tal* (*Garel of the Blooming Valley*), is a direct response to Der Stricker's *Daniel*. Several motifs or incidents echo or reverse similar ones in Der Stricker's romance. As in *Daniel*, for example, the hero's adventures begin with a challenge delivered by a giant from a lord with a grievance against Arthur. But here the giant is courtly and not rude and strange. Like Daniel, Garel rides out before Arthur's forces must fight; but, in a reversal of the motif in *Daniel*, through his knightly valour more than his cunning he earns the allegiance of numerous noblemen, who then assist Garel in his battle against Arthur's enemy Ekunaver. There are, to be sure, some marvels, such as the sea monster who is half man and half horse and who has a shield with a head depicted on it that kills anyone who looks at it. Garel overcomes this monster by calling on the dwarf king Albewin, who steals the shield and hides it, thereby giving Garel the opportunity to kill the beast. But it is not a trick that allows Garel to triumph: it is the loyalty he has earned from Albewin through his valour. Due to other allegiances he has secured, Garel is able to assemble a large army and defeat Ekunaver's force.

Der Pleier also wrote two tales of knightly adventure in which love is the moving force. *Tandareis und Flordibel* tells of the coming of Flordibel, the daughter of the King of India, to Arthur's court with the condition that if any man loves and marries her, Arthur will kill him. Tandareis, a youth in Arthur's service, falls in love with her and she with him. Eventually Tandareis and Flordibel run off together; and Arthur, angry at the betrayal, condemns Tandareis to die. Since the lovers have not married, Tandareis has not fulfilled the conditions that would require his death. Though spared because of this technicality, Arthur decrees that he must seek adventure in foreign lands and not return until summoned by the king. Tandareis soon wins fame through such typical knightly deeds as rescuing maidens, killing giants, and defeating large numbers of knights. When he finally returns to Arthur's court, he is a knight of great reputation. Claudin, a woman he has rescued, and Antonie, a woman who has rescued him from imprisonment and death by starvation, both claim Tandareis as a husband. In a formal pleading, they present their cases, as does Flordibel. Arthur decides that they all have a claim and tells Tandareis that he must choose among them. Of course, he chooses Flordibel, but he asks Arthur to arrange worthy marriages for the other two.

Der Pleier's *Meleranz* is the story of the son of Arthur's sister Olimpia and the King of France, who is named Meleranz but called The Breton 'out of affection for Arthur' (370). The young prince leaves his father's court to seek out Arthur's. On the way, he meets the maiden Tydomie at a beautiful bath, which is described with courtly splendour. They fall in love and Meleranz, after being knighted by Arthur, sets out to win the fame that will make him worthy of Tydomie's love. He proves himself by defeating knights who have never been beaten before, by coming to the aid of Tydomie's cousin, and then by regaining from an invader the meadow where the splendid bath is located.

Meleranz, like Der Pleier's other romances, is somewhat reactionary, full of conventional courtly motifs and narrative elements. Nevertheless, Der Pleier's works must have had a degree of popularity, as a series of murals in the summer house built at Castle Runkelstein near Bolzano, Italy, demonstrates. The castle, built in 1237, was acquired by Nikolaus and Franz Vintler in 1385. Nikolaus had a summer house built and decorated, probably in the first five years of the 1400s (Rushing 247), with murals depicting scenes from romance as well as the *Nine Worthies and other heroes. In addition to scenes from *Wigalois* and the Tristan story, there is a series of murals based on *Garel*, including one portraying a scene from the romance in which the Round Table is set up outdoors.

The anonymous thirteenth-century German romance *Wigamur* tells of the kidnapping of the youth Wigamur, another non-traditional hero, by a wild woman named Lespia. Much of the romance involves the hero's search for information about his lineage. It also borrows motifs from great earlier romances. Wigamur, for example, is educated in knighthood in a manner similar to 'Parzival's education by *Gurnemanz'; he fights for a woman named Eudis to defend her inheritance of a wondrous fountain, an episode 'echoing Hartmann's *Iwein*'; and like Iwein he assists a noble beast, in this case an eagle fighting a vulture, which becomes a faithful companion and gives him a new name, the Knight of the Eagle (Meyer 99, 100).

Written in the late twelfth century by the same author who wrote *De ortu Waluuanii* (discussed in Chapter 5), the Latin romance *Historia Meriadoci, regis*

Cambrie (*The Story of Meriadoc, King of Cambria*) is the tale of Meriadoc, son of Caradoc, King of Cambria, who is treacherously killed by his brother Griffin. Griffin also tries to kill Caradoc's children, Meriadoc and Orwen; but they are saved by the faithful Ivor and his wife. After defending Arthur's claim to various lands in judicial combat against three knights and gaining their allegiance by asking Arthur to restore to them the land they claimed, Meriadoc goes to fight for the emperor of the Alemanni. He has adventures in a strange castle that causes a maddening fear in all who enter, escapes the castle through his boldness, and wins the release of the emperor's daughter. Even though Meriadoc is promised her hand in marriage because of his valour, he is betrayed again, this time by the emperor, who has also promised his daughter to the King of Gaul in order to secure a peace with him. Claiming that Meriadoc has forcefully violated his daughter, he imprisons his champion. But Meriadoc escapes and joins the King of Gaul, ultimately killing the emperor and marrying his daughter.

Two English metrical romances also have non-traditional heroes. The hero of *Sir Degrevant* (*c.*1400) would hardly be considered an Arthurian knight were it not for the fact that the text calls him a knight of the Round Table. *Degrevant's lands are despoiled by an earl while he is off fighting in the Holy Land; he must regain his lands as well as his beloved, the earl's daughter Melidore, who has been promised to Duke Gerle. Degrevant defeats the duke in combat and wins Melidore. He then inherits the lands of the earl; and he and Melidore live together happily for many years and have seven children before she dies. Returning to the Holy Land, Degrevant dies fighting a sultan. The typical return to Arthur's court does not occur, and there is no other link to Arthur or his knights.

The late fourteenth-century *Sir Cleges* is noteworthy as the only romance to be set at the court of *Uther Pendragon rather than Arthur. Cleges is a hero different from those of classical Arthurian romance. He is said to be meek as a maid, and he and his wife are praised for being great 'almusfolke' (givers of alms) (377, 378). In fact, Cleges's almsgiving leads to the problem of the romance: he and his wife are so generous that they become impoverished. But God rewards them by having a cherry tree in their garden bear fruit on Christmas Eve. When they bring the fruit to Uther, he too rewards them, by giving them Cardiff Castle and other gifts. So unusual is the setting at Uther's court that when the tale was adapted in 1924 as *Sir Cleges*, a short play for children by Frances Chesterton (1875–1938), wife of G. K. Chesterton, she changed the setting to Arthur's court.

LANVAL AND LAUNFAL

Another knight known for his generosity became quite popular in medieval literature. *Lanval or Launfal, while not one of the famous knights like Lancelot, Gawain, Tristan, and Perceval, who dominate medieval romance, was nevertheless internationally known. In the latter half of the twelfth century, Marie de France wrote a Breton lay called *Lanval*. Marie's lay is believed to have been translated into Middle English in a version now lost. This translation influenced the Middle English poem *Sir Landevale* (written in the first half of the fourteenth century), which in turn influenced Thomas Chestre's late fourteenth-century *Sir Launfal*. The lost translation is believed also to have influenced two sixteenth-century English versions of the tale, *Sir Lambewell* and the fragmentary *Sir Lamwell*, a rendition of the tale with Scottish dialectical traits.

Marie's *Lanval* is a Breton lay, a term that designates a short verse tale claiming to be based on a Celtic theme as sung by Breton harpers. Marie tells a tale similar to the one found in another lay, *Graelent*, which is not set at the court of Arthur but at the court of a king of Brittany. Marie's Lanval is a knight who receives nothing from King Arthur and thus slips into poverty. In the countryside, he encounters a fairy maiden who gives him her love and great wealth, which he distributes liberally to others. The maiden's only condition for her love is that it never be revealed, lest he lose her forever. Lanval abides by this condition until he is propositioned by Arthur's queen. He refuses her by saying he will not betray Arthur; but when she charges that he is 'not interested in women' and has 'taken [his] pleasure' with the young men he trains, he retaliates by declaring that he loves a lady 'whose poorest serving girl is more worthy' than the queen (38). In her anger, she accuses him of having propositioned her and then of insulting her. When he is tried, Arthur's barons demand that he produce his beloved to prove his claim about her beauty. At the last moment, the fairy maiden rides up and vouches for Lanval's account of his encounter with the queen. Lanval, acquitted, leaps on his lady's horse, and they ride off to Avalon.

While *Sir Landevale* is a fairly close translation of its original and serves as a source for Thomas Chestre's *Sir Launfal*, the latter poem also adds a good bit of material not in the earlier versions. It includes scenes in which the mayor of the town fails to show hospitality to Launfal because of his poverty. It adds a demonstration of Launfal's prowess when he is challenged by a knight named Valentyne, who is said to be fifteen feet tall and whom he kills in battle. It also expands on the picture of Gwennere (Guinevere) as an unfaithful, proud, vengeful woman. Said to be the daughter of King Ryon of Ireland, Gwennere proclaims that her eyes should be put out if Launfal can produce a fairer woman. When his beloved, here named Tryamour, arrives and all agree that she is indeed fairer, the fairy woman blows on her such a breath that Gwennere is blind ever after.

The lays of Marie and other anonymous lays were translated as part of the initiative of King Hákon Hákonarson of Norway. Twenty-one lays in all comprise the *Strengleikar*, the collection of lays translated into Norse. *Lanval* was translated into Norse as *Janual* (or *Januals ljóð*), a fairly close rendition of Marie's lay with occasional variations and stylistic traits typical of the Norse adaptations of romance literature.

Lanval has not often figured in literature after the Middle Ages. He was, however, the protagonist in the popular American poem 'The Vision of Sir Launfal' (treated at length in Chapter 4). Edward George Bulwer-Lytton (1803–73), who wrote an epic poem about King Arthur (discussed in Chapter 3), also wrote a short poem called 'The Fairy Bride' (1853) which tells the story of a knight named Elvar, who loses his fairy lover when he breaks his pledge never to speak of her. Though his Genevra (Guinevere) has none of the vices of her medieval counterpart, Bulwer-Lytton's poem is no doubt a reworking of the traditional tale. Lanval is also the subject of the play *Lanval* (1908) by British author T. E. Ellis, which combines elements from the chronicle tradition and from other romances with the traditional Lanval story. Arthur is fighting the Picts and the Saxons; Geraint is a friend and a champion of Lanval; and Agravaine is his enemy. The play dramatizes Lanval's encounter with the fairy Triamour and, after a stay in her realm, his desire to return to the world. There he is favoured by his lover until he reveals her existence. When he is condemned in an act of expediency rather than justice and is banished, Triamour does not appear to save him from the judgement; but she does reappear as he wanders disgraced in the woods to ask sarcastically if he is content 'With all the honours, merits and rewards' the world has given him. When he learns from her that Geraint, the one knight who recognized his worth, is dead, he grants to her his 'being' in return for which she says she will give him 'the kindest gift of all— | Release' from life (126, 129). He dies without the vindication that he receives in the medieval tales and without any disclosure of the queen's guilt.

CHASTITY TESTS

A theme popular in several romances and tales is that of the chastity test involving a horn that only a man whose wife is faithful can drink from without spilling its contents, or a glove or a mantle that will fit correctly only a faithful wife, or even a bridge that only a true spouse can cross. The theme sometimes appears as an episode in a longer romance and sometimes as the sole subject of a shorter tale.

Robert Biket's Anglo-Norman *Lai du cor* (*Lay of the Horn*), written in the latter part of the twelfth century, tells of a wondrous gift to Arthur, a horn with two special qualities. The first is that it has a hundred small bells that make sweet music whenever anyone touches it. The other is more ominous. As an inscription on the horn explains, no man can drink from the horn without spilling its contents upon himself unless his wife is completely faithful in deed and in thought. When Arthur tries to drink from it and spills the wine, he becomes enraged and grabs a knife 'with which he intended to stab the queen' (214) but is restrained by his knights. The queen explains that her one fault was to give a ring to a young man who killed a giant who had made an accusation against Gawain. Arthur's anger subsides when all the kings and counts in attendance spill the wine they attempt to drink. Only one knight, Caradoc (Garaduc in the French text), is able to drink cleanly from the horn, for which Arthur rewards him by giving him the horn and confirming his lordship of Cirencester.

A similar tale is told about a cloak or mantle in *Le Mantel mautaillié* (*The Ill-Fitting Cloak*). Written in French verse in the late twelfth century, the tale substitutes for the drinking horn a cloak that will fit only a woman who is perfectly faithful to her husband or lover. As in Biket's lay, first the queen and then all the ladies of the court are tested. They try on the cloak; and it fits all of them poorly though in different ways—ways which are sometimes related, in fairly crude jokes, to the manner of the woman's infidelity. In the end, only Caradoc's wife is able to wear the cloak without disgrace.

A number of longer romances include chastity tests as a small part of their action. In the First Continuation to Chrétien's *Perceval*, for example, a knight brings to Arthur's court a drinking horn named Boënet that can change water to wine; but only a man whose beloved has been faithful can drink from it without spilling the wine. Arthur drinks from the horn despite Guinevere's urging that he not do so, and, like almost all his knights, spills the wine. Only Carados can drink cleanly, but his success causes him to send his beloved Guinier away from the court because of the envy her faithfulness has inspired (121–2). In the lays about the horn and the cloak, Caradoc's beloved is unnamed; but in her edition of the Welsh *Triads*, Rachel Bromwich has associated Guinier with Tegau Eurvron, known in Welsh literature as a model of fidelity and beauty (cf. her note, pp. 512–14), who appears in Triad 66 as one of the 'Three Faithful Wives of the Island of Britain' (174).

The chastity test was also quite popular in German literature. *Der Mantel*, a version of the *Mantel mautaillié*, has been ascribed to Heinrich von dem Türlin, though his authorship is a matter of controversy. The text is incomplete but is of interest for including Erec and Enite among those tested by the mantle. The chastity test appears elsewhere in German literature. In Ulrich von Zatzikhoven's *Lanzelet*, a lady in the service of the mermaid or water-fey who raised Lanzelet brings a mantle to Arthur's court. The garment does not fit Ginover (Guinevere), who is said to be 'courtly and good' but who has 'erred in thought' (105). It fits some of the ladies, like Kay's wife, very poorly. On the other hand, it comes close to fitting Walwein's ladylove and Enite (Enid), and 'they could well have had it' (108) were it not for the fact that it fits perfectly Lanzelet's beloved, Yblis. Two chastity tests also figure in Heinrich von dem Türlin's *Diu Crône* (discussed in Chapter 5). And in a poem called 'König Artus mit der Ehbrecher-brugk' ('King Arthur and the Adulterers' Bridge'), written in 1545 by Hans Sachs (1494–1576), a bridge can be safely crossed only by the faithful. Contrary to all other chastity-test tales, Guinevere is the one woman who passes the test.

Möttuls saga (*The Tale of the Mantle*), a version of *Le Mantel mautaillié* in Norse prose, was written in the thirteenth century as part of King Hákon Hákonarson's translation initiative. Though generally a fairly close translation, the saga occasionally adds information to the original or omits details from it. To the simple statement at the beginning of the French tale that the events recounted occurred at the court of good King Arthur, for example, the Norse adds a long statement on

Arthur's renown and virtues and notes that many deeds that happened to Arthur and his court have been recorded, some of them about 'illustrious events', some about 'valiant deeds of chivalry', and some about 'other curious matters'. The tale is 'about a curious and amusing incident' (7), an explanation obviously designed to prepare the reader or listener for something other than the more courtly tales associated with Arthur. As in the French, only one woman, the beloved of Karadin, passes the test.

The saga of the mantle was adapted into Icelandic verse in the fourteenth century *Skikkju rímur* (*Mantle Rhymes*). Aside from the radically different form which uses stylistic devices typical of Icelandic verse, such as alliteration and kennings, the poem adds or changes details. The cloak, for example, is said to have taken three elf-women more than fifteen years to weave (291), and the faithful maiden is given the name Kardon (309). But the basic story in which the cloak fits only this one maiden remains the same.

In Malory's *Morte d'Arthur* (discussed fully in the next chapter), there is a version of the drinking horn test in 'The Book of Sir Tristram', an episode that Malory adapted from the French *Prose Tristan*. Morgan le Fay sends a testing horn to Arthur's court because of her enmity for Guinevere and Lancelot. Lamerok discovers the plot and diverts the horn to Mark's court because Tristram had jousted with him, at Mark's insistence, when he was weary from other battles and knocked down horse and man; Lamerok sees the horn as the means by which to repay Tristram for the dishonour. At Mark's court, Isode and a hundred other ladies drink from the horn, and only four pass the test. Mark wants to burn Isode and the others who failed the test but is dissuaded by his barons, who convince him that the punishment should not be inflicted on the women because of a horn made by sorcery and sent by an enemy of true lovers (269–70).

Another English version of the chastity test involving a drinking horn is found in the fifteenth-century English tale called *Syre Corneus* because the text says that a knight of Arthur's court named Sir Corneus wrote the tale and 'namyd it after hys awne name' (9)—though early editions bore a different title, *The Cokwolds Daunce*. The poem is light-hearted, asserting that Arthur loved cuckolds since he himself was one and that he owes a debt to the man who lay with his queen and thus helped him while he, Arthur, was away by cheering his wife since 'women louys wele play' (women love fooling around) (8).

BALLADS

The chastity test theme also appears in a ballad in *Reliques of Ancient English Poetry*, the collection of early ballads compiled in 1765 by Bishop Thomas Percy (1729–1811). Percy's collection was one of the most important and influential of those produced by the antiquarian movement that sought to preserve and to make available native romances and ballads. In his defence of medieval 'romance' (a term he uses almost interchangeably with 'ballad') in his introduction to the third volume of the collection, Percy writes that although romances are 'full of the exploded fictions of Chivalry', they 'frequently display great descriptive and inventive powers' and they 'exhibit no mean attempts at Epic Poetry' (p. xii). This linking of the romances—which Percy feels often contain the 'rich ore of an Ariosto or a Tasso' buried 'among the rubbish and dross of barbarous times' (p. ix)—with the epic is a way of using eighteenth-century critical standards to argue for the quality of the medieval material. Percy contends that 'Nature and common sense had supplied to these old simple bards the want of critical art, and taught them some of the most essential rules of Epic Poetry' (p. xii). Summarizing the Arthurian romance 'Libius Disconius' (better known as *Libeaus Desconus*) to show the courage and nobility of Gawain's son, he concludes that the romance is 'as regular in its conduct, as any of the finest poems of classical antiquity' (p. xvi).

Percy's collection contained a wide range of material from the Middle Ages and the Renaissance, including six ballads that treated various aspects of the Arthurian legends. 'Sir Lancelot du Lake' recounts Lancelot's fight with Tarquin; 'King Ryence's Challenge' relates Ryence's demand that Arthur send his beard as a sign of submission; 'King Arthur's Death: A Fragment' describes Arthur's final battle with Mordred and his being taken off in a barge after Excalibur is returned to a river; and 'The Legend of King Arthur' is a synopsis of the chronicle version of the story of Arthur. 'The Marriage of Sir Gawaine' tells of Gawaine's marriage to a loathly lady who becomes fair, an analogue of the story told by the Wife of Bath in Chaucer's *Canterbury Tales*. 'The Boy and the Mantle' contains a version of the chastity test: putting on a mantle that 'shall never become that wiffe, | That hath done amisse'. Guinevere, of course, fails the test, as does Sir Kay's wife. Only the wife of Sir Craddocke, after confessing to the fault of having kissed her husband before their marriage, can wear the garment. While Guinevere, out of malice, accuses Craddocke's loyal wife of infidelity, two other tests, one with a carving knife and one with a drinking horn, ultimately confirm the mantle's judgement.

'The Ylle Cut Mantell', an American poem which appeared anonymously in *The Democratic Review* in May 1844, purported to be 'A Romaunt of the Tyme of Gud Kynge Arthur Done Into English from an Authentic Version' by a 'daughter of Eve' (467), an indication of a female author. The authentic version referred to is 'The Boy and the Mantle', from Bishop Percy's *Reliques*. The American poem, however, transforms the ballad in some fascinating ways. Considerably longer than the earlier ballad, it presents the mantle as the only test of fidelity. As in the ballad, Guinevere fails the test; but in a departure from its source, the wife of 'Caradois', here called Ella, also fails: the robe is too short on her 'by half an ell' because 'she had been faithless and untrue' (471). There is no mitigating explanation, as in the ballad, that she had merely kissed her future husband. Following Ella's discomfiture, two hundred other ladies, all the women of Arthur's court save one, also fail. That one young woman, Coralie, had been brought to court to marry a lord named Hubert before 'envious lips and lying tongue' had poisoned his mind against her. The remarkable thing is that Coralie is 'a Norman peasant's child', a point emphasized when the handsome young knight who brings the mantle announces that 'the magic robe was woven | for the poor Norman peasant girl' and proclaims her 'of maids the pride and pearl' (473, 475). In this way, 'The Ylle Cut Mantell' rejects worth based on birth and underscores the notion that virtue is more important than rank or wealth, a lesson Hubert appears to learn when he takes Coralie back to her native village to wed her there rather than in the pomp of court.

The ballad 'The Boy and the Mantle' is the source for 'The Magic Mantle' (1903) by Stephen Jackson (pseudonym of John Stevenson (b. 1853)). Jackson's story suggests that the tests of virtue described in the ballad, which only Sir Craydock and his wife pass, were devised by Merlin as a way of delaying the ultimate doom of Arthur's court. The second half of the story tells how the thirteenth-century descendant of Craydock and his bride prove themselves worthy of carrying on the family name, in part by undergoing the test of the mantle.

Another important medieval ballad not published in the *Reliques* but, like most of the Arthurian ballads found there, coming from Bishop Percy's folio manuscript is 'King Arthur and King Cornwall'. This tale, fragmentary because of the damage to the paper manuscript that Percy salvaged from the home of a friend where pieces of it were used to light the fire, begins with Guinevere claiming that she knows of a Round Table better than Arthur's. Because she is unwilling to say where it is located, Arthur and a group of knights set off in quest of it. Arriving at the court of King Cornwall, who boasts that he has had a daughter by Arthur's queen, they learn of a steed that in a day can go three times the distance that Arthur's horse can and of other magical objects owned by the king. In Cornwall's palace, Sir Bredbeddle, the Green Knight, who also figures in the romance *The Greene Knight*, a reworking of *Sir Gawain and the Green Knight* (discussed in Chapter 5), fights a fiend named Burlow Beanie. His weapons shatter in the battle with the fiend, who has seven heads and one body; Bredbeddle, however, uses the Bible to subdue the fiend and to force him to help them obtain other of Cornwall's magical objects. One of these is a sword that Arthur uses to behead his adversary, King Cornwall. The existing portion of the ballad does not describe the fulfilment of Gawain's vow to take Cornwall's daughter back to Brittany, where Arthur's court is located in this ballad, and to work his will with her, or the completion of the quest for the better Round Table, which may have been another of the objects won at King Cornwall's court.

A number of later authors return to the form that helped to initiate the modern interest in Arthurian poetry by consciously imitating the early ballads. Sometimes reproducing the traditional ballad stanza of alternating lines of iambic tetrameter and trimeter rhyming xaxa, sometimes using a variation of it, the modern ballad-makers are concerned with the simple direct narrative and the folk or supernatural elements that typify the form. In 1881, an anonymous work addressed to children, *Six Ballads about King Arthur*, recounted events from the legend from Arthur's begetting to his death, including King Ryence's challenge and the quest for the Grail. Victorian poet John Davidson (1857–1909), in 'The Last Ballad' (1899), portrayed a Lancelot maddened by his unintentional betrayal of Guinevere that led to the birth of Galahad. Years later, Lancelot is cured by his son but remains torn between his desire for 'a vision of the cup' and what he actually sees, 'a vision of the Queen' (21). This struggle seems to suggest that human blindness leads people to view as a flaw that which is actually their strength. John Masefield, in addition to using the ballad form for some of the poems in *Midsummer Night*, wrote about Bors's quest for the Grail in 'The Ballad of Sir Bors' (1910). And in 'The Ballad of King Arthur' (1926), G. K. Chesterton describes Arthur's victory at *Badon, where he fought with the image of the Virgin on his shield. The poem then discusses the fame he achieved after his death and suggests that the queen who will stand 'at his right hand | If Arthur comes again' (17) is that same Virgin.

American poet Edgar Lee Masters (1868–1950) published two Arthurian ballads in his collection *Songs and Satires* (1916). In 'The Ballad of Launcelot and Elaine', he recounts the begetting of Galahad; and in 'The Death of Sir Launcelot', he describes Launcelot's final days and holy death. Both poems contain touches that are worthy of the form they imitate. The former describes *Elaine's maid Dame Brisen as 'the subtlest witch | That was that time in life; | She was as if Beelzebub | Had taken her to wife' (143). And in the latter, after Launcelot turns to religion, there is an evocative description of his armour: 'His shield went clattering on the wall | To a dolorous wail or wind; | His casque was rust, his mantle dust | With spider webs entwined' (151). Some years later, another American poet, Laurence Pratt (b. 1890), wrote a 'Ballad of White Magic' in *New American Legends* (1958), which tells of a messenger from Merlin who brings the magician Houdini to the castle where *Vivien has entrapped Merlin. In response to Vivien's charms and potions and her calling on harpies and sirens against him, Houdini uses 'ordered reason and clear-eyed science' (77–8) and defeats her.

BIBLIOGRAPHY

Chrétien de Troyes and the Beginnings of the Romance Tradition
Andreas Capellanus. *The Art of Courtly Love*, trans. John Jay Parry, ed. and abridged Frederick W. Locke. New York: Frederick Ungar, 1957.
Chrétien de Troyes. *The Complete Romances of Chrétien de Troyes*, trans. David Staines. Bloomington: Indiana University Press, 1990.
—— *Lancelot or The Knight of the Cart (Le Chevalier de la Charrete)*, ed. and trans. William W. Kibler. New York: Garland, 1981.
—— *Les Romans de Chrétien de Troyes I: Erec et Enide*, ed. Mario Roques. Paris: Librairie Honoré Champion, 1978.
Dronke, Peter. ' "Andreas Capellanus" ', *Journal of Medieval Latin*, 4 (1994), 51–63.
Frappier, Jean. *Chrétien de Troyes: The Man and his Work*, trans. Raymond J. Cormier. Athens: Ohio University Press, 1982.

Graelent and Guingamor: Two Breton Lays, ed. and trans. Russell Weingartner. New York: Garland, 1985.

Keen, Maurice. *Chivalry*. New Haven: Yale University Press, 1984.

Kelly, Douglas. *The Art of Medieval French Romance*. Madison: University of Wisconsin Press, 1992.

Lacy, Norris J. *The Craft of Chrétien de Troyes: An Essay on Narrative Art*. Leiden: E. J. Brill, 1980.

Lull, Ramón. *The Book of the Orde of Chivalry: From the 1926 Early English Text Society Publication of William Caxton's The Book of the Ordre of Chyvalry (in Late Middle English) as Translated from a French Version of Ramón Lull's Le Libre del Odre de Cauayleria*, trans. Robert Adams. Huntsville, Tex.: Sam Houston State University Press, 1991.

Newman, F. X. (ed.). *The Meaning of Courtly Love*. Albany: State University of New York Press, 1968.

Uitti, Karl D., with Freeman, Michelle A. *Chrétien de Troyes Revisited*. New York: Twayne, 1995.

Ulrich von Liechtenstein. *Service of Ladies*, trans. J. W. Thomas. Chapel Hill: University of North Carolina Press, 1969.

The Influence of Chrétien de Troyes

Barron, W. R. J. *English Medieval Romance*. London: Longman, 1987.

Blumenfield-Kosinski, Renate. 'Arthurian Heroes and Convention: *Meraugis de Portlesguez* and *Durmart le Galois*', in Norris J. Lacy, Douglas Kelly, and Keith Busby (eds.), *The Legacy of Chrétien de Troyes*, vol. ii. Amsterdam: Rodopi, 1988: 79–92.

Claassens, Geert H. M., and Johnson, David F. 'Arthurian Literature in the Medieval Low Countries: An Introduction', in Geert H. M. Claassens and David F. Johnson (eds.), *King Arthur in the Medieval Low Countries*. Leuven: Leuven University Press, 2000: 1–34.

Entwistle, William J. *The Arthurian Legend in the Literatures of the Spanish Peninsula*. 1925; repr. New York: Phaeton Press, 1975.

Erec: Roman Arthurien en Prose, ed. Cedric E. Pickford. Geneva: Librairie Droz, 1959.

Erex saga and Ívens saga: The Old Norse Versions of Chrétien de Troyes's Erec and Yvain, trans. Foster W. Blaisdell, Jr., and Marianne E. Kalinke. Lincoln: University of Nebraska Press, 1977.

Erex saga Artuskappa, ed. Foster W. Blaisdell. Copenhagen: Munksgaard, 1965.

Ferguut, ed. and trans. David F. Johnson and Geert H. M. Claassens. Arthurian Archives, Dutch Romances II. Cambridge: D. S. Brewer, 2000.

Füetrer, Ulrich. *Iban*, in *Das Buch der Abenteuer*, ed. Heinz Thoelen, 2 vols. Göppingen: Kümmerle, 1997: ii. 220–77.

Gereint Son of Erbin, in *The Mabinogion*, trans. Gwyn Jones and Thomas Jones, rev. edn. London: Dent, 1974: 229–73.

Guillaume le Clerc. *Fergus of Galloway: Knight of King Arthur*, trans. D. D. R. Owen. London: J. M. Dent, 1991.

—— *The Romance of Fergus*, ed. Wilson Frescoln. Philadelphia: William H. Allen, 1983.

Hart, Jack. *The Lady of the Fountain*. Independence, Mo.: The International University Press, 1986.

Hartmann von Aue. *Erec*, trans. J. W. Thomas. Lincoln: University of Nebraska Press, 1982.

—— *Erec*, ed. Albert Leitzman, rev. Ludwig Wolff, 6th edn. prepared by Christoph Cormeau. Tübingen: Max Niemeyer, 1985.

—— *Iwein*, trans. J. W. Thomas. Lincoln: University of Nebraska Press, 1979.

—— *Iwein*, ed. G. F. Benecke, K. Lachmann, and L. Wolff, trans. Thomas Cramer, 7th edn. Berlin: Walter de Gruyter, 1981.

Hasty, Will. *Adventures in Interpretation: The Works of Hartman von Aue and their Critical Reception*. Columbia, SC: Camden House, 1996.

Herbert, Kathleen. *Bride of the Spear*. New York: St Martin's, 1988.

Herr Ivan: Kritisk Upplaga, ed. Erik Noreen. Uppsala: Almqvist & Wiksells, 1931.

Hunt, Tony. 'The Medieval Adaptations of Chrétien's *Yvain*: A Bibliographical Essay', in Kenneth Varty (ed.), *An Arthurian Tapestry: Essays in Memory of Lewis Thorpe*. Glasgow: Dept. of French, University of Glasgow for the British Branch of the International Arthurian Society, 1981: 203–13.

Ívens saga, ed. Foster W. Blaisdell. Copenhagen: C. A. Reitzel, 1979.

Ívens saga, in *Erex saga and Ívens saga: The Old Norse Versions of Chrétien de Troyes's Erec and Yvain*, trans. Foster W. Blaisdell, Jr., and Marianne E. Kalinke. Lincoln: University of Nebraska Press, 1977: 37–83.

Kalinke, Marianne E. *King Arthur North-by-Northwest: The Matière de Bretagne in Old Norse-Icelandic Romances*. Copenhagen: C. A. Reitzels, 1981.

Konrad von Stoffeln. *Der Ritter mit dem Bock. Konrads von Stoffeln 'Gauriel von Muntabel'*. Tübingen: Max Niemeyer, 1997.

Meyer, Matthias. 'Intertextuality in the Later Thirteenth Century: *Wigamur, Gauriel, Lohengrin* and the Fragments of Arthurian Romances', in W. H. Jackson and S. A. Ranawake (eds.), *The Arthur of the Germans: The Arthurian Legend in Medieval German and Dutch Literature*. Cardiff: University of Wales Press, 2000: 98–114.

Middleton, Roger. '*Chwedl Geraint ab Erbin*', in Rachel Bromwich, A. O. H. Jarman, and Brynley F. Roberts (eds.), *The Arthur of the Welsh: The Arthurian Legend in Medieval Welsh Literature*. Cardiff: University of Wales Press, 1991: 147–57.

Muir, Lynette R. 'A Reappraisal of the Prose *Yvain* (National Library of Wales MS. 444-D)', *Romania*, 85 (1964), 355–65.

'Nunca fuero caballero', in James Young Gibson (trans.), *The Cid Ballads and Other Poems and Translations from Spanish and German*, ed. Margaret Dunlop Gibson. London: Kegan Paul, Trench, Trübner, 1898: 385–6.

Ormerod, James. 'Meliagrance and Guenevere', in *Tristram's Tomb and Other Poems*. London: Elkin Mathews, 1928: 79–100.

Owain (The Lady of the Fountain), in *The Mabinogion*, trans. Gwyn Jones and Thomas Jones, rev. edn. London: Dent, 1974: 155–82.

Prose Yvain. Edition by Norris J. Lacy (in progress).

Rawe, Donald R. *Geraint: Last of the Arthurians*. Padstow: Lodenek Press, 1972.

Reynolds, Marion Lee. *Geraint of Devon*. Boston: Sherman, French, 1916.

Rhys, Ernest. *Enid: A Lyric Play*, music by Vincent Thomas. London: J. M. Dent, 1908.

Sala, Pierre. *Le Chevalier au lion*, ed. Pierre Servet. Paris: Honoré Champion, 1996.

Thompson, Raymond H. 'Interview with Kathleen Herbert', www.lib.rochester.edu/camelot/intrvws/herbert.htm.

Thomson, R. L. '*Owain: Chwedl Iarlles y Ffynnon*', in Rachel Bromwich, A. O. H. Jarman, and Brynley R. Roberts (eds.), *The Arthur of the Welsh: The Arthurian Legend in Medieval Welsh Literature*. Cardiff: University of Wales Press, 1991: 159–69.

Ywain and Gawain, in Mary Flowers Braswell (ed.), *Sir Perceval of Galles and Ywain and Gawain*. Kalamazoo, Mich.: Medieval Institute Publications, 1995: 77–202.

Lancelot and Guinevere

Benson, Larry. *Malory's 'Morte Darthur'*. Cambridge, Mass.: Harvard University Press, 1976.

Burns, E. Jane. *Arthurian Fictions: Rereading the Vulgate Cycle*. Columbus, Oh.: State University Press for Miami University, 1985.

Claassens, Geert H. M., and Johnson, David F. 'Arthurian Literature in the Medieval Low Countries: An Introduction', in Geert H. M. Claassens and David F. Johnson (eds.), *King Arthur in the Medieval Low Countries*. Leuven: Leuven University Press, 2000: 1–34.

Dante. *The Divine Comedy*, trans. Laurence Binyon, in *The Portable Dante*. New York: Viking, 1947: 3–544.

Frappier, Jean. *Étude sur la Mort le roi Artu, roman du XIIIe siècle*. Geneva: Droz, 1972.

Gardner, Edmund G. *The Arthurian Legend in Italian Literature*. London: J. M. Dent, 1930.

L'Illustre et famosa historia di Lancilotto dal Lago. Venice: Michele Tramezzino, 1558–9.

Kelly, Douglas. *Medieval French Romance*. New York: Twayne, 1993.

King Artus: A Hebrew Arthurian Romance of 1279, ed. and trans. with cultural and historic commentary by Curt Leviant. New York: KTAV Publishing House, 1969.

Lacy, Norris J. 'The Mort Artu and Cyclic Closure', in William W. Kibler (ed.), *The Lancelot–Grail Cycle: Text and Transformations*. Austin: University of Texas Press, 1994: 85–97.

Lancelot, in *Lancelot–Grail: The Old French Arthurian Vulgate and Post-Vulgate in Translation*, gen. ed. Norris J. Lacy, vols. ii and iii. New York: Garland, 1993 and 1995. (*Lancelot* is translated by Samuel N. Rosenberg, Carleton W. Carroll, Roberta L. Krueger, and William W. Kibler.)

[*Lancelot-Compilatie.*] *Roman van Lancelot (XIII eeuw)*, ed. W. J. A. Jonckbloet. 2 vols. The Hague: W. P. van Stockum, 1846–9.

Lancelot do Lac: The Non-Cyclic Old French Prose Romance, ed. Elspeth Kennedy. 2 vols. Oxford: Clarendon, 1980.

[*Lancelot do Lac*, trans. as] *Lancelot of the Lake*, trans. Corin Corley. Oxford: Oxford University Press, 1989.

Lancelot of the Laik, in Alan Lupack (ed.), *Lancelot of the Laik and Sir Tristrem*. Kalamazoo, Mich.: Medieval Institute Publications for TEAMS, 1994: 1–141.

McClelland, Nicola. *Ulrich von Zatzikhoven's Lanzelet: Narrative Style and Entertainment*. Cambridge: D. S. Brewer, 2000.

Mort Artu (The Death of Arthur), in *Lancelot–Grail: The Old French Arthurian Vulgate and Post-Vulgate in Translation*, gen. ed. Norris J. Lacy, vol. iv. New York: Garland, 1995: 89–160. (*The Death of Arthur* is translated by Norris J. Lacy.)

[*Prosa-Lancelot.*] *Lancelot: Nach der Heidelberger Pergamenthandschrift Pal. Germ. 147*, ed. Reinhold Kluge. 3 vols. Berlin: Akademie, 1948, 1963, 1974.

Stanzaic Morte Arthur, in Larry D. Benson (ed.), *King Arthur's Death*, rev. Edward E. Foster. Kalamazoo, Mich.: Medieval Institute Publications for TEAMS, 1994: 9–128.

Ulrich von Zatzikhoven. *Lanzelet: A Romance of Lancelot*, trans. Kenneth G. T. Webster, rev. Roger Sherman Loomis. New York: Columbia University Press, 1951.

—— *Lanzelet: Eine Erzählung*, ed. K. A. Hahn. Berlin: Walter de Gruyter, 1965.

Vogel, Bertram. 'Secular Politics and the Date of *Lancelot of the Laik*', *Studies in Philology*, 40.1 (Jan. 1943), 1–13.

Witkowski, Jacek. *Szlachetna a wielce żałosna opowieść o Panu Lancelocie z Jeziora: Dekoracja malarska wielkiej Sali wieży mieszkalnej w Siedlęcinie*. Wrocław: Wydawnictwo Universytetu Wrocławskiego, 2002.

Woods-Marsden, Joanna. *The Gonzaga of Mantua and Pisanello's Arthurian Frescoes*. Princeton: Princeton University Press, 1988.

Romances with Non-traditional Heroes

Chesterton, Frances. *The Children's Crusade, Sir Cleges, The Christmas Gift*. London: Samuel French, 1924.

[*Claris et Laris*.] *Li Romans de Claris et Laris*, ed. Johann Alton. Tübingen: Litterarischer Verein in Stuttgart, 1884.

Floriant et Florete, ed. Harry F. Williams. Ann Arbor: University of Michigan Press, 1947.

[*Historia Meriadoci*.] *The Story of Meriadoc, King of Cambria (Historia Meriadoci, regis Cambrie)*, ed. and trans. Mildred Leake Day. New York: Garland, 1988.

Hunt, Tony. 'Texte and Prétexte: *Jaufre* and *Yvain*', in Norris J. Lacy, Douglas Kelly, and Keith Busby (eds.), *The Legacy of Chrétien de Troyes*. 2 vols. Amsterdam: Rodopi, 1988: ii. 125–41.

Jaufre: An Occitan Arthurian Romance, trans. Ross G. Arthur. New York: Garland, 1992.

Jaufré: Roman Arthurien du XIIIe siècle en vers Provençaux, ed. Clovis Brunel. 2 vols. Paris: Société des Anciens Textes Français, 1943.

Kelly, Douglas. *Medieval French Romance*. New York: Twayne, 1993.

Melion, in *Les Lais anonymes des XIIe et XIIIe siècles: Édition critique de quelques lais Bretons*. Geneva: Droz, 1976: 289–318.

Melion, in Isabel Butler (trans.), *Tales from the Old French*. Boston: Houghton Mifflin, 1910: 73–92.

Meyer, Matthias. 'Intertextuality in the Later Thirteenth Century: *Wigamur, Gauriel, Lohengrin* and the Fragments of Arthurian Romances', in W. H. Jackson and S. A. Ranawake (eds.), *The Arthur of the Germans: The Arthurian Legend in Medieval German and Dutch Literature*. Cardiff: University of Wales Press, 2000: 98–114.

Der Pleier. *Garel von dem blünden Tal*, ed. Wolfgang Herles. Vienna: Karl M. Halosar, 1981.

—— *Garel of the Blooming Valley*, in *The Pleier's Arthurian Romances: Garel of the Blooming Valley, Tandareis and Flordibel, Meleranz*, trans. J. W. Thomas. New York: Garland, 1992: 1–196.

—— *Meleranz*, ed. Karl Bartsch. 1861; repr. Hildesheim: G. Olms, 1974.

—— *Meleranz*, in *The Pleier's Arthurian Romances: Garel of the Blooming Valley, Tandareis and Flordibel, Meleranz*, trans. J. W. Thomas. New York: Garland, 1992: 367–490.

—— *Tandareis und Flordibel*, in *The Pleier's Arthurian Romances: Garel of the Blooming Valley, Tandareis and Flordibel, Meleranz*, trans. J. W. Thomas. New York: Garland, 1992: 197–366.

—— *Tandareis und Flordibel: Ein höfischer Roman von dem Pleiaere*, ed. Ferdinand Khull. Graz: Styria, 1885.

Rushing, James A., Jr. *Images of Adventure: Ywain in the Visual Arts*. Philadelphia: University of Pennsylvania Press, 1995.

Sir Cleges, in Anne Laskaya and Eve Salisbury (eds.), *The Middle English Breton Lays*. Kalamazoo, Mich.: Medieval Institute Publications for TEAMS, 1995: 367–407.

[*Sir Degrevant*.] *The Romance of Sir Degrevant: A Parallel-Text Edition from Mss. Lincoln Cathedral A.5.2 and Cambridge University Ff.1.6*, ed. L. F. Casson. EETS os 221. London: Oxford University Press for the EETS, 1949; repr. 1970.

Der Stricker. *Daniel von dem blühenden Tal*, ed. Michael Resler. Tübingen: Max Niemeyer, 1983.

—— *Daniel of the Blossoming Valley (Daniel von dem blühenden Tal)*, trans. Michael Resler. New York: Garland, 1990.

Wallbank, Rosemary E. 'Three Post-Classical Authors: Heinrich von dem Türlin, Der Stricker, Der Pleier', in W. H. Jackson and S. A. Ranawake (eds.), *The Arthur of the Germans: The Arthurian Legend in Medieval German and Dutch Literature*. Cardiff: University of Wales Press, 2000: 80–97.

Wigamur, ed. Danielle Buschinger. Göppingen: Kümmerle, 1987.

[*Yder.*] *The Romance of Yder*, ed. and trans. Alison Adams. Cambridge: D. S. Brewer, 1983.

Lanval and Launfal

Bulwer-Lytton, Edward. 'The Fairy Bride', in *Dramas and Poems*. 1853; repr. Boston: Roberts Brothers, 1874: 270–84.

Chestre, Thomas. *Sir Launfal*, ed. A. J. Bliss. London: Thomas Nelson, 1960.

Ellis, T. E. *Lanval: A Drama in Four Acts*. London: Privately printed by John & Ed. Bumpus, 1908.

Graelent and Guingamor: Two Breton Lays, ed. and trans. Russell Weingartner. New York: Garland, 1985.

Janual, in *Strengleikar: An Old Norse Translation of Twenty-One French Lais*, ed. and trans. Robert Cook and Mattias Tveitane. Oslo: Norsk Historisk Kjeldeskrift-Institut, 1979: 212–27.

Marie de France. *Lanval*, trans. Norris J. Lacy, in Alan Lupack and Barbara Tepa Lupack (eds.), *Arthurian Literature by Women*. New York: Garland, 1999: 35–42.

—— *Lanval*, in *Lais*, ed. Alfred Ewert. Oxford: Basil Blackwell, 1960: 58–74.

Sir Lambewell, in John W. Hales and Frederick J. Furnivall (eds.), *Bishop Percy's Folio Manuscript: Ballads and Romances*. 3 vols. London: N. Trübner, 1867: i. 142–64.

Sir Lamwell, in F. J. Furnivall (ed.), *Captain Cox, his Ballads and Books; or, Robert Laneham's Letter*. London: For the Ballad Society, 1871: pp. xxx–xxxiii.

Sir Landevale, in Thomas Chestre, *Sir Launfal*, ed. A. J. Bliss. London: Thomas Nelson, 1960: 105–28.

Chastity Tests

Biket, Robert. *Lai du cor*, in Philip Bennett (ed.), *Mantel et Cor: Deux lais du XIIe siècle*. Exeter: University of Exeter, 1975: 41–87.

—— *The Lay of the Horn*, in Richard White (ed.), *King Arthur in Legend and History*. London: J. M. Dent, 1997: 211–17.

Dentzien, Nicole. 'Hans Sachs's Arthurian Chastity Test', *Arthuriana*, 13.1 (Spring 2003), 43–65.

The First Continuation, in *Perceval: The Story of the Grail*, trans. Nigel Bryant. Cambridge: D. S. Brewer, 1982: 98–135.

Malory, Sir Thomas. *Works*, ed. Eugène Vinaver, 2nd edn. London: Oxford University Press, 1971.

Der Mantel, Bruchstück eines Lanzeletromans des Heinrich von dem Türlin, nebst einer Abhandlung über die Sage vom Trinkhorn und Mantel und die Quelle der Krone, ed. Otto Warnatsch. Breslau: Wilhelm Koebner, 1883.

Mantel mautaillé (or *Le Lai du cort mantel*), in Philip Bennett (ed.), *Mantel et Cor: Deux lais du XIIe siècle*. Exeter: University of Exeter, 1975: 1–39.

Möttuls saga, in Marianne E. Kalinke (ed. and trans.), *Norse Romance*, vol. ii. Arthurian Archives 4. Cambridge: D. S. Brewer, 1999: 6–31.

Skikkju rímur, in Marianne E. Kalinke (ed. and trans.), *Norse Romance*, vol. ii. Arthurian Archives 4. Cambridge: D. S. Brewer, 1999: 267–325.

Syre Corneus: Ein mittelenglisches Gedicht, ed. Hermann Hedenus. Erlangen: K. b. Hof-und Univ.-Buchdruckerei von Junge & Sohn, 1904.

Trioedd ynys Prydein: The Welsh Triads, ed. Rachel Bromwich. Cardiff: University of Wales Press, 1978.

Ulrich von Zatzikhoven. *Lanzelet: A Romance of Lancelot*, trans. Kenneth G. T. Webster, rev. Roger Sherman Loomis. New York: Columbia University Press, 1951.

Ballads

Chesterton, G. K. 'The Ballad of King Arthur', in *The Queen of the Seven Swords*. London: Sheed & Ward, 1926: 15–17.

Davidson, John. *The Last Ballad and Other Poems*. London: John Lane, 1899.

Jackson, Stephen. 'The Magic Mantle', in *The Magic Mantle and Other Stories*. New York: Greene, 1903: 1–251.

'King Arthur and King Cornwall', in Thomas Hahn (ed.), *Sir Gawain: Eleven Romances and Tales*. Kalamazoo, Mich.: Medieval Institute Publications for TEAMS, 1995: 419–36.

Masters, Edgar Lee. *Songs and Satires*. New York: Macmillan, 1916.

Percy, Thomas (comp.). *Reliques of Ancient English Poetry*. 3 vols. London: J. Dodsley, 1765.

Pratt, Laurence. 'Ballad of White Magic', in *New American Legends*. Mill Valley, Calif.: The Wings Press, 1958: 74–9.

Six Ballads about King Arthur. London: Kegan Paul, Trench, and Co., 1881.

'The Ylle Cutt Mantell: A Romaunt of the Tyme of Gud Kynge Arthur (Done into Modern English from an Authentic Version)', *Democratic Review* (May 1844), 465–76.

Malory, his Influence, and the Continuing Romance Tradition

The romance tradition flourished throughout the Middle Ages and remained vital into the modern period. Though many of the medieval romances have influenced modern works and have been adapted to modern genres and media, no romance has been more influential or more often adapted and reworked, particularly in the English-speaking world, than *Le Morte d'Arthur* (completed 1469–70) by Sir Thomas Malory. While there has been some debate about which of the several men named Thomas Malory who appear in medieval records wrote the *Morte*, it is now generally accepted that Sir Thomas Malory of Newbold Revell in Warwickshire (1414/18–1471) was the author. One of the great literary achievements of the Middle Ages, Malory's book has remained a dominant force in literature and an important factor in the continuing interest in *Arthur and his knights.

Malory's *Le Morte d'Arthur* was first printed by William Caxton in 1485, and Caxton's text was substantially reproduced by Wynkyn de Worde in two editions in 1498 and 1529. Two other editions followed in the sixteenth century: by William Copland in 1557 and by Thomas East in 1578. The edition published by William Stansby in 1634 was the last before the revival of interest in Malory led to the publication of two new editions in 1816 and another in 1817 (cf. Gaines 3–19). All editions of Malory were based on the text printed by Caxton, until a manuscript was discovered in the library of Winchester College by W. F. Oakeshott in 1934. The *Winchester manuscript was edited by Eugène Vinaver, who noted differences from what is found in the Caxton edition. Caxton's edition had added chapter headings and divisions and had thus altered the structure of the text as it appeared in the manuscript. It also changed some of the wording, especially in the story of Arthur's continental wars, which had its source in the *Alliterative Morte Arthure* and had reproduced a good deal of the alliteration of the original. This section had been changed in the Caxton edition to make the style and diction less dependent on the source and more consistent with the rest of the text. The structural changes were, however, the ones that attracted the most attention and controversy. Vinaver believed that by deleting colophons and dividing the material of the romance into twenty-one books, which were in turn divided into chapters, Caxton had taken what were essentially eight separate romances on Arthurian themes and made of them one book. And so when Vinaver edited the first edition based on the Winchester manuscript (which was first published in 1947), he did not use the standard title of *Le Morte d'Arthur* but called it simply the *Works* of Malory.

Vinaver had thrown down a critical gauntlet, and his challenge was accepted by several critics. A number of British scholars saw the matter differently from Vinaver. C. S. Lewis, for example, suggested that the very question of whether there is one book or eight might be prejudiced by a modern view: 'I do not for a moment believe that Malory had any intention of writing a single "work" or of writing many "works" as we should understand the expressions. He was telling us about Arthur and the knights. Of course his matter was one—the same king, the same court. Of course his matter was many—they had many adventures' (22). Derek Brewer also argued for the 'connectedness' and 'cohesion' of the tales and demonstrated some of the ways in which they were bound together: 'by the unity of atmosphere and continuous moral concern; by the chronological continuity of the main events and characters . . . by significant references back and forward to important characters and events; and by links between the various tales' (42, 61). An American critic who disagreed with Vinaver's assessment, Robert Lumiansky, assembled a team of scholars to examine, in a book called *Malory's Originality*, each of the eight tales in Vinaver's edition. By comparing the tales to their sources and looking at the changes made and the interconnections among the tales, they argued that Malory wrote one book, not eight. In fact, study of the text makes it clear that Malory meant the tales to be thought of in some sense as part of a whole and that by seeing them as related to one another the *Morte* becomes more than the sum of its parts.

In creating the *Morte*, Malory drew on several sources, including various parts of the *Vulgate and Post-Vulgate cycles, the *Prose Tristan*, and the *Alliterative Morte Arthure* and the *Stanzaic Morte Arthur*; but he was not a slavish translator. He reshaped his originals, omitted much that was not relevant to his purpose, and even created new sections to advance his themes. One of the ways that Malory reworked earlier texts was by bringing *Lancelot into prominence and making him the central character, more important even than Arthur in the overall scheme of the book. John Steinbeck, who began a modernization of Malory, made a perceptive comment about Lancelot in the *Morte*. He said that 'it is nearly always true that a novelist, perhaps unconsciously, identifies himself with one chief or central character in his novel. Into this character he puts not only what he thinks he is but what he hopes to be. We can call this spokesman the self-character.' Steinbeck believed 'that Malory's self-character would be Launcelot. All of the perfections he knew went into this character, all of the things of which he thought himself capable. But being an honest man he found faults in himself, faults of vanity, faults of violence, faults even of disloyalty and these would naturally find their way into his dream character' (518–19). Though the *Morte* is also the story of Arthur from his birth to his death, Arthur provides, as he often does in medieval romance, a symbolic centre from which Lancelot and the other knights operate. The *Morte* is a 'historical tragic narrative' of Arthur's rise and fall interwoven with a more ' "comic" narrative . . . that leads to the vindication of Arthurian chivalry' (Benson 209). And it is Lancelot who is the highest exemplar of that chivalry.

One of the things that makes Lancelot such a significant and interesting character is that, in his attempt to live up to his reputation as the best of knights, he strives for perfection in all of the codes that a knight should be subject to. He is more chivalric and courtly than any other knight: he seeks adventure, champions women and the oppressed, acts in a courtly manner, and serves his king at home and abroad to a degree unachieved by anyone else. He is the truest of all lovers, never even considering another woman—something that cannot be said about *Tristram, the other great lover of the book. And he strives to perfect himself spiritually as he seeks the Holy *Grail. Of course, he fails to be perfect in all these areas—partly because they place conflicting demands on him. By being a true lover to *Guinevere, he fails in the quest for the Grail and he is less than loyal to his king. But the attempt to adhere to the conflicting codes is what gives Lancelot his grandeur; and the very fact of those conflicts is what makes him the sort of character with whom readers for centuries have been able to identify, even as they recognize his failings—or perhaps because they recognize his failings—in the great enterprise he has undertaken. Lancelot's prominence does not negate the centrality of Arthur or the roles of the vast cast of other fascinating characters in the *Morte*. Indeed, it is the wealth of characters and tales in the book that has made it such a treasure trove for future artists. But Lancelot's character and conflict are central unifying elements in the book; and he is the one against whom all the others are measured.

Malory begins his account of Arthur in 'The Tale of King Arthur' with the story of *Uther's desire for *Igraine. Transformed by *Merlin's magic so that he looks like the Duke of Cornwall, Uther sleeps with Igraine and begets Arthur. As recompense, Uther promises to give the baby to Merlin, who enlists the help of Sir *Ector and his wife in raising him. Brought up in seclusion, Arthur must later prove his identity and his right to the throne by removing a sword stuck through an anvil and into a stone. This sword—as well as *Excalibur, the sword given to Arthur by the *Lady of the Lake when the sword drawn from the stone breaks—becomes an iconic symbol in the book and throughout the Arthurian tradition. Despite this sign of his right to the throne, Arthur must put down a rebellion by a group of kings who are reluctant to accept a young boy as their ruler. In the war, *Lot, one of the rebellious kings and the father of *Gawain and his brothers, is killed by *Pellinore, a deed that sows the seed of future conflict between the two families.

The feud between the families of such powerful knights is one of the factors that lead eventually to the end of Arthur and his glorious reign. Another is the disappearance of Merlin. Having become enamoured of Nyneve, the wise mage becomes a foolish lover. Even though he knows the outcome of his infatuation, he pursues her and gives her a charm which allows her to seal him up forever. Nyneve acts not out of enmity towards Arthur, whom she saves from the plot in which *Morgan gives Excalibur to her lover *Accolon to use against the king, but because she tires of Merlin's attention and because she fears him since he is known to be 'a devyls son' (77).

Another tale with ominous overtones is related in the opening section of the *Morte*, the tale of *Balin, who is known as the Knight with Two Swords. Balin is a worthy knight who is imprisoned for killing one of Arthur's relatives. When a lady comes to Arthur's court wearing a sword that can be removed only by a surpassingly good knight, Balin is able to remove it and thus to prove himself. Nevertheless, he is involved in a series of incidents in which he intends good but causes disastrous consequences. He beheads the Lady of the Lake at Arthur's court because she slew his mother. When Balin is banished for the slaying, he is pursued by a knight named Launceor, whom he kills. Then, when Launceor's beloved wishes to kill herself out of grief, Balin tries to stop her. But for fear of hurting her, he releases her, at which point she commits suicide. Merlin informs Balin that because of her death, he will strike 'a stroke most dolerous' that will hurt the most worthy man alive and bring ruin to three kingdoms (45). After a series of misadventures, Balin ultimately kills his own brother *Balan in a combat in which neither recognizes the other. The story of the hapless Balin, which comes immediately after Arthur has established himself as king, may seem a digression from the main action; but in fact it is thematically significant in that it shows both the tragedy and the glory of Arthurian knighthood. A knight of great virtue and prowess, Balin dies tragically, killing his own brother in the process. The figure of a knight with two swords who tries to do good but dies in battle with his own relative parallels Arthur himself.

But 'The Tale of King Arthur' is not only an ominous foreshadowing of the downfall of Arthur's kingdom. It is also the beginning of the glory of Arthur's reign. Arthur's future success in war is suggested by his quelling of the rebellion against him. And despite the missteps of new knights and a young society, much is learned. In the triple quest of Gawain, *Torre, and Pellinore, the knights make some mistakes; but, as a result, a code to which all the knights of the *Round Table swear is established: they will not commit murder or other crimes, will avoid treason, will give mercy to those who request it, will protect ladies and widows, and will not fight in a wrongful cause for either love or profit (75).

Malory's 'Tale of the Noble King Arthur that Was Emperor Himself . . .' elevates Arthur from king to emperor. In response to a demand by the Roman Emperor *Lucius for tribute, Arthur raises an army and wages a war of epic scope against the Romans and their allies. During the war, Arthur demonstrates his personal prowess as well as his power. Malory's source for much of what appears in this book is the *Alliterative Morte Arthure*; and, as in that work and other accounts of Arthur's continental wars in the chronicle tradition, Arthur himself fights and slays the *Giant of St Michael's Mount. In Malory's account, the giant has ravished and killed the Duchess of Brittany, who is said to be the wife of Arthur's relative

Howell. The affront to Arthur is further personalized by the fact that the giant desires Arthur's wife (120–1). In addition to his sexual offences, the giant eats babies. Arthur sees damsels the giant has forced into service and whom he intends to rape turning spits upon which twelve infants are being cooked as one would roast birds ('broched in maner lyke birdis'). Before killing the giant, Arthur provides punishment appropriate to his offences by cutting his genitals asunder and then doing the same to his stomach (121–2). Arthur's personal valour is also emphasized by his killing of Lucius in battle, as he does in Malory's immediate source but not generally in the chronicle tradition. Malory has adapted his source so that Arthur's victories on the continent are the greatest achievement of the king and his knights and not a prelude to the end of his kingdom.

Among his knights, Lancelot rises to prominence in this tale. In the *Alliterative Morte*, Lancelot is mentioned a few times, but Gawain is the greatest of Arthur's knights and performs the greatest deeds. In Malory's account, Lancelot does such deeds that 'the knyghthode of sir Launcelot were mervayle to telle' (130). This second book begins, in fact, with Lancelot and Tristram coming to court but distinguishes Lancelot by noting that he was 'passyng wrothe' at Tristram for staying behind in Cornwall 'for the love of La Beale Isode' while Arthur waged war on the continent (113, 118). Thus Lancelot's valour in war and sense of duty to his king are established.

The focus shifts to Lancelot and his accomplishments in Malory's 'A Noble Tale of Sir Launcelot du Lake'. A statement at the beginning of the tale asserts that Lancelot surpassed all other knights, a judgement confirmed at the end when he is said to have 'the grettyste name of ony knyght of the worlde' (149, 173). In the tale, Lancelot demonstrates his prowess and courtesy as a knight errant. One of his greatest triumphs is his combat with Sir *Tarquyne, who has defeated and imprisoned sixty-four of Arthur's knights. So eager is Lancelot to encounter Tarquyne and free the prisoners that when he finds a basin set up for knights to strike to signal their willingness to fight, he beats on it with the butt of his spear so hard and so often that its bottom falls out. *Gaheris, the most recent prisoner of Tarquyne, witnesses the contest and after Lancelot's victory calls him 'the beste knyghte in the worlde' (159), a phrase that echoes throughout much of the *Morte*. Lancelot frees the prisoners and gives them whatever treasures they find in the castle, a generosity similar to that of Arthur, who distributed among his followers the vast treasure of the Giant of St Michael's Mount. In a parallel scene a short time later, Lancelot rescues sixty ladies held in servitude by two giants who force them to do 'all maner of sylke workys' (162). Lancelot kills the giants, frees the ladies, and gives them the treasure hoarded by their captors. By these deeds, Lancelot proves his service and generosity to knights and ladies.

Lancelot's role as a lover is also introduced in this third book. He is captured by Morgan and three other queens, who ask him to choose one of them as his lover; but he rejects them all, and they admit that no lady but Guinevere can win his love. The suggestion of the illicit love between knight and queen, apparently before anything has happened between them, introduces a note of suspicion. Another supernatural lady also hints at the love. When Lancelot goes to the Chapel Perilous to retrieve a sword and a cloth that will cure the wounds of Sir Melyot de Logyrs, he is commanded by thirty knights and a lady to leave the objects in the chapel. He refuses, after which the lady, *Hallewes the Sorceress, tells him that if he had left the sword he would never have seen Guinevere again. When Lancelot refuses to give Hallewes a kiss, she tells him the kiss would have killed him. Since she realized, as did the queens, that no woman but Guinevere can have his love, slaying him would have allowed her to keep his body, embalmed and wrapped, so that she could have him always with her and could kiss and hug him every day 'despyte of queene Gwenyvere' (168). These suggestions notwithstanding, at this point in the book Lancelot's service to the queen seems above reproach. He sends defeated knights to her as a sign of honour; but it is apparently accurate when he calls her 'the treweste lady unto hir lorde lyvynge' (152).

While much of the third book is based on the Vulgate *Lancelot*, the following 'Tale of Sir Gareth of Orkney' has no known source, though some have postulated a lost French tale about *Gareth on which it might be based. Whether or not this hypothetical tale existed, it is clear that Malory has his own agenda in telling of Gareth. The fact that Lancelot knights Gareth sets up a special bond between them. At times, Gareth even refuses to take the part of his own brothers because they are acting unchivalrously or against the interests of Lancelot. In a tournament, Gareth will fight against Gawain but not against Lancelot, whom he loves more than any other knight and in whose company he wishes to be whenever he can (224). This close relationship has particular poignancy in the final book of the *Morte*. As Terrence McCarthy has observed, 'we need a life of Gareth because his death means so much' (26).

This tale of Gareth is, however, comic. It outlines the development of Gareth, who must work for a year in Arthur's kitchen under the scornful Sir *Kay before being knighted. Gareth is also scorned by *Lynet, who comes to court to ask for a great knight to help her sister *Lyones against a fearsome knight who besieges her but is given instead the help of this young man right out of the kitchen. Here as elsewhere, Malory, is able to exploit the great comic potential of the situation. Lynet is sharp-tongued, telling Gareth that he stinks of the kitchen and insultingly calling him a 'turner of brochis, and a ladyll-wayscher' (turner of spits and a ladle-washer) (182). After Gareth defeats a series of knights and then falls in love with Lyones, the two 'brente bothe in hoote love' and intend to satisfy their desire. But their intentions are discovered by Lynet, who decides to preserve their honour by sending an armed knight to interrupt their tryst. Gareth beheads the knight and, though wounded, is so 'hoote in brennyng love' (hot with burning love, 206) that he returns to his beloved's bed, but the knight appears again. This time Gareth cuts the head into a hundred pieces and throws them out the window; the resourceful Lynet gathers up the pieces, puts them together, and sends the knight back. But the tale is a comedy, and love is only temporarily frustrated. After proving himself further, Gareth marries Lyones in the same ceremony in which Gaheris marries Lynet and *Agravaine marries a wealthy woman named Lawrell.

The comic tale of Sir Gareth is followed by a tragic one, 'The Book of Sir Tristram de Lyones', which tells the story of Tristram, beginning with the sorrowful birth in which his mother dies and including many of the deeds of Tristram and numerous other knights. The popularity of the Tristan legend in the Middle Ages (see Chapter 7) no doubt caused Malory to recount so much of his history. But the tale is also crucial to the exploration of knightly fellowship and the envy and treachery that result when fellowship is absent (cf. Lynch 98). Noble knights like Tristram and Lamerok and Lancelot respect each other; but baser emotions can lead even normally good knights to do evil deeds. The family feud between the house of Lot and the house of Pellinore erupts in the treacherous slaying of Lamerok by Gawain and his brothers—except for Gareth. The ominous nature of the attack and its implications for the larger Arthurian tragedy are suggested by the fact that *Mordred gives Lamerok his fatal wound in his back (428).

Much of what is best in knights is reflected in Lancelot and much of what is worst contrasts sharply with Lancelot's actions. When Tristram's fame is generally acknowledged and 'the name ceased of sir Launcelot', Lancelot's kin display the same feuding instincts as the sons of Lot: they want to slay Tristram. But Lancelot says that he will kill anyone who harms Tristram (476–7). Here, as elsewhere in the tale and in the *Morte* as a whole, Malory works by comparison and contrast, a parallelism of detail or incident analogous to the parallelism between larger structural units that is so important to the architecture of the *Morte*. Good knights are compared with one another and contrasted with those who are less worthy. The same principle applies to the knights as lovers and to kings as rulers and worthy men.

Tristram's book is not only an exploration of knightly fellowship; it is also an exploration of the adherence to another code, that of courtly love. The story of Tristan and *Isolt is one of the great love stories of all time, and their tale could not be told without a consideration of matters of the heart. At one point in Malory's tale, Isode sends *Palomides, the Saracen knight who loves her but who never quite matches Tristram in prowess or in passion, to Guinevere with the message that there are only four lovers (that is, these are the truest lovers) in the land: Lancelot and Guinevere and Tristram and Isode. And Lancelot's love is greater than Tristram's. Throughout the *Morte*, Lancelot never loves any other woman, though many offer him their affection. Tristram, on the other hand, vies with *Mark for the love of the wife of Sir *Segwarydes, a competition that occurs after he has met Isode but before they drink the love potion. When Tristram goes so far as to marry another woman, *Isode of Brittany, Lancelot is furious with him for betraying his 'fyrst lady' and says that though he has loved Tristram, he now considers him his 'mortall enemy' (273). While Tristram's first love triumphs, as Guinevere predicted it would (274), it must be judged inferior to Lancelot's unwavering love.

Just as Lancelot and Tristram are compared as lovers, so are Arthur and Mark compared as kings. As Lamerok says, 'the honour of bothe courtes be nat lyke' (276). Mark is depicted as jealous, mean-spirited, and treacherous. Unlike Arthur, who takes joy in the accomplishments of his knights, Mark is distressed when Tristram wins honour (333). A cowardly Mark falls from his horse rather than fight with Lancelot (365). He swears falsely, counterfeits letters from the pope, and is said to be 'but a murtherer' (375, 413, 357); and indeed his treacherously murderous tendencies are demonstrated several times in the book. Mark kills his own brother *Bodwyne because he has won honour defeating the Saracens who attacked Mark's lands. Thus, though Bodwyne has defended Mark's interests, Mark slays him out of jealousy. And later he kills Bodwyne's son, *Alexander the Orphan (388, 398). Mark also intends to have Tristram killed or to kill him himself by wiles or treason, and ultimately he does slay Tristram (251, 353, 398).

The comparison between Arthur and Mark, like that between Lancelot and Tristram, heightens the final tragedy in which Lancelot's love and Arthur's honour come into conflict and the fellowship of the Round Table is broken. Much of what happens in the fifth book is designed to anticipate the end. For this reason, the story of Tristram, in contrast to virtually all the medieval and modern versions of the tale, does not conclude with the death of the lovers. Although there is a mention of the fact that Mark will kill Tristram and another report of his death in 'The Book of Sir Launcelot and Queen Guinevere', the event is not enacted in all its tragic grandeur. Malory's focus is on the tragedy that is the main subject of his whole book, and he does not want to undercut it by describing in detail the tragic end of Tristram.

Left with the problem of completing the book centring on Tristram without describing his death, Malory links Tristram's tale to the next one, 'The Tale of the Sankgreal', by telling of the birth of *Galahad. Lancelot is able to free *Elaine of Corbenic from a tub of boiling water, a sign that he is destined to father the Grail knight. Realizing this, Elaine, daughter of King *Pelles who is of the family of *Joseph of Arimathea, tricks Lancelot into sleeping with her. Elaine's maidservant Dame *Brusen, a great enchantress, devises a potion to dull Lancelot's senses enough that he believes he is with Guinevere rather than Elaine; from their union, Galahad is born. At the end of the book, Palomides is christened; and then he and Tristram, who serves as one of his godfathers, go to a feast at Arthur's court, the same feast at which Galahad arrives at *Camelot and sits in the *Siege Perilous.

These events, two appearances of the Grail (495, 500), and the introduction of adventures by *Percival and *Bors at the end of 'The Book of Sir Tristram' set the stage for the Grail quest. Malory's source is the Vulgate *Queste*, but his omission of much of that romance's 'moralizing and allegorizing commentary, which provides the principal coherence of the French tale, thus shifts the source of coherence from the hermits to the knights, especially Lancelot, the one knight who appears throughout the entire tale' (Benson 217). The quest for the Grail is different from other knightly quests. Lancelot is repeatedly called the best knight of the world, but the virtually redundant tag 'of the world' takes on a new meaning in the context of the Grail. It comes to mean 'worldly', as Lancelot is told that he is still the best 'of ony synfull man of the worlde' but that there is 'now one bettir' (520). Lancelot, who has symbolized knightly energy, is reduced to inaction. He sleeps outside a chapel while a sick knight is cured by the Grail; because of his sin, he has no power to rise. The link between the spiritual and the chivalric is made clear when the cured knight takes Lancelot's helmet, sword, and horse, the symbols of his knighthood. It is not until he confesses to a hermit who gives him new arms and a horse that Lancelot is able to win back his own mount.

An even greater paralysis comes upon Lancelot when he reaches the Grail chapel. While a priest consecrates a host, Lancelot has a vision of two men placing a third young man in the priest's hands. Fearing that the priest will fall under the weight, Lancelot enters the chamber forbidden to him and is struck by a divine fire. The blast leaves him unconscious for twenty-four days, as a punishment for the twenty-four years he has sinfully loved Guinevere. This marks the end of the quest for Lancelot (597–8).

Just as Lancelot's arms have symbolic implications, so too does Galahad's shield. Before he obtains the shield destined for him, Galahad fights in a tournament without a shield, and no one is able to harm him because he is divinely protected. The shield he ultimately uses is the shield of *Evelake on which the son of Joseph of Arimathea painted a red cross with his own blood. It protects Galahad but not other knights who try to use it.

Like arms, knightly adventures have symbolic value in this book. Perceval, Bors, and Galahad have many adventures because they are destined to achieve the Grail, but other knights have none. When Gawain asks a hermit why he and *Ector have not met with as many as they are accustomed to, he is told that the adventures of the Grail quest are not for sinners. The hermit adds, however, that though Lancelot will not achieve the Grail because he is not 'stable', he will 'dye ryght an holy man' (563)—a somewhat irrelevant response to Gawain's question but an important statement that Lancelot is not spiritually irredeemable. His fault is that he is likely to turn again to his sin, that is, to his love for Guinevere. While this fault makes him less than 'stable' as a Grail knight, it suggests that he is quite 'stable' as a lover, which is a virtue in the chivalric world that Malory creates.

Because he is single-focused, Galahad is successful where Lancelot is not. Galahad is concerned only with the spiritual and does not have the conflicting demands of the codes of chivalry and love to distract him. He has not been diverted from his quest by earthly pleasures or the demands of becoming part of a society. In fact, when Galahad has achieved the Grail, he prays to leave the world, which for him is 'wrecched' (606). Of the three Grail knights, only Bors returns to Camelot and becomes involved in the intrigues that lead to the destruction of the Round Table fellowship.

The last two books of the *Morte* focus on the relationship between Lancelot and Guinevere and its results. 'The Book of Sir Launcelot and Queen Guinevere' begins with an episode in which the queen is falsely accused of having poisoned Sir Patryse at a dinner she arranged. In fact, the poisoned apple Patryse ate was intended for Sir Gawain by Sir Pyonell, a kinsman of Lamerok who was trying to avenge one treacherous slaying with another. Revenge for a family member also plays a part in the accusation of Guinevere by *Mador de la Porte, cousin of Patryse, who demands justice—that is, the death of Guinevere. Fortunately, Lancelot, dismissed by Guinevere as a common lecher (612) because ladies sought his company, learns of the queen's plight and arrives in time to defend her in a trial by combat, after which Nyneve reveals the identity of the murderer.

Guinevere's jealousy is seen again in the tale of *Elaine of *Astolat, a young maiden whose token Lancelot agrees to wear in a tournament not out of love for her but so that he, who was known for never wearing a lady's token, will be unrecognized. His plan works so well that even his own kin do not know who he is and attack him. Seriously wounded by Bors, he is nursed by Elaine. Guinevere, hearing that Lancelot has honoured another lady and believing him to have taken another lover, is so angry that she says that she does not care if he dies ('no forse, though he be distroyed' (632)) and then that she is sorry he will live (637). But Lancelot is faithful to the queen and, refusing Elaine's request that he marry her or be her lover, returns to find Guinevere unwilling to speak to him—until a barge arrives at Camelot with the body of Elaine, a letter clutched in her hand. The scene is so pitiful that even Guinevere, after hearing the letter read and realizing that Lancelot did not love Elaine, says that he might have shown her 'som bownté and jantilness' and so have saved her life; but Lancelot responds that 'love muste only aryse of the harte selff, and nat by none constraynte' (641). Before her death, Elaine had told her confessor that God made her so that she loved Lancelot and that 'all maner of good love comyth of God' (639). Her statement, combined with Lancelot's explanation that love comes from the heart, comments on—and to a degree exonerates—the love of Lancelot for Guinevere. That their true love qualifies as a 'good love' is confirmed by the judgement made about Guinevere a little later that 'whyle she lyved she was a trew lover, and therefor she had a good ende' (649).

After the account of Elaine's death, Malory describes a great tournament, an account which has no known source. Malory uses this tournament to recall the special relationship between Gareth and Lancelot. Gareth fights in the party of Lancelot against his own brothers; and Gawain himself recognizes that 'no man shall make hym be ayenste sir Launcelot, bycause he made hym knyght' (647).

The tournament is followed by Malory's version of the tale of the Knight of the Cart, in which Guinevere goes a-maying and is kidnapped by *Mellyagaunt. When Lancelot's horse is killed as he pursues the kidnappers, he insists that he be driven in a cart and even slays one of the two carters who would prevent him. Hearing a lady declare that the knight riding in the cart must be a condemned man going to a hanging, Guinevere considers the comment 'fowle-mouthed' (634), and nothing further is said about Lancelot's riding in the cart. Seeing Lancelot, Mellyagaunt asks the queen to protect him, which she does. Lancelot comes that evening to the queen's chamber and must remove iron bars to reach her, cutting his hands in the process and bleeding on the queen's sheets. Mellyagaunt sees the blood and accuses her of treason, that is, of sleeping with one of the wounded knights captured with her, a charge he must prove in trial by combat with Lancelot. Treacherously imprisoned by Mellyagaunt, Lancelot is freed by a lady just in time to fight and kill the queen's accuser. When accused earlier by Mador, Guinevere was innocent; this time, she is innocent only on the technicality that she did not sleep with one of the wounded knights.

The final section of 'The Book of Sir Launcelot and Queen Guinevere' is another tale that has no known source, the healing of Sir *Urry, a Hungarian knight who has been wounded by Sir Alpheus, a knight he ultimately slays. But Alpheus' mother, a sorceress, has worked a spell so that Urry's wounds will not be healed until the best knight of the world searches them. After seeking this knight for seven years, Urry comes to Arthur's court. All the knights except Lancelot attempt unsuccessfully to heal him—an occasion which allows Malory to list many of the knights of the Round Table and to recount some events or add details to events already recounted, such as that Mark killed Tristram as he sat harping before Isode and that the son of Alexander the Orphan avenged the death of his father and of Tristram by killing Mark (666). Lancelot, knowing his own failings, is reluctant to try, but Arthur asks him to do it 'for to beare us felyshyp' (668) and so, after praying that he might heal the suffering knight by the grace and power of God, he cures him. Then 'sir Launcelote wepte, as he had bene a chylde that had bene beatyn' (668), says Malory. Lancelot weeps because he knows his own failings and the great gift he has been given in performing this miracle. The grace of God, undeserved in his eyes, is like a punishment that makes him aware of his own misdeeds. But the very fact that he is able to heal Sir Urry is a sign that, now that the Grail quest is over and Galahad has passed from this world, he is once again the best knight; it is also a sign of God's blessing on the knight who strives for perfection in all of the codes to which he adheres.

Malory's final book, 'The Most Piteous Tale of the Morte Arthur', begins with the plotting of Agravain and Mordred, the son whom Arthur unwittingly conceived with his half-sister *Morgause, to expose the love of Lancelot and Guinevere. Gawain and his other brothers want no part of this plot; and Gawain even declares that he will not oppose Lancelot, who rescued him from Carados and who rescued Agravain and more than sixty other knights from Tarquyne (673). But the two malicious brothers persist in their plot and trap the lovers in the queen's chamber. Though, in making his escape, Lancelot kills Agravain and twelve other knights, including two of Gawain's sons, Gawain still defends him. It is only when, in the rescue of the queen from execution at the pyre, Lancelot kills Gareth and Gaheris that Gawain turns against him. In Gawain's eyes, the slaying of Gareth, who loved Lancelot beyond all other knights, is an unforgivable offence. This deed, which Lancelot committed without even knowing that Gareth was a member of the guard or that he went unarmed because he did not wish to be there but could not disobey the command of his king, is an example of the human blindness that lies behind so many of the actions in the *Morte*. In fact, human blindness is a motif that extends back to the deeds of Balin in the first book.

Gawain's adamancy forces Arthur to besiege Lancelot. In the siege, Lancelot proves his chivalric nature and his loyalty by refusing to fight Arthur and by refusing to let the king be killed when Bors has him at his mercy. The intervention of the pope forces the return of Guinevere to Arthur, but Gawain persists in his desire for revenge, compelling Arthur to mount an expedition and attack Lancelot in France. This gives Mordred the opportunity to forge letters saying that Arthur is dead, to claim the throne, and to demand that Guinevere marry him. She avoids that fate by fleeing to the Tower of London and ultimately to the nunnery at *Almesbury. The usurpation forces Arthur to return and to fight Mordred. In the final battle, Arthur wounds his son with a spear but receives a fatal blow in return. The dying Arthur entrusts Excalibur to *Bedivere to return to the water, and a barge arrives to carry him away. Although Malory makes mention of the inscription on Arthur's tomb, he also notes that many believe Arthur will come again.

But the book does not end with the death of Arthur. Lancelot visits the queen in the nunnery and she, still unaware of the full depth of his love, suggests that he return to France and take a wife. In a moving speech, he declares that he will devote himself to the same life to which she has committed herself. When she says she fears he will turn to the world again, he replies that were it not for his love for her, he would have surpassed all other knights, except Galahad, in the quest for the Grail. By adopting a life like hers and in effect bearing her fellowship, Lancelot is able to 'renounce the world . . . without renouncing his faithful love for the queen' (Benson 245). Both of the true lovers remain true to their holy lives and die holy deaths.

In this way, Lancelot can, like a saint, be taken to heaven by angels (724), but he can also be praised by Ector as the most courteous knight, the truest lover, the most gentle man, and the sternest knight when facing a foe (725). Lancelot is in the end a holy man and still the highest example of chivalric virtue and courtly love.

FROM MALORY TO TENNYSON

Editions of Malory and other medieval romances were published throughout the Renaissance. Medieval romance also influenced the Renaissance epic. In Italy, for example, Matteo Maria Boiardo (1441–94) looked to the romances of Charlemagne for inspiration but also infused his *Orlando innamorato* (begun in 1475 and left unfinished) with the spirit of medieval Arthurian romance and courtly love. Boiardo's Orlando (the Roland of the medieval Charlemagne legend) is driven not by the epic concerns of reputation and heroic action with national implications but by love. Of those great men 'who conjoin warfare with love', Boiardo lists Tristan who loved Isolde, Lancelot who loved Guinevere, 'But most of all, bold

Count Orlando, | Who loved the fair Angelica', the daughter of the King of Cathay (302).

Boiardo's theme is taken up by Ludovico Ariosto (1474–1533) in his great poem *Orlando furioso* (first published in 1516 and then in revised editions in 1522 and 1532). Like Boiardo, Ariosto was influenced by Arthurian romance, including such works as the Italian *Vita di Merlino* and the *Tavola Ritondo*, and the French *Palamedes*, the *Prose Tristan*, and the Vulgate *Lancelot* (cf. Gardner 284–94). In addition to telling the continuing story of Orlando who has become 'furioso' or maddened by his love for Angelica, the poem aggrandizes the house of Este, the future greatness of which is predicted in canto 3 by Merlin's spirit from the cave where the 'Lady of the Lake betrayed him' (i. 160).

Influenced by the Italian epics of Boiardo and Ariosto, the English poem *The Faerie Queene* by Edmund Spenser (1552–99) carries the spirit of medieval romance into the English Renaissance. Just as Ariosto used his epic to praise the Estes, so Spenser used his to glorify Elizabeth and her Tudor heritage. Begun in the 1570s, the poem was only a little more than half finished when Spenser died in 1599. Of the twelve books traditionally found in an epic, he completed six and part of a seventh, each of which dealt with a particular virtue (holiness, temperance, chastity, etc.).

Spenser's poem is an allegory, with each of the main characters representing a virtue or vice or some abstract quality. Even though he appears only sporadically throughout the poem, Arthur is a key figure in Spenser's scheme since he represents magnificence, or the quality of being great-souled, which contains within it all the other virtues. After having had a vision of the Fairy Queen (Gloriana, who represents 'Glory' but also stands for Queen Elizabeth), Arthur sets out in search of her and so rides as a knight errant through the allegorical world Spenser has created.

Book I begins with an account of how the Red Cross Knight, accompanied by Una (a symbol of revealed Truth), rides in search of a dragon that the Fairy Queen has ordered him to slay. Arthur plays no role until canto vii, when he comes upon Una and learns that her companion has been imprisoned by the giant Orgoglio. Arthur agrees to free the Red Cross Knight, which he does after killing the giant. Then Arthur leaves the scene and is absent from the rest of book I, which proceeds with the slaying of the dragon by the Red Cross Knight. Arthur makes similar cameo appearances in the later books, and Merlin is introduced; but otherwise there is little that is recognizable as Arthurian in Spenser's epic. Ultimately, had the poem been completed, Arthur was to have been united with Gloriana. The union of the two would have alluded to the Tudor myth of descent from Arthur and suggested that Elizabeth had brought back to England the glory of her famous ancestor.

Despite its relatively small Arthurian content, *The Faerie Queene* is important in the Arthurian tradition. At a time when the traditional medieval romances were considered old-fashioned and therefore no longer a viable form, Spenser revitalized the Arthurian material by structuring it around the largely Aristotelian concepts of virtue and thus appealing to the classical interests of his age and adapting it to the political concerns of his day.

Though the period between the Renaissance and the nineteenth century is usually thought of as a time when Arthurian literature was in decline and while it is true that Malory was not printed or frequently adapted between 1634 and 1816, much interesting Arthurian material was in fact produced. Renaissance plays, ballads, topographical poems, chronicles, satires, popular almanacs, antiquarian explorations—all kept the Arthurian legends alive and paved the way for the burst of creative activity in the Victorian age.

Alfred, Lord Tennyson

When Pre-Raphaelite artists and Victorian writers rediscovered Malory as a source of inspiration, major works based on the *Morte* were produced. The greatest and most influential of these was the *Idylls of the King* by Alfred, Lord Tennyson (1809–92). Tennyson's Arthurian interest spanned his career. He wrote at least a part of the short poem called 'Sir Launcelot and Queen Guinevere' in 1830 (though it was not published until 1842). The important poem 'The Lady of Shalott' was first published in 1833 and then in a revised form in 1842. The well-known 'Sir Galahad' also appeared in 1842. And his 'Merlin and the Gleam' was published in 1889. In addition to these short poems, Tennyson worked on his *Idylls of the King* for most of his career. This epic poem that began with the notebook version of 'Morte d'Arthur' in 1833 (a poem published in 1842 that later formed part of the idyll 'The Passing of Arthur') was virtually finished in 1885 with the publication of the 'Balin and Balan' idyll in *Tiresias and Other Poems* (although he was still making small changes as late as 1891). In between, the poems that comprise the finished epic appeared in various stages. The first was in 1859 with the publication of *Idylls of the King*, a volume containing four idylls: 'Enid', 'Vivien', 'Elaine', and 'Guinevere'. Later the names were changed ('Elaine' becoming 'Lancelot and Elaine', for example); and 'Enid' was divided into two idylls, as Tennyson strove for the twelve parts conventional in an epic. The 1859 volume was followed in 1869 by the publication of 'The Coming of Arthur', 'The Holy Grail', 'Pelleas and Ettarre', and 'The Passing of Arthur'; then in 1872 by 'Gareth and Lynette' and 'The Last Tournament'; and finally in 1885 by 'Balin and Balan'. Malory was Tennyson's source for all of these idylls, except the two devoted to *Enid and *Geraint, which take their inspiration from the translation of the *Mabinogion* published by Lady Charlotte Guest in 1849.

As the *Idylls of the King* grew from the 'Morte d'Arthur' to the completed sequence, Tennyson created a thematic and structural consistency that not only is compelling in its own right but also seems to be a perfect reflection of the Victorian age. In addition to—and probably more essential than—his stated theme of soul at war with sense, Tennyson consistently balances appearance and reality, and 'the true and the false' (initially intended to be the subtitle of the 1859 *Idylls of the King* and actually used as the subtitle of the 1857 trial volume *Enid and Nimüe*, which was recalled and of which only one copy is known still to exist); and he presents characters who must cope with the fact that things are sometimes better and often worse than they initially seem. The resulting tensions thus have a universal significance at the same time that they are a metaphor for an age that was itself torn between faith and doubt, hope and despair.

The Victorian age saw in the very scientific, technological, and intellectual advances that brought hope of bettering the human condition a darker side, an undermining of faith (expressed so well in Matthew Arnold's poem 'Dover Beach'), and a possibility of exploitation that called into question the notion of progress. This duality, which Tennyson represents in a form well suited to it, lasts even to the present day and helps to explain the popularity of Arthurian material among modern poets. The Arthurian world, like the modern world, has great potential for improving the human condition; but it seems that such an ideal is always frustrated by the failings and imperfections that are inherent in the world and in those who inhabit it.

The first task for Arthur in the *Idylls* is to bring order to a devastated land overrun with beasts and beast-like men, the condition described at the very beginning of the poem (15). In fact, the poem sets up a scheme that combines medieval and Renaissance ideas of the chain of being with nineteenth-century notions of evolution. The *Idylls* is replete with animal imagery—Jerome H. Buckley says such imagery is 'omnipresent' (185)—suggesting the beastly nature that men must overcome if they are to advance morally and move towards the level of the angels. The highest example of such progress is found in Arthur.

Though Arthur himself is prominent primarily in 'The Coming of Arthur' and 'The Passing of Arthur', the two idylls that frame the body of the work, his symbolic presence hovers over all the idylls. Tennyson's Arthur is idealized almost to the point of unreality, in part because of a central event in the poet's life, the death of his beloved friend Arthur Hallam at the age of 22 in 1833. Hallam's death led directly to Tennyson's writing of one of the greatest English elegiac poems, *In Memoriam* (published in 1850 but begun shortly after Hallam's death in 1833). As John D. Rosenberg has so perceptively observed, it is no coincidence that a draft of Tennyson's 'Morte d'Arthur' 'appears in the same notebook that contains the earliest sections of *In Memoriam*. The first-composed but last-in-sequence of the *Idylls* is sandwiched between Section XXX of *In Memoriam*, which commemorates the Tennyson family's first desolate Christmas at Somersby without Hallam, and Section XXXI, which depicts Lazarus rising from the dead. The physical placement of the "Morte" graphically expresses the poet's longing' (229).

Tennyson's Arthur is the 'stainless King' and the 'blameless King' (118, 120). So perfect is he that Tennyson first defies his source by making Uther and Igraine conceive him after the death of Gorloïs and then by creating an alternative story of a mystical coming of Arthur. *Bellicent (the name Tennyson gives to the mother of Gawain and his brothers) reports that *Bleys, Merlin's 'master', told her that on the night that Uther died, he and Merlin saw a ship 'Bright with a shining people on the decks' (23), followed by waves washing the shore. The ninth wave carried a baby to Merlin's feet, a baby whom the mage recognized as an heir for Uther.

In the evolutionary scheme of the *Idylls*, Arthur has evolved beyond most men and thus can be an example to them. In the symbolic description of Camelot in the 'Holy Grail' idyll, scenes carved around the castle depict Arthur's role and his superior nature:

> And four great zones of sculpture, set betwixt
> With many a mystic symbol, gird the hall:
> And in the lowest beasts are slaying men,
> And in the second men are slaying beasts,
> And on the third are warriors, perfect men,
> And on the fourth are men with growing wings,
> And over all one statue in the mould
> Of Arthur, made by Merlin, with a crown,
> And peaked wings pointed to the Northern Star.
> And eastward fronts the statue, and the crown
> And both the wings are made of gold, and flame
> At sunrise till the people in far fields,
> Wasted so often by the heathen hordes,
> Behold it, crying, 'We have still a King'. (176)

Arthur has slain the beasts in his kingdom and the beast in himself, and he has progressed—or evolved—beyond most men so that he approaches the level of the angels.

At the beginning of 'Geraint and Enid', Tennyson comments on the blindness of men who create trouble for themselves 'By taking true for false, or false for true' (79). A pattern of mistaking appearance for reality is evident throughout the *Idylls*. Early in the poem, 'evil may prove illusion; the reality may be fairer than the appearance' (Buckley 178). This is certainly the case in the two idylls devoted to Enid and Geraint, in which Geraint believes his wife less true than she really is. In fact, as Merlin tells Gareth when he approaches the city of Camelot, 'there is nothing in it as it seems | Saving the King' (33). Merlin of course recognizes that Gareth himself is not what he seems and tells him so in one of the many dramatic confrontations that are so essential to the *Idylls* and through which Tennyson often advances the story of Arthur and the knights and ladies of his court. Gareth discovers that appearance can be worse than reality in his quest, as he fights ever fiercer knights. When he reaches the one who is most terrifying and whose very appearance makes a maiden swoon, he discovers that the knight is just a boy in gruesomely decorated armour. Similarly Lynette, who has insulted Gareth throughout the idyll, realizes that he is a far better knight than she imagined.

'Balin and Balan', the last of the idylls to be written, crystallizes the problem of dealing with the beastly side of one's nature in a world where appearances can be deceptive. Arthur suggests that, in order to help him control his violent tendencies,

Balin, known as 'the Savage', should worship the queen and replace the image of the 'rough beast' on his shield with her 'crown-royal' (103, 106). When *Garlon refers to the image as the 'crown-scandalous' (110), Balin, who has observed Lancelot and Guinevere alone in a garden, is enraged and kills him. Later, hearing *Vivien lie about witnessing Lancelot and the queen kissing, Balin remembers seeing them alone and, in a rage, stamps on the image on his shield and throws it into 'the forest weeds' (114). Hearing Balin's cry of anguish, his brother Balan believes him to be the demon of the forest that he has been seeking in furtherance of Arthur's goal of driving the beastly out of his realm; and the two brothers fight and kill each other. Ironically, by killing his brother, Balan has indeed destroyed an element of the beastly in the realm.

In 'Merlin and Vivien', an idyll in which reality is unquestionably worse than appearance, Vivien's deceitfulness is prominent. Though she pretends to be a friend of Arthur and his court, she is lying and deceptive, often compared to a serpent in Tennyson's pattern of animal imagery. She gains a place at court because she says her father died fighting for the king when in fact he died 'in battle against the King' (118, 117). Not only does she spread rumours about good knights, but she even flirts with Arthur himself. When she is laughed at by those who hear from a witness that she tried to tempt the blameless king, she turns to Merlin, who is flattered by her attention. Vivien plots to acquire a charm in his book of magic, a book whose history and contents Tennyson brilliantly describes. Merlin succumbs to her when a storm in the forest of *Broceliande frightens her and she clings to him but does not forget 'her practice in her fright' (138). She then uses the charm he gives her to seal him in a hollow oak. Unlike Malory's Nyneve, Tennyson's Vivien is irredeemably false. She does nothing to further Arthur's goals but merely defames good knights and tells lies. And because of her, Merlin is 'lost to life and use and name and fame' (138).

Just as Merlin is lost because of his affection for Vivien, so Elaine of Astolat is lost because of her love for Lancelot. Although, as Lancelot says to Arthur, she was as pure 'as you ever wish your knights to be', she 'lived in fantasy' (169, 147), believing that Lancelot loved her. When he leaves Astolat, he 'glanced not up, nor waved his hand' to the innocent maiden. And he rides off without her sleeve, worn in tournament only as a disguise and not as the token of love she thought it to be. He also leaves behind the cover she has sewn for his shield (160–1), the same cover that her brothers drape over her when she is placed in the barge that carries her body to Camelot (164). This image is typical of Tennyson's concern, in the epic scope of his poem, for the significant detail. Another fine example of this concern occurs when Lancelot brings to Guinevere the necklace made of nine diamonds that he has won in nine tournaments. Because Guinevere has heard that Lancelot wore another woman's favour in the tournament, she is so filled with anger and jealousy that she tells Lancelot to give it to his 'new fancy' but changes her mind and throws the precious necklace out her window and into the river that flows past Camelot. The necklace strikes the water, and from the surface flash up 'Diamonds to meet them', drops of water that glisten in the sun. Then Guinevere sees passing over the very spot where the necklace has sunk, 'the barge | Whereon the lily maid of Astolat | Lay smiling' (166), an image that captures Guinevere's jealousy, Lancelot's fidelity to her, and Elaine's innocent but unrealistic love.

If love can be a deceptive illusion, so too can the Grail. Tennyson did not believe in the mystic experience of the Grail, and he saw the quest for it as a distraction from the practical duties to which knights should attend. That is why Arthur does not undertake the quest and is critical of it. In fact, the idyll calls into question the very reality of the Grail. 'The Holy Grail' alone of all the idylls is narrated by one of the characters, Percivale, who is not always a reliable narrator, and from whose account a reader can infer things of which Percivale appears to be unaware. Arthur is critical of Percivale's vow, the first to be sworn and the one that prompts all the other knights to make a similar promise. When Arthur remarks that had he (Arthur) been present, the knights would not have sworn the vow, Percivale asserts that Arthur himself would have done so had he been there. Arthur's response is significant; he asks, 'Art thou so bold and hast not seen the Grail?' (177). For, in fact, Percivale has made his commitment primarily on the basis of his sister's vision. A. Dwight Culler contends that 'Tennyson treats the quest for the Holy Grail as an example of mass hysteria. The whole thing originated, he makes perfectly clear, in the frustrated sexual desires of a young woman [*Percivale's sister] who had been disappointed in love and gone into a nunnery' (228). It is because of his sister's vision that Percivale interprets the strange experience at Camelot when Galahad sat in the Siege Perilous—a 'blast', thunder, a beam of light, and something covered with 'a luminous cloud'—as a visitation by the Grail and vows to quest until he sees it as his sister had. Arthur, significantly omitting Percivale, says that the vision is for such as Galahad and is troubled because the quest in which most of the knights 'follow but the leader's bell' (179) marks the beginning of the end of his Round Table.

Though Arthur's admission that the quest is for someone like Galahad suggests that he accepts the possibility of the validity of this sort of mystical experience, he considers the quest an indulgence for virtually all the others who undertake it. Not only is the truly spiritual nature of the quest in doubt but most of the knights do not return—'scarce return'd a tithe' (191)—and thus the work of the kingdom that they should have done is left undone. Arthur complains that Percivale, having 'beheld it far off', now, after the quest, leaves 'human wrongs to right themselves, | Cares but to pass into the silent life' (191). Indeed, Percivale avoids the world at every turn. In a rather melodramatic scene, he encounters his former lover, now widowed, who offers herself and all her wealth to him, and her people plead with him to rule over them and 'be as Arthur in our land'. But Percivale's vow makes him flee from her. The monk Ambrosius, to whom Percivale tells his tale, recognizes the pathos of the act. He declares it a 'pity | To find thine own first love once more' and then to 'cast her aside . . . like a weed' (185).

The vision Percivale claims to have had does not enlighten him either about the spiritual world or about earthly matters. The readers of the idyll know more than this narrator, whose last comment is an admission of ignorance. Thus, in his 'Holy Grail' idyll, Tennyson has captured and expressed through the character of Percivale much of the tension between doubt and faith, appearance and reality, that is so much a part of the *Idylls* and that, in fact, makes Tennyson's poem a reflection of the Victorian age.

The two tales which follow in the finished sequence, 'Pelleas and Ettarre' and 'The Last Tournament', are emblematic of the decline of the society that Arthur has tried to build. Gawain betrays *Pelleas, as in Malory; but since Vivien is a far different character from Nyneve, there is no saving love for Pelleas. He is driven mad by the experience and, in a frenzied ride, he tramples a begging cripple, a sign that Arthur's purpose has lost its meaning for him. As he passes Camelot, he calls it a 'Black nest of rats' and says of its architecture, 'ye build too high'—that is, the symbolism of the towers reaching towards the heavens is false. Pelleas's unknightly trampling of the beggar is paralleled in 'The Last Tournament' by the breaking of 'the laws that ruled the tournament' in the aptly named 'Tournament of the Dead Innocence' (210, 209). This idyll contains Tennyson's version of the story of Tristram and Isolt, in which their love loses all its romance. Tristram suggests that he will no longer love Isolt when she gets old, and she tells him that he has become like a wild beast (221). Even *Dagonet, Arthur's fool, says that Tristram, known throughout the Arthurian tradition as a skilled harper, makes 'broken music', so Dagonet will not dance when Tristram plays. Given the way Tristram is depicted, his death at the hands of Mark, who 'clove him thro' the brain' as he presents the ruby necklace won in the tournament to Isolt and kisses her, hardly seems tragic.

The 'Guinevere' idyll, the only one of the original four to whose title Tennyson did not add a male name before that of the woman who is its central character, depicts the queen in the nunnery. The idyll is dramatic rather than narrative. Guinevere's guilt and anguish are revealed as she listens to a young novice, who, not knowing to whom she speaks, prattles about the king's sorrows, for which she blames 'the sinful Queen' (231). Guinevere's anguish is even greater in another dramatic meeting that Tennyson introduces into the tradition, an encounter with Arthur who visits her at Almesbury. Arthur, the blameless king, forgives Guinevere and says that he still loves her, but he forgives 'as Eternal God | Forgives!' (236). And even as he does, he reminds her that she has 'spoilt the purpose of my life' (235). While Arthur speaks, Guinevere adds to the drama if not by words then by her body language—she grovels and, when he pauses in his speech to her, she creeps 'an inch | Nearer' and lays 'her hands about his feet' (237). It is only when Arthur is riding off into the mist that Guinevere regains her voice and cries out 'O Arthur!' (239). She then admits that she thought she 'could not breathe in that fine air, | That pure severity of perfect light' because she 'yearn'd for warmth and color', which she found in Lancelot; but she realizes that it was her 'duty to have loved the highest', and it would have been her 'profit' and her 'pleasure' had she only known and seen more (239–40).

Arthur is too far above average women and men for them to live up to his standards. Even the vows to which he makes his knights swear are such 'as is a shame | A man should not be bound by, yet the which | No man can keep' (33). But it is precisely his impossible idealism that gives Arthur his symbolic power in the *Idylls* and in parts of the later Arthurian tradition influenced by them.

In the last idyll, Arthur passes from the world as 'The old order changeth, yielding place to the new', a line that repeats one at the end of the first idyll (251, 26). But in the 'Passing', as opposed to the 'Coming', Tennyson adds the lines 'And God fulfils himself in many ways, | Lest one good custom should corrupt the world'. The paradox Arthur uses to console Bedivere—how, after all, can a *good* custom corrupt the world?—seems to suggest the need for change, growth, evolution. Stagnation is the enemy of the human spirit: without change there is no growth from the level of the beasts towards the level of the angels. Just as Arthur brought a time of glory that remains as an example, so, Arthur implies, something new will evolve. Bedivere feels desolate and alone—how could he not?—as he watches the barge carrying Arthur disappear, but it vanishes 'into light, | and the new sun rose bringing the new year' (253). Like Arthur's comment to Bedivere, this ending suggests not only the end of the old order, but the beginning of something new.

LADY OF SHALOTT / ELAINE OF ASTOLAT

Elaine, the Lily Maid of Astolat, is a variant of the figure of the *Lady of Shalott, whose tragedy formed the subject of an early poem by Tennyson, 'The Lady of Shalott' (1833, reprinted in a revised form in 1842). The Lady spends her life weaving and viewing 'shadows' of the real world through a mirror; but after seeing in the mirror Sir Lancelot riding by, she is drawn from her loom and her world is thrown into chaos: 'Out flew the web and floated wide; | The mirror cracked from side to side', and she realizes that ' "The curse is come upon me" ' (265). The intrusion of Lancelot, who represents the world of love and adventure, contrasts sharply with the Lady, who represents the artist, destined to be lonely and unappreciated. As Jerome Buckley has pointed out, 'The curse upon her is the endowment of sensibility that commits her to a vicarious life. Confined to her island and her high tower, she must perceive actuality always at two removes, at a sanctifying distance and then only in the mirror that catches the pictures framed by her narrow casement' (49). How unaware Lancelot is of what he is causing is captured in the lines: ' "Tirra lirra," by the river | Sang Sir Lancelot' (265). In contrast to his casual singing is that of the Lady of Shalott as she floats down to Camelot in a boat, and 'Singing in her song she died' (266).

The image of the maiden who dies for love of Lancelot and whose dead body arrives in a boat at Camelot captured the Victorian imagination and was often reprinted and illustrated. In the paintings and drawings of the tragic maiden and certainly in the public consciousness, the Lady of Shalott and Elaine of Astolat sometimes merge, though their stories are different in detail and come from different sources. The Lady of Shalott has her origin in 'La damigella di Scalot,' tale 82 of Il novellino, a collection of Italian tales (written about 1300), rather than in Malory. Tennyson does, however, add to this source the distinctive elements of 'The Lady of Shalott', particularly the weaving and the viewing of the outside world through a mirror.

Indeed, the image of the Lady of Shalott or the Lily Maid of Astolat in the boat is one of the most commonly depicted scenes in all Arthurian art. A number of artists also drew or painted the Lady of Shalott in her tower. Pre-Raphaelite artist William Holman Hunt (1827–1910) first drew the lady ensnared by threads from the unravelling tapestry in The Lady of Shalott in 1850. Another version of the drawing appeared in 1857 in the collection of Tennyson's Poems known as the Moxon Tennyson (because it was published by Edward Moxon), the same collection for which Dante Gabriel Rossetti (1828–82) illustrated the arrival of the Lady in her barge at Camelot. Hunt's drawings evolved into a painting of the Lady (completed in 1905) (cf. Poulson 179–84).

John William Waterhouse (1849–1917) painted the well-known Lady of Shalott (1888, now in the Tate Gallery) showing the Lady in a barge. The painting is rich in the sort of detail of which the Pre-Raphaelites were so fond. Waterhouse completed two other paintings of the Lady of Shalott, one in 1894, showing her ensnared in the threads from her weaving in much the same manner as in Hunt's works. Another, done in 1915 and called I Am Half-Sick of Shadows, depicts the Lady musing as she sits before her loom.

Numerous other artists found inspiration in the plight of the Lady or Elaine. Like Waterhouse, Sidney Harold Meteyard (1868–1947) created a painting, 'I Am Half-Sick of Shadows' Said the Lady of Shalott (1913), of the Lady distressed by the shadow world in which she lives. Others, like Sophie Anderson (b. 1823) in Elaine (1870), depicted the dead maiden in the barge, as did American artist Toby E. Rosenthal (b. 1848) in a work also called Elaine (1874). Rosenthal's painting was extremely popular and attracted great attention when it was exhibited in San Francisco in 1875; and in 1876, a poem called 'Rosenthal's Elaine' by W. H. Rhodes (1822–76) declared that the painting 'sheds immortal fame on ROSENTHAL' (61). Many illustrators (some of whom will be discussed in detail below) also took up the theme. Among them was Howard Pyle, whose second book, an early attempt at colour illustration, provided the text of 'The Lady of Shalott' in two versions, one printed in a pseudo-medieval type and the other incorporated into illustrations with elaborate initials imitative of a medieval manuscript.

Elaine and the Lady of Shalott even made their way into the new medium of photography. Under the influence of the Pre-Raphaelites (cf. Harker 31–3), Henry Peach Robinson (1830–1901) staged and photographed images of Elaine Watching the Shield of Lancelot (1859) and The Lady of Shalott (1861) in her barge. Another early photographer, Julia Margaret Cameron (1815–79), provided photographic illustrations to a group of the *Idylls* (1875). Included with images of Enid, Gareth and Lynette, Merlin and Vivien, Galahad and Percivale's sister, Lancelot and Guinevere, Guinevere and the novice, and Arthur in armour and in the barge that will take him to *Avalon are three images of Elaine: 'Elaine the Lily Maid of Astolat', which shows Elaine with Lancelot's shield; 'Elaine in the Barge'; and 'The Corpse of Elaine in the Palace of King Arthur'. So popular was the tragic tale of Elaine that several early silent films, *Launcelot and Elaine* (Vitagraph, 1909; dir. Charles Kent) and two films titled *The Lady of Shalott* (Hepworth, 1912; dir. Edwin Neame; and Vitagraph, 1915; dir. C. Jay Williams), none of which is extant, were based on Tennyson's idyll and poem.

Besides Tennyson's, the earliest modern literary treatment of the story, or more precisely an analogue of the story, is by Letitia Elizabeth Landon (1802–38), a poet and novelist who wrote under the pseudonym L.E.L. Her poem 'A Legend of Tintagel Castle', first published in 1833, offers a fascinating variant of the Elaine of Astolat story, with a nymph dying of unrequited love for Lancelot. The nymph takes Lancelot to her cave where 'They might have been happy' if, like the flowers, they could have dwelled in their own private place. But Lancelot hears 'the sound of the trumpet', a symbol for the call of the world. As a result, he abandons the wood-nymph, who waits, like Elaine of Astolat, for him to return, thinking that 'every sun-beam that brightened the gloom' is 'the waving of Lancelot's plume' (9). Lancelot's love, however, is for 'Genevra', and when the lady realizes that, she dies. Like the Lily Maid's, her body floats down to Camelot in a barge. Lancelot weeps at the sight. But the author, who recognizes the waste in the nymph's death, observes that 'Too late we awake to regret but what tears | Can bring back the waste to our hearts and our years!' (9).

The theme of the Lady of Shalott was also taken up by Owen Meredith (pseudonym of Edward Robert Bulwer-Lytton (1831–91), the son of Edward George Bulwer-Lytton) in two poems originally published in 1855. In 'Elayne le Blanc', Meredith describes the loneliness of the woman called 'the White Flower of Astolat', who sits in her tower and sings songs that reflect her sad state. The poem does not end with the death of Elayne but merely with her sighting of Lancelot riding to Camelot, where each knight fights in tournament with 'his lady's sleeve upon his helm' (382). Meredith, who in his poem 'Queen Guenevere' praised the beauty of the queen, wrote another poem called 'The Parting of Launcelot and Guenevere', the parting being when Launcelot leaves for the tournament in which he wears the favour of Elaine of Astolat. But as in 'Elayne le Blanc', Meredith does not bring the episode to the point that is the climax in his source. He is concerned with the actual parting, made difficult because of tension in the relationship between the lovers. Despite the queen's aloofness, Launcelot kisses her and their passion resurfaces. Yet Meredith depends for the effect of his poem on the larger story. The tension, Guenevere's insecurities, Launcelot's sense of being misunderstood by her—all are present in the action of this poem; but the reader familiar with Malory knows that they are small matters compared with the crises that arise as a result of the tournament.

A number of other poets have also written short lyric poems about the tragic character of Elaine. Edna St Vincent Millay's 'Elaine' (1921), a monologue by the title character, is notable less for its picture of Elaine's devotion than for revealing the desperation of her love, which even her studied composure cannot hide, and for the way that love hints at her impending tragic end: as Elaine pleads to an absent Lancelot to return, she promises to be so unobtrusive that 'You needs must think—if you should think— | The lily maid had died' (57). As in Landon's poem, the shift of focus to the dying woman garners sympathy for her plight.

American author Elizabeth Stuart Phelps's 'Elaine and Elaine' (1883), despite its title, deals with only one Elaine, the Lily Maid who dies for love of Lancelot. Like the title, the poem itself is somewhat cryptic: it seems to argue paradoxically for silence in the face of the tragedy. The two sections of the poem end with questions about whether we should speak about Elaine if the steersman of her barge 'speaketh not a word' and whether 'If she [Elaine] | Sayeth nothing, how should we?' (35). It may be that Phelps wishes her readers to be silent so they can reflect on the fact that Elaine's position is representative, as is the fate of the Lady of Shalott in Aline Kilmer's poem 'For All Ladies of Shalott' (1921), in which the circumstance of the towered lady becomes emblematic of that of many women. Another poet, W. M. Letts, describes the thraldom imposed on Elaine by love while Lancelot passes nonchalantly from her life in 'Elaine at Astolat' (1917).

The story of Elaine from Tennyson's idyll is reinterpreted in *Launcelot and Elaine* (1920) by American dramatist Edwin Milton Royle (1862–1942). Faithful in the main events to Tennyson's version and even using lines directly from the *Idylls* (though sometimes from idylls other than 'Lancelot and Elaine'), Royle also adds to his source such things as an alliance among Gawain, Mordred, and Vivian, and Vivian's attempt to kill Launcelot by telling Elaine that a poisoned drink she gives her is a love potion. British dramatist Morley Steynor, who also reworked the events of the final tragedy in his play *Lancelot and Guenevere* (1904, published 1909), bases his *Lancelot and Elaine* (1904, published 1909), an account of Elaine's love and death, primarily on Malory but adds details drawn from Tennyson.

A more interesting reinterpretation of the Elaine character is found in another work by Elizabeth Stuart Phelps, the short story 'The Lady of Shalott' (1879), which translates Tennyson's poem of that name into a nineteenth-century context. The title character, a 17-year-old woman, was crippled at the age of 5 when her drunken mother threw her down a flight of stairs. This bit of information, the author adds, is one 'fact which I think Mr. Tennyson has omitted to mention in his poem' (48). The alcoholic mother dies a few years later, leaving the Lady of Shalott with only a sister, Sary Jane, for support. Her life becomes still more pathetic because her immobility prevents her from weaving—or from doing anything else. In Phelps's story, the weaver is not the title character but her sister Sary Jane, who does piecework while hunched under the eaves of the small garret room in which the young women live, and the earnings from her labour barely allow the two to subsist.

Phelps's Lady of Shalott is trapped by her disability in a tower of sorts, for her room opens directly onto a flight of stairs so steep that in times of emergency they become a death trap rather than an escape route. But the primary correspondence between the poem and the story is the mirror through which Phelps's character sees her surroundings and the doctor, her Lancelot figure, who might have been her salvation. The smallness of her world is symbolized by the size of her mirror: 'All the world came for the Lady of Shalott into her little looking-glass,—the joy of it, the anguish of it, the hope and fear of it, the health and hurt,—ten by six inches of it exactly' (51). As in Tennyson's poem, the cracking of the mirror (in this case, by a rock thrown by a street urchin) foreshadows the Lady of Shalott's death. Her body, however, does not float to a castle in a barge but is carried down the steep flight of stairs on a pine board. The plight of Phelps's Lady of Shalott is caused by a variety of social ills—her mother's alcoholism, the labour laws that allow her sister to be paid so little, the lack of adequate health care for the poor, and the slum conditions in which the woman is forced to live. Phelps's purpose undoubtedly is to call attention to these ills by means of analogy to Tennyson's familiar poem and by deromanticizing one of the most romantic and most recognizable images of the nineteenth century—that of the Lady of Shalott floating down to Camelot.

A story written a few years earlier, 'A Southern Lady of Shalott' (1876) by an author identified only as Latienne, similarly translates Tennyson's Lady into the nineteenth century but in a romantic tale with a happy ending. Because of a misunderstanding with her lover, a woman moves to the country and lives an isolated life with only her art, painting, to occupy her time. When she gathers flowers, puts them into a boat, loses her oars, and faints, she presents an image similar to the Lady of Shalott. She is, however, rescued by her lover, and, their misunderstanding resolved, they are reunited.

Another use of the Lady of Shalott in modern fiction is found in *Tirra Lirra by the River* (1978) by Australian novelist Jessica Anderson. Set in the twentieth century, the novel uses Tennyson's poem as a controlling allusion to describe the life of a woman who is creative and imaginative enough that, even as a child, she had already made the romantic landscape of Tennyson's verse a region of her mind. Though she escapes from a small town in Australia to Sydney and to London, she returns to her childhood home and examines her life in an attempt to find her own identity. By weaving, through her memories in the novel, the tapestry of her life, she approaches an understanding of herself and her friends and family that is more important to her than the nonsense song of Lancelot. In fact, she comes to see that her romantic notions are an escape from reality. In the closing pages of the novel, she recalls a black cloth being placed over her, not a shroud for a body on a barge but a mourning dress put on for her father's funeral; and the plumes she recalls are not from Lancelot's helmet but the plumes on the horses at the funeral (140–1).

Both Elaine and the Lady of Shalott appear as different characters in *Kairo-kō: A Dirge* (1905) by Japanese novelist Natsume Sōseki (1867–1916). The Lady, seeing Lancelot in her mirror, looks out on the real world where he rides, only to have her mirror crack and the threads from her loom ensnare her, an image reminiscent of the paintings by Hunt and Waterhouse. With her dying breath, she curses Lancelot, who rides past Shalott to Astolat, where Elaine falls in love with him and gives him a sleeve from her robe as a favour. When he fails to return to the Lady of Shalott, she dies and her body is put in a boat with a letter proclaiming her love for Lancelot clasped in her hand. As she arrives at Camelot, the thirteen knights who have accused Guinevere of infidelity see the body and 'turned and looked at one another' (126). This last image of the dirge suggests that one tragedy has, temporarily, averted another and places the tragic death of the maiden in the larger context of the Arthurian story; but the curse of the Lady of Shalott still echoes in the background.

OTHER VICTORIAN POETS

Other Victorian poets besides Tennyson contributed to the Victorian revival of interest in Arthurian literature. Before the first instalment of Tennyson's *Idylls* appeared, Edward George Bulwer-Lytton (1803–73) wrote the epic poem *King Arthur* (1848). *King Arthur*, which James Merriman has called 'the last of the eighteenth-century epics', incorporates most of the expected epic devices into its twelve episodic books. Arthur, a Welsh king who would rather die than surrender his freedom, symbolizes the love of freedom of the British people. While this theme is worthy of epic treatment, the vagaries of the plot and the sometimes bizarre details undermine its seriousness. For example, Arthur is led on his journey for the sword and shield needed to defend his throne by a dove which, from time to time, perches on his helmet and even brings Arthur, as he journeys through the Arctic regions, a plant which cures scurvy. The plot, which owes little to Malory or any other Arthurian work, is replete with elements that seem closer to some of the absurdities of Gothic novels than to the true spirit of either epic or romance. Arthur fights with walruses as well as Saxons, and Gawain is threatened with being burned by Vikings as a human sacrifice. Though elements in the poem, like the episodes in the Polar regions, appealed to contemporary popular interest, it is far less successful than Tennyson's *Idylls* in capturing the spirit of its age.

Shorter Victorian poems did, however, achieve distinction. Perhaps the most important Arthurian poem of the age besides the *Idylls* was William Morris's 'The Defence of Guenevere' (1858), which borrows much from Malory but also changes details for dramatic effect. The poem appeared in the volume *The Defence of Guenevere and Other Poems* (1858), a collection that was also reprinted by Morris at his Kelmscott Press in 1892. Whereas the 1859 *Idylls* gave women a central place in Arthurian stories, Morris's poem lets Guenevere speak for herself in her own defence and thus begins a tradition that is usually identified with much later works. In 'The Defence of Guenevere', the queen uses various rhetorical strategies to explain her actions and to defend them and herself. As she describes the birth of the passionate attraction between herself and Launcelot and reminds Gauwaine of the fatal outcome of his own mother's passion, she links herself to Morgawse as a device for evoking sympathy at the same time that she suggests the disastrous results of an inability to accept human nature or to pity a wrongdoer. Moreover, early in the poem Morris puts into her mouth a revealing metaphor: the comparison of her decision to a choice offered by an angel between two cloths, one representing heaven and one hell, shows how difficult and arbitrary life's choices sometimes are and how momentous an apparently small decision can be. Guenevere also recalls the accusations made by Mellyagraunce, as a warning and a threat to those who would accuse the woman championed by Launcelot.

There is some doubt as to what Guenevere actually believes to be true and what she says for effect. She tells Gauwaine that he lies in his accusation of her, but it is not clear what she means by this. Perhaps she means that she never intended to be treasonous, to undermine Arthur and his realm. Perhaps she is suggesting that on the night she and Launcelot were surprised in her chamber, they had not slept together. Or perhaps she is merely denying the accusation to buy time until Launcelot comes to her rescue, as she knows he will. However the ambiguity is resolved, it is clear that Morris's Guenevere stands in sharp contrast to the grief-stricken queen who grovels at Arthur's feet in Tennyson's *Idylls*. She is a proud woman who 'never shrunk, | But spoke on bravely' (4).

In another poem in the same volume, 'King Arthur's Tomb' (1858), Morris shows first Launcelot's and then Guenevere's perspective on their relationship before bringing them together for a final meeting at Arthur's tomb. In addition to the poignance he attains in this last encounter, Morris skilfully uses imagery to convey meaning, as when he describes an arras on which 'the wind set the silken kings a-sway' (26), an image that recalls the instability and ultimate collapse of Arthur's realm.

As in his retelling of the Tristan legend (discussed, along with other Victorian poems on the subject, in Chapter 7), Algernon Charles Swinburne (1837–1909) used fate as an overpowering force in his *Tale of Balen* (1896). The author did not have to alter Malory's version of Balin's story very much to show how destiny governs human life. Even in Malory, Balin is buffeted by fortune as harshly and as clearly as Oedipus, and there is something of the feel of a Greek tragedy about the tale. But whereas in Malory Balin's story is preparatory to subtler tragedies that follow and dissipate its effect, in Swinburne's version this is not the case, and so the reader feels the full power of fate.

Among Swinburne's shorter poems, two are analogous to Morris's 'Defence of Guenevere' and 'King Arthur's Tomb'. 'The Day before the Trial' and 'Lancelot' form a diptych depicting the relationship between Arthur and Guenevere in one panel and between Lancelot and Guenevere in the other. In both poems, there is a play between the Grail and Guenevere. In the former, Arthur's monologue is virtually framed by the thought of 'My wife that loves not me' (299 and 300). In addition to watching her love turn toward another, he is precluded by his marriage to her from the vision of the Grail. He says, 'No maid was I, to see | The white Sangreal borne up in the air'. He speaks ironically of his 'honours', which were to be found at Camelot, not *Carbonek: 'I had the name of king to bear, | And watch the eyes of Guenevere, | My wife, who loves not me' (300).

In the 'Lancelot' frame of the diptych, which presents a dream of a dialogue with an angel, a vision of the Grail is adumbrated by 'a shadow on my sight' (306). The shadow that blots out the light of the Grail is Guenevere. The intensity of Lancelot's passion for her is conveyed in images reminiscent of those created by Pre-Raphaelite painters. Though Lancelot has intimations of the Grail, he, like Arthur, fails in his quest because of Guenevere. And in his vision Lancelot speaks lines that echo Arthur's from 'The Day before the Trial', an echo that makes clear the intentional diptych nature of the pair of poems. Lancelot says, 'All my love avails not her, | And she loves not me' (311). While the two poems are very different in form and content, they combine thematically related scenes to reveal the tragedy of Camelot as experienced by Arthur and by Lancelot.

PARODIES AND CRITICISMS OF TENNYSON

Because of the popularity of Tennyson's Arthurian poems, they were an easy target for satire. Generally, the parodies were humorous, but in some cases the reactions to Tennyson had a more serious side. Elizabeth Stuart Phelps, who reworked 'The Lady of Shalott' for purposes of social commentary, also provided a different perspective on the fate of the Guinevere of the *Idylls* in a remarkable story, 'The True Story of Guenever' (1876). In Phelps's version, which she declares to be 'the true story of Guenever the Queen' (80), Arthur is called 'the blameless king' (65); but obviously Phelps lays some of the blame for Guenever's actions upon him, for he fails to understand that she is 'a delicate, high-strung, impulsive creature, a trifle mismated to a faultless, unimpulsive man' (65). Phelps's Arthur is translated into a master carpenter of the nineteenth century, just as her Launcelot, 'as all scholars of romantic fiction know, was the young bricklayer to whom Arthur and Guenever had rented the spare room when the hard times came on' (68–9). And her Guenever is mismated not, as in Tennyson, because Arthur is so far above the average man that he is unable to understand human needs and desires, but rather because he is typical of the average man who, for Phelps, is unable to understand a woman's needs and desires.

In Phelps's 'true story', when Guenever departs with Launcelot, she finds herself alone with him in a stormy wilderness. When she has a vision of 'The Man whose stainless lips were first to touch the cup of the Holy Grael, which all poor souls should after Him go seeking up and down upon the earth', he tells her she can be forgiven. Yet, in a striking reversal, almost as if the word of Christ cannot be trusted, she finds no redemption. She is in the same position towards Christ that she is towards Arthur in Tennyson's *Idylls*: 'she groveled on the ground where the sacred Feet had stood' (78). Waking to find herself in Arthur's sheltering arms, Guenever has been redeemed by the storyteller's suggestion that her running off with Launcelot occurred in a nightmare induced when the queen mistakenly took laudanum for a toothache. Thus she can wake, morally unblemished, to a loving Arthur. This ending raises Guenever from the convent floor. The price she must pay, however, is certainly high: she must accept the limitations that a relationship with a man with typical nineteenth-century attitudes implies. Guenever has attained a modicum of peace and respectability, but she has not achieved the Holy Grail of female fulfilment.

While Phelps's criticism of Tennyson's portrayal of Guinevere is quite harsh and pointed, other authors reacted to Tennyson with a lighter touch. Even before the *Idylls* were completed, they were being parodied in the anonymously published *The Coming K—: A Set of Idyll Lays* (1873). Ascribed to Samuel Orchart Beeton (1831–77), George R. Emerson, and others, the series of idylls, named mockingly after those of Tennyson, is set in and comments on the nineteenth century. Thus there are, for example, sections devoted to 'Vilien', in which Vilien buys from the charlatan magician Herlin the 'charm' of how he makes a table rap, which 'all depends on the wrist' and the rest is 'humbug all of it' (81); and to 'Loosealot and Delaine', in which 'Delaine the fair, Delaine the flirty one' (85), rejected by Loosealot, returns to him his love letters and the umbrella he had left with her and marries another.

Another poem, George du Maurier's 'A Legend of Camelot', which first appeared in *Punch* in 1866, tells of the deaths of two women with extremely long hair. While the humour and the satire are heavy-handed, the poem 'makes fun of both the subject-matter and the form of such poems as "The Lady of Shalott" and Morris's *Defence of Guenevere* poems' as well as of the 'type-image of the Pre-Raphaelite woman' (Taylor and Brewer 148).

In America, where Tennyson's poems were widely known and quite popular, they were also parodied. In his *Post-Laureate Idyls*, Oscar Fay Adams (1855–1919) responds to Tennyson in a similarly mocking tone. Adams's 'idyls' appeared in two volumes, ten of them in *Post-Laureate Idyls and Other Poems* (1886) and four more in a sequence called 'Post-Laureate Idyls, Second Series', in the volume *Sicut Patribus and Other Verse* (1906). The poems are a strange conglomeration of forms, themes, influence, and originality. Imposing upon himself the demands of Tennysonian blank verse, Adams not only weaves into his poems lines from Tennyson's *Idylls* but also begins each idyl with a verse from a nursery rhyme, which he calls an 'Argument' for the poem and which appears to be a driving force for its plot. Although—even in combination—they do not retell the whole Arthurian story, Adams's idyls treat some of the story's more sad and human elements, including the romance of Tristan and Isolt, the passing of Arthur, Guinevere in the nunnery, and the aftermath of the final battle. Typical of American Arthurian literature, they also shift the focus to everyday concerns, frequently to the tragedy behind seemingly simple events and to characters not central to the tales.

Another American, Edgar Fawcett (1847–1904), wrote a burlesque play called *The New King Arthur* (1885), which has a mock dedication to Tennyson. The new version of the story of Arthur, however, strips the characters of all their grandeur, heroism, and romance. The plot revolves around attempts by various characters to steal Excalibur, which will give them control over Merlin, who possesses two cosmetic products, which Lancelot describes to Guinevere in terms that might be suitable for an advertisement. One of the products is a 'face-wash that shall lend those blooming cheeks | A pearlier beauty than of mortal tint'; the other is a 'hair-dye that shall stain each silken strand | Of those rich tresses into sunnier sheen' (32). Lancelot encourages Guinevere to steal Excalibur, which he will use to force Merlin to give Guinevere the cosmetics she covets; and then Lancelot and Guinevere will run off together. Vivien also covets the magic cosmetics because she loves the pompous Galahad and wants to become more like the vision of an angelic woman with golden hair that he once described to her (cf. p. 77) by changing herself from a brunette to a blonde. But Modred, who in turn loves Vivien and wants the hair-dye to tempt her, plans to steal Excalibur from Guinevere after she has stolen it from Arthur. The final irony is that Dagonet the Fool, the one person true to Arthur, steals Excalibur from Guinevere before Modred does so that he can return it to the king. Dagonet is then accused of the crime by all of the conspirators and is confined in a monastery as a lunatic. Fawcett introduces a note of the mundane into Camelot and thus creates his new King Arthur as well as a new approach, combining parody and realism, to the tales that Tennyson had romanticized and the characters that he had idealized.

The humorous and satiric treatment of the Arthurian legends was also taken up by the well-known American humourist Max Adeler (a pseudonym for Charles Heber Clark (1841–1915)). Adeler wrote a long story called 'The Fortunate Island' (1882, published earlier as 'Professor Baffin's Adventure'), which recounts the adventures of Professor E. L. Baffin and his daughter Matilda, who are shipwrecked as Baffin is on the way to lecture in England and Scotland. Trusting to his own rubber life-raft rather than the ship's lifeboats, Baffin and his daughter reach an island that 'in the time of King Arthur' was 'separated from the rest, and drifted far out upon the ocean' with hundreds of inhabitants (24). Much of the humour of the piece comes from the fact that the inhabitants have maintained the customs and beliefs of their ancestors. This leads to some obvious discrepancies between the values and customs of the inhabitants of the island and the newcomers. Adeler anticipates Mark Twain in poking fun at medieval values and superstitions by contrasting them with American attitudes and in using modern inventions and gadgets to generate humour and interest. An examination of the similarities between Adeler's and Twain's stories led one critic to conclude that Adeler's story 'inspired *A Connecticut Yankee in King Arthur's Court*' (Ketterer 31).

Mark Twain's *Connecticut Yankee*

Whether or not Mark Twain (pseudonym of Samuel Langhorne Clemens (1835–1910)) knew the work of Adeler, it is obvious that he made much better comic and serious use of the juxtaposition of the nineteenth and sixth centuries. Twain's *A Connecticut Yankee in King Arthur's Court* (1889) began as a burlesque inspired by the thought of a practical nineteenth-century American finding himself in the midst of a society that is socially, technologically, and morally backward by his standards. As a means of poking fun at British culture and values, he included passages from Malory as examples of tedious storytelling and exaggerated the absurdities of medieval romance. But as Twain satirized the British nobility and such notions as advancement by birth and title rather than by natural ability, he realized that there were disturbing similarities between that system and economic and social conditions in America. These similarities are sometimes spelled out more explicitly in the illustrations drawn by Dan (Daniel Carter) Beard (1850–1941) for the first edition of the novel, illustrations with which Twain was very pleased and in which Merlin, the representative of medieval superstition, is given the face of Tennyson. Beard's illustrations called attention to the parallels between the feudal system in sixth-century Britain, in which those who do the work receive little profit, and both slavery in the South before the Civil War and the capitalism of robber barons in the late nineteenth century.

When a blow to the head during a fight propels him back to sixth-century Camelot, Hank *Morgan, the practical Yankee protagonist of the book, sets out to undermine the society into which he has been thrust. Hank is in many ways a larger-than-life superhero who can 'make anything a body wanted—anything in the world, it didn't make any difference what; and if there wasn't any quick new-fangled way to make a thing, I could invent one—and do it as easy as rolling off a log' (15; all citations, except where otherwise noted, will be to the Signet edition). But he is also 'practical' to a fault and 'nearly barren of sentiment, I suppose—or poetry, in other words' (14). It is precisely this lack of sentiment or poetry that is Hank's fatal flaw, a flaw that is not immediately apparent because his abilities and his espousal of democratic ideals make him seem like the prototypical American democrat at odds with tyranny and social codes that deny equality of opportunity.

On one level, Hank fulfils this latter role. There is undeniable satire of advancement by birth rather than by talent in *Connecticut Yankee*, and Hank at times speaks and acts nobly in defence of a more just system. He establishes Man Factories to train those who could not otherwise rise to positions of power in the rigidly structured political, military, and social hierarchy of Arthur's Britain; and he recognizes that 'there is nothing diviner about a king than there is about a tramp' (252–3). Hank also seems genuinely concerned about the plight of the poor. He observes that England is like 'a corporation where nine hundred and ninety-four of the members furnished all the money and did all the work, and the other six elected themselves a permanent board of direction and took all the dividends'. His hope is to change the situation so that the 'nine hundred and ninety-four dupes' get 'a new deal' (85). The idea seems so democratically fair that President Franklin D. Roosevelt took the phrase and applied it to his plans for economic recovery because, he wrote, 'I felt the same way about conditions in America as the Yankee did about those in ancient Britain' (quoted in Cyril Clemens 19–20). In certain ways, in fact, Hank seems such a representative of American ideals that in the first edition of the book Dan Beard portrayed him, in a couple of illustrations, dressed like Uncle Sam. (See p. 525 for the clearest example and p. 575, where the Uncle Sam figure astride Thomas Paine's *Common Sense* uses a quill pen to joust with an overweight nobleman.)

There is, however, another side to this champion of democracy and the common man. After suggesting that 'unlimited power *is* the ideal thing when in safe hands' (64) and that despotism would be the best form of government except that a perfect despot must die and be succeeded by someone less perfect, Hank declares that his own 'works showed what a despot could do with the resources of a kingdom at his command' (64–5). In the final analysis, this statement is highly ironic. Hank's actions do indeed show what a despot can do: he can destroy a world and turn an Eden into a *wasteland.

Hank's failings as a champion of democracy are seen in various ways in Twain's novel. He is so upset, for example, at seeming to be bested in an argument by 'an ignorant country blacksmith' (236) that he makes the man fear for his life because he has inadvertently admitted that he paid a worker more than the allowable wages. Throughout the novel, Hank uses his scientific and technical knowledge much as Merlin, his arch-enemy, uses magic—as a means of controlling and manipulating people and events to his own advantage. Hank is willing to destroy all those who disagree with him and who would be a danger to his political plan. It is no wonder that one critic refers to Hank's disregard for the lives of his opponents as his 'final solution' (Miller 131). In preparation for the battle of the Sand Belt, Hank tells his fifty-two faithful followers that they should not be worried about the upcoming battle because, although the whole of England is marching against them, they will have to fight only the 30,000 armed knights and then 'the civilian multitude in the rear will retire' (307). The undemocratic sentiment underlying his statement is striking. Hank's cold-blooded side is also demonstrated in the battle itself. He plans to give the knights of Britain an unexpected blow so devastating that it will destroy the very institution of knighthood. As he prepares for the encounter, Hank proves just how cheaply he has come to regard human life. In checking the electrified fences that will slaughter the knights, he is primarily concerned that Clarence has set up the connections in a way which will waste energy (cf. 302). This attitude is surely as much an abuse of Hank's intellectual power over the people of the sixth century as it is an abuse of electrical power. Ultimately, Hank shows himself to be much worse than those whose policies he has decried: he is more dictatorial than any of the nobles he has encountered; he has less regard for human life than Morgan le Fay; and he uses his technological wizardry of electric wires and Gatling guns more ruthlessly than Merlin, from whose cave Hank directs the slaughter at the battle of the Sand Belt, ever used his phoney magic. In the end, Hank is no longer a representative of the common man. He has the Yankee ingenuity to boss the nation but not the simple values and the 'sentiment' that would allow him to avoid being corrupted by the power he achieves.

Twain's *Connecticut Yankee* in Film

Twain's *Connecticut Yankee*, the central text in the American Arthurian tradition, has influenced the ways in which a number of later authors interpret the legends. In addition, Twain's text itself has often been reproduced or reinvented. Particularly attractive to film-makers, it first came to the screen in 1920 in *A Connecticut Yankee at King Arthur's Court*, a silent film directed by Emmett J. Flynn and starring Harry C. Myers as Martin Cavendish, a wealthier version of Twain's protagonist. The film was remade in 1931 as *A Connecticut Yankee* (dir. David Butler) starring Will Rogers as the Yankee, Maureen O'Sullivan, and Myrna Loy, and again in 1949 as *A Connecticut Yankee in King Arthur's Court* (dir. Tay Garnett), a musical which starred Bing Crosby as a crooning Yankee. A 1979 Disney film, *Unidentified Flying Oddball* (dir. Russ Mayberry; released in Britain as *The Spaceman and King Arthur*), sends a NASA robotics engineer and his lookalike robot (both played by Dennis Dugan) back to King Arthur's time with such gadgets as a laser weapon and a lunar rover. Twain's book has also been reworked in several television movies. The 1952 Westinghouse Studio One version starred Boris Karloff as King Arthur and Tom Mitchell as a middle-aged Hank Martin. In a 1989 television movie, the Yankee was transformed into a young Connecticut girl named Karen Jones (Keisha Knight Pulliam). And in *A Knight in Camelot* (1998), Whoopi Goldberg played Dr Vivien Morgan, a physicist who combines traits of the Connecticut Yankee and of Vivien from the Merlin story.

In the remakes of Twain's book, which, in addition to films and television movies, include also a Rodgers and Hart musical (1927), revived in 1943 with the Yankee as a naval officer, and a play by John G. Fuller (1941), there is little recognition of the dark side of the original character. And technology, which in Twain's book has as much potential for destruction as for advancing civilization, becomes a gimmick updated with each new version. Thus the novel becomes an entertainment, a comedy, sometimes a children's story, and even a Bugs Bunny cartoon (*A Connecticut Rabbit in King Arthur's Court* (Chuck Jones Enterprises/Warner Bros., 1977), renamed *Bugs Bunny in King Arthur's Court* in 1979); and the heroes of these various reworkings lose the complexity and ambiguity of Twain's character.

ARTHURIAN YOUTH GROUPS AND THEIR INFLUENCE

Despite the fact that Tennyson's high moral tone and medieval subject matter were easy targets for some critics and parodists, others embraced those very qualities in his work. In 1893, a minister named William Byron Forbush (1868–1927) established the first of what was to become a national network of clubs for boys called the Knights of King Arthur. Forbush was concerned about what he called 'the boy problem' and sought a positive outlet for the energies and inclinations of adolescent boys. He saw in the legends of the knights of the Round Table as interpreted by Tennyson a model that could inspire boys to manly courage and moral virtue.

The organization was made up of local clubs, called Castles, which were designed to channel what was believed to be the instinctive tendency in adolescent males to form gangs into a means of doing good deeds and developing character. Each Castle, Forbush wrote, is 'a fraternity, private but not secret, self-governing and under the control of the local church. It is based upon the oldest English Christian legend, that of the Round Table. It is a revival of the nobler side of medieval chivalry. The thought is to fulfill the prophecy of King Arthur that he would return to re-establish a kingdom of righteousness, honor and service.' In the course of his membership in Forbush's clubs, a boy progressed through the ranks of Page, Esquire, and finally Knight (Forbush and Forbush 4). In order to help him focus on particular virtues, each boy took the name of a knight or of some other hero, ancient or modern, and tried to emulate him.

Each club was guided by an adult adviser, called a Merlin; but the meetings were run by one of the boys elected to be the King Arthur for that Castle. A particular honour was reserved for the member who performed exceptional service. That boy would be allowed to adopt the name of Sir Galahad and to sit in the Siege Perilous for an evening. Each Castle was to have such a seat, and the honour of occupying it could be conferred only by the unanimous consent of the members.

A female parallel to the Knights of King Arthur known as the Queens of Avalon (originally, Queens of Avilion) was established by Forbush in 1902, nine years after the Knights. Whereas the boys were directed by a Merlin, the girls were guided by a Lady of the Lake. As did the Knights, the Queens of Avalon strove to revive values. The society 'represents itself as the revival of the group of royal ladies, who, in the Arthurian legends, lived on the magic island of Avalon, the land of flowers and fruit, of peace and purity, of wholesomeness and healing, and ministered to humanity with graciousness and beauty. It is the Kingdom of Ideal Womanhood' (Forbush, *The Queens of Avalon* 7).

Another American minister, Perry Edwards Powell, founded a very similar organization called the Knights of the Holy Grail. But more influential was the Knighthood of Youth, a programme run through the schools and designed to provide moral training in a manner analogous to the training in hygiene provided in the schools. And, of course, there were numerous other societies for youngsters, some of them based on chivalric virtues and some not. The most successful and long-lasting was the Boy Scouts, whose founder, Sir Robert Baden-Powell, modelled his club largely on Forbush's Knights of King Arthur and on another American group, the Woodcraft Indians. Scouts, in fact, were encouraged to read stories of chivalry; and many of the virtues espoused by the Scouting movement derived from Baden-Powell's notions of chivalry (Girouard 254–5).

One of the lasting effects of these groups is in the literature created for them. The clubs inspired retellings of the legends, which they advised their members to read, as well as original novels. Horace M. Du Bose's *The Gang of Six* (1906), for example, describes the efforts of a young man to transform six street urchins by founding a club modelled on the Round Table. Two didactic novels, each with the same title *Little Sir Galahad*, take a similar approach. The earlier of the two (1904), by Lillian Holmes, is the story of a crippled boy named David. His friend Arthur Bryan plays at being King Arthur (18) and laments to his mother that David cannot play knight because of his disability. But Mrs Bryan offers the example of Galahad and quotes from Tennyson's poem 'Sir Galahad': 'My strength is as the strength of ten, | Because my heart is pure.' The second of the *Little Sir Galahad* novels was written by Phoebe Gray in 1914. The little Sir Galahad of the title is a boy named Charlie who, as in Holmes's story, is crippled. He is enrolled by a young friend, Mary Alice Brown, in a group called the Galahad Knights and ultimately proves himself an exemplar of Grail Knighthood, which is based on moral, not physical, strength.

Symbolic notions of the Grail and of knighthood also play a part in *Two Little Knights of Kentucky* (1899), a novel in the Little Colonel series by one of the most popular turn-of-the-century American authors of juvenile literature, Annie Fellows Johnston (1863–1931), in which two young boys befriend an abandoned lad. So that he can stay in the care of a kindly but poor old professor, the youngsters raise money by organizing a benefit that consists of readings from Lowell's *The Vision of Sir Launfal* and Tennyson's *Idylls*, accompanied by tableaux in which children don the garb of knights and ladies. Johnston also wrote a short prose work called *Keeping Tryst: A Tale of King Arthur's Time* (1906), which tells the story of a page-boy named Ederyn who wants to become a knight. Ultimately he achieves his goal by passing a series of tests of his faithfulness and by keeping tryst despite obstacles and temptations. The notion that a young person becomes a knight of the Round Table because of moral integrity rather than prowess or nobility of birth is the very basis for the Arthurian clubs and for the symbolic knighthood in the other literature inspired by them.

More than in such popular novels, the influence of the youth groups was felt in the widespread reading of the stories of Arthur and his knights and in the writing of many new adaptations of Malory and Tennyson for children. Forbush instructed the Merlins of his clubs to have available a library of books, including such titles as *The Boy's King Arthur* by Sidney Lanier, the *Idylls of the King* and other Arthurian poems (like 'Sir Galahad', which presented an idealized model of virtue) by Tennyson, Thomas Bulfinch's *Age of Chivalry*, and the Arthurian ballads from Percy's *Reliques of Ancient English Poetry*. They were also instructed to provide images of works such as reproductions of Edwin Austin Abbey's Holy Grail paintings for the Boston Public Library and G. F. Watts's *Sir Galahad*. Through such reading and viewing, the various youth groups were a means of spreading knowledge of the Arthurian stories to hundreds of thousands of children.

Adapting and Illustrating the Arthurian Legends for Children

The model of moral knighthood that was influenced largely by Tennyson and adapted in the American Arthurian youth groups and in related literature was no doubt behind the interest, in the latter part of the nineteenth century and the early twentieth century, in abridgements and retellings of the Arthurian legends for young people, especially young boys. Even before the youth groups boosted the readership for Arthurian stories, Sidney Lanier's (1842–81) *The Boy's King Arthur* had already become popular. First published in 1880 with illustrations by Alfred Kappes (1850–94), *The Boy's King Arthur* was reissued in 1917 with illustrations by N. C. Wyeth (1882–1945), a student of Howard Pyle (and again in 1950 under a different title with illustrations by Florian).

The Boy's King Arthur is an abridged, modernized version of Malory. Lanier notes that, with the exception of words used to explain unfamiliar or archaic terms (like 'hight' or 'mickle') and connective passages to 'preserve the thread of a story which could not be given entire', 'every word in the book...is Malory's, unchanged except that the spelling is modernized' (1880 edn., p. xxii). But, as is typical of retellings for young people, certain elements of the story are omitted or glossed over. Uther's rape of Igraine, for example, has no place in an edifying tale, so Lanier's story begins with the birth of Arthur, who is delivered, without explanation, to Merlin. Other examples of sexual impropriety are similarly disregarded, and new explanations are created for matters that would otherwise require some tarnishing of the knights who are meant to be models for the young readers. For instance, Lanier obviously deems Malory's account of Launcelot's madness unsuitable. To avoid the sordid details, Lanier concocts an excuse that makes the queen's anger seem a misunderstanding: 'it happened that Queen Guenever was angered with Sir Launcelot, yet truly for no fault of his, but only because a certain enchantress had wrought that Sir Launcelot seemed to have shamed his knighthood' (1880 edn., 79). The explanation clearly suggests that Launcelot is maligned through no failing of his own, and Guenever is not the jealous lover she appears to be in Malory but rather a queen rightly concerned with knightly honour.

Noble deeds make the Arthurian stories as retold by Lanier appropriate models for young boys to emulate. Lanier comments on this aspect of the book in his introduction. After discussing how the besieged Lancelot refuses to kill Gawaine and how he will not allow the unhorsed Arthur to be slain, Lanier observes that 'Larger behavior is not shown us anywhere in English literature' (1880 edn., p. xxi). Launcelot's large or greatly generous and chivalric behaviour is, for Lanier, precisely the point of the story.

Of even more significance than Lanier is Howard Pyle (1853–1911). Recognized as one of the greatest illustrators America has produced, Pyle was well known in his day as an illustrator of articles on American history for magazines such as *Scribner's* and *Harper's*, and he made his reputation as an illustrator and writer of children's books with his version of the story of Robin Hood (1883). Moreover, he was prolific, illustrating more than four hundred magazine articles or stories (nearly half of which he wrote himself), writing and illustrating more than twenty books, and contributing illustrations to more than a hundred books by other authors.

In four books that he wrote and illustrated—*The Story of King Arthur and his Knights* (1903), *The Story of the Champions of the Round Table* (1905), *The Story of Sir Launcelot and his Companions* (1907), and *The Story of the Grail and the Passing of Arthur* (1910)—Pyle retold the Arthurian stories from Arthur's birth to his death. Unlike Lanier, who edited Malory with a good deal of abridging and bowdlerizing, Pyle was not an editor. Nor was he even a reteller in the sense of one who merely simplifies an old story for young readers. Instead, Pyle created a new version of the legends, a version intended for children without patronizing them. He took the basic form from Malory but changed it to suit his purposes, combined material from other sources (the *Mabinogion*, French versions of the legends, and ballads), and added scenes and characters from his own imagination. He also used his own illustrations to complement the text.

Pyle suggests that the knights of his stories provide models of behaviour. Early in *The Story of King Arthur*, just after Arthur has drawn the sword from the anvil, Pyle writes: 'Thus Arthur achieved the adventure of the sword that day and entered into his birthright of royalty. Wherefore, may God grant His Grace unto you all that ye too may likewise succeed in your undertakings. For any man may be a king in that life in which he is placed if so he may draw forth the sword of success from out of the iron of circumstance. Wherefore when your time of assay cometh, I do hope it may be with you as it was with Arthur that day, and that ye too may achieve success with entire satisfaction unto yourself and to your great glory and perfect happiness' (35). The conclusion to the final adventure in *The Story of King Arthur*, a retelling of the story of Gawaine and the *Loathly Lady (discussed in detail in Chapter 5), provides a similar link between the reader and the inhabitants of Camelot. When Gawaine marries the loathly lady, Pyle advises: 'when you shall have become entirely wedded unto your duty, then shall you become equally worthy with that good knight and gentleman Sir Gawaine; for it needs not that a man shall wear armor for to be a true knight, but only that he shall do his best endeavor with all patience and humility as it hath been ordained for him to do. Wherefore, when your time cometh unto you to display your knightness by assuming your duty, I do pray that you also may approve yourself as worthy as Sir Gawaine approved himself in this story' (312). In Pyle's retelling, Arthur and his knights are not ideals from another time and place for which there are no parallels in the modern world. They are examples of certain virtues that can be translated into the modern world by the reader in his or her personal life.

Howard Pyle trained a generation of artists who eventually became some of the most famous and prolific illustrators in America. Though he taught in various places, it was a summer location at Chadd's Ford, Pennsylvania, on the Brandywine River that gave to his followers the name of the Brandywine School. A number of his students illustrated Arthurian retellings, including not only N. C. Wyeth, whose son Andrew later provided portraits of several Arthurian characters for *Arthur Pendragon of Britain* by John W. Donaldson, but others as well. Two of Pyle's students, Frank E. Schoonover (1877–1972) and Henry C. Pitz (1895–1976), illustrated editions of the abridged version of Malory by Henry Frith that first appeared in London in 1884 and that was reprinted many times. In 1949, Pitz also illustrated another version of Malory, the popular retelling by Mary Macleod, which first appeared in 1900 and was reprinted often with illustrations by various artists.

Illustrating Malory and Tennyson

Many other artists have illustrated editions and adaptations of Malory's *Morte* and of Tennyson's *Idylls*, some intended for children and some for adults. The long tradition of illustrating Malory's book began with woodblock illustrations in the earliest editions. When Malory was rediscovered in the nineteenth century, he was at first edited with little illustration beyond frontispiece and title page. But the edition published by Dent in 1893–4 with illustrations by Aubrey Beardsley (1872–98) began a trend of producing more elaborately illustrated editions. Beardsley's illustrations—in which knights are sometimes indistinguishable from ladies, and border decorations and chapter headings are exotic and bizarre, containing satyrs, nymphs, and hermaphrodites—were quite different from those in the adaptations for children, which presented models of heroic achievement.

Whereas Beardsley parodies the Pre-Raphaelites, the illustrations of William Russell Flint (1880–1969) for another edition of Malory (1910–11) are influenced by their rich use of detail. 'Then Was She Girt with a Noble Sword Whereof the King Had Marvel', for example, shows careful attention both to architectural details and to the clothing of the lady with the sword that will be removed by Balin. Though Flint illustrates some of the classic scenes from Malory, he also depicts some less well-known episodes. Such originality is apparent in his 'Morgan le Fay Was Put to School in a Nunnery, and There She Learned So Much that She Was a Great Clerk of Necromancy', in which the young Morgan conjures up an image to frighten one of the nuns.

Arthur Rackham (1867–1939), another important illustrator of an edition of Malory (*The Romance of King Arthur and his Knights of the Round Table*, abridged by Alfred W. Pollard in 1917), had a talent for conveying through colour and composition a mood or an emotion, as in the fiery brilliance of his Grail maiden or the festive green of the clothing of Guinevere and her entourage in 'How Queen Guenever Rode A-Maying into the Woods and Fields Beside Westminster'. Working as he did during the First World War, Rackham had a keen sense of the chaos and devastation of war, as is seen in his 'How Arthur Drew his Sword Excalibur for the First Time' and even more grimly in 'How Mordred was Slain by Arthur, and How by him Arthur Was Hurt to the Death', in which Arthur and his son kill each other on a battlefield strewn with bodies of knights and horses under an ominous sky in which carrion birds fly.

The first complete edition of Malory's *Morte* (*Le Morte D'Arthur*, ed. John Matthews) to be illustrated by a woman, Anna-Marie Ferguson, was published in 2000. In her watercolours and black and white drawings, Ferguson includes some scenes not often illustrated, like the crucial healing of Sir Urry, as well as a number of expected scenes, like Arthur's receiving of Excalibur from the Lady of the Lake and Elaine in the barge. But many of her images combine to offer a reading of the text by making her audience aware of the many roles women play in this romance. She depicts victimized or mistreated women—like Elaine of Astolat, Elaine of Corbenic being rescued by Lancelot, *Brangwaine bound in the forest, and Percivale's sister dying after having been bled—as well as women of power, like *Nimue beguiling Merlin, Morgan le Fay, and the four queens (one of whom is Morgan) who capture Lancelot. In addition, Ferguson portrays other women important to the story, such as the three ladies who lead Gawaine, *Uwaine, and *Marhaus on their quests, Isoud's mother discovering the notch in Tristram's sword, and the damsel who arms herself and gives Sir Alisander a buffet to wake him from his stupor and prevent him from being shamed.

As with Malory's *Morte*, there are some distinctive illustrated editions of Tennyson's *Idylls*. The very Romantic drawings of Gustave Doré (1832–83) illustrating the first four idylls present imposing scenes in which the characters are dwarfed by the grandeur and sublimity of nature, and Gothic touches abound: Yniol's magnificently ruined castle, the head of the earl separated from the falling body in 'Geraint Slays Earl Doorm', the decayed corpses in 'King Arthur Discovering the Skeletons of the Brothers', the brothers of Elaine overcome with grief as her body begins its journey to Camelot. Doré's ominous Gothicism is evident in both exterior and interior scenes. The oak tree in 'Vivien and Merlin Repose' has roots that seem to be tentacles about to ensnare the old magician. And in the 'Cloister Scene', Guinevere in the nunnery sits beneath mysteriously receding Gothic arches in a room with a crypt in the floor.

Another artist influenced by the Pre-Raphaelites, Eleanor Fortescue Brickdale (1872–1945), produced beautiful and insightful illustrations of the *Idylls*. Her depiction of Elaine sewing a cover for Lancelot's shield, for example, uses colour and detail brilliantly. The contrast between the rather drab colour of her dress and the red cover with blue and gold details that Elaine is sewing suggests the excitement that Lancelot has brought into her life. His shield is propped up in such a way that it receives the light from the chamber's window and can be seen from Elaine's bed, a detail that symbolizes her devotion to Lancelot. And in Brickdale's depiction of Guinevere in the nunnery, Guinevere is not confined to a dark cloister but appears outdoors. The image is replete with texture, from the rough stones of the low wall behind her to the tiles on the roof. These simple details combine with the beautiful flowers and the loaves of bread in the basket she holds to give a sense that life goes on even after the tragedy she has endured, the sadness of which can be seen in her face.

The illustrations executed by George Wooliscroft Rhead (1854–1920) and Louis Rhead (1857–1926) for an American edition of the *Idylls* published in 1898 often capture high drama. They depict the moment when Guinevere is about to throw into the river the necklace made of the diamonds that Lancelot won for her in tournament. The barge bearing Elaine is just coming into view; on the floor of Guinevere's chamber are leaves torn in jealous anger from the vine growing outside the window. Other moments of high drama that they illustrate include Geraint's misunderstanding of Enid's words, Vivien clinging to Merlin when she is frightened by lightning, and the parting kiss of Lancelot and Guinevere. Like Doré (but not Brickdale), they also depict Guinevere grovelling at Arthur's feet.

In addition to these and other illustrated editions and adaptations, various artists produced paintings, stained-glass windows, even tiles depicting Arthurian scenes based on the Arthurian works of Malory and Tennyson. For the commission he received to decorate the Queen's Robing Room in the New Palace at Westminster, William Dyce (1806–64) chose scenes from the *Morte d'Arthur* to represent virtues. Generosity, for example, is represented by *King Arthur Unhorsed Spared by Launcelot* and Mercy by *Sir Gawaine Swearing to Be Merciful and Never Be Against Ladies*. Dyce also completed frescos representing Religion (*The Vision of Sir Galahad and his Company*), Courtesy (*Sir Tristram Harping to la Beale Isoud*) and Hospitality (*The Admission of Sir Tristram to the Fellowship of the Round Table*). He did not, however, live to finish two other planned scenes: Courage, represented by the combat between Arthur and three of his knights against five kings, and Fidelity, symbolized by Lancelot's rescue of Guinevere from Meliagrance.

In 1862, the firm owned by William Morris was commissioned to create stained-glass windows for the house of merchant William Dunlop in Yorkshire. Morris employed a group of Pre-Raphaelite artists, including Dante Gabriel Rossetti and Edward Burne-Jones, to create scenes from Malory's story of Sir Tristram. Another ambitious stained-glass project was undertaken for the Milbank Choir in the Chapel at Princeton University. The windows representing four Christian epics by Bunyan, Milton, Dante, and Malory were designed in the 1920s by the architectural firm of Cram (that is, Ralph Adams Cram, author of the play *Excalibur*) and Ferguson and executed by Boston stained-glass artist Charles J. Connick. *Le Morte d'Arthur* is located in the central bay of the north wall. Various panels depict scenes from the *Morte*, including a group from the quest for the Grail. Some of the scenes present the knights or their deeds as examples of virtue, and one of the panels shows Malory in prison writing his great book (cf. Stillwell 59–75).

Tennyson's *Idylls of the King* was also the subject of twelve tiles designed (c.1875) by John Moyr Smith for Minton. On the tiles are portrayed key scenes and characters from the poem, including Arthur's receiving Excalibur, Gareth, Lynette, Enid, Geraint, Pelleas, *Ettarre, Elaine, Vivien, Isolt, Guinevere grovelling before

Arthur, and the Death of Arthur. These tiles, which were used in fireplaces, furniture, and trivets, brought scenes from Tennyson into Victorian homes.

THE CONTINUING ROMANCE TRADITION IN POETRY

Not just an important source for artistic representation, Malory and Tennyson and elements of the continuing romance tradition, especially the love between Lancelot and Guinevere and the rebellion of Mordred, had a great influence on all genres of Arthurian literature from the nineteenth century to the present.

Even before Tennyson wrote his Arthurian poems, Reginald Heber (1783–1826) began a poem called 'Morte D'Arthur' (1812). Never finished and published only in fragmentary form, the poem borrows from Malory and adds freely from other sources and from Heber's own imagination. Though she is the 'heir of Carmelide' (139), Ganora (Guinevere) is raised as a village maid. Before marrying Arthur, she meets and falls in love with Lancelot, who is posing as a forester, and does not learn his identity until, as queen, she comes upon a chapel containing the Grail and a series of murals depicting the deeds of the knights. Heber's poem also shows the influence of Malory by recounting Balin's pulling a sword from a sheath carried by a lady and, with significant changes, the episode in which a white hind enters Arthur's court pursued by hounds and a lady. Ganora protects the hind, not knowing that it is Morgue (Morgan le Fay) transformed. Morgue, the mother of Modred, became the enemy of the king when Arthur slew her lover. Throwing herself from a cliff in grief, she floated on an 'enchanted wind', and was considered a 'kindred spirit' by the fays (164). The poem ends with an account, similar to that found in the Vulgate *Lancelot*, of Lancelot's being taken and raised by the Lady of the Lake. Though the poem is incomplete, Heber clearly intended complications that, as in Malory, involved the love of Lancelot and Ganora and the enmity of Morgue and Modred.

In his *Lays of the Round Table* (1905), Ernest Rhys (1859–1946) adapts episodes from Malory in a series of poems about characters from the *Morte d'Arthur*, a text which Rhys had edited in 1892. Included are two songs from his play *Gwenevere* as well as poems about Launcelot on the Grail quest, his death, and 'The Lament of Sir Ector de Maris' for Launcelot. In 'Sir Launcelot and the Sancgreal', the blast of divine light, which in Malory keeps Launcelot from seeing the Grail and puts him into a coma for twenty-four days, is a kind of blessing because it transforms the sinner. Rhys also writes of characters such as Dagonet and Alisander le Orphelin. In 'The Lay of King Mark', he constructs the mocking lay supposed to have been made by *Dinadan about Mark; and in 'The Sermon of the Gentlewoman . . .', he reworks the explanation of Percivale's sister about the sword left on Solomon's ship for Galahad. Though Rhys does not attempt to reconstruct the entire history of Arthur, he uses both major and minor events from Malory as the basis for his poems.

A less ambitious response to Malory is 'The Parting of Launcelot and Guinevere' (1908) by British poet and playwright Stephen Phillips (1868–1915). This short poem describes Launcelot's last meeting with Guinevere at the convent and the difficulty and sorrow of their final parting.

Another writer who adapted Malory to verse was S. Fowler Wright (1874–1965). His *The Song of Arthur* (the title for his combined Arthurian works) is impressive in that it attempts to retell all of Malory. Fowler Wright published three books containing parts of this massive work: *Scenes from the Morte d'Arthur* (1919, written under the pseudonym Alan Seymour); *The Ballad of Elaine* (1926), a retelling of the story of Lancelot and Elaine of Astolat; and *The Riding of Lancelot* (1929), which reworks the sixth book of Caxton's edition, in which Lancelot and *Lionel set out on a quest and Lancelot has numerous adventures, including his battle with Tarquyne. Wright adapted and added to the material in these books for most of his life. In 1941, when he had nearly finished the work, his manuscript was destroyed by a bomb and he began reconstructing the text. (The reconstructed *Song of Arthur* is now available on-line.)

A more recent response to Malory is found in a sequence of twenty-three poems titled *Arthurian Notes*, which appeared in the volume *Seatonian Exercises* (2000) by eminent Arthurian scholar Derek Brewer. The sequence begins with 'Lancelot's First Memory', which is of his being taken into the realm of the Lady of the Lake. A number of the poems deal with the character and relationships of Lancelot; others examine the relationship between Merlin and Ninive, treat the Grail quest, and explore Arthur's thoughts before the last battle. The final poem, 'Work and Sleep', links Arthur and Merlin, so different in life, in the inevitable fate of every person as 'Stone blanketed [both] their graves' (241).

Canadian poet Charles G. D. Roberts (1860–1943) retold in 'Launcelot and the Four Queens' (1880) the story of Launcelot's capture by Morgan and her sister queens, who insist that he select one of them as a lover. Declaring that there is no gain if 'one's body live | An' his dear honor die' (31), the knight refuses to choose any of them. He escapes with the help of King *Bagdemagus' daughter when he agrees to fight for her father in a tournament. The poem combines narrative details from Malory with the moral tone of Tennyson. A later Canadian author, Margaret Atwood (b. 1939), wrote a sequence of seven short Arthurian poems early in her career. 'Avalon Revisited' (1963) contains lyric poems focusing on such topics as the betrayal of Merlin by Vivien, the betrayal of Arthur, the death of Elaine, and the false belief that Arthur is in Avalon—'He is not there' (13). The sequence emphasizes the sorrow and loss inherent in the legend. Another Canadian poet, Frank Davey, uses the legend of Arthur as a metaphor for a modern relationship in the series of short poems in free verse that comprise *King of Swords* (1972). The deromanticized view of the legend finds its counterpart in modern society—'& the death of Arthur continues', Davey says, in modern strife and war (36)—and in the narrator's relationship with the woman to whom the poem is addressed: 'Then your adultery' (37). The poem sees the romantic view of life and love fostered by the Arthurian story as deceptive.

Under the influence of Tennyson and Malory, a number of American poets have also written on Arthurian themes. In the long poem *Accolon of Gaul* (1889), the prolific American poet Madison Cawein (1865–1914) retells Malory's story of the affair between Morgane and Accolon and the treachery of Morgane in duping Arthur with a copy of Excalibur. In broad outline, Cawein follows Malory; but the few changes he makes are significant. Nimue, who rescues Arthur in Malory's version and uses her magic to force Accolon to drop Excalibur, does not appear in Cawein's poem. Instead, Arthur, who realizes after his counterfeit blade shatters that Accolon has the true sword, picks up 'the truncheon of a bursten lance' (48) and strikes Accolon on the wrist as he seizes Excalibur. Since Cawein is telling the story of Morgane and Accolon and not the intricate, extended story that Malory recounts, his exclusion of Nimue seems to be for purposes of narrative compression. Nevertheless, the change makes this climactic moment in the struggle ordinary and almost comic.

Another innovation introduced by Cawein is the motivation of Morgane, who appears intent on having a passionate love affair. Morgane 'felt she'd loved' Urience (Malory's *Uriens) until she hears of the passionate loves of Tristram and Isoud and Launcelot and Guinevere. She would have Accolon crowned so that the emphasis of the kingdom will shift from war to love (cf. pp. 55–6). However, the love motif not only seems imposed on the tale but also fails to explain the ending of the poem: when two knights drop the dead body of Accolon at Morgane's feet and tell her that it comes from the king, she flees to Avalon and is not heard of again until she comes to bear 'The wounded Arthur from that last fought fight | Of *Camlan in a black barge into night' (64). Given Morgane's 'morbid hatred' (54) of her brother, there is no reason why she should perform this final act.

Cawein also wrote a dozen shorter poems on Arthurian subjects in the volume called *Accolon of Gaul with Other Poems*; and in some of these shorter lyrics, he used the legendary material more skilfully and demonstrated the talent that made him so widely published even in some of the most innovative magazines of his day. Cawein's 'Waste Land', which appeared in *Poetry* in 1913, may even have influenced the creation of T. S. Eliot's *The Waste Land*. In an essay in the *Times Literary Supplement*, Robert Ian Scott notes similarities between Eliot's imagery and Cawein's and argues that Cawein provided some of the imagery as well as 'the emotional geography on which Eliot's poem, its effect and much of his fame are based' (14).

Another short lyric poem, 'Launcelot' (originally published in the *Yale Literary Magazine* in 1904), was a youthful venture by novelist Sinclair Lewis (1885–1951). The poem uses an autumn day that is 'chill and drear' to reflect the mood of Launcelot as he rides 'thinking Guenevere | Proves almost unkind' (245).

A longer study of the queen's lover appears in *Lancelot* (1920) by Edwin Arlington Robinson (1869–1935), who makes Camelot a symbol of the modern world. Robinson's poem comments on war and destruction and the end of personal dreams, with an obvious contemporary application. The most important thematic element in the poem is the Light that haunts Lancelot. The Light is, in terms of the traditional story, the light of the Grail; but in Robinson's interpretation it is demystified into a kind of moral goal, though still difficult to attain. On the quest for the Grail, Lancelot was 'blinded' by the Light (9) and now feels 'There is no place for me save where the Light | May lead me' (9–10). And yet, as Guinevere perceptively comments, 'There is a Light that you fear more today | Than all the darkness that has ever been' (31). What Lancelot fears is the total commitment that following the Light requires.

As in Malory, following this Light means abandoning his love for Guinevere. As she says to him, 'Another light, a longer time ago, | Was living in your eyes, and we were happy' (31). This lower-case 'light' is, of course, the light of his love for her, which distracts him from his pursuit of the loftier ideal. It is a sign of how divided Lancelot is that ultimately, despite his near obsession with the Light, Guinevere, who is far more decisive than he, must make the decision that allows him to pursue the spiritual goal. Even when she enters the convent at Almesbury, Lancelot goes to her and asks her to journey with him to France. She is the one who must decline: 'I shall not come | Between you and the Gleam that you must follow, | Whether you will or not' (174). The notion of 'following the Gleam' is an obvious echo of a line from Tennyson's 'Merlin and the Gleam'. Though Robinson diverges radically from Tennyson's versions of the stories of the Arthurian characters, he was nevertheless greatly influenced by the *Idylls* and by Tennyson's other Arthurian poems.

Robinson's *Lancelot* is a study of an individual who has had a glimpse of a way of life that he recognizes as a good higher than anything he has achieved or can achieve by pursuing any other goal. But there is another dimension to the poem. *Lancelot*, like its companion piece *Merlin* (1917, discussed in Chapter 6), also implies a less private, more universal spiritual salvation. Robinson suggests in both poems a formula for the improvement or advancement of the world. It is one of Robinson's innovations that he looks on Camelot not as an ideal but as a stage in the development of the world. Gawain tells Lancelot, 'you might have had no Gleam had I been King, | Or had the Queen been like some queens I knew' (151). As in Tennyson's *Idylls*, there is a sense that in some ways Arthur's kingdom took men a step beyond where they were, but that step was surely not a final one; further evolution is necessary.

Robinson also published separately in 1929 *Modred*, a fragment deleted from *Lancelot*. This poem is a dramatic scene in which Modred manipulates Colgrevance so that he will help with the unsavoury work of trapping Lancelot and the queen. Modred's ability to control the basically noble knight by using his virtues, fearlessness and sense of duty, against him makes Modred a fascinatingly dangerous and despicable villain.

Other American poets have treated the love of Lancelot and Guinevere in shorter poems. In 'The Flight of Guinevere' (1921), George V. A. McCloskey (1883–1933) constructs a triptych in which Arthur, Guinevere, and Lancelot all speak of their love. Arthur finds the death of love 'bitterer than all other death'; Guinevere declares that she saw a 'new world of freedom' in her love for Lancelot; and Lancelot tells how love banished guilt and fear, and hopes that death will 'unite whom life divides' (18, 23, 30–1).

'Launcelot in Hell' (1961), a poem by John Ciardi (1916–86), is a modern treatment of the love between Launcelot and Guinevere and of the final days of Camelot. Ciardi deromanticizes the events. His Launcelot has killed Arthur in the final battle and then thrown the king's sword into a swamp where 'No fairy arm reached out of the muck to catch it' (48). Worst of all, from the romantic perspective, is Launcelot's attitude towards the queen. He refers to her as a 'mare' (47) that he mounted and is disgusted by her turning to religion. This harshly realistic view of the bitter end of the Arthurian realm seems to justify Launcelot's statement that 'There is no moral' (49); and yet the title provides an ironic comment that demonstrates that Ciardi's Launcelot does not fully comprehend, or at least does not fully explain, the events even in their demystified form.

Several American women have explored Guinevere's position as a woman married to a king who places political above personal affairs. For example, in 'Guenevere' (1911) by Sara Teasdale (1884–1933), a monologue in the tradition of Morris's 'Defence of Guenevere', the queen complains of being 'branded for a single fault'; describes vividly her meeting with Lancelot; and reveals, with great emotion, her frustration with those who expect her to play a particular role, to 'be right fair, | A little kind, and gownèd wondrously' (27–8). Teasdale's accent grave on the e in 'gownèd' highlights, simultaneously, the word itself and the artificiality of the role into which Guenevere is forced. The whole poem, in fact, can be read as a woman's rejection of the demand to conform. A woman is valued, the speaker of the poem seems to be saying, not for her own ideas or emotions but for her doll-like elegance.

'Guinevere at her Fireside' (1931) by Dorothy Parker (1893–1967) presents a very different kind of woman. Parker's thoroughly modern and more cynical queen respects the king but is unhappy that her bed has become just 'a thing to kneel beside' (42). Arthur's lack of attention to her because he is too involved with ruling and his inability to champion her because he is king (a motif found, for example, in Malory) are translated into sexual terms. As Parker's Guinevere explains in her own words, she decided to turn to Lancelot in order to compensate for Arthur's neglect. Tristram, in her estimation the better catch, 'was busied otherwhere' (43).

The tradition of giving voice to Guinevere is continued by contemporary writer Wendy Mnookin (b. 1946). In *Guenever Speaks* (1991), Guenever gives her own account of her actions and emotions, an account significantly different from the usual male-oriented versions of her story. Mnookin's poems treat subjects that are far removed from or neglected in more conventional tellings. In one poem, Guenever prays for a child and then loses the baby. 'Guenever Retreats to Almesbury after Arthur's Death' describes the simple sensuous act of working in the convent's herb garden and the subsequent modest activities of Guenever's day, which are charged with emotion and meaning because of the contrast they offer to her former life. And in the poem 'Guenever Returns from the Garden', the queen declares her intention never to leave the nunnery or to look again on Lancelot, not because of an asceticism she has learned through the consequences of their love but because she 'cannot lose him | again' (49).

THE CONTINUING ROMANCE TRADITION IN DRAMA, MUSIC, AND FILM

Drama

The earliest Arthurian plays generally draw material from the chronicle tradition. From the Romantic period onward, however, themes and characters from the romance tradition receive dramatic treatment. John Thelwall (1764–1834), a radical thinker and a friend of Coleridge, wrote a play called *The Fairy of the Lake* (1801). The play is set in the time of the Saxon invasions and identifies Arthur as the British champion but not a king until the very end; yet the importance of Arthur's love for Guenever, said to be the daughter of *Vortigern, and the prominence of the Lady of the Lake suggest that the play is in the romance more than the chronicle tradition. Thelwall's Arthur pines for Guenever. In his 'vacant agony' (51), he lays aside his arms, including Excalibur, which was given to him earlier by the Fairy of the Lake. Without the protection of the magic sword, he is ensnared by a troop of demons commanded by the Saxon queen and sorceress *Rowenna; and one of the demons takes Excalibur. The villain of the play, Rowenna is driven by her love of Arthur to poison Vortigern, whom Thelwall identifies as her husband and a man with an incestuous passion for his daughter Guenever. The Fairy of the Lake must help Arthur regain the sword. Later, when Rowenna sets fire to the tower in which Guenever and Tristram have taken refuge, Arthur is again less than heroic. All he can do is set the castle ablaze in an act of desperate vengeance. The Fairy of the Lake must intervene again, arriving quite literally as a *dea ex machina*, to save Guenever.

Though Thelwall may have had a political agenda in presenting the model of British monarchy as a rather ineffective hero, a play written several decades later, *Launcelot of the Lake* (1843) by C. J. Riethmüller (d. 1895), is pure melodrama. In Riethmüller's play, Morgan le Fay, the mother of Mordred, seeks vengeance on Arthur for impregnating and then abandoning her. Gwenever had pledged herself to Launcelot before her marriage to Arthur, but when the young knight took up the quest for the Grail and did not return to her, she believed he had forgotten her. Not realizing Morgan's animosity towards Arthur, Gwenever confides in her; and though Launcelot and Gwenever are innocent of any wrongdoing, Morgan schemes to have Launcelot visit the queen before leaving the court at Gwenever's request. Launcelot must then rescue the queen, who has been condemned largely because of the false testimony of Morgan. As he saves the queen from unjust punishment, Launcelot kills Gareth and Gaheris and earns the enmity of Gawin.

While Arthur is fighting Launcelot, Mordred, at Morgan's instigation, seizes the throne. To make her vengeance sweeter, Morgan tells Arthur that she had arranged the meeting between the queen and Launcelot and that they were innocent. After Arthur is slain in battle with Mordred, Launcelot returns to kill Mordred but is given a mortal wound.

Though many of Riethmüller's details, such as Gawin's refusal to be part of the guard bringing the queen to her punishment and the threat of interdict by the pope, come directly from Malory, he also adjusts the narrative for his own purposes. He makes Morgan the mother of Mordred to provide motivation for the plot against the queen. He justifies the love between Launcelot and Gwenever by their prior commitment; yet he makes that love innocent. And, in keeping with his focus on the title character, he has Launcelot, not Arthur, kill Mordred.

By the end of the nineteenth century and through the first half of the twentieth, the combined influence of Tennyson's *Idylls*, which were themselves very dramatic, and new editions and adaptations of Malory prompted the writing of numerous Arthurian plays. In 1895, there appeared two plays called *Mordred*, one (written in 1893 but first published in 1895) by Canadian poet Wilfred Campbell (1858?–1918) and another by British poet Henry Newbolt (1862–1938). Campbell's hunchbacked Mordred is initially a good person who loves his father. Arthur, however, is so put off by his son's deformity that when he first sees him, he faints. And both Guinevere and Launcelot insult him, she calling him a 'monster' and Launcelot calling him 'Toad! Abortion!' (48). Encouraged by Vivien, a character clearly influenced by Tennyson (though much of the action has its source in Malory), Mordred ultimately repays them for the insults by trapping Launcelot and Guinevere and undermining Arthur's kingdom.

Also influenced by Malory and Tennyson, Newbolt makes the story of Pelleas and Ettarre an important element in his plot. (Their story is retold again in the dramatic poem *The Tragedy of Etarre* (1912) by American scholar and author Rhys Carpenter (1889–1980), who recounts this episode without reference to the larger tragedy of Arthur's realm.) In Newbolt's play, though Arthur feels bound by justice to condemn his nephew Gawain for his betrayal of Pelleas, he is convinced not to do so by Mordred. Arthur's decision is influenced by Mordred's subtle threat to reveal the story of his own birth. Fearing that the knowledge of his incestuous affair would destroy the Order that he has established, Arthur betrays his principles, an act that leads to Guinever's turning from him since it was his adherence to his ideals that she most admired. Almost as if in response to Tennyson's portrayal of her, she says to Lancelot, 'Shall he be pure | And Guinever break troth' and proclaims that while Arthur is king of himself, 'no less will I be queen' (19). But when he is no longer the blameless king, she is without the moral example that keeps her true to him. Arthur's passionate desire to maintain his Order becomes the tragic flaw which undermines that Order. Newbolt's king, more flawed and more human than Tennyson's Arthur, comes close to tragic stature as he sacrifices his life for his kingdom and makes his last act the giving of a ring to Bedivere as a token of authority so that the stability of the state may be preserved.

More popular and influential than Newbolt's play was *King Arthur* (1895) by J. Comyns Carr (1849–1916), a spectacular production that captured the attention of the public as well as of other writers. Not only did it star two of the most famous actors of the day, Henry Irving as Arthur and Ellen Terry as Guinevere, but its sets and costumes were designed by Edward Burne-Jones and its music scored by Sir Arthur Sullivan. The play, which makes extensive use of dramatic spectacle, had a long run in England and toured the United States and Canada 'and might well have been revived if an 1898 fire had not destroyed the scenery' (Goodman 255).

The scope of the play, which treats Arthur's career from the time he receives Excalibur until his death, requires considerable condensing of the traditional material; but Carr maintains unity by focusing on a few principal characters. His primary interest is in Arthur, Guinevere, and Mordred, who is at times Iago-like in his deceit and manipulation. Carr's Lancelot is less interesting and less heroic than is usual. Because he fears that Mordred will reveal to Arthur the love between him and the queen, Lancelot delays reporting to the king a threat to the kingdom. But, in a dramatic touch lacking in Malory or Tennyson, he redeems himself by slaying Mordred after the villain has given Arthur his fatal wound. Like Newbolt, Carr blends elements from Malory, Tennyson, and Shakespeare and adds touches of his own imagination to create a spectacular new version of the Arthurian story.

Another British dramatist, Graham Hill (1865–1934?), wrote the play *Guinevere* (1906), in which Mordred and his wife Vivien plot to reveal the love of Launcelot and the queen. Guinevere's love for Launcelot is intensified when he defends her against Mador's charge that she poisoned Sir Patrise. Later, the lovers are caught together by Arthur and his knights; but punishment is postponed while Arthur, with Launcelot protecting him, fights against the rebellious Mordred and Mark. Arthur and Mordred both die; and although Launcelot receives a fatal wound, he lives long enough to reach Guinevere in the convent, where, despite the moral warning of the abbess, she takes him in her arms, declaring that 'For him, or with him, would I burn for ever!' (106). Launcelot dies, but a final image of the lovers walking arm in arm into a forest suggests that their love lasts beyond death.

Francis Coutts (Francis Burdett Money-Coutts, 1852–1923) wrote in 1897 three plays which he revised for the book called *The Romance of King Arthur* (1907). The later volume includes an introductory poem on 'Uther Pendragon' and a concluding poem on 'The Death of Launcelot'. The two poems flank two plays, *Merlin* and *Launcelot du Lake*. In Coutts's sequence, Uther and Igraine are married long after her first husband's death and 'Without enchantment' (29). Morgan, the mother of Mordred, plots against Arthur so her son, Arthur's nephew, can rule. It is Morgan who gives to Nivian the spell that seals Merlin in a cave; she also encourages Mordred to trap Launcelot and Gueneuere. As in Malory, Coutts's main source, the lovers lead holy lives after the fall of Arthur's kingdom.

British playwright and poet Laurence Binyon's (1869–1943) tragedy *Arthur* (1923) is also concerned with Mordred's treachery and the end of Arthur's reign, as well as the tragic love of Elaine of Astolat for Launcelot, whom she nursed back to health after he was wounded by a hunter's arrow. As in Malory's version of the story, Elaine's declaration that she is an 'earthly woman' and 'cannot help my love' and Launcelot's explanation that 'Love cannot be constrained' (38, 65) comment on the love between Launcelot and Guenevere as much as on that of Elaine. Despite the tragic results of that love, in the end Arthur recognizes Launcelot's nobility and forgives him. In a scene influenced by Tennyson's Arthur's encounter with the queen in the nunnery, Arthur visits Guenevere before his battle with Mordred. Very different from Tennyson, however, is Arthur's asking her for forgiveness. Though Arthur and Mordred kill each other in the final battle, there is triumph in the ending since, as the king said to Guenevere in their last meeting, 'something, surely, shall remain. | A seed is sown in Britain' (122).

In *Lancelot* (1944) by James Bridie (1888–1951), Merlin assists in the plot to have Lancelot father Galahad on Elaine, the daughter of King Pelleas. Merlin is trying to preserve knighthood as 'the perfect state of mankind' (29)—even though he recognizes that Arthur's court is 'a parcel of bullies and strumpets ruled over by a dolt' (52). Pelleas insists that Lancelot and his daughter be married before Lancelot sleeps with her, and so Lancelot is drugged and made to believe he is engaging in a ceremony with the queen so he does not think he is offending his religious host. When Guenevere hears of this, she rejects Lancelot, who consequently runs mad from Camelot. Years later, Agravaine brings him back from Corbenic to see the queen, only to betray him and cause the final tragedy. Merlin's comment to Lancelot that he put all his trust in chivalry and honour and forgot he was a man (51) is echoed in the ending when the spirit of Lancelot speaks to Guenevere, confirming that their love is the enduring part of Camelot.

The relationship between Lancelot and Elaine is central to a short play by American author Mildred Weinberger. Her *Elaine* (1923) is set during a garden party at a country house in modern Brittany, where two characters seem to re-experience the relationship between Lancelot and Elaine of Corbenic. In the play, Lancelot loves Elaine and marries her, but Guinevere's anger deranges him. Vivienne, who has learned a charm from Merlin and used it to put him to sleep, employs the same charm on Lancelot when he refuses her advances. Elaine calls on the power of the Grail to overcome the charm, cure Lancelot, and wake him.

A number of other American plays are also grounded in the romance tradition. In *Excalibur: An Arthurian Drama* (written in 1893 though not published until 1909) by Ralph Adams Cram (1863–1942), a prominent neo-Gothic architect, Arthur is a doting lover; and Lancelot, who expressed his love before Guenever became queen, accuses her of betraying him with Arthur. This accusation leads to a fight between knight and king, which is ended only when Merlin intervenes, against Arthur's will. Later in the play, Arthur's love blinds him to the dangers to his kingship and causes him to lose Excalibur to a scheming Morgan. Instead of being oblivious to the relationship between his wife and his knight and paying more attention to his kingdom than to his queen, as is traditional, Arthur is so deeply enamoured of Guenever that he risks losing his kingdom. Consequently, Lancelot and Arthur are presented as squabbling, jealous rivals rather than as courtly lovers.

The role and character of Merlin are significant in Cram's play. Merlin is the controlling force and tells Arthur he is merely 'a crownèd jester' without the 'prop of wisdom' that Merlin represents (99). In the final scenes, Arthur is deceived into thinking he is meeting Guenever, but he in fact meets and yields his sword to Morgan. Arthur must appeal to Merlin: 'Give me back my lady and I do thy will' (155), he says. Thus, in Cram's play, Merlin and not Arthur is the focal point, the moral centre, intent on establishing order.

Like Cram, Richard Hovey (1864–1900) recasts the relationships among the three principals. Hovey intended to write a sequence of nine plays, collectively titled *Launcelot and Guenevere, A Poem in Dramas*. The nine projected plays were to be divided into three groups, each consisting of a masque 'foreshadowing the events to follow', a tragedy, and a third play that provided a 'reconciliation and solution' (*The Holy Graal* 23). But only four of these works were completed, two masques (*The Quest of Merlin* (1891) and *Taliesin* (1900)) and the two plays of the first group (*The Marriage of Guenevere* (1899) and *The Birth of Galahad* (1898)).

In *The Quest of Merlin*, seeking knowledge about what will come from the upcoming marriage between Arthur and Guenevere, Merlin goes to a cavern in the bowels of the earth where he compels the Norns to predict the future; and their predictions are dire. But, at the end of the masque, 'three forms like unto the Angels' predict a harmonious outcome to the strife caused by the love triangle: Launcelot 'will prevail' and Guenevere 'will leave a name beyond Time's scorn' (78, 79). The ultimate fate of the Arthurian dream does not negate the love of Launcelot and Guenevere. Both the destructive and the creative aspects of their love are parts of the created world. From Hovey's cosmic perspective, that love, despite the initial destruction that it causes, is a positive force.

As Hovey's sequence progresses, he adds other radical deviations from received tradition. In *The Marriage of Guenevere*, Launcelot tells of how, almost at the point of death, he travelled without food through rough terrain on his way to Camelot and was rescued by a lady, whom he later learns to be the queen. The fact that their love began at this time, before her marriage to Arthur, represents to them a prior commitment so that Guenevere considers Launcelot to be her true, though not legally recognized, husband. (Such justification of a love that transcends the restrictions of society was essential not only to Hovey's view of the legend but also to him personally because he himself had an affair with a married woman, Henrietta Russell, who later divorced her husband and married him.) Guenevere also complains about the restrictions put on her as a woman who 'must be quiet, | Demure—not have her freedom with the boys'. She complains that a princess and a peasant woman labouring in the fields are both 'bondslaves by their sex!' and observes that by marrying Arthur, 'I have ordered a new pair of manacles' (41–2).

This use of Guenevere to reflect new attitudes towards women foreshadows later feminist interest in the queen and other Arthurian women.

Hovey's *The Birth of Galahad* develops his notion of a new world-view. The play portrays Launcelot as the Grail knight's father, as is usual; however, it makes his mother not Elaine (or Ylen, as she is called in the play) but Guenevere. Of course, this device is essential to Hovey's purpose in his sequence: the glorification of love and the presentation of a new world order based on the harmony of which true love is a symbol.

Hovey's sequence of plays was supposed to lead up to the death of Arthur; but this was not to have been Hovey's final statement on the legend. In *The Holy Graal and Other Fragments by Richard Hovey*, Mrs Hovey observed that 'the evolution of mythologies running through the masques makes it seem likely that all the people of [Hovey's] earth-world and his unreal world as well should have assembled, each making some essential part of the completed harmony' (127), which was to be presented in the final play, *Avalon: A Harmonody*. Hovey apparently regarded Avalon as a spiritual symbol. In his wife's words, 'Somewhere in eternity, not regarding place, all stages of the human race must coexist regardless of their place in time, and their relation or absence of relation or their experiences. This condition he uses as a place, and calls Avalon' (128). Thus Hovey's Arthurian world was to be transformed into an Avalon where everyone lived in harmony.

Like Hovey and Cram, Southern playwright and poet Stark Young (1881–1963) dramatized the relationship between Launcelot and Guenevere. His play *Guenevere* (1906), based largely on Malory, focuses on Guenevere and makes her internal struggle the centrepiece of the drama. At her trial, Young's Guenevere tells Arthur that since he is 'ideal, they that love thee love | Thee as a mystic symbol' and that he tries her for no 'husband's | Nor no lover's jealousy' but because of 'the jealous eye the king bends on the crystal | Perfectness of his long-dreamed-of court' (59). Moreover, she admits that while she loves him 'as men love saints' (58), she also loves Launcelot in a more romantic way.

Even in the convent Guenevere feels the pull of two worlds. Having given up the world of the court, she still dreams of a tournament at Camelot, a dream that makes her fear that she can 'be neither | Spiritual nor fleshly, saint nor queen' (66). When Arthur visits her, she wishes to leave with him and return to Camelot, a situation that is impossible because of the events that she has helped to cause. She is so torn that her body can no longer take the strain; the result is her fatal illness. Although she never returns to Camelot, in the end Guenevere is for Launcelot a symbol of its glory, a reminder, as he says, of 'the peerless ventures and sweet courtesy | Of this the summer of all time' (76). But she is also a woman destroyed by the clash between her spiritual and her physical desires.

The year after Young's play appeared, two lesser-known authors published plays exploring the relationship between Lancelot and Guinevere. John William Conway (b. 1851) wrote *Lancelot and Guinevere* (1907), a play about the lovers and, in fact, about love as a force more powerful than hatred. When Guinevere is falsely accused of poisoning the brother of Mador, Arthur refuses to light the fire that is to burn her. After Lancelot defeats Mador, and Mordred and Agravaine are implicated in the murder, Lancelot forgives them because 'To hate is crime'. Guinevere proclaims that though Lancelot is turned aside from the quest for the Grail, he has found another chalice with sacred contents, 'Woman's love' (109). Another approach to the lovers is taken by Hermann Hagedorn (1892–1964), a poet, playwright, and biographer of Edwin Arlington Robinson and others. In his one-act play *The Silver Blade*, Hagedorn depicts a Guinevere who realizes she is in love with Launcelot, Arthur's emissary, and not the king and is driven to contemplate suicide with a dagger. The silver blade of the title is both the heraldic device of her family and the knife with which she nearly kills herself.

A number of plays for children have also been derived from the Arthurian story as told by Malory and Tennyson. Among these, Arthur's pulling of the sword from the stone is an especially popular motif. It is the subject of *The Youth of King Arthur* (1935) by W. Marlin Butts (b. 1904), which concludes with Arthur's drawing the sword and then reciting the lines from Tennyson's 'Guinevere' idyll in which Arthur recounts the vows required of the knights of his order. It is also the climactic event in *Arthur and the Magic Sword* (1949) by Keith M. Engar and *King Arthur's Sword* (1959) by Margery Evernden. In *The Life and Death of King Arthur* (1930) by British author Frank H. Jones (b. 1854), the pulling of the sword from the stone is the subject of the first of four scenes, the others taking up the quest for the Grail and the passing of Arthur. In his note on the play, Jones acknowledges basing the first three scenes on Malory and 'lifting' the fourth from Tennyson. Another British author, J. C. Trewin, in *A Sword for a Prince* (1960), tells of Arthur's receiving Excalibur from the Lady of the Lake, not on the lake but in a castle where he is about to be taken prisoner by the raider Sir Brun.

Music

Like the treatment of Arthurian material in literature, the use of characters and themes from the legend in music is broad and varied in form and content. The wealth and variety of Arthurian music can only be suggested by the representative examples discussed here. (Fuller lists of such music can be found in the 'Arthurian Music' section of the general bibliography accompanying the Introduction to this volume.)

Just as Sir Arthur Sullivan composed music for Carr's play *King Arthur*, so Sir Edward Elgar (1857–1934) wrote music (recorded as the *King Arthur Suite*) for Laurence Binyon's play *Arthur*. In 1937, Benjamin Britten (1913–76) also provided music for a dramatization of D. G. Bridson's story of Arthur for radio. Britten's suite *King Arthur* includes a wedding anthem, Grail music, and a lively fanfare for a tournament which is echoed in the final battle music.

Another play, Francis Coutts' *Merlin*, is the basis of the libretto for the opera *Merlin* (1898) by Spanish composer Isaac Albéniz (1860–1909). The opera, intended as the first part of a trilogy based on the three plays written by Coutts in 1897, is noteworthy for its variety: the rousing music when Arthur pulls the sword from the stone, the different moods as Gawain and the other knights call for the condemnation of Mordred and Morgan and then Arthur grants them clemency, the lyrical Maytime music of Act III, the Arabic tones associated with Nivian that make a virtue of the absurdity of Coutts's describing her as a Saracen dancing-girl, and Nivian's joyous proclamation of her freedom when she seals Merlin in the cave.

Ernest Chausson (1855–1899) wrote both the music and the libretto for one of the best Arthurian operas, Le Roi Arthus (first performed in 1903). In Chausson's retelling of the story of the tragedy caused by the love of Lancelot and Guinevere, Lancelot wounds and thinks he has killed Mordred, who has caught the lovers together. But Mordred lives and, when Arthur and Lancelot engage in battle, declares himself king. Feeling abandoned and betrayed by Lancelot, who says that he will end the struggle against the king by surrendering, Guinevere strangles herself with her own hair. Lancelot, who has thrown down his sword, is grievously wounded when he tries to stop the combatants from fighting. Believed dead, he wakes for a moment to ask Arthur to slay him. Though Arthur refuses, Lancelot dies of his wound. Arthur too wishes for unending rest and is told by heavenly voices that he will sleep but will return to continue his great work because he believed in the Ideal.

British composer Rutland Boughton (1878–1960) distinguished between opera and what he called music drama, which he defined as 'a story of the symbolic type which can only be adequately expressed in the continuous emotional mood of music'. Of this highest form of drama, Wagner 'gave us a taste' but did not bring the form to perfection (17, 24). Boughton composed a number of these symbolic music dramas, including five that told the story of Arthur, a project on which he worked from 1908 until 1945. He began with The Birth of Arthur (originally called Uther and Igraine) and The Round Table, on both of which he collaborated with poet Reginald R. Buckley (b. 1882). These were followed by The Lily Maid, Galahad, and Avalon.

American composer Elinor Remick Warren (1900–91) also found inspiration in Arthur's tragedy. Her choral symphony The Legend of King Arthur, which had its world première in 1940, is based on Tennyson's Idylls. In fact, the work was originally called The Passing of Arthur, after the idyll that is its narrative source. But the name was changed to put more emphasis on the spiritual elements of Arthur's story than on his death.

A more popular attempt at a musical version of the Arthurian legends is found in Rick Wakeman's 1975 album The Myths and Legends of King Arthur and the Knights of the Round Table. The seven tracks on the album translate the story of Arthur into rock music and lyrics and are devoted to characters like Arthur, the Lady of the Lake, Guinevere, Merlin, and Galahad, or events like Lancelot's battle with another knight and Arthur's last battle. In a more recent rock opera, Once and Future King (2003), Gary Hughes reworks the legend from the birth of Arthur to his passing and the prediction that he will return at a time of need for his people.

One of the finest examples of modern popular music based on the legends is *The Trial of Lancelot* (2000) by Canadian songwriter and singer Heather Dale. In addition to songs inspired by Welsh poetry—'The Prydwen Sails Again' and the sprightly 'Culhwch and Olwen', which captures wonderfully the mood of the original—Dale sings of the tragedy of Arthur's realm. Her songs include the lament 'The Lily Maid' and 'Morgan's Lullaby', sung by Morgan to her son Mordred and chilling in its contrast between medium and message. 'Hawthorn Tree' tells of Merlin's entrapment. And several songs tell of the end of Arthur's realm: the title track; 'Miles to Go', Guinevere's words from the nunnery; 'Tarnished Silver', Lancelot's response to Guinevere's death; and 'Measure of a Man', a final response to Arthur's passing, which declares that 'The measure of a man | Stands or falls with what he leaves behind.'

Film

In the second half of the twentieth century, although quite a few Arthurian plays were still being written, many more people saw the legend interpreted on the screen than in the theatre. Among the movies influenced by the romance tradition, some owed a debt to the spirit of that tradition and to the concepts of love and chivalry but took very little of their plot from a specific source. Perhaps the most unusual of these was *The Black Knight* (1954), produced by the British company Warwick but distributed by Columbia, with an American director (Tay Garnett), screenwriter (Alec Coppel), and star (Alan Ladd). In the film, Arthur resides at Camelot, his knights gather at the Round Table, and a few familiar characters appear; but the hero is John, a blacksmith in the service of the Earl of Yeonil. John loves the earl's daughter Linet (Patricia Medina) but is told by the earl that no relationship can ever develop between them because of the difference in their stations. The threat to John's personal happiness is paralleled by a threat to Camelot. John learns that Palamides and his Saracens, who are in league with King Mark's Cornishmen to take over Arthur's kingdom, have been masquerading as Viking raiders, creating panic and instability in Britain. In order to prove his accusation of treason against Palamides, John must acquire the skills of a knight as well as a secret identity as the Black Knight. Ultimately, through his innate ability and with a sword he himself forged, John saves both the woman he loves and the kingdom he serves from the foreign threat; and, as a result, he is knighted and is granted the hand of Lady Linet in marriage.

The unprecedented plot of *The Black Knight*, with pagans about to sacrifice Christians at *Stonehenge and Saracens attacking Camelot, seems strange indeed. But Tay Garnett, who had directed the Crosby musical remake of *Connecticut Yankee* five years earlier, was creating a version of the Arthurian legends that reflects perennial American values and ideals as well as specific American concerns of the 1950s. John's rise from rags to riches, without nobility of birth or inherited wealth but only through his own courage, resourcefulness, and hard work, symbolized by the sword he made with his own hands, represents the American Dream. And the threat to Camelot both from a foreign invader and from treason within is a thinly disguised allegory for the Communist threat.

Similarly grounded in the spirit of Arthurian romance rather than a specific source is *Knightriders* (United Films/Laurel Entertainment, 1981; dir. George Romero). The film's Arthur figure is Billy Davis (played by Ed Harris), leader of a troupe of entertainers who travel throughout twentieth-century Pennsylvania staging medieval tournaments on motorcycles. The troupe espouses old-fashioned, even utopian, values: loyalty, integrity, community. Principle is paramount to Billy and to the society that he has created, and he feels compelled to fight any challenge to that order. 'It's real hard', he reminds the members of his court, 'to live for something you believe in.' Billy's idealism links him to the legendary Arthur. Like Arthur's fellowship, however, Billy's soon begins to crumble. A disgruntled Morgan signs on with a promoter who promises to book him in Las Vegas; other members of the group are lured away by prospects of profit and fame; and Alan (the Lancelot figure in the film), Billy's good friend and staunchest supporter, rides off with a young woman (a latter-day Elaine) whom he met at a tournament. Although Morgan and the others eventually return, Billy realizes that his dream of an ideal society is tarnished. When Morgan wins his crown in a tournament, Billy allows his queen Linet and Alan a chance for happiness together. Billy rides off on the open highway, where he is crushed by a truck—but not before being transformed into a medieval knight on a charger riding against an unseen enemy. Like Arthur, Billy holds on to his vision of an ideal kingdom (and of a kingdom of ideals) until the very end; and, by accepting his defeat with integrity, he provides an example to the society of misfits that he has created and a reason for them to endure.

More traditional romance material is found in several films. The love between Lancelot and Guinevere is the theme of Robert Bresson's *Lancelot du Lac* (Mara Films, 1974). The prologue that scrolls across the screen at the film's opening recounts much of the legend in summary fashion: marvellous adventures, the quest for the Grail to which Merlin pledged the knights before his death, Perceval's precedence in the quest. The film proper begins with the return of those knights who survived the quest, including Lancelot, who says he will not fight in a tournament against the knights of Escalot, but then does so. He defeats all he encounters but is severely wounded. After being nursed back to health, he rescues Guinevere, who has been accused by Mordred. In the fighting, however, Lancelot unknowingly kills Gawain, who has been a friend and supporter. Though Lancelot returns the queen, Mordred rebels against Arthur's rule and causes a bloody final battle.

Bresson's camera shots, sometimes focusing on the horses's hooves and knights' feet rather than their bodies or faces, tend to depersonalize the characters and the action and thus to undercut the tragic conflicts. But the film uses symbols well. For example, Guinevere leaves a scarf at her meeting place with Lancelot. Later, the scarf appears in Mordred's tent; and then Gawain, as an act of friendship, returns it to the queen. Relationships are not developed at length but are revealed in brief encounters or conversations. Thus, the film does not have the narrative directness of many Arthurian films; rather, it tells its story through the visual and the symbolic.

Lancelot and Guinevere (Emblem Productions, 1963; dir. Cornel Wilde), released in the United States as *The Sword of Lancelot*, starred Cornel Wilde as Lancelot, who falls in love with Guinevere (Jean Wallace) as he brings her to be Arthur's bride. Though recognizing that there is 'no kinglier man, no manlier king' than Arthur, Lancelot is unable to resist his love. The night before he plans to leave for France, he meets Guinevere and is trapped by Mordred, killing Gareth and thus earning Gawain's enmity in the process. Lancelot rescues Guinevere from the pyre to which she has been condemned, but the queen is ultimately sent to a convent in order to end the war. Some time later, Gawain finds Lancelot in France and tells him that Modred has killed Arthur. Lancelot returns and slays Modred, after which he seeks out Guinevere in the nunnery. Learning from her that she will take vows as a nun, he decides he must atone and pray, but the film ends without reaching the point of their holy deaths. Basically an adventure film and a romance, *Lancelot and Guinevere* is unusual in that it ends sadly with the final parting of the lovers.

While parts of *Lancelot and Guinevere* are influenced by Malory, *Knights of the Round Table* (MGM, 1953; dir. Richard Thorpe) claims to be 'based on Sir Thomas Malory's *Le Morte D'Arthur*'; and indeed many of the traditional characters are featured in the film, though often in some untraditional situations. Morgan le Fay, for example, supports Modred, whom she wants to install as king and with whom she plots to destroy her half-brother. Here, Arthur (Mel Ferrer) is an adult, not a boy, when he first pulls the sword from the stone; and, after fighting for many months to prove with deeds rather than words his right to rule, he draws Excalibur from the stone again, this time at 'the ring of stones', before the council of lords. In this film, Elaine is not only the sister of Percival but also the wife of Lancelot (Robert Taylor), who married her, at the suggestion of Guinevere (Ava Gardner), to quell the gossip at court. Together, Lancelot and Elaine move to the north country, where he grows genuinely fond of her, and they live happily for a time, until she dies giving birth to their son Galahad. After Elaine's death, Lancelot returns to Camelot, where Modred exploits and exposes his rather chaste affection for Guinevere; and, although Arthur banishes him, Lancelot returns again for a reconciliation with his dying king and friend—and even, at Arthur's request, to cast Excalibur into the sea. The film ends with Percival and Lancelot at the now-empty hall of the Round Table, where the former sees the Grail and the latter is told in voice-over to take comfort because 'nothing is lost', Lancelot's own sins have been forgiven, and his son Galahad will be the greatest knight of all.

Director John Boorman's *Excalibur* (Orion, 1981) also claims to be 'adapted from Malory's *Le Morte Darthur*', though it borrows as much from Tennyson and introduces some original material as it tries to tell the whole story of Arthur, from Uther's lust for Igraine to the final battle with Mordred and the return of Excalibur to the water—in this case, by Perceval. For example, Arthur becomes the wounded king who must be healed by the Grail, which is achieved by Perceval alone. After Arthur's healing and before the final battle, he rides to the nunnery to ask Guinevere to accept his forgiveness and to put her heart at rest. He proclaims that he has always loved her and that he still does, to which she responds: 'I loved you as king, sometimes as husband' and then adds, 'One cannot gaze too long at the sun'. Even though the dynamic between the characters is completely different from that in the *Idylls*, the meeting in the nunnery and Guinevere's comment are obviously derived from Tennyson's depiction of Arthur's visit to Almesbury and Guinevere's question in the 'Lancelot and Elaine' idyll: 'But who can gaze upon the Sun in heaven?' Guinevere does not grovel silently but speaks her mind and even voices mild criticism of Arthur. And instead of spoiling the purpose of his life, which Tennyson's Arthur says Guinevere did, she helps him to fulfil it by returning to him the sword that will allow him to 'defend what was and the dream of what could be' in his final battle. The visual beauty of certain scenes, the conception of some of the characters (Merlin and Morgan, for example), and the controlling theme—the notion that the king and the land are one—make this one of the finest examples of Arthurian cinema.

THE CONTINUING ROMANCE TRADITION IN FICTION

While film assumed some of the function of drama in transmitting the romance tradition of the Arthurian legends, fiction also became a popular vehicle for reworking the Arthurian story in the twentieth century. Several major authors and many genre authors or minor novelists undertook the retelling of that story in part or in whole. Among these retellings, one of the most important and certainly the most influential was T. H. White's *The Once and Future King*.

T. H. White

Terence Hanbury White (1905–64) published *The Once and Future King* in parts. *The Sword in the Stone*, *The Witch in the Wood*, and *The Ill-Made Knight* were each published separately. White then added *The Candle in the Wind* as the final part when he published *The Once and Future King* in 1958. At one point in the writing, he planned a five-part book that would conclude with *The Book of Merlyn*, which, though not published in the 1958 volume, is essential to understanding White's plan. White originally thought of his book as a classical tragedy and even wrote *The Candle in the Wind* first as a play; but his conception shifted as he 'suddenly discovered' that 'the central theme of Morte d'Arthur is to find an antidote to war' (letter of 6 Dec. 1940, in *Letters to a Friend* 120) and, no doubt, as he got very negative reactions to the play.

There is throughout White's sequence of books an awareness of time, the most obvious example of which is the fact that Merlin lives backwards in time. Because of this unusual quality, White is able to introduce any number of anachronisms into the novel. White's playing with time is not, however, just for purposes of humour and satire; it is part of the very fabric of the book. White, in fact, reflects the ageing of his characters in the macro-structure of his book. In a rather brilliant structural experiment, at the same time that the characters age in the sequence, the book itself is growing up with them.

In *The Sword in the Stone* (1938), Arthur's nickname Wart marks him as a different figure from the hero of romance, a child who must learn to be king by learning about the world around him, the animals that live in that world, and from them and their political systems about man and his. In *The Witch in the Wood* (1939, retitled *The Queen of Air and Darkness* in the 1958 edition), Gawain and his brothers continue the childhood theme, sometimes with a darkness that it did not have in the earlier book. With a mother who is more of a figurative than a literal witch but who nonetheless casts a spell over her children, most of the brothers become psychopaths. Arthur, who is called 'the young king of England' (220), is beginning to mature. He arrives at the idea of Might for Right; and Merlin says 'the first few words of the Nunc Dimittis' (248) because his pupil has begun to think for himself and what he thinks is noble.

The Sword in the Stone is a children's book. The turning of Arthur into various animals, the adventure with Robin Hood, the talking owl Archimedes, Merlin's botched spells—all are the stuff of a tale for young readers. The distance from this book to the almost pessimistic philosophizing of *The Book of Merlyn* seems great, but part of White's artistry is to make the process gradual, like ageing itself. *The Queen of Air and Darkness* also has elements of a children's book—though ultimately a darker and more ominous one than *The Sword in the Stone*. Arthur is the young king learning to think for himself; but much of the book is set in the Gaelic world of Lothian. The killing of the griffin from *The Sword in the Stone* is paralleled by the hunting of the unicorn in *The Queen of Air and Darkness*. Both are adventures with a fabulous beast, but the latter—a revolting slaughter of a beautiful animal, an offence against the nature that Wart learns to love and respect in the first book, and a double travesty because it is done to please an uncaring and unpleasant mother—is a sign of the deep dysfunctionality of the Lothian clan. This is then a step beyond the idyllic world of the first book but, despite ominous foreshadowing, the characters have not yet reached the world of adult trouble that later books depict. It seems as if White was trying in this second part of his pentalogy to write a *Bildungsroman* in which Arthur comes of age and is no longer in need of his tutor but also to link it through both comic and disturbing elements to the part that came before.

Early in *The Ill-Made Knight* (1940), when 'Guenever was twenty-two', White introduces a long passage on the development of a seventh sense in middle age. This seventh sense is a sense of balance that is gained with experience of the world. It is the reason 'Middle-aged people can balance between believing in God and breaking all the commandments, without difficulty' (378). White speaks of this quality before Guenever or Lancelot has developed it because it is precisely this ageing and balancing process that is the subject of the third and central book of his Arthuriad. Midway through *The Ill-Made Knight*, Lancelot has fathered Galahad, lived with Elaine for a time, and returned to Camelot and resided there for fifteen more years. White calls attention to the new generation at court 'for whom Arthur was not the crusader of a future day, but the accepted conqueror of a past one' (421). Towards the end of this instalment of his book, he writes that 'Now the maturest or the saddest phase [of Camelot] had come, in which enthusiasms had been used up for good, and only our famous seventh sense was left to be practised' (477). The characters have reached mature, worldly-wise, and a bit world-weary middle age. *The Ill-Made Knight* was also conceived as belonging to a different genre. As Elisabeth Brewer points out, White repeatedly wrote in his letters to L. J. Potts, his former tutor at Cambridge, and others that it was to be a 'Romance' (76). With the adventures and quests and especially the love interest that that genre usually implies, the book concerns itself with love and religion and strife.

In *The Candle in the Wind*, the sequence ages again with the characters as it moves from romance to tragedy. Lancelot and Arthur share a love for each other that is almost as strong as their love for Guenever. Arthur is very much aware of the affair between his wife and his champion; and yet he chooses to overlook it because he puts the good of his kingdom and of his friend above his own pride. But when the king is confronted with an accusation and his entire system of law and justice depends on his condemning those he loves, he can no longer look the other way. Later, Arthur is prevented from reconciling with Lancelot by Gawain's anger and Mordred's innate iniquity. Mordred, like all true scoundrels, uses against the one he would destroy that person's own goodness.

The pattern of ageing continues into *The Book of Merlyn* where, on the first page, Arthur is said to have 'an old man's misery' (3) and is repeatedly described as old. In this book, the sequence moves from the tragedy of the fourth part to a philosophical dialogue. The change in genre is a key to White's structural experimentation. It is the capstone in the construction of the sequence, a speculative reflection on the nature of man and on the problem of Might. And it is the last stage in the ageing of White's book, which mirrors the ageing of the characters. Thus, in the five parts of White's Arthuriad, the book's genres 'mature' from a children's story to a *Bildungsroman*, to a romance, to a tragedy, to a philosophical treatise.

But White's publisher objected to including this last section, in part because *The Book of Merlyn* is so different from all the books that preceded it in White's cycle. Elisabeth Brewer suggests that 'Interesting as *The Book of Merlyn* is, it would have made a strange ending to the story of Arthur. . . . For what reader, after reaching the tragic end of the story, when Arthur, old and defeated, faces death at the hand of his own son, really wants to attend a Privy Council of animals, including the sentimental and sentimentalised hedgehog, for another dose of polemic and facetious humor at the end?'—even though the return to the animals 'creates a circular pattern' that would have some structural merit (Brewer 150, 152).

While *The Book of Merlyn* has some merit, it is hard to imagine a better ending than that of the 1958 version—for several reasons. First of all, the omission of *The Book of Merlyn* forced White to move its chapters about the ants and the geese to *The Sword in the Stone*, where they are more suitable as part of Arthur's education about man's role as a political animal. The 1958 ending also seems appropriate to the concern with time throughout the sequence. In the end, time, so essential to the book, is part of its ultimate theme. There is not enough time to solve the great problems like war and human iniquity and to learn to deal with the tragic consequences that result from them, and not enough time to teach the things that make it possible to solve these problems, not even enough time for someone like Merlin, who lives many lifetimes. Thus art and culture, embodied in the young Tom Malory who wishes to fight for Arthur but whom the king commands to run from the battle and write about Camelot and what it represents, become crucial so that one is not always starting at the beginning, so that values and ideals can be preserved and absorbed even when Merlin or some Merlin figure like T. H. White is not around to teach.

White's Merlin said that 'the best thing for being sad . . . is to learn something' (183). The ending of the 1958 *The Once and Future King* implies that the best answer to macrocosmic sorrows like war is indeed to learn something—from the examples of books like Malory's *Morte d'Arthur* and White's own sequence. At the end of the 1958 novel, White writes of a youth, not Wart but a young Tom Malory, who will learn and then inspire others to learn. In this ending, White suggests a different kind of return of Arthur from that hinted at in Malory, a return of the sort seen over and over again—in the literature and music and art that have been written through the ages, a tradition to which White himself adds an innovative and experimental novel.

White's book became extremely popular in England and in America and was adapted for film and stage. An animated version of *The Sword in the Stone* (Walt Disney Productions, 1963; dir. Wolfgang Reitherman) focuses on Merlin's education of Wart, the young Arthur, and culminates in Arthur's drawing the sword from the stone and accepting, reluctantly, the kingship for which the wizard has been preparing him. The drawing of the sword was a perfect subject for a children's story, as the plays which use that theme indicate. The triumph of a youth who has grown up in the shadow of others is a perennial theme in children's literature; and it is made all the more appealing by the outstanding animation for which Disney is rightly famous.

White's book was also adapted as the play *Camelot* (1960) by Alan Jay Lerner, with music by Frederic Loewe. The play emphasizes the glorious ideal that Camelot represents and that survives the human tragedy. This theme, along with the tragic love of Lancelot and Guinevere, the pageantry, and the enduring music, has inspired many productions of the play as well as a cinematic version, *Camelot* (Warner Brothers, 1967; dir. Joshua Logan), which starred Richard Harris, Vanessa Redgrave, and Franco Nero.

Partly because of his fondness for the play *Camelot*, coupled with an interest in the legends that originated with his childhood reading of a version of Malory, John F. Kennedy's presidency has been referred to as 'Camelot'. Actually, the identification between Kennedy and Camelot first occurred soon after Kennedy's death, when Jacqueline Bouvier Kennedy urged her friend, reporter and historian Theodore H. White, to label her late husband's historical myth in specifically Arthurian terms. In a chapter of his memoirs entitled 'Camelot', White recalls, 'she urged my using the word "Camelot" to describe it all. And her message was his message—that one man, by trying, may change it all' (538). And over the years presidential historian William Manchester and others increasingly associated Kennedy with the legend of Arthur—so much so, in fact, that 'The New Frontier' was perceived as an analogue of Arthur's dream and the Peace Corps as a 'group of Kennedy's knights who went on their individual quests, fighting the dragons of poverty and helping populations in distress, enduring hardships for noble causes in strange and foreign lands' (Knight 31).

John Steinbeck

Another writer who reworked Malory's book was the great American novelist John Steinbeck (1902–68), who wanted to modernize Malory's *Morte* so it would be accessible to an American audience. Steinbeck had been fascinated by Malory's tale since childhood. As he noted in the introduction to the *Acts of King Arthur*, it was a version of Malory designed for youngsters from which he developed 'my sense of right and wrong, my feeling of noblesse oblige, and any thought I may have against the oppressor and for the oppressed' (4). Thus Malory's *Morte* helped to shape all of Steinbeck's work, even his novels of social concern.

The Arthurian influence is evident in the Grail motif in Steinbeck's first novel *Cup of Gold* (1929) (discussed in Chapter 4) and in *Tortilla Flat* (1935), in which Steinbeck translates the Arthurian realm into the modern world by creating an overlay of Arthurian allusion to ennoble the lower-class characters of the novel. Steinbeck himself said in a letter written in 1934 that *Tortilla Flat*, 'has a very definite theme. I thought it was clear enough. I have expected that the plan of the Arthurian cycle would be recognized, that my Gawaine and my Launcelot, my Arthur and Galahad would be recognized. Even the incident of the Sangreal in the search in the forest is not clear enough I guess. The form is that of the Malory version, the coming of Arthur and the mystic quality of owning a house, the forming of the round table, the adventure of the knights and finally, the mystic translation of Danny [the King Arthur figure in the book]' (*Steinbeck: A Life in Letters* 96–7). To make the link more obvious, therefore, Steinbeck added chapter headings that imitated those in the Caxton edition of Malory. Steinbeck also added a sentence to the preface to make the Arthurian connection more explicit: 'For Danny's house was not unlike the Round Table, and Danny's friends were not unlike the knights of it' (9). Danny, who shelters his friends, takes on the role of Arthur in medieval romance by providing a focal point for his followers and a starting point for all their adventures. Danny's companion Pilon, who advises him, is the story's Merlin. Despite the use of the Arthurian material to ennoble his characters, Steinbeck never idealizes or overly romanticizes them—although they do have their own code of ethics and do champion those in distress.

Like *Tortilla Flat*, Steinbeck's novel *Sweet Thursday* (1954) re-enacts portions of the Arthurian story in the modern world; but instead of following the tragic pattern of Malory's romance, as the earlier novel does, *Sweet Thursday* offers a deliberate and comic reversal of that pattern. The Arthur figure in *Sweet Thursday* is Doc, a biologist who makes his living gathering marine specimens and preparing them for use in research and who is essential to the health and well-being of his community. To counteract the malaise that has descended on Doc, his friends, who live in the Palace flophouse, decide to find him a wife. In this endeavour, they are led by one of the modern knights from the Palace, a man named Hazel, Doc's champion and the Lancelot figure of the book. After a disastrous attempt to get Doc together with a woman named Suzy, Hazel realizes that Suzy's pride prevents her from renewing her relationship: only if she feels that Doc needs her will she go to him. By breaking Doc's arm with a baseball bat just as he is about to set out on a trip to gather much-needed marine specimens to replenish his diminished stock, Hazel forces Suzy to act. His plan works: Suzy rushes to Doc, offering to drive him on his trip and turn over rocks for him so he can find his specimens. The reversal of Malory's tragedy is complete when Doc tells Suzy of his love for her and she responds, 'Brother... you got yourself a girl' (270). Instead of the fatal wound that Malory's Arthur suffers, Doc receives a wound that gives his life meaning. Instead of having his closest companion betray him by loving his wife, Doc's friends bring him together with the woman he loves. And in another reversal, the knights of the Palace flophouse rig a raffle so that Doc wins the building in which they dwell. Therefore, instead of causing the destruction of Camelot, Doc's friends make him the possessor of the Palace.

The ending offers yet another inversion of the traditional story. Doc and Suzy depart after she, never having driven before, gets a quick driving lesson. Steinbeck seems to be thinking of the ending of Tennyson's *Idylls* where Bedivere, alone on the shore, watches the barge carrying Arthur and the mystic maidens become smaller and smaller until it disappears into the light of the dawn. Steinbeck's departure scene suggests the different tone of his novel: 'Doc turned in the seat and looked back. The disappearing sun shone on his laughing face, his gay and eager face. With his left hand he held the bucking steering wheel' (273). Doc, wounded but joyful, sets out towards the water—never mind that they are heading for La Jolla rather than Avalon—with Suzy driving the car for their festive rather than funereal trip.

Steinbeck's fascination with the legend led him not only to incorporate Arthurian themes into his novels but also to undertake a modernization of Malory, which was posthumously published in 1976 as *The Acts of King Arthur*. It began as a fairly straightforward translation of Malory's language into modern English. But the novelist in Steinbeck soon took over, and he started to alter his source. Some of the changes are merely editorial. 'Malory removed some of the repetition from the Frensshe books,' Steinbeck wrote. 'I find it necessary to remove most of the repetition from Malory' (*Steinbeck: A Life in Letters* 558). But as he progressed, he began making revisions that went far beyond the editorial. He wanted to update and Americanize the characters and events, so he elaborated on Malory's text by providing more explanation and commentary than Malory did. When Malory's Merlin tells of his own fate, Arthur advises him to use his 'crauftes' to prevent it. Merlin simply replies that it cannot be. Steinbeck's Merlin responds that he cannot save himself 'Because I am wise. In the combat between wisdom and feeling, wisdom never wins' (122). Similarly, Steinbeck feels the novelist's need to explain character. As Kay is transformed from a brave knight to a petty, sniping critic who never sees the true worth of others, Steinbeck explains that Kay changed because as seneschal he must pay attention to the 'important littleness' of day-to-day matters, 'all greatness eaten away by little numbers as marching ants nibble a dragon and leave picked bones' (321–2).

In addition to the emphasis on characterization, Steinbeck modernizes his account of Arthur's realm in the way he treats the women of the story. The expanded tale of the temptations by the four queens is just one example of his attempt to individualize some of Malory's stock characters. Steinbeck also gives women richer and more complex roles, and it seems likely that, had the book been finished, a character like Guinevere would have been prominent. Steinbeck's Guinevere wishes that she could be a man because her 'only adventures are in the pictures in colored thread of the great gallant world. My little needle is my sword. That's not a very satisfying conflict' (252). Surely had her character been fully developed, she would have had a tremendous influence on the events at Camelot and in her own life.

Even though Steinbeck did not totally realize his new intention, the *Acts* is a significant addition to the Arthurian tradition by a major American novelist. Steinbeck's achievement in the *Acts* is largely a result of his focus on Lancelot, a character he said (in a letter dated 25 July 1959) he loved because he 'is tested, he fails the test and still remains noble'. Steinbeck takes what is a given in Malory's romance, Lancelot's greatness, and analyses it. Not content simply to assert that greatness, Steinbeck explores it, showing both how ridiculous total dedication can be to those who do not understand it and how inspiring it can be to those who do. Steinbeck had come to understand Lancelot, or at least to understand how he wanted to portray Lancelot. 'He's my boy,' Steinbeck wrote in the same letter. 'I can feel him. And I'm beginning to feel Guinevere and out of that I will get to feel Arthur' (*Acts* 437–8). What he seemed to appreciate most about Lancelot was that he was struggling toward an unachievable but ennobling perfection. Steinbeck believed that 'strength and purity lie almost exclusively in the struggle—the becoming' (*Steinbeck: A Life in Letters* 741). It is this quality of struggle towards an unattainable goal rather than his prowess in battle that, for Steinbeck, makes Lancelot a hero who is as relevant to the modern world as he was to the medieval.

Thomas Berger

Another American novelist who attempts to tell the whole story of Arthur is Thomas Berger (b. 1924). His *Arthur Rex* (1978) demonstrates a great admiration for the legend of Arthur as told by Malory and others; but he also modernizes, at times parodies, and radically revises the received version of the story. Like the legend itself, Berger's novel is full of paradoxes and ironies. For instance, after Arthur pulls the sword from the stone and assumes the throne, he quickly discovers the burden of kingship. One of the first of those discoveries is that a monarch has fewer liberties than his subjects do. 'Captive of many laws, ordinances, traditions, customs, and moreover, prophecies', all of which conspire to guarantee that he 'is never free to do his will' (65), Arthur feels that he is 'fundamentally a slave' (78).

Kingship reveals to Arthur other unpleasant realities, such as the fact that doing good may lead to evil. His marriage shatters in large part because of his own selfless actions. Arthur extols Launcelot's virtues to Guinevere and assigns Launcelot not to the quest, for which he longs, but to the queen's side as her protector and defender. The dissolution of Arthur's household mirrors the dissolution of his fabled Order, a noble concept that leads ultimately to war and to the deaths of every knight of the Round Table. 'For this', according to Berger, 'was the only time that a king had set out to rule on principles of absolute virtue, and to fight evil and to champion the good, and though it was not the first time that a king fell out with his followers, it was unique in happening not by wicked design but rather by the helpless accidents of fine men who meant well and who loved one another dearly' (447). In various other ways, good leads to evil. Conversely, the renouncing of evil does not necessarily lead to good, as illustrated by the example of Sir Meliagrant. Enamoured of Guinevere, whom he has detained and imprisoned, the notoriously wicked knight decides to change himself in order to win her affection. But 'whereas he had been fearsome when vile, he was but a booby when he did other than ill' (174). The newly reformed Meliagrant is soon robbed and wounded by a beggar (who, insultingly, purchases the weapon he uses against Meliagrant with the gold that the knight had earlier given to him in charity) and then is killed in a fight with Launcelot. Before he dies, however, Meliagrant concedes—with some understatement—that 'This honor can be a taxing thing' (175).

Interestingly, Berger's female characters seem best able to articulate his notion of the pursuit of the dangerous ideal. Late in the novel, for instance, when Launcelot says that his war with Arthur is not the result of any hatred between the two, Guinevere thinks to herself, 'Nay, it hath happened because of men and their laws and their principles!' (442). In effect, she implies that idealism itself is responsible for many of the world's problems. This notion is echoed by Morgan la Fey, Arthur's half-sister and his greatest nemesis. Throughout the novel, Morgan repeatedly seeks to undermine Arthur's kingdom. Finally, however, Morgan enters the Convent of the Little Sisters of Poverty and Pain, for after a long career in the service of evil she comes to believe that corruption 'were sooner brought amongst humankind by the forces of virtue, and from this moment on she was notable for her piety' (453). She even becomes mother superior of the convent that Guinevere eventually joins.

Similarly, the Lady of the Lake, who serves as the antithesis to Morgan's villainy, tells Arthur and his knights that no quest should be conducted blindly. The principles of chivalry, she suggests, must admit some alteration; otherwise, those principles become mere abstractions. And the knights—even the kings—who grow obsessed with 'adherence to the letter' (312) stop being men and become instead 'abstract example[s] for-argument's-sake' (431). To have a noble purpose is good, she says; 'but to be so intent upon it as to see only its end is folly. Never to be distracted is to serve nothing but Vanity' (105). The Lady of the Lake appears again to instruct the wounded king on the battlefield at Salisbury Plain. When Arthur wonders if he could have ruled more wisely, she reassures him, 'Thou couldst not have done better than thou didst. . . . Thine obligation was to maintain power in as decent a way as would be yet the most effective, and a Camelot without Guinevere, a Round Table without Launcelot, were inconceivable, as would be an Arthur who put to death his best friend and his queen. All human beings must perform according to their nature' (484).

Yet the recognition, and ultimately the appreciation, of the dangerous ideal is not restricted to the women in Berger's novel. Merlin, for one, is quite aware of it, especially as he instructs and assists Arthur in the early chapters. The young king, with the zeal of youth, wants to burn the 'strumpet residents' of a nearby brothel called the Nunnery of St Paul's and have the 'trollops [sent] to a proper convent'; but Merlin 'cast a spell upon Arthur, in which he seemed to see smoke and flames arising from the stews' (33). Just as Malory's Merlin uses a spell to save Arthur in a battle with Pellinore, here Berger's Merlin uses a spell to save Arthur from a moral battle that will bring him only harm. Later, after defining his principles of chivalry, Arthur expresses his concern about wielding the enchanted sword Excalibur against his enemy King *Ryons, who is armed with only a 'conventional weapon'. Merlin says it is 'never justice, but rather sentimentality, to deal mildly with intruders' (39–40).

Berger's use of the central theme of the dangerous ideal provides a means of exploring the great paradox of Malory's text, the destruction of a noble ideal through the flaws of noble men. It is a theme, perhaps *the* theme, of *Arthur Rex* that extreme adherence to moral rules can be more damaging than lapses in morality. This is not to suggest that Berger finds the desire to be better and to make things better wrong. But in Berger's novel, the desire to make things *perfect* without admitting human failings usually causes more trouble than outright imperfection does.

Donald Barthelme

Another intriguing retelling of the Arthurian story—though one less ambitious and successful than Berger's *Arthur Rex*—occurs in Donald Barthelme's (1931–89) last novel. Posthumously published, *The King* (1991) is both a parody of medieval myth and a political allegory that conflates a familiar legend with modern history, both factual and imaginary. Barthelme's novel contains numerous references to people and events of the Second World War. The knights in *The King* seek a Grail—the atomic bomb—that will ostensibly destroy the very notion of the quest. The 'Grail-as-bomb' (79), once achieved, can never be unachieved. Throughout *The King*, the characters undercut their own mythic significance by contrasting their current circumstances with the 'old days'. One of the main differences between the 'old days' for which the characters long and the current times is the inherent value of the causes that they espouse and the principles that they defend. And most of the major characters in the novel fall short of the mythic stature of their medieval counterparts.

Barthelme's Arthurian world in *The King*, in which Arthur gets called to jury duty, King Unthank produces pornographic films starring his wife, and brazen knights actually wear brown armour with black horses, is quite modern. It is also mythic, almost postmythic, the way Barthelme's fiction is sometimes labelled postmodern. Yet Barthelme's use of Arthurian motifs suggests that for him, as for so many other contemporary American novelists, the legendary world provides an excellent vantage point from which to survey and to parody contemporary events.

Lancelot and Guinevere in Fiction

A number of other novels focus on the love of Lancelot and Guinevere as a cause of the tragic end of Arthur's reign. *The Queen's Knight* (1920) by Chester Keith, which recounts the story of Lancelot from his boyhood to his death, has been called a 'stuttering redaction of Malory with a dash of Tennyson' (Starr 42). In *Launcelot* (1926), Lord Ernest Hamilton (1858–1939) combines Malory with Tennysonian morality and writes in deliberately archaic language. His Launcelot is beyond reproach: even though Gueneviere professes her love for him and tries to seduce him, he resists her advances. The honourable knight is married to Elaine, daughter of Pelles, their son Galahad being born in lawful wedlock. When Launcelot and the queen are trapped in her chamber, they are innocent. He is there only because Agravaine sent a message saying that she needed to see him 'touching some weighty matter' (272).

Philip Lindsay (1906–58) explores the role of love in the Arthurian tragedy in his novel *The Little Wench* (1935). Adapted primarily from Malory, the novel tries to capture the spirit of the Middle Ages by describing tournaments, hawking, and siege warfare, and by presenting love as a courtly game modelled on notions of courtly love. Lancelot's love develops from this innocent beginning into a passion that leads to tragic consequences. Lindsay alters some of the relationships in Malory, making Mordred the son of Morgain and a cousin, but not a brother, to Gawain. And the depiction of Lancelot is initially rather unattractive. He disciplines his son Galahad by punching him, and before falling in love with Guinevere, he thinks of women as 'only beasts with a voice' (34). After Lancelot has rescued Guinevere and been besieged by Arthur and Gawain, he returns to help Arthur but arrives after the king's death. He searches years for Guinevere, who has become a reclusive nun; when he finally finds her hermitage, she refuses to speak to him, a decision that torments Lancelot but which he finally realizes was correct.

Also much influenced by Malory is *Launcelot, my Brother* (1954) by Dorothy James Roberts (1903–90). The novel is narrated by Bors, who is here said to be the brother of Launcelot, and thus depicts in detail Launcelot's motivations and actions as well as those of Bors and their youngest brother Blamor. As in Malory, the feud between the houses of Lot and Pellinore is important to the plot. Gawaine, troubled by the offences to the honour of his family, participates in the slaying of *Lamorak and is manipulated by Mordred to accuse Lancelot and the queen. Despite his love for Guinevere, Launcelot remains loyal to Arthur and tries to prevent the collapse of his kingdom. Though Arthur's realm ends in bloodshed and tragedy and though Arthur dies and is buried, Bors understands the stories that claim he has not died because 'Arthur would return, the goodness, the pride, the glory we could not attain, yet must hope for'. Bors realizes that these qualities and 'the desire to be better than we are' are inherent in all men and thus 'Arthur was I, I was Arthur'. To pass on this realization, Bors tells his story (373).

Marvin Borowsky (1907–69) also tells the story of Launcelot and Guinevere in his novel *The Queen's Knight* (1955). Arthur is 'a rustic lout Merlin brought . . . to be Mordred's poppet'. They assume he will be a 'straw-king' easily manipulated by Mordred and the council of nobles who control Britain (9). But Arthur is concerned about the hunger among the people and the high taxes that burden them. He has sympathy for the common man and a vision of offering 'a new hope' (86), a vision which wins over Merlin and some of the lords. Launcelot helps Arthur to overcome those who oppose him, but the affair between Launcelot and the queen forces the king to condemn them. When Mordred attacks, Arthur postpones the sentence and Launcelot fights beside the king, who kills Mordred but is himself fatally wounded and dies after declaring amnesty for all who fought against him and naming *Constantine his successor. Launcelot declares that he will defend the Northern Wall, thus continuing Arthur's defence of Britain.

The Arthurian tragedy is the focus of *A Camelot Triptych* (1997) by Norris Lacy, noted Arthurian scholar and general editor for the first complete translation of the Lancelot–Grail Cycle. Lacy's tale adopts some of the complex style of narration of that cycle. The three frames of the triptych are told from the perspectives of three participants—Merlin, Guinevere, and Mordred—who relate their stories, respectively, to Blaise, to a nun in the convent, and to a scholar named John of Carlisle. In addition, Mordred's version of events is said to be 'an account of John's account of Mordred's account of his brief, unhappy life'(60). As the various reports, sometimes of the same events, unfold, the complexity of the tale and the ways in which it varies depending on who is telling it become the focus and point of the narrative.

As happens with other elements of the Arthurian tradition, the affair between Lancelot and Guinevere is sometimes translated into a modern setting. Such is the case in *Guinevere's Lover* (published in Britain as *The Sequence 1905–1912*) (1913) by British novelist Elinor Glyn (1864–1963); *Launcelot & the Ladies* (1927) by Will Bradley, in which the modern hero sees visions of the Arthurian world and marries not the Guinevere figure but the woman who parallels Elaine; and *Guinever's Gift* (1977) by Nicole St John, which involves a search for Arthur's grave and two generations of characters who re-enact the Arthurian love triangle. The best of such novels is *The Lyre of Orpheus* (1988) by Canadian novelist Robertson Davies (1913–95), in which Arthur and Maria Cornish and their friend Geraint Powell re-enact the Arthurian triangle as the foundation funded by Arthur's uncle Francis Cornish provides funds to a brilliant but eccentric graduate student to finish the music for a purported unfinished opera by E. T. A. Hoffmann about King Arthur, *Arthur of Britain, or the Magnanimous Cuckold*. The tragic ending of the Arthurian opera contrasts with the comic outcome of the modern triangle.

The Arthurian triangle and other elements of the tradition are also prominent in the trilogy known as The Fionavar Tapestry by Canadian author Guy Gavriel Kay. The trilogy involves five people from modern Canada who are drawn into the alternative world of Fionavar, where the powers of Light and Dark struggle for supremacy. One of those characters, Jennifer, turns out to be Guinevere. Though the Arthurian elements do not come into play in *The Summer Tree* (1984), in the second novel, *The Wandering Fire* (1986), Arthur is drawn from his rest to assist in the struggle. He leads an expedition to Cader Sedat, the equivalent in Fionavar of Caer Sidi, the Celtic underworld, to destroy a cauldron that is supposed to bring life but that is being misused by the forces of the Dark. In Cader Sedat, Arthur finds Lancelot and brings him back to life to aid him in the conflict. Much is made of the fact that Arthur slaughtered children in his attempt to kill Mordred, and because of this act he is fated to return and repeat the pattern of his death. In the third novel, *The Darkest Road* (1986), there is a final struggle on a field called Camlann. Arthur thinks it is his fate to fight the champion of the forces of the Dark and to die doing so, but one of the inhabitants of Fionavar takes on that task. When the forces of the Dark are defeated without Arthur's death, the old pattern is broken. Guinevere is reunited with Arthur, and they ask Lancelot to accompany them on their journey in the ship *Prydwen 'upon waters of a sea that belonged to no world and to all of them' (394).

Lancelot himself is the main character in the short story 'The Mill' (1902) by Henry Van Dyke (1852–1933), which uses bits of narrative derived from Malory as the foundation for a totally original tale about a young man named Martimor, whom Lancelot encounters in a land called Beausejour. Lancelot trains Martimor as a knight and sends him off on a quest to name the blue flower Lancelot has had painted on his shield. On his quest, Martimor meets a miller and his daughter Lirette, who are plagued by 'three foul churls' (55). Martimor eventually ends their troubles by killing the churls; he also saves Pellinore's daughter from three knights, for which, Lancelot tells him, Pellinore would reward him with a castle and a noble lady for a wife. But in a resolution typical of American Arthurian literature, he chooses to remain at the mill with Lirette. Concerning his quest for the name of the blue flower, he tells Lancelot that the one who 'names it shall never find it . . . and he that finds it needs no name' (72).

Mordred

Because of the interest in and importance of the final events of Arthur's reign, a number of authors have made Mordred the central character in their novels. The best of the Mordred novels was written by Mary Stewart (b. 1916), author of a Merlin trilogy (discussed in Chapter 6). *The Wicked Day* (1983) combines elements of the chronicle and romance traditions, drawn primarily from Geoffrey of Monmouth and Malory, to tell of a Mordred who comes to be branded a traitor but who is actually a reasonable man and loyal supporter of the king. He does not join his brothers Agravaine and Gaheris in the slaying of Lamorak; and he tries to prevent bloodshed when his brothers trap Guinevere and Bedwyr (rather than Lancelot) in the queen's chamber. His only act of vengeance is the killing of his mother Morgause's lover, who burned his foster-parents in the hut in which they lived.

When Mordred assumes control of Britain, he does so because he has had a report that Arthur was killed in the battle against the Roman forces under the command of Lucius; and he is carrying out instructions given by Arthur in the event of his death. But Constantine, who believed he would be Arthur's successor, sends messages to Arthur suggesting that Mordred has betrayed him and Britain. As the king and his son meet to discuss peace, a soldier stung by an adder draws his sword and the battle begins on this 'wicked day of destiny' (336), a phrase that, like the incident with the adder, is borrowed from Malory. Although Arthur and Mordred kill each other, Stewart implies that their deaths are caused by fate rather than by the wilful actions of either of them.

Haydn Middleton tells Mordred's story in the three novels of The Mordred Cycle: *The King's Evil* (1995), *The Queen's Captive* (1996), and *The Knight's Vengeance* (1997). The cycle creates a dark picture of the Arthurian world, in which the legend of Arthur is spread by his followers, called merlins, in assemblies called Round Tables. In the second instalment, Mordred has an affair with Morgan, his own mother, and has a son by her. Arthur brings about a Great Remaking in which Albion is transformed into *Logres but is ultimately undone by Mordred.

In his fantasy novel *The Book of Mordred* (1988), American author Peter Hanratty tells the story of Mordred's youth and his quest for and winning of the Grail in the company of Lancelot and Galahad. An earlier novel by Hanratty, *The Last Knight of Albion* (1986), is more science fiction than fantasy. In that novel, Percivale seeks Mordred to punish him for using an atomic bomb that wasted the land in the last battle. Mordred justifies the use because Merlin, 'Arthur's chief Druid', was trying to create even worse weapons of mass destruction, including a biological weapon that would cause 'a plague so virulent that it would have destroyed half the inhabitants of the Eastern Kingdom within a few days' (234).

American fantasy novelist Nancy Springer (b. 1948) also tells Mordred's story in *I Am Mordred* (1998). The novel describes Mordred's youth; his conflict between loving Arthur, encouraged by Nyneve, and hating him, encouraged by Morgan le Fay; and his attempt to come to terms with the fate predicted by Merlin—his killing of Arthur. Though Mordred learns that fate cannot be avoided, he attempts to entrust his soul to Arthur in a Druid ceremony. Instead, it is transferred to a raven. After the final battle, Arthur is taken to Avalon to be healed; and during his long sleep, he is watched over by that raven. Thus Mordred fulfils his destiny but follows the advice of Vivien, the Lady of the Lake, who has said he can only fight his destiny with love.

Excalibur

The sword Excalibur is an important symbol in a number of Arthurian works. *Excalibur: A Tale for American Boys* (1865)—published anonymously but written by Moncure Daniel Conway (1832–1907) and appearing earlier in a variant version in *The Dial* (1860) as 'Excalibur: A Story for Anglo-American Boys'—creates a history for Excalibur, the 'sword that never struck but for justice and honor' (5). After Bedivere threw it into the sea, it was fished out by a Bavarian peasant who gave it to Frederick the Great. After using it to fight 'the evils of the Hapsburg Dragon' (12), Frederick bestowed it on George Washington. Later it is wielded by John Brown in his struggle against slavery, Brown and his sons being called 'modern Knights of the Round Table' (18). Upon Brown's death, the people gave the sword to Abraham Lincoln, who used it to cut the head from the 'Dragon of Slavery' (23). At his death, the sword passed to Andrew Johnson. A more recent American work, the fantasy novel *Excalibur* (1973) by Sanders Anne Laubenthal, also brings Excalibur to America. The sword and the Grail, transported to the New World by the Welsh Prince Madoc, become central to a struggle between the forces of good and evil.

In *Any Old Iron* (1989), British novelist Anthony Burgess recounts some of the great events of the twentieth century. Intertwined with these events is the discovery of Excalibur, the sword said to have belonged to Attila, passed to a Roman general and then to *Ambrosius Aurelianus. For Reginald Jones, the Welshman who has stolen it from the Russians, who stole it from the Nazis, who stole it from the Benedictine monks who were holding it in trust for the British people, the sword becomes a symbol of the romantic past and Welsh heritage. Eventually, however, Jones returns it to the water because he finds the 'chunk of the romantic past' to be 'rust' and because he has to fit himself 'for the modern age' (338).

Feminist Retellings

The female characters—Nyneve, Morgan le Fay, Morgause—play a large role in modern novels such as Nancy Springer's novel about Mordred and Laubenthal's about Excalibur. This prominence is consistent with a trend in modern Arthurian fiction to emphasize the women and to retell the legend through them or from their perspectives.

One of the most successful and influential of these novels is Marion Zimmer Bradley's (1930–99) *The Mists of Avalon* (1982), which relates the Arthurian story from the viewpoint of the women: Igraine, the wife of *Gorlois; Morgaine, their daughter and the central figure and primary voice of the book; Morgause, Igraine's half-sister, and later the wife of King Lot; Viviane, Igraine's half-sister and Lady of the Lake, who is a priestess of the Holy Isle of Avalon and mother to Lancelet; Niniane and Nimue, Viviane's descendants; and Gwenhwyfar, queen and wife of Arthur.

Though *The Mists of Avalon* is usually read as a feminist tale, not all of the women are admirable. For most of the book, Gwenhwyfar is a nagging agoraphobe who tries to inflict her religious beliefs on everyone around her, including Arthur and therefore the people of his realm. First seen as a weeping child lost in the mists of Avalon, she dutifully marries Arthur and with her uncompromising piety draws him, and all of Britain, under the powerful sway of the Christian priests. She even believes in making 'such laws as would keep my people from sin' (420). It is she who insists that Arthur abandon the Pendragon banner because of its ties to the ancient religion of Britain and has him carry instead a Christian banner. By failing to fight under the Pendragon banner, Arthur breaks the vow he made to Viviane as Lady of the Lake when she presented him with the sword Excalibur and its scabbard, crafted by Morgaine and enchanted so it will prevent him from bleeding while he wears it.

This struggle between a matriarchal Avalon and a patriarchal Christianity becomes the central conflict of the novel. But the contrast between Avalon and Christianity is symbolic of something more integral to the book than the feminist theme. As Raymond Thompson has noted, 'The basic conflict is waged between tolerance and intolerance' (132), which is couched primarily in terms of the struggle between the natural and liberating Goddess worship of Avalon and the restrictive and constrictive rules of Christianity. Throughout the novel, those who practise the religion of Avalon are generally tolerant of Christianity and object mainly to its attempt to declare all other religions heresy. A basic principle of the religion of Avalon is that 'all the Gods are one' (779), a notion that echoes throughout the *Mists*. It is preached by *Taliesin, the first of two 'Merlins'—here a title rather than a name—who appear in the book, and by his successor, Kevin, who tries to accommodate the new religion in ways that seem to Morgaine such a betrayal that he must be put to death. It is a similar sacrilege by Arthur, his using Excalibur as a cross on which to swear an oath to the Saxons, that prompts Morgaine to give the sword to Accolon, her lover (and the son of her husband Uriens), to use against Arthur, who is himself more interested in peace in his realm and his marriage than in doctrine.

More important, however, than the discord between Morgaine and Kevin or Morgaine and Arthur is that between Gwenhwyfar and Morgaine. Morgaine is initially a priestess who is possessed of the Sight. She is also a tormented woman, torn, as Gwenhwyfar is, by love for Lancelet and also by her failures as a mother, sister, and wife; and it is her tragic and heroic fate to bring down Arthur, her brother, lover, and foe. Against this continuing conflict, Bradley tells the traditional story—of Arthur's conception; his fathering of Mordred by his half-sister; his marriage to Gwenhwyfar; his establishing of the Round Table; the love between Gwenhwyfar and Lancelet; the affair between Lancelet and Elaine and the resulting birth of Galahad; the Grail quest, including Galahad's achieving of it; and Arthur and Mordred's final battle—albeit in an often untraditional way. For example, Lancelet's love for Gwenhwyfar is tinged with homosexual desire for Arthur; and the half-sister and mother of Mordred, whose birth name is Gwydion, is not Morgause but Morgaine.

But even the rivalry between Gwenhwyfar and Morgaine is softened by a natural bond between the women. Morgaine recognizes that 'in spite of all old enmities, there was love too' between her and Gwenhwyfar (725). And in the end Gwenhwyfar can think of Morgaine 'with a sudden passion of love and tenderness' (864). Though it takes most of the book for this rapprochement to develop, both become a little more forgiving of each other and of what each represents. Through her love for Lancelet, a love she chooses and not a relationship that is thrust upon her, Gwenhwyfar finally overcomes her fear of being out in the open, which is really a fear of life. Just as she learns to love her newfound freedom, however, she realizes that because of the love she has for Lancelet and the obligation, paralleling Morgaine's, that she has to Britain, she must forgo her chance for personal happiness and retire to the nunnery at *Glastonbury. The sense of enclosure in the cloister, which had once made her feel 'so safe, so protected', now almost overwhelms her as she feels the walls 'closing her in, trapping her' (864). But she is willing to endure the maddening sense of imprisonment because her sacrifice will prevent the kingdom from being torn apart as Troy was because of Helen (862). Though Gwenhwyfar is still sacrificing her happiness for others, it is now her choice to do so, a mature sacrifice for a higher good rather than a frightened child's acquiescence to authority figures.

Morgaine too matures, as does her view of the worship of the Goddess as the feminine principle in the world. As Avalon fades more and more into the mists and Morgaine feels that it might be lost forever to the outside world, she brings to Glastonbury cuttings from Avalon's thorn tree, which grew originally from the staff of Joseph of Arimathea, so that something of Avalon will remain. At Glastonbury, she learns that nuns pray for Viviane, to whose burial at Glastonbury rather than Avalon Morgaine had objected. Once thought to be an evil sorceress by the Christian priests, Viviane, or at least her memory, is now treated with respect by the nuns of Glastonbury, who also drink from the Chalice Well so sacred to the old religion and pray to Brigid as a saint though she is in fact 'the Goddess as she is worshipped in Ireland' (875). Morgaine realizes that the nuns know 'the power of the Immortal' (875) and that the Goddess is not only within those who worship her but within the world as well. Morgaine's ability to accept the nuns of Glastonbury as representatives of the Goddess is a broadening of her awareness of the presence and power of the divine force she worships. With this new awareness, she understands that 'I did not fail. I did what she had given me to do. It was not she but I in my pride who thought I should have done more' (876). (Bradley's novel *Lady of Avalon* (1997) is a prequel to the *Mists*.)

As in Bradley's *Mists of Avalon*, so too in British novelist Fay Sampson's Daughter of Tintagel series Morgan is the central character. Sampson's series is comprised of five books chronicling the life of Morgan le Fay from her childhood to the end of her life. Each of the books has a different narrator; in the first four, the narrator is someone who is devoted to Morgan but whom she manipulates: her governess, a nun, a blacksmith, and the bard Taliesin. *Wise Woman's Telling* (1989) describes Morgan's strong attachment to her father and her hatred of Uther and Arthur after her father is killed. This hatred leads to her banishment to the nunnery at *Tintagel. *White Nun's Telling* (1989) is a skilful character study depicting the power of Morgan's personality even as a child, as she manipulates a nun at the convent who has been charged with controlling her but who cannot keep her from participating in the rites of the old religion. In *Black Smith's Telling* (1990), Morgan marries Urien and controls a blacksmith named Teilo, who loves her. She ruins him, like most of those who love her, forcing him to dress like a woman and serve her. In *Taliesin's Telling* (1991), Taliesin is the bard to Urien and Morgan and as such witnesses their raising of Modred. Even the bard loves Morgan and is used by her. The novel also tells of Modred's love for Gwenhyvar, which, like most other events in the series, is brought about by Morgan's machinations. *Taliesin's Telling* ends with the tragic result of that love, the final battle between Arthur and Modred. The last book, *Herself* (1992), is told from Morgan's own point of view. She comments on the events of the first four books as well as on the way her character is treated in literary tradition from medieval chronicles and romances to modern novels, including a suggestion that even 'Fay Sampson is using me here for her own ends' (306).

Morgan is not only a central character but also the lover of Arthur and the mother of Mordred in Joan Wolf's *The Road to Avalon* (1988), a novel set in the fifth century but clearly in the romance and not the chronicle tradition. Wolf's Morgan is Merlin's daughter by Nimue; and Arthur is Merlin's grandson; thus, though in love, they cannot marry. Arthur knows of his wife Gwenhwyfar's affair with Bedwyr but does not mind since he continues his affair with Morgan. Mordred, Morgan's son, is not the villain who causes the battle in which Arthur dies; rather, it is Agravaine who manipulates Mordred into declaring himself king and then leads the army that opposes Arthur at Camlann. Arthur is not slain by Mordred but is mortally wounded and brought to Morgan at Avalon. Although she is unable to heal him, she hides the fact that his wound is fatal so that his people expect his eventual return. In the tradition of modern romance novels, Morgan and Arthur believe they will be together after death.

The attention to the women of the Arthurian legend is evident in a number of other novels, including trilogies focusing on Guinevere, which have become a popular means of reworking the legend, as is demonstrated by Sharan Newman's Guinevere Trilogy (*The Chessboard Queen*, 1983; *Guinevere*, 1981; *Guinevere Evermore*, 1985), Persia Woolley's sequence (*Child of the Northern Spring*, 1987; *Guinevere: The Legend in Autumn*, 1991; *Queen of the Summer Stars*, 1990); Helen Hollick's Pendragon's Banner Trilogy (*The Kingmaking*, 1994; *Pendragon's Banner*, 1995; and *Shadow of the King*, 1997), in which the role of Gwenhwyfar is central to Arthur's story; Rosalind Miles's Guenevere Novels (*Guenevere, Queen of the Summer Country*, 1998; *The Knight of the Sacred Lake*, 2000; and *The Child of the Holy Grail*, 2001); and Alice Borchardt's The Tales of Guinevere (a projected trilogy begun with *The Dragon Queen*, 2001, and *The Raven Warrior*, 2003). Two of the four Arthurian books by Nancy McKenzie—*The Child Queen* (1994) and *The High Queen* (1995)—tell the story of Guinevere (her other novels, *Grail Prince* (2003) and *Prince of Dreams* (2004), focus on Galahad and Tristan and Essylte). In *Avalon* (1991), a lesbian romance by Mary J. Jones, Gwenhyfar's child Argante ('brilliant one') grows to womanhood with her soul-friend Elin and becomes the Lady of the Lake, a Daughter of the Goddess whose duty it is to watch over the Celtic Realms. And Barbara Ferry Johnson's *Lionors* (1975) focuses on a woman mentioned briefly by Malory as having an affair with Arthur and bearing him a child—the son in Malory's account becoming a daughter in Johnson's novel.

BIBLIOGRAPHY

Sir Thomas Malory's *Morte d'Arthur*

Benson, Larry D. *Malory's Morte Darthur*. Cambridge: Harvard University Press, 1976.

Brewer, D. S. ' "the hoole book" ', in J. A. W. Bennett (ed.), *Essays on Malory*. Oxford: Clarendon Press, 1963: 41–63.

Field, P. J. C. *Romance and Chronicle: A Study of Malory's Prose Style*. London: Barrie & Jenkins, 1971.

Gaines, Barry. *Sir Thomas Malory: An Anecdotal Bibliography of Editions, 1485–1985*. New York: AMS Press, 1990.

Lewis, C. S. 'The English Prose *Morte*', in J. A. W. Bennett (ed.), *Essays on Malory*. Oxford: Clarendon Press. 1963: 7–28.

Lumiansky, R. M. (ed.), *Malory's Originality: A Critical Study of Le Morte Darthur*. Baltimore: The Johns Hopkins Press, 1964.

Lynch, Andrew. *Malory's Book of Arms: The Narrative of Combat in 'Le Morte Darthur'*. Cambridge: D. S. Brewer, 1997.

McCarthy, Terrence. *An Introduction to Malory*. Cambridge: D. S. Brewer, 1991.

Malory, Sir Thomas. *Works*, ed. Eugène Vinaver, 2nd edn. London: Oxford University Press, 1971.

Steinbeck, John. *Steinbeck: A Life in Letters*, ed. Elaine Steinbeck and Robert Wallsten. New York: Viking, 1975.

From Malory to Tennyson

Ariosto, Ludovico. *Orlando furioso (The Frenzy of Orlando)*, trans. Barbara Reynolds. 2 vols. London: Penguin Books, 1973.

Boiardo, Matteo Maria. *Orlando innamorato*, trans. Charles Stanley Ross. Oxford: Oxford University Press, 1995.

Buckley, Jerome H. *Tennyson: The Growth of a Poet*. Boston: Houghton Mifflin, 1960.

Culler, A. Dwight. *The Poetry of Tennyson*. New Haven: Yale University Press, 1977.

Gardner, Edmund M. *The Arthurian Legend in Italian Literature*. London: J. M. Dent, 1930.

Rosenberg, John D. 'Tennyson and the Passing of Arthur', in Christopher Baswell and William Sharpe (eds.), *The Passing of Arthur: New Essays in Arthurian Tradition*. New York: Garland, 1988: 221–34.

Spenser, Edmund. *The Faerie Queene*, ed. Thomas P. Roche, Jr., with the assistance of C. Patrick O'Donnell, Jr. New Haven: Yale University Press, 1981.

Tennyson, Alfred, Lord. *Idylls of the King and a Selection of Poems*. New York: Signet / New American Library, 1961.

Lady of Shalott/Elaine of Astolat

Anderson, Jessica. *Tirra Lirra by the River*. South Melbourne: Macmillan, 1978.

Buckley, Jerome H. *Tennyson: The Growth of a Poet*. Boston: Houghton Mifflin, 1960.

Cameron, Julia Margaret. *Illustrations to Tennyson's 'Idylls of the King and Other Poems'*. London: Henry S. King, 1875.

'La Damigella di Scalot', Tale 82 of *Il Novellino*, in Cesare Segre and Mario Marti (eds.), *La Prosa del duecento*. Milan: Riccardo Ricciardi, 1959: 868–9.

Harker, Margaret F. *Henry Peach Robinson: Master of Photographic Art, 1830–1901*. Oxford: Basil Blackwell, 1988.

Kilmer, Aline. 'For All Ladies of Shalott', in *Vigils*. New York: George H. Doran Co., 1921: 37.

Landon, Letitia Elizabeth. 'A Legend of Tintagel Castle', *Fisher's Drawing Room Scrapbook* (1833), 8–9.

Latienne. 'A Southern Lady of Shalott', *Harper's*, 53 (June–Nov. 1876), 582–8.

Letts, W. M. 'Elaine at Astolat', in *The Spires of Oxford and Other Poems*. New York: E. P. Dutton, 1917: 66–7.

Meredith, Owen [pseudonym of Edward Robert Bulwer-Lytton]. *The Poetical Works of Owen Meredith (Robert, Lord Lytton)*. Boston: Houghton Mifflin, n.d.

Millay, Edna St Vincent. 'Elaine', in *Second April*. New York: Mitchell Kennerley, 1921: 56–7.

Phelps, Elizabeth Stuart. 'Elaine and Elaine', *Independent*, 35 (7 June 1883), 1. (Repr. in *Songs of the Silent World*. Boston: Houghton Mifflin, 1891: 77–8.)

—— 'The Lady of Shalott', in *Sealed Orders*. 1879; repr. New York: Garret Press, 1969: 48–64.

Poulson, Christine. *The Quest for the Grail: Arthurian Legend in British Art 1840–1920*. Manchester: Manchester University Press, 1999.

Pyle, Howard (ill.). *The Lady of Shalott* [by Alfred Tennyson]. New York: Dodd, Mead & Co., 1881.

Rhodes, W[illiam] H[enry]. 'Rosenthal's Elaine', in Daniel O'Connell (ed.), *Caxton's Book: A Collection of Essays, Poems, Tales and Sketches*. San Francisco: A. L. Bancroft, 1876: 60–2. (Repr. with a new introd. by Sam Moskowitz. Westport, Conn.: Hyperion Press, 1974.)

Royle, Edwin Milton. *Launcelot and Elaine: A Dramatization of Tennyson's Poem*. New York: Samuel French, 1929.

Sōseki, Natsume. *Kairo-kō: A Dirge*, trans. with commentary by Toshiyuki Takamiya and Andrew Armour. *Arthurian Literature*, 2 (1982), 92–126.

Steynor, Morley. *Lancelot and Elaine: A Play in Five Acts*. London: George Bell and Sons, 1909.

—— *Lancelot and Guenevere: A Play in a Prologue and Four Acts*. London: George Bell and Sons, 1909.

Tennyson, Alfred, Lord. 'The Lady of Shalott', in *Idylls of the King and a Selection of Poems*. New York: Signet/New American Library, 1961: 262–6.

Other Victorian Poets

Bulwer-Lytton, Sir Edward. *King Arthur*. 2 vols. 1848; repr. Leipzig: Tauchnitz, 1849.

Merriman, James D. 'The Last Days of the Eighteenth-Century Epic: Bulwer-Lytton's Arthuriad', *Studies in Medievalism*, 2.4 (Fall 1983), 15–37.

Morris, William. *The Defence of Guenevere and Other Poems*. 1858; repr. London: Longmans, Green, 1900.

Swinburne, Algernon Charles. *Arthurian Poets: Algernon Charles Swinburne*, ed. James P. Carley. Woodbridge: The Boydell Press, 1990.

Parodies and Criticisms of Tennyson

Adams, Oscar Fay. *Post-Laureate Idyls*. Boston: D. Lothrop and Co., 1886.

—— *Sicut Patribus, and Other Verse*. Boston: Printed by W. B. Jones for the Author, 1906.

Adeler, Max. *The Fortunate Island and Other Stories*. Boston: Lee and Shepard, 1882.

Clemens, Cyril. *Mark Twain and Franklin D. Roosevelt*, with a foreword by Eleanor Roosevelt. Webster Groves, Mo.: International Mark Twain Society, 1949.

The Coming K——: A Set of Idyll Lays. London: n.p., 1873.

du Maurier, George. *A Legend of Camelot, Pictures and Poems, Etc*. New York: Harper and Brothers, 1898.

Fawcett, Edgar. *The New King Arthur: An Opera without Music*. New York: Funk & Wagnalls, 1885.

Fuller, John G. *Mark Twain's A Connecticut Yankee in King Arthur's Court: A Comedy in Three Acts*. Boston: Walter H. Baker Co., 1941.

Ketterer, David. ' "Professor Baffin's Adventures" by Max Adeler: The Inspiration for *A Connecticut Yankee in King Arthur's Court?*', *Mark Twain Journal*, 24.1 (Spring 1986), 24–34.

Miller, Robert Keith. *Mark Twain*. New York: Frederick Ungar, 1983.

Phelps, Elizabeth Stuart. 'The True Story of Guenever', *Independent*, 28 (15 June 1876), 2–4. (Repr. in *Sealed Orders*. 1879; repr. New York: Garret Press, 1969: 65–80.)

Taylor, Beverly, and Brewer, Elisabeth. *The Return of King Arthur: British and American Arthurian Literature since 1900 [i.e. 1800]*. Cambridge: D. S. Brewer, 1983.

Twain, Mark. *A Connecticut Yankee in King Arthur's Court*. New York: Charles L. Webster, 1889.

—— *A Connecticut Yankee in King Arthur's Court*, with an afterword by Edmund Reiss. New York: Signet/New American Library, n.d.

Arthurian Youth Groups and their Influence

Donaldson, John W. *Arthur Pendragon of Britain: A Romantic Narrative by Sir Thomas Malory as Edited from 'Le Morte Darthur'*, ill. Andrew Wyeth. New York: G. P. Putnam's, 1943.

Du Bose, Horace M. *The Gang of Six: A Story of the Boy Life of Today*. Nashville, Tenn.: Publishing House of the M. E. Church, South; Smith & Lamar, Agents, 1906.

Forbush, William Byron. *The Queens of Avalon*, 4th edn. Boston: The Knights of King Arthur, 1925.

—— and Forbush, Dascomb. *The Knights of King Arthur: How to Begin and What to Do.* Oberlin, Oh.: The Knights of King Arthur, 1915.

Frith, Henry. *King Arthur and his Knights*, ill. Frank Schoonover. Garden City, NY: Garden City Publishing Co., 1932.

—— *King Arthur and his Knights*, ill. Henry C. Pitz. Garden City, NY: Garden City Publishing Co., 1955.

Girouard, Mark. *The Return to Camelot: Chivalry and the English Gentleman*. New Haven: Yale University Press, 1981.

Gray, Phoebe. *Little Sir Galahad*. Boston: Small, Maynard and Co., 1914.

Holmes, Lillian. *Little Sir Galahad*. Chicago: David C. Cook, 1904.

Johnston, Annie Fellows. *Keeping Tryst: A Tale of King Arthur's Time*. Boston: L. C. Page and Co., 1906.

—— *Two Little Knights of Kentucky: Who Were the 'Little Colonel's' Neighbours*. Boston: L. C. Page and Co., 1899.

Lanier, Sidney. *The Boy's King Arthur*, ill. Alfred Kappes. New York: Charles Scribner's Sons, 1880.

—— *The Boy's King Arthur*, ill. N. C. Wyeth. New York: Charles Scribner's Sons, 1917.

—— *King Arthur and his Knights of the Round Table*, ill. Florian. New York: Grosset & Dunlap, 1950.

Macleod, Mary. *The Book of King Arthur and his Noble Knights*. Philadelphia: J. B. Lippincott, 1949.

Powell, Perry Edwards. *The Knights of the Holy Grail: A Solution of the Boy Problem*. Cincinnati: Press of Jennings & Graham, 1906.

Pyle, Howard. *The Story of King Arthur and his Knights*. New York: Charles Scribner's Sons, 1903.

—— *The Story of Sir Launcelot and his Companions*. New York: Charles Scribner's Sons, 1907.

—— *The Story of the Champions of the Round Table*. New York: Charles Scribner's Sons, 1905.

—— *The Story of the Grail and the Passing of Arthur*. New York: Charles Scribner's Sons, 1910.

Illustrating Malory and Tennyson

Gilbert, Henry. *King Arthur's Knights: The Tales Re-told for Boys & Girls*, with 16 illustrations in colour by Walter Crane. Edinburgh: T. C. & E. C. Jack, n.d.

Malory, Thomas. *The Birth Life and Acts of King Arthur of his Noble Knights of the Round Table their Marvelous Enquests and Adventures the Achieving of the San Greal and in the End the Morte Darthur with the Dolorous Death and Departing out of This World of Them All*, ill. Aubrey Beardsley, with an introd. by Prof. John Rhys and a note on Aubrey Beardsley by Aymer Vallance. 2 vols. London: J. M. Dent, 1893.

—— *Le Morte D'Arthur*, ed. John Matthews, ill. Anna-Marie Ferguson. London: Cassell, 2000.

—— *Le Morte Darthur: The Book of King Arthur and of his Noble Knights of the Round Table*, ill. Russell Flint. 4 vols. London: Philip Lee Warner, 1910–11.

—— *The Romance of King Arthur and his Knights of the Round Table*, ill. Arthur Rackham, abridged by Alfred W. Pollard from Malory's *Morte d'Arthur*. London: Macmillan, 1917.

Stillwell, Richard. *The Chapel of Princeton University*. Princeton: Princeton University Press, 1971.

Tennyson, Alfred. *The Idylls of the King*, ill. Eleanor Fortescue Brickdale. London: Hodder and Stoughton, n.d. [1911].

—— *Idylls of the King*, ill. George Wooliscroft Rhead and Louis Rhead. New York: R. H. Russell, 1898.

—— *Idylls of the King*, ill. Gustave Doré. London: Edward Moxon, 1868.

The Continuing Romance Tradition in Poetry

Atwood, Margaret. 'Avalon Revisited', *The Fiddlehead*, 55 (Winter 1963), 10–13.

Brewer, Derek. *Seatonian Exercises and Other Verses*. London: Unicorn Press, 2000.

Cawein, Madison J. *Accolon of Gaul with Other Poems*. Louisville, Ky.: John P. Morton & Co., 1889.

—— *The Poems of Madison Cawein*. 5 vols. Boston: Small, Maynard & Co., 1907.

Ciardi, John. 'Launcelot in Hell', in *In the Stoneworks*. New Brunswick, NJ: Rutgers University Press, 1961: 47–9.

Davey, Frank. *King of Swords*. Vancouver: Talonbooks, 1972.

Heber, Reginald. 'Morte D'Arthur: A Fragment', in *Poetical Works*. Boston: Little, Brown, 1853: 136–91.

Lewis, Sinclair. 'Launcelot', 1904; repr, in Alan Lupack (ed.), *'Arthur, the Greatest King': An Anthology of Modern Arthurian Poetry*. New York: Garland, 1988: 245.

McCloskey, George V. A. 'The Flight of Guinevere', in *The Flight of Guinevere and Other Poems*. 1921; 2nd edn. New York: Authors and Publishers Corp., 1928: 15–31.

Mnookin, Wendy. *Guenever Speaks*, ill. Deborah Davidson. Rochester, NY: Round Table Publications, 1991.

Parker, Dorothy. 'Guinevere at her Fireside', in *Death and Taxes*. New York: Viking, 1931: 42–43.

Phillips, Stephen. 'The Parting of Launcelot and Guinevere', in *New Poems*. London: John Lane, 1908: 105–7.

Rhys, Ernest. *Lays of the Round Table and Other Lyric Romances*. London: J. M. Dent, 1905.

Roberts, Charles G. D. 'Launcelot and the Four Queens', in *Orion and Other Poems*, ed. Ross S. Kilpatrick. 1880; repr. London, Canada: Canadian Poetry Press, 1999: 25–34.

Robinson, Edwin Arlington. *Lancelot: A Poem*. New York: Thomas Seltzer, 1920.

—— *Modred: A Fragment*. New York: Edmond Byrne Hackett, The Brick Row Bookshop, 1929.

Scott, Robert Ian. 'The *Waste Land* Eliot Didn't Write', *Times Literary Supplement*, 8 Dec. 1995: 14.

Seymour, Alan [pseudonym of S. Fowler Wright]. *Scenes from the Morte d'Arthur*. London: MacDonald, 1919.

Teasdale, Sara. 'Guenevere', in *Helen of Troy and Other Poems*. New York: Macmillan, 1911: 27–9.

Tennyson, Alfred, Lord. *Idylls of the King and a Selection of Poems*, ed. George Barker. New York: Signet/New American Library, 1961.

Wright, S. Fowler. *The Ballad of Elaine*. London: The Merton Press, 1926.

—— *The Riding of Lancelot*. London: Fowler Wright, Ltd., 1929.

—— *The Song of Arthur*. www.sfw.org.uk/books/arthurchapters.html (accessed 17 Dec. 2002).

The Continuing Romance Tradition in Drama, Music, and Film

Binyon, Laurence. *King Arthur: A Tragedy*. Boston: Small, Maynard and Co., 1923.

Boughton, Rutland, and Buckley, Reginald R. *Music-Drama of the Future: Uther and Igraine; Choral Drama*. London: William Reeves, 1911.

Bridie, James. *Lancelot*, in *Plays for Plain People*. London: Constable, 1944: 1–78.

Butts, W. Marlin. *The Youth of King Arthur: A Legendary Play in Five Scenes*. East Boston: W. Marlin Butts, 1935.

Campbell, Wilfred. *Mordred: A Tragedy in Five Acts*, in *Poetical Tragedies*. Toronto: William Briggs, 1908: 9–123.

Carpenter, Rhys. *The Tragedy of Etarre: A Poem*. New York: Sturgis & Walton, 1912.

Carr, J. Comyns. *King Arthur: A Drama in a Prologue and Four Acts*. London: Macmillan, 1895.

Conway, John William. *Lancelot and Guinevere*. Norton, Kan.: The Champion Press, 1907.

Coutts, Francis. *The Romance of King Arthur*. London: John .ʳ ᵉ 1907.

Cram, Ralph Adams. *Excalibur: An Arthurian Drama*. Boston. .. ..ːrd G. Badger, 1909.

Engar, Keith M. *Arthur and the Magic Sword*. Anchorage, Ky.: The Children's Theatre Press, 1952.

Evernden, Margery. *King Arthur's Sword*. Chicago: Coach House Press, 1959.

Goodman, Jennifer R. 'The Last of Avalon: Henry Irving's *King Arthur* of 1895 ', *Harvard Library Bulletin*, 32.3 (Summer 1984), 239–55.

Hagedorn, Hermann, Jr. *The Silver Blade: A Drama in One Act*. Berlin: Alfred Unger, 1907.

Hill, Graham. *Guinevere: A Tragedy in Three Acts*. London: Elkin Mathews, 1906.

Hovey, Richard. *The Birth of Galahad*. Boston: Small, Maynard, and Co., 1898.

——— *The Holy Graal and Other Fragments by Richard Hovey: Being the Uncompleted Parts of the Arthurian Dramas*, ed. with an introd. and notes by Mrs Richard Hovey and a preface by Bliss Carman. New York: Duffield & Co., 1907.

——— *The Marriage of Guenevere: A Tragedy*. Boston: Small, Maynard and Co., 1899.

——— *The Quest of Merlin*. 1891; repr. Boston: Small, Maynard and Co., 1898.

——— *Taliesin: A Masque*. Boston: Small, Maynard and Co., 1900.

Jones, Frank H. *The Life and Death of King Arthur*. London: Macmillan, 1930.

Newbolt, Henry. *Mordred: A Tragedy*. London: T. Fisher Unwin, 1895.

Riethmüller, C. J. *Launcelot of the Lake: A Tragedy in Five Acts*. London: Chapman and Hall, 1843.

Thelwall, John. *The Fairy of the Lake. A Dramatic Romance, in Three Acts*, in *Poems Chiefly Written in Retirement. The Fairy of the Lake, a Dramatic Romance; Effusions of Relative and Social Feeling: and Specimens of The Hope of Albion; or, Edwin of Northumbria: An Epic Poem*. Hereford: W. H. Parker, 1801: 1–92.

Trewin, J. C. *A Sword for a Prince*, in *A Sword for a Prince and Other Plays for a Young Company*. London: Elek Books, 1960: 9–54.

Weinberger, Mildred. *Elaine: A Poetic Drama*. Poet-Lore, 34 (1923), 72–110.

Young, Stark. *Guenevere: A Play in Five Acts*. New York: The Grafton Press, 1906.

The Continuing Romance Tradition in Fiction

Barthelme, Donald. *The King*. New York: Harper and Row/An Edward Burlingame Book, 1990.

Berger, Thomas. *Arthur Rex: A Legendary Novel*. New York: Delacorte Press/Seymour Lawrence, 1978.

Borchardt, Alice. *The Dragon Queen*. New York: Del Rey, 2001.

——— *The Raven Warrior*. New York: Del Rey, 2003.

Borowsky, Marvin. *The Queen's Knight*. New York: Random House, 1955.

Bradley, Marion Zimmer. *Lady of Avalon*. New York: Viking, 1997.

—— *The Mists of Avalon*. New York: Knopf, 1982.

Bradley, Will. *Launcelot & the Ladies*. New York: Harper & Brothers, 1927.

Brewer, Elisabeth. *T. H. White's The Once and Future King*. Cambridge: D. S. Brewer, 1993.

Burgess, Anthony. *Any Old Iron*. London: Hutchinson, 1989.

Crane, John K. *T. H. White*. New York: Twayne, 1974.

Davies, Robertson. *The Lyre of Orpheus*. New York: Viking, 1989.

Excalibur: A Tale for American Boys. Philadelphia: King & Baird, 1865.

French, Warren. *John Steinbeck's Fiction Revisited*. New York: Twayne, 1994.

—— 'Steinbeck's Use of Malory', in Tetsumaro Hayashi (ed.), *Steinbeck and the Arthurian Theme*. Steinbeck Monograph Series 5. Muncie, Ind.: The John Steinbeck Society of America, Ball State University, 1975: 4–11.

Glyn, Elinor. *Guinevere's Lover*. Auburn, NY: The Authors' Press, 1913.

Hamilton, Ernest. *Launcelot: A Romance of the Court of King Arthur*. London: Methuen, 1926.

Hanratty, Peter. *The Book of Mordred*. Lake Geneva, Wis.: New Infinities Productions, 1988.

—— *The Last Knight of Albion*. New York: Bluejay Books, 1986.

Hollick, Helen. *The Kingmaking*. London: Heinemann, 1994.

—— *Pendragon's Banner*. London: Heinemann, 1995.

—— *Shadow of the King*. London: Heinemann, 1997.

Jones, Mary J. *Avalon*. Tallahassee, Fla.: Naiad Press, 1991.

Kay, Guy Gavriel. *The Darkest Road*. New York: Arbor House, 1986.

—— *The Summer Tree*. New York: Arbor House, 1984.

—— *The Wandering Fire*. New York: Arbor House, 1986.

Keith, Chester. *The Queen's Knight*. London: George Allen & Unwin, 1920.

Kinney, Arthur F. 'The Arthurian Cycle in *Tortilla Flat*', *Modern Fiction Studies*, 11.1 (Spring 1965), 11–20. (Repr. in Robert Murray Davis (ed.), *Steinbeck: A Collection of Critical Essays*. Englewood Cliffs, NJ: Prentice-Hall, 1972: 36–46.)

Knight, W. Nicholas. ' "Lancer": Myth-Making and the Kennedy Camelot', *Avalon to Camelot*, 2.1 (1986), 26–31.

Lacy, Norris. *A Camelot Triptych*. Rochester, NY: Round Table Publications, 1997.

Lerner, Alan Jay. *Camelot*, music by Frederic Loewe. New York: Random House, 1961.

Lindsay, Philip. *The Little Wench*. London: Ivor Nicholson and Watson, 1935.

McKenzie, Nancy. *The Child Queen: The Tale of Guinevere and King Arthur*. New York: Del Rey, 1994.

—— *Grail Prince*. New York: Del Rey, 2003.

—— *The High Queen: The Tale of Guinevere and King Arthur Continues*. New York: Del Rey, 1995.

—— *Prince of Dreams*. New York: Del Rey, 2004.

Middleton, Haydn. *The King's Evil*. London: Little, Brown, 1995.

—— *The Knight's Vengeance*. London: Little, Brown, 1997.

—— *The Queen's Captive*. London: Little, Brown, 1996.

Miles, Rosalind. *Guenevere, Queen of the Summer Country*. New York: Crown, 1998.

—— *The Knight of the Sacred Lake*. New York: Crown, 2000.

—— *The Child of the Holy Grail*. New York: Crown, 2001.

Mitchell, Robin C. 'Steinbeck and Malory: A Correspondence with Eugène Vinaver', *Steinbeck Quarterly*, 10 (Summer–Fall 1977), 70–9.

Newman, Sharan. *The Chessboard Queen*. New York: St Martin's, 1983.

—— *Guinevere*. New York: St Martin's, 1981.

—— *Guinevere Evermore*. New York: St Martin's, 1985.

Roberts, Dorothy James. *Launcelot, my Brother*. New York: Appleton-Century-Crofts, 1954.

St John, Nicole. *Guinever's Gift*. New York: Random House, 1977.

Sampson, Fay. *Black Smith's Telling*. London: Headline, 1990.

—— *Herself*. London: Headline, 1992.

—— *Taliesin's Telling*. London: Headline, 1991.

—— *White Nun's Telling*. London: Headline, 1989.

—— *Wise Woman's Telling*. London: Headline, 1989.

Springer, Nancy. *I Am Mordred: A Tale from Camelot*. New York: Firebird, 1998.

Starr, Nathan Comfort. *King Arthur Today: The Arthurian Legend in English and American Literature 1901–1953*. Gainesville: University of Florida Press, 1954.

Steinbeck, John. *The Acts of King Arthur and his Noble Knights*, ed. Chase Horton. New York: Ballantine/Del Rey, 1977. (Originally published in 1976 by Farrar, Straus and Giroux.)

—— *Cup of Gold: A Life of Sir Henry Morgan, Buccaneer, with Occasional Reference to History*. New York: Covici Friede, 1936.

—— *Steinbeck: A Life in Letters*, ed. Elaine Steinbeck and Robert Wallsten. New York: Viking, 1975.

—— *Sweet Thursday*. New York: Viking, 1954.

—— *Tortilla Flat*. New York: Grosset & Dunlap, 1935.

Stewart, Mary. *The Wicked Day*. London: Hodder and Stoughton, 1983.

Thompson, Raymond H. *The Return from Avalon: A Study of the Arthurian Legend in Modern Fiction*. Westport, Conn.: Greenwood Press, 1985.

Van Dyke, Henry. 'The Mill', in *The Blue Flower*. New York: Grosset & Dunlap, 1902: 41–72.

Warner, Sylvia Townsend. *T. H. White: A Biography*. London: Jonathan Cape with Chatto & Windus, 1967.

White, T. H. *The Book of Merlyn: The Unpublished Conclusion to 'The Once and Future King'*, prologue by Sylvia Townsend Warner. Austin: University of Texas Press, 1988.

—— *Letters to a Friend: The Correspondence between T. H. White and L. J. Potts*, ed. François Gallix. New York: G. P. Putnam's Sons, 1982.

—— *The Once and Future King*. 1958; repr. New York: Berkeley Medallion, 1966.

—— *The White/Garnett Letters*, ed. David Garnett. New York: Viking, 1968.

White, Theodore H. *In Search of History: A Personal Adventure*. New York: Harper & Row, 1978.

Wolf, Joan. *The Road to Avalon*. New York: New American Library, 1988.

Woolley, Persia. *Child of the Northern Spring*. New York: Poseidon Press, 1987.

—— *Guinevere: The Legend in Autumn*. New York: Poseidon Press, 1991.

—— *Queen of the Summer Stars*. New York: Poseidon Press, 1990.

The Holy Grail

The legend of the Holy *Grail became extremely popular in the Middle Ages, was relatively ignored for several centuries thereafter, and, like many things Arthurian, had a revival in the nineteenth and twentieth centuries. The concept, if not the original stories, of the Grail is now so well known that the unique object of knightly quest has become virtually a cliché: 'Holy Grail' is used to denote any kind of great goal or achievement or anything eagerly sought after, from championships in sports to exceptional computer equipment. The Grail of medieval legend, however, has a more specific connotation: it is usually said to signify the cup from which Christ drank at the Last Supper or the cup which caught his blood as he hung on the cross, though this is not the only or even the earliest form the Grail takes.

Early scholars attempted to explain the origin of the stories and the development of this signification in various ways. Jessie Weston thought the Grail stories to be a Christianization of pagan fertility rituals, with the cup and the lance having sexual significance and the wounded king who is healed being analogous to the king who must die and be reborn to give life to his land. But the theory formulated in her once influential book *From Ritual to Romance* (1920) is no longer accepted by scholars. Another theory, popularized by Roger Sherman Loomis, most notably in his book *The Grail: From Celtic Myth to Christian Symbol* (1963), saw the origins of the Grail in Celtic story and legend. Yet, while Loomis and others pointed out interesting and important analogies between Celtic tales and medieval romances, it is an over-simplification to consider the tale of the Grail as merely a development of earlier Celtic material. Perhaps the origin of the Grail stories will never be precisely defined; but what is clear is that the fertile imagination and narrative brilliance of one writer, Chrétien de Troyes, inspired a host of others to take up the tale.

CHRÉTIEN DE TROYES'S *PERCEVAL* AND ITS CONTINUATIONS AND TRANSLATIONS

Chrétien de Troyes's *Perceval* or *Le Conte du Graal*
The earliest and still the most intriguing Grail romance is Chrétien de Troyes's *Perceval* or *Le Conte du Graal*. Written in the 1180s, *Perceval* was left incomplete,

perhaps because Chrétien died before it was finished (though it may also be that he abandoned it as he did the *Lancelot*). The romance's incompleteness intrigued subsequent authors and prompted a number of them to try to create an ending for it; but like its incompleteness, the questions left unanswered—and unasked— were also a part of the story's appeal. In this his final work, Chrétien explored, as he did in his earlier romances, the nature of the chivalric ideal itself and put it into conflict not (or not only) with the ideal of love but also with a spiritual ideal. In so doing, he created a pattern that inspired much subsequent Arthurian literature.

Perceval opens with the hero of the tale as a youth living in a secluded forest with his mother, whose other two sons were killed in knightly combat and whose husband, himself wounded in battle, subsequently died of grief. Because of this family history, *Perceval's mother wants him never to see a knight, and so keeps him ignorant of all those things that his noble nature calls him to. A chance meeting with a group of knights introduces him to knighthood in one of several comic scenes that base their humour on Perceval's naïveté. In a passage that exemplifies Chrétien's masterful use of imagery, Perceval first hears the knights coming: 'As they neared their armor made a loud clamor since branches of oaks and hornbeams often struck against their equipment. All the hauberks jingled; the lances knocked against the shields; the wood of the lances resounded; and the steel of the shields and hauberks reverberated' (340; all citations are to Staines' translation). When Perceval sees the knights, he believes them to be angels led by God because of the beauty of their armour. After he discovers that they are knights and not angels, he asks a series of questions about what they are wearing and carrying. When he learns of a hauberk's ability to protect from javelins or arrows, he responds, 'God keep the does and stags from such hauberks, for I could never race after and kill them' (343).

While the scene is humorous, it also has serious implications. Perceval ignores a question asked of him by one of the knights while insisting on answers to his own questions. Such self-centred lack of regard for others is part of a pattern. When Perceval leaves his mother to go to *Arthur's court to ask for arms like those of the knights he has encountered, he rides off even though he watches his mother collapse in grief, from which, it is later revealed, she dies. He misinterprets his mother's advice about how to treat ladies so that he takes from a lady in a pavilion a ring, a kiss, and food. The lady is punished for Perceval's transgressions even though she is guiltless. Perceval later amends the injustice done to the lady when her jealous lover punishes her by making her ride a nag and allowing her no new clothing; but it is only after he has begun his process of maturation that he rights this wrong. Similarly, when Perceval comes to Arthur's court, he is concerned only about the immediate gratification of his desire for arms. He rides his horse directly into the king's court and even knocks the cap from Arthur's head with his horse's tail, so little regard does he have for decorum. When Arthur tells of the insult done to his court and his queen by the Red Knight, Perceval 'did not care a chive for anything the king said or related to him, nor did he care about the queen's sorrow or her shame' (351), but insists on being made a knight and given arms.

At Arthur's court, a maiden who has not laughed in more than six years and who would not laugh until she saw the greatest knight, laughs when she sees Perceval. When *Kay, with his typical boorishness, slaps her, Perceval does not defend her, though later, as soon as he dons armour, he vows to avenge her and eventually does. Perceval's problem is not a failure of strength or courage—he easily kills the Red Knight with a javelin—but rather a failure of concern for others besides himself. As Keith Busby has pointed out, the prologue which praises Chrétien's patron, Philip of Flanders, introduces a theme of charity that is central to the romance itself (13–14). And just as Perceval must learn about chivalry, so too must he learn about charity. His education in knightly matters comes from a worthy man named *Gornemant of Gohort. After some training, Perceval shows concern for his mother for the first time. It is unclear exactly how the instruction in arms, at which Perceval has a natural talent, changes the young knight but perhaps the suggestion is that knighthood implies obligation. Before he departs, he is given advice by Gornemant, including the admonition not to keep citing his mother as the source of his knowledge and also the critical advice to 'take care not to be too talkative or too inquisitive' (360).

On his journey, he comes to the castle of *Blancheflor, which is besieged by the forces of Clamadeu, who wants to take her for his bride against her will. Perceval defeats Anguiguerron, Clamadeu's seneschal, and then Clamadeu himself; and he falls in love with Blancheflor. Not only does he act in service of another, but he sends the defeated knights to Arthur with the message that he will avenge the lady whom Kay struck. As he continues his journey to his mother, he meets a man fishing, the *Fisher King, who offers him hospitality. In his castle, Perceval learns that the Fisher King suffers from a wound, and he witnesses the Grail procession: a young man carries a lance with a drop of blood falling from its tip; he is followed by two attendants carrying candelabra; then a young lady passes by carrying a grail, which causes 'such brilliant illumination' that 'the candles lost their brightness just as the stars and the moon do with the appearance of the sun' (379); she, in turn, is followed by a woman carrying 'a silver carving platter' (379). Through all of this, Perceval, remembering Gornemant's advice, remains silent even though he is curious about what he sees. Perceval's childish insistence early in the romance on asking a series of questions 'contrasts strikingly with his failure to ask the single question which would have saved the Fisher King' (Lacy 111).

As is revealed later, had he asked about what he saw—about the meaning of the lance and the Grail and about who is served by the Grail—he could have cured the wounded Fisher King. Although Chrétien never explains why asking the question will effect the cure, the testing of the hero seems to involve his ability to go beyond even the advice of the worthy man who instructed him and thus to act truly independently and empathetically. As the cousin Perceval meets after leaving the castle tells him, his failure is 'because of your sin against your mother, for she died of grief for you' (384). Though there appears to be no logical connection between the two events, there is a suggestion that his lack of concern for his mother is analogous to his lack of concern or compassion for the terrible wound of the Fisher King.

Perceval's failure leaves unexplained just what the Grail is and what its function is. When the Grail first appears, it is not 'the' Grail but 'a' grail. 'The use of the indefinite article *un* (v. 3186) implies the *graal* was not an unknown object in Chrétien's day. . . . this is the earliest significant use of the object (and word) in Old French literature.' Chrétien's grail 'appears to be a slightly concave serving dish, not dissimilar in shape to a modern soup dish . . . which, we learn later, contains a single Host' (Uitti 149 n.3). Jean Frappier has stated unequivocally that 'Nothing authorizes us to believe that Chrétien imagined the *graal* . . . in any other way except as a wide and hollow dish.' Yet this does not mean that it is without religious significance (140–1). In later versions of the story, the Grail is described as the cup used to catch Christ's blood when he hung on the cross, and the lance is identified as *Longinus' spear, with which he pierced Christ's side; but even in later centuries, these interpretations are by no means universal. Some of the master-pieces of Grail literature, like Wolfram von Eschenbach's *Parzival*, adopt a radically different interpretation of the Grail.

Because of the service Perceval has performed by killing the knight who stole a cup from the king's table and insulted the queen, Arthur sets out in search of him. Not far from where the king and his knights pitch their pavilions after the day's journeying, Perceval witnesses a falcon attacking a goose. The wounded bird sheds three drops of blood, which fall on the snow. Perceval is reminded by the red and white 'of the fresh hue on his beloved's face, and he mused until he forgot himself' (391). Squires report the presence of a strange knight to Sir *Sagremor the Unruly, who tries to bring him back to court. In his contemplation, Perceval does not hear Sagremor's command that he go to court and he looks up just in time to see the knight charging at him. When Sagremor is mocked by Kay because Perceval has bested him, Arthur sends his seneschal to fetch Perceval. Kay suffers an even worse fate than Sagremor when he is unhorsed: his collarbone is dislocated and his arm broken in his fall—and in the process Perceval avenges the slap given to the maiden who laughed when he first came to Arthur's court. *Gawain (Gauvain in the French) then accomplishes through courtesy what the others have failed to do with brute force.

This scene is significant for several reasons. It shows a development in the character of the hero since, when Perceval contemplates the three drops of blood on the snow, 'This amorous ecstasy, almost involuntary, is his first sign of introspection' (Frappier 135). The blood is also part of a masterful pattern of analogies in Chrétien's romance. As Norris Lacy notes, 'the blood on the point of the lance prefigures the three drops of blood on the snow, while the bleeding lance reminds us of the one which wounded the Fisher King' (109). The scene also brings together Perceval and Gawain; and the relationship between them, which is 'articulated in this scene, will become a functional element of the plot later in the *Conte du Graal* and, more generally, in much of the Grail corpus' (Armstrong 147).

The bond between Perceval and Gawain remains strong for the rest of the romance. When the two return to Arthur's court and receive praise for their deeds, their moment of triumph is short-lived. A loathly damsel enters to berate Perceval. Chrétien's description of her supports his summary that 'there never was a creature so totally foul, even in hell' (396): her neck is blacker than iron; her eyes small as a rat's; her nose like that of a cat or monkey, and her ears like those of a donkey or cow. In addition, she has yellowed teeth, a beard like a goat's, and a body twisted and deformed. She criticizes Perceval, as his cousin had, for not asking the questions about the lance and Grail that would have healed the Fisher King and prevented his kingdom from becoming a *wasteland. Hard upon this accusation, a knight named Guinganbresil enters and accuses Gawain of treacherously killing his lord.

Consequently, both knights must set out on a quest, Perceval to ask and learn the answers to the questions and Gawain to answer the charge. Their departure begins a long series of adventures for Gawain, in which he performs deeds that no other knight has been able to achieve. For the love of an ill-tongued maiden, he crosses the Perilous Ford. He also endures the test of the Bed of Marvels. After entering the marvellous bed in a castle he has come to, Gawain uses his shield to protect himself from numerous crossbow bolts and arrows shot by unseen archers. When the arrows stop coming, he is attacked by a fierce and hungry lion, which, as Chrétien recounts in a typically apt image, 'planted all its claws in his shield as if it were wax' (433). But in one stroke, Gawain cuts off the lion's paws and its head. By enduring these tests, he dispels the enchantment that has kept a group of ladies, including his mother and Arthur's, prisoners in the castle. Such tests that prove the unique superiority of a knight might be the kind at which the Grail knight would be expected to succeed; but here they are tests that prove the prowess of Gawain and mark him as an exceptional model of chivalry.

While a modern reader might see these adventures of Gawain as a digression from the main plot, they are actually essential. David Fowler has argued that the poem's meaning lies in Perceval's attempt to resolve the conflict between the ideals of prowess and charity (3). In the poem, Gawain is the epitome of courtly values: his courage and courtesy are beyond reproach. But just as Chrétien combines adventures of Gawain and *Lancelot in his *Knight of the Cart* to demonstrate that Lancelot's devotion to the queen is even greater than that of the bravest and most loyal knight, so here Gawain's excellence highlights the area in which Perceval will ultimately surpass him. As Keith Busby has noted, combining the adventures of Perceval with those of Gawain suggests that 'The profane ideal of chivalry needs to be supplemented and completed by spiritual concerns, not destroyed and supplanted' (88).

Perceval must learn the spiritual values, especially charity, that will allow him to put others before himself. After he is berated by the loathly damsel at Arthur's court, he wanders for five years gaining chivalric honour by sending 'as prisoners fifty thousand esteemed knights to King Arthur's court' (415) but forgetting God and failing to do anything to win God's mercy. When he meets five knights escorting a group of ladies on Good Friday, they criticize him for wearing armour on such a holy day. In one of those analogies that, as Norris Lacy has demonstrated, give the poem form and meaning (111) and are part of its very fabric, a reader is reminded of the five knights who directed the young Perceval to Arthur's court and thus initiated his knightly adventures. The knights he meets on Good Friday direct him to a hermit who will begin his spiritual instruction. Just as Perceval had to learn to put on his armour and acquire knightly skills and virtues, so now, as part of the pattern of subjugating his own desires to the needs of others, he must learn to take off his armour and thus to render service to God. The hermit, Perceval's uncle, reminds him that his failure to ask the questions at the Grail castle was due to the fatal grief he caused his mother and gives him penance. Just as Gornemant taught the young knight to go beyond his mother's instruction, so now his uncle teaches him to go beyond even that of the worthy man Gornemant, to look beyond the worldly to the spiritual. Obviously he succeeds, since 'On Easter, Perceval received communion with a pure heart' (418). Whereas in Chrétien's earlier romances, knights had to learn to balance chivalry and love, in his *Perceval* the balance is between chivalric and spiritual values. As one critic has observed, 'the extraordinarily beautiful human *amor* felt by Lancelot for Guenevere, which that protagonist learns to understand in all its implications during the history of his rescue of the queen, is, in *Le Conte du Graal*, transformed into the *caritas*—the highest form of love—according to which Perceval learns to govern his life' (Uitti 124–5).

Chrétien's unfinished romance breaks off in the middle of one of Gawain's adventures and before Perceval can return to the Grail castle, ask the appropriate questions, and heal the Fisher King. But the intriguing story Chrétien created called out for completion; and a number of medieval writers answered that call.

The Continuations and Prologues to Chrétien's *Perceval*
The First Continuation
The first attempt to continue Chrétien's *Perceval* takes up the story where it broke off, in the middle of Gawain's adventures. In fact, this continuation, written around 1200, virtually ignores Perceval. It tells of Gawain's conflict with Guiromelant, his bitter enemy but also the lover of Gawain's sister *Clarissant. Towards the end of the *Perceval*, the two had arranged to meet for combat, in which they now engage. When Guiromelant begins to weaken, Clarissant asks Arthur to stop the battle; but, because of the rules of chivalry, he refuses. At his sister's request, Gawain postpones the battle but says they will fight again the next morning unless Guiromelant retracts his accusation of treachery, which he does not do. Arthur, however, allows Clarissant and Guiromelant to be married, thus forcing peace between the combatants, much to Gawain's chagrin.

To fulfil a promise he had made in the *Perceval*, Gawain then sets off in search of the bleeding lance. After finding the Grail castle and the maimed king and witnessing the Grail procession, he asks the meaning of the lance and the Grail and why the young woman who carried the Grail was weeping; but the king will give him the answers only if he can join the parts of a broken sword. Gawain succeeds in putting the pieces together, but since they can be pulled apart again, his host tells him he has 'not yet achieved enough as a knight to be able to know the truth about these things' (trans. Bryant 113).

Unable to secure the bleeding lance, Gawain returns to Escavalon, where he is to fight with Guigambresil, another knight who accused him of treachery in Chrétien's romance. But on the way he meets and fights with a knight named Disnadaret. Because he is losing, Disnadaret proposes that they suspend the combat until they can meet in front of a court so one of them can win renown. In Escavalon, both Disnadaret and Guigambresil demand the right to combat with Gawain, so the peers of the town rule that he must fight both of them at once. Again Arthur makes peace through marriage, this time by marrying two grand-daughters to the knights.

Gawain has other adventures related to the Grail, including a visit to a chapel where a ghastly hand snuffs out a candle, and another visit to the Grail castle, where he again fails to mend the broken sword. But he does learn that the bleeding lance is 'the very lance with which the son of God, undoubtedly, was struck in the side, right to the heart, on the day when He was hung on the cross. The one who struck Him was called Longinus' (trans. Bryant 113). Gawain is, however, overcome with sleep before he can hear the meaning of the Grail.

In addition to the adventures of Gawain, the First Continuation is noteworthy for an exchange of blows episode analogous to that found in *Sir Gawain and the Green Knight* but involving Carados, not Gawain. As with Gawain in the later Middle English romance, Carados decapitates the challenger, who picks up his severed head and reminds Carados that he will be back in a year. When the knight returns, he reveals to Carados that he is his father and does not return the blow. Carados also participates in a chastity test involving a drinking horn which spills wine on any man who does not have a faithful wife. Only Carados is successful; but afterward, out of fear for *Guinevere's jealousy, he sends his wife away from court.

The First Continuation is, as the varied adventures of Carados and Gawain suggest, quite episodic. Matilda Tomaryn Bruckner has said that the cycle of romances that begins with Chrétien's *Perceval* and progresses through four continuations 'produces a "conte du graal" more interested in middles than ends, a Grail story in which you can always find something more to sandwich in before the inevitable end' (34).

The Second Continuation
The Second Continuation, written shortly after the first (perhaps by the Gauchiers de Dondain, who is identified as the author (cf. l. 31421 in Roach's edition)), returns

to the adventures of Perceval. On his journey, he returns to his mother's house and is 'seized by pity' for her (149)—perhaps a sign that the author is well aware of the spiritual development that was begun by Chrétien—before going back to his uncle for further instruction and penance. Among the things Perceval learns is that he should not be proud of killing other knights, even though the incident that prompts this instruction involves Perceval's fighting to protect his sister.

In a long series of adventures, including combat with Gawain's son, who is called 'the *Fair Unknown', Perceval distinguishes himself; and in one adventure he proves himself to be the best knight. On Mont Dolerous, there is a pillar built by *Merlin for *Uther Pendragon so that 'he could identify. . . the finest knight in his land' (trans. Bryant 186). The test is simple: only the finest knight can tether his horse to the pillar. Many knights had tried and were either grievously injured or driven mad, but Perceval accomplishes the task. Perceval also demonstrates his excellence by crossing an unfinished bridge, which ends halfway across a river. When he rides onto the bridge, the foot of the structure tears itself from one bank and swings around to the other so that he can cross safely, another feat which no one else had been able to achieve.

The Second Continuation culminates in Perceval's return to the Grail castle, where he puts together the broken sword. But there remains 'a very small notch'. This, like Perceval's earlier achievements, confirms that while there is no greater knight 'in combat or in battle', he has 'not yet done enough' to have God bestow on him the traits that would allow him to be considered 'of all knights . . . the most endowed with all high qualities' (192–3).

Gerbert de Montreuil's Continuation
Gerbert de Montreuil's Continuation, sometimes referred to as the Fourth Continuation, was written at about the same time as Manessier's Third Continuation (discussed below), c.1230, but in some manuscripts it is placed between the Second and Manessier's Continuation. In fact, there are various versions and placements of the Continuations in different manuscripts, so the combined texts should not be considered one fixed work. It is also important to recognize that 'the Perceval manuscripts contain no obvious signals to indicate when we pass from Chrétien to the First, Second, or Third Continuation' (Bruckner 37). The result is that some medieval readers read or heard the story as if it were a single work and not a series of different tales.

Gerbert's Continuation begins at the Grail castle after Perceval has put the sword together but left the small notch. Until he can repair the notch, the Fisher King will not tell him about the lance and Grail. But Perceval discovers in his travels after leaving the castle that by asking about the Grail and lance, he has restored a wasted land where 'every spring and river was dry' (198) even though he has not yet learned the answers and cured the king's wound. In this continuation, Perceval performs many new and wondrous deeds, including the passing of new tests to prove that he is the Grail knight. For example, he returns to Arthur's court and sits in an empty seat which has already swallowed up six other knights. Not only does Perceval sit without harm, but the earth opens and restores the six.

The romance contains both a series of adventures, including a lengthy *Tristan episode (referred to as *Tristan menestrel* (*Tristan the Minstrel*)), and a good bit of allegorizing and moralizing, such as attacks on homosexuality and talking in church, before Perceval returns once again to the Fisher King's castle and repairs the notch in the sword as a sign that he is worthy to learn about the Grail and lance.

Manessier's Continuation

About 1230, Manessier wrote his continuation to *Perceval*, sometimes called the Third Continuation. In this conclusion to the story, Perceval learns that the lance of the Grail procession was the one which Longinus used to pierce Christ's side as he hung on the cross, that the Grail was the vessel that *Joseph of Arimathea used to catch the blood that flowed from the wound made by the lance and that was later brought to England, and that the silver trencher was used to cover the Grail so that Christ's blood would be protected. Perceval also learns that the sword he repaired was the one that Partinial the Wild used to kill the Fisher King's brother and which broke from the force of that fatal blow. In his grief over his brother's death, the Fisher King wounded himself in the thighs and was destined to remain helpless until the murder is avenged.

This continuation includes a series of adventures by Perceval, Gawain, and other knights. Perceval once again proves his uniqueness and his sanctity by exorcizing the demonic Black Hand from a chapel, a deed that more than three thousand other knights could not accomplish. Ultimately Perceval meets and defeats Partinial, who is killed because he refuses to ask for mercy. Returning to the Fisher King's castle, Perceval finds him cured. When the Fisher King dies some time later, he leaves his lands to Perceval, who rules for seven years and then retires to a hermitage. The Grail and lance follow him and remain with him until his death, when they follow him again, this time to heaven.

Eric Rohmer's *Perceval le Gallois*

A modern film, Eric Rohmer's *Perceval le Gallois* (1978), provides its own continuation of Chrétien's romance. Of all Arthurian films, Rohmer's is perhaps the closest to its medieval source. In fact, Rohmer was concerned with reproducing 'the Old French text as literally as possible without taxing the modern public's powers to understand the medieval idiom' (Grimbert 34). Gawain's adventures are abbreviated but Perceval's are presented fairly faithfully, in a modernization (with some abridgement) of Chrétien's text, even when that faithfulness requires the characters to shift between third and first person in recounting the narrative.

Rohmer uses simplified, stylized scenery, the effect of which seems appropriate to the continuation/conclusion that he supplies. Following the instruction by his uncle on Good Friday, Perceval observes a pageant depicting the Passion of Christ before he rides off to continue his quest, a quest which is not completed in the film.

Thus the pageant is the final significant action of the film. By ending this way, Rohmer suggests that Perceval has undergone a spiritual rebirth and that 'Chrétien's poem is as implicitly Christian as the prose writers who reworked his romances in the following centuries would have us believe' (Grimbert 40–1). Even the Grail that is carried in procession at the Fisher King's castle seems to reflect the Christianized ending at the same time that it tries to be faithful to the medieval text. The Grail stands on a base like a chalice but is much larger than a drinking cup would be; more like a bowl, it is a cross between the serving dish that is the original meaning of 'grail' and the chalice that it becomes in some versions. Like the medieval continuators, Rohmer provides an ending that takes some of the mystery out of the original poem but that helps to fulfil the director's desire to make the tale accessible to a modern audience.

The *Elucidation*

In addition to the Continuations to *Perceval*, there is a short poem of fewer than five hundred lines called the *Elucidation* which is, as its editor calls it, 'a prologue' to Chrétien's poem. Written early in the thirteenth century, the *Elucidation* tells how the kingdom of *Logres becomes desolate and wasted (87) because a king named Amangon and his vassals deflowered the maidens who served water to travellers at wells and stole the maidens' golden cups. One result of this outrage is that the court of the Fisher King is lost. The knights of the *Round Table must avenge the maidens and find the Fisher King's castle, which Perceval and Gawain do.

Bliocadran

Bliocadran, another early thirteenth-century verse prologue to *Perceval*, elucidates not motifs surrounding the Grail but rather the story of Perceval's father Bliocadran. His fate, in turn, explains why Perceval's mother is so distraught when her son learns about knighthood and decides to leave her protective care and seek out Arthur's court. In spite of having lost eleven brothers to knightly pursuits, Bliocadran is unable to resist fighting in yet another tournament, in which he is killed. Several months later, his wife takes her newborn son to the remote forest so he will be free from the knowledge and influence of knighthood. *Bliocadran* differs in some details from Chrétien's brief account, where Perceval's father, already living in the waste forest, dies from grief when his two sons are killed in combat. But, as the poem's editor comments, 'It makes no difference to the story whether he [Perceval] had two brothers or eleven uncles. They existed only to motivate the mother's terror of chivalry in either account' (Wolfgang in *Bliocadran* 11). Like the *Elucidation*, *Bliocadran* explains only a few of the questions raised by Chrétien's complex poem, but both texts show the interest and popularity of *Perceval* and its importance as a cornerstone of French—and indeed of all later—Grail literature.

Translations and Adaptations of Chrétien's *Perceval*

Chrétien's *Perceval* was translated from French verse into the Old Norse prose *Parcevals saga*, presumably as one of the translations commissioned by King Hákon

Hákonarson, who ruled Norway from 1217 to 1263. The translation is interesting not only as an example of the popularity of Chrétien's work but also because of its approach to the material. Perhaps the most striking feature of the translation is that, though Gawain plays a role in the *Parcevals saga*, a number of his adventures are separated out in a tale called *Valvens þáttr* (*The Tale of Gawain*). This separation may reflect a different view of narrative structure in the saga, which follows the general practice of Old Norse translators of romances by reducing the source 'considerably, especially when it comes to soliloquy, dialogue, descriptive passages', such as descriptions of nature and 'the trappings of courtly society' (Campbell 23). Chrétien's romance and the saga differ in other ways as well. The saga 'lacks not only the wealth of Christian detail and reference of the French version; it lacks genuine religious commitment and shows from the start a predilection for the heroic' (Campbell 34–5).

The saga writer, not content to leave the tale unfinished, wraps things up neatly at the end. After five years of advancing himself in chivalry, Parceval receives instruction from a hermit, then marries Blankiflúr and becomes 'a splendid ruler' who fights and defeats 'all the fiercest knights who were alive in his day' (181–3). He neither returns to the Grail castle nor cures the Fisher King, perhaps in part because the translator did not know what to make of the Grail and its implications. When the Grail appears in the procession in the Fisher King's castle, the translator says that a maiden carried 'in her hands, just as though it were a gospel-book ['*textus*' in the Norse], something which they call in the French language a grail ['*braull*' in the Norse text, which may be a misreading for the word 'Graull' (cf. Kalinke in *Parcevals saga* 213)]' (149). But, the translator adds, 'we may call [it] "processional provision ['*ganganda greiða*' in the Norse]" '. Concerning this explanation, Marianne Kalinke has commented that 'The mystery of the grail is in fact conveyed by the very unintelligibility of the passage, so that a Norwegian or Icelandic audience would have reacted with as much puzzlement as we' (Kalinke 77). At any rate, the tale of Parceval concludes and *Valvens þáttr* opens with the statement that 'the story begins a second time and tells of the great deeds of Sir Gawain and of his travels' (185).

A Dutch translation of *Perceval*, a romance known as *Perchevael*, is one of the cycle of romances called the *Lancelot Compilation. Since this translation is made part of the larger group of tales, it omits the opening sequences depicting the hero's youthful foolishness. More emphasis is placed on the adventures of Wale-wein (Gawain), which are 'supplemented with Gauvain episodes taken from the First *Perceval* Continuation' (Besamusca 89), than on those of Chrétien's hero.

La Nef, a contemporary Canadian group, has adapted Chrétien's romance to a musical setting as *Perceval: la quête du graal*. Using a simplified version of Chrétien's text, the group has created a modern rendition that highlights the main incidents from its source but which sounds at times medieval and at times like modern Gaelic folk music. In her notes to the recording, Katherine A. Dory has observed that the composition is a 'collage' that borrows elements 'from Medieval Play,

Baroque Opera, and more contemporary musical styles' (6). La Nef's *Perceval*, like Rohmer's *Perceval le Gallois*, offers a good example of the way that traditional Arthurian material has been adapted to popular culture.

ROBERT DE BORON AND THE PROSE ADAPTATIONS OF HIS WORK

At some time in the last decade of the twelfth century or the first few years of the thirteenth, Robert de Boron wrote in octosyllabic French verse a romance called *Joseph d'Arimathie*, which is of great importance in the development of the Grail legend and of the Arthurian tradition in general. He also wrote, or at least began, a romance called *Merlin* and perhaps a *Perceval*. One manuscript of the *Joseph* survives, and only a fragment of the *Merlin*; if the verse *Perceval* was written, it is not extant. There are, however, prose adaptations of all three romances. The prose version of the *Joseph*, which survives in fifteen manuscripts and which has been translated into Middle Dutch by Jacob van Maerlant as the *Historie van den Grale*, was 'made in all probability shortly after the composition of the poem' (cf. O'Gorman 450).

Robert's *Joseph* is the first romance to turn Chrétien's mysterious Grail into the now familiar Holy Grail by linking it to the cup used by Christ at the Last Supper and subsequently by Joseph of Arimathea to collect the blood of the crucified Christ. In the process, 'Robert combined and adapted New Testament apocrypha in order to provide an "origin legend" for the Grail and prepare the way, in retrospect, for the guardianship of the sacred vessel to pass into the West and ultimately to Perceval' (Gowans 1). At the end of the *Joseph*, Robert says that he will tie together the various strands of his story, including the fate of *Alain, the son of *Bron (also called Hebron); reveal where the Fisher King went; and tell about Alain and his heir, that is, Perceval (trans. Rogers 59). Robert thus projects for the first time a cycle of romances. Whether or not he actually completed a *Perceval*, he nevertheless outlined a series of stories leading to the completion of the Grail quest, an innovation that led not only to great compilations like the *Vulgate (or Lancelot–Grail) Cycle of French romances but also ultimately to the multi-volume series of novels that are so popular in the twentieth and twenty-first centuries.

The *Perceval* portion of the prose cycle has been referred to as the Didot *Perceval* because one of the two surviving manuscripts of the work, the one first edited (in 1875), was owned by Ambroise Firmin-Didot. Other names (*Perceval or the Quest of the Holy Grail*, the *Prose Perceval*) have been applied to the romance, but Didot *Perceval* is still commonly used, despite the fact that most recent scholars agree that the other manuscript (Modena Biblioteca Estense, E.39) is superior to the Didot. Because the Didot *Perceval* incorporates a 'significant amount of material reworked from Chrétien de Troyes and the Second (*Perceval*) Continuation' and other sources, at least one critic considers it 'a minor masterpiece in its own right' and not just of interest for what 'remnants of a hypothetical lost work by Robert de Boron' it might contain (Pickens 493, 510).

As the cycle develops in the prose version, it tells the history of the Grail and recounts the pre-Arthurian history of Britain, the rise of Arthur to kingship, the quest for the Grail, and even the downfall of Arthur's kingdom through *Mordred's treachery. The *Joseph* begins with a reference to the Fall and the Redemption (trans. Bryant 15), which sets the entire story in the context of sacred history, just as the reference to the fall of Troy at the beginning of *Sir Gawain and the Green Knight* sets that tale in the context of Britain's heroic past. This context suggests the much more Christian interpretation of the Grail and of the story of Arthur and his knights that informs the cycle. Joseph is said to be a soldier in the service of Pontius Pilate, who, as a reward for his loyalty, is allowed to bury the body of Christ after the Crucifixion. Pilate also gives Joseph the vessel used by Christ at the Last Supper. After Christ is taken from the cross, Joseph gathers the blood dripping from his wounds in this vessel, which is thus sanctified and becomes the Holy Grail. Other relics of the Crucifixion also play a vital part in the cycle. The cloth with which Veronica wiped the face of Jesus cures Vespasian, the son of the Emperor Titus, of leprosy and leads them to free Joseph from imprisonment and to punish the Jews responsible for the Crucifixion. And it is revealed in *Perceval* that the bleeding lance of the Grail procession is the spear with which Longinus pierced Christ's side while he hung on the cross (trans. Bryant 155). Even the Round Table is linked to the Grail and to spiritual history: it is modelled after the table of the Last Supper and the table of the Grail company established by Joseph of Arimathea. Just as one seat at the original table was left open because of Judas's betrayal, so one seat at Joseph's table was kept empty. When the unworthy Moyse sits in it, the earth opens and swallows him. Similarly, the *Siege Perilous at the Round Table remains empty— until Perceval sits in it. Since Perceval has not yet demonstrated the necessary virtue and prowess to achieve the Grail, the earth groans and splits, and the stone will not be mended where he sat until he perfects himself. A voice tells Arthur and the court that only because of the goodness of Perceval's father and grandfather was he saved from falling into the abyss and dying the terrible death that Moyse did (trans. Bryant 118).

In the second part of the cycle, the birth of Merlin becomes incorporated into the sacred history of the Grail. The devils, angered that Christ has harrowed hell and led the souls of the just to heaven, plot to have one of their number impregnate a woman on earth so that she can bear a child who will help them 'to deceive men and women alike, just as the prophets worked against us' by warning people to lead holy lives in preparation for Christ's incarnation (trans. Bryant 46). The woman the devils select to impregnate—after destroying her parents, her brother, and her two sisters—is actually a good woman who is instructed by a holy confessor. But one night, angry with her sister, she forgets to make the sign of the cross before going to bed, thus giving a demon the opportunity to impregnate her. The plan of the devils goes awry, however, when the child, Merlin, free to decide 'which way he inclined', chooses good rather than evil. As the son of a devil, Merlin has knowledge of the past; and he is given knowledge of the future by God because 'Our Lord . . . did not wish to punish the child for his mother's sin' (trans. Bryant 55). Nor is the mother punished, since her young son's wisdom and knowledge of past and future save her from condemnation. Her confessor, named *Blaise, is directed by Merlin to retire to Northumberland and to write the history that Merlin periodically reports to him. The *Merlin* portion of the cycle also tells the story of the sword in the stone and has Merlin continue to advise the royal family in the person of Arthur after Uther's death.

The account of Arthurian prehistory in which Merlin assists Uther and his brother Pendragon and the story of Merlin's birth, youth, and revelation to *Vortigern that his tower will not stand because of the red and white dragons battling beneath it are significant additions to the sacred history of the Grail. They demonstrate that Robert's poems and the prose adaptations of his work rely not only on Grail material but also on a variety of sources that they combine into a fairly well-unified cycle.

The cycle's *Perceval* uses material from Chrétien as well as from the Second Continuation but includes much that is in neither of these sources. Before his death, Perceval's father Alain told him about Arthur's court; and although Perceval has a certain naïveté when he first arrives there, he is nothing like the fool Chrétien depicts. He greets Arthur 'most nobly' and not with the childish insistence on his own demands that Chrétien's Grail hero displays. He is also said to grow 'much in wisdom and courtesy' at Arthur's court because 'when he left his mother's house he knew nothing' (trans. Bryant 115), though there is no narrative demonstration of that ignorance.

Perceval does require two visits to the Grail castle to achieve his quest. As in Chrétien, he fails to ask the appropriate question on his first visit because, 'remembering how his mother had told him not to talk too much or ask too many questions', Perceval 'was afraid of upsetting his host' (trans. Bryant 141). After spending seven years seeking the Fisher King but giving no thought to God, he meets pilgrims on Good Friday and comes to his spiritual senses. But even after a visit to his hermit uncle, he is distracted by the lure of a tournament until Merlin reminds him that he has broken his vow not to stay more than one night in the same place until he reaches the Fisher King's castle again. Leaving immediately, Perceval arrives there directly, this time asking the questions without hesitation and then assuming the role of Fisher King.

The achieving of the Grail is not, however, the end of the story. For this romance returns to Arthur, who is shown conquering France and killing its king. The Emperor of Rome is enraged by such treatment of his vassal and demands tribute from Arthur, who responds by leading an expedition to the continent. The religious aspect of the cycle is not totally ignored in this section: the emperor allies himself with the sultan, who brings 50,000 Saracens to assist in the fight against Arthur; and the emperor 'transgressed mightily against God and Holy Church, for he took the Sultan's daughter for his wife—a beautiful woman indeed, but an infidel' (trans. Bryant 165–6). In the ensuing battle, both the emperor and the sultan are killed; but the triumphal march to Rome, where Arthur is to be crowned as emperor, is forestalled by news of Mordred's treachery. Arthur's nephew has married Guinevere, allied himself with the Saxons, and even 'banned the singing of mass or matins'. During the landing on Britain's shore, Gawain is killed when 'a Saxon wielding an oar dealt him a blow to the head that struck him dead' (trans. Bryant 169–70). Ultimately, Arthur pursues Mordred to Ireland and slays him but is himself grievously wounded and taken to *Avalon to be healed by his sister *Morgan. So strong is the belief in his return that the people of Britain wait forty years before naming another king.

Sacred and secular history are combined as the story of the Grail becomes part of the story of Arthur and his knights in a cycle which, despite its scope, has numerous wonderful narrative details. For example, when the Fisher King Bron dies, Perceval looks up and sees 'David with his harp and a great host of angels with censers waiting to receive Bron's soul' (trans. Bryant 155–6). When Arthur fights Floire, the King of France, the entire battle is brilliantly described. One mighty blow from Floire is presented almost in slow motion: he strikes Arthur's shield, splitting it and cutting off a chunk of it; as Floire's sword crashes down, 'it smashed three hundred rings from Arthur's mailcoat and cut into his thigh, taking with it a handful or more of flesh, and down it came still, severing a spur and three toes from his foot before it plunged a full yard into the earth' (trans. Bryant 159). By uniting the story of the Grail with an account of Arthur's life from birth to death, Robert de Boron and the prose adaptation of Boron's work made a significant contribution to the development of the Arthurian legend.

PERLESVAUS

Perlesvaus

Perlesvaus, also known as The High History of the Holy Grail, is a prose romance probably written in the first decade of the thirteenth century (though there are a variety of opinions about its date) which claims to be translated into French from a Latin original written by Josephes. Perlesvaus (meaning 'he lost the vales') is so named by his father, Alain le Gros, so that his name will be a reminder that 'the Lord of the Fens had taken from him the greater part of the Vales of Kamaalot' (30), which is not the *Camelot where Arthur held court, as the author explains (197). And ultimately Perlesvaus does punish the Lord of the Fens for his appropriation of the family lands.

It is true that 'Perlesvaus is, in one sense at least, a "sequel" ' to Chrétien's Perceval, even though there are 'major differences between the two works' (Kelly 25). For example, Perlesvaus's mother is alive through most of the narrative. The romance begins, however, after great misfortune has befallen Britain because of 'just a few words which [a good knight] neglected to say' (19). Yet while recognizably influenced by and following from *Perceval*, *Perlesvaus* differs in tone and theme from its predecessor. The Grail is clearly the cup in which Joseph of Arimathea gathered Christ's blood, and the poem is explicitly, sometimes militantly, Christian. The spreading of the New Law and the protection of the Grail family justify a great deal of bloodshed. As Peggy McCracken has observed, 'There are an astonishing number of human heads requested, offered, carried around, and disputed in the *Perlesvaus*' and 'Decapitation is only one dismemberment among many in...a romance...obsessed with blood, murder, decapitation, dead bodies, and their mutilation' (339, 341). In fact, reading *Perlesvaus*, one is struck by the brutality of the work, in which even the Grail knight kills and tortures, almost with glee. When Perlesvaus learns that the Lord of the Fens is attacking his mother's castle, he defeats him in combat, cutting off his right arm in the process; but he does not kill him immediately. First he has eleven of the lord's knights beheaded and collects their blood in a large vat. Then Perlesvaus has the lord hung by his feet over the vat, immersed up to his shoulders, and 'held there until he drowned to death' (151–2).

Perlesvaus is an interesting development in Arthurian romance because it contains not only the adventures of Perlesvaus and of Gawain (Gavain in the French text) but also those of Lancelot, one of which is a beheading contest analogous to that in *Sir Gawain and the Green Knight*. After cutting off the head of his challenger, Lancelot must undergo a similar blow a year later (although this is delayed). It is not the knight Lancelot has struck but his brother who, like the Green Knight, is sharpening his axe on a whetstone and who strikes a blow from which Lancelot flinches. As the knight prepares to deliver a second blow, a maiden whom Lancelot has assisted begs for his life and the knight grants her wish. He tells Lancelot that twenty other knights have begun a similar contest against members of his family but not one came to receive the return blow. Had Lancelot not been true to his word, his family would have, for some unexplained reason, lost their city and castles forever.

As Lancelot prepared for the blow, he wept, for only the second time since he became a knight, at the thought of never seeing Guinevere again. The inclusion of the love of Lancelot and Guinevere is a noteworthy feature of this Grail romance. As he nears the Grail castle, Lancelot confesses to a hermit, to whom he admits that he repents of all his sins but one, his love of the queen. When the hermit criticizes him, Lancelot says that 'never again' will he 'confess it to any man on earth' (110), an amazing statement in this very religious romance. Because of his intransigence, when Lancelot comes to the Fisher King's castle, the Grail does not appear at the feast, even though it appears when Gawain, who is linked with Lancelot by the Hermit King as 'the finest knights in the world but for their lust' (167), visits. Thus Lancelot's lust—or, from another perspective, his love—is greater. Lancelot's major role in the adventures and the emphasis on his love for Guinevere are clear steps towards those longer cycles and romances, like the Vulgate Cycle and Malory's *Morte d'Arthur*, in which Lancelot's love is central.

As in many of the romances in which Gawain is prominent, Kay is also an important figure. In *Perlesvaus*, however, his role extends beyond that of the rude and boastful knight who is a poor judge of character. Here he kills *Loholt, Arthur and Guinevere's son, who has slain a giant, and claims the glory himself by cutting off the giant's head and bringing it back to court as proof that he did the deed (141). Later, when his crime is discovered, Kay flees to Brittany where he allies himself with Arthur's enemy, Brien of the Isles, and even participates in an attack on Arthur's kingdom before retiring to his own castle, Chinon, in Brittany.

Despite moving towards a cycle of stories encompassing all of Arthurian history, *Perlesvaus* remains a Grail romance. As such, it contains stories of sacred relics like the crown of thorns set in gold and precious gems; Joseph of Arimathea's shield, acquired by Perlesvaus, which has special protective properties because some of Christ's blood and a piece of his clothing are sealed in its boss; and the sword that beheaded St John the Baptist, which bleeds each day at noon because that is the hour at which John was killed (131, 162, 69). But it is a strange Grail romance, not only because its hero can be more brutal than Grail knights are expected to be, but also because Perlesvaus does not even entertain the possibility of curing the Fisher King, who dies before Perlesvaus has an opportunity to return to his castle a second time to ask the healing questions (147). Yet Perlesvaus demonstrates his worthiness to be the Grail knight in many adventures throughout the romance, by remaining chaste throughout his life (a virtue that becomes even more crucial in later Grail literature), and in the end by recovering the Grail castle from his one wicked uncle, the King of the Castle Mortal, who, when he realizes that Perlesvaus has triumphed, climbs to the highest part of the castle and 'stabbed himself right through the body and tumbled over the wall and into the river, swift and deep' (171).

After more adventures, Perlesvaus returns to the Grail castle where he remains until a voice tells him to divide its sacred relics among holy hermits; then a ship with a red cross on its white sail comes to take him away, 'and from that time forth no earthly man ever knew what became of him' (264). Because *Perlesvaus* deviates quite radically from the Grail stories told by Chrétien and Malory, it has not been the most influential of romances, though parts of it have been adapted in several works. *Perlesvaus* may have had some influence on the French romance *Mériadeuc* and was the source of one episode in *Fouke Fitz Warin*; and it may have been one of many sources used by Malory (cf. Field). In addition, it was translated into Welsh and was the source for a modern novel.

Y Seint Greal

Y Seint Greal, a Middle Welsh prose Grail romance, translates two French Grail stories. The first part is a rendition of the Vulgate *Queste del Saint Graal*, and the second of *Perlesvaus*, which despite 'their incompatibilities—Galaad is the Grail hero in the *Queste*, Perlesvaus in the second romance, and the concepts of Christian and knightly duty are strikingly different—... are presented as two parts of a single whole' (Lloyd-Morgan 195–6). At least, the *Perlesvaus* portion declares itself to be 'the second part' (*Y Seint Greal* 547) of the story of the Grail. But since *Peredur (the Welsh name given to Perceval) has just died and been buried by Bort (*Bors), it is difficult to think that the translator did not recognize and expect his reader to recognize the great differences in the two tales and see them, as contemporary readers do, as two stories united only by the fact that they both focus on the Grail and both include Peredur as a Grail knight.

Dorothy James Roberts's *Kinsmen of the Grail*

In addition to the medieval works influenced by *Perlesvaus*, one modern novel, Dorothy James Roberts's *Kinsmen of the Grail* (1963), draws much of its material from the romance. The novel tells of Gawin's fateful encounter with the young Percival, who has been kept ignorant of knights and chivalry by a mother who fears that he, like her husband and her other sons, will be killed in combat. Of course, nothing can prevent Percival from fulfilling his destiny. With Gawin's help, he becomes a knight; and he pulls a sword from a pillar, a deed that marks him as the chosen Grail knight. Although initially he fails to ask the question that will allow him to achieve the Grail, he ultimately succeeds. *Kinsmen of the Grail* has a multifaceted view of the Grail, which Percival says is 'a cup, first the cup of earth's bounty, then the cup of the shed blood of death, then the cup of the seed of resurrection. And at last is it the cup of the divine union of death and resurrection' (282–3). Thus Roberts blends interpretations of the Grail as fertility symbol and Christian icon.

The Grail quest is set against a background of political intrigues, in which Kei, as in the French romance, is the villain who murders Arthur and Guinevere's son Loholt. In the end, Gawin seems destined not to continue his quest for the Grail but to serve Arthur and Britain as a warrior; and so he and *Yvain swear an oath to destroy Kei. The focus and the conclusion of the novel are different from those of its source, yet it is an interesting adaptation of a medieval romance to the form and conventions of modern fiction.

PEREDUR AND SIR PERCEVAL OF GALLES

Peredur

The Welsh romance *Peredur* survives in four manuscripts from the fourteenth century, but the text was probably written in the thirteenth century and draws on elements that are even older. Part of the story is analogous to material in Chrétien's *Perceval*, though there are also portions unlike anything in the French romance. Peredur is raised in seclusion by his mother because her husband and six other sons have been killed in battle. When Peredur encounters three knights and determines to leave the refuge of his mother's home, she advises him to go to Arthur's court. As in *Perceval*, Peredur takes a ring and a kiss from a lady, for which she is punished until the hero can set things right. At court, two characters speak, in this case a male and a female dwarf, who have not spoken for a year. Cei strikes the male and kicks the female; and Peredur must ultimately avenge them. The young hero gets his armour by killing with his spear a knight who has insulted Arthur and Gwenhwyfar by stealing a goblet and pouring its contents on the queen. Also like Perceval, Peredur is instructed by two men as he moves from following his mother's advice to acting on his own; and he contemplates drops of blood on the snow, which remind him of his beloved. Gwalchmei (the Welsh equivalent of Gawain) is accused of treachery, just as Peredur is berated by a hag, and has other adventures, though not nearly so many as in *Perceval*.

On the other hand, many things mark *Peredur* as different from *Perceval*. As Ian Lovecy has observed, *Peredur*'s style, though not consistent throughout the romance, 'is in general much less discursive and descriptive than the French' (176). But the most obvious difference is that *Peredur* is not a Grail romance. Peredur encounters a kind of Fisher King, a lame man sitting on a cushion on the shore while youths fish in a boat. This man, who is Peredur's uncle, advises him not to ask questions if he sees strange things and tells him that 'Not upon thee will the fault be, but upon me, for I am thy teacher' (*Peredur* 191). Peredur then comes to the hall of another uncle, where he sees a strange procession, parallel to but different from the Grail procession in *Perceval*. He watches as two youths bear a large spear with 'three streams of blood along it' followed by two maidens carrying a great salver with a man's head on it 'and blood in profusion around the head' (192). As instructed by the first uncle, Peredur does not inquire about this strange sight even though everyone in the hall is shrieking in lamentation. As in *Perceval*, when the hero returns to Arthur's court, an ugly maiden rides in and berates Peredur for not asking the meaning of the marvels since that would have given health to the lame king (thus confusing or conflating the two uncles, because the one who was lame was not the same one in whose hall the procession took place) and brought peace to the kingdom. Her criticism seems stranger here than in *Perceval* or Wolfram's *Parzival* since he was not only warned that he should not ask about strange things but also assured that he would receive no blame for not asking. Even stranger still is the fact that at the end of the romance, Peredur's male cousin says that it was he who came 'in the guise of' the hag to Arthur's court (226).

Peredur ends abruptly with the hero slaying the witches of Caer Loyw, who taught him to ride and to handle his weapons (199) and who had slain one of Peredur's cousins, whose head was carried on the salver (226). These and other details of the story suggest that its author was drawing on various sources. For example, at one point Peredur rules with the Empress of Constantinople for fourteen years. In other episodes, he fights mythic beasts. Thus the world of *Peredur* seems less stable and consistent than that of Chrétien's romances, more the realm of a fairy tale or a dream. Clearly, *Peredur* differs from *Perceval* even as it shares with the French romance so many episodes and details that it must be, at the least, drawing on some of the same narratives that inspired Chrétien.

Sir Perceval of Galles

The Middle English verse romance *Sir Perceval of Galles*, like *Peredur*, has much in common with Chrétien's account of Perceval but omits any reference to the Grail. This omission has prompted the question of whether or not the tale's author knew Chrétien's version of the story. David Fowler contends that the author of *Sir Perceval of Galles* was indeed familiar with Chrétien's romance and that his omission of the Grail episode 'represents a daring innovation, an intentional change' (6), but Fowler's opinion is not universally held.

Elements of the romance are analogous to ones found in Chrétien's *Perceval*; but the English poem has a comic tone, a simplicity of verse, and a simplification of the plot and the themes that mark it as a different kind of work. For example, 'not only is the hero's spiritual progress ignored, but his initiation into knighthood, such an important theme of Chrétien's work, is hardly even hinted at' (Busby 601). The only education in knighthood occurs when Perceval learns that the horse he is riding is called a mare. This becomes a running joke in the text as Perceval thinks all horses are called mares; in the midst of his climactic battle with the sultan, he hears the word 'steed' for the first time (52) and ponders the name deeply, in a scene perhaps inspired by Perceval's contemplation of his beloved when he sees the drops of blood on the snow in *Perceval* (Fowler 17).

Even before Perceval kills the sultan, his prowess is amply demonstrated. He slays so many of the sultan's Saracens besieging the castle of Lufamour, who later becomes his wife, that their skulls bounce like hailstones (their 'hede-bones | hop als dose hayle-stones', in the nicely alliterative Middle English) (39). And his first demonstration of his knightly ability is, as in Chrétien, the killing of the Red Knight. In the English poem, the Red Knight has killed Perceval's father and thus his slaying is also an act of vengeance, though Perceval is not aware of it. In addition to avoiding the complications that a revenge theme might create, the author also makes the scene a comic tour de force. Perceval is able to kill the Red Knight with a javelin through his eye because he raises his visor the better to see the simpleton clad in goat skins who has challenged him. When the knight falls dead, Perceval speaks to him as if he were still alive, and then, believing that the Red Knight would continue the fight if he had his 'mare', Perceval runs after it on foot because his own mare is pregnant and cannot run fast enough. When the knight still does not move, Perceval decides to take his armour but cannot get it off, so he makes a fire to burn him out of it. After Sir Gawain arrives and helps Perceval remove the armour, he throws the Red Knight in the fire anyway, a fortunate decision since his mother is a witch who could have brought him back to life had his body not been burned.

This scene exemplifies what critics have called the 'liveliness' (Eckhardt 218 and Braswell in *Sir Perceval* 2) of *Sir Perceval of Galles*, which is an appealing tale even if its verse and themes do not rise to the level of Chrétien's. It is also a 'symmetrically constructed' poem (Eckhardt 216), in which the hero returns to the forest and the clothing of his youth, as he seeks, finds, and cures his mother Acheflour, King

Arthur's sister in this romance, who was driven mad when she believed him dead. In his humbling of himself and returning to his roots, David Fowler has suggested, there occurs a 'secularization of the Grail theme' (18). Whether or not its author knew Chrétien and whether or not he intentionally secularized the Grail story, *Sir Perceval of Galles* is an often comic and always entertaining reworking of the story of Perceval.

Tyolet and Related Tales

Tyolet

Tyolet, a sometimes funny, sometimes bloody French lay from the late twelfth century, was obviously influenced by *Perceval*. The title character is a youth who, like Chrétien's hero, is brought up in seclusion by his mother after the death of his father. Tyolet has been taught by a fairy to attract animals with a whistle, but he has learned nothing of the ways of the world. When he encounters a knight by chance and desires to become a knight himself, his mother does not discourage him but rather gives him armour and advises him to go to Arthur's court. There, a maiden enters and offers herself to the knight who will cut off the white foot of a stag. Many knights fail in this quest but Tyolet whistles seven times and the stag stands still, at which point he cuts off its foot. The stag's cry brings the seven lions which guard it. Tyolet slays the lions, is badly wounded, and entrusts the white foot to a knight who rides up. But the knight treacherously stabs Tyolet, leaves him for dead, and rides off to claim the maiden. Gawain, suspicious when the brachet the maiden gave Tyolet to hunt the stag returns without him, finds Tyolet, arranges for a leech to heal him, and returns to accuse the villainous knight. Just as Gawain is about to meet the knight's challenge, Tyolet returns. Rather than risk death in combat, his attacker confesses and is pardoned by Tyolet, who in turn marries the beautiful maiden.

The lay has in common with the story of Perceval the youth's sheltered upbringing, the death of the father, a quest that only the hero can achieve, and the sharing of the adventure with Gawain. Of course, *Tyolet* is not an account of a Grail quest; but it is an instance of an author's adapting motifs from the Perceval story or a tale analogous to it to another knight.

Lanceloet en het hert met de witte voet

Tyolet or a Middle Dutch version of it (see Claassens 173) was adapted as the Dutch verse romance *Lanceloet en het hert met de witte voet* (*Lancelot and the Stag with the White Foot*), which tells of the maiden's request to Arthur that a knight acquire the white foot of a stag. In this case, Lanceloet obtains the foot and entrusts it to a treacherous knight. As in the French romance, Walewein (Gawain) finds his wounded companion and reveals the treachery; but it is also Walewein who kills the wicked knight. Since Lanceloet wins the hand of the maiden by completing the quest, the plot demands that the marriage be deferred.

Moriaen

The Middle Dutch romance *Moriaen*, which dates from the latter half of the thirteenth century, presents a title character who is a member of the family of Perceval (Perchevael in the Dutch), the son of Perceval's brother *Agloval (Acglavael in the Dutch); and some critics contend that 'in an earlier version of the *Moriaen*, Perchevael was the hero's father' (Haan 43). Whether or not this is the case, much of the action takes place while Lancelot and Gawain are searching for Perchevael, and their quest is paralleled by Moriaen's quest for his father.

Gawain is a central figure in the narrative, as he is in most of the Dutch Arthurian romances. Described repeatedly as the 'Father of Adventure' (60, 61, 67, etc.), he is presented as a knight who can read and who is skilled at healing as well as one who does great deeds of valour. Moriaen's rescue of Gawain, who has been treacherously deprived of his sword and his horse, is one of the principal ways he proves himself a worthy member of Arthurian society, despite the fact that his black skin colour (like his armour, his skin is 'blacker than soot or pitch' (115)) and great size make him an object of fear to many he meets.

Lancelot too has a major role in the narrative, in an adventure similar to that in *Lancelot and the Stag with the White Foot*, though in this instance he slays 'the most fell beast ever man heard or read of', a beast that is 'the Foul Fiend himself' (46). A maiden who lives in the land ravaged by the beast has promised to wed whoever kills it. When Lancelot does so, a traitorous knight wounds the weakened Lancelot and cuts off the right foot of the beast to prove that he was its slayer. Gawain arrives just as the villain is about to ride off and, at Lancelot's request, kills him. Gawain then brings Lancelot to a hermit's hut, where Moriaen awaits and where Gawain's brother Gariët has brought news that Arthur has been captured and the queen is besieged by the King of Ireland.

Moriaen, Lancelot, Gawain, and Perceval arrive just in time to defeat the attackers in a battle in which Moriaen leads the vanguard and to capture the King of Ireland, whom they force to surrender Arthur. Moriaen then leads Agloval, who has promised to wed the woman he left years before, back to 'the Moorish land' (145). The romance does not end with the wedding, however, as might be appropriate; but since it is part of the large collection known as the *Lancelot Compilation*, it acknowledges in its conclusion the return of Gawain and Lancelot to Camelot for the Pentecost feast at which *Galahad is knighted and sits in the Siege Perilous and then goes on to achieve the Grail. So even though *Moriaen* is a romance that focuses on the family of Perceval and has as its central character Agloval's son, it recognizes that primacy in the Grail quest was passing to Lancelot's son.

Clemence Housman's *The Life of Sir Aglovale de Galis*

While Agloval is generally a minor character, as in *Moriaen* and Malory's *Morte d'Arthur*, in one modern novel, *The Life of Sir Aglovale de Galis* (1905) by Clemence Housman (1861–1955), sister of A. E. Housman, he is the protagonist. Housman builds her novel on the frame of the relatively few references to Aglovale provided by Malory, whom she acknowledges as her source and to whom she repeatedly refers as 'my most dear Master' or 'he whom I love so much'. Though flawed, Aglovale is a worthy knight who is not recognized as such because he puts truth above reputation. He is also free of the petty grudges that motivate so many of the other knights. After *Agravaine and *Gaheris try to make him a victim of the feud between their family and the family of *Pellinore by drowning him, he saves the two brothers from a similar fate and never reveals his magnanimous deed. When, much later, Gaheris learns that it was Aglovale who rescued them, he says to him 'Hell would be an empty hole, if only God Almighty can be as greatly merciful as you' (285). Though Aglovale is sometimes at odds with the ways of knighthood, the best of the knights come to realize that he lives by a code that is superior to theirs. He also proves himself worthy of his relationship to the Grail knight Percivale, whom he raised.

George Moore

Another British novelist, George Moore (1852–1933), tells, as does *Tyolet*, of a character analogous in many ways to Perceval. In *Peronnik the Fool* (1926), Moore writes of the simple Peronnik, who is able to succeed in a quest in which many other knights have failed, obtaining from the sorceress Redemonde a Diamond Spear and a Golden Bowl that provides food and drink and all kinds of wealth. He is successful in large part because he is a fool, unschooled in the ways and the desires of the more worldly knights. The spear he retrieves is instrumental in restoring the wasteland that his native region has become. The tale was originally part of Moore's *Héloïse and Abélard* (1921), where it is said that Héloïse wrote it to teach French to her son, who spoke Breton; but the Peronnik section was excised from that novel because it distracted from the main plot.

WOLFRAM VON ESCHENBACH AND HIS INFLUENCE

Parzival

One of the masterpieces of medieval Arthurian literature is Wolfram von Eschenbach's Grail romance *Parzival*, composed in rhyming couplets in the first decade of the thirteenth century. Wolfram says he is writing his tale because Chrétien 'did not do justice' to the story of the Grail (430), presumably because he left his tale incomplete and as a result many things, even the nature of the Grail itself, were not clarified. Though much of his romance is based on Chrétien's, Wolfram claims to be working from a better version of the story, one written by a poet named Kyot. Wolfram identifies this almost assuredly fictional author as a Provençal poet writing in French a version of a story originally composed in Arabic (224).

Among the most obvious changes that Wolfram makes to Chrétien's version of the Grail story is to supply an ending, in which Parzival returns to the Grail castle

*Munsalvaesche and brings the quest to completion. He also adds two books to the beginning of the story detailing the history and exploits of Parzival's father Gahmuret. Chivalry and love are essential parts of Gahmuret's story, as they are of the entire romance, including the deeds of Parzival, the Grail knight. Gahmuret has an insatiable desire for knightly adventure, which leads him to leave his own land and to fight in the cause of Belcane, Queen of Zazamanc, with whom he falls in love. The result of their union is a child *Feirefiz, who, because his mother was black and his father white, is piebald.

Despite his love, Gahmuret leaves Belcane in search of further adventure. His travels take him to Wales, where he wins Herzeloyde and her lands in a tournament. After marrying her, he continues his quest for adventure and dies fighting again in the east, in support of the Baruch of Baghdad. His death is the result of treachery: a knight poured 'a tall glass filled with he-goat's blood...on the diamond helmet [of Gahmuret], whereat the helmet became softer than a sponge' (59) and left him vulnerable to a fatal blow.

The death of her husband causes Herzeloyde to withdraw from the world, to raise Parzival in isolation, and to keep him ignorant of knighthood and combat. But by chance the boy encounters a man named Karnahkarnanz, whom he thinks must be God. When Parzival discovers that Karnahkarnanz is a knight, he sets out to become a knight himself. Leaving his sheltered home with only his mother's advice to guide him, Parzival must learn about the world, about knighthood, and ultimately about the Grail before he can fulfil his destiny. He is instructed by a knight named Gurnemanz, who tells him, among other things, not to ask too many questions, a fateful bit of advice since Parzival remembers it in the presence of the wounded Grail King *Anfortas and thus refrains from asking the question that would cure him.

In the course of his narrative, Wolfram explains much more than Chrétien did about the nature of the Grail and about Anfortas, the wounded king. The Grail is not the vessel that it is in Chrétien's romance; nor is it the cup of the Last Supper. Rather it is a stone called 'lapsit exillis', a phrase which has inspired much commentary and explanation. (These views are summarized in Friedrich Ranke's essay on 'The Symbolism of the Grail in Wolfram von Eschenbach'; Ranke suggests that the name comes from the 'lapis exilis' in an episode of the Alexander legend, which is a reminder to the conqueror of the need for humility (371–3).) The stone is so powerful that it allows the phoenix to rise from its own ashes; and anyone who sees it will not die within a week, no matter how ill he or she might be. Nor will that person age or change in appearance. The Grail also provides food and drink of any sort. Every Good Friday, a dove from Heaven deposits a small white wafer on the stone, from which the Grail gets its power (351–2).

It is by the power of the Grail that Anfortas has been sustained despite being wounded by a poisoned spear when he fought in the service of love rather than of the Grail. In the ethic of this romance, love inspires and ennobles—Parzival himself says that he suffers grief 'for the Grail, after that, for my own wife' (251); and the narrator comments that 'the Grail's power will sustain him. Love, too, will afford him protection' (385)—but the Grail King, though permitted to be married, should have been fighting only in service of the Grail. Wounded by a heathen, Anfortas returned to Munsalvaesche, where his life was preserved by the Grail but his pain became so great that he wished he could die. At times when the wound is particularly painful, Anfortas is carried to a lake 'for the sake of the sweet air and for the sake of his bitter, gaping pain. . . . From this came the rumor that he was a fisherman' (262) and the designation 'Fisher King'; but just as the painful wound prevents him from standing or lying, it also prevents him from actually fishing.

Parzival learns about the Fisher King, as he must learn of spiritual matters, from the hermit Trevrizent (brother of Parzival's mother and of Anfortas), who teaches him what he needs to know to complete his quest. Trevrizent's instruction balances that given by Gurnemanz in worldly and chivalric matters. That Parzival needs such instruction is made clear first of all by his failure to ask the question that will heal the wounded king. 'Both Trevrizent and Parzival, when he finally realizes his sin (488, 17), consider the crime to consist in a lack of feeling in the face of true sorrow' (Sacker 54). Indeed, the change Wolfram makes in the question Parzival is expected to ask is indicative of this failing: 'If the question which Chrestien's Perceval failed to ask was one of information ("Who is served with the Grail?" "Why does the lance bleed?"), the question that Wolfram's Parzivâl failed to ask was one of compassion, i.e., a question as to the nature of the Grail King's suffering (namely: "Uncle, what is it that troubles you?")' (Poag 61). Parzival surely has the innate qualities necessary to achieve the quest. A knight cannot fight his way to the Grail castle; he must be called there by heaven, and Parzival is the chosen knight. Yet on his first visit to the castle, he does not ask the question and as a result is subjected to much criticism and even abuse, particularly from *Cundrie, who is the messenger or spokesperson for the Grail.

When Parzival arrived at Arthur's court, Cunneware, who could not laugh until she saw him to whom the highest praise is given, laughed; and Antanor, who similarly would not speak, spoke. For these acts, they were struck by Keie (Kay). On his return to Arthur's court, Parzival punishes Keie for those blows, and he is made a knight of the Round Table. At this moment of great personal triumph, the hag Cundrie rides in on her mule and berates him. Though Cundrie is extremely learned, with knowledge of languages, dialectic, geometry, and even astronomy, and richly dressed, she has 'hair so long that it touched the mule. It was black and hard. . . . She had a nose like a dog's, and two boar's teeth stuck out from her mouth, each a span in length. Both eyebrows were braided. . . . Cundrie had ears like a bear's and no lover could desire a face like hers, hairy and rough.' And her fingernails are like a lion's claws (169–70). Even more shocking than her appearance is the message she brings: that Parzival is not worthy of the honours bestowed upon him, that he is 'so shy of manly honor and so sick in knightly virtue that no physician can cure' him, that he is unworthy of the sword his host gave him, that he is guilty of 'the sin supreme', and that his 'fame has turned to falseness' (171). Nor is

Cundrie the only one to berate Parzival for his failing; his own cousin Sigune, whose tragic love for Schionatulander is alluded to several times, echoes Cundrie's sentiments.

Cundrie's criticism spurs Parzival to embark on another quest so he can set right that which has caused him shame. Parzival still has much to learn. He even acknowledges a hatred for God, whom he blames for causing his sorrow (242). And yet he has enough faith to give his horse free rein in the hope that God will show him the way that is best for him. This act embodies the trust in Divine Providence that underlies all errantry: Divine Providence directs the wanderings of the knight to make them purposeful and to lead him where he is meant to be. This is just what Parzival's mount does, as he bears him to the dwelling of 'the pious Trevrizent' (243), who explains that instead of hating God, Parzival should put his trust in him. Trevrizent also leads Parzival to a confession that he was the one who failed to ask the question that would have cured Anfortas, the account of whose suffering seems instrumental in causing the young knight to accept his guilt and to move toward the humility he needs to complete his quest.

The result of Trevrizent's instruction is apparent when Parzival encounters Feirefiz, not knowing that he is his half-brother. As the two fight, Parzival is hard pressed; but he 'had faith in God since departing from Trevrizent, who had so earnestly counseled him to seek help from Him Who can confer joy in the midst of trouble' (387). Though the two are reconciled before either is killed, Parzival's faith is a sign of a new maturity. Shortly after their battle Cundrie rides up and announces that an inscription has appeared on the Grail naming Parzival as the new Grail King.

Wolfram's Parzival, who initially declares his hatred of God and who is engaged in the world, both in terms of his reputation and as a lover, is a strange Grail King. Parzival's love for *Condwiramurs seems at times more important to him than the Grail. Wolfram includes the well-known episode in which three drops of blood from a goose struck by a falcon fall on the snow and Parzival contemplates them because they remind him of the red cheeks and chin on the white face of his wife. So distracted is he by thoughts of her that he does not realize he is being challenged. His horse's motion at the sound of the attacker distracts him long enough to unhorse his opponent. Keie is next to challenge him, and similarly it is only when his horse turns him away from the drops of blood that he is even aware of his opponent. Again he is victorious: he gives Keie a fall in which the carping knight breaks his arm and leg. When the ever-courteous Gawan realizes the reason for Parzival's distraction and covers the drops of blood, Parzival goes to Arthur's court and joins the fellowship of the Round Table.

Unlike the chaste Galahad of later romances, Parzival has a lover and as Grail King is married. This is the supreme example of the medieval concept of the ennobling nature of love. But, as the sad tale of Anfortas suggests, the Grail King cannot then devote his knightly deeds to love. Nor can he, like Gahmuret, serve many women. But the qualities that make a man a true lover, a true knight, and a true servant of God are not very different. 'Wolfram sees the world, including that of the spirit, in categories of the knightly calling. Courage is necessary to face battle against an enemy on horseback, but it is also necessary to face the battle within one's heart. Courage is required to cope with incomprehensible passions and incomprehensible judgments of God' (Poag 91). And faithfulness is necessary in all three areas.

The episode of the three drops of blood is also significant because it exemplifies the unfailing courtesy of Gawan. Following a pattern set by Chrétien and imitated in turn by other authors, including those who wrote a number of the Middle English alliterative romances, Wolfram contrasts Keie's boorishness with Gawan's courtly manners. So much of the romance is devoted to Gawan and his adventures that at times it seems as if he is the hero. In fact, some of his trials are comparable to those a Grail knight might undergo. For example, in the Castle of Wonders ('Schastel Marveile'), Gawan finds a group of ladies, including his own mother and Arthur's mother, imprisoned by the magic of *Clinschor, a knight turned malevolent magician after being castrated by a jealous lover. In order to free the ladies, Gawan must endure the test of the Bed of Wonders ('Lit Marveile'), created by Clinschor. When Gawan enters the bed, it races around the room, slamming into the walls with such force that the castle shakes. When it stops, 500 slings hurl stones at Gawan, and then 500 crossbows shoot at him. Next he is attacked by a lion as big as a horse. The beast strikes Gawan's shield so violently that his claws are embedded in it. Gawan cuts off the foot, leaving it stuck in the shield, and then slays the lion.

Gawan's prowess, like his courtesy, is exemplary, as he proves over and over again. And one of the ways that Parzival's character is revealed is through comparison with Gawan as they pursue their various quests and adventures and intersect at key points. For example, just after Cundrie has berated Parzival, another messenger to the court, a knight named Kingrimursel, enters and accuses Gawan of basely killing his lord Kingrisin (173). Unlike Chrétien, Wolfram 'differentiates strikingly' between the two principal knights in this scene. Whereas 'Parzival is pounded into despair by his public disgrace,' Gawan's 'mood of confidence and calm acceptance of his misfortune' allows him 'to consider Parzival's predicament rather than his own' (Wynn 146–8; see also Sacker 147–9 for parallels between Parzival's story and Gawan's). Thus Gawan already possesses a quality that Parzival must learn. Moreover, both knights are inspired by and do great deeds in the name of the women they love. For Parzival, Condwiramurs is as much of an inspiration as the Grail; and Gawan performs many heroic acts to win the love of Orgeluse. Also, just as Parzival must ultimately heal the wounded Anfortas, so Gawan is presented as a healer when he comes upon a wounded knight and performs a kind of battlefield surgery; being 'no fool in the matter of wounds' (270), Gawan bandages the knight and speaks 'a healing spell' (271).

The comparisons between Parzival and Gawan function to show qualities of a mature knight that the younger knight must develop. In the end, however, they also serve to emphasize the greatness of the hero who develops those qualities and who finally achieves that which even the great and noble Gawan cannot.

Titurel

Wolfram expanded upon his account of the love of Parzival's cousin Sigune and Schionatulander in his *Titurel*, which is incomplete. The Titurel of the title is the first Grail King, father of Frimutel and grandfather of Anfortas, Parzival's mother Herzeloyde, and three other children. But the surviving fragments of the romance are concerned primarily with the love between Sigune and Schionatulander, whose death Sigune mourns in *Parzival*. The second fragment of Titurel recounts the finding of a dog named Gardeviaz by the lovers. The dog has a magnificent collar but also a leash 'twelve fathoms long, made up of band-silk of four colors', whose strips were adorned with precious stones and held together by 'rings decorated with pearls' (41–3). But of even more interest to Sigune is the text written on the leash, which tells the history of the dog: it was given by a queen to a prince. In her eagerness to read the entire text, Sigune unties the dog, who then runs off. When she promises her love to Schionatulander if he retrieves the leash, he goes in quest of it. Though the fragment ends before giving an account of the actual quest, there are ample hints that he will die trying to retrieve the leash. In *Parzival*, we learn that Sigune becomes a hermitess, is fed by the Grail, and ultimately dies praying over the body of her beloved.

Just as Wolfram and others attempted to complete Chrétien's Grail romance, so a thirteenth-century writer named Albrecht (formerly, but no longer, thought to be Albrecht von Scharfenberg) expanded greatly on *Titurel* in his long poem *Der jüngere Titurel* (*The Later Titurel*, c.1270), which gives a history of Titurel and of the Grail as well as a detailed account of Schionatulander's quest for the leash, his death in that quest, and the avenging of his death.

Richard Wagner

Wolfram's *Parzival* was the inspiration for Richard Wagner's (1813–83) operas *Lohengrin* (completed 1848, first produced 1850) and *Parsifal* (first produced 1882). The Arthurian content of the former is slight. It is only at the end of the opera that *Lohengrin reveals that he is the son of Parsifal, who guards the Grail in Monsalvat. His purpose in coming to the royal court is to clear the name of Elsa of Brabant, who has been accused of killing Gottfried, her younger brother. Gottfried in fact has been turned by the sorceress Ortrud into a swan, the swan who pulls Lohengrin's boat. In answer to Lohengrin's prayer, the dove of the Grail descends and restores Gottfried to his own form. Since Elsa has broken her vow not to enquire about Lohengrin's identity by insisting that he reveal his name and lineage, he must return to Monsalvat.

In terms of music and of Arthurian content, *Parsifal* is a much more interesting opera. Parsifal leaves his mother, thus causing her death, and makes his way to the Grail castle. There Gurnemanz, one of the Grail knights, hopes he will be the holy fool destined to bring about the cure of Amfortas, who succeeded Titurel as keeper of the Grail and the Spear of Longinus. Amfortas lost the spear to the sorcerer Klingsor and was wounded by it; his wound can only be cured by that same spear. Parsifal, however, does not understand what he sees at the castle and is thrust out by Gurnemanz.

When Parsifal makes his way to Klingsor's castle, he is tempted by Kundry, who has been cursed for mocking Christ. Because Parsifal resists her temptations, she calls to Klingsor for help. When he hurls the sacred spear, it stops over Parsifal's head. The young knight takes it and makes the sign of the cross with it, at which point Klingsor's enchanted castle and pleasure garden are destroyed. After much wandering, Parsifal returns to the Grail castle, arriving on Good Friday. Amfortas wishes for death to end his suffering, but Parsifal touches his wound with the spear and heals him physically and spiritually. He also baptizes Kundry and frees her from her sin, though she dies shortly thereafter. Parsifal then remains at Monsalvat as the new Grail king. Only small parts of Wolfram's text were used in the opera's plot. Wagner 'had little use for the chivalric adventure' in *Parzival* and borrowed principally the 'scenes of ritual', which were his primary dramatic concern (Haymes 183).

Works Influenced by Wolfram and Wagner

Wolfram and Wagner influenced a number of writers and artists who dealt with the Grail. In Germany where their influence is especially strong, they have inspired literature as diverse as the plays *Der heilige Gral* (*The Holy Grail*) (1912) by Richard von Kralik (1852–1934), and *Der Gral* (1976) by Arthur Maximilian Miller (1901–92); the epic poem *Parzival* (1922) by Albrecht Schaeffer (1885–1950); the novel with a modern setting, *Professor Parsifal* (1985) by Frido Mann; novels with a medieval setting such as Werner Heiduczek's *Die seltsamen Abenteuer des Parzival* (*The Curious Adventures of Parzival*) (1974) and *Der rote Ritter* (*The Red Knight*) (1993) by Swiss-German author Adolf Muschg (b. 1934); and the children's tales *Lohengrin* (1913) and *Parsival* (1914) by Gerhart Hauptmann (1862–1946).

Wagner's opera was also adapted to film as *Parsifal* (1982) by director Hans Jürgen Syberberg. Syberberg employs a variety of innovative techniques: he uses puppets in telling the story of Parsifal; at times he allows a death mask of Wagner to dominate the setting and distract from the medievalism of the opera; and his Parsifal is played by both a male and a female actor, who embrace at the end of the opera, an action that 'may be read as a Jungian allegory of the reunified soul' but also as a symbol of 'the reunion of East and West Germany, and a victory over both Nazism and Communism in a Germany made new and newly whole' (Hoffman 51).

The Grail in the Vulgate (or Lancelot–Grail) and the Post-Vulgate Cycles and Henry Lovelich's Translation

Estoire del Saint Graal (*The History of the Holy Grail*)

Though written after some of the other parts of the Vulgate Cycle (or Lancelot–Grail Cycle), the *Estoire del Saint Graal* (*History of the Holy Grail*) begins the narrative account that develops throughout the sequence of romances. It recounts the events by which the Grail was brought to Britain, and it predicts and paves the way for the quest that will occur during Arthur's reign. Strikingly, this first part of the cycle is presented, in an elaborate prologue, as a book written by Christ himself and copied by the narrator at Christ's instruction; and later in the story, the narrator asserts that 'you will never find a clerk bold enough to say that He [Christ] ever wrote anything after the Resurrection other than the high writing of the Holy Grail' (76). Thus the tale, which tells of the Crucifixion and the fate of the Grail after Christ's death, becomes in effect an extension of sacred history. The assertion of divine authorship is part of the elaborate pattern throughout the cycle of what E. Jane Burns has called 'a fiction of authority [and authorship] that is both cultivated and actively undermined' (41).

The history of the Grail begins after the Crucifixion when Joseph of Arimathea preserves the dish used by Christ at the Last Supper and collects in it some of the blood of Christ after he is laid in the tomb that Joseph provides for his body. Imprisoned in 'the most hideous and filthy prison ever seen' (10) because of the respect he has shown to Christ's body, Joseph is sustained for forty-two years by the Grail in such a manner that he thought himself incarcerated only from Friday until Sunday. As in Robert de Boron's account of these events, Vespasian, son of the Emperor Titus, is cured by Veronica's cloth and determines to avenge Christ's shame.

When Joseph is freed by Vespasian, Christ appears to him and tells him to preach in his name, so he journeys to *Sarras, the city from which 'came the first Saracens' and from which the Saracens got their name (15). *Josephus, Joseph's son and the first bishop (consecrated by Christ), assists King *Evalach of Sarras in defeating his enemy Tholomer by making a cross of red silk on Evalach's shield and telling him to cover it and to reveal it only when he is in desperate straits. In the battle, when Evalach is wounded and being led from the field, he uncovers the cross, at which point a white knight appears on the battlefield and turns the tide of the battle by striking down Tholomer and allowing Evalach to take him prisoner and by doing other wondrous deeds of chivalry.

After the battle, the image on Evalach's shield is transformed into a cross with a crucified man. When a soldier with a severed hand touches the image, his hand is restored, a miracle which causes Evalach's brother-in-law *Seraphe to be baptized and to take the Christian name *Nascien; subsequently Evalach is baptized as *Mordrain. A series of adventures tests and confirms the faith of these two converts, including the transportation of each to mysterious places, the Rock of the Perilous Port and the Turning Isle. While Nascien is on the Turning Isle, he is visited by Solomon's ship, the story of which explains symbols and prepares for events significant in the later quest for the Grail.

The ship was built by Solomon because he foresaw that the last of his line would be a knight (Galahad) who would surpass all others and because Solomon wanted to convey to this descendant the fact that he knew about him. Solomon's wife advised him to build 'a ship of wood that cannot rot from water or any other thing for four thousand years' and to prepare a weapon for the knight. The sword, she instructed, should be that of King David, 'the richest and most marvelous sword ever forged, and the sharpest ever found or wielded by a knight'; and it should have a marvellous hilt and scabbard. When Solomon wanted to provide an equally rich belt for the sword, his wife offered a poor and ugly one made of hemp, knowing that in the time of Galahad a woman would make one much more splendid. The improvement by a later woman (*Perceval's sister) on what Solomon's wife did is, in the highly allegorical style of the *Estoire*, seen as symbolic of Mary's reparation of the wrong done by Eve (83–4). On the ship, Solomon prepared a bed on which the sword was to be laid and which was framed with three spindles cut from the tree that grew from the little branch of the Tree of Life that Eve held in her hand when she was expelled from the Garden of Eden. When she planted the branch in the ground, it grew white; after she and Adam lay together and conceived Abel, it turned green; and when Cain killed Abel, it turned red. It is from this tree in its various colours that the three spindles are taken. Along with the sword, Solomon placed on the bed a letter explaining the ship and its contents and advising the knight for whom it was intended to 'protect yourself from woman's ruse' (84). Solomon's ship both 'symbolizes Holy Church' (86) and is literally the ship that will take the last man of Nascien's lineage, Galahad, with the Holy Grail to Sarras (116), thus completing the circular journey of the Grail and the kin of Joseph of Arimathea.

Having prepared for the Grail quest, the romance goes on to explain how the Grail came to Britain. A heavenly voice directed Josephus to spread his under-tunic on the sea. The cloth grew larger as each of 150 Christians stepped on it; and then it carried them over the ocean to Britain. There they continued their proselytizing and Christianized much of Britain, including the city of Camelot. Joseph died in Britain and was buried in the Abbey of the Cross in Scotland. Before his son Josephus died, he used blood from his bleeding nose to paint a red cross on Mordrain's shield, the shield that is destined for 'Galahad, the very good knight, the last in Nascien's line' (157). The history of the Grail before the quest is completed when the sacred vessel is passed on to Alan, who brings it to the Land Beyond, where a castle named *Corbenic is built for it, the castle in which the Grail remains until the days of King Arthur.

The *Estoire del Saint Graal* thus bridges the gap between the time the sacred vessel is used by Christ at the Last Supper and by Joseph of Arimathea to collect Christ's blood and the time the Grail arrives in Britain. In addition, it gives a history to the sword and shield that Galahad will use in his quest.

Queste del Saint Graal (*The Quest for the Holy Grail*)

After the story of Merlin, who is in effect a prophet of the Grail, and an account of the deeds of Lancelot and his companions and of his love for the queen, the cycle progresses to the quest for the Grail. Parts of the *Queste del Saint Graal* depict the fulfilment of events predicted or foreshadowed in the *Estoire*. Galahad (Galaad in the French) receives the sword and finds the letter left for him by Solomon and the shield on which a red cross was painted with the blood from Josephus' nose. Perceval's sister makes a belt for the sword from gold and silk and her own hair, an event foretold by Solomon's wife. There is also some recounting of information already told in the *Estoire del Saint Graal*, such as the building of the ship and the nature of the spindles on the bed within it.

It seems clear that the *Estoire* was designed in part to flesh out the background and symbolism of the Grail already presented in the *Queste*, which contains a good deal of religious instruction and interpretation of events and dreams. Once thought to have been written by a Cistercian monk because a number of 'the practices and beliefs presented in the romance are also to be found in Cistercian writings', the *Queste* is now generally seen as the product of someone who 'was familiar with and had a special interest in' the Cistercians and their doctrines but who was not a monk (Pratt 87).

The quest begins when Galahad is brought to Arthur's court and is able to sit in the Siege Perilous and pull a sword from the stone floating in the river beside Camelot. These feats mark him as the best knight, a point emphasized by the arrival of a lady at court who tells Lancelot that now 'there's a better knight than you' (7). That better knight is, however, not the Perceval of earlier Grail literature but Lancelot's own son Galahad. Modern readers who have come to know the story of the Grail through Malory and Tennyson may not be struck by how radical a change and how important a development in the Arthurian tradition this is. Emmanuèle Baumgartner has called the creation of Lancelot's son Galahad, descended through his father from Joseph of Arimathea and through his mother from David, as the hero of the Grail quest a 'masterstroke' and adds that 'another masterstroke is to have substituted for a single hero, Perceval, a triad made up of two "older heroes", Bors and Perceval, and a "newcomer", Galahad, and to have invented a hierarchy that relegates the traditional hero Perceval to the background while giving an unexpected role to Bors, Lancelot's cousin and "double" in the prose text' (Baumgartner 19–20).

Perhaps equally striking are the roles that Gawain and Lancelot play in the romance. Gawain, the first to swear to seek the Grail, enquires of a hermit why he has no adventures and is told that the adventures on this quest are signs of the Grail and so 'will never appear to sinners or anyone surrounded by sin' (51). (Gawain is blamed in the *Mort Artu* for killing eighteen of the thirty-two knights who did not return from the quest, so it seems that he had a certain kind of adventure.) Thus his role shifts from that of a model of chivalry in the earlier Grail stories to a worldly and unworthy knight. Lancelot, who does not figure in the earlier Grail stories, becomes a major participant in the quest, his exploits being interlaced with those of the three successful questers. And he is the only knight other than those three who makes a sincere effort at betterment: he confesses his sins, does penance, and even renounces his love for the queen and swears that he will never again 'sin with her or any other woman' (24). For keeping that vow for the duration of the quest, he is rewarded with a partial vision of the Grail. He sees it covered with red silk and 'around it ministering angels' and then witnesses a mass in which he views the miracle of transubstantiation; when the priest raises the host, he observes three men above him, two of them placing the third in the priest's hands. Lancelot, rushing forward to help the priest who seems about to fall under the burden, is blasted by a fiery wind and is unable to hear or see or control his limbs for twenty-four days, which correlate to the twenty-four years he had 'been in the devil's service', that is, had loved the queen (80–1). While Lancelot is rebuked for disobeying the divine injunction against entering the chapel and though he has been and will again be a sinner, he nevertheless has a spiritual adventure unlike that of any other of the knights except the chosen three, two of whom, it is important to remember, are his relatives.

Galahad, Perceval, and Bors take the Grail to Sarras on Solomon's ship, thus bringing it and its history full circle. Galahad becomes King of Sarras and, after a year, looks into the sacred vessel and sees in it 'the source of great deeds and the cause of all prowess' as well as 'mysteries that surpass all other mysteries' (87); then he dies. Angels carry his soul to heaven and, because of the worldliness of the people of Logres, the Grail and the lance are taken up by a hand from heaven, never to be seen on earth again. Perceval lives as a hermit for a year and three days after Galahad's death, at which time he dies and Bors returns to Arthur's court.

The Post-Vulgate *Queste del Saint Graal*

In the Post-Vulgate Cycle, the *Estoire del Saint Graal* is close to the Vulgate version. The *Queste*, however, differs considerably from its predecessor, especially in the addition of material adapted from the *Prose Tristan* and other sources. Some of this material is included as preparation for the final section of the cycle and the collapse of Arthur's kingdom. Much is made of Gawain's wicked nature and even more of Mordred's. The Loathly Damsel berates Gawain—not Perceval, as in earlier Grail literature—and links him in treachery to Mordred when she says: 'you and your brother Mordred were born only to do bad and dolorous deeds' (125). Perhaps to foreshadow his role as an adversary of Lancelot in the events leading to the downfall of Camelot, Gawain is presented as a vengeful knight who kills *Bademagu and other knights of the Round Table; who lies to Perceval about having killed his father, Pellinore, and his brothers; and who treacherously stabs *Palamedes. Thus he is markedly different from the Gawain of earlier French literature and of much later literature. Despite the criticism Gawain receives, even he is appalled at the unchivalrous actions of his brother Mordred. At one point, Gawain has sworn to protect Mordred, without knowing his identity, from a pursuing knight, who turns out to be their brother *Gaheriet. Gaheriet has followed Mordred because of an act of treachery he has seen him commit— dragging a maiden at his horse's tail. Though Gawain is fighting for him, Mordred rides down Gaheriet; then, when Gawain objects to the cowardly act, Mordred rides down and tramples him as well. Indeed, Gaheriet calls him 'the most treacherous knight I know today' (191).

Another noteworthy feature of the Post-Vulgate *Queste* is the role played by characters associated with the Tristan legend. Tristan himself seeks the Grail; Palamedes tracks the *Questing Beast and actually kills it, something that could not be done until the chosen Grail knight had come; and *Mark invades Arthur's realm when he hears a rumour that all of his knights have been killed on the quest. Mark first assaults *Joyous Guard, seizes Iseut, and sends her back to Cornwall. He then attacks Camelot, wounds Arthur, and nearly triumphs until Galahad, Arthur the Less (Arthur's illegitimate son), *Esclabor, and Palamedes rout the attackers.

Galahad, Perceval, and Bors achieve the quest for the Grail, take the sacred vessel on Solomon's ship to Sarras, and live there until Galahad and Perceval die. Bors then returns to Camelot, where he discovers strife between the family of King *Ban and the family of *Lot. There is also much talk of the infidelity of Lancelot and Guinevere and an ominous prediction that Agravain will reveal their crime to the king.

Henry Lovelich's *The History of the Holy Grail*

The *Estoire del Saint Graal* from the Vulgate cycle was translated into Middle English verse couplets by Henry Lovelich, a member of the London Company of Skinners, sometime between 1425 and 1450. Though Lovelich's *History of the Holy Grail*, like his translation of the Vulgate *Merlin*, has generally been ignored or dismissed by critics as the work of an unskilled poet whose verse is tedious and whose translation is too literal, it is nonetheless remarkable that a man of the middle class would write a poem of this length (nearly 24,000 lines of the poem survive and the first eleven chapters are lacking). And, though it must be admitted that the poem is not a masterpiece, it is in a number of ways typical of English verse romances, many of which have been seen as cruder than their French originals. Despite the poem's length, there is occasionally a reduction in the French text and sometimes a directness that its source lacks. For example, when Nasciens finds the sword on Solomon's ship, the writing on the scabbard omits the reference to the maiden's making of another belt from which it will hang; and where the French text says that the writing warns that if the sword is drawn by someone unworthy of it, he 'will find the most to blame in me [the sword] at a moment of great need' (78), the English text declares bluntly, 'he schal be the ferst that schal be ded' (Lovelich i. 360, chapter 28). Lovelich is not above making occasional small changes to his source, as when the French romance says that Joseph of Arimathea's body is brought to 'the Abbey of Urglay' in Scotland (157), but Lovelich asserts that he is buried in 'thabbey of Glays . . . which Abbey of Glaystyngbery now men hald' (Lovelich ii. 324, chapter 54), a detail that reflects the interest in Joseph's connection to *Glastonbury found in other English works about him.

JOSEPH OF ARIMATHEA

Sone de Nausay

An important figure in the history of the Grail as developed in medieval romance, Joseph of Arimathea is also the subject of a number of popular accounts after the Middle Ages. In the French romance *Sone de Nausay*, written in the second half of the thirteenth century and generally not treating Arthurian matter, Sone visits an abbey called Galoches off the coast of Norway and hears the story of Joseph of Arimathea's placing Christ's body in a sepulchre, an act for which he is imprisoned but is visited by Christ, who brings him the Grail. He remains imprisoned until freed by Vespasian. Joseph eventually comes to Norway, where he slays the pagan king but falls in love with his daughter. Although Joseph has her baptized before he marries her, God, in punishment, wounds him in his loins (123). To relieve his pain, he goes fishing in a boat and thus acquires the name of Fisher King ('Rois peschieres', 125). He suffers for many years—and as long as he suffers, his land of Logres, now called Norway, is as a wasteland—until a knight, unnamed in the text, heals him. At the abbey, Sone is shown the Grail and the bleeding spear.

Joseph of Arimathea

The Middle English *Joseph of Arimathea*, an alliterative romance, probably written in the latter half of the fourteenth century, is a rendition, with the severe reductions typical of English adaptations of French romances, of a portion of the Vulgate *Estoire del Saint Graal*. The English poem blends traditional romance battle scenes with preaching and debate to produce a self-contained account of the power of God.

The beginning of the romance is lacking, but perhaps it contained the story of Titus and Vespasian since the existing portion opens with the baptism of Vespasian. The text then recounts how the voice of Christ tells Joseph to preach God's word. Though he protests that he is not a clerk, Joseph is told that the Holy Spirit will direct his words; so he proceeds to Sarras, where he attempts to convert King Evalak by teaching him about the Immaculate Conception, the Slaughter of the Innocents, and the mystery of the Trinity. When one of the king's clerks disputes Joseph's teaching, the clerk's eyes fly from his head and the images of his gods are unable to cure him.

Joseph wins the king to Christianity not just by his preaching but by his assistance in Evalak's battle against his enemy King Tholomer of Babylon: he makes a red cross of cloth for Evalak's shield, to be uncovered at a desperate moment in the battle. On the uncovered cross, Evalak sees a child and prays for his help, at which point a White Knight appears, who gives strength to Evalak and his allies and slays Tholomer. Afterwards, Evalak and his brother-in-law Seraphe are baptized by Joseph and given the baptismal names of Mordreyns and Naciens; and then Josaphe, Joseph's son, baptizes 5,000 more before he and Naciens set out to convert others. At this point, the romance concludes rather abruptly although no material seems to be missing at the end.

One of the most striking elements of *Joseph of Arimathea* is what has been called a 'de-emphasis of the Holy Grail' (Lagorio 94) and 'the perfunctory treatment accorded the Grail' in a number of episodes, which reflects the poet's 'intention to transform the Grail romance which he had taken as his source into a saint's legend focusing upon the missionary career of Joseph of Arimathea' (Noble 7). Clearly, *Joseph of Arimathea* is a romance with a limited but definite agenda. As an independent romance, it does not pave the way for the later story of the Grail or the glories of Arthur's realm as its French source did but instead uses an account of part of the life of a holy man to set forth some of the mysteries of Christianity and to extol and exemplify the power of God.

Later Accounts of the Life of Joseph of Arimathea

Several short narratives of the life of Joseph of Arimathea survive only in print and not in manuscript. A brief prose *Lyfe of Joseph of Armathy*, printed by Wynkyn de Worde, perhaps in 1511, tells how Joseph was delivered from captivity by Jesus when four angels lifted up the house he was in. After being baptized by St Philip, Joseph converted many people and then came to Great Britain. When Joseph was imprisoned by the 'kynge of Northwales', God directed King 'Mordrams' to deliver him (31–2). This brief life is said to contain true assertions concerning the antiquities of the monastery of Our Lady in Glastonbury (27).

Glastonbury is also central to the fascinating verse *Lyfe of Joseph of Armathia*, printed in 1520 by Richard Pynson, which begins with a very brief account of Christ's birth and death, followed by the story of Joseph's burial of Christ, during which he collects two cruets of the holy blood. When Joseph is imprisoned by the Jews, Jesus himself lifts the house and frees him. After spending fifteen years with Mary, Joseph travels to France with St Philip, who sends him and his son Josephas to England, where the King of Wales imprisons him; but Christ appears to 'Mordrayous' and tells him to free Joseph (41). Joseph then goes to Britain, where King Averagas grants him Avalon ('avilonye'), which is 'now called Galstenbury'. After some time, the Angel Gabriel tells Joseph to build a chapel in honour of Mary's Assumption, and he himself makes an image of Mary, which is still at Glastonbury in 'the same churche' (43). When Joseph dies, he is buried at Glastonbury, where many miracles are done for those who pray to him. Of particular interest in this poem is the recounting of some of those miracles, with the names of the people who were healed or brought back to life and the dates on which these events purportedly happened. Thus the author demonstrates to pilgrims the benefits of visiting Glastonbury. The verse *Lyfe* is followed by an epilogue called 'A Praysyng to Joseph' which is, as its title suggests, an encomium to the saint. Picking up on a theme from the preceding life, it praises Joseph who, without pills, drugs, potions, or other medicine, can cure festering sores, plague, insanity, fever, jaundice, gout, and dropsy (51).

Joseph is also the subject of an eighteenth-century chapbook, *The History of That Holy Disciple Joseph of Arimathea*, which gives a brief history of Joseph's life without any mention of the Grail. It recounts how Joseph, not a knight but just a holy man, receives the body of Christ from Pontius Pilate, buries it, and then, after being made one of the seventy-two disciples by Peter, travels to Rome and intercedes with the Empress Poppeia to free Christians. Upon returning to the Holy Land, he is sent by the apostles to preach in England, where he gains favour with King Ethelbertus and other nobles, baptizes prodigious numbers of converts, and founds an abbey at Glastonbury which is said to be 'the first Christian church in the world' (8). While there is no reference to the Grail, the story of Joseph's staff sprouting into a thorn which blooms on Christmas Day is told twice in the short chronicle, the second time with the comment that though 'the time of superstitious popery' has passed, thousands of people go each year to Glastonbury to see this 'curiosity' (8).

Two twentieth-century British poems also focus on Joseph. In the dramatic poem 'St. Joseph of Arimathæa' (1928), James Ormerod presents Joseph in conversation with Arviragus, the heathen prince whom he converts and who gives Joseph land on which to build a wattle church. Joseph recalls the events of Christ's Crucifixion, burial, and Resurrection that he has witnessed and then says that he brought the Grail with him to Glastonbury. The legend that Joseph of Arimathea, as a trader in tin, brought the young Christ to Britain is related in *The Legend of Glastonbury* (1948) by A. G. Chant. In this poem, Glastonbury Tor is a place of human sacrifice until Christ, causing lightning to 'split the altar stone' (36), ends the custom. Years later, when an ageing Joseph returns and plants his staff, it blossoms into the Glastonbury thorn tree.

The Glastonbury Thorn figures prominently in the novel *The Thorn of Arimathea* (1959) by Frank G. Slaughter (1908–2001). Because the Emperor Tiberius is gravely ill, Quintus Volusianus, a Roman centurion and physician, journeys to the Holy Land to find the man who is reputed to cure the sick. There he meets Veronica; through her and her father, he comes to know Joseph of Arimathea, Veronica's uncle in the novel, who tells him of Christ. Quintus himself is healed by the veil of Veronica. The novel being primarily a story of romance, Veronica and Quintus marry. Tiberius dies before the veil can be brought to him; and Quintus and Veronica must survive a series of political intrigues and separation before being reunited in Avalon, where Joseph and Veronica have been preaching and where the thorn tree blooms in winter as a symbol of their message.

Joseph also brings Jesus to Britain in the American novel *Refuge in Avalon* (1962) by Marguerite Steedman. After providing a tomb for Jesus, Joseph, bearing the cup used by Christ at the Last Supper, seeks refuge in Glastonbury, where he is greeted by *Taliesin, whom Jesus had befriended years earlier. When Joseph plants the thornwood staff carved by Jesus on a hill at Glastonbury, it flowers; and Joseph is cured of the limp that has plagued him for years.

The Grail from Malory to Victorian England

Sir Thomas Malory's 'Tale of the Sankgreal' (discussed in Chapter 3) took much of its material from the *Queste* in the Vulgate Cycle and established Galahad as the primary Grail knight in the English and American traditions. Between the time of Malory and the nineteenth century, the Grail and many other elements of the Arthurian tradition virtually disappeared from literature. Renaissance literature on the legends was largely historical or political; and the Age of Reason used the Matter of Britain largely for satire and parody. The late eighteenth century saw the beginnings of a renewed interest in medieval Arthurian romance, which blossomed in the nineteenth century, largely due to the influence of Wagner and Tennyson. When the Grail re-emerged as a significant theme in England, it was largely under the influence of Malory.

William Wordsworth
In the Romantic age, the Grail remained elusive. Grail knights and stories were nowhere to be found until William Wordsworth (1770–1850) published the improbably titled Arthurian poem 'The Egyptian Maid or The Romance of the Water Lily' in 1835. In this poem Merlin, through blind malice, sinks the barge bearing an Egyptian maid to Arthur's realm, where she is destined to wed one of his knights. Nina, the Lady of the Lake, arranges for the maid's seemingly lifeless body to be retrieved from the sea and brought to Arthur's court, where Merlin devises a test to determine 'What Bridegroom was for her ordained by Heaven' (127). As in Malory's tale of the healing of Sir *Urry, all the knights touch the stricken body; but in this case, to Guinever's delight, it is *not* Lancelot who is the chosen one. Wordsworth, who acknowledges his debt to Malory, is aware of Percival's traditional role and includes him among the knights who make the attempt. Called the 'devoutest of all Champions' (127), Percival crosses himself three times; but he is unsuccessful. It is only when Galahad, wearing the very mantle he wore when he sat in the Siege Perilous, touches the maid's hand that she returns to life; a streak of colour tinges her cheek, her lips redden, and she breathes 'a soft and flower-like breath' (129). Soon Galahad and the Egyptian maid marry.

J. H. Shorthouse
In J. H. Shorthouse's (1834–1903) Victorian novel *Sir Percival: A Story of the Past and the Present* (1886), one of the characters, the Duke of Cressy and de la Pole, observes that 'Sir Percival was hardly treated in the "Morte d'Arthur". In the French books he had a romance all to himself, and occupied the same position that Sir Galahad does in the English romance, but that when Sir Thomas Mallory [sic] undertook to translate these French romances into one book, he would not omit any one of them, and was therefore obliged to cut out all the deeds of poor Sir Percival, which were identical with those of Sir Galahad, and leave him in a very secondary position' (98). What His Grace the Duke of Cressy and de la Pole says of Percival's position in Malory is equally true of his role in Victorian literature.

Shorthouse, like many modern novelists, translates Arthurian characters and themes into a modern setting. He focuses on a nineteenth-century knight, Percival Massareen, who leaves the woman he loves for service on the west coast of Africa, where he is presented with an opportunity to give his life for God and country. He volunteers for a dangerous assignment, the rescue of an English bishop who had been trying to convert 'fierce and warlike tribes' (278). With colonial hubris, Percival ventures forth 'accompanied only by trusty natives' because he hopes 'that the presence of an English officer might overawe the natives and their king' (278). But they are not overawed: the bishop is killed by his captors after taking a communion of three blades of grass with Percival, and then Percival is slain as an 'idol sacrifice' (298), but only after he has a final vision of England, the woman he loves, and Christ.

Victorian Poets

Among the Victorian poets who looked to the stories of the Grail for their subject matter were Robert Stephen Hawker (1803?–1875), who wrote 'The Quest of the Sangraal' (1864); and Thomas Westwood (1814?–1888), who published in 1866 'The Sword of Kingship', which tells of Arthur's youth and his pulling the sword from the anvil, and 'The Quest of the Sancgreall' (1868). Hawker felt, with some justification, that Westwood borrowed from his Grail poem. Hawker, who treats the Grail as a mystical symbol, describes its spiritual history, back to the time of Joseph of Arimathea when the Grail 'as though it clung to some etherial chain, | Brought down high heaven to earth at Arimathèe' (184). Hawker's Arthur, who has no children, feels that his name will live on if his knights can succeed in their quest for the Grail. This is a very different view from that taken by Tennyson, who visited Hawker in 1848, before either of them had written a Grail poem, and who was troubled by the quest and ultimately cast doubt on the reality of the Grail. Hawker agrees with Tennyson, however, that Arthur does not participate in the quest because of his sense of duty. Hawker's Arthur says 'the true shepherd must not shun the fold' (196).

Perhaps even more influential in popularizing Galahad than Tennyson's 'Holy Grail' idyll was his poem 'Sir Galahad' (published 1842, but written in 1834). Tennyson's Galahad, who says of himself, 'My strength is as the strength of ten, | Because my heart is pure', is moral perfection personified. He is also a character who, like the Arthur of the *Idylls*, is beyond human passion because 'all my heart is drawn above' (151). In his short poem, Tennyson provided a model of ideal, moral knighthood which inspired other literature and art and influenced social theories about the moral training of children, particularly in the United States (discussed more fully in Chapter 3).

The poem 'The Romaunt of Sir Floris' (1870) by John Payne (1842–1916) was influenced by Tennyson's 'Sir Galahad'; but though Galahad plays a major role in the poem, a knight named Floris is the central figure. A valiant knight, Floris hears a voice in a dream calling him. He rises and follows a holy bird to 'a place of flowers' (154), where he is tested in battle by a series of beasts, including a lion, a leopard, a snake, a vulture, a bear, a dragon, and a creature with two dog heads and the back part of a 'worm' or dragon. As he kills each one, a flower blooms. As in a Victorian book on the language of flowers, the significance of each blossom is explained; for example, the lily represents chastity, the marigold largesse. After slaying all the threatening beasts, Floris is visited by Galahad, who invites him to go to Sarras where a band of knights guards the Grail. There he finds Titurel, Percivale, Bors, Lohengrin, and many other unnamed knights. On the Grail temple, he sees depicted the story of the quest for the Grail, his own fight with the beasts in the garden, and, surprisingly, even the stories of the love of Tristan and *Ysolde and Lancelot and Guenevere. As the poem explains, there was nothing there that suggested what 'ancient doctors teach', that is, that 'All pleasant things' are 'Unloved of God'. This notion that the beauties and pleasures of the natural world are good seems to be thematic in a poem which delights in the natural world, naming and describing beasts, flowers, and rocks; and it is underscored by the motto accompanying the depictions of the lovers on the temple which declares (in French): Whoever loves, even though a sinner, is pleasing to God (212–13). Thus it is significant that Floris is sent back to the world of everyday duties to await another call to serve the Lord before a final summons to his eternal reward. Floris awakens thinking all had been a dream, but he finds the emblem of a dove with eyes of gold emblazoned on his helmet and shield and the celestial sword he was given in Sarras as proof that he truly experienced the wonders described in the poem.

Victorian Artists

Not only Victorian writers but also Victorian artists used Grail themes fairly frequently (cf. Poulson 74–141); and one of the best known images, 'Sir Galahad' (1862, now in the Fogg Art Museum, Harvard University) by G. F. Watts (1817–1904), was often associated with Tennyson's 'Sir Galahad', although the artist himself denied that the painting was inspired by the poem. The depiction of the young knight standing in full armour next to his white steed suggested the purity of heart that gave Tennyson's Galahad the strength of ten and became an icon of moral knighthood used to inspire both members of American Arthurian youth groups (discussed in Chapter 3) and young British men about to fight for their country in the First World War (cf. Burns).

The Grail quest also inspired numerous works by the Pre-Raphaelites. Edward Burne-Jones (1833–98), who was enthralled by the story of the Grail, was able to treat the subject in a variety of media, sometimes under the auspices of William Morris's company. Burne-Jones designed a series of stained-glass panels originally intended for his house at Rottingdean in 1886 (though in fact given to a neighbour). Two of the panels depict the failures of Gawain and Lancelot before showing the success of Galahad and the Grail in Sarras. In 1890–1, Burne-Jones was the primary designer of the tapestries that Morris and Company executed for W. K. D'Arcy's

Stanmore Hall in Uxbridge. As in the stained-glass panels, two of the tapestries focus on the failures of Lancelot and of Gawain and Ewain. The first two depict with epic brilliance the summons of the knights to the quest and the arming and departure of the knights. The series ends with a depiction of the ship that carries Galahad and the Grail to Sarras and 'The Achievement of the Grail' in which Galahad, flanked by lilies, kneels before the Grail altar, with three angels and Perceval and Bors behind him. Other depictions of material from the Grail legend by Burne-Jones include a drawing called *Sir Galahad* (1858, now in the Fogg Art Museum, Harvard University), the oil painting *Launcelot at the Chapel of the San Grael* (1896), and the frontispiece to the Kelmscott Press edition of *Syr Percyvelle of Gales* (1895) showing the young Perceval and his mother.

Another member of the Pre-Raphaelite brotherhood drawn to the Grail stories was Dante Gabriel Rossetti (1828–82), who produced a short poem called 'God's Graal' which was intended to be part of a larger work that was never completed. The Grail, however, figured prominently in his Arthurian art. In 1857, when he was commissioned to provide a series of murals for the Union Debating Hall at Oxford University, Rossetti decided to depict Arthurian themes. He enlisted a team of artists, including Morris and Burne-Jones, to help with the project. While his colleagues undertook depictions of Arthur receiving *Excalibur from the *Lady of the Lake, the death of Merlin, the death of Arthur, the jealousy of Palomedes, *Pelleas and *Ettare, and Gawain meeting three ladies at the well, Rossetti himself painted the two Grail scenes, *Lancelot's Vision of the Sangrael* and *How Sir Galahad, Sir Bors and Sir Percival Saw the Sangrael*, as well as *Launcelot in the Queen's Chamber*. He also painted the watercolours *The Damsel of the Sanct Grael* (1857, now in the Tate Gallery), an image of a maiden with the dove of the Holy Spirit above her as she carries a chalice with a long, thin stem containing the sacred blood and a basket containing the host draped with a white cloth, and *How Sir Galahad, Sir Bors and Sir Percival Were Fed with the Grael; but Sir Percival's Sister Died by the Way* (1864, now in the Tate Gallery), vibrant with reds and golds and featuring a glowing lily, symbolizing the purity of the Grail knights. The presence of the body of Percival's sister demonstrates the detailed knowledge of Malory that lay behind the art of Rossetti and the other Pre-Raphaelites.

Numerous other Victorian artists interpreted the Grail stories. A common motif was the portrayal of Galahad on horseback in a rugged landscape, symbolizing the difficulties of his quest. Such is the case in *Sir Galahad* (1870, now in the Walker Art Gallery, Liverpool) by Arthur Hughes (1832–1915), *Sir Galahad* (1879, now in a private collection) by Joseph Noël Paton (1821–1902), and *Sir Galahad and his Angel* (1885, now in a private collection), also by Paton. As the title of the last of these works suggests, Galahad is given divine guidance to help him deal with the rigours of his quest. Significantly, in each of these three paintings he is accompanied by one or more angels, which symbolize divine assistance.

These paintings are reminiscent of the poem 'Sir Galahad, a Christmas Mystery' (1858) by William Morris (1834–96), which presents a lonely, weary Galahad who is fully aware of what he is missing and fears that all will come to naught and that he will be found 'Dead in my arms in the half-melted snow' (74). But a divine voice assures him of success in the quest, and an angel tells him he will be brought to Solomon's ship and that he will soon have the company of his father and then of Percival, Bors, and Percival's sister.

AMERICAN INTERPRETATIONS OF THE GRAIL

James Russell Lowell's *The Vision of Sir Launfal*

A view of moral knighthood similar to that in Tennyson's poem 'Sir Galahad' can be seen in *The Vision of Sir Launfal* (1848) by American poet James Russell Lowell (1819–91). This poem, though out of favour with modern critics largely because of its overtly moral purpose, was extremely popular in its day. It was widely taught and memorized in schools, acted out in pageants, and reissued in a new edition or a reprint of an earlier one virtually every year from its publication until the turn of the twentieth century.

In Lowell's poem, *Launfal falls asleep in the first stanza of part I; and all of the poem's action, including the entire quest and the learning of the true meaning of the Grail, occurs in the vision that comes to him as he sleeps. Since the reader sees Launfal only as he is setting out on the quest and then returning, the poem is neither a narrative nor a romance in the medieval sense. *The Vision of Sir Launfal* is most reminiscent of the dream vision, in which a lesson is learned—in this case, a lesson about the true meaning of charity.

Even as a dream vision, however, *Launfal* suffers from structural problems, since Lowell tries to combine the medieval form with the style and description of an American romantic nature poem. Such Americanizing of the Arthurian world may well be a reason for the poem's popularity among its nineteenth-century audience. In Lowell's poem, Nature becomes a teacher. The line—'And what is so rare as a day in June?' (4–5)—has become such a cliché that its original importance is easily overlooked: the glory of a June day, a rare and therefore valuable thing, is freely bestowed upon men by Nature and Nature's God. Launfal must learn to bestow his charity just as freely and as lovingly on others.

Lowell creates a most untraditional Grail knight—a Grail hero to be found nowhere else in Arthurian legend. Though Launfal appears in other works, he is usually little more than one of the members of Arthur's court and certainly not one of the elite group of Grail knights. Marie de France's *Lanval* and the Middle English *Sir Launfal* (discussed in Chapter 2) have no mention of a Grail quest, though in each, the title character's generosity is crucial to the plot; and it is precisely generosity, or the Christianized version of the virtue, charity, that Lowell's Launfal must acquire. Lowell's hero learns a true charity that allows him not simply to toss a coin to a beggar but to empathize with his fellow man so fully that his castle becomes home to any other person who wants or needs it.

In his choice of Launfal as Grail hero, Lowell was deliberately attempting to distance himself from tradition. This is clear from the note Lowell placed at the beginning of his poem: 'The plot (if I may give that name to any thing so slight) of the following poem is my own, and, to serve its purposes, I have enlarged the circle of competition in search of the miraculous cup in such a manner as to include, not only other persons than the heroes of the Round Table, but also a period of time subsequent to the date of King Arthur's reign.' The note is instructive not only because its reference to the slightness of the plot recognizes that the poem is different from traditional narratives, but also because it deliberately divorces the Grail legend from Arthur (though no part of the poem proper dates it outside Arthur's reign). Lowell sets *The Vision of Sir Launfal* after the time of Arthur because he wants to dissociate the Grail from its connections to nobility, even the admirable nobility of Arthur and the Grail knights. Such disassociation allows Lowell to make the north country where Launfal's castle is located a world unto itself, a world that can become a sort of new Eden as a consequence of the natural charity that Launfal learns from his vision. It also implies that the achieving of the Grail—which, in this poem, is the acquiring and practising of true charity—is not something limited to Arthur's time and place or to the exclusive group that Arthur gathered about him. Rather, the achieving of the Grail comes within the reach of all men, surely a democratic notion appropriate to an American poem. Although Lowell was the most popular early American writer to reinterpret the Grail story, he was not the only one.

J. Dunbar Hylton's *Arteloise*

Arteloise (1887) by J. Dunbar Hylton (1837–93), a New Jersey physician and writer of epic poems, introduces several original elements into the Grail story. The hero of *Arteloise* is a knight named Beau de Main, in whom are combined the valour of Lancelot and the purity of Galahad. Beau de Main is led on a series of quests by a guide, none other than the Wandering Jew. The valiant knight's adventures include the slaying of a dragon, the freeing of the castle Arteloise from the power of the evil prophet who controls it, the obtaining of superhuman arms and armour from Vulcan, and the freeing of Merlin's daughter Ursula from the enchantment placed on her by Polar spirits.

Clearly, in his poem Hylton conflates medieval and nineteenth-century popular motifs with little regard for historical accuracy or literary tradition—though neither the medieval nor the contemporary motifs account for his innovative and surprisingly feminist handling of the Grail theme. In the course of his adventures, Beau de Main meets a woman named Griselda. She is 'a maiden knight' (139), who boasts of her prowess (140). Not only does Griselda ride and fight as a knight errant but she is also in quest of the Grail. And, contrary to any tradition, she actually achieves it: an angel brings the sacred vessel to her and Beau de Main after they have demonstrated their courage and have, despite their love for each other, remained chaste. Griselda is still clutching the Grail in the final scene when the Wandering Jew, by his power as a rabbi, joins her and Beau de Main in wedlock.

Katrina Trask

Another non-traditional approach to the Grail is found in the poem 'Kathanal' by Katrina Trask (1853–1922). Author of the volume *Under King Constantine* (first published in 1892 and reprinted in 1893), which contains three poems set in the reign of *Constantine, who is said by Malory to reign after the passing of Arthur, Trask admits that these poems 'have no legendary warrant' (3). In her poems, there is no evidence of the civil strife that has wracked Britain; King Constantine rules a kingdom where there is the leisure for typical knightly pursuits.

In 'Kathanal', the title character is not drawn to the quest by divine vision but has it imposed upon him by Leorre, the wife of his 'patron knight', as a way of sublimating the forbidden love they feel for each other. 'Kathanal' is a poem that cries out for a Freudian interpretation. Frustrated by his as yet unspoken love for Leorre, Kathanal tears the plume from his helmet and tosses it into the sea. With his 'knightly symbol lost', he feels dishonoured as a knight, and his boyhood dream of being 'a knight like Galahad, pure and true', seems unattainable (74–5). Soon they both admit their love to each other and suggest their desire. Lest their love become 'inglorious' (81) like that of Tristram and Isoud or Launcelot and Guenever, Leorre asks Kathanal to undertake the quest for the Grail. To replace the purple plume from his helmet, Leorre gives him a 'spotless scarf, the girdle from [her] robe' (85). He wavers but resists temptation and so ultimately achieves the Grail through self-denial. Kathanal learns the lesson that 'All love should be a glory, not a doom; | Love for love's sake, albeit bliss-denied' (90).

Sophie Jewett's 'The Dwarf's Quest'

In 'The Dwarf's Quest: A Ballad' (1905), another American woman, Sophie Jewett (1861–1909), retells the story of the Grail quest by placing the focus on *Dagonet the dwarf, King Arthur's fool. The object of derision and even physical abuse by knights such as Kay, Dagonet believes that he is not meant to undertake the quest. But a divine voice informs him that 'There waits one vision of the Cup | For thee and Galahad' (55). This injunction to seek the holy cup comes despite the fact that Dagonet, feeling excluded from the quest, has 'cursed' the Grail. Yet the King of Heaven, like the King of Camelot, forgives the biting words of the jester.

Dagonet's physical deformity is less important than his inner qualities, qualities which are revealed in the poem when he comes upon Lancelot seriously wounded and stops to care for him. As Dagonet tends to the unconscious knight, he sees a bright light and then four maidens, one of whom bears the Holy Grail. He tries to wake Lancelot because he thinks the vision has appeared for him. When Dagonet cannot rouse him, his 'answered prayer is punishment | Since my lord might not see!' (58). And while Lancelot is cured by the appearance of the Grail, he has not achieved the quest because he has not witnessed its appearance, as Dagonet has.

When Dagonet returns to Camelot, he is mocked again for setting out on the quest 'Till something in the rider's eyes | Silenced the merry jest' (59).

Sara Hawks Sterling

A Lady of King Arthur's Court (1907) by Sara Hawks Sterling, like other American Grail literature, introduces an unexpected Grail knight, *Anguish of Ireland. Loved by Dieudonnée, Anguish feels a sense of guilt that causes him to leave her just after their wedding. But since she loves him, Dieudonnée disguises herself as a monk, accompanies him on his quest, and helps him to avenge himself on the wicked Hellayne, who beguiled him, and then to achieve the Grail. After the quest and after Arthur's kingdom has fallen, Dieudonnée, whom Anguish has come to love more deeply than ever during what he believes to be his absence from her, reveals herself and tells him 'Life is before us'. They depart together, he now realizing that she is his 'perfect wife, perfect love' (261–2). Thus the Grail quest becomes secondary to the story of their love.

Edwin Austin Abbey's Grail Murals

In the Delivery Room of the Boston Public Library at Copley Square is a remarkable interpretation of the Grail: a series of murals, *The Quest and Achievement of the Holy Grail* (1895–1902), by Edwin Austin Abbey (1852–1911). Inspired by Tennyson, Abbey depicts Galahad as the ideal Grail knight, but Abbey's reinterpretation combines elements from the medieval stories of both Galahad and Perceval and includes some events that are nowhere else associated with Galahad. The frieze consists of fifteen panels, beginning with 'The Vision, or The Infancy of Galahad', in which Galahad's mother is visited by a dove carrying a golden censer and an angel carrying the Grail, and 'The Oath of Knighthood', in which Galahad receives his spurs from Lancelot and Bors. In the third panel, 'The Round Table of King Arthur', Galahad takes his seat in the Siege Perilous before embarking, in 'The Departure', on the quest with other knights. In 'The Castle of the Grail', he encounters the wounded Amfortas but fails to ask the question that might heal him, a failure for which he is assailed in 'The Loathly Damsel', elements of the story that derive from the versions in which Perceval, not Galahad, is the Grail knight. The next three panels—'The Key to the Castle', 'The Conquest of the Seven Deadly Sins', and 'The Castle of the Maidens'—depict other adventures leading up to the wedding of Galahad to 'Blanchefleur', whom he leaves (in 'Galahad Parts from his Bride: Blanchefleur') to return to the Grail castle, where, in another borrowing from the Perceval story, he finally asks the required question. In 'Galahad the Deliverer', 'Solomon's Ship' (or 'The Voyage to Sarras'), and 'The City of Sarras', Galahad passes from the land onto Solomon's ship, which bears him to Sarras; and, in the final panel, 'The Golden Tree and the Achievement of the Grail', he is made king and builds a golden tree for a year until it is perfect (Greenslet 77). When the tree is complete, Joseph of Arimathea appears, Galahad's kingly trappings fall away, and his spirit—along with the Grail—ascends to heaven. Abbey's murals achieved great popularity, and the images from them were often reproduced. No doubt they inspired Linwood Taft's *Galahad: A Pageant of the Holy Grail* (1924), which exhibits some of the same blending of the stories of Galahad and Perceval that the murals do. They also inspired a poem by Sara Teasdale, 'Galahad in the Castle of the Maidens' (1911), which is addressed 'To the maiden with the hidden face in Abbey's painting'. And the renowned early film-maker D. W. Griffith planned, though never actually produced, *The Quest of the Holy Grail*, a film based on the Abbey murals (Harty 6).

Irwin St John Tucker's *The Sangreal*

While works like Lowell's *Vision of Sir Launfal* and Abbey's Grail murals were seen as providing moral examples, some writers used the story of the Grail to comment on political or social issues. Irwin St John Tucker (1886–1982) incorporated his socialist views into his play *The Sangreal* (1919). Early in the play, Pinel, the court fool, argues with some of Arthur's knights about the worth of knights and by extension knighthood. He suggests that without 'serfs and smiths and tanners and such folk' to farm and make armour and weapons and pay ransom for captured knights, chivalry could not exist (8). In the course of the play, nobility and the type of religion which supports it lead to war and killing. After the final battle in which Arthur dies, Launcelot, to whom the king has bequeathed the crown in spite of his betrayal, refuses to rule and becomes a priest. The crown passes to Galahad, who promises to build a court comprised of 'artisans and blacksmiths and serfs and poets' and without noblemen, just as Christ chose for his followers 'fishermen and scorned the Pharisees' (100). The archbishop who sanctified the folly of the nobility is displaced in favour of *Torre, who has lived a simple life as a hermit; and the jester Pinel is made Galahad's chancellor.

John Erskine's *Galahad*

John Erskine (1879–1951), a professor of English literature at Columbia University, wrote a novel called *Galahad: Enough of his Life to Explain his Reputation* (1926), which comments on the role of women in society. Erskine deliberately eliminates the legendary elements that he sees as the elaborations of poets and minstrels. Choosing instead to focus on realistic events, he tells 'the story as it happened in our world, to people like ourselves or only a little better' (16). The people who are most like 'ourselves', that is, the people of the 1920s, are the women of the story. Erskine says that 'the plot is composed of three women and one coincidence' (16), the coincidence being that two of the women who play major roles in the story are named Elaine, the first *Elaine of Corbin, the daughter of *Pelles, and the second *Elaine of *Astolat, who plays a relatively minor part in the novel. The third woman is Guinevere.

In the world created by Erskine, there are, as Lancelot tells Galahad, no ladies in distress (164). Guinevere and the Elaine who gives birth to Galahad are representative of the new woman. A free-thinking and bold-speaking individual, Elaine, who has a respectable suitor, Sir Bromel, deplores the traditional wifely role. When she falls in love with Lancelot, she determines to give him a child although the thought of giving birth out of wedlock shocks Bromel and ultimately makes that very child, Galahad, turn away from her.

Guinevere is a woman of vision. She describes her marriage to Arthur as one in which her wishes were not consulted, but she married him because she knew that as a woman she 'can't do stirring things' and so wanted to assist Arthur, who she thought would achieve greatness. When she saw him become complacent with what he had accomplished, she turned to Lancelot hoping, she tells Arthur, that he would complete Arthur's work and 'encouraged him—all I could' (104). Too devoted to the king, Lancelot not only shares Arthur's values but also follows him even in matters that Guinevere considers trivial rather than reserving his knightly skills for weightier matters. Her conclusion is that neither Arthur nor Lancelot will achieve the legendary greatness she had hoped for.

In Galahad, Guinevere sees the potential for such greatness, and she takes it upon herself to mould him in a way that she could not do with her husband her lover. In his early years Galahad is a spoiled, self-centred, and difficult and; but when he comes to Camelot, Guinevere, who once thought of 'Lancelot's noble work and his splendid name' as her 'children' (134), adopts Galahad so she can make of him the 'masterpiece' that she could not make of Arthur or Lancelot. The content of the masterpiece is to be 'an absolutely new kind of man, an original type' (198). To create this 'new kind of man', Guinevere teaches Galahad to resist the charms of women, to fight only in defence of what is right, to 'have some passion or vision' in his life, and, when he has chosen 'one dream', to 'be faithful to that' (216, 218–19).

The pursuit of this ideal comes at a cost. It requires Galahad to reject anyone who loves him, including his parents and ultimately Guinevere herself. But it is precisely this single-mindedness that makes his reputation. When he disappears from court, people say that he is 'devoting his life . . . to the search for the holiest treasure in the world' (339). In one sense this is true: the purity he seeks is beyond what is reasonable to expect in the real world and so is worthy of description in the superlative degree. Such talk is also, as Lancelot says, 'how stories grow' (339), tales like that of the quest for the Holy Grail. The rumour that grew into Galahad's storied success in this quest explains his reputation.

Jack Spicer

The Holy Grail (originally published in 1962) by California poet Jack Spicer (1925–65) comments not on a political or social issue, but on the role of poetry in the modern world. Spicer's poem is a sequence of seven short 'books', each containing seven stanzas in free verse and each devoted to a different Arthurian character. The poem combines images and events from the modern and medieval worlds. At first, the unusual content of this poem seems at odds with the traditional Arthurian characters; but the contrast is intentional in a poem that explores the nature of poetry itself, the clash between the real and the ideal, and the real quest that people must undertake and which a poem can help them understand—if not achieve—

better than the Grail can. Spicer comments that 'The grail is the opposite of poetry | Fills us up instead of using us as a cup the dead drink from'. Of the relationship between poem and Grail, he says 'The poem. Opposite. Us. Unfullfilled' (188). Spicer never precisely defines what the Grail represents, but he does say that it is 'as common as rats or seaweed' (209).

John Steinbeck's *Cup of Gold*

The Grail quest is a controlling metaphor in a number of twentieth-century American novels set in times other than the Middle Ages. In John Steinbeck's first novel, *Cup of Gold* (1929), the cup of gold that the novel's protagonist Henry Morgan seeks is Panama, a city of great wealth and the ultimate prize of pirate plundering. But besides its fabled wealth, Panama contains another treasure, a woman of such beauty that 'men fall before her as heathen kneel before the sun'. Though none of the pirates has ever seen her, they all dream of 'La Santa Roja' and address prayers to her. As her legend grows, 'She became to every man the quest of his heart, bearing the image of some fair young girl left on a European beach to be gloriously colored by the years. And Panama was to every man the nest of his desire' (123). Like the Holy Grail that provides everyone with the sustenance he most desires, La Santa Roja becomes the woman every man idealizes in his memory. And for Morgan himself she becomes 'the harbor of all my questing' (175).

To take Panama, Morgan leads his men on an arduous overland journey reminiscent of the questers' struggles in search of the Holy Grail. Although they suffer various trials, including fatigue, hunger, and thirst, ultimately they take the prize. But when Morgan finds himself conqueror of Panama, he is not filled with peace; in fact, he has lost more than he has gained. Although he is the captor of La Santa Roja, his dream of winning her love proves illusory: she recognizes that he does not 'carry a torch' for her and that she does not 'burn' with love for him. Therefore, instead of finding the ultimate reality at the end of his quest, he realizes that he had gone 'sailing and sailing looking for something—well, something that did not exist, perhaps' (241). The achieving of his Grail turns out to be an ironic reversal of the traditional motif. After taking the Cup of Gold and being rejected by La Santa Roja, he experiences a spiritual and emotional dryness of the sort that success in the traditional Grail quest would have eradicated.

Bernard Malamud

The Perceval story is used as a controlling metaphor in three important American novels set in the modern world: *The Natural* (1952) by Bernard Malamud (1914–86), *Lancelot* (1977) by Walker Percy (1916–90), and *In Country* (1985) by Bobbie Ann Mason (b. 1942). *The Natural*, Malamud's first novel, is the story of Roy Hobbs, a remarkable baseball player who, late in life, has a chance to play for the Knights, a major league team. Roy is a 'natural' not just in the modern sense of possessing an outstanding innate talent but also in the medieval sense of being an innocent fool like Perceval.

Because of his own blindness, Roy ultimately fails both in his quest for Knightly fame and in his quest to help others, including the Fisher King, Pop Fisher. When Roy first meets him, Pop, the team's manager and part owner, is seated at the edge of a 'dusty field' complaining, literally and metaphorically, that 'it's been a blasted dry season. No rains at all. The grass is worn scabby in the outfield and the infield is cracking. My heart feels as dry as dirt' (45). And he has a wound (athlete's foot on his hands) that will not heal. As Roy begins winning games for the Knights, the rains come; Knights Field grows green again; and Pop's physical and spiritual wounds heal. During the final game to determine the winner of the pennant, however, after Roy deliberately strikes out, 'a breeze blew dust all over the place' (221); and Pop recognizes that his last hope is gone. Roy destroys Pop's dream along with his own, until all that remains is the dusty field after yet another losing season and the dashed hopes in the eyes of the little boys who had once aspired to be Knights themselves.

Malamud enhances the pathos, if not the tragedy, of Roy's situation by suggesting that his potential was like that of Perceval but that, in contrast to the legendary figure on whom he is based, he wastes even his second chance to achieve something of value, to heal the wounded king, and to revitalize the modern wasteland. Roy also contrasts sharply with the Hollywood character he becomes in the film version of *The Natural* (dir. Barry Levinson, 1984), which in typical Hollywood fashion has Roy (played by Robert Redford) hit a home run to win the pennant for the Knights.

Walker Percy

Walker Percy's novel *Lancelot* (1977), set in twentieth-century Louisiana, is the story of Lancelot Andrewes Lamar, the narrator of the tale. *Lancelot* is virtually a monologue, but the presence of the priest Percival, who is silent for the most of the novel (he utters 'no' once and 'yes' a few times on the last two pages of the text), is central to the narrative. Percival serves as both psychiatrist and confessor to his old friend Lancelot. It is to him that Lancelot recounts his discovery that his would-be actress wife Margot, with whom he had lived happily for a time in the Joyous-Gard-like sanctuary called Belle Isle, has been unfaithful with Robert Merlin, a film director. Disillusioned and maddened by the betrayal, Lancelot begins a quest for pure evil because 'If there is such a thing as sin, evil, a living malignant sore, there must be a God' (52). Thus Lancelot considers himself a 'Knight of the Unholy Grail' (138).

Lancelot is able to relate the details of his experiences to his old friend only because Percival is a fellow quester seeking to fill a void in his own life and to discover his own version of the Grail. Indeed Percival, who shares Lancelot's sense that something in contemporary life is deficient or, at best, awry, comes to know the nature of his own quest only when he hears the story of Lancelot's. It is clear that Walker Percy and his character are aware of the bond that is created by the allusions to the Arthurian legends; and in fact Percy makes that bond between

Lancelot and Percival closer than it is in the traditional stories. 'Do you think I was named Lancelot for nothing?' Lancelot asks. 'The Andrewes was tacked on by him [Lancelot's father Maury] to give it some Episcopal sanction, but what he really had in mind... was Lancelot du Lac, King Ban of Benwick's son, knight of the Round Table and—here was the part he could never get over—one of only two knights to see the Grail (you, Percival, the other)' (116). This reinterpretation (or misremembering) of Lancelot and Percival as the only two knights ever to see the Grail is unique to Percy and, in fact, is central to his retelling.

When Lancelot sets off a methane gas leak that causes Belle Isle to explode, killing his wife and everyone else inside, he soon realizes the error of his actions: left 'cold', he acknowledges that there was 'nothing at all, not even any evil... there is no answer. There is no question. There is no unholy grail just as there was no Holy Grail' (253). So, after a year of incarceration in a hospital, he chooses to make a 'new beginning' in a world of his own creation with his new Eve, the mental patient Anna who has been raped back into innocence. Percival, meanwhile, commits himself to the pursuit of his own Grail by setting out for a small church in Alabama. Yet, although the two old friends ultimately go in different directions, both find a source of grace and redemption, a way of filling their spiritual voids, a justification for their struggles, and above all, an affirmation of their hopes.

Bobbie Ann Mason

Another contemporary American treatment of the Perceval figure occurs in Bobbie Ann Mason's first novel *In Country* (1985), the story of the quest of Samantha ('Sam') Hughes for knowledge about her father Dwayne, who was killed in Vietnam. Like Perceval, she can establish her own identity only through her quest, and she must discover the right questions to ask before she can achieve her goal.

In Mason's novel, Sam's uncle Emmett Smith is a type of the Fisher King. Emmett returns from Vietnam to Hopewell, Kentucky, a wounded and broken man who simply does not fit into the society he had so recently left. Initially, Sam suspects that Emmett has been sexually maimed, that his manhood was destroyed by some kind of physical injury suffered in combat; and she raises the question of Emmett's wounding with all of her friends and family. But Emmett's wound is more psychic than physical, a guilt caused by the fact that he lived while his buddies died, that he survived by pretending that he too was dead, by hiding all night and all day under their corpses, until he, the lone survivor, felt dead inside.

While Emmett is the Fisher King, in an interesting gender twist Sam is the Grail knight who eventually restores him, and those around him, to health. To do this, she, like the traditional Grail knight, must ask the questions that will effectuate the healing. Sam embarks on a journey, first metaphorical, later literal, to find the answers she needs. Like Perceval, she is told not to ask too many questions. It is only from her father's letters and his diary that she begins to see what Vietnam meant and what effect it had on those who served there. Disturbed by what she reads, she runs away to nearby Cawood's Pond, where she intends to relive a small part of her father's experience and discover the purpose men believe they have in going to war. Alone in the swamp, like the Grail knight keeping his solitary vigil, she spends the night 'walking point' (211) and imagining the face of the Viet Cong in every raccoon she sees and their presence in every sound of nature she hears. But it is not until morning, when Emmett finds her, that she learns his long-held secret of how he survived by hiding for hours under the bodies of his comrades. Sam's disappearance, says Emmett, duplicated for him the horror of that event; it was 'like being left by myself and all my buddies dead' (225). The confrontation that Sam has forced allows Emmett to begin his healing. Having uttered the unutterable, having spoken his secret, he can begin to heal from his wound. This process and Sam's education are completed by a visit to the Vietnam Memorial in Washington.

Sam's quest to understand the meaning of the Vietnam War, which created deep political and philosophical divisions in America, is as noble as any quest in medieval literature, and its achievement helps to heal the war-wounded Emmett and others around her as well. As in the Grail legend, the healing of the land and the healing of the individual are inseparable. Through the use of the Perceval legend to undergird her narrative, Mason, like Malamud and Percy, adds a mythic dimension to a very contemporary and very American tale.

JESSIE WESTON AND T. S. ELIOT

The most influential Grail poem since Tennyson's 'Sir Galahad' and Lowell's 'The Vision of Sir Launfal' was T. S. Eliot's (1888–1965) *The Waste Land* (1922), which responded directly and immediately to the plight of the post-war world by describing the wasteland of contemporary society. What makes Eliot's poem interesting and still meaningful more than three-quarters of a century later is that he found a way to see in the condition of the world a reflection of the human condition and of rampant spiritual decline. And what allowed him to make this connection was the myth he found in Jessie Weston's *From Ritual to Romance* (1920). Weston, who herself wrote a Grail poem, 'Knights of King Arthur's Court', that celebrated Perceval's spirituality, had a wide-ranging knowledge of texts and was more conversant with medieval romance than almost any other scholar of her day. Although her approach—seeing the Grail stories as Christianized versions of a pagan fertility rite—and most of the conclusions of her book have since been rejected, in its day *From Ritual to Romance* was a monument of research. Eliot was undoubtedly drawn to the cultural fluency displayed in the book and derived from its use of myths and texts from different periods and cultures a paradigm for the use of imagery and allusion in *The Waste Land*. In his notes to the poem, Eliot says that 'Not only the title, but the plan and a good deal of the incidental symbolism of the poem were suggested by Miss Jessie L. Weston's book on the Grail legend: *From Ritual to Romance*' (47). Though Eliot himself came to regret the fact that this and his other notes led so many to search for allusions as if they were solving a puzzle, he was right to acknowledge his debt to Weston, whose account of the wasteland offers insights into the meaning of his poem. In her study, Weston observed that 'the "Waste Land" is really the very heart of our problem; a rightful appreciation of its position and significance will place us in possession of the clue which will lead us safely through the most bewildering mazes of the fully developed tale' (*From Ritual to Romance* 63–4). Eliot no doubt recalled this statement or at least the concept behind it, the centrality of the wasteland to a series of myths, for which the idea of the wasted land and the need for its restoration serves as a unifying motif.

Eliot, moreover, surely adopted the approach suggested by this notion as a means of consolidating a host of otherwise disparate stories, characters, and images. As George Williamson observed, 'The most important idea for Eliot in Miss Weston's scheme was that the Grail story subsumes a number of myths; this provided him with both a central myth and a basic system of metaphor'. Thus Eliot had a complex of stories and ideas, a multi-layered system of suggestion and metaphor, or, as Williamson calls it, a 'subsumptive myth' (119–20), to provide material and meaning for his poem. Through this method, Eliot brings together a wealth of allusion that allows him to contrast the rich intellectual and emotional life of past ages with the sterile and passionless people of the present. As a result, the Grail myth is all important to the poem even though there are few *specific* Grail allusions in the text. It is worth commenting, in fact, that although *The Waste Land* is one of the most influential Arthurian poems in America, its actual Arthurian content is slight. Aside from the use of the Grail story as a 'subsumptive myth', *The Waste Land* contains only a few references to the Fisher King, the general symbol of the wasteland, and a couple of allusions to the story of Tristan and Isolt.

Following Weston's lead, Eliot placed the Fisher King at the centre of the poem. Since the basic premise of the theory that links the Fisher King to vegetation and fertility rituals is that the king and the land are bound together and the fate of one is dependent upon the other, a wounded king means a wounded land—the land that is wasted until, in terms of the ritual, the new season brings new growth, or, in terms of the romance, the Grail knight cures the king and thus restores the land. Moreover, the link between king and land allows both geography and character to reflect the same condition. There is sterility of all kinds in the wasteland of modern society, which Eliot emphasizes in both the form and the content of his poem.

Just as all of the people in the poem partake of the sterility of the wasteland, so all the male characters share the metaphoric wound of the Fisher King. The typist's young man is carbuncular, but that physical condition, like the wound of the Fisher King, hints at a more serious affliction that affects him and results in his passionless lovemaking. It also affects his land, the modern city of London. When Eliot alludes to the Fisher King, his picture bespeaks a languid and debilitated world that is far from either ritual or romance.

Even spring and water, traditional signs of fertility, are suspect in the poem, where 'April is the cruellest month' (Eliot 29), not the month of hope for renewal. What traditionally makes April the beginning of a season of hope is the coming of the spring rains that bring life to dormant vegetation and, as a result, to those who depend on that vegetation for life. But Eliot has Madame Sosostris, his 'famous clairvoyante', advise her client to 'Fear death by water' (30–1). And the fourth section of the poem is called 'Death by Water'.

Such paradox raises the question of whether any redemption is possible: if water, the life-giving force in vegetation myths, is to be feared, what then offers hope? The overriding pessimism arising from this attitude towards water is perhaps reflected as well in the lack of a Grail knight in the poem. Though Eliot quotes one line from Verlaine's 'Parsifal' in the poem—'Et O ces voix d'enfants, chantant dans la coupole' (37)—the line does not refer in any substantive way to the Grail knight himself. And although Eliot alludes to the Chapel Perilous, he makes no mention of Galahad or of any other Grail knight enduring the trials the Chapel traditionally presents. Weston observes that the hero of the Grail romance often 'meets with a strange and terrifying adventure in a mysterious Chapel, an adventure which, we are given to understand, is fraught with extreme peril to life. The details vary: sometimes there is a Dead Body laid on the altar; sometimes a Black Hand extinguishes the tapers; there are strange and threatening voices, and the general impression is that this is an adventure in which supernatural, and evil, forces are engaged' (From Ritual to Romance 175). But in The Waste Land, 'There is the empty chapel, only the wind's home. | It has no windows, and the door swings, | Dry bones can harm no one' (Eliot 44). With the Chapel divested of the dangers and trials through which a knight could prove himself worthy and without even a questing knight, there is little hope that the wounded king will be healed and his land restored.

Although the Fisher King's rebirth or regeneration is crucial to the restoration of life and fertility, Eliot's poem ends on a note of ambiguity. The final image of the Fisher King fishing and the barrage of quotations at the end do not resolve the problem of whether renewal is even possible. But perhaps some hope is offered by the final two lines with their suggestion of a formula for spiritual renewal in the Sanskrit injunctions: 'Datta. Dayadhvam. Damyata.' The result of following this formula—Give, Sympathize, Control—may be 'shantih', which Eliot's note translates as 'the Peace which passeth understanding'. If so, though, it is a peace that is gained, the poem implies, by cultural tradition and individual spirituality, by personal trial and triumph, not by those of a rescuer or Grail knight. The Fisher King, who merges with many of the other characters in the poem, is a kind of Everyman or at least Every Modern Man, for whom, Eliot's poem seems to say, redemption in a sterile world must come from within.

The Influence of *The Waste Land*

Eliot's treatment of the wasteland and of the figure of the wounded Fisher King had a tremendous impact on later writers, particularly novelists, who saw in the myth Eliot had adapted the perfect symbol for modern society and its ills. The novelists of the Lost Generation found in these images a symbol for the troubles of their age and incorporated them into some of the most significant fiction they wrote. Among the numerous authors and works of this era directly influenced by the Fisher King, wasteland, and Grail imagery of Eliot's poem were F. Scott Fitzgerald in *The Great Gatsby*, Ernest Hemingway in *The Sun Also Rises*, William Faulkner in *Soldier's Pay*, and John Steinbeck in *The Winter of our Discontent*. These authors were, in turn, major influences on the novelists of the succeeding generations, who also adapted the imagery Eliot had appropriated from Jessie Weston.

Twentieth-Century British Interpretations of the Grail

In addition to the Americans who found inspiration in the story of the Grail, British authors have adapted the legend or parts of it in drama, verse, and fiction. And like their American counterparts, they set their works both in the Middle Ages and in the modern world.

R. C. Trevelyan

Edwardian playwright R. C. Trevelyan (1872–1951) wrote three verse dramas, one set in the Middle Ages and two in the modern world, that rework the story of Perceval. *The Birth of Parsival* (1905), as its title suggests, focuses more on the parents of Parsival, here said to be Frimutel and Herzeloida, than on the Grail knight himself. By loving Herzeloida and putting that love before his duty, Frimutel rebels against his role as keeper of the Grail. Believing that he acted reasonably, he breaks with tradition, declares that the impulse to deliver the Grail from 'ignoble superstition' (12) came from God, and exalts Reason over the superstition that the Grail represents. Kundry, the prophetess of the Grail, predicts that God will bless the parents through their child, Parsival (49), and Frimutel hopes to live to see the glory of the 'child of [his] rebellion' (102). Yet while Frimutel is resigned to having his son serve the Grail for a time, he feels certain that Parsival too in his turn will abjure service to the Grail.

Trevelyan again takes up the Grail knight (now called Parsifal) in *The New Parsifal: An Operatic Fable* (1914), which is far from a continuation of the plot of the earlier play. Rather than a serious or reverent drama of the quest, it is a burlesque, as the opening makes obvious: an examiner of plays discusses with a Lord Chamberlain a manuscript he has received for a play called *The New Parsifal*; and over the objection of the ghost of Wagner to the text's blasphemy against 'the sanctitude | Of the Bayreuthian Grail', they pass the 'stupid play' (3, 6).

The play itself recounts the arrival of Klingsor and a band of followers on the island of Circe. The conflict between Circe's magic and the power of the Grail is complicated by the appearance of a twentieth-century pilot named Percival Smith, the Perceval figure of the play. *The New Parsifal* is a satiric burlesque, critical of the aesthetic values of its day; but Percival Smith could only be a Grail knight in the mock-heroic world that play creates, a world where he must reject the Grail to be worthy. The same character appears in another play by Trevelyan, *The Pterodamozels* (1916), which lacks the specific references to the Grail found in the two earlier plays; but in a sense its Percival Smith is more of an achiever and a healer than is the protagonist of *The New Parsifal*. The title refers to a race of winged female creatures created by Prometheus to destroy and replace his earlier creation, mankind, who have become debased and wicked. Percival argues to Prometheus and his new creations that it is not mankind but a few politicians and captains of industry who cause all the trouble, like the world war that is raging. When these world leaders are kidnapped, peace breaks out. A worldwide federation of free republics is declared, and Percival is chosen as 'Provisional President | Of the whole world' (57–8). Prometheus, disowning both man and the Pterodamozels, causes the island to begin to sink; but Percival insists that everyone, even the world leaders, be saved before he will leave. While the play has a comic conclusion with a hymeneal song to celebrate the wedding of Percival to Parthenope, one of the Pterodamozels, his 'live and let live' (63) attitude is in the end foolish because it preserves the very scoundrels from whom he has delivered the world by achieving the Grail of world peace and harmony.

E. S. Padmore

The play *The Death of Arthur* (1936) by E. S. Padmore is equally unconventional in its presentation of the Grail. Arthur becomes disillusioned with his own virtue and abdicates. Nevertheless, Mordred challenges him and kills him. As Arthur dies, he sees *Vivien, earlier identified as the Grail maiden, carrying the sacred vessel, which turns into the face of her son by *Dynadan. Arthur's final realization is that 'little children' are 'the living cup—the living blood' because 'of such is the kingdom of heaven' (54–5).

Evelyn Underhill

The Column of Dust (1909) by Evelyn Underhill (1875–1941), better known for her writings on mysticism and her editions of *Cloud of Unknowing* and Walter Hilton's *Scale of Perfection* than for her fiction, brings the Grail into the modern world. The novel is the story of Constance Tyrrell, a clerk in a London bookstore who uses a book of magic to conjure up a spirit. The spirit remains with her, indeed becomes a part of her, for the rest of her life. Referred to as the Watcher, this spirit comments on the world in which people live, a world it refers to as a dream of the Idea, or true spiritual reality; and Constance often engages in dialogues and debates with it.

When Constance, who has intentionally had an illegitimate child named Vera, is holidaying in a remote part of England, her horsecart overturns and she sees a light, towards which the Watcher urges her to go. She discovers that it is the light of the Grail, kept by a priest named Martin in a remote chapel. The Grail is 'a rough glass cup, without a base, and with one clumsy handle', something like 'a kitchen teacup' (139), before which Constance kneels in reverence without understanding why. Later, Martin, aware of his impending death, passes the Grail on to Constance, who keeps it in her London flat.

Vera becomes ill, and the Watcher struggles to force Constance to let the child die, a fate which seems to it natural, just another side of the veil. He also says that Vera is 'twisted, imperfect: she will never grow, never be beautiful, never transmit the Idea' (270), an assessment with which Constance cannot disagree. The only way to save Vera is to free the Watcher by allowing herself to die. Realizing that 'the Secret of the Grail' is to sacrifice 'oneself for the unworthy' (275), she makes the sacrifice that 'was commonplace enough' and that 'took no heroic rank amongst the sublime adventures of the dust' (302).

The Column of Dust presents an unsentimental view of children and a realistic view of people at the same time that it depicts a vital spiritual world. It is particularly interesting for its unconventional depiction of an unmarried mother as the keeper of the Grail.

Arthur Machen

Underhill's novel is dedicated to Arthur Machen (1863–1947) and his wife. Machen himself subsequently wrote two tales in which the Grail serves as a source of spiritual revitalization in the modern world. In the novella *The Great Return* (1915), the Grail makes a return to Llantrisant, a Welsh village, in the twentieth century. Its presence is revealed through a series of strange events: a great bell sounds and a light glows fiery red; a tubercular girl on the verge of death is cured; a mean dog becomes tame; a sheep dog and a fox frolic together; a sense of well-being and kindness prevails; the sensual world is 'quickened and glorified and full of pleasures' (63); and the people of the town witness a Grail mass.

In the novel *The Secret Glory* (1922), the protagonist Ambrose Meyrick attends a public school named Lupton, where he never quite fits in. Recognizing the superficiality of what he is learning, he seeks out the Gothic architecture that his father has taught him to love. When he returns late from one such jaunt, he is cruelly beaten by his uncle, who is high usher of Lupton and who dreams of becoming headmaster and raising the reputation and the revenues of the school by creating a past through rumours of antiquity and of attendance by famous men. For a time, Ambrose endures his situation, in part because of his memory of a visit with his father to a farmer named Cradock, who was 'the last, in direct descent, of the hereditary keepers of the holy cup' (102). At Cradock's farm, Ambrose has a vision of the Grail, in which he experiences its secret glory. He feels 'ineffable rapture', has a vision of a castle which he knows to be 'Corabennic', and later learns from his father that he has seen 'the cup of wonders and mysteries, the bestower of visions and heavenly graces' (98–9, 102).

Ambrose runs away from school and spends some time with a common woman whom he sees as 'a miracle' (187), which is part of his realization of the goodness of the physical world. He ultimately concludes that 'Every day of our lives we see the Graal carried before us in a wonderful order, and every day we leave the question unasked, the Mystery despised and neglected' (257). When Cradock dies, Ambrose himself becomes keeper of the Grail. He brings it to 'a certain concealed shrine in Asia' and gives it to someone who would 'hide its glories for ever from the evil world'. On his return trip, he is martyred, crucified by 'the Turks or the Kurds—it does not matter which', and thus achieves 'the most glorious Quest and Adventure of the Sangreal' (307–9).

John Cowper Powys's *A Glastonbury Romance*

Like Arthur Machen, John Cowper Powys (1872–1963) wrote a novel in which the Grail appears in modern Britain. In *A Glastonbury Romance* (1932), Powys tells the story of John Geard, a modern Merlin figure, who wants to revitalize Glastonbury and to make it 'the centre of the Religion of all the West' (292). To that end, he organizes a pageant which presents scenes from Arthurian legend, a Passion play, and material from 'ancient Cymric Mythology' (594–5). In the course of the novel, Sam Dekker, the son of the local minister, has a vision of the Grail as 'a globular chalice that had two circular handles. The substance it was made of was clearer than crystal; and within it there was dark water streaked with blood, and within the water was a shining fish' (982). In a motif reminiscent of one found in Machen's *The Great Return*, common objects and experiences give Sam great joy after his vision.

The appearance of the Grail is not the climax, however, of this rambling novel with its Dickensian cast of characters. The focus shifts frequently from one character or group of characters to another. In the end, however, John Geard, who has himself used the power of Chalice Well to cure a woman of cancer, drowns while saving Philip Crow, the industrialist whose vision of Glastonbury is diametrically opposed to his, during a flood that destroys much of the city. As he dies, he apparently has his own vision of the Grail. But more than the quest for or even the visions of the Grail, Glastonbury as a presence, a symbol, and a place of power from pre-Christian times to the twentieth century gives the novel its unity and controls its structure.

Charles Williams

In Charles Williams's (1886–1945) works, as in Machen's, the Grail's mystical power is 'concentrated in Christian belief' rather than Celtic primitivism (Starr 150). For Williams, the Grail is unquestionably the cup from the Last Supper, 'which in its progress through the imagination of Europe was to absorb into itself so many cauldrons of plenty and vessels of magic' (Williams in *Arthurian Torso* 13). But the Grail cup is not so much a physical object as the symbol of divinity taking on humanity.

Williams, who, as a number of critics have noted, has written some of the most original Arthurian poetry of the twentieth century (see, for example, Göller 121–2), also created one of the few versions of the Grail story in that century that is informed by a faith and a belief system comparable to what is found in the medieval versions. Williams believed that the Grail is central to the Arthurian legends and that retellings of those legends are the less if they do not make it so. As he observed, Tennyson 'meant to make the Grail an episode, and he did. He said it was only for certain people, and he modified the legend accordingly. If it is to be more, it must take the central place. Logres then must be meant for the Grail.... This indeed must be the pure glory of Arthur and Logres' (*Arthurian Torso* 83). In *Taliessin through Logres* (1938) and its companion *The Region of the Summer Stars* (1944), Williams created a complex of symbols centring on the Grail in a cycle of poems telling the story of Logres, Arthurian Britain, and its inhabitants.

Much of the Arthurian background to which Williams alludes is based on Malory, but the notion of an anarchic state that must be redeemed by the order of Camelot derives from Tennyson. Other aspects of Tennyson's work, however, such as his opposition of the true and the false and his condemnation of the passions of the body, are at odds with Williams's view of the goodness of the material world because of the Redemption.

Williams's concern with uniting the spiritual and the natural is reflected in the poem 'The Crowning of Arthur'. In *Arthurian Torso* (111–12), C. S. Lewis observed that in this poem: 'Externally all is well: nay, more than well, all is gorgeous. The poem is full of torch-light, flute music, heraldry. The heraldic beasts on the shields, conventionalized into symbols of honour and order, are an expression of the long desired union between *Broceliande and Byzantium'; but, he concluded, 'the union is precarious'. Merlin, seeing the events from the perspective of Byzantium, also sees—or rather foresees—the destructive elements of Arthur's court, such as the affair between *Lamorack and *Morgause (which another poem in Williams's cycle, 'Lamorack and the Queen Morgause of Orkney', depicts as lacking any element of true spiritual love) and the love of Lancelot and Guinevere. In 'The Departure of Merlin', which comes later in the sequence of events of Williams's poems than Merlin's beguilement does in Malory, Arthur's adviser leaves the world 'better and worse, more redeemed and more condemned', as Lewis says (*Arthurian Torso* 172) and as the images of a despairing sailor and of Galahad sitting in the Siege Perilous suggest.

The focal characters in the cycle are Taliessin and Galahad. The significance of the former is evident in 'Mount Badon', in which Taliessin is both 'king's poet' and 'captain of horse in the wars' (33). The dual roles merge because Taliessin the warrior is engaged in a battle to bring order to Logres just as the poet is always engaged in an attempt to bring the order of the Logos (for Williams, the written word and Christ) to Arthur's realm. This coalescence is emphasized by Taliessin's vision of Virgil seeking 'the word' and 'the invention of the City' (34), that is, the order of civilization that both the city and poetry represent. The vision comes to Taliessin as he attempts to find a weakness in the enemy's defences. Poetry and battle, pen and sword, become mixed in the poem's imagery because at this moment they are one, both means of imposing order. Williams writes that Taliessin saw 'the hexameter spring and the King's sword swing', thus equating the verse of Virgil with the sword wielded by Arthur. And when Taliessin 'fetched the pen of his spear from its bearer' (34), his functions as poet and military leader blend.

Taliessin also plays a significant role in another poem of special importance in the sequence, 'The Coming of Galahad', which again reflects Williams's concern with uniting the spiritual and the natural. The occasion of the poem is the arrival of Galahad, the chosen knight who is able to sit in the Siege Perilous and thus complete the circle of knights at the Round Table. But most of the poem is devoted to a conversation Taliessin has with Gareth and a slave girl. When Gareth asks who has been allowed to sit in the forbidden seat, Taliessin speaks of 'the double dance of a stone and a shell' (76), a notion that Williams took from Wordsworth. In The Prelude, Wordsworth wrote of a dream in which an Arab shows him a stone that represents geometric truth and a shell that represents poetry, two images that suggest the typical Romantic opposition between reason and imagination, science and poetry. Williams extends the meaning of these symbols to the natural and the supernatural, which are united by Galahad as Grail knight. His sitting in the 'perilous sell' (76) is like the fitting of the stone to his shell.

This union is an important concept in 'The Coming of Galahad' and indeed in Williams's poetry in general. The strange site of the conversation, 'among the jakes and latrines' (75), is appropriate because the baser elements, as much a part of the natural world as the porphyry stair in the palace, are necessary to the achieving of the Grail, as Taliessin's words imply: 'without this alley-way how can man prefer? | and without preferences can the Grail's grace be stored?' (77). The union of the natural and the spiritual in Galahad is alluded to again in the image of his hands: 'when he washed his hands, the water became phosphorescent'. The 'sanctity' implied here is absent from Guinevere, whose hand 'lying on her heart' is quite the opposite. Her fingers are like claws, and represent 'the stone | fitting itself to its echo' (Williams, Arthurian Poets 78–9) and not to the shell. Though Guinevere's sin is a symbol for the fall of man, 'Williams also asserts, through the women in the cycle, the intrinsic beauty and goodness of the flesh appropriately disciplined, as reflection of the divine beauty, source of inspiration, and constant delight. It is in and through the flesh that we learn: through the scar on the slave's back, through the arm of Iseult' (Brewer 113).

Williams's symbolism can be difficult, even cryptic at times, but the cycle developed in Taliessin through Logres and The Region of the Summer Stars is a significant contribution to Arthurian poetry; the volumes present a very different picture of the Grail from that in T. S. Eliot's Waste Land, the other major modern poetic treatment of the subject. Whereas Eliot uses the myth to emphasize the sterility of modern society, Williams uses it to suggest the possibility of finding the grace of the Grail by integrating the natural and supernatural worlds.

Williams's novel *War in Heaven* (1949) also uses the Grail as a central symbol. The title is taken from the Book of Revelation 12: 7, which says that there was war in heaven in which Michael fought against the dragon. The novel, which develops a similar struggle between good and evil, is in part a murder mystery, beginning with the discovery of a body in a London publishing house. The murderer is Gregory Persimmons, the father of the current director of the firm. Persimmons is also involved in a plot to steal the Grail, which a manuscript sent to the firm revealed to be housed in a church in the town of Fardles. Though the location of the Grail is excised from the printed book at the author's insistence, the archdeacon in Fardles realizes from a copy of the proofs that an old chalice in his care is actually the Grail. Persimmons and his unsavoury accomplices steal the Grail and use its power in black-magic rituals. Ultimately they are foiled by *Prester John, who declares himself to be 'the Grail and the Keeper of the Grail' (214) and who arrives in time to assist the archdeacon and a couple of associates in their struggle against the forces of evil.

C. S. Lewis's 'Launcelot'

Charles Williams's colleague C. S. Lewis (1898–1963), who like Williams wrote a novel that contained Arthurian themes in the context of a struggle between good and evil, also wrote 'Launcelot', an Arthurian poem centring on the quest for the Grail. Lewis's poem is fascinating in its account of the sense of loneliness and loss that hangs over Arthur's hall and of the effect of the quest on the knights who undertook it. When Launcelot, the focus of the poem, returns, he delays visiting the queen; and when he finally sees her, he stares into the fire (perhaps a reminder of the eternal fires of hell) as he tells of his adventures at the dwelling of a lady who had prepared coffins for Lamorake, Tristram, and Launcelot, the 'three best knights of Christendom' (100). The lady hoped to get the living knights to lie in the coffins, which contain a device that will drop a 'razor-keen' blade on their necks. After killing them, she planned to 'Keep those bright heads and comb their hair and make them lie | Between my breasts and worship them until I die' (103). These chilling lines, the last in the poem, explain the change in Launcelot, who has been made to confront an extreme and perverted form of the worldliness of which he himself has been guilty. Though the differences between his love for the queen and the lady's desire to possess the three earthly knights are obvious, so too are the differences between the way chosen by the three best knights of Christendom, the Grail knights, and that chosen by Launcelot and the other 'earthly knights'.

Naomi Mitchison

To the Chapel Perilous (1955) by Naomi Mitchison (1897–1999) tells the story of the Grail as covered by two reporters, Dalyn from the *Northern Pict* and Lienors from the *Camelot Chronicle*. What they learn is that although there is only one Grail, it takes many forms. Gawain's Grail is a bowl or cauldron; Peredur's, a stone; Lancelot's, a silver cup; Bors's, the dish used at the Last Supper; Galahad's, a vessel full of blood which he keeps near his heart but whose blood does not spill. The variety of interpretations, deriving in part from the variety of forms the Grail takes in Arthurian tradition, makes each quester important since each helps to define what the Grail is.

Mitchison's novel is, however, more than just a commentary on spiritual quests; it is also a satire of power and the manipulation of information. Taking into account not only the various interpretations of the Grail but also the fact that, at least in the English tradition, Galahad has generally supplanted Percival as the Grail knight, Mitchison suggests that both the Church and economic forces have a vested interest in having a single Grail knight, a single version of the story. Thus they manipulate the facts, fake photographs of Galahad's triumph, and coerce reporters into supporting the deception. In its anachronistic portrayal of Arthurian story and its postmodern scepticism about the reliability of a received story, *To the Chapel Perilous* foreshadows later works like Barthelme's *The King*.

Jim Hunter

One of the best Arthurian Grail novels is *Percival and the Presence of God* (1978) by Jim Hunter (b. 1939). Hunter has said that in early drafts of the novel 'I had a twentieth-century narrator taking airplane flights and thinking about the issues'. The issues that the ultimately discarded narrator considered are large ones, for this tale is not the typical late medieval fantasy. It is really an exploration of the state of the modern world, as is demonstrated by the fact that Hunter originally thought of the book as 'a gloss on T. S. Eliot's *Waste Land*' (Thompson, 'Interview with Jim Hunter').

The Percival of Hunter's tale is a questing knight, but since his story is a novel and not a romance, the action is often realistic rather than heroic. Percival's tutor Mansel, for example, is killed not in knightly combat but in an ambush by 'petty robbers' who strip him of his armour and leave his naked body lying in the mountain pass where they attacked him. They care nothing for his knighthood or for the fact that he was taught the knightly code 'by one who had been with Arthur' (20). Even Arthur is part of the book's realistic fabric. In fact, the Arthur of the novel, who never appears and is never found by Percival, is much like the Arthur of modern scholarly study: some people believe in him, others do not. He is the subject of stories, but his reality is never confirmed.

Percival's quest is for a way of life, or rather for a way of living in the world, and thus the quest and the question of the novel are about the modern world as much as the world of Arthurian knights. The way Percival seeks is defined by the 'code' in which he has been instructed by Mansel. While not specifically defined, the code is a moral guide that Percival follows 'because it *has* to be followed. Because of what I see of men without the code.' It is, as Percival says in a sentiment that seems to echo Tennyson, 'what we must have, to draw us away from the beast' (23). This code makes Percival continue his second quest, to return to the castle of the fisher-lord, even after he gives up his quest for Arthur. Having visited the fisher-lord once and, as in the traditional version of the story, having failed to ask the sympathetic question that would free the wounded lord, Percival realizes that he must persist and fulfil his destined role by 'reducing the *time* he [the fisher-lord] must suffer' (137).

Percival has been prepared for this more important quest both by his instruction in the code and by his seeking of Arthur. The process of changing the focus of his quest from Arthur to the fisher-lord becomes part of the pattern that defines Percival's life and gives him faith in the presence of God. Ultimately, his faith in a plan is more essential than his faith in a person. While Percival seeks Arthur throughout much of the book, in the end he himself admits, 'I no longer believe in Arthur, it being all I can manage to believe in God' (140). Hunter has said that his book has a 'hero who is chosen without particularly willing it' (Thompson, 'Interview with Jim Hunter'). This quality makes him a type of the modern Everyman searching for a defining purpose not because he chooses to but because it is the only way to make sense of the otherwise incomprehensible world.

Anthony Powell

Novelist Anthony Powell (1905–2000) uses elements of the Grail myth in *The Fisher King* (1986), a novel whose central character, Saul Henchman, is compared explicitly to the Fisher King by the other passengers on a cruise ship touring Britain. Henchman, injured during the war, is accompanied by beautiful ballet dancer Barberina Rookwood, who gave up her career to tend to him. On the cruise, Barberina becomes enamoured of Robin Jilson, a sort of Perceval figure who travels with his mother but who, unlike Perceval, has trouble leaving her. He suffers from a muscular illness that leaves him extremely tired and thus unsuited for certain kinds of work. On this 'Arthurian cruise' (180), there is also a Loathly Damsel, Lorna Tiptoft, a blend of Cundrie and *Ragnell. But in the inversion of Arthurian story that underlies the novel, the Loathly Damsel keeps Powell's Perceval from fulfilling himself with Barberina and never turns into a beautiful maiden; Jilson has no Grail to achieve; and the Fisher King leaves the cruise to fish in the Orkneys with no hope of a return of the Grail knight or of healing. Therefore, the novel is less ambiguous in the pessimism of its ending than Eliot's *Waste Land*, which influenced it.

Peter Vansittart

Like Hunter, Mitchison, and Powell, another British novelist, Peter Vansittart (b. 1920), writes a tale that is meant to be a comment on the modern world. Because of Vansittart's belief that 'the figure of Parsifal is not bound particularly by time and space,' his *Parsifal* (1988) follows the title character from 'about the time Rome is being founded' to Nazi Germany (Thompson, 'Interview with Peter Vansittart'). Vansittart's Parsifal is a character in whom people see what they want rather than one who performs heroic deeds or achieves moral perfection. Right to the end of the book, where Heinrich Himmler considers him the 'supreme embodiment of purity' (254), he is always less than what he is perceived to be.

THE GRAIL IN POPULAR CULTURE

The Grail has become a symbol as omnipresent in modern culture as it was rare and elusive in medieval romance. In almost every field, from computing to sports and business, there are Holy Grails to be attained; and references to the Grail abound in magazines, newspapers, and other media. The Grail also appears frequently in popular fiction and film and in other aspects of popular culture, such as New Age speculation.

The Grail in Popular Literature
In literature, the Grail is found not only in fantasy fiction but also in romances, mysteries, and humorous and juvenile novels. American author Richard Monaco's (b. 1940) fantasy series of Parsival novels, loosely based on Wolfram von Eschenbach's *Parzival*, depicts an Arthurian world without the spiritual values of the medieval romances. The violence of the tales is greater and more senseless than that found in the sequence's predecessors, including *Perlesvaus*. In *Parsival* (1977), *The Grail War* (1979), *The Final Quest* (1980), and *Blood and Dreams* (1985), murder, rape, destruction, and even cannibalism are all used in part to deromanticize the stories of knights and quests and the Grail. Against this background of gratuitous violence, Parsival's quest for the Grail does not lead to fulfilment or enlightenment. In *Grail* (1982), a horror novel by Philip Michaels (pseudonym of Canadian author Philippe van Rjndt), a cup made by demons as a 'life force' was lost by them and remade into the cup used by Christ. When it is removed from the Vatican, modern Fisher Kings try to prevent the demons from regaining it and using its power to multiply and to take over the world. In the tradition of those modern fantasy writers who focus on the female characters of the legends, Susan Shwartz (b. 1949) makes Kundry the central figure in *The Grail of Hearts* (1992), a novel which draws its inspiration from Wagner's *Parsifal*. In *Grail* (1997), Stephen Lawhead recounts Arthur's miraculous renewal by the sacred relic, which mysteriously vanishes and must be recovered by the king and his Dragon Flight. *The Serpent and the Grail* (1999) by A. A. Attanasio (b. 1951) combines Norse and Arthurian lore in a tale in which Arthor is helped by his mother *Ygrane and by Merlin as he attempts to recover the Grail which protects Britain. In an earlier novel, *Kingdom of the Grail* (1992), Attanasio introduced an ageing baroness whose lands are seized by her wicked son. Years later, a beautiful young woman returns claiming to be the baroness restored to youth by the Holy Grail.

In *The Grail: A Novel* (1963), Babs H. Deal links modern sports and medieval combat and questing by transposing the Arthurian story to the world of American college football, a world in which a season without a loss is the Holy Grail. Arthur, Guenevere, and Launcelot are transformed into Coach Arthur Hill of Castle University, his wife Jennie, and his star quarterback Lance Hebert. In fact, virtually all of the traditional characters appear in the novel, usually as players and their sorority girlfriends. The coach, hailed as king for his career successes, seems well on the way to achieving his dream, until Lance falls in love with Jennie and disrupts the unity of the team, which loses its final game.

British novelist Tom Holt's *Grailblazers* (1994) is a humorous novel about Sir Boamund, a knight of Arthur's court, who wakes from an enchanted sleep to lead a group of knights (*Bedevere, Turquine, Pertelope, Lamorak, and Galahaut) on three quests which must be accomplished before they can undertake the quest for the Holy Grail. Holt presents the Grail as a 'terracotta washing-up bowl', which was transformed into blue plastic after Christ used it to wash the dishes dirtied at the Last Supper (337–8). Though, even from a comic perspective, the novel is not one of the more interesting modern treatments of the Grail legend, Holt's Monty-Pythonesque humour produces some very funny scenes.

The Grail figures in several mysteries or detective novels that draw, often obliquely, on Arthurian legend. In Jonathan Gash's (pseudonym of John Grant, b. 1933) novel *The Grail Tree* (1979), an antique dealer/detective named Lovejoy finds the ultimate antique, the Grail, for which its keeper, Reverend Henry Swan, has been murdered. The murderer and thief committed his crimes because the Grail was housed in a priceless tree-shaped casket enhanced over the centuries by famous jewellers, from a seventeenth-century artisan to Fabergé. In Richard Ben Sapir's *Quest* (1987), the hero, worldly-wise Detective Arthur ('Artie') C. Modelstein seeks the gold, gem-encrusted salt cellar that incorporates the Holy Grail and that was originally created for Queen Elizabeth I to celebrate the victory over the Spanish Armada. Artie's quest takes him inside the criminal world of international gem dealers. The Grail in one form or another also figures in Nelson DeMille's *The Quest* (1975) and James P. Blaylock's *The Paper Grail* (1991).

The Grail is also a common theme in novels written for children, which often provide a lesson for the young readers. In *In the Court of King Arthur* (1918) by Samuel E. Lowe, a page to Sir Percivale named Allan proves his worth by being 'tireless in the performance of [his] duty' (126), is singled out by Joseph of Arimathea who asks Launcelot to help guide him, and ultimately is knighted and given the name Galahad. After much seeking, he finds the Grail in a scene reminiscent of Lowell's *The Vision of Sir Launfal*, when he is charitable to a beggar and learns that the Grail was always near to home.

Another sort of lesson is taught in *Brother to Galahad* (1963) by Gwendolyn Bowers. Hugh of Alleyn leaves his ancient castle of Brannlyr, where he lives with his mother after the death of his father in a seclusion similar to that of Perceval. After travelling to Glastonbury, Hugh learns of its history and of Alleyn, the first Fisher King. He also discovers that he is descended from the line of Joseph of Arimathea and thus is related to Galahad. Hugh gives to Galahad the treasure of Brannlyr, the cloth to cover the red-cross shield that only Galahad can bear; becomes Galahad's squire on the Grail quest; and is knighted by him. Yet even after Galahad has achieved the Grail, Hugh's quest continues. He remembers Galahad's words: 'For you too follow the Grail—by another road' (Bowers 186).

After witnessing Arthur's battle with Modred and his departure for Avalon, Hugh vows to renew the spirit of Camelot at Brannlyr.

In Eleanore Myers Jewett's *The Hidden Treasure of Glaston* (1946), another Hugh, this one a lame young oblate at the monastery of Glastonbury whose father was one of the murderers of Thomas Becket, has a vision that leads to the discovery of Arthur's body. Later, when he risks his life to rescue one of the monks during a fire that destroys Glastonbury Abbey, he is granted a vision of the Grail which cures him of his lameness. The lesson he learns is that the spirit of Glastonbury is to build and to give and that 'to the builders and the givers will come the vision—when God so wills it!' (287).

The Sparrow Child (1958), by British author Meriol Trevor (1919–2000), tells of a modern quest for the Grail at a home in Cornwall called Corben, where family lore says the Grail was brought by an ancestor who was a monk at Glastonbury at the time of the dissolution of the monasteries by Henry VIII. When the Glastonbury Chalice is found, it does not cure the physical ills of family members, but it does bring about a reconciliation; and Philip Sparrow, the young boy who is central to the story, learns that the Grail is in Corben, in England, in 'the world of mankind', and in each heart (241).

Elements of the Perceval story—the need to ask the right questions, the need to heal the land as well as individuals, the need to find answers about a past denied to a child because of the death of a father—underlie the structure of one of the best of modern Arthurian children's novels, *Park's Quest* (1988) by Katherine Paterson (b. 1932). Paterson's Parkington Waddell Broughton the Fifth ('Park' for short) embarks on a quest to learn about his father, who died in Vietnam when Park was just a baby. Park's quest takes him first to the Vietnam Memorial in Washington and then to the farm where his father was raised, where he discovers the family secrets that his mother has withheld from him and discouraged him from asking about—that she divorced his father just before his second tour of duty in Vietnam, during which he was killed; that his grandfather, a career military officer called simply 'the Colonel', had suffered his first stroke when he heard the sad news; and the deepest secret of all, that Thanh, the Vietnamese girl who lives on the farm and who is a kind of Grail maiden in the novel, is actually his half-sister. The very contemporary Park is therefore much like the traditional Perceval, whose mother kept him ignorant of chivalry, which she blamed for his father's death; who, learning of the existence of knights, ignored his mother's grief and left for court; who, in a castle, is witness to a strange procession but, as advised, never questions what he sees; and who eventually asks the question that cures the infirm Fisher King.

Another of Paterson's novels is based on Wolfram von Eschenbach's *Parzival*. In her *Parzival: The Quest of the Grail Knight* (1998), she recounts Parzival's sheltered youth, his knighting, his marriage to Condwiramurs, and his failure to ask the question that would heal Anfortas. After learning that posing the question is a sign of compassion for the suffering king, Parzival ultimately returns and cures him.

The story of the Grail quest is also retold in Rosemary Sutcliff's (1920–92) *The Light Beyond the Forest* (1979), which is essentially a modernization and a simplification of parts of Malory's account of the quest. When Galahad arrives at Arthur's court early in the tale, the older knights who had felt 'the high and shining days were over' now believe there is 'something ahead of them again', something that Lancelot calls 'a light beyond the forest' (20).

The Grail in Film

Since the era of silent movies, film-makers have recognized the cinematic potential of the Grail. In *The Light in the Dark* (Vitagraph, 1922; dir. Clarence L. Brown; also known as *The Light of Faith*), Lon Chaney stars as Tony Pantelli, a gangster in love with a girl who is restored to health through the powers of the Holy Grail and who, in the end, is reconciled with her millionaire boyfriend, from whom Tony stole the Grail in order to cure her. The silent film, shot in black and white, was dyed for the story of the quest for the Grail, which is told in flashback.

A somewhat later production, *The Adventures of Sir Galahad* (Columbia, 1949; dir. Spencer Gordon Bennet), a fifteen-part serial, suggests just how adaptable the legends are to cinematic conventions. Though the episodes have no connection to the Grail story, Galahad (George Reeves) is the hero who, as a young knight, is blamed for the disappearance of Excalibur and who ultimately recovers it to save his reputation. The episodes follow the cliffhanger formula: at the beginning of each new episode, Galahad must escape from an apparent tragedy that ended the previous one.

More recent films have made use of the Grail theme to comment on the violence, greed, and absurdity of modern society. In *The Fisher King* (Columbia, 1991; dir. Terry Gilliam), Jack Lucas (Jeff Bridges), a shock disc jockey, is partly responsible for the death of the wife of Henry Sagan (Robin Williams), a professor of medieval history. When she is killed, Sagan goes insane and believes himself to be on a quest for the Holy Grail. 'I'm a knight on a special quest,' Henry (who now calls himself Parry) tells Jack, 'and I need your help.' But, in fact, it is Jack, like Parry both a Fisher King and a Grail knight figure, who needs Parry's help. After retrieving from a Fifth Avenue apartment a trophy cup that Parry thinks is the Grail, Jack is able not only to heal his friend but also to assume responsibility for his own actions, to resurrect his career, and to rebuild his personal relationships, thus revitalizing his own life as well.

Indiana Jones and the Last Crusade (Lucasfilm/Paramount, 1989; dir. Steven Spielberg), the third instalment of the popular Indiana Jones trilogy, takes archaeologist Indiana Jones (Harrison Ford) on a quest, first for his father (Sean Connery), an archaeological scholar who has disappeared while tracking the hiding place of the Holy Grail, and then for the Grail itself. Alerted by wealthy collector Walter Donovan to his father's disappearance and guided by the elder Jones's notebooks on the sacred vessel, Indy rescues his father from the Nazis who are holding him captive, and ultimately they and the others seeking the Grail locate the place where it has been protected for centuries. Donovan, however, mortally wounds Dr Jones, forcing Indy to undergo a series of tests to achieve the Grail, which alone can save his father. The last protector of the Grail, a knight who has survived since the Middle Ages, tells them they must choose the real Grail from among scores of goblets. After Donovan chooses a rich cup and drinks from it, he disintegrates. In a classic understatement, the knight says, 'He chose poorly.' Indy chooses well and restores his father to health. But Donovan's companion Elsa tries to remove the Grail from the temple, against the knight's admonition. She plunges to her death trying to retrieve it from the chasm into which it has fallen. Indy, after failing to rescue her, ignores his own warning and tries himself to retrieve the Grail, which has fallen onto a ledge in the chasm just beyond his reach. He then must do something as hard as achieving the Grail; he must follow his father's counsel to 'let it go'.

Perhaps the most popular Grail film is *Monty Python and the Holy Grail* (Python Pictures, 1975; dir. Terry Gilliam and Terry Jones). Its popularity derives not only from its outrageous humour but also from the many motifs its creators adapt from medieval literature. The fabulous beasts, the dangerous trials, the perilous bridge crossing, the combat that continues when one knight is severely wounded, the rescue of a maiden imprisoned in a tower, the fabulous ship that takes the knights to the Grail castle—all these stock motifs from medieval romance are parodied in the film. Also parodied is the kind of anachronism found both in medieval literature and in modern renderings of the medieval. The medieval political structure is turned into the subject of a debate between Arthur and a peasant; a Holy Hand Grenade is used to kill a vicious rabbit. The consciousness of such anachronism is emphasized by having 'a famous historian' comment on the narrative, only to be killed by a knight. The film ends not with the successful completion of the quest but with the arrest of Arthur and Bedivere by modern policemen, who appear a couple of times earlier to investigate the historian's death. Perhaps this ending is just one more way the film creates humour by having the modern world intersect the medieval; or perhaps it is meant to indicate that the modern mindset so intrudes on our reception of medieval story that it is impossible for us not to imprison the original narrative in our own preconceptions.

Esoteric and New Age Approaches to Glastonbury and the Grail

The elusive and spiritual nature of the Grail and the associations of Glastonbury with this sacred object and its history are favourite subjects among those who delve into or dabble in mystical, psychic, or eccentric theories. Among the most important and influential of these writers was Dion Fortune (pseudonym of Violet Mary Firth, 1890–1946), who worked to make Glastonbury a spiritual and cultural centre. Her book *Avalon of the Heart* (1934) claimed that Glastonbury can be approached not only through history and through legend but also through 'the Mystic Way', which leads to the 'Avalon of the Heart', and spoke of Glastonbury as 'a gateway to the Unseen' (1, 2). Her assertion that 'There is spiritual power in Glastonbury' (47) is surely behind the many people and books that see the place as a source of some sort of psychic, spiritual, or natural energy. And her definition of 'the two Avalons, the Christian and the pagan', seems to have influenced Marion Zimmer Bradley's novel *The Mists of Avalon*. In fact, Fortune describes the 'mist' which local folk call 'the Lake of Wonder' when it thickens over Glastonbury until 'Avalon is an island again'; and she talks of how the legends of Arthur and the Lady of the Lake are evoked when 'the Lake of Wonder rises from its faery spring under the Hunter's Moon' (66, 61, 62).

When Fortune writes of the Grail stories, it is sometimes hard to differentiate history from romance: she recounts the legends of Joseph of Arimathea and the Glastonbury Thorn as if they were part of the actual history of Glastonbury. She is, in this respect, like the medieval chroniclers and like many of those modern authors who write about Glastonbury or the Grail.

Even before Fortune wrote her book and established Glastonbury as an esoteric centre of Britain, Frederick Bligh Bond (1864–1945), an architect appointed as director of excavations at Glastonbury Abbey, recorded in *The Gate of Remembrance* (1918) automatic writing said to have been controlled by the spirits of monks who had served at Glastonbury. These accounts led to the excavation of several previously unknown buildings—but also, eventually, to Bond's dismissal from his position. A subsequent volume, *The Company of Avalon*, 'carries on, or rather, carries back, the story of the building and the builders of the great monastery to other times' (p. v). In the preface to this volume, Bond asserts that he witnessed the automatic writing of a script containing an account of the 'missionary journeys of Philip the Evangelist, who claimed to have been one of the company of Joseph of Arimathea', and another purporting 'to be an account by St. Joseph himself of the institution of the religious House of Glaston' (p. xix).

A later writer, K. E. Maltwood (1878–1961), in *A Guide to Glastonbury's Temple of the Stars*, posits a giant zodiac laid out in the region surrounding Glastonbury by primitive people and suggests that clues to these ancient monuments can be found in the adventures of the knights on the quest for the Grail in *Perlesvaus* and other Grail romances.

The Grail itself is redefined in *The Holy Blood and the Holy Grail* (1982) by Michael Baigent, Richard Leigh, and Henry Lincoln, who analyse a range of documents and tales, from medieval to modern, to construct a hypothesis that Mary Magdalene 'was in fact Jesus's wife', that they may have had 'at least one child', and that Mary Magdalene and her child went to Gaul after the Crucifixion. Thus, the authors argue, there might have been 'an hereditary bloodline descended directly from Jesus' which may be the true '*sang réal*' or royal blood (275). That line, they conjecture, had its descendants in the Merovingian kings and has been maintained down to the present. This notion of Mary Magdalene as the wife of Jesus and their descendants as the Grail also underlies the popular novel *The Da Vinci Code* (2003) by Dan Brown.

For Gareth Knight, in *The Secret Tradition in Arthurian Legend* (1983), the Arthurian legends 'enshrine a secret Mystery Tradition'. He refers to the Lesser Mysteries as the 'Grade of the Powers of Arthur', the 'Grade of the Powers of Merlin', and the 'Grade of the Powers of Guenevere', all of which deal in one way or another with the material or conscious world. Beyond these are the 'Greater Mysteries of the Quest and Achievement of the Holy Grail'. The stories of the Grail 'describe the transcendent forces behind the Elemental creation'. Knight believes that we all 'have the Grail within us' and so the quest for the Grail 'is, in a sense, a voyage or journey of self re-discovery' (13–15).

The ideas formulated or interpreted by Knight are the basis for a host of spiritual self-help books, ranging from the crazy to the comforting, in which the Grail is a symbol for personal development. *The Sangreal Tarot* (1988) by William G. Gray, for example, uses the tarot as an aid to achieving 'what might be termed a Sangreal-state of spiritual awareness' (p. vii), a method that assumes the Grail to be 'a new type of consciousness' brought by beings from another planet and impelling humans towards some higher spiritual existence (2). In *The Cup of Destiny* (1988), Trevor Ravenscroft views Wolfram's *Parzival* as a document initiating its reader into the knowledge of the three stages 'in a radical evolution of conscious-ness' through which humanity must pass: from dullness to doubt to blessedness (15). *Crossing to Avalon* (1994) by Jean Shinoda Bolen sees the re-emergence of interest in the Goddess, the transformative and healing feminine principle, as the return of the Grail in the modern world. John Matthews and Marian Green provide in their *Grail Seeker's Companion* (1986) a guidebook to the Grail quest, which they define as an attempt to correct the overemphasis on material things in our society by seeking inner values and spiritual worth. To this end, they have written 'a reference book of Grail-ology, including history, ritual meditation, advice and instruction' (11).

BIBLIOGRAPHY

Chrétien de Troyes's *Perceval* and its Continuations and Translations

Armstrong, Grace. 'The Scene of the Blood Drops on the Snow: A Crucial Narrative Moment in the *Conte du Graal*', *Kentucky Romance Quarterly*, 19 (1972), 127–47.

Besamusca, Bart. 'The Damsel of Montesclare in the Middle Dutch *Lancelot Compilation*', in Geert H. M. Claassens and David F. Johnson (eds.), *King Arthur in the Medieval Low Countries*. Leuven: Leuven University Press, 2000: 87–96.

Bliocadran: A Prologue to the Perceval of Chrétien de Troyes: Edition and Critical Study, ed. Lenora D. Wolfgang. Tübingen: Max Niemeyer, 1976.

Bruckner, Matilda Tomaryn. 'Looping the Loop through a Tale of Beginnings, Middles and Ends: From Chrétien to Gerbert in the *Perceval* Continuations', in Keith Busby and Catherine M. Jones (eds.), *'Por le soie amisté': Essays in Honor of Norris J. Lacy*. Amsterdam: Rodopi, 2000: 33–51.

Busby, Keith. *Chrétien de Troyes: Perceval (Le Conte du Graal)*. Critical Guides to French Texts 98. London: Grant and Cutler, 1993.

Campbell, Ian. 'Medieval Riddarasögur in Adaptation from the French: *Flóres saga ok Blankiflúr* and *Parcevals saga*', *Parergon*, 8.2 (Dec. 1990), 23–35.

Chrétien de Troyes. *Li Contes du Graal*, ed. Rupert T. Pickens, trans. William W. Kibler. New York: Garland, 1990.

—— *Perceval* (translated as *The Story of the Grail*), in *The Complete Romances of Chrétien de Troyes*, trans. David Staines. Bloomington: Indiana University Press, 1990: 339–449.

Continuations of Perceval, in *Perceval: The Story of the Grail*, trans. Nigel Bryant. Cambridge: D. S. Brewer, 1982. (Contains abridged translations of the Continuations to *Perceval*.)

The Continuations of the Old French 'Perceval' of Chrétien de Troyes, ed. William Roach. 5 vols. Philadelphia: University of Pennsylvania Press/American Philosophical Society, 1949–83.

The Elucidation: A Prologue to the Conte del Graal, ed. Albert Wilder Thompson. New York: Institute of French Studies, 1931.

Fowler, David. *Prowess and Charity in the Perceval of Chrétien de Troyes*. Seattle: University of Washington Press, 1959.

Frappier, Jean. *Chrétien de Troyes: The Man and his Work*, trans. Raymond J. Cormier. Athens: Ohio University Press, 1982.

Gerbert de Montreuil. *La Continuation de Perceval*, vols. i and ii ed. Mary Williams and vol. iii ed. Marguerite Oswald. Paris: Champion, 1922, 1925, 1975.

Grimbert, Joan Tasker. 'Distancing Techniques in Chrétien de Troyes's *Li Contes del Graal* and Eric Rohmer's *Perceval le Gallois*', *Arthuriana*, 10.4 (Winter 2000), 33–44.

Kalinke, Marianne E. *King Arthur: North-by-Northwest: The Matière de Bretagne in Old Norse-Icelandic Romances*. Copenhagen: C. A. Reitzels, 1981.

Lacy, Norris J. *The Craft of Chrétien de Troyes: An Essay on Narrative Art*. Leiden: E. J. Brill, 1980.

La Nef. *Perceval: La Quête du graal (The Quest for the Grail)*. 2 compact discs, booklet by Katherine A. Dory. Troy, NY: Dorian Recordings, 1999, 2001.

Parcevals saga and *Valvens þáttr*, in *Norse Romance*, vol. ii, ed. and trans. Marianne E. Kalinke. Cambridge: D. S. Brewer, 1999: 108–220.

Uitti, Karl D., with Freeman, Michelle A. *Chrétien de Troyes Revisited*. New York: Twayne, 1995.

Robert de Boron and the Prose Adaptations of his Work

The Didot Perceval: According to the Manuscripts of Modena and Paris, ed. William Roach. Philadelphia: University of Pennsylvania Press, 1941.

Gowans, Linda. 'The Grail in the West: Prose, Verse and Geography in the *Joseph* of Robert de Boron', *Nottingham French Studies*, 35.2 (Autumn 1996), 1–17.

O'Gorman, Richard. 'The Prose Version of Robert de Boron's *Joseph d'Arimathie*', *Romance Philology*, 23 (1970), 449–61.

Pickens, Rupert T. ' "Mais de çou ne parole pas Crestiens de Troies . . . ": A Re-examination of the Didot-*Perceval*', *Romania*, 105 (1984), 492–510.

Robert de Boron. *Joseph d'Arimathie: A Critical Edition of the Verse and Prose Versions*, ed. Richard O'Gorman. Toronto: Pontifical Institute of Medieval Studies, 1995.

—— *Joseph d'Arimathie: A Romance of the Grail*, trans. Jean Rogers. London: Rudolf Steiner Press, 1990.

—— *Merlin and the Grail: Joseph of Arimathea, Merlin, Perceval: The Trilogy of Prose Romances Attributed to Robert de Boron*, trans. Nigel Bryant. Cambridge: D. S. Brewer, 2001.

—— *Merlin: Roman du XIIIe siècle*, ed. Alexandre Micha. Geneva: Droz, 1980.

Skeels, Dell (trans.), *The Romance of Perceval in Prose: A Translation of the E Manuscript of the Didot Perceval*. Seattle: University of Washington Press, 1961.

Perlesvaus

Field, P. J. C. 'Malory and *Perlesvaus*', *Medium Ævum*, 62 (1993), 259–69.

Le Haut Livre du Graal: Perlesvaus, ed. William A. Nitze and T. Atkinson Jenkins. 2 vols. Chicago: University of Chicago Press, 1932, 1937.

The High Book of the Grail: A Translation of the Thirteenth Century Romance of Perlesvaus, trans. Nigel Bryant. Cambridge: D. S. Brewer, 1978.

Kelly, Thomas E. *Le Haut Livre du Graal: Perlesvaus: A Structural Study.* Geneva: Droz, 1974.

Lloyd-Morgan, Ceridwen. '*Breuddwyd Rhonabwy* and Later Arthurian Literature', in Rachel Bromwich, A. O. H. Jarman, and Brynley F. Roberts (eds.), *The Arthur of the Welsh: The Arthurian Legend in Medieval Welsh Literature*. Cardiff: University of Wales Press, 1991: 183–208.

McCracken, Peggy. 'Damsels and Severed Heads: More Linking in the *Perlesvaus*', in Keith Busby and Catherine M. Jones (eds.), '*Por le soie amisté*': *Essays in Honor of Norris J. Lacy.* Amsterdam: Rodopi, 2000: 339–55.

Roberts, Dorothy James. *Kinsmen of the Grail.* 1963; repr. Oakland, Calif.: Green Knight, 2000.

Y Seint Greal, Being the Adventures of King Arthur's Knights of the Round Table, in the Quest of the Holy Greal, and on Other Occasions. Originally Written about the Year 1200, ed. and trans. Robert Williams. London: Thomas Richards, 1876.

Peredur and Sir Perceval of Galles

Busby, Keith. 'Chrétien de Troyes English'd', *Neophilologus*, 71 (1987), 596–613.

Eckhardt, Caroline D. 'Arthurian Comedy: The Simpleton-Hero in *Sir Perceval of Galles*', *Chaucer Review*, 8 (1973–4), 205–20.

Fowler, David C. '*Le Conte du Graal* and *Sir Perceval of Galles*', *Comparative Literature Studies*, 12 (1975), 5–20.

Historia Peredur vab Efrawc, ed. Glenys Goetinck. Cardiff: University of Wales Press, 1976.

Lovecy, Ian. '*Historia Peredur ab Efrawg*', in Rachel Bromwich, A. O. H. Jarman, and Brynley F. Roberts (eds.), *The Arthur of the Welsh: The Arthurian Legend in Medieval Welsh Literature*. Cardiff: University of Wales Press, 1991: 171–82.

Peredur, in *The Mabinogion*, trans. Gwyn Jones and Thomas Jones, rev. edn. London: Dent, 1974: 183–227.

Sir Perceval of Galles, in Mary Flowers Braswell (ed.), *Sir Perceval of Galles and Ywain and Gawain*. Kalamazoo, Mich.: Medieval Institute Publications, 1995: 1–76.

Tyolet and Related Tales

Claassens, Geert H. M. 'The Narrator as a Character in *Lanceloet en het hert met de witte voet*', in Geert H. M. Claassens and David F. Johnson (eds.), *King Arthur in the Medieval Low Countries*. Leuven: Leuven University Press, 2000: 173–85.

Guingamor, Lanval, Tyolet, Bisclaveret: Four Lais Rendered into English Prose from the French of Marie de France and Others, trans. Jessie Weston. London: David Nutt, 1900.

Haan, M. J. M. de. 'A Philological Paternity Test', *Dutch Studies*, 1 (1974), 37–43.

Housman, Clemence. *The Life of Sir Aglovale de Galis.* 1905; repr. Oakland, Calif.: Green Knight, 2000.

Le Lai de Tyolet, in Prudence Mary O'Hara Tobin (ed.), *Les Lais anonymes des XIIe et XIIIe siècles: Édition critique de quelques lais Bretons*. Geneva: Droz, 1976: 227–53.

Lanceloet en het hert met de witte voet, in David F. Johnson and Geert H. M. Claassens (eds. and trans.), *Dutch Romances*, iii: *Five Interpolated Romances from the Lancelot Compilation*. Cambridge: D. S. Brewer, 2003: 524–61.

Moore, George. *Peronnik the Fool*. Mount Vernon, NY: William Edwin Rudge, 1926.

Moriaen, ed. H. Paardekooper-van Buuren and M. Gysseling. Zutphen: N. V. W. J. Thieme, 1971.

Morien: A Metrical Romance Rendered into English Prose from the Mediæval Dutch, trans. Jessie L. Weston. Arthurian Romances Unrepresented in Malory's 'Morte d'Arthur' 4. London: D. Nutt, 1901.

Wolfram von Eschenbach and his Influence

Albrecht. *Albrechts von Scharfenberg: Jüngere Titurel*, ed. K. A. Hahn. Quedlinburg: G. Basse, 1942.

Groos, Arthur. *Romancing the Grail: Genre, Science, and Quest in Wolfram's Parzival*. Ithaca, NY: Cornell University Press, 1995.

Hasty, Will (ed.). *A Companion to Wolfram's Parzival*. Columbia, SC: Camden House, 1999.

Hauptmann, Gerhart. *Lohengrin*. Berlin: Ullstein, 1913.

—— *Parsival*. Berlin: Ullstein, 1914.

Haymes, Edward R. 'From Romance to Ritual: Wolfram, Arthur, and Wagner's *Parsifal*', in Debra N. Mancoff (ed.), *The Arthurian Revival: Essays on Form, Tradition, and Transformation*. New York: Garland, 1992: 174–90.

Heiduczek, Werner. *Die seltsamen Abenteuer des Parzival: Nach Wolfram von Eschenbach neu erzählt*. Berlin: Neues Leben, 1974.

Hoffman, Donald L. 'Re-framing Perceval', *Arthuriana*, 10.4 (Winter 2000), 43–56.

Kralik, Richard von. *Der heilige Gral*. Trier: Petrus, 1912.

Mann, Frido. *Professor Parsifal: Autobiographischer Roman*. Munich: Ellermann, 1985.

Miller, Arthur Maximilian. *Der Gral*. Kempten: Allgäuer Zeitundsverlag, 1976.

Muschg, Adolf. *Der rote Ritter: Eine Geschichte von Parzivâl*. 3 vols. Frankfurt am Main: Suhrkamp, 1993.

Parshall, Linda B. *The Art of Narration in Wolfram's Parzival and Albrecht's Jüngere Titurel*. Cambridge: Cambridge University Press, 1981.

Poag, James F. *Wolfram von Eschenbach*. New York: Twayne, 1972.

Ranke, Friedrich. 'The Symbolism of the Grail in Wolfram von Eschenbach', in Dhira B. Mahoney (ed.), *The Grail: A Casebook*. New York: Garland, 2000: 367–77.

Sacker, Hugh. *An Introduction to Wolfram's Parzival*. Cambridge: Cambridge University Press, 1963.

Schaeffer, Albrecht. *Parzival*. Leipzig: Insel, 1922.

Weigand, Hermann J. *Wolfram's Parzival: Five Essays with an Introduction*, ed. Ursula Hoffmann. Ithaca, NY: Cornell University Press, 1969.

Wolfram von Eschenbach. *Parzival*, ed. Karl Lachmann; rev. Eberhard Nellman, trans. (into modern German) Dieter Kühn. 2 vols. Frankfurt: Deutscher Klassiker Verlag, 1994.

—— *Parzival*, trans. Helen M. Mustard and Charles E. Passage. New York: Vintage Books, 1961.

—— *Titurel and the Songs*, ed. and trans. Marion E. Gibbs and Sidney M. Johnson. New York: Garland, 1988.

Wynn, Marianne. 'Parzival and Gawan—Hero and Counterpart', *Beiträge zur Geschichte der Deutschen Sprache und Literatur*, 84 (1962), 142–72.

The Grail in the Lancelot–Grail (or Vulgate) and the Post-Vulgate Cycles and Henry Lovelich's Translation

Baumgartner, Emmanuèle. 'From Lancelot to Galahad: The Stakes of Filiation', in William H. Kibler (ed.), *The Lancelot–Grail Cycle: Text and Transformations*. Austin: University of Texas Press, 1994: 14–30.

Burns, E. Jane. *Arthurian Fiction: Rereading the Vulgate Cycle*. Columbus: Ohio State University Press for Miami University, 1985.

Estoire del Saint Graal, in *Lancelot–Grail: The Old French Arthurian Vulgate and Post-Vulgate in Translation*, gen. ed. Norris J. Lacy, vol. i. New York: Garland, 1993: 1–163. (*Estoire del Saint Graal* is translated by Carol J. Chase.)

Kibler, William W. (ed.). *The Lancelot–Grail Cycle: Text and Transformations*. Austin: University of Texas Press, 1994.

Lovelich, Henry. *The History of the Holy Grail*, ed. Frederick J. Furnivall. 5 vols. EETS ES 20, 24, 28, 30, 95. 1874, 1875, 1877, 1878, 1905; repr. Woodbridge: Boydell and Brewer for the EETS, 1996 (bound as 2 vols., in 1, with new pagination in each volume).

The Post-Vulgate *Queste del Saint Graal*, in *Lancelot–Grail: The Old French Arthurian Vulgate and Post-Vulgate in Translation*, gen. ed. Norris J. Lacy, vol. v. New York: Garland, 1996: 111–289. (The Post-Vulgate *Quest for the Holy Grail* is translated by Martha Asher.)

Pratt, Karen. 'The Cistercians and the *Queste del Saint Graal*', *Reading Medieval Studies*, 21 (1995), 69–96.

Queste del Saint Graal, in *Lancelot–Grail: The Old French Arthurian Vulgate and Post-Vulgate in Translation*, gen. ed. Norris J. Lacy, vol. iv. New York: Garland, 1995: 1–87. (*Queste del Saint Graal* is translated by E. Jane Burns.)

The Vulgate Version of the Arthurian Romances, ed. H. Oskar Sommer. 8 vols. Washington: The Carnegie Institution of Washington, 1908–16.

Joseph of Arimathea

Chant, A. G. *The Legend of Glastonbury*, ill. Horace J. Knowles. London: The Epworth Press, 1948.

The History of That Holy Disciple Joseph of Arimathea. [London]: Printed and sold in Bow-Church-yard, London, [1770?].

Joseph of Arimathea: A Critical Edition, ed. David A. Lawton. New York: Garland, 1983.

Lagorio, Valerie M. 'The *Joseph of Arimathie*: English Hagiography in Transition', *Medievalia et Humanistica*, NS 6 (1975), 91–101.

Lyfe of Joseph of Armathia and 'A Praysyng to Joseph', in *Joseph of Arimathie: Otherwise Called The Romance of the Seint Graal, or Holy Grail: An Alliterative Poem Written about A. D. 1350, and Now First Printed from the Unique Copy in the Vernon MS. at Oxford. With an Appendix, Containing 'The Lyfe of Joseph of Armathy,' Reprinted from the Black-Letter Copy of Wynkyn de Worde; 'De Sancto Joseph ab Arimathia,' First Printed by Pynson A.D. 1516; and 'The Lyfe of Joseph of Armathia,' First Printed by Pynson A.D. 1520*, ed. Walter W. Skeat. EETS OS 44. 1871; repr. New York: Greenwood, 1969.

The Lyfe of Joseph of Armathy, in *Joseph of Arimathie: Otherwise Called The Romance of the Seint Graal, or Holy Grail: An Alliterative Poem Written about A. D. 1350, and Now First Printed from the Unique Copy in the Vernon MS. at Oxford. With an Appendix, Containing 'The Lyfe of Joseph of Armathy,' Reprinted from the Black-Letter Copy of Wynkyn de Worde; 'De Sancto Joseph ab Arimathia,' First Printed by Pynson A.D. 1516; and 'The Lyfe of Joseph of Armathia,' First Printed by Pynson A.D. 1520*, ed. Walter W. Skeat. EETS OS 44. 1871; repr. New York: Greenwood, 1969.

Noble, James. 'The Grail and its Guardian: Evidence of Authorial Intent in the Middle English *Joseph of Arimathea*', *Quondam et Futurus*, 1.2 (Summer 1991), 1–14.

Ormerod, James. 'St. Joseph of Arimathæa', in *Tristram's Tomb and Other Poems*. London: Elkin Mathews, 1928: 117–27.

Slaughter, Frank G. *The Thorn of Arimathea*. New York: Doubleday, 1959.

Sone von Nausay, ed. Moritz Goldschmidt. Tübingen: Litterarischer Verein in Stuttgart, 1899.

Steedman, Marguerite. *Refuge in Avalon*. Garden City, NY: Doubleday and Co., 1962.

The Grail from Malory to Victorian England

Burns, James. *Sir Galahad: A Call to the Heroic*. London: James Clarke, n.d. [1915].

Hawker, Robert Stephen. *The Quest of the Sangraal: Chant the First*. 1864; reprinted in *Cornish Ballads and Other Poems*. Oxford: James Parker and Co., 1869: 180–203.

Morris, William. 'Sir Galahad, a Christmas Mystery', in James P. Carley (ed.), *Arthurian Poets: Matthew Arnold and William Morris*. Woodbridge: The Boydell Press, 1990: 73–9.

Payne, John. 'The Romaunt of Sir Floris', in *The Masque of Shadows and Other Poems*. London: Basil Montagu Pickering, 1870: 143–223.

Poulson, Christine. *The Quest for the Grail: Arthurian Legend in British Art, 1840–1920*. Manchester: Manchester University Press, 1999.

Rossetti, Dante Gabriel. 'God's Graal', in *The Works of Dante Gabriel Rossetti*, ed. William M. Rossetti. London: Ellis, 1911: 239. (The poem was written in 1858 but first published in this 1911 edition of Rossetti's poems.)

Shorthouse, J. H. *Life, Letters, and Literary Remains*, edited by his wife. 2 vols. London: Macmillan and Co., 1905.

—— *Sir Percival: A Story of the Past and the Present*. London: Macmillan, 1886.

Tennyson, Alfred Lord. 'Sir Galahad', in Alan Lupack (ed.), *Modern Arthurian Literature: An Anthology of English and American Arthuriana from the Renaissance to the Present*. New York: Garland, 1992: 151–3.

Westwood, Thomas. *The Quest of the Sancgreall, The Sword of Kingship, and Other Poems*. London: John Russell Smith, 1868.

—— *The Sword of Kingship: A Legend of the 'Mort d'Arthure'*. London: Whittingham and Wilkins (for private circulation), 1866.

Wordsworth, William. 'The Egyptian Maid or The Romance of the Water-Lily', 1835; repr. in Alan Lupack (ed.), *Modern Arthurian Literature: An Anthology of English and American Arthuriana from the Renaissance to the Present*. New York: Garland, 1992: 119–31.

American Interpretations of the Grail

Erskine, John. *Galahad: Enough of his Life to Explain his Reputation*. Indianapolis: Bobbs-Merrill, 1926.

Greenslet, Ferris. *The Quest of the Holy Grail: An Interpretation and a Paraphrase of the Holy Legends . . .*, with *Illustrations from the Frieze Decoration in the Boston Public Library by Edwin Austin Abbey, R.A.* Boston: Curtis & Cameron, 1902.

Harty, Kevin J. 'The Arthurian Legends on Film: An Overview', in Kevin J. Harty (ed.), *Cinema Arthuriana: Essays on Arthurian Film*. New York: Garland, 1991: 3–28.

Hylton, J. Dunbar. *Arteloise: A Romance of King Arthur and Knights of the Round Table*. Palmyra, NJ: The Hylton Publishing Co., 1887.

Jewett, Sophie. 'The Dwarf's Quest: A Ballad', in *Persephone and Other Poems: By Members of the English Literature Department, Wellesley College, for the Benefit of the Wellesley Library Fund*. Boston: The Fort Hill Press, 1905: 53–61.

Lowell, James Russell. *The Vision of Sir Launfal*. Cambridge: George Nichols, 1848.

Malamud, Bernard. *The Natural*. New York: Farrar, Straus & Giroux, 1952.

Mason, Bobbie Ann. *In Country*. New York: Harper & Row, 1985.

Percy, Walker. *Lancelot*. New York: Farrar, Straus & Giroux, 1977.

Spicer, Jack. *The Holy Grail*, in *The Collected Books of Jack Spicer*, ed. Robin Blaser. Los Angeles: Black Sparrow Press, 1975: 185–213.

Steinbeck, John. *Cup of Gold*. 1929; repr. New York: Bantam, 1953.

Sterling, Sara Hawks. *A Lady of King Arthur's Court: Being a Romance of the Holy Grail*. Philadelphia: George W. Jacobs, 1907.

Taft, Linwood. *Galahad: A Pageant of the Holy Grail*. New York: A. S. Barnes, 1924.

Teasdale, Sara. 'Galahad in the Castle of the Maidens', in *Helen of Troy and Other Poems*. New York: Macmillan, 1911: 85.

Trask, Katrina. *Under King Constantine*, 2nd edn. New York: Anson D. F. Randolph and Co., 1893.

Tucker, Irwin St John. *The Sangreal*. Chicago: Published by the Author, 1919.

Jessie Weston and T. S. Eliot

Eliot, T. S. *The Waste Land and Other Poems*. New York: Harvest Books, 1963.

Weston, Jessie. *From Ritual to Romance*. 1920; repr. Garden City, NY: Doubleday Anchor Books, 1957.

—— 'Knights of King Arthur's Court', in *The Rose Tree of Hildesheim and Other Poems*. London: David Nutt, 1896: 47–58.

Williamson, George. *A Reader's Guide to T. S. Eliot: A Poem-by-Poem Analysis*, 2nd edn. New York: Octagon Books, 1979.

Twentieth-Century British Interpretations of the Grail

Arthurian Torso: Containing the Posthumous Fragment of The Figure of Arthur by Charles Williams and a Commentary on the Arthurian Poems of Charles Williams by C. S. Lewis. London: Oxford University Press, 1948.

Brewer, Elisabeth. 'Women in the Arthurian Poems of Charles Williams', in Brian Horne (ed.), *Charles Williams: A Celebration*. Leominster: Gracewing, 1995: 98–115.

Göller, Karl Heinz. 'From Logres to Carbonek: The Arthuriad of Charles Williams', *Arthurian Literature*, 1 (1981), 121–73.

Heath-Stubbs, John A. *Charles Williams*. Writers and their Work 63. London: Longmans, Green & Co. for The British Council and the National Book League, 1955.

Hunter, Jim. *Percival and the Presence of God*. London: Faber and Faber, 1978.

Lewis, C. S. 'Launcelot', in *Narrative Poems*, ed. Walter Hooper. London: Geoffrey Bles, 1969: 93–103.

Machen, Arthur. *The Great Return*. London: Faith Press, 1915.

—— *The Secret Glory*. London: Martin Secker, [1922].

Mitchison, Naomi. *To the Chapel Perilous*. 1955; repr. Oakland, Calif.: Green Knight, 1999.

Padmore, E. S. *The Death of Arthur: The Story of the Holy Grail*. London: Herbert Jenkins, 1936.

Powell, Anthony. *The Fisher King*. London: Heinemann, 1986.

Powys, John Cowper. *A Glastonbury Romance*. New York: Simon and Schuster, 1932.

Starr, Nathan Comfort. *King Arthur Today: The Arthurian Legend in English and American Literature 1901–1953*. Gainesville: University of Florida Press, 1954.

Taylor, Beverly, and Brewer, Elisabeth. *The Return of King Arthur: British and American Literature since 1900 [i.e. 1800]*. Cambridge: D. S. Brewer, 1983.

Thompson, Raymond H. 'Interview with Jim Hunter', www.lib.rochester.edu/camelot/intrvws/hunter.htm (accessed 23 Dec. 2001).

—— 'Interview with Peter Vansittart', www.lib.rochester.edu/camelot/intrvws/vansitrt.htm (accessed 1 Feb. 2004).

Trevelyan, R. C. *The Birth of Parsival*. London: Longmans, Green, and Co., 1905.

—— *The New Parsifal: An Operatic Fable*. London: Printed for the Author at the Chiswick Press, 1914.

—— *The Pterodamozels: An Operatic Fable*. London: Printed for the Author at the Pelican Press, 1916.

Underhill, Evelyn. *The Column of Dust*. London: Methuen, 1909.

Vansittart, Peter. *Parsifal*. London: Peter Owen, 1988.

Williams, Charles. *Arthurian Poets: Charles Williams*, ed. David Llewellyn Dodds. Woodbridge: The Boydell Press, 1991. (Contains *Taliessin through Logres*, originally published in 1938, and *The Region of the Summer Stars*, originally published in 1944, and other published and previously unpublished poems by Williams.)

—— *War in Heaven*. New York: Pellegrini & Cudahy, 1949.

The Grail in Popular Culture

Attanasio, A. A. *Kingdom of the Grail*. New York: HarperCollins, 1992.

—— *The Serpent and the Grail*. New York: HarperPrism, 1999.

Baigent, Michael, Leigh, Richard, and Lincoln, Henry. *The Holy Blood and the Holy Grail*. London: Jonathan Cape, 1982.

Blaylock, James P. *The Paper Grail*. Norwalk, Conn.: The Easton Press, 1991.

Bolen, Jean Shinoda. *Crossing to Avalon: A Woman's Midlife Pilgrimage*. San Francisco: HarperSanFrancisco, 1994.

Bond, Frederick Bligh. *The Company of Avalon: A Study of the Script of Brother Symon, Sub-Prior of Winchester Abbey in the Time of King Stephen*. Oxford: Basil Blackwell, 1924.

—— *The Gate of Remembrance: The Story of the Psychological Experiment which Resulted in the Discovery of the Edgar Chapel at Glastonbury*. Oxford: B. H. Blackwell, 1918.

Bowers, Gwendolyn. *Brother to Galahad*. New York: Henry Z. Walck, 1963.

Brown, Dan. *The Da Vinci Code*. New York: Doubleday, 2003.

DeMille, Nelson. *The Quest*. New York: Manor Books, 1975.

Fortune, Dion. *Glastonbury: Avalon of the Heart*. 1934; rev. and expanded edn. Wellingborough: The Aquarian Press, 1986. (Originally published under the title *Avalon of the Heart*.)

Gash, Jonathan. *The Grail Tree*. London: Collins, 1979.

Gray, William G. *The Sangreal Tarot: A Magical Ritual System of Personal Evolution*. York Beach, Me.: Samuel Weiser, 1988.

Holt, Tom. *Grailblazers*. London: Orbit, 1994.

Jewett, Eleanore M. *The Hidden Treasure of Glaston*. New York: Viking, 1946.

Knight, Gareth. *The Secret Tradition in Arthurian Legend*. Wellingborough: The Aquarian Press, 1983.

Lawhead, Stephen R. *Grail*. Book Five in the Pendragon Cycle. New York: Avon Books, 1997.

Lowe, Samuel E. *In the Court of King Arthur*. Racine, Wis.: Whitman Publishing Co., 1918.

Maltwood, K. E. *A Guide to Glastonbury's Temple of the Stars: Their Giant Effigies Described from Air Views, Maps, and from 'The High History of the Holy Grail'*. Greenwood, SC: The Attic Press, 1964.

Matthews, John, and Green, Marian. *Grail Seeker's Companion: A Guide to the Grail Quest in the Aquarian Age*. Wellingborough: The Aquarian Press, 1986.

Michaels, Philip. *Grail*. New York: Avon, 1982.

Monaco, Richard. *Blood and Dreams*. New York: Berkley, 1985.

—— *The Final Quest*. New York: Putnam's, 1980.

—— *The Grail War*, ill. David McCall Johnston. New York: Wallaby, 1979.

—— *Parsival or a Knight's Tale*, ill. David McCall Johnston. New York: Macmillan, 1977.

Paterson, Katherine. *Park's Quest*. New York: Lodestar Books/E. P. Dutton, 1988.

—— *Parzival: The Quest of the Grail Knight*. New York: Lodestar Books, 1998.

Ravenscroft, Trevor. *The Cup of Destiny*. 1981; repr. York Beach, Me.: Samuel Weiser, 1982.

Sapir, Richard Ben. *Quest*. New York: E. P. Dutton, 1987.

Shwartz, Susan. *The Grail of Hearts*. New York: TOR, 1992.

Sutcliff, Rosemary. *The Light beyond the Forest: The Quest for the Holy Grail*. London: The Bodley Head, 1979.

Trevor, Meriol. *The Sparrow Child*. London: Collins, 1958.

5

Gawain

*Gawain plays a significant role in *Grail romances, where he is one of the questing knights (though rarely does he actually achieve the Grail); and he—along with his brothers—also plays a large role in those works that treat the tragic events caused by the love between Lancelot and Guinevere. Gawain is important too in the chronicle tradition, where, as *Arthur's nephew and boldest knight, he is instrumental in Arthur's continental victories. Gawain has an equivalent in Welsh literature: the hero Gwalchmai who, at some point, becomes Arthur's nephew and is identified with Gawain. In many other medieval romances—more, in fact, than those in which *Lancelot is the protagonist—as well as in some of the modern works based on them, Gawain is the central character, his adventures are the focal point, and he defines knightly courtesy, love, and valour.

GAWAIN ROMANCES OTHER THAN ENGLISH

The Youth of Gawain

Gawain is the hero of the Latin romance *De ortu Waluuanii nepotis Arturi* (*The Rise of Gawain, Nephew of Arthur*), written in the twelfth century by the same author (sometimes identified, but with no real certainty, as Robert de Torigny (d. 1186), abbot of Mont Saint-Michel) who wrote the *Historia Meriadoci* (discussed in Chapter 3). According to the romance, Gawain is born to *Anna and *Loth, a hostage at *Uther's court, before their marriage. To hide the birth, Anna entrusts the child to a group of merchants. But a fisherman named Viamundus steals Gawain and the rich possessions Anna has provided for him, and takes him to Rome. Viamundus pretends to be a nobleman, but before his death he tells the truth about Gawain to the emperor, who raises the boy and knights him. On his way to Jerusalem to do single combat for the emperor with the champion of a pagan king, Gawain, called the Knight of the Surcoat because he wears a crimson tunic over his armour, stops to hunt on an island and finds that its ruler Milocrates has abducted the emperor's niece. Gawain frees her, kills Milocrates, and defeats his forces; and then, as he sails off, he defeats the fleet commanded by Milocrates' brother, even though his enemies use the feared Greek fire.

After reaching Jerusalem and fighting a fierce three-day battle with Gormundus, the pagan champion, Gawain wants more action, and so he journeys to Britain to aid Arthur in his battles. Yet, even after Gawain unhorses *Kay and Arthur, the king says he will accept him as his knight only if he accomplishes something that all his army has failed to do. The opportunity arises when the lady of the Castle of Maidens is carried off by a pagan king. Arthur's army is routed by the pagan forces; but Gawain charges them, kills their king, rescues the lady, and disperses the king's guard. Returning with the pagan king's head, he is received by Arthur as his knight. Gawain's identity as the king's kinsman is finally revealed; and his progress from 'the Boy with no Name' to 'the Knight of the Surcoat' to Gawain, the nephew and best knight of King Arthur, is complete.

The story of Gawain's youth is also related in the early thirteenth-century French romance *Les Enfances Gauvain* (*The Youth of Gawain*). The surviving fragments of this romance tell of Gawain's birth to Morcades (*Morgause) and Lot, and of his being set adrift and found by a fisherman who takes him to Rome, where he is knighted by the pope.

French Romances

Many French romances recount the exploits of Gawain (Gauvain in the French) and represent him as the model of chivalry and valour. Some romances, however, seem to react against the traditional characterization or use it for comic or satiric purposes.

Two short French verse romances with Gawain as hero were written in the very late twelfth or the early thirteenth century. One of them, *La Mule sans frein* (*The Mule without a Bridle*), claims to be by Paien de Maisières, generally considered a pseudonym. In the romance, a lady rides to Arthur's court on a mule which has no bridle and asks that a knight retrieve the bridle for her. Kay undertakes the quest and passes through a wood where lions, tigers, and leopards instil in him 'a fear so great that never was a greater' (29). But the beasts kneel to the mule the lady has given him to ride and do not harm him. He also passes serpents and snakes but turns back when he comes to a turbulent river with only a very narrow iron bridge spanning it.

As is typical in Gawain romances, Gawain must complete the task at which Kay has failed. After encountering the same dangers as Kay and crossing the treacherous bridge, Gawain comes to a revolving castle. There, he forces the mule to leap for the door and gains entry. Inside he encounters a hairy churl, who proposes a beheading contest analogous to the one in the later English romance *Sir Gawain and the Green Knight*, 'probably the earliest appearance of this theme in romance' (Busby 259–60). Gawain chops off the churl's head and must withstand his return blow the next morning; but the churl spares him because 'he had so well kept his promise' (35). Gawain then must fight with and kill two ferocious lions, encounter a fierce knight, and slay two dragons. After Gawain passes all these tests, the lady of the castle, who is the sister of the lady seeking the bridle, offers herself and her thirty-nine castles to him if he will stay with her. He refuses and returns, past rejoicing people who have been freed from fear of the lions he has killed, to give the lady who sent him on the quest her bridle. The 'messianic overtones' of Gawain's adventure and freeing of the people, 'suggestive of the Harrowing of Hell', are part of the 'gentle humorous burlesque' (Busby 262) of the poem.

A second short verse romance, *Le Chevalier à l'épée* (*The Knight of the Sword*), is anonymous but shares a number of characteristics with *Mule* and is sometimes considered to be by the same author. In the main action, Gawain, lost in a forest, meets a knight who takes him to his castle and puts him to bed with his courteous and beautiful daughter. But above the bed is a sword which descends to strike anyone who attempts to make love to her. When Gawain makes advances to the lady, he is struck by the sword. Since he receives only a slight cut, the test proves Gawain to be the best knight (49). As a result, he marries the lady and they set off together from her father's castle.

The second part of the romance, which, the editors conjecture, 'appears to have its source in . . . a lost *lai* . . . or some popular, fabliau-type tale' (3), recounts the couple's encounter with a knight who abducts Gawain's new wife. Gawain wants to arm himself and fight, but the knight refuses his challenge and suggests instead that the lady decide with whom she will go. She chooses the stranger and then asks her new knight to retrieve her dogs from Gawain since they, unlike the faithless wife, have chosen to remain with him. This occasions 'a violent anti-feminist outburst' from Gawain 'in the course of which comparisons are drawn between women and dogs, comparisons not entirely to the advantage of women' (Busby 256). When Gawain defeats the knight, his wife wants to return to him, but he leaves her and goes back to court.

Gliglois, a verse romance of the first half of the thirteenth century, takes a different approach: it makes Gawain a foil to the young hero of the tale. Gliglois is the accomplished and courtly son of a German chatelaine, who sent him to Arthur's court to serve and learn from Gawain. When a maiden named Beauté arrives at court, Gawain almost immediately professes his love for her, but she rejects him. To try to win her love by honouring her, Gawain instructs Gliglois to serve her. Gliglois too falls in love with her but is troubled by feelings of disloyalty. When a tournament is called, Beauté refuses to go as Gawain's beloved; but Gliglois finds a knight to escort her. Not wishing to remain behind, Gliglois follows them on foot and suffers greatly from the heat and the hard ground; Beauté will not, however, let her companion provide him with a mount.

After seeing his devotion, Beauté sends Gliglois with a letter to her sister instructing her to provide the young man with arms and a company of knights. So equipped, he attends the tournament, proves himself courageous and skilled by winning the tournament prize of a falcon, and learns that Beauté loves him and has been testing him. Gliglois is then made a member of Arthur's court and is betrothed to Beauté. By suffering for love, Gliglois proves himself a true practitioner of 'fine amor' (152) and thus earns the rewards of love. Gawain, who does not earn such rewards, nevertheless shows his nobility by giving his approval to the marriage and asking the king to increase the young man's wealth.

Gawain, though not the primary hero, plays an important role in two romances written during the first two decades of the thirteenth century, *Meraugis de Port-lesguez* and *La Vengeance Raguidel*, the former certainly and the latter probably written by Raoul de Houdenc. *Meraugis de Portlesguez* begins with two friends, Meraugis and Gorvain, vying for the love of a lady named Lidoine. When *Guinevere and her ladies rule that Meraugis has a better claim, he must prove himself worthy by finding Gawain, who has been long absent. He meets Gawain on an island and fights him because of a custom that demands that a knight remain and fight intruders until he is defeated. However, by imprisoning the lady of the castle and dressing in her clothes to summon the boat that will take them off the island, Meraugis gains freedom for himself and Gawain. In this incident and in a later combat between Gawain and Meraugis, Gawain is less clever than and at best of equal valour to the new knight.

The main concern of *La Vengeance Raguidel* is achieving vengeance for the slain knight Raguidel. Gawain, the only knight who can remove the truncheon from Raguidel's body, must seek to avenge the death; but when he sets out, he forgets the lance point that is needed for the vengeance. Moreover, the vengeance can only be accomplished with the help of the man who can remove five rings from the dead knight's fingers, a task accomplished by *Yder. The romance deflates the romance hero in other ways. 'The ease with which Gauvain falls in love is comic', and the excesses of the passage in which his infatuation is described 'combine to form what can be little else than a burlesque of the traditional description of a man falling in love' (Busby 283–4). The humour is even greater when, given a choice between him and another knight, Gawain's beloved Ydain chooses the stranger. Love at Arthur's court in general is disparaged by the inclusion of an account of a chastity test which, as is conventional, only the beloved of Caradoc passes (113). Though Gawain is said to be a great hero and performs heroic deeds, a 'comic tone pervades *La Vengeance Raguidel* . . . and the humor is often at Gauvain's expense' (Busby 293). (Sometime in the first half of the thirteenth century, the romance was adapted into Middle Dutch as *De Wrake van Ragisel*.)

The thirteenth-century verse romance *Hunbaut* also presents a Gawain who is less than perfect. When Arthur asks him to force the King of the Isles to do homage, Gawain wants a companion for the journey. Unable to spare a knight, Arthur sends Gawain's sister with him. Hunbaut, one of Arthur's knights, advises the king that Gawain is not diplomatic enough for such a mission—a striking statement given the reputation of Gawain in many romances (the English romances discussed below, for example) for being so courteous that he often sets right situations worsened by Kay's bluntness. Hunbaut joins Gawain and tells his sister to have a passing knight accompany her back to court. (Unfortunately, she encounters an enemy of Gawain's, is kidnapped, and must be rescued in a later adventure.) On their journey, Gawain acts somewhat like Kay when he takes food from a knight by force.

At the entrance to the castle of the King of the Isles, Gawain is challenged to a beheading contest by a churl. Gawain strikes off his head and holds his enchanted body to prevent him from retrieving it. After a time the magic of the enchantment fails and the churl dies, so Gawain does not have to endure a return stroke. Afterwards, Gawain and Hunbaut deliver Arthur's message to the King of the Isles, who is in a reverie and does not realize until later what they have demanded. Since the romance is incomplete, whether or not the King ultimately does homage to Arthur is not known. In the romance, however, Gawain is presented as a brave knight and a lover—even inspiring one lady to have constructed a lifelike statue of him which she keeps near her bed—but not as the model of courtesy.

In the verse romance *Mériadeuc* (edited and translated as *Le Chevalier aux deux épées* (*The Knight of the Two Swords*)), written in the second quarter of the thirteenth century, Gawain again shares the central role with another hero. The romance begins with an adventure analogous to that of *Balin as recounted in the Old French *Suite du Merlin* and in Malory's *Morte d'Arthur*. King Ris has demanded Arthur's beard to trim a cloak which is lined with the beards of nine other kings. Ris is invading Arthur's lands and has already taken the castle of the Lady of Cardigan, who frees herself and her people by retrieving a sword from a dead knight and then seeking at Arthur's court the great knight who will be capable of ungirding it and who will, according to her request to Arthur, become her husband. No one but a nameless knight can accomplish the task, a feat which earns him the epithet of the Knight with Two Swords—only at the end of the romance is his name revealed to be Mériadeuc—but he rides off and Arthur must send four knights to bring him back. After Mériadeuc defeats the four knights Arthur has charged to bring him back, the Knight with Two Swords earns even more fame when he sends to Arthur the wounded Ris and many of his men.

On his quest to find Mériadeuc, Gawain encounters Brien of the Isles, who loves the Queen of the Isles. She will marry Brien only if he can kill Gawain, the greatest knight. In order to meet this condition, Brien jousts with Gawain, even though the latter is without armour, and after wounding him seriously, leaves him for dead. When Gawain is healed, he seeks Brien to punish him for his treachery. At his coronation, Brien declares that he has slain Gawain and is therefore the best knight. But the Knight with Two Swords disputes Brien's claim and says that if Gawain is dead, then he is now the best knight. Gawain in turn disputes Mériadeuc's claim and the two fight; but when Gawain reveals his name, they end their combat, at which point Gawain challenges Brien, defeats him, and sends him to Arthur's court.

It is soon revealed that Gawain slew Bleheri, Mériadeuc's father, but only because he was tricked into the combat by a knight named Brien de la Gastine, who then took control of Bleheri's lands. Bleheri, moreover, was the knight whose sword was retrieved by the Lady of Cardigan and which his son now wields. An angry Mériadeuc parts company with Gawain and slays Brien de la Gastine, an act that causes Brien's son Galien to attack Bleheri's widow. After Gawain fights in her defence and kills Galien, the widow reveals that her husband knew that Gawain was tricked into fighting him and forgave Gawain before his death. Gawain's defence of Mériadeuc's mother and her declaration of his father's forgiveness lead to a reconciliation between the two knights, who become companions on a quest to a fountain where Mériadeuc obtains another sword, which he uses to cure a wounded knight.

Following yet another adventure, Gawain and Mériadeuc return to court, where Mériadeuc is married to the Lady of Cardigan and Gawain is married to a woman whose love he won during his adventures. The nameless knight who became the Knight with Two Swords finally realizes his full identity and potential and is named 'King Meriadeuc' (182). Although Gawain's assistance is central to Mériadeuc's attaining knighthood, regaining his heritage, and being crowned a king, Mériadeuc is the figure of primary interest in the romance and Gawain's role is only a supporting one.

There are, however, other French romances of the thirteenth century in which Gawain is the true hero and not the subject of humour or parody. One such romance, *The Perilous Cemetery* (*L'Atre périlleux*), written *c.*1250, is influenced by both Raoul de Houdenc and Chrétien de Troyes. Gawain's adventures begin when a knight named Escanor abducts a lady who has requested that she be made Arthur's cupbearer. Gawain delays in rescuing her, and Kay, who calls Gawain a coward, rides after her, only to be unhorsed and injured in the attempt. Following the typical pattern, Gawain must set right what Kay could not. Gawain soon comes upon three women, who tell him that the great knight Gawain has been killed and dismembered and that a squire who tried to help him has been blinded. Gawain then begins a quest to regain his identity and his literal and figurative name.

Before encountering the slayers of the man believed to be Gawain, the hero undergoes another series of adventures, including the one from which the romance takes its name. Unable to gain entrance to a castle, Gawain goes to a chapel with a cemetery, where he intends to spend the night. A young man informs him that the place is called the Perilous Cemetery and that no knight has taken refuge there for a hundred years without being found dead in the morning since each evening the devil comes to meet with a woman over whom he has gained control by offering to cure her of the madness that she suffered because of an enchantment. To free her, Gawain must fight the devil who arrives fully armed. Gawain prevails with the help of the lady, who reminds him to look at a cross every time his strength weakens.

Gawain then overtakes Escanor, who had abducted the cupbearer so he might have the opportunity to fight the famous knight. In defeating Escanor, Gawain wins his allegiance and his assistance in overcoming the knights who claimed to have killed Gawain and who have offered to fight anyone who disputes their assertion. Escanor accepts the challenge of one of them, Gomeret, and Gawain of the other, the Proud Magician. Both Escanor and Gawain are victorious; and, to avoid being killed, the Proud Magician promises to restore the life of the slain and mutilated knight and the sight of the squire.

A fascinating romance, *The Perilous Cemetery* deals with questions of reputation and knightly identity. It begins almost as if it were another comic treatment of Gawain, who is in a quandary as to whether or not he should wait until the meal is finished before setting out to rescue the kidnapped lady. But after he has 'questioned Gauvain's reputation, the *Atre* poet tries to restore it by righting the wrongs committed against the two innocent men', the knight and the squire, and ultimately 'he tries to turn Gauvain into a real hero' (Walters 8).

The Marvels of Rigomer (*Les Merveilles de Rigomer*), an episodic verse romance written about 1250 by an author who refers to himself as Jehan, reverses the pattern of a work like Chrétien's *Lancelot*, in which Lancelot succeeds at a quest also undertaken by Gawain. In *The Marvels of Rigomer*, Lancelot sets out for Rigomer, 'a castle created by spell' (150). He has many adventures and defeats many opponents, including the giant Knight of Triple Arms, who wears three helmets and has three swords. Lancelot is told repeatedly that all who seek Rigomer 'will be either dead or vilified and locked away in prison, or severely wounded' (88). Despite Lancelot's proven greatness and his ability to pass the dragon that guards the entrance to Rigomer by stunning it with a giant cudgel, he becomes the victim of enchantment and is made a prisoner, one of 140, by having a gold ring put on his finger that robs him of memory and ability. He is then reduced to beastly behaviour and is made to cook in the castle.

When those whom Lancelot defeated on his journey to Rigomer begin arriving at Arthur's court and reveal that Lancelot is imprisoned, all the knights want to set out to free him; but Arthur will allow only sixty of them, led by Gawain, to go. Some of the great knights, such as Engrevain (*Agravain), Bliobeheris (Bleoberis), *Yvain, *Cligés, and Waheriés (*Gareth), experience individual adventures. But it is Gawain who is the pre-eminent knight; and it is he who is destined to end the treacherous marvels of Rigomer. Gawain wins the love of a damsel named Lorie, who provides him with a hundred knights to fight with him in a great tournament on the plain outside Rigomer. When Gawain approaches the dragon guarding the castle, the creature kneels before him and does not oppose his entry; and he frightens the maiden who intends to place the enchanting gold ring on his finger and causes her to run off. Upon finding Lancelot (who, in one of the many humorous touches in the poem, is now chief cook and who offers his friend bread, cheese, and wine), Gawain breaks the enchanting ring off his finger and removes the rings from all the other knight prisoners. With the enchantment ended, Rigomer abounds 'with great joy and cheer' (312). Just as the romance seems to have reached a natural conclusion, Arthur and Lancelot assist the Lady of Quintefuelle in resisting a relative's claim to her land 'because it never passed to a woman before' (340). The manuscript breaks off as Arthur and Lancelot come to a fountain, where new adventures are about to begin.

Roman van Walewein

To an even greater degree than the French romances that give pre-eminence to Gawain, the Dutch *Roman van Walewein* (c.1350) presents Walewein (Gawain) as the model of chivalric virtue. The romance was begun but left incomplete by an author who identifies himself as Penninc; the ending, about 3,300 of the romance's 11,200 lines, was supplied by Pieter Vostaert. As in other Dutch romances, Gawain is called the 'Father of Adventure' (161), a title he earns by achieving a series of interwoven adventures that require almost superhuman ability. He is also said to comfort damsels in distress (377) and always to give mercy to his enemies if they request it (247–9), to pray for slain enemies, to heal wounds, and to offer spiritual counsel. Walewein's adventures in this romance begin when a chess-set flies through the window of Arthur's court at Caerleon. After settling for a time, it flies off again. Arthur wants someone to retrieve the wondrous set, but no one offers to do so until Arthur says he will pursue it himself. Then Walewein takes the challenge and is taunted by Kay as he sets off.

The motif of Kay's foolish and insulting words, common in romance, is, in fact, the controlling motif in another Dutch romance, *Walewein ende Keye* (*Gawain and Kay*), which is found in the **Lancelot Compilation*. In this romance, the sharp-tongued seneschal falsely accuses Walewein of boasting for saying 'that in one year he would have more adventures than all the other knights of the *Round Table together', and he enlists a group of companions to support his lie. In what has been called 'the most idealized . . . Walewein portrait in Arthurian romance' (Hogenbirk 165, 164), Walewein, the chivalric opposite of Keye, not only is joined in defeating Keye and his companions by those from whom he has won allegiance in a series of adventures, but also compels Keye's followers to admit that 'everything Keye had said | about Walewein was a lie' (523).

The *Roman van Walewein* also presents an idealized depiction of its hero. As he pursues the chess-set, Walewein must fight a nest of baby dragons and then their mother. After killing all the creatures in what is one of the greatest dragon-slaying scenes in all literature, he reaches the Castle of Wonders, where the King of Wonders and his son are playing a game with the set. The king, whose castle is truly full of wonders such as a bed that heals the wounds of whoever sleeps in it, agrees to give the chess-set to Walewein if he will bring him the Sword with Two Rings from King Amoraen. That sword can be used only by a chosen knight; anyone else trying to wield it will be cut in two by it.

As Walewein sets out in search of the sword, he encounters a young squire who must be knighted in order to avenge the slaying of his brother. On his way to Arthur's court, the squire is robbed of his horse and armour. Walewein lends him his own beloved horse Gringolet, an act that prompts the narrator to comment that Walewein was a knight 'from whom one could learn much | about virtue and honor' (93). When the young man returns and kills his enemy, he is beset by the man's friends; but Walewein comes to his aid and helps him slay hundreds.

Walewein seeks the Sword with Two Rings at Ravenstene, the castle of King Amoraen, who promises to give him the sword, but only—in the pattern of adventure begetting adventure that defines much of the structure of this romance—if Walewein will win for him the beautiful Ysabele, daughter of King Assentijn, who is held in a castle surrounded by twelve heavily guarded walls. Walewein agrees and sets off with the sword, which he uses to slay a Red Knight and two other wicked knights who have been abusing ladies. Before the Red Knight dies, Walewein advises him to repent and gives him a symbolic communion by placing 'a handful of earth' (199) in his mouth.

Proceeding in search of Ysabele, Walewein comes to a river which burns everything that enters it. Over it hangs a razor-sharp bridge. Walewein fears that he must turn around until he encounters a talking fox named Roges, who, he learns, was a man enchanted by his stepmother and who can return to his human form only if he looks on four people all together: the King of Wonders and his son, Walewein, and Ysabele. Roges shows Walewein a trapdoor leading to a tunnel under the river. As he reaches the castle with the twelve gates, Walewein slips through an open gate in the first wall, uses the fearsome Sword with Two Rings to slay many of the defenders, and follows the remainder as their comrades guarding the second wall give them refuge. Walewein makes his way through ten of the gates, slaying hundreds of defenders along the way; but finally he is struck on his arm and drops the wondrous sword, after which he is overwhelmed by a host of the enemy and captured.

King Assentijn, furious at the slaughter of so many of his knights, plans a cruel death for Walewein; but his daughter asks that he be placed in her chamber for the night, ostensibly so she can inflict tortures on him. Instead, having fallen in love with him, she washes and feeds him; and the two engage in love play. When a spying knight reports this treachery, the king and hundreds of knights break down the door and imprison Walewein and Ysabele; but before their execution, they are rescued by the ghost of the Red Knight, whose soul Walewein saved. The ghost, able to open locks merely by touching them, leads the prisoners to a place where the fox awaits them.

On his return to Amoraen with Ysabele, Walewein encounters and slays a haughty knight who wishes to abduct her; then he takes shelter in the pavilion of a duke who is, in fact, the father of the slain knight. When the son's body is brought to the pavilion and begins bleeding again, the duke knows from this sign that Walewein is the slayer. Imprisoned again, Walewein breaks his chains when the jailer strikes Ysabele and makes her bleed, slays the jailer, and then escapes with Ysabele. Together they reach Ravenstene, where, fortunately (since the two are now in love), Amoraen has died. Thus Walewein fulfils his pledge of bringing Ysabele to Ravenstene but can ride off with her and the sword to the Castle of Wonders, where the fox is restored to his human form and Walewein is given the chess-set.

The romance is ambiguous about whether Walewein and Ysabele marry and whether Walewein rules after Arthur, the reward promised to the knight who brings the king the chess-set. But those details are tangential to the romance which surely restores Walewein to a position of pre-eminence, perhaps, as the poem's editors suggest, in 'conscious reaction against' the decline in his reputation in some romances in the French tradition (5–6). The *Roman van Walewein*, a romance full of brilliant detail, interesting characters, exciting adventures, and examples of chivalric virtue, is one of the great Arthurian works of the Middle Ages. (Gawain's exploits and pursuit of the chessboard provide the basis for the Dutch novel *Het zwevende schaakbord* (*The Floating Chessboard*, 1923) by Louis Couperus (1863–1923), in which Gawain dies just after delivering the chessboard to Arthur.)

Heinrich von dem Türlin's *Diu Crône*

In Heinrich von dem Türlin's long verse romance *Diu Crône* (*The Crown*, c.1225), as in the *Roman van Walewein*, Gawein (Gawain) is a hero beyond reproach, though the German romance differs in tone and approach from the Dutch text. The 'crown' of the title is the romance itself. At the end of his tale, Heinrich says that even if he had more to say, he would not add to his text because 'it is not fitting to add base lead to such a well-crafted crown, which has embellished beautiful gems by setting them in gold, as art and skill can do with precious stones'; and he speaks of 'the crown that my hands wrought skillfully as I conceived it from a model' (333–4).

The romance recounts a number of adventures of Gawein and of Arthur's court. Early in the tale, the first of two chastity tests—this one, reminiscent of the *Lai du cor*, with a tankard—is described. None of the ladies is proved totally blameless, though Ginover (Guinevere) comes closest to passing the test. The knights are also called upon to drink from the tankard, and all are shown to have faults ranging from the insignificant to the serious. Only Arthur is able to drink without spilling any of the wine, and so the tankard remains in his possession. Later in the romance, there is another test, this time with a glove which will make invisible one side of the body of a perfectly virtuous person. All the ladies and knights try it on and various parts of their bodies remain visible, indicating flaws that Keii (Kay) comments on in sometimes quite bawdy terms as he fulfils his typical role of being rude and insulting. The glove fits perfectly and conceals the entire half of the body only for Arthur and Gawein. (Some scholars believe Heinrich to be the author of another account of a chastity test, the German tale known as *Der Mantel*, though his authorship is a matter of debate.)

Gawein's pre-eminence is evidenced by many adventures in the romance. He must rescue Ginover from an abductor, Gasozein de Dragoz, who claims that she was promised to him long before she married Arthur. Gawein arrives just in time to save the queen from being disgraced by Gasozein, who behaves in a less than courtly manner: he 'turned his hands loose on her bare hips. Once he had felt her body, there could be no truce .... After the knight had grasped her hip, his hand wandered here and there at will until he came to where Lady Love's mountain lies hidden and the palace that she alone rules' (131). As demonstrated in the chastity test, Heinrich's men and women are subject to real desires, even if they do live in a world full of wonders and marvellous creatures.

Gawein also recovers a bridle in an episode that is clearly influenced by some version of the story of *La Mule sans frein* (*The Mule without a Bridle*). Here, as in the French tale, Gawein succeeds where Keii fails; and he undergoes a beheading challenge and fights with lions, a knight, and dragons before he succeeds in retrieving the bridle for the damsel Sgoidamur, who needs it to regain her inheritance from her sister Amurfina. The hero's other adventures include the slaying of a giant; a visit to Lady Fortune (remarkable in that she is presented as a noble lady at whose castle a knight can be entertained); and the recovery of several items—the ring that Fortune gave to Arthur, two gloves of invisibility won by the king as a result of the chastity test, and a protective stone—all of which were stolen by the Knight with the Goat for Giramphiel, from whose lover Gawein acquired the stone. Perhaps most noteworthy of all Gawein's undertakings is his achieving the quest for the Grail by asking the question that Parzival did not (328), even though for him this 'is not a profound mystery, much less the spiritual climax' of the hero's life (Wallbank 88).

Heinrich's account of the Grail borrows elements from Wolfram's and Chrétien's Grail romances, just as his poem borrows episodes from Chrétien's other romances, from various French tales, and from Ulrich von Zatzikhoven, Hartmann von Aue, and Robert Biket. He knows well the Arthurian texts of his age and uses them freely. He also frequently inserts comments about morals, literature, and behaviour into the text; and sometimes he ascribes such comments to the characters of the romance. Moreover, his narrator has a presence in the text, and this narrator's opinions help to ground it in everyday reality despite the marvellous deeds it describes.

The Irish Tale *The Story of the Crop-Eared Dog*

The Irish tale *Eachtra an Mhadra Mhaoil* (*The Story of the Crop-Eared Dog*), the earliest manuscripts of which date from the seventeenth century, tells of the adventures of Gawain (erroneously referred to as *Galahad in the only translation of the work) with the son of the King of India, whose stepmother has transformed him into a dog so that her son, the Knight of the Lantern, may rule. When the Knight of the Lantern defeats and binds all the knights of Arthur's court except Gawain, who is said to be a 'beardless boy' (11), Gawain and the dog set out after him. The Knight uses magic to escape them many times; he changes himself into various creatures, ranging from a gnat to a lion, but his pursuers win the lantern from which he gets his name and some of his magic powers and, after further adventures, capture him. To save his life, the Knight of the Lantern agrees to restore the dog to his human form. The romance is full of wonders, magic, and tales explaining names or details, such as how the dog's ears and tail came to be cropped.

ENGLISH GAWAIN ROMANCES

Sir Gawain and the Green Knight

The greatest of English verse romances is the alliterative poem *Sir Gawain and the Green Knight* (*SGGK*), which was written in a north-west Midland dialect late in the fourteenth century and survives in a single manuscript, Cotton Nero A.x, which contains three other poems—*Pearl, Cleanness,* and *Patience*—believed to be by the same author. Written in alliterative stanzas of irregular length with a rhyming bob and wheel (a short one-stress line followed by four three-stress lines, rhyming ababa) at the end, *SGGK*, one of the most elaborately structured medieval poems, employs intricate patterns of parallelism through which its meaning is revealed. Narrative elements reflect one another and interweave to bind the poem together much as the alliterating syllables bind lines together. Symbols are also paired for purposes of comparison and contrast.

SGGK begins in *Camelot at Christmastime. As often happens in Arthurian romance, something strange from outside the court intrudes and challenges its people and its values. A knight, green not just in his livery but also in his person and astride a green horse, enters with contrasting symbols, a holly bob indicating peace and a great axe. Interpreted by critics as everything from a force of nature to a demon, the Green Knight proposes to the court a beheading contest: he will endure a stroke of the axe and then give one in return. The challenge and the reluctance of anyone to accept it, which prompts a taunt from the Green Knight, introduces a controlling theme of the poem, that of renown. As Larry Benson's study of *SGGK* and its analogues demonstrates, one of the main concerns of the *Gawain*-poet is 'renown': 'The poet carefully added this theme to each episode of the narrative, and the theme of fame ... unifies the entire poem' (Benson 209). In accepting the Green Knight's challenge, Gawain says that he is the weakest and the least of Arthur's knights (10), but he uses as the device on his shield the pentangle which suggests perfection. Later in the poem, *Morgan le Fay, the old lady Gawain meets in Bertilak's castle, is said to have instigated the challenge in order to test the Round Table and to frighten Guinevere.

It is significant that when Gawain arms himself before setting out to find the Green Knight, there is an extended account of the symbolism of the pentangle, which represents a host of virtues interconnected like the lines of the pentangle (18–19). In order to keep his vow, Gawain endures the dangers of travel through lands outside the protection of Arthur's authority and the hardships of winter. When he prays that he might find lodging where he can hear mass on Christmas Day, almost immediately he sees a castle belonging to a lord named Bertilak, where he is well received and honoured because he is the famous Gawain. At the castle, he enters into a second bargain, which parallels the beheading contest begun at Camelot and which is closely related to it. He agrees to an exchange of winnings with Bertilak, who goes out hunting each of the three mornings that Gawain is a guest. In return for the game Bertilak brings home, Gawain must give him whatever he wins during the day.

On each of the three days, while his host hunts a deer, a boar, and a fox, respectively, Gawain is tempted by the wife of Bertilak (or Bercilak). As Henry Savage has suggested, there is a relationship between the animals being hunted by Bertilak and the actions of Gawain as he is being tempted by his host's wife. On the first day, he is shy and elusive like the hart; on the second day, he faces his pursuer and resists like the boar; and on the third day, he is deceitful like the fox (Savage 31–48). The theme of renown becomes 'even more important in the scenes at Bercilak's castle than it is at Arthur's court' (Benson 218). Bertilak's wife's temptations are based upon Gawain's reputation as the most famous knight. She praises his fame, and he is appropriately self-deprecating; but when she says that she can hardly believe he is Gawain because a man such as Gawain is reputed to be could not have spent time with a lady without asking for a kiss (36), he does kiss her, once the first day, twice the second, and three times on the third. On the third day, the lady asks for a gift from Gawain; and he is able to say truthfully that he has nothing with him that is worthy of her. She offers him a ring, which he refuses; then she offers her ominously green belt or girdle and tells him that it will protect him from harm. Seeing a chance to save his life, he accepts the gift. Each evening when Bertilak returns, Gawain gives him the kisses in exchange for the game he has brought home. But when he exchanges the winnings with the lord on the third evening, he breaks the established pattern in which Bertilak offers his winnings and then Gawain bestows the kisses. Instead, Gawain initiates the exchange, an indication of the guilt he feels because he intends to hold back the green girdle. The variation from the pattern emphasizes the fault and the guilt of keeping the girdle.

When Gawain goes to meet the Green Knight, he is armed again; but in this instance, the arming culminates not in his taking of the shield with the device symbolic of virtue but in his putting on the green girdle, perhaps an indication of a lack of faith or at least a shift in faith from virtue to magic. As he rides to meet his fate, he undergoes another temptation, this time of his courage. The guide Bertilak has given him to take him to the Green Chapel suggests that he ride away without meeting the Green Knight and swears not to tell anyone what Gawain did. But Gawain refuses to be a coward and so rides on.

As he prepares to receive the blow from the Green Knight's axe, however, Gawain flinches. The Green Knight says he cannot be Gawain, who never feared any opponent, because he flinches before he feels the blow. The attack on Gawain's reputation steels him, and he does not move as the axe descends a second time; but it stops before striking him. The third time, the stroke nicks Gawain's neck and draws blood but does no real harm. The three strokes reflect the three days of temptation and exchanges. On the first two, Gawain preserved his honour and kept his word. On the third, he was not completely true to his bargain, and so he receives a slight wound. Though Gawain, whose heraldic device is a symbol of perfection, is greatly ashamed at his failing, Bertilak says he only 'lakked a lyttel' (was slightly at fault, 65). Nevertheless, Gawain says he will now wear the green girdle 'in syngne of my surfet' (as a symbol of my failing, 67).

When Gawain returns to Camelot, the court views the adventure much as Bertilak did. Arthur orders that the green girdle be worn by each member of the court in recognition of the fame that Gawain has brought to the Round Table. Like the displaying of the axe with which he beheaded the Green Knight so all men might see it and know of Gawain's deed, this act is another visible sign of the honour in which he is held. But the girdle that the court considers a sign of his renown, Gawain perceives as a sign of his shame. Thus he has come to the realization that virtue is not a matter of public recognition and that knowledge of his own deeds is more important than the regard of others.

Other English Gawain Romances

Gawain is the central character in two other English poems in alliterative verse and a number of rhyming verse romances. The late fourteenth-century northern poem *The Awntyrs of Arthur at the Terne Wathelyn* (*The Adventures of Arthur at Tarn Wathelene*) contains two episodes. The first is concerned with the warning given to Gaynour (Guinevere) by the ghost of her mother, who is suffering the torments of purgatory because of the way she lived her life. The queen is advised to avoid pride and to be meek and charitable. The ghost also says that Arthur is too covetous (186) and predicts the treachery of *Mordred and the downfall of the Round Table as part of the general admonition that everyone, no matter how powerful, will have to atone for his or her sins in the afterlife.

The second part of the poem begins with a description of a lavish feast at Arthur's court, which stands in stark contrast to the charitable giving recommended by the ghost. A lady enters and asks that Arthur treat with reason and right her beloved Sir Galerone, who accuses Arthur of winning his lands in war 'with a wrange wile' and giving them to Gawain (189, 191). Galerone offers to fight for his heritage, and Gawain volunteers to accept the challenge, thus placing his right to the lands in dramatic opposition to Galerone's. Although neither knight wins the battle, each is influenced by the other. Galerone is so impressed by Gawain's courage that he renounces his claim. Arthur, in turn, is so impressed with Galerone's respect for knightly valour over material wealth that he offers Gawain an impressive list of lands and castles in return for yielding the disputed territory to Galerone, a gesture that Gawain willingly makes. As a further reward, Galerone is married to his lady and made a member of the Round Table, and tranquillity is restored. In the final stanza, Gaynour has priests say 'a mylion of Masses' for her mother, an essential conclusion since, for the poem to end on the desired note of harmony, the troubled soul, like the troubled knight and the troubled state, must be brought to peace.

The two frames of the *Awntyrs* are connected by the weakest of narrative links but are bound thematically as a kind of diptych. (On the diptych principle in the alliterative Gawain romances and in other poems of the *Alliterative Revival, see

Lupack 53–102 and throughout.) The same is true of the fifteenth-century Scottish alliterative poem *Golagros and Gawain*, the two parts of which have their source in the First Continuation of Chrétien's *Perceval*. The significant action of the first part of the English poem involves Arthur's attempt to obtain provisions for his troops. When he arrives at a castle, he sends Kay to buy the needed supplies. Upon entering the castle, Kay sees a dwarf cooking small birds and, instead of fulfilling his mission, he takes food for himself. When the lord of the castle accuses him of unknightly behaviour, Kay insults the lord, who knocks Kay down with a punch. Gawain then undertakes the mission and acts in stark contrast to the seneschal. He courteously states his purpose and, when the lord refuses to sell food, merely asserts that it is right that he be 'lord of your aune' (239). Because of Gawain's courtesy, the lord is willing to forgive Kay's boorishness, to provide food an· shelter for Arthur's knights, and even to offer Arthur fresh troops if he needs them.

Kay's impetuous actions are much like Arthur's impetuous vow when he hears of the independence of Golagros, a knight whose castle they pass. Arthur swears to make Golagros do homage after the pilgrimage is completed. On his return, Arthur again sends Gawain as an emissary with an offer of gifts if Golagros will swear allegiance to him. Golagros refuses because no lord of his land ever acknowledged an overlord. As with the lord in the first part of the poem, he wants to be lord of his own.

A number of Golagros's men fight with Arthur's knights and most of them lose. As a result, Golagros decides to champion his own cause. When he and Gawain meet, they fight long and hard; but ultimately Gawain has his opponent at his mercy. Yet, since he does not want to be shamed, Golagros refuses to yield. Gawain tries to help him save his honour and is told that the only way would be to deny his own victory and to act as if Golagros had defeated him. By agreeing to this unprecedented request, Gawain proves his courtesy to be exceptional. Because Gawain has made him lord of his own, Golagros reveals that Gawain was actually the victor and pledges loyalty to Arthur, who shows his magnanimity by releasing Golagros from his pledge. Arthur leaves him 'Fre as I the first fand' (As free as I first found you, 277). In both parts of the poem, it is Gawain's courtesy rather than the use of force that obtains the desired results.

In addition to the alliterative Gawain romances, there are several that were composed in tail-rhyme stanzas (stanzas ending with a shorter 'tail' line and typically employing twelve-line stanzas rhyming aab aab ccb ddb, though length and rhyme scheme vary). There are also poems about Gawain in ballad stanzas or other verse forms.

The fifteenth-century tail-rhyme romance *The Jeaste of Sir Gawain*, like *Golagros and Gawain*, has its source in the First Continuation of Chrétien's *Perceval*; but the author of the *Jeaste* bases his tale on 'precisely those episodes of the Libre du Chastel Orguelleus rejected by the author of *Golagrus and Gawain* as dishonorable, his seduction of the Damoisele de Lis and the inconclusive combat with her brother Bran' (Barron 166). In the *Jeaste*, Gawain defeats the father of the lady and two of her three brothers. Brandles, the oldest brother, challenges Gawain; and they fight a fierce battle which must be postponed because of darkness. The two swear to fight to the death when next they meet, but 'they never mette more' (413). Gawain returns to court without having won a victory over the fiercest of the brothers and without even protecting his mistress, who leaves after being beaten and called a 'harlot' by Brandles and is never seen again (412–13). Gawain therefore seems less than perfect both in valour and in love.

The Avowing of King Arthur, Sir Gawain, Sir Kay, and Baldwin of Britain, a romance of the late fourteenth century written in sixteen-line tail-rhyme stanzas, describes the vows made by Arthur and three of his knights. Arthur swears to slay a fierce boar, which he does. Kay promises to ride the forest all night and fight whoever he meets, but is defeated and taken prisoner by a knight named Menealfe. Gawain, who has vowed to spend the night at the lake known as Tarn Wathelene, must defeat Menealfe and free Kay. As in a number of the Gawain romances, the mysterious and threatening stranger is then made a knight of the Round Table.

Half of the poem is devoted to the vows of Baldwin, the third knight, who has sworn never to be afraid for his life, never to deny food to anyone who needs it, and never to be jealous of his wife. Despite tests by Arthur and his knights that would lead most men to break these vows, Baldwin is true to them all. When asked how he could be so trusting, generous, and unafraid, he tells several tales—about how a wicked woman amended much even after committing a serious fault, about how a man who hid from battle was killed while those who fought bravely survived, and about how a siege was lifted when Baldwin lavishly entertained a messenger with the last of his garrison's food and made him believe that they had more provisions than they actually did.

Another tail-rhyme romance, Sir Gawain and the Carle of Carlisle, which was written about 1400, and the poem The Carle of Carlisle, written in rhyming couplets in the sixteenth century, tell similar stories of an encounter of the three knights who figured in The Avowing of King Arthur—Gawain, Kay, and Baldwin—with a giant Carl from whom they seek lodging. Kay's and Baldwin's discourtesy is contrasted with Gawain's respect for the Carl and his sovereignty in his own home. In both versions, Kay and Baldwin mistreat the Carl's horse in order to give their own horses better shelter and food. Gawain, however, tends to the Carl's horse, in the later poem even covering it with his own cloak. In both poems, the Carl instructs Gawain to thrust at his face with a spear and Gawain obeys his host, though the Carl ducks and avoids the blow. And in both, the Carl commands Gawain to get in bed with his wife, then stops him from having intercourse with her, but rewards him for his obedience by letting him sleep with his daughter.

In Sir Gawain and the Carle of Carlisle, the Carl says he vowed that anyone who lodged with him and did not do his bidding would be killed, and he shows Gawain ten cartloads of bones of men he has slain. Because Gawain has been courteous and compliant, the Carl now ends his wicked ways and welcomes all who come to his castle. He gives gifts to the three knights and allows his daughter to become

Gawain's wife. The Carl, another outsider integrated into courtly society, does homage to Arthur and is made a knight of the Round Table.

In *The Carle of Carlisle*, after Gawain has slept with the daughter, the Carl asks him to cut off his head with a sword. Though reluctant, Gawain obeys his host. Following the beheading blow, the Carl stands before Gawain as a man of normal height, not as the seventy-five foot giant he formerly was, and explains that he had been enchanted into the form of a giant until a knight of the Round Table beheaded him. Many had failed in the test and were killed by the Carl, who now mends his ways. Gawain marries the Carl's daughter, and the Carl becomes a knight of the Round Table. As the most recent editor of these poems has observed, 'Gawain's role is to bring the strange, the threatening, and the resistant within the ambit of the Round Table' (Hahn 83).

Gawain plays a similar role in *The Turke and Sir Gawain*, written about 1500 in six-line tail-rhyme stanzas. The Turke of the title comes to Arthur's court and proposes an exchange of blows. After he survives Gawain's buffet, the Turke takes Arthur's knight with him first to a strange castle and then to the Isle of Man, where a heathen sultan is king. With the Turke's help, Gawain survives a number of trials at the king's castle, after which the Turke kills the king and asks Gawain to cut off his head, an act that transforms the Turke into the knight Sir Gromer. Gromer suggests that Arthur make Gawain King of Man, but the knight refuses and recommends that Gromer be given that honour instead.

In the English Gawain romances, Gawain's courtesy, virtue, and valour are often tested. And he generally shows himself to be without peer, though not always perfect, as *Sir Gawain and the Green Knight* and *The Jeaste of Sir Gawain* demonstrate. Nevertheless, he endures chastity tests and beheading contests that other knights do not dare to undertake and is the hero against whom others are measured.

REWORKINGS OF *SIR GAWAIN AND THE GREEN KNIGHT*

The Greene Knight

Although the fact that *Sir Gawain and the Green Knight* (*SGGK*) survives in only one manuscript suggests that the romance was not widely known in its day, an interesting romance called *The Greene Knight* was obviously influenced by the earlier masterpiece. Written about 1500 in six-line rhyming stanzas rather than alliterative verse, the poem contains many of the motifs of its predecessor, including the beheading contest, the exchange of winnings, the hunts and temptations, and the green girdle or 'lace' (325). The lord in this poem, called Bredbeddle, is enchanted by his mother-in-law Agostes because his wife loves Gawain, and her mother wants to bring the famous knight into her presence to test his knightly qualities. *The Greene Knight* does not, however, employ the elaborate patterns that are found in the alliterative poem. The blow with the axe, for instance, is repaid with a stroke of a sword; and there is only one hunt and one temptation, encouraged by Agostes. Interested in narrative economy, the later romance gets right to the point—the keeping of the lace that Gawain believes will protect him. Following the one return blow, Bredbeddle accompanies Gawain to Arthur's court. The poem ends abruptly with a statement that this, the story of the green lace, is why Knights of Bath wear the lace until they have won their spurs, a parallel to the inclusion of the motto of the Order of the Garter at the end of *SGGK*.

Though *The Greene Knight* is the only direct survival in the Middle Ages, quite a few modern authors have responded to the earlier poem or reworked it in verse, drama, opera, fiction, and film. Such adaptation, however, did not begin until early in the twentieth century. *Sir Gawain and the Green Knight* was virtually unknown until it was edited for the first time in 1839 by Frederic Madden (1801–73), one of the great medieval scholars of the nineteenth century. In *Syr Gawayne: A Collection of Ancient Romance-Poems of Scotish and English Authors*, his collection of Gawain romances that brought together English-language treatments of Sir Gawain, Madden provided the name that has remained attached to the poem ever since. Of course, it was some time after Madden's edition before the poem was widely read and recognized as the masterpiece that it is.

Poetry

Charlton Miner Lewis (1866–1923), a poet and a professor of English literature at Yale, wrote *Sir Gawayne and the Green Knight* (1903), which the author calls 'a plain, straightforward man's unvarnished word' that is 'part sad, part sweet,—and part of it absurd' (64). Some elements of the story are indeed absurd: the fairies that Lewis introduces, for example, or the Green Knight who can walk away after being decapitated. But the tone and the similes and metaphors also contribute to the spirit of absurdity. When Gawayne chops off the Green Knight's head, the author struggles to describe the flowing blood and finally compares it to a flood of crème de menthe (31). Moreover, when the Green Knight leaves the castle, his green horse's hoofs strike the floor and produce green sparks. And when Gawayne arrives at the Green Chapel, its inhabitant offers to brew him 'a cup of hot green tea' (100).

Lewis subtitles his poem 'A Fairy Tale', a phrase that is to be taken literally since Lewis's major innovation in his rendition is a subplot involving the young woman Elfinhart. After her mother, widowed in 'the dark days before King Arthur came', makes her way to the shore of 'the Murmuring Mere, in Fairyland' (38), where she dies, the infant Elfinhart is taken in by the fairies, who raise her. The poem tells of Gawayne's love for Elfinhart, which prompts the testing by the Green Knight, who is sent by the fairies to prove Gawayne's courage and his affection for their charge. Though there are many dangers to Elfinhart in the world of humans, it is love that the fairies fear the most. So the exchange of blows and the temptations by the lady of the castle not only are a reflection of the whimsical nature of the fairies but also are designed to determine if Gawayne is a fit protector and husband for Elfinhart. As in the medieval poem, the hero lacks only a little—'Your fault was small', the

Green Knight tells him (104)—and the poem ends with the union of the couple and the suggestion that, as in a fairy tale, they will live happily ever after.

Of the other Americans who wrote lyric poems responding to SGGK, the best known is Yvor Winters (1900–1968), whose 'Sir Gawaine and the Green Knight' (1937) depicts the Green Knight as a natural force in contrast to the things made by men. Loren Eiseley's 'New Men, New Armor' (1973) similarly presents the Green Knight as a symbol of nature which persists while men like Arthur and Gawain die and Arthur's 'great board lies splintered'; but equally persistent is the death and destruction of battles, which though fought with 'new men, new armor' still cause the ravens to 'circle' and 'swoop' on the bodies of the slain (106). And Vince Gotera employs the rhythms and language of rap to retell SGGK in six quatrains in 'Gawain's Rap' (1989), a poem that refers to Camelot as 'King Arthur's crib' and the Green Knight's home as 'Hulk's castle' (29).

SGGK has also been adapted into blank verse by British poet Marilyn Bechely in Gawain and the Green Knight (2001), which follows the plot of the medieval romance fairly closely. It includes the Green Knight's challenge, the exchange of blows, the three temptations and three hunts, Gawain's receiving only a small wound for accepting the girdle, and his return to Camelot. The most striking difference is in the explicit comments on what Gawain has learned from the experience. His wound heals, Bechely writes, but 'the pain of knowing [that he was less than perfect] does not' (71). Of all those at court, only Guinevere understands what he is feeling; only she knows 'What a hard birth this has been | in the winter hills' and 'what certainties will never be certain again'. Consequently, Gawain feels as lonely in Arthur's court 'as ever he was in the wilderness' (76–7).

Drama

The spectacle and dramatic elements of SGGK make it a natural subject for plays. British dramatist Nicholas Stuart Gray's Gawain and the Green Knight (1969) combines the story of the *Loathly Lady (a motif discussed below) with the events of SGGK, which are presented against a background of battles with the Saxons, historical material that seems at odds with the magic and mystery of the two stories from romance. The play is also conscious of the link between the hunts and Gawain's behaviour during the temptations and specifically compares him to the animals being hunted. In contrast to the complications of Gray's plot, American dramatist Dennis Scott simplifies the story in The Fantasy of Sir Gawain & the Green Knight (1978), a short play which focuses on the testing of Gawain. Scott's play interlaces the hunts and the temptations, making the animals characters who recount some of the action; and it includes a Conteur, who describes scenes and events. Though Gawain is shamed by his flaw in not surrendering the green belt, Bercilak reminds him that 'Life is precious! You are right to cherish it' (29).

The verse play Gawain (1991) by David Harsent was written as a libretto for music by Harrison Birtwistle. The play allows for various types of music, from lullabies to chant, and includes interesting effects, such as the interweaving of the changing of the seasons with the arming of Gawain. Morgan le Fay is introduced in the beginning of the play as the instigator of the events. In the end, Gawain, who wears the pentangle on his shield, recognizes that he 'wanted fame' and is 'guilty of cowardice' (71). When he comes back to court and is asked to relate his great deeds, he says repeatedly, 'I'm not that hero' (79, 80, 81, 82, 83, 85). As the members of the court come to realize, things seem to have returned to normal with the return of Gawain, but the experience has changed him and all of them: 'All as it was, all completely changed' (84).

Fiction

Several British and American authors, including popular genre writers, have adapted SGGK to fiction, either as an episode in a larger tale or as the main plot. These adaptations range from novels set in the Arthurian period to those with more modern settings which use the medieval story as a controlling device.

An episode of American novelist Thomas Berger's Arthur Rex (1978; discussed in Chapter 3) retells SGGK in a thoroughly modern fashion. Largely because of its bawdy scenes, the tale was originally published in Playboy before being incorporated into the novel. The *Lady of the Lake teaches a valuable lesson to Gawaine, who is detained at Liberty Castle—Berger's version of Bertilak's castle in SGGK—a mysterious place where 'the freedom of [the] guest is absolute' (201). In keeping with this directive, the castle is full of luxuries and pleasures, including scantily clad young women (or young men, for those so inclined) and exotic foods like 'lark's eyes in jelly', 'coddled serpent-eggs', and 'pickled testicles of tiger'. Gawaine tries nobly to resist the temptations by rejecting sexual pleasures and preferring, in good British fashion, 'cold mutton and small beer' (203) to the unusual delicacies.

At last, however, he succumbs to the advances of the woman he believes to be his host's wife. Since the terms of his bargain with the host require the exchange of whatever each man has won during the day, Gawaine decides to lie: he chooses to say that he gained nothing that third day rather than return to a man the pleasure he received from a woman. Whereas in the medieval poem Gawain tries to save his own life by keeping a green girdle presumed to have magical powers, for Berger the issue is preserving one kind of virtue by yielding another. The dilemma that Gawaine faces—lying *to* his host rather than lying *with* his host—highlights the moral complexity of Berger's tale of the Green Knight in particular and of Arthur Rex as a whole.

The Green Knight, whom Gawaine encounters after leaving Liberty Castle (and who is actually the Lady of the Lake, in one of her several disguises), recognizes that Gawaine's failing is small and so gives him, as in the medieval poem, a nick on the neck rather than the beheading Gawaine expects. At the same time, she explains to him that 'a knight does better to break his word than, keeping it, to behave unnaturally. And a liar, sir, is preferable to a monster.' Not only does the Lady of the Lake illustrate rather graphically to the young knight the danger of rigid adherence to abstract ideals defined by others; she also sanctions his conclusion that 'sometimes justice is better served by a lie than by the absolute and literal truth' (215).

The lessons of the Lady of the Lake serve Gawaine well. Her tutoring, Berger implies, helps turn Gawaine from a notorious lecher into Arthur's 'best knight' and allows him to engage in his most noble act of all, his marriage to Lady *Ragnell and his subsequent acknowledgement of her sovereignty (see the discussion of the Loathly Lady below). In refusing to exercise the power of husband as 'lord and master' over his wife—'Thou art not an object which I possess like unto a suit of armor' (325–6), he declares—Gawaine not only breaks the spell Morgan la Fey cast on Ragnell but also, and perhaps more importantly, gains an even greater power.

British novelist Iris Murdoch (1919–99) sets her novel *The Green Knight* (1993) primarily in modern London, but the events of *SGGK* serve as a controlling motif. The central incident in a complex tale with a large cast of characters is the attempt by Lucas Graffe to kill his brother Clement with a bat. A stranger, Peter Mir, intervenes and takes the blow. Declared dead, Mir is revived by doctors and later visits Lucas, who falsely claims that he acted in self-defence because he believed the stranger was trying to rob him. Mir is the Green Knight figure: he wears a green tie and a suit that is 'sort of green', carries a green umbrella, and is even a member of the Green Party (194). When he recovers, he asks the brothers for 'exactly appropriate payment' (123) for the injury he has suffered, which affects his memory and prevents him from working. Eventually, he uses a knife concealed in his umbrella to inflict 'the merest pinprick' (321) on Lucas in order to bring about reconciliation between them. At one point, Clement recalls the plot of *SGGK* and draws comparisons between it and the events of their lives, though he admits 'it's all mixed up' (431–2) since there is no exact parallel but many similarities.

Another British novelist, Vera Chapman (1898–1996), retells the story of Gawain and the Green Knight and makes the family of Gawain central to her Three Damosels trilogy. In *The Green Knight* (1975), Chapman has as her hero not Gawain the son of Lot but his nephew Gawain le Jeune, a young knight who is the son of Gareth and Leonie of Lyonesse. Gawain asks to be allowed to take up the challenge of the Green Knight, who is also Sir Bertilak, a good knight unable to resist the magic of Morgan le Fay. Morgan initiates the beheading contest because she is trying to frighten the pregnant Guinevere into miscarrying. Ultimately the plot fails because Arthur does not take up the challenge, and later in the novel Guinevere gives birth to a daughter. The young Gawain is loved by and comes to love Vivian, the daughter of Blaisine, who is in turn the child of *Merlin and *Vivian. The younger Vivian is forced by Morgan to marry Bertilak and then to tempt Gawain. When Gawain passes the test, Morgan, posing as Merlin and claiming that the act is necessary to save Arthur's life, sacrifices the young lovers at *Stonehenge; but Merlin arrives in time to use lightning to shock them back to life. Chapman's retelling borrows motifs from the medieval poem: the beheading contest, the involvement of Morgan, the temptations, the three blows; but it adds fanciful material typical of modern fantasy novels.

In *The King's Damosel* (1976), Chapman focuses on *Lynett, who marries *Gaheris after bringing Gareth to rescue her sister Leonie of Lyonesse from Ruber, the Knight of the Red Lands. The journey of Lynett and Gareth is merely alluded to; the novel is more concerned with Lynett after her marriage. Neither she nor Gaheris is happy with the union, and they separate immediately after their wedding night, without consummating the marriage. Lynett, who loves her sister's husband Gareth, is encouraged by Merlin to become a messenger for Arthur. Since the king cannot knight a woman, he gives her the title of King's Damosel. Her first mission is to bring a message to Bagdemagus, a knight who raped her as a child. After refusing Arthur's offer of peace, Bagdemagus imprisons Lynett and tortures her for information; but Lancelot rescues her and, though Bagdemagus begs for mercy, beheads the wicked knight at her request.

Later, some of Bagdemagus' men capture Lynett, but she escapes and is assisted by a blind man named Lucius, with whom she falls in love. When she learns that Lucius is dying and can be helped only by the Grail, she undertakes the quest with *Perceval, *Bors, and Lancelot. Arriving at the *Fisher King's castle, she alone, though unfaithful to her husband and no longer a virgin, asks the healing question and then is given the Grail to use to heal Lucius. She is told, however, that he can use it for only one boon, to cure either his illness or his blindness but not both. He chooses sight, so that he can see the woman he loves. A short time later, Lucius dies and Lynett returns to the castle of her sister and Gareth so she can pass on to their son (Gawain le Jeune, the hero of *The Green Knight*) what her father taught her about chivalry.

The King's Damosel is the novel on which the animated film *Quest for Camelot* (Warner Bros., 1998; dir. Frederic Du Chau) was, very loosely, based. The film renames the young heroine Kayley, portrays her seeking *Excalibur rather than the Grail, and introduces a comical two-headed dragon; but it maintains her attraction to a blind man, here named Garrett, and the name Ruber for the villain, who, in this version, wants to take over Arthur's kingdom.

Chapman's third novel, *King Arthur's Daughter* (1976), is the story of Morgan and Mordred's attempt to prevent Arthur's daughter Ursulet from ruling or to force her to marry Mordred's wicked elder son. Mordred, who survived the battle with Arthur, is opposed by Ambris, the son of Gawain le Jeune and Vivian. In a climactic battle, Ambris loses his right hand but kills Mordred. Despite Mordred's death, Ursulet does not get the chance to rule because the Saxons have taken over the country; but she and Ambris must 'raise the lineage from which all Arthur's true followers are to grow... along the distaff line' and they must realize that Arthur will conquer 'not by war, nor by one kingship, that soon passes away, but by the carriers of the spirit that does not die' (153).

In *The Enchantresses* (1998), a prequel to her trilogy, Chapman treats the three sisters Morgan, Morgause, and Vivian, respectively representatives of evil, of the neutral but sensual (and therefore easily drawn to the bad), and of good. Vivian, who marries Merlin and assists him in obtaining *Caliburn (Excalibur) for Arthur, is killed by Morgan, but not before she has a daughter, Blaisine, who inherits her magical powers and her instinct for the good.

In American novelist Anne Eliot Crompton's *Gawain and Lady Green* (1997), another fantasy novel based on *SGGK*, Gawain rides into a northern village, where he is pulled from his horse and forced into the role of May King. The May Queen, Lady Green, falls in love with him and, because of his promise to marry her, agrees to help him escape the village; but he abandons her and returns alone to Arthur's court. To repay him for this betrayal, Lady Green and the Druid who loves her design the challenge of the Green Knight. When Gawain keeps the green girdle, they have succeeded in breaking his pride. Lady Green is content with that humiliation and marries the Druid, whose love would not have survived had she demanded Gawain's death and thus surrendered to evil.

An especially unusual reworking of *SGGK* is the Western novel *Ride South to Purgatory* (1999) by American author James C. Work. A mysterious stranger named Hochland, wearing a blackish green hat and a green scarf, arrives during a Christmas party at the Keystone ranch of Art Pendragon and his wife Gwen and issues a challenge: someone will take three shots at him with a pistol, and a year later that person must seek him out and let Hochland take three shots at him. Hochland has come to Keystone because he has heard that there 'cowboys still stood for courage and chivalry like the knights of old' (58); and indeed Art is trying to bring civilization and law to the territory. Art's nephew Pasque accepts the challenge and shoots the stranger, who is unhurt by the bullets. To keep his part of the bargain, the following year Pasque makes a difficult journey, plagued by mountain lions and wounded by renegade Apaches. He is cared for and tempted by a woman whose husband is away hunting buffalo and who offers him the secret of invulnerability—a ghost-dance shirt which some Indian tribes believe protects them from harm—in exchange for kisses. When Pasque finally meets Hochland, he flinches at the first shot and the second is a misfire. Before the third shot, Pasque tells Hochland about the shirt and removes it. Hochland then wounds but does not kill him because 'in the end, you dealt square with me' (218). The novel asserts that the story of the encounter and the values implied in it will spread through the West and become part of the civilizing process.

Film

SGGK has twice been adapted to film, both adaptations directed by Stephen Weeks and neither doing justice to the great medieval poem. *Gawain and the Green Knight* (United Artists and Scancrest, 1973), starring rock singer Murray Head as Sir Gawain, inserts into the middle of the events of the medieval poem an episode borrowed from Chrétien's *Yvain*. After pouring water from a spring onto a stone, Gawain is confronted by a knight whom he wounds mortally and follows to his castle. There, Gawain receives a ring of invisibility from Linet (Ciaran Madden), with whom he falls in love and who gives him a green sash which she says will protect him. The film presents the Green Knight as someone sent by the nature gods 'to ripen his [Gawain's] untutored youth and reveal to him . . . the mystery of life: to each his seasons, his moments of defeat and glory, of loving and losing, of death and joyful rebirth that his time on this earth might be fulfilled with courage and the purity of heart that befits a man'. After the return stroke, the Green Knight literally returns to the earth.

A decade later, Stephen Weeks remade his version of *SGGK* as *Sword of the Valiant: The Legend of Gawain and the Green Knight* (Cannon Films, 1983). Starring Sean Connery as the Green Knight and Miles O'Keeffe as Sir Gawain, *Sword of the Valiant* varies from the 1973 film in a few details, the most noticeable of which is an elaborate riddle the Green Knight poses. By solving the four parts of the riddle, Gawain can save himself from the return stroke, but he solves only three, realizing the answer to the fourth part only after he has endured the return blow. The riddle is designed to teach the young knight about life and therefore to assist in his development. Weeks also omits the closing statement about the mystery of life, though the Green Knight remains a force of nature and, as in the earlier film, returns to the earth at the end.

SGGK was also adapted to television as *Gawain and the Green Knight* (Thames Television, 1991; dir. John Michael Phillips). Though the initial events of the poem are told in flashback, this version is more faithful to the original poem than the films by Weeks; and its 'recasting of the tale as a psychological adventure allows the film to remain true to the poem's larger themes' (Blanch and Wasserman 193).

THE LOATHLY LADY

The popular story of a loathly lady who saves Arthur on the condition that she marry his best knight Gawain was the basis for a romance and a ballad as well as for tales by Chaucer and Gower and several modern reworkings. The fifteenth-century tail-rhyme romance *The Wedding of Sir Gawain and Dame Ragnelle*, which P. J. C. Field has suggested may have been written by Sir Thomas Malory, relates Arthur's encounter with Sir Gromer Somer Joure, a knight whose lands Arthur has appropriated and given to Gawain. Dressed for hunting, not battle, Arthur finds himself at Gromer's mercy and manages to save his life only by promising to return in a year to tell Gromer what women most desire. If his answer is incorrect, Arthur will forfeit his life. Over the next months, Arthur and Gawain ride throughout the realm, each compiling from those they question a book of answers, none of which is satisfactory. With only a little time left before the year's end, Arthur meets a foul hag, Dame Ragnelle, who tells him she can give him the correct answer if, as her reward, she can have Gawain for her husband. The courteous knight asserts that he would marry her even if she were a fiend and 'as foulle as Belsabub' so that he might save Arthur's life (56).

The response Ragnelle gives the king—that women desire 'sovereynté' (58)—is indeed correct, and Arthur's troubles end; but Gawain's begin. He must now marry the hag. At the wedding feast, she eats enough for six people; and on the wedding night, Gawain cannot even look at her, until she reminds him of his duty. But when he turns to kiss her, he finds Ragnelle transformed into a beautiful lady. Telling him that she can be fair either at night when they are alone together or by day when they are at court, but not both, she asks her husband to decide which it should be. His refusal to make the decision for her grants her sovereignty or control of her own fate and thus breaks the spell that her wicked stepmother had cast. Henceforth, she will be beautiful both day and night. The romance, which has elements of the fairy tale, is another expression of the supreme courtesy and loyalty of Gawain.

A similar tale is told in 'The Marriage of Sir Gawain', one of the ballads printed by Bishop Thomas Percy in his *Reliques of Ancient English Poetry*. Working from a defective manuscript, Percy himself, in a manner typical of the eighteenth-century antiquarians, reconstructed the missing text so as to print a complete story. Therefore, his version, unlike those found in scholarly editions, is more 'complete' but less original. The events of the ballad as reconstructed by Percy are similar to those of the romance, but some details vary. The description of the hag is as graphic but makes her even more foul, with, for example, her eye appearing where her mouth should have been. The ballad also introduces the motif of the sharp-tongued Kay, who says that he would rather be slain than wed to this lady. And in the ballad, the wicked stepmother bewitches both the hag and her brother, who is the churlish knight who threatens Arthur. But both ballad and romance include the crucial question, a similar answer (which, in the ballad, is that 'A woman will have her will'), the decision about when to be fair, the granting of the choice to the lady, and her transformation.

Before these two versions of the tale were written, two of the greatest of medieval English authors, John Gower (1330?–1408) and Geoffrey Chaucer (c.1342–1400), wrote their own Loathly Lady tales. Gower's 'Tale of Florent' (written between 1386 and 1390) in book I of the *Confessio Amantis* almost certainly draws on earlier material. Gower's tale does not have an Arthurian setting but tells instead of a knight named Florent who slew Branchus, whose grandmother wants to avenge the death without incurring blame. She frees Florent on the condition that he return to tell her what women most desire. A hag offers Florent the answer, but only if he consents to marry her. Thinking that the old woman will live just a short time, he agrees and is given the answer: that all women want to be 'soverein of mannes love' (144). When he is freed from his obligation to Branchus' grandmother and married to the hag, Florent lets her choose whether to be fair by day or by night. Giving her sovereignty ends the spell cast on her by her stepmother, and she is revealed to be the daughter of the King of Sicily. In the pattern of advice to the lover and the moral scheme developed in the *Confessio*, the tale provides an example of how 'Obedience in love availeth | Wher al a mannes strengthe faileth' (138).

When Chaucer reworked the story of the Loathly Lady for 'The Wife of Bath's Tale' (probably written after 1392) in his *Canterbury Tales*, he set it in Arthur's court. The life of Arthur, however, is not threatened; nor is Sir Gawain involved. Instead, the tale is adapted to its teller, the Wife of Bath, and is very different from moral Gower's handling of the theme. In Chaucer's version, an unnamed knight rapes a maiden. The queen and her ladies offer him a chance to save himself by telling them what women most desire. The answer he receives from a hag is that women desire 'sovereynetee' and 'maistrie' over their husbands and lovers (119). In return for the life-saving response, the knight must marry the hag. When he is less than eager to enjoy the marriage bed because she is old, ugly, and low-born, she lectures him on true gentility, which she says lies in deeds rather than possessions, and advises that old age should be honoured and that her foulness will prevent him from being cuckolded.

She then offers him a choice which is different from that in all other versions. She can be foul and old but a true and faithful wife; or she can be beautiful, but he will be uncertain about her dealings with other men. Unable to make the decision, he grants her 'maistrie' or control, because of which she asserts that she will be both fair and good. The tale and its ending are a reflection of the Wife of Bath's character, suggesting her desire to regain youth and beauty and to have control over men, as is seen in the summary of her dealings with her husbands in her prologue. The tale is also woven into a complex pattern of interaction with tales told by some of the other characters.

Chaucer's version of the Loathly Lady theme was adapted in the play *The Riddle: A Pleasant Pastoral Comedy* by Walter Raleigh (1861–1922). A variant version of the tale was told by Reginald Heber (1783–1826) in 'Fragments of The Masque of Gwendolen' (1816). Gwendolen is a beautiful woman loved by Merlin. When she refuses to marry him and says that she wishes she were ugly so he would not be attracted to her, his demonic heritage inspires him to transform her into a hideous hag. The spell will last until she is married by a youth 'Sprung from *Brutus' ancient line' (197). After Merlin is sealed in a tomb by 'his elfin paramour' and dies (199), Gwendolen assists Gawain who, because of a rash oath made by Arthur, has lost his earldom and has had his friend Llewellin condemned to die unless he can tell Arthur what women most crave. Gwendolen gives Gawain the answer: 'Power is their passion' (204). In return, he must agree to marry her. The fragmentary masque ends with Gwendolen claiming a kiss from the knight and asking him to turn to her, presumably to see her transformed into a beautiful woman.

American poet Benjamin F. Leggett also retells the story in 'The Ballad of the King' (1887), in which Arthur is imprisoned through enchantment. Freed for a year and a day to discover what women most desire, he meets a hag who, in return for being wed to one of Arthur's knights, informs him that 'What woman values more than earth | Is but her own sweet will!' (9). When Arthur tells the court of his pledge, 'Gewain' volunteers to marry the hag, who turns into a beautiful woman on their wedding night. By allowing her to decide whether she will be fair by day or by night, Gewain dissolves the spell upon her and so she remains always beautiful. The poem concludes that 'Love still retains the potent charm | It held in days of old!' (13). Thus the moral of the experience is changed from the importance of granting women their will to the power of love.

A similar transformation in the moral of the story of Gawaine and the Loathly Lady occurs in the final adventure in *The Story of King Arthur* (1903) by Howard Pyle. When Gawaine does what is required and marries the Loathly Lady, only to have her transformed into a beautiful woman, Pyle advises: 'when you shall have become entirely wedded unto your duty, then shall you become equally worthy with that good knight and gentleman Sir Gawaine; for it needs not that a man shall wear armor for to be a true knight, but only that he shall do his best endeavor with all patience and humility as it hath been ordained for him to do' (312). Thus Pyle uses the tale as an exemplum to instruct the children reading his book.

The tale is reworked again for children in Marguerite Merington's play *The Testing of Sir Gawayne* (1913). Gawayne passes three tests of chivalry: he agrees to marry the hag, here called Déliverance La Belle Pilgrim, so that Arthur can learn the answer to the riddle posed by a giant churl; he is true to his promise; and he gives the hag her own will in the matter of when she will be fair.

A recent adaptation of the motif occurs in 'Gawain and the Loathly Lady' (2001), a poem in blank verse by British poet Marilyn Bechely. Like Bechely's *Sir Gawain and the Green Knight*, the poem is fairly faithful to the story found in its medieval source. But in a major departure from *The Wedding of Sir Gawain*, Arthur is helpless against Sir Gromer because Morgan le Fay has enchanted the land. After Gawain's faithfulness breaks the spell upon Ragnell and her brother Gromer, there comes a golden age when it is 'as though a fountain sprang from one great love' which brings peace, prosperity, and a period of seven years in which the arts and learning thrive, a period said to be 'the glory of the reign of Arthur | and the gift of the Lady and Gawain' (117).

THE FAIR UNKNOWN

The author of the fifteenth-century romance *The Wedding of Sir Gawain and Dame Ragnelle* notes that Ragnelle bore Gawain a son named Gyngolyn. Several earlier medieval romances tell the story of that son, whose name is sometimes a variant of Gyngolyn, sometimes not. He is also referred to as the *Fair Unknown because in several of these romances his identity is not revealed or even known by the young man himself when he first comes to Arthur's court but is discovered only after he has proved his worth. This pattern is found in the verse romance *Le Bel Inconnu* (*The Fair Unknown*) written in the very late twelfth century by an author who gives his name as 'Renals de Biauju' (372) or Renaut de Beaujeu, who has been identified by the most recent editor of the poem as Renaut de Bâgé, 'the Seigneur de Saint-Trivier who flourished between 1165 and 1230' (p. x). Like so many French romances, *Le Bel Inconnu* was influenced by Chrétien.

In the romance, the Fair Unknown comes to Arthur's court and asks a boon: that he be allowed to undertake the quest initiated by Helie, a maiden who has requested a great knight to rescue her lady, the daughter of King Guingras. Though Helie initially scorns the young knight, she soon recognizes his valour as he defeats more seasoned warriors, rescues a maiden from two giants, and ends the custom of a castle that requires all who pass to fight a wicked knight. After he accomplishes this last task, the lady of the castle says she will marry him; but he steals away to fulfil his original quest. At the castle of Helie's mistress, the Fair Unknown must fight two enchanters, Mabon and Evrain the Cruel, and then undergo the trial of the Fearsome Kiss, which involves being kissed by a terrifying serpent. When he succeeds in the trial, the serpent is turned into a beautiful woman, Blonde Esmeree, who wants to marry her champion; and he learns that he is *Guinglain, the son of Gawain and Blanchemal the Fay.

Unfortunately, just as he wins this beautiful damsel, he realizes he loves the first woman he won, the Maiden of the White Hands, whom he left in order to complete his quest. Putting off Esmeree by saying he needs Arthur's approval before marrying, he returns to his first love who, after tormenting him with illusions she conjures up using her knowledge of magic, takes him back but insists that he always act in accordance with her will. He agrees to this condition, but when he hears that Arthur has called a great tournament, he resolves to take part in it, even though his beloved warns him that if he returns to court, he will marry another. Guinglain goes to sleep in her castle but wakes in the forest and realizes he has lost his lady.

After distinguishing himself at Arthur's tournament, Guinglain is married to Blonde Esmeree. The romance, written by Renaut for his own beloved, concludes with a suggestion that the ending is malleable according to her wishes. If she shows Renaut 'a gracious countenance', he will continue the tale so that Guinglain will find his first love again; if she does not, then Guinglain 'must bear the sorrow | of never finding her again' (373).

Other French versions of the Fair Unknown story include the thirteenth-century verse romances *Beaudos* by Robert de Blois; *Gogulor*, which survives only in a fragment of fewer than 140 lines that recount a battle by a young knight with the giant Gogulor; and the early sixteenth-century prose tale *L'Hystoire de Gigalan, filz a messire Gauvain* by Claude Platin, which borrows from *Le Bel Inconnu* and the Provençal romance *Jaufre* (cf. Kirsop 116–18). There is also an Italian version of the motif, *I cantari di Carduino* (1370s), in which the hero Carduino is the son of Dondinello, a knight who is murdered by lords jealous of the great favour shown him by Arthur. The youth of Carduino resembles that of Perceval in that his mother takes him away from court, to which he eventually returns and, with a maiden whose sister has been transformed into a serpent by a magician, undertakes a quest, during which he has other adventures comparable to those in *Le Bel Inconnu*.

A German version of the tale of the Fair Unknown is found in the romance *Wigalois* (written in the first decade of the thirteenth century) by Bavarian poet Wirnt von Grafenberg. In addition to the basic plot of a young man coming to Arthur's court and asking to be allowed to undertake a dangerous adventure for which the messenger requesting aid thinks him unsuitable until he proves himself, *Wigalois* shares a number of adventures with Renaut's *The Fair Unknown*, including the fight with two giants who are about to ravish a maiden, the encounter with a lord who requires a knight to joust with him before he gives hospitality, the defence of a lady whose prize for beauty has been taken from her, and the joust with the owner of a hunting dog.

Wigalois, however, differs from *The Fair Unknown* in several significant ways. It begins, for example, with an account of how Gawain, defeated by a knight wearing a belt with protective powers, accompanies him to his land. There, Gawain meets and marries the beautiful maiden Florie and conceives a son before leaving the land for what he promises will be a short time. But he stays away longer than he told Florie that he would, and when he tries to return he realizes he is unable to enter without the belt which he left with her. Twenty years later, his son *Wigalois comes to Arthur's court and immediately proves himself by sitting on a stone on which only a faultless person can sit. Gawain provides Wigalois with arms, including a helmet with a wheel on top, a device which earns him the name the Knight of the Wheel.

Wigalois soon sets out to regain his heritage. On the way, he has many adventures, such as the slaying of a dragon with a lance brought by an angel; and he is freed through prayer and divine intervention from the bonds of the bestial woman Ruel. God also has a hand in allowing him to achieve his quest to restore the lands of Larie, daughter of King Lar of Korntin, which were stolen when Lar was slain by Roaz. To correct this wrong—and in the process to win the hand of Larie—Wigalois must cross a bridge over a deadly swamp; but the bridge is protected by a wheel turned by flowing water to which are attached swords and maces that will kill anyone who tries to cross. By driving a dense fog into the water causing it to stop running and thus stilling the wheel, God allows Wigalois to cross. When he reaches the castle, Wigalois slays the usurper Roaz, who has given his soul to the devil in order to have his aid; and Roaz's soul is carried off by demons. As these adventures suggest, Wigalois not only serves as a model of chivalry but he is also favoured and aided by God.

Wigalois has been called 'a hero who undergoes no crisis' and 'who pursues his course with one-dimensional single-mindedness' (Honemann 146–7). Indeed, he does not even face the problem of choosing between two lovers that Guinglain experiences in *The Fair Unknown*. Nevertheless, the tale of Wigalois is full of marvellous adventures, a military expedition led by Gawain after the main quest is completed, courtly descriptions, strange and supernatural creatures, and a character who is unwavering in his dedication to chivalric and moral virtues— qualities that no doubt explain the popularity of the romance, which survives in forty-one manuscripts, a number large enough to suggest that it was widely known. *Wigalois* was later abridged and adapted into the prose tale *Wigoleis vom Rade* (*Wigoleis of the Wheel*), first published in 1493. It was also adapted and translated into Yiddish verse in a version known as *Widuwilt* (sometimes called *Artus hof* [*Arthur's Court*]) that survives in sixteenth-century manuscripts but may actually have been written in the fifteenth (Honemann 152).

An English version of the Fair Unknown theme appears in the stanzaic romance *Lybeaus Desconus*, believed to have been written by Thomas Chestre, author of *Sir Launfal*, in the latter half of the fourteenth century. Like the Italian *Carduino*, *Lybeaus* depicts a young man—ultimately revealed to be Gyngelayne, son of Gawain—sheltered by his mother from knighthood. After taking the armour from a dead knight, he travels to Arthur's court at *Glastonbury and asks to be made a knight and given the next battle. Since he does not know the young man's name, Arthur calls him Lybeaus Desconus, the Fair Unknown. When the maiden Elene arrives and asks for help for her lady, the Queen of Synadowne, Lybeaus claims the adventure. Elene, initially displeased because of her champion's youth, soon sees his valour, as he defeats Sir William and his three nephews, rescues a maiden from two giants, wins a falcon by challenging Sir Jeffron's claim that his lady is the loveliest, and kills the giant Maugis, who is thirty feet tall (153), and thereby liberates Dame Amoure. Using sorcery, Amoure keeps Lybeaus with her for a year before Elene berates him for being false and abandoning the queen of Synadowne.

Recalled to his duty, Lybeaus comes to the castle where the lady is held under a spell by the enchanters Mabon and Yrayn. He fights them, killing Mabon and grievously wounding Yrayn, and then receives a fearsome kiss from a dragon, who is thus freed from a spell that could only be broken by kissing Gawain or one of his kin. The dragon's tail and wings fall off, and she is revealed to be the beautiful Queen of Synadowne. Together they return to Arthur's court where they are married.

The Fair Unknown story was widely known. The versions in French, Italian, German, and English incorporate some of the same adventures and the same basic motif, one similar to that found in Malory's 'Tale of Sir Gareth of Orkney', of an exceptional young man who proves his worth and his worthiness despite reservations about his youth and abilities.

GAWAIN AND HIS FAMILY IN LATER LITERATURE

Gawain and his brothers are, of course, important though not central figures in Malory's *Morte d'Arthur* and in many of the works, such as T. H. White's *The Once and Future King*, that recount the love of Lancelot and Guinevere and the tragic end of Arthur's realm that their love causes. Besides reworkings of the stories of Gawain's encounter with the Green Knight or the Loathly Lady, however, there are relatively few noteworthy modern works in which Gawain or someone connected to him is the protagonist.

As opposed to the numerous trilogies which retell the story of Lancelot and Guinevere or the final events of Arthur's reign, there is only one trilogy, written by Gillian Bradshaw, which narrates the life and deeds of Gwalchmai (Gawain). In *Hawk of May* (1980), the young Gwalchmai (a name meaning 'the Hawk of May') has skill only in riding and harping and not in martial matters. His mother Morgawse intends, therefore, to teach him sorcery and make him a servant of the Darkness. When he learns that she will also teach sorcery to his young brother Medraut (Mordred), Gwalchmai flees in horror, spends some time in a fairy realm where he is given the sword Caledvwlch, and ultimately enters Arthur's service, where his ability to ride makes him one of the best of Arthur's cavalry.

In the sequel, *Kingdom of Summer* (1981), Gwalchmai, now famous for his military prowess, searches for a woman named Elidan, whom he loved but could not marry because he had slain her brother. Elidan lives in a convent with Gwyn, the son Gwalchmai fathered but does not know exists. With the assistance of his faithful servant Rhys ap Sion, from whose perspective the story is told, Gwalchmai resists the sorcery and machinations of Morgawse and Medraut, who wish to steal his magic sword and use it for evil. By chance, Rhys and the woman he loves arrive at Elidan's convent after they have been subjected to Morgawse's sorcery and brutality. From Rhys, Gwalchmai learns Elidan's whereabouts; but despite asking for forgiveness and expressing his love for her, she will not come away with him.

In *Winter's Shadow* (1982), the final book of the trilogy, is told by Gwynhwyfar (Guinevere). Medraut has discovered that he is Arthur's son and comes to *Camlann, Arthur's central court, to begin plotting to undermine his father and seize power. Gwalchmai's son Gwyn also comes to court and, since he can read, serves Gwynhwyfar as he trains to be a warrior. It is only when Elidan writes a letter to Gwalchmai just before her death that he learns the boy is his son. When Medraut uses the affair that develops between *Bedwyr and Gwynhwyfar to split Arthur's followers, Bedwyr is exiled and the queen is sent to her own land, which is ruled by a cousin who bears only enmity towards her. In trying to save her from living a life he knows will be harsh, Bedwyr frees Gwynhwyfar from her guards but in so doing kills Gwyn, thus earning the hatred of Gwalchmai. While Arthur wages war on the continent to capture and punish Bedwyr, Medraut claims the throne and forces Arthur to return for a final battle, in which Medraut is slain by one of Arthur's allies, and Arthur is killed. Bedwyr becomes a monk, and Gwynhwyfar retires to a convent to write her account of the tragic events, an account that ends with the realization that 'what we had in Camlann was the dream that the hearts of all men have ever longed for' (377).

Surprisingly few modern poems have been written about Gawain. *The Wraith of Gawain* (1948) by E. H. Tax (b. 1910) is a long poem that combines, sometimes incoherently, tales from Malory, from the *Mabinogion*, and from Irish works referred to in Roger Sherman Loomis's *Celtic Myth and Arthurian Romance*. The best part of the poem is the conclusion, in which a wounded Gawain fights on the beach as Arthur returns after Mordred's treachery, a scene perhaps influenced by the author's own wartime experiences. In the landing, Gawain is killed, an act that the author calls a great deed done by an 'obscure hand' (288). The wraith of Gawain appears to Arthur in a dream to warn him against fighting until Lancelot brings aid; but fate does not allow that. Arthur, who had expressed the hope that he might, like Gawain, 'fall with grace, not from it' (297), is fatally wounded while slaying Mordred in the final battle.

Prince Valiant

The concept of building a story for children around a young page or squire—to Sir Gawain or some other knight—who proves himself worthy underlies a number of juvenile Arthurian tales. Such is the case in two stories by Eugenia Stone (1879–1971), *Page Boy for King Arthur* (1949), in which Tor, a peasant boy, rescues Lancelot and is rewarded by being made a page to Galahad, and *Squire for King Arthur* (1955), in which Tor rescues the son of *Pellinore from the Saxons, warns Arthur of a Saxon invasion, and is rewarded by being made Pellinore's squire. It is also the case in *The Squire's Tale* (1998) by Gerald Morris, in which Gawain's squire, who comes to the realization that he is the son of an enchanter and thus has fairy blood, helps Gawain on a number of quests, assists Arthur in his struggle against the rebellious kings, and ultimately saves Arthur's life by ending the enchantment that Morgause is using to kill him.

The most famous of Gawain's squires, however, is Prince Valiant. Created by Harold R. (Hal) Foster (1892–1982) and appearing in the weekly comic strip *Prince Valiant* since 1937 (drawn since 1980 by John Cullen Murphy (1919–2004) and since 2004 by Gary Gianni), Valiant is an exiled prince who becomes Gawain's squire and eventually earns knighthood. Foster's Prince Valiant has been the subject of numerous books, games, and toys, an animated television series (*The Legend of Prince Valiant*, 1991), and two movies: *Prince Valiant* (Twentieth-Century Fox, 1954; dir. Henry Hathaway) and *Prince Valiant* (Constantin Film, 1997; dir. Anthony Hickox), which was adapted into a novel by Martin Delrio. In both films, Valiant regains his kingdom and wins the woman he loves, Alita in the former and Ilene in the latter. In the 1954 film, as in *The Black Knight*, there is a championing of Christian values as well as echoes of the McCarthy era: one of the evil Vikings, for instance, tries to get Valiant to name the Christian Vikings at the court of the pagan Sligon. In the 1997 film, Valiant recovers Arthur's Excalibur, which was stolen by the Vikings, and not the Singing Sword that is rightfully his, as in the earlier film. The 1997 film is also noteworthy because Morgan le Fay is in league with the Vikings, who capture and kill Gawain. Both films take a comic strip approach to characters and plot; the later film even uses comic strip images to introduce some of its scenes.

Gareth

Gawain's brother Gareth, a young boy whose worth is not recognized initially but who goes on to prove his superior virtue and valour, has been a popular subject in juvenile literature. Malory's 'Tale of Sir Gareth' has been retold for young readers in works such as *The Kitchen Knight* (1965) by Barbara Schiller and *The Kitchen Knight: A Tale of King Arthur* (1990) by Margaret Hodges, but Gareth is also featured in a number of other stories. In *King Arthur's Wood* (1904), written and illustrated by Elizabeth Stanhope Forbes (1859–1912), for example, young Myles Morris meets a 'little Brown Spirit of the Woodlands' and hears from him the deeds of Sir Gareth as a 'shining... example' (31, 39). Forbes's account of Gareth's deeds is based on Malory's 'Tale of Sir Gareth of Orkney'; and the Spirit who relates it to Myles is the dwarf who accompanied Gareth on his quest. That Spirit teaches Myles to love the creatures of the woods, to be kind to all things weaker than himself, and, through the story of Gareth, to be honest and brave. Thanks to the Spirit's advice, Myles grows into a good and successful man. The elaborate illustrations, moreover, make Forbes's book an art object in its own right.

Gareth of Orkney (1956), a novel for young adults by E. M. R. (Edith Margaret Robertson) Ditmas (b. 1896), also retells Gareth's story largely as found in Malory and Tennyson. It does, however, add characters like Father Basil, a former knight turned monk who advises Gareth on moral matters, and a wicked aunt Morgan le Fay, who tries to get Gareth to poison Basil. The novel details Gareth's work in Arthur's kitchen for a year, a condition his mother, who wants him to become a priest, imposes on him. He then claims as a boon from Arthur the mission of freeing the Lady of Lyonnesse from the Red I ...,t, undergoes Linet's scorn, eventually proves himself as knight and lover, and marries the rescued lady.

In *The Sword in the Tree* (1956) by Clyde Robert Bulla, a young boy named Shan goes to Arthur's court for help when his wicked uncle Lionel takes over his father's castle and position after what Lionel claims was a hunting accident. Arthur sends Gareth to help Shan, who must prove his identity by recovering from a hollow in an oak tree his father's sword, which he hid there from his uncle. After Gareth defeats Lionel, a faithful servant reveals to Shan that his father has been imprisoned in the castle dungeon. All ends happily as the family members are reunited and resume their former way of life.

BIBLIOGRAPHY

Gawain Romances Other than English
Busby, Keith. *Gauvain in Old French Literature*. Amsterdam: Rodopi, 1980.
Le Chevalier à l'épée, in *Two Old French Gauvain Romances*, ed. R. C. Johnston and D. D. R. Owen. New York: Barnes and Noble, 1973: 30–60.
Couperus, Louis. *Het zwevende schaakbord*. Amsterdam: L. J. Veen, 1994.
Eachtra an Mhadra Mhaoil/Eachtra Mhacaoimh-an-Iolair (The Story of the Crop-Eared Dog/The Story of Eagle-Boy): Two Irish Arthurian Romances, ed. and trans. R. A. Stewart Macalister. Irish Texts Society 10. London: David Nutt, for The Irish Texts Society, 1908; repr. 1998, with new introduction by Joseph Falaky Nagy.

'Les Enfances Gauvain: Fragments d'un poème perdu', ed. Paul Meyer, *Romania*, 39 (1910), 1–32.

Gliglois: A French Arthurian Romance of the Thirteenth Century, ed. Charles H. Livingston. Cambridge, Mass.: Harvard University Press, 1932.

Heinrich von dem Türlin. *Diu Crône*, ed. Gottlob Heinrich Friedrich Scholl. 1852; repr. Amsterdam: Rodopi, 1966.

—— *The Crown: A Tale of Sir Gawein and King Arthur's Court*, trans. J. W. Thomas. Lincoln: University of Nebraska Press, 1989.

Hogenbirk, Marjolein. 'A Perfect Knight: Walewein in the *Walewein ende Keye*', in *King Arthur in the Medieval Low Countries*, ed. Geert H. M. Claassens and David F. Johnson. Leuven: Leuven University Press, 2000: 163–72.

The Marvels of Rigomer (Les Merveilles de Rigomer), trans. Thomas E. Vesce. New York: Garland, 1988.

[*Mériadeuc.*] *Li Chevaliers as deus espees: Altfranzsöischer Abenteuerroman*, ed. Wendelin Foerster. Halle: Max Niemeyer, 1877.

[*Mériadeuc.*] *The Knight of the Two Swords: A Thirteenth-Century Arthurian Romance*, trans. Ross G. Arthur and Noel L. Corbett. Gainesville: University Press of Florida, 1996.

Les Mervelles de Rigomer, ed. Wendelin Foerster and H. Breuer. 2 vols. Dresden: Gesellschaft für romanische Literatur, 1908–15.

Paien de Maisières. *La Mule sans frein*, in R. C. Johnston and D. D. R. Owen (eds.), *Two Old French Gauvain Romances*. New York: Barnes and Noble, 1973: 61–89.

[Paien de Maisières. *La Mule sans frein.*] Translated as *The Girl with the Mule, or the Mule without a Bridle*, trans. Elisabeth Brewer, in *From Cuchulainn to Gawain: Sources and Analogues of Sir Gawain and the Green Knight*. Totowa, NJ: Rowman and Littlefield, 1973: 28–42.

Penninc and Pieter Vostaert. *Dutch Romances, i: Roman van Walewein*, ed. and trans. David F. Johnson and Geert H. M. Claassens. Arthurian Archives VI. Cambridge: D. S. Brewer, 2000.

The Perilous Cemetery (L'Atre périlleux), ed. and trans. Nancy B. Black. New York: Garland, 1994.

Raoul de Houdenc. *Meraugis von Portlesguez*, ed. Mathias Friedwagner. Halle: Max Niemeyer, 1897.

—— *La Vengeance Raguidel*, ed. Mathias Friedwagner. Halle: Max Niemeyer, 1909.

The Rise of Gawain, Nephew of Arthur (De ortu Waluuanii nepotis Arturi), ed. and trans. Mildred Leake Day. New York: Garland, 1984.

The Romance of Hunbaut: An Arthurian Poem of the Thirteenth Century, ed. Margaret Winters. Leiden: E. J. Brill, 1984.

Walewein ende Keye, in David F. Johnson and Geert H. M. Claassens (eds. and trans.), *Dutch Romances, iii: Five Interpolated Romances from the Lancelot Compilation*. Arthurian Archives X. Cambridge: D. S. Brewer, 2003: 368–523.

Wallbank, Rosemary E. 'Three Post-Classical Authors: Heinrich von dem Türlin, Der Stricker, Der Pleier', in W. H. Jackson and S. A. Ranawake (eds.), *The Arthur of the Germans: The Arthurian Legend in Medieval German and Dutch Literature*. Cardiff: University of Wales, 2000: 81–97.

Walters, Lori. 'The Creation of a "Super Romance": Paris, Bibliothèque Nationale, fonds français, MS 1433', *Arthurian Yearbook*, I (1991), 3–25.

Die Wrake van Ragisel, in David F. Johnson and Geert H. M. Claassens (eds. and trans.), *Dutch Romances*, iii: *Five Interpolated Romances from the Lancelot Compilation*. Cambridge: D. S. Brewer, 2003: 50–195.

English Gawain Romances

The Awowyng of Arthur, in Thomas Hahn (ed.), *Sir Gawain: Eleven Romances and Tales*. Kalamazoo, Mich.: Medieval Institute Publications for TEAMS, 1995: 113–68.

The Awntyrs off Arthur, in Thomas Hahn (ed.), *Sir Gawain: Eleven Romances and Tales*. Kalamazoo, Mich.: Medieval Institute Publications for TEAMS, 1995: 169–226.

Barron, W. R. J. *English Medieval Romance*. London: Longman, 1987.

Benson, Larry D. *Art and Tradition in Sir Gawain and the Green Knight*. New Brunswick, NJ: Rutgers University Press, 1965.

Brewer, Elisabeth (comp.), *Sir Gawain and the Green Knight: Sources and Analogues*. Cambridge: D. S. Brewer, 1992.

The Carle of Carlisle, in Thomas Hahn (ed.), *Sir Gawain: Eleven Romances and Tales*. Kalamazoo, Mich.: Medieval Institute Publications for TEAMS, 1995: 373–91.

The Greene Knight, in Thomas Hahn (ed.), *Sir Gawain: Eleven Romances and Tales*. Kalamazoo, Mich.: Medieval Institute Publications for TEAMS, 1995: 309–35.

Hahn, Thomas (ed.), *Sir Gawain: Eleven Romances and Tales*. Kalamazoo, Mich.: Medieval Institute Publications for TEAMS, 1995.

The Jeaste of Sir Gawain, in Thomas Hahn (ed.), *Sir Gawain: Eleven Romances and Tales*. Kalamazoo, Mich.: Medieval Institute Publications for TEAMS, 1995: 393–418.

The Knightly Tale of Gologras and Gawain, in Thomas Hahn (ed.), *Sir Gawain: Eleven Romances and Tales*. Kalamazoo, Mich.: Medieval Institute Publications for TEAMS, 1995: 227–308.

Lupack, Alan. 'Structure and Tradition in the Poems of the Alliterative Revival', diss., University of Pennsylvania, 1974.

Savage, Henry. *The Gawain-Poet: Studies in his Personality and Background*. Chapel Hill: University of North Carolina Press, 1956.

Sir Gawain and the Carle of Carlisle, in Thomas Hahn (ed.), *Sir Gawain: Eleven Romances and Tales*. Kalamazoo, Mich.: Medieval Institute Publications for TEAMS, 1995: 81–112.

Sir Gawain and the Green Knight, ed. J. R. R. Tolkien and E. V. Gordon, 2nd edn., rev. Norman Davis. Oxford: Clarendon Press, 1967.

The Turke and Sir Gawain, in Thomas Hahn (ed.), *Sir Gawain: Eleven Romances and Tales*. Kalamazoo, Mich.: Medieval Institute Publications for TEAMS, 1995: 337–71.

Reworkings of *Sir Gawain and the Green Knight*

Bechely, Marilyn. *Gawain and the Green Knight*, in *Gawain the White Hawk*. Winchester: George Mann Publications, 2001: 7–77.

Berger, Thomas. 'Arthur Rex', *Playboy* (Sept. 1978), 102–5, 110, 232–4, 236.

—— *Arthur Rex: A Legendary Novel*. New York: Delacorte Press/Seymour Lawrence, 1978.

Blanch, Robert J., and Wasserman, Julian (eds.). 'Gawain on Film (The Remake), Thames Television Strikes Back', in Kevin J. Harty (ed.), *Cinema Arthuriana: Twenty Essays*. Jefferson, NC: McFarland, 2002: 185–98.

Chapman, Vera. *The Enchantresses*. London: Victor Gollancz, 1998.

—— *The Green Knight*. London: Rex Collings, 1975.

—— *King Arthur's Daughter*. London: Rex Collings, 1976.

—— *The King's Damosel*. London: Rex Collings, 1976.

Crompton, Anne Eliot. *Gawain and Lady Green*. New York: Donald I. Fine Books, 1997.

Eiseley, Loren. 'New Men, New Armor', in *The Innocent Assassins*. New York: Charles Scribner's Sons, 1973: 105–6.

Gotera, Vince. 'Gawain's Rap', *Wooster Review*, 9 (Spring 1989), 29.

Gray, Nicholas Stuart. *Sir Gawain and the Green Knight: A Play*. London: Dennis Dobson, 1969.

The Greene Knight, in Thomas Hahn (ed.), *Sir Gawain: Eleven Romances and Tales*. Kalamazoo, Mich.: Medieval Institute Publications for TEAMS, 1995: 309–35.

Harsent, David. *Gawain*. London: Universal Edition, 1991.

Lewis, Charlton Miner. *Sir Gawayne and the Green Knight: A Fairy Tale*. Boston: Houghton, Mifflin and Co., 1903.

Madden, Frederic (ed.), *Syr Gawayne: A Collection of Ancient Romance-Poems of Scotish and English Authors Relating to That Celebrated Knight of the Round Table*. London: Richard and John E. Taylor, 1839.

Murdoch, Iris. *The Green Knight*. London: Chatto and Windus, 1993.

Scott, Dennis. *The Fantasy of Sir Gawain & the Green Knight*. New Orleans: The Anchorage Press in association with The O'Neill Center's The National Theater of the Deaf, 1978.

Winters, Yvor. 'Sir Gawaine and the Green Knight', in *Collected Poems*. Denver: Alan Swallow, 1952: 113–14.

Work, James C. *Ride South to Purgatory*. Unity, Me.: Five Star, 1999.

The Loathly Lady

Bechely, Marilyn. *Gawain and the Loathly Lady*, in *Gawain the White Hawk*. Winchester: George Mann Publications, 2001: 79–119.

Chaucer, Geoffrey. 'The Wife of Bath's Prologue and Tale', in *The Riverside Chaucer*, ed. Larry D. Benson, 3rd edn. Boston: Houghton Mifflin, 1987: 105–22.

Field, P. J. C. 'Malory and *The Wedding of Sir Gawain and Dame Ragnell*', in *Malory: Texts and Sources*. Cambridge: D. S. Brewer, 1998: 284–94.

Gower, John. 'The Tale of Florent', in *Confessio Amantis*, vol. i, ed. Russell A. Peck. Kalamazoo, Mich.: Medieval Institute Publications for TEAMS, 2000: 139–50.

Heber, Reginald. 'Fragments of The Masque of Gwendolen', in *Poetical Works*. Boston: Little, Brown, 1853: 192–207.

Leggett, Benj. F. 'The Ballad of the King', in *A Sheaf of Song*. New York: John B. Alden, 1887: 7–13.

'The Marriage of Sir Gawain', in Thomas Hahn (ed.), *Sir Gawain: Eleven Romances and Tales*. Kalamazoo, Mich.: Medieval Institute Publications for TEAMS, 1995: 359–71.

Merington, Marguerite. *The Testing of Sir Gawayne*. 1913; repr. in Montrose J. Moses (ed.), *A Treasury of Plays for Children*. Boston: Little, Brown, and Co., 1926: 105–36.

Pyle, Howard. *The Story of King Arthur and his Knights*. New York: Charles Scribner's Sons, 1903.

Raleigh, Walter. *The Riddle: A Pleasant Pastoral Comedy Adapted from 'The Wife of Bath's Tale' as It Is Set Forth in the Works of Master Geoffrey Chaucer*, in John Drinkwater, Sir Walter Raleigh, Lady Gregory, Laurence Binyon, 'Saki' (H. H. Munro), Eden Phillpots, and Lord Dunsany, *Modern Short Plays*. London: University of London Press, 1930: 33–56.

The Wedding of Sir Gawain and Dame Ragnelle, in Thomas Hahn (ed.), *Sir Gawain: Eleven Romances and Tales*. Kalamazoo, Mich.: Medieval Institute Publications for TEAMS, 1995: 41–80.

The Fair Unknown

I cantari di Carduino giuntovi quello di Tristano e Lancielotto quando combattettero al petrone di Merlino, ed. Pio Rajna. Bologna: Gaetano Romagnoli, 1873.

Chestre, Thomas. *Lybeaus Desconus*, ed. M. Mills. EETS os 261. London: Oxford University Press for the Early English Text Society, 1969.

[*Gogulor.*] Charles H. Livingston (ed.), 'Fragment d'un roman de chevalerie', *Romania*, 66 (1940–1), 85–93.

Honemann, Volker. 'The Wigalois Narratives', in W. H. Jackson and S. A. Ranawake (eds.), *The Arthur of the Germans: The Arthurian Legend in Medieval German and Dutch Literature.* Cardiff: University of Wales, 2000: 142–54.

Kirsop, Joan Lindblad. 'Claude Platin, *vir obscurissimus inter obscuros*', *Australian Journal of French Studies*, 17.1 (Jan.–Apr. 1980), 86–120.

Platin, Claude. *L'Hystoire de Gigalan, filz a messire Gauvain* . . . Lyon: Claude Nourry, [1530?].

Renaut de Bâgé. *Le Bel Inconnu (Li Biaus Descouneüs; The Fair Unknown)*, ed. Karen Fresco, trans. Colleen P. Donagher, music ed. Margaret P. Hasselman. Garland: New York, 1992.

Robert de Blois. *Beaudos*, vol. i of *Sämmtliche Werke*. 1889; repr., with 3 vols. bound as 1, Geneva: Slatkin Reprints, 1978.

Schofield, William Henry. *Studies of the Libeaus Desconus.* Harvard Studies and Notes in Philology and Literature 4. Boston: Ginn and Co., 1895.

[*Widuwilt.*] *Ritter Widuwilt: Die westjiddische Fassung des Wigalois des Wirnt von Gravenberc: Nach dem jiddischen Druck von 1699*, ed. Siegmund A. Wolf. Bochum: N. Brockmeyer, 1974.

Wirnt von Grafenberg. *Wigalois: The Knight of Fortune's Wheel*, trans. J. W. Thomas. Lincoln: University of Nebraska Press, 1977.

—— *Wigalois: Der Ritter mit dem Rade*, ed. J. M. N. Kapteyn. Bonn: F. Klopp, 1926.

Gawain and his Family in Later Literature

Bradshaw, Gillian. *Hawk of May.* New York: Simon and Schuster, 1980.

—— *In Winter's Shadow.* New York: Simon and Schuster, 1982.

—— *Kingdom of Summer.* New York: Simon and Schuster, 1981.

Bulla, Clyde Robert. *The Sword in the Tree*, ill. Paul Galdone. New York: Thomas Y. Crowell, 1956.

Delrio, Martin. *Harold R. Foster's Prince Valiant.* New York: Avon Books, 1998.

Ditmas, E. M. R. *Gareth of Orkney.* London: Faber and Faber, 1956.

Forbes, Elizabeth Stanhope. *King Arthur's Wood.* London: Simpkin, Marshall, Hamilton, Kent, n.d. [1904].

Hodges, Margaret. *The Kitchen Knight: A Tale of King Arthur*, ill. Trina Schart Hyman. New York: Holiday House, 1990.

Morris, Gerald. *The Squire's Tale.* Boston: Houghton Mifflin, 1998.

Schiller, Barbara. *The Kitchen Knight*, ill. Nonny Hogrogian. New York: Holt, Rinehart and Winston, 1965.

Stone, Eugenia. *Page Boy for King Arthur.* Chicago: Wilcox and Follett, 1949.

—— *Squire for King Arthur.* Chicago: Follett, 1955.

Tax, E. H. *The Wraith of Gawain.* Prairie City, Ill.: The Press of James A. Decker, 1948.

Merlin

Like *Gawain, *Merlin is integral to both the romance and chronicle traditions; he is also a figure who appears often in popular culture. Though sometimes thought of as Merlin the Magician, in various works he is a prophet, a bard, an adviser, a soldier, and a lover, as well as a wizard. The earliest references to him—or more properly to the figure who develops into the Merlin of later romance—occur in Celtic literature. Several Welsh poems allude to the tragic story of Myrddin, possibly a historical person whose lord Gwenddolau was killed in the battle of Arfderydd (c.575) by his enemy Rhydderch. Consequently, Myrddin, maddened and uttering prophecies, leads a life of exile in the Caledonian Woods.

The Celtic Merlin Figures

The earliest Myrddin poems appear in the manuscript known as the Black Book of Carmarthen (c.1250); others are found in manuscripts written considerably later. (All of these poems are conveniently translated in the section on 'Myrddin in Early Welsh Tradition' in Goodrich.) Some of the material contained in these poems, however, dates to a time significantly earlier than when the manuscripts were written. One of the oldest of the poems is 'Yr Afallennau' ('The Apple Tree Stanzas'), which includes, amidst prophecies by Myrddin, allusions to the battle at Arfderydd. Myrddin speaks of his fifty years of outlawry after the battle because he is 'hateful to Gwasawg, Rhydderch's supporter' (23) and presumably hunted by him. Myrddin also suggests that in the battle he killed the son of Gwenddydd, who is identified in other of the poems as Myrddin's sister.

In 'Yr Oianau' ('The Little Pig Stanzas'), Myrddin addresses the piglet that is his sole companion in the woods. As in 'Yr Afallennau', he alludes to his fifty years of exile and to being hunted by Rhydderch, even as he utters prophecies about the future of Britain that predict a troubled history with moments of glory. His personal situation is, however, unchanged: he grows old living in poverty while his enemy Rhydderch feasts in his hall, and 'Gwenddydd visits me not' (28).

In 'Ymddiddan Myrddin a Thaliessin' ('The Conversation of Myrddin and Taliesin'), Myrddin and *Taliesin speak of 'a battle fought by the men of Dyfed against an invading host led by Maelgwn ... at some time during the first half of the sixth century'; but the subject of the poem shifts, in the twenty-third of its thirty-eight lines, to the battle of Arfderydd (Jarman, 'The Merlin Legend' 120). There are allusions to the carnage of the battle but not to the role of Myrddin or his personal tragedy.

The verse dialogue 'Cyfoesi Myrddin a Gwenddydd ei Chwaer' ('The Dialogue of Myrddin and Gwenddydd, his Sister') also refers to 'Gwenddolau's death in the bloodshed of Arfderydd' (32) in the midst of a series of prophecies by Myrddin about future rulers of Britain. Gwenddydd calls Myrddin 'my lordless brother' and suggests that he is both poet and warrior (38, 39). Another prophetic poem, 'Gwasgargedd Fyrddin yn y Bedd' ('The Separation-Song of Myrddin in the Grave'), predicts a troubled future for Britain and alludes both to Myrddin's former status as one who 'drank wine from fair glass | with grim lords of war' (47) and to his decline, by means of allusions to Gwasawg and Gwenddydd. Similarly, 'Peirian Faban' ('Commanding Youth') mentions 'the memory of Gwenddolau' and incorporates allusions to Gwenddydd, Rhydderch, and Gwasawg into 'a vaticinatory poem' which 'gives prominence to the name of the Scottish Dalriadic king Aedán mac Gabráin (Aeddan ap Gafran), who was a contemporary of Rhydderch Hael' (Jarman, 'The Merlin Legend' 120).

The Welsh Myrddin poems demonstrate the existence both of a prophetic tradition and of a lost 'saga, whether oral or written, in which Myrddin's overlord Gwenddolau figured prominently' (Jarman, 'The Merlin Legend' 120). Analogous tales exist in Irish and Scottish tradition. The Irish *Buile Suibhne* (*Frenzy of Suibhne* [Sweeney], *c*.1200) tells of the hero's madness after he is cursed and his death by a spear is predicted. A closer analogue to the story of Myrddin's madness is found in the Scottish wild man named Lailoken who dwells in the forest and utters prophecies. Lailoken appears in two tales 'preserved in a fifteenth-century copy which probably derived from an earlier twelfth-century *Life of St. Kentigern* than that by Joceline' (Jarman, 'The Merlin Legend' 122). *Kentigern and Lailoken* tells of an encounter between St Kentigern and Lailoken, 'a madman, naked, hairy, and wretched' who some say 'was Merlin, the famous seer among the Britons' (5). When, in the midst of a battle, a voice tells Lailoken that he alone is 'guilty of the blood of all your slain comrades' (5), he goes mad. Known for obscure predictions and wild behaviour, Lailoken asks Kentigern to give him the Eucharist and the Last Rites on the day he knows he will die. Lailoken predicts three different deaths for himself: by stones and clubs, by a sharp wooden spear, and by drowning. After Lailoken's senses are restored in answer to Kentigern's prayers and he receives the sacraments, Lailoken meets his death when he is stoned and beaten by shepherds of King Meldred, falls onto a stake in a fish pond, and dies with his head beneath the water, thereby fulfilling the three different predictions of his own death. *Meldred and Lailoken* also uses the motif of the triple death which Lailoken predicts for himself. Meldred's queen, whose adultery Lailoken has revealed, incites shepherds to attack him. He is beaten, pierced, and drowned, thus fulfilling his seemingly impossible prophecy and giving credence to his accusation of the queen.

A. O. H. Jarman has speculated on the stages in the development of the Merlin figure from Celtic myth and poetry to Geoffrey of Monmouth's writings: basic themes, such as that of the wild man, are linked to the battle of Arfderydd, to Lailoken, and to St Kentigern; then the legend is transferred from the north of Britain to Wales and Lailoken is identified with Myrddin; subsequently the legend develops in Wales and is associated with 'the national tradition of prophecy'; finally Geoffrey of Monmouth transforms Myrddin into the Merlin figure who plays a role in 'international literature' (Jarman, 'Early Stages' 327).

Geoffrey of Monmouth
As noted in Chapter 1, Geoffrey of Monmouth, in his *History of the Kings of Britain* (completed *c.*1138), combined the figure of the youth Ambrosius Aurelianus from Nennius and the Celtic figure of Myrddin in his character Ambrosius Merlin, and in doing so created the figure of Merlin as he appears in virtually all later Arthurian literature. Geoffrey also introduced into the tradition the story of Merlin's being fathered by an incubus and he assigned to Merlin the subsequent encounter with *Vortigern, in which Merlin explains that Vortigern's tower will not stand because of a struggle between a red and white dragon beneath the foundation, and after which he proceeds to utter a series of increasingly obscure predictions. Geoffrey makes Merlin an adviser to British kings, though not to *Arthur, and describes the transformation of *Uther into the shape of the Duke of Cornwall so that he might conceive Arthur.

Another of Geoffrey's works was ultimately much less influential than his *History*, but it demonstrates a knowledge of the Celtic traditions about Myrddin. The *Vita Merlini* (*Life of Merlin*), written in verse around 1150, recounts the battle of Arfderydd but, in contrast to the Myrddin poems, presents Merlin as an ally of Rodarch (Rhydderch), along with whom he fought in support of a prince named Peredur in his campaign against Gwenddolau. Grief over the deaths of 'three brothers of the prince' (55) drives Merlin mad, and he flees to the woods and lives like a wild animal. Merlin's sister Ganieda, who in Geoffrey's account is married to Rodarch, sends men in search of her brother. One of them finds him and uses music to restore his senses. But when Merlin's madness recurs, Rodarch chains him to prevent his running off to the woods again.

Because of this restriction, Merlin is despondent; but upon seeing Rodarch remove a leaf from his wife's hair, he laughs. When Rodarch asks for an explanation of the laughter, Merlin says he will give it only if he is freed, to which Rodarch agrees. Merlin reveals that Ganieda got the leaf in her hair by lying in the undergrowth with her lover. To try to convince her husband that Merlin's charge is just the raving of a madman, Ganieda asks her brother to predict how a certain boy will die. Merlin responds that he will fall from a high rock. She has the boy disguise himself and asks Merlin how the apparently different boy will die. Merlin says 'he will meet a violent death in a tree through misjudgment'. Then, after dressing the boy in woman's clothing, she asks Merlin how the 'girl' will die. Merlin says that she will drown in a river (69). The three different answers convince Rodarch that Merlin's accusation of Ganieda is false. But Merlin's prophecies are fulfilled when the youth, while hunting, falls from a precipice in such a way that one of his feet is caught in a tree overhanging a river and most of his body is submerged in the water.

After Merlin returns to the woods and his wife Guendoloena remarries, Merlin kills her new husband with a stag's horns, an act for which he is captured and imprisoned once again. But when he laughs at three events, Rodarch again agrees to free him if he explains the reason for his laughter. Merlin does so and returns to the woods, where he makes predictions about the future of Britain, predictions which he says he once made at even greater length to Vortigern (89). When Taliesin visits, they discuss such things as the nature of winds and rainstorms, the properties of certain types of fish, and other elements of natural history and geography, including a description of the 'Island of Apples' or 'The Fortunate Island' where Morgen and her eight sisters dwell. The Morgen of the *Vita Merlini*, a far different figure from the wicked *Morgan le Fay of some later literature, is skilled in healing and astrology and is able to shift her shape and even to fly. It is to her that Arthur is brought for healing after the battle at *Camlann.

Merlin recounts for Taliesin the history of the Saxon invasions and Arthur's reign, including Vortigern's allowing the invaders to enter the country, the struggles of *Ambrosius and Uther against them, Arthur's victories in Britain and abroad (against Frollo and *Lucius), and *Mordred's treachery. Thus the Merlin of the *Vita* combines elements of the Welsh Myrddin and of the Merlin of Geoffrey's history. Geoffrey presents him as living beyond Arthur's time to the time of the battle at Arfderydd and afterwards. In the *Vita*, the final picture is of him in his forest retreat, accompanied by Maeldin, a friend from his youth, Taliesin, and Ganieda, who has now been given the gift of prophecy that once was Merlin's.

Although modern authors generally do not write in the tradition of the Welsh Myrddin and Geoffrey's *Vita Merlini*, there are a few notable exceptions. German Romantic poet Ludwig Uhland (1787–1862), in his poem *Merlin der Wilde* (*Merlin the Wild Man*, 1829), retells the story of the *Vita Merlini*, which he knew from the summary in George Ellis's *Specimens of Early English Metrical Romances* (1805). Merlin's retreat to the woods 'expresses beautifully Uhland's conception, attitude, and worship of nature' (Weiss 95, 98). Scottish Victorian poet John Veitch (1829–1894), in an introductory note to his poem 'Merlin' (1889), observes that he is writing about 'Merlin Caledonius, known also as Merlin Wylt and Silvestris' (5). Veitch's Merlin laments the loss of his prince Gwenddoleu, of 'well-lovëd Gwendydd's son', and of all the 'dead of Ardderyd' (15). Part of the poem, like one of the early Welsh Myrddin poems, is a dialogue with his sister. Merlin dies when a band of rustics attacks and drowns him because he is the devil's son. His former lover

Hwimleian, 'The Gleam', appears to him; and their spirits are united with each other and with the natural world. Veitch's Gleam, who represents unity with the natural world, is a very different symbol from that employed by Tennyson in 'Merlin and the Gleam' (discussed below), but one that works perfectly in a poem rich in natural imagery. British poet Laurence Binyon (1869–1943) also draws on Geoffrey's *Vita* and the Welsh Myrddin poems in his dramatic poem *The Madness of Merlin* (1947), in which Merlin rushes from battle, maddened by his own killing of three princes. Binyon uses the motif of Merlin's laughter at the transgression of Redderech's wife, here Langoreth and not Merlin's sister Gwyndyth. But Binyon's work was left unfinished, and there is no indication of Merlin's ultimate fate.

PROPHECIES OF MERLIN

Geoffrey of Monmouth's *History* was tremendously influential in the development of the character of Merlin in several ways, including the popularization of a tradition of prophecies attributed to Merlin that often have political or religious implications for the time in which the prophecies were actually written. Geoffrey drew on the Celtic tradition of a prophetic Merlin (or Myrddin) in his *Prophetiae Merlini* (*Prophecies of Merlin*), originally written as a separate book in 1130 and then incorporated into the *Historia* as book 7. These prophecies predict numerous events, including the victories and glory of Arthur and the ultimate triumph of the Saxons in Britain, and continue with a series of cryptic utterances to a final apocalyptic vision. Because of the difficulty of interpreting them, the prophecies were not always translated or adapted with the rest of Geoffrey's work. Wace, for example, omitted them. And while they were translated into Icelandic as *Merlinus spa* (*c.*1200) by Gunnlaugr Leifsson (d. 1218 or 1219), they appear in only one of the manuscripts of the *Breta sögur*, the Icelandic translation of Geoffrey's *History*.

Despite, or in some cases because of, their obscurity, Geoffrey's prophecies influenced other collections of prophecies attributed to Merlin, such as the *Prophécies de Merlin*, written in the 1270s and ascribed, probably spuriously, to Maistre Richart d'Irlande. The *Prophécies* commented on political and religious matters, as did many other prophecies from the Middle Ages and the Renaissance, when such predictions were used to support various causes, including Welsh nationalism and the Reformation. There is also an anonymous fifteenth-century English translation of and commentary on Geoffrey's prophecies.

In later literature, Merlin figures as a prophet in Ben Jonson's masque *The Speeches at Prince Henries Barriers*. The 'Barriers' were a celebration (at the Christmas festivities of 1609) in honour of the investiture of Henry, eldest son of James I, as Prince of Wales in 1610. The Stuarts, like the Tudors, traced their lineage back to Arthur. As James Merriman observed, 'Like the Tudors before him, James I was quick to see the usefulness of Arthur in bolstering his throne. Through both the Tudor and the Stuart lines, he was able to trace himself to Arthur's blood, and by his relinquishment of separate titles to the two realms of Scotland and England and his taking instead the title of King of Great Britain, James made possible the assertion by his supporters that his accession fulfilled Merlin's prophecy that under the name of Brutus England and Scotland would be united once more as they had been under Arthur' (49). Thus it is fitting that the *Lady of the Lake and Merlin instruct James's son as he becomes Prince of Wales. In the masque, the Lady of the Lake presents a shield to Meliadus (who represents Henry) and then calls on Merlin to explain to him the shield's images. The allusion to the shield of Achilles is obvious; and other classical echoes occur throughout (cf. Peacock 175). Merlin's reading of the shield is in effect a prediction of the glories of Arthurian and English history, including the accomplishments of the Tudor and Stewart monarchs and a final prophecy about the glory of James and his line.

In 1641, Thomas Heywood's (1574?–1641) *Life of Merlin* used purported prophecies of Merlin as the basis for a history of England up to the beginning of the reign of Charles I. Merlin's name was also frequently used by astrologers and writers of almanacs in the seventeenth century. In 1644, William Lilly (1602–81) began publishing almanacs under the names of Merlinus Anglicus Junior, later Merlinus Anglicus; and in the late seventeenth and early eighteenth centuries, John Partridge (1644–1715) produced an almanac under the name of Merlinus Liberatus and Merlinus Redivivus.

Jonathan Swift (1667–1745) parodied these prophecies by predicting in the Bickerstaff Papers that John Partridge would die on 29 March 1708, and then writing after that date that the prediction had in fact proved true (though Partridge did not actually die until 1715). Swift also mocked the abuse of prophecies attributed to Merlin in 'A Famous Prediction of Merlin, the British Wizard, Written above a Thousand Years Ago and Relating to the Present Year 1709', in which he created a prophecy with the obscure language and animal imagery typical of the genre and twisted its language so that he could wring from it any meaning he wanted by proclaiming that such obscurity is 'after the usual manner of old astrological predictions' (82).

The tradition of using prophecies of Merlin for political purposes was, however, strong enough that even Swift's biting satire could not end it. In 1807, Joseph Leigh, a Welsh-born American author, wrote *Illustrations of the Fulfilment of the Prediction of Merlin: Occasioned by the Late Outrageous Attack of the British Ship of War the Leopard on the American Frigate Chesapeake, and the Measures Taken by the President, Supported by the Citizens Thereon*. Leigh's treatise takes the form of a prophecy of Merlin which purportedly predicted both the attack of the British ship *Leopard* on the American vessel *Chesapeake*, seen by modern historians as a significant event leading to the War of 1812, and dire consequences for Britain unless reparations are made for the attack.

British poets also continued to use the notion of prophecy, as Jonson did, to 'predict' a magnificent reign for the ruling monarch. In 1838, the year after Victoria ascended to the throne, George Darley's (1795–1846) 'Merlin's Last Prophecy' predicted the glories of Victoria and the British Empire. Several decades later, Canadian poet John Reade (1837–1919) wrote 'The Prophecy of Merlin' (1870), in which Merlin foretells to *Bedivere, despondent at Arthur's passing, that Victoria and Albert will restore the values that Arthur represented. The prophecy makes reference to specific details of their reign, including the construction of the Crystal Palace, the birth of a son named Arthur, and the grief of Victoria at the death of her husband (in 1861).

The notion of Merlin as a prophet, which is found in some of the earliest references to the character, persisted in popular culture even in those centuries when Arthurian literature was less prominent than in the Middle Ages or the Victorian period. Merlin's prophetic powers are also central in some of the key texts in twentieth-century Arthurian literature, including the novels of T. H. White and Mary Stewart.

MERLIN IN MEDIEVAL ROMANCE

Merlin in French Romance

The story of Merlin created by Geoffrey was significant not only because of the prophetic tradition that it inspired. Geoffrey's Merlin also influenced Robert de Boron as he incorporated into the account of Arthurian prehistory in his *Grail cycle the story of the attempt by the devils to counter the good done by the birth of Christ by having one of their number impregnate a human woman. Their plan to create an Antichrist is frustrated when Merlin is baptized and uses the powers he possesses as the son of a devil for good rather than evil. (See Chapter 4 for a fuller account of Robert de Boron's treatment of Merlin and the Grail story.) The story that came through Geoffrey, Robert de Boron, and the prose renditions of Boron's work is the basis for the history of Merlin in the *Vulgate Cycle.

In the Vulgate (or Lancelot–Grail) Cycle (c.1215–35), Merlin is presented as a prophet of the Grail but also as an architect of Arthur's reign, during which the Grail quest is achieved. The Estoire de Merlin (Story of Merlin) begins with a council of devils complaining about Christ's redemption of sinners and plotting to bring into the world a man sired by one of their kind in order to win back those who had turned to Christ. The devils destroy the livestock of a wealthy man, kill his son, and cause his wife to take her own life. When the man grows ill from grief and dies, his three daughters are left alone. The devil undoes two of the daughters, but the third, counselled by a holy man, resists temptation until, one evening when she is angered by the loose living of her sister, her wrath allows an incubus to enter her chamber and impregnate her as she sleeps. When her condition is discovered and she is imprisoned, she seeks the advice of her confessor. Following his instruction, she baptizes her son Merlin as soon as he is born and thus frustrates the devils' plan to make him a servant of evil. Nevertheless, Merlin retains the devils' power of knowing all things past; in addition, God grants him the power of foreseeing the future.

The Vulgate *Merlin* includes Merlin's encounter with Vortigern, who has been told that only the death of a child with no father will keep the tower he is building from collapsing. The strange circumstances of Merlin's birth mark him for sacrifice. But he reveals the two dragons fighting beneath the foundation, interprets them as representing Vortigern and the sons of Constant (*Constantine), and predicts Vortigern's death. After Pendragon is killed and his brother Uther assumes the kingship, Merlin assists Uther in satisfying his lust for *Ygraine and in return is promised custody of Arthur, the child of that union. Merlin entrusts the child to *Antor and his wife to raise until Uther's death, when Arthur proves his right to rule by drawing a sword from a stone. With the help of Kings *Ban and *Bors, Arthur defeats those kings who were unwilling to accept him and secures his rule.

The influence of the chronicle tradition is clear not only in the account of Merlin's early history but also in the emphasis placed on the battles with the Saxons, in which the king's nephew Gawainet (Gawain) distinguishes himself and swears loyalty to Arthur, despite his father *Lot's refusal to accept Arthur as king. Also recounted is Arthur's expedition to Gaul. After fighting the *Giant of St Michael's Mount, he defeats the Romans in a battle in which Gawainet, using *Excalibur, kills the emperor. Merlin advises Arthur not to proceed to Rome and instructs him that before returning to Britain, he must cross to the other side of the Lake of Lausanne to slay a giant cat possessed by the devil who destroys the countryside and kills the people of the region. After a fierce battle, Arthur slays the cat.

The climax of the Vulgate *Merlin* is the story of Merlin's love for *Viviane (or Niniane—the name appears with various spellings in the Vulgate and Post-Vulgate texts), a lady to whom he teaches magic. When she asks him to share with her the spell whereby she could imprison a man 'without a tower or walls or irons, but through wizardry, so that he could never get away but through me', Merlin is 'overcome by love' and must do her bidding even though he knows she will use the knowledge against him. Sitting beneath a hawthorn bush, Viviane works the spell so that when Merlin awakes he seems to be in a beautiful tower (416). Viviane, who earlier pledged her love to Merlin (283) and actually cares for him, can enter and leave the tower as she wishes. She promises to visit him often, and in fact keeps her word, 'for few days or nights went by when she was not with him' (417).

The *Suite du Merlin* (*The Merlin Continuation*), the Post-Vulgate account of Merlin's history, was the source for Malory's 'The Tale of King Arthur'; and therefore many of its incidents are familiar to those whose primary knowledge of the Arthurian story comes from Malory. The *Suite* recounts Arthur's receiving Excalibur from the Lady of the Lake; the tragic history of *Balin and his use of *Longinus' spear to strike the *Dolorous Stroke; Arthur's marriage to *Guinevere; the triple quest undertaken by Gawain, Tor, and *Pellinor; and Morgan's treachery in giving Excalibur to her lover Accalon to use in combat against Arthur.

Perhaps most significant for the development of traditions surrounding Merlin is the way the *Suite* handles the relationship between Merlin and Viviane, which is in sharp contrast to the treatment found in the Vulgate *Merlin*. Although Viviane wants to learn magic from Merlin, she does not love him because she 'couldn't love the son of the devil for anything in the world'. She uses the magic he teaches her to enchant him so that he can be sealed in the tomb of two lovers whose long-buried bodies are now 'ugly and horrible', and she has Merlin 'thrown upside down into the hole where the two lovers lay' (iv. 260). The gruesome fate puts Merlin face to face with the decaying bodies but is also an ironic reminder of the love he sought but will never have. Since this was the account of Merlin's entombment known to Malory, the tradition that is passed on to English and American readers is primarily that of the Viviane who does not love Merlin and who entombs him because she tires of his advances.

In the latter half of the thirteenth century, an author identified in the text as Heldris de Cornuälle wrote the romance *Silence*, in which Merlin plays a role analogous to that in the Grisandole episode in the Vulgate *Merlin* (cf. chapter 35, pp. 321–9) (an episode that later becomes the basis for 'The Story of Grisandole' (1987) by John Matthews). The title character of the medieval romance is Silence, a girl raised as a boy because the English king Evan had decreed that women may not inherit and her parents want to pass their land on to her. When the king's wife Eufeme makes advances to Silence, whom she thinks to be a handsome young man, and then accuses Silence of attacking her when he/she rejects the queen, Silence is sent to France where she becomes a knight. Returning to England to help Evan put down a rebellion, Silence is again accused by Eufeme and is sent away on a mission to find Merlin, which the king and queen believe she will never accomplish since there is a prophecy that he can only be captured by a woman. But Silence does in fact bring Merlin back to court. One of the traditional motifs that Heldris uses is Merlin's laughter at various incidents, which the king commands him to explain and which becomes the device by which the truth is revealed in the romance. Merlin says that he laughed at a peasant who bought a new pair of shoes because he would die before wearing them; at a leper who was begging because a treasure was buried beneath his feet; at a man who was weeping at the funeral of a child because the priest was the real father of the child; and at a nun who was really a man. He also laughed at Silence, the king and the queen, and himself because the queen dishonoured the king by making advances to Silence, and Silence deceived them because she is in fact a woman and not a man. As a reward for Silence's loyalty, Evan decrees that women may once again inherit.

Merlin in English Romance

The Vulgate *Estoire de Merlin* was popular in England and was adapted in a number of verse and prose English works. The thirteenth-century romance *Arthour and Merlin*, for example, is based on the Vulgate *Merlin*. Aside from the obvious change of the French text's prose into verse, *Arthour and Merlin* follows a common pattern of adaptation from French sources and omits or condenses a number of episodes. It tells of the sons of Costaunce (Constantine) and of Fortiger's (Vortigern's) treachery and invitation of the Saxons into Britain, the role of the devil in Merlin's birth, Fortiger's attempt to build a castle which will not stand, and Merlin's revelation of the dragons fighting beneath its foundation. Aurilis' (Aurelius') role in winning back the kingdom is downplayed while Uther's is emphasized.

Merlin is an adviser to kings and the engineer of Arthur's birth and reign, but not, as in the Vulgate, a prophet of the Grail. He assists Uther in satisfying his lust for Igerne by smearing him with herbs so he takes on the appearance of her husband, the Duke of Cornwall. When Merlin receives the baby born of that union, he entrusts his upbringing to Antor. Arthur later proves his right to rule by drawing the sword from the stone, here called 'Estalibore' (i. 185), which he uses to overcome rebellious kings and dukes, defeat invaders, and conduct a long battle against the forces of Rion and his supporters. In the course of these wars, Arthur gains the support of Wawain (Gawain) and his brothers; of Galathin, son of Igerne's daughter Blasine; and of 'Bast [Bastard] Ywain' (i. 311), the illegitimate son of *Uriens, who also has a legitimate son named *Ywain. After twice rescuing *Leodegan, father of Guenor (Guinevere), Arthur wins her in marriage.

The longest version of *Arthour and Merlin* (that found in the famous Auchinleck Manuscript) ends after the great victory of Arthur over the forces of Rion; yet that event does not seem to bring a satisfactory resolution. Perhaps the author intended to add further material, though it is impossible to know with certainty. There are also several fifteenth-century manuscripts which contain a shorter version of the poem that ends before Uther conceives Arthur and that offers no account of Arthur's reign. The climactic event in this version is the death of Uther's brother Aurilis. The shorter version is also the basis for *A Lytel Treatyse of þe Byrth and Prophecye of Marlyn*, printed by Wynkyn de Worde in 1510, which in turn seems to have been the source of the *Historie van Merlijn*, a Dutch chapbook printed between 1534 and 1544 (cf. Besamusca 195).

In the middle of the fifteenth century, Henry Lovelich translated the Vulgate *Merlin* into English verse couplets, as he did with the Vulgate *Estoire del Saint Graal* (see Chapter 4). Lovelich's *Merlin* is fairly close to his French source, but the sole manuscript in which it appears is incomplete, ending in the midst of the battle with King *Claudas. Whereas *Arthour and Merlin* contains only an allusion to Niniame who 'Begiled the gode clerk Merlin' (228) and not the full story of their relationship, Lovelich tells of the meeting of Merlin and Nimiane. Merlin begins to teach her magic in return for her swearing to be his 'Owne Al Only' and plighting her troth to him (iii. 570, 574); however, the text ends before his entrapment, which presumably would have followed the Vulgate version in which Nimiane loves him and returns to visit him.

Another translation of the Vulgate *Merlin* into Middle English, the anonymous *Prose Merlin*, was also written in the middle of the fifteenth century and is also a fairly close rendition of its source. Though the text of the romance breaks off before the end, the *Prose Merlin* does include the beguiling of Merlin by Nimiane. Merlin is so 'supprised [overwhelmed] with hir love' (ed. Conlee 320) that he is unable to deny her anything. As in the French source, Nimiane requites his love and visits him often in the tower that she has constructed with the magic he taught her.

Although the period from the Renaissance until the renewal of interest in medieval literature in the Romantic and Victorian ages is often said to be the nadir of Arthurian literature, Arthurian material survived and even, in some genres, thrived. Arthurian themes are found in chronicles, epic poetry, drama, prophecy, and satire. Perhaps the most popular Arthurian character in this period, Merlin appears not only in the political prophecies attributed to him and satirized by Jonathan Swift but also in versions of the story of *Tom Thumb who was associated with Merlin and Arthur's court in chapbooks and ballads and who was the subject of another eighteenth-century satire, a play by Henry Fielding.

TOM THUMB

Henry Fielding's (1707–54) burlesque play *Tom Thumb* (1730) is a satiric tour de force that criticized everything from politics, doctors, and lawyers to printing practices and the heroic and romantic conventions of the drama of his day. As part of his parody of the Arthurian legends, Fielding takes as his hero Tom Thumb, the chapbook character, the minuscule protagonist who was 'by Merlin's Art begot' and who is called by Arthur 'Hero, Giant-killing Lad, | Preserver of my Kingdom' (Fielding 23–4). But the greatest example of Tom Thumb's valour in the play is his killing of a bailiff who wants to arrest Tom's friend Noodle.

Fielding satirizes not only the debased form of valorous action found in contemporary chapbooks and heroic drama but also the love interest found in both. Because of his services to the country, Tom has been promised the hand of Princess Huncamunca. His decision to leave martial pursuits for 'Hymeneal' ones is compared, in a mock-heroic epic simile, to a chimney sweeper washing his face and hands and changing his shirt before he lies with his wife (Fielding 26). The love plot is complicated by the fact that Arthur's queen, in this version not Guinevere but Dollalolla, is also in love with Tom.

Both loves are frustrated when Tom is swallowed by a cow, but his ghost returns, only to be killed by a character named Grizzle, who has a grievance against him. Huncamunca then kills Grizzle and is herself killed by Doodle, who is then killed by the queen. In quick succession, Noodle kills the queen and is killed by a character named Cleora, who is killed in turn by one Mustacha. Arthur kills this last murderer and, to complete the parody of bloody dramatic endings, kills himself.

Fielding expanded his original play in 1731 as *The Tragedy of Tragedies*, which introduced new characters. Glumdalca, the Queen of the Giants, who is in love with Tom Thumb and is loved by Arthur, adds to the buffoonery. A Parson wishes that Tom and Huncamunca might propagate like maggots in a Cheshire cheese. And Merlin himself, who did not appear in the earlier version, explains his role in Tom's birth by quoting from the ballad 'The Life and Death of Tom Thumb'. In the printed version of his play, Fielding adds numerous footnotes quoting lines from other works which are echoed in his burlesque, thus emphasizing the artificial rhetoric of contemporary drama. The play, however, ends with the same series of multiple homicides and Arthur's suicide as in the earlier version. Fielding's selection of the story of Tom Thumb, traditionally linked to Merlin and Arthur, is probably due more to its mock-heroic possibilities than to any particular dislike for the legend of Arthur, which was at a low point anyway in his day, since eighteenth-century rationalism rejected many of the fantastic events of medieval romance.

Fielding's play was reworked as *The Opera of Operas; or, Tom Thumb the Great* by Eliza Haywood (1693?–1756) and William Hatchett (*fl.* 1730–41) with music by Thomas Arne (1710–78), composer of the music for 'Rule, Britannia'. As the title implies, this version adds numerous 'airs' or songs. It also introduces the ghost of Tom's father, Gaffer Thumb, who warns Arthur of Grizzle's rebellion. And it expands the role of Merlin. The seer predicts that Tom will be swallowed by a cow, but Tom is content because, as Merlin tells him, this 'heroic Act' will be memorialized in a 'tunefull Opera' (Haywood and Hatchett 36–7).

After the series of deaths, repeated as in Fielding, two characters, Sir Crit-Operatical and Modely, discuss the opera; and the former criticizes it for its tragic ending, which he believes an Italian opera would never have. But Modely tells him there is more to come. Merlin then appears and uses 'emetick Power' to force the cow to spit up Tom, after which he restores all the other characters to life and enchants them so that their strife is ended and Arthur and Dollalolla, Tom and Huncamunca, and Grizzle and Glumdalca are all happy in love. Thus the opera offers the kind of resolution Sir Crit-Operatical desires.

Another adaptation of Fielding's play, *Tom Thumb the Great* by Kane O'Hara (1714?–1782), was first produced in 1780 (though not printed until 1805). O'Hara follows the scheme of Haywood and Hatchett, including the appearance of Merlin as a *deus ex machina* to restore life and harmony at the end, but without the intrusion of the modern commentators on the apparent tragic ending.

In his plays about Tom Thumb, Fielding was drawing on earlier ballads and chapbooks. The first surviving text to tell the story of Tom Thumb and to link the diminutive hero and King Arthur was the prose *History of Tom Thumbe* (1621) by Richard Johnson (1573–1659?), although 'accounts of his [Tom's] life must have been circulating widely throughout England for many decades prior to the first publication of this tract' (Bühler in Johnson p. ix). Indeed, Johnson's own text suggests earlier versions.

In Johnson's tale, Tom's father, who is King Arthur's husbandman, advises his wife to go to Merlin to find out the cause of their childlessness and help them to correct the problem. Merlin, described as 'a man, rather a diuell or spirit, cunning in all Arts and Professions, all sciences, secrets and discoueries, a coniurer, an inchanter, a charmer, hee consorts with Elues and Fayries, a Commaunder of Goblins, a worker of Night-wonders' (Johnson 4), arranges for the couple to have a son in accordance with the father's wish for a child even if he were no bigger than his thumb. Tom's size allows for adventures such as tumbling into his mother's pudding, being ingested and excreted by a cow (here given a laxative, in contrast to the emetic magic that Merlin works in Haywood and Hatchett's version of the story), being carried off by a raven, falling down a giant's chimney, and being swallowed by the giant and then vomited into the sea when his activity makes the giant feel as if the devil is playing tennis in his stomach. When Tom is discovered, after being swallowed by a fish which is caught and given to King Arthur, he is made Arthur's dwarf and delights the ladies of the court and the king himself. Later, after visiting his parents and carrying three pence for them on his back, he meets with the giant Gargantua, from whom he escapes by enchanting him so he is unable to move. The tale promises a sequel with further adventures of Tom, but either it was never written or it has not survived.

Some of the material in Johnson's tale is also found in the earliest surviving ballad to treat the diminutive hero, *Tom Thumbe, his Life and Death* (1630), in which Tom is begotten and born, with Merlin's help, in half an hour; within four minutes, he grows to his full height of one inch. Many of his adventures are the same as in Johnson's *History of Tom Thumbe*, including being swallowed by a cow, carried off by a raven, eaten by a giant and then a fish. He arrives at Arthur's court inside the fish, becomes a favourite, and ultimately dies, his body carried to the land of the Fairy Queen, who had supplied him with his clothing when he was born.

Fielding drew on the popular tale for his play, but he was not the first to see the satiric possibilities of Tom Thumb. William Wagstaffe (1685–1725), in *A Comment upon the History of Tom Thumb* (1711), parodied the enthusiasm for ballads in the criticism of his day. Wagstaffe compares verses and events from the ballad to lines and scenes from Virgil and Ovid. Tom's father's consulting Merlin is said, for example, to be like Aeneas's consulting the oracle at Delphi, and Tom's being carried off by the raven is 'almost the same Story as that of *Ganimede,* and the Eagle in *Ovid*' (Wagstaffe 9, 13). The ballad is also given mock-moral seriousness when Wagstaffe observes that 'the Design was undoubtedly to recommend Virtue, and to shew that however any one may labour under the Disadvantages of Stature or Deformity, or the Meanness of Parentage, yet if his Mind and Actions are above the ordinary Level, those very Disadvantages, that seem to depress him, shall add a Lustre to his Character' (Wagstaffe 5). Thus, it is clear that Fielding had predecessors in the satiric as well as the literary use of the character of Tom Thumb.

Besides Fielding's, one of the most remarkable interpretations of the Tom Thumb stories was that of Victorian novelist Charlotte Yonge (1823–1901), whose *The History of Sir Thomas Thumb* (1855) incorporates more Arthurian material into the narrative than any other version. It also adds numerous notes which are recommended to the children for whom the book is intended because they include 'some of the choice passages of English fairy poetry' and they 'give a few sketches from the romances of King Arthur's Court, often a subject of much youthful curiosity, not easily gratified' (Yonge p. iv).

In addition to recounting some of the traditional ballad material, Yonge makes the tale a moral for the young by having Tom learn from his youthful indiscretions not to be mischievous like the fairies but instead to be 'steady and trustworthy' (Yonge 35), qualities that serve him well at Arthur's court and that provide an appropriate lesson for young readers. Yonge's story also weaves Tom Thumb into the larger Arthurian narrative in several ways. After Merlin arranges with Mab, queen of the fairies, for Tom's birth, Yonge observes that Merlin may have intended to watch over Tom's parents because of the hospitality they gave him, but he was unable to because of the disaster—his imprisonment by Viviana, Lady of the Lake—that befell him. Similarly, when Tom arrives at Arthur's court, there is an account of how Arthur had just returned from killing 'the wicked giant Ryence, of North Wales' (Yonge 39), a story which, as told here, combines Ryence or Ryons and the Giant of St Michael's Mount into one character.

After Tom is made Arthur's page, he captures a mouse as a steed and hunts spiders, wasps, gnats, and other insects so they will not disturb the ladies of the court. When the magpie that belongs to Tom's wicked aunt steals a jewel that Sir Cradocke intended for his wife, Tom assaults the bird and makes it drop the gem. He is then attacked by his aunt's cat, but Sir *Tristrem's hound *Petticrewe barks and awakens the knight and scares off both bird and cat. For his courage and service, Tom is made a knight and accompanies Arthur on his quest to the Castle of Terne Wadling, where a giant has captured a lady's lover; but as the two approach, they lose their strength. As a result, Arthur must agree to answer a riddle or be killed. Thus begins the story of Sir Gawayne and the *Loathly Lady.

This account, in turn, allows Yonge to contrast Gawayne with another of Arthur's nephews, Mordred. The evil nephew tries to steal Arthur's signet ring so he can use it to raise an army of rebellion. At first, he is thwarted by Tom; but the second time, Mordred succeeds and severely wounds the diminutive knight, who is taken to the realm of the fairies for healing. There he consults with the trapped Merlin, who advises him not to eat the fairy food. Tom follows the advice but discovers that the seven days in the fairy realm were actually seven human years. He goes back to the world of men just in time to see the dead Mordred and to join Bedivere in watching Arthur being taken off in the barge. Returning to Caerleon to report the sad events to Guenever, Tom is appalled at the state of the castle and the *Round Table. When he sees a spider weaving a web on Arthur's throne, Tom attacks but is slain by its venomous bite. Although he is buried in the shadow of Mount Snowdon, some people believe that when Arthur returns, Tom will return with him.

Yonge makes the tale of Tom Thumb unquestionably a story for children. By including suitable morals and using the tale to demonstrate that 'manfulness lies in the spirit, not the height' (Yonge 50), she foreshadows much later literature for children wherein knighthood becomes a moral and not a physical or social quality.

In 1863, in *The Fairy Book*, Dinah Maria Mulock Craik (1826–87) retold a number of fairy tales from various sources, including what she called 'the few real old English fairy tales' such as *Tom Thumb* and *Jack the Giant Killer*, both of which associate their heroes with King Arthur's court. She clearly intended these fairy tales 'for the delight of all children' (Craik p. vii) and therefore follows Charlotte Yonge in transforming the story of Tom Thumb from the popular entertainment or satire that it had been originally into the children's story it has been since the Victorian era, as the numerous illustrated retellings geared specifically to young readers attest. Craik tells the tale according to the ballad tradition, describing in her prose Merlin's role in the birth of Tom and many of Tom's traditional adventures, including being eaten by a cow and swallowed by a fish. Craik also accounts for Tom's death by having him killed by a spider, although, in her tale, Tom's demise has nothing to do with defending the honour of Arthur and the Round Table.

MERLIN IN DRAMA

In addition to his role in works in the chronicle and romance tradition discussed in previous chapters, Merlin also appears in post-medieval plays, which range from masques and lyrical dramas set to music to one-act and multi-act dramas. Some of these interpretations are based heavily on traditional accounts; others use traditional motifs but interpret them in original ways; and some are totally original.

One of the most interesting of the Renaissance Arthurian plays to use chronicle material is *The Birth of Merlin* (c.1620), attributed in its first printed edition of 1662 to William Rowley (1585?–1642?) and William Shakespeare (1564–1616), although no one now believes that Shakespeare collaborated in its writing. The play (which was translated into German by Ludwig Tieck (1773–1853) as *Die Geburt des Merlin*) has a comic plot which overwhelms the historical to such a degree that it seems inappropriate to call it a 'subplot'. The comic action involves a search by Merlin's mother for the father of her child. In this play, she is not the holy woman of medieval romance but a simple woman called Joan Goe-too't. Having gone to it with a stranger and bearing his child, Joan enlists the help of her brother, identified only as a 'Clown', to find the father. Though the devil is described in the stage directions as having 'horrid' (32) head and feet, she is unable to describe him, except to say that he was a gentleman who wore rich clothing and had a gilt sword and 'most excellent hangers' (14), 'hangers' being the loops or straps from which a sword was hung, but also having vulgar connotations as used by Joan and the Clown. Her lack of discernment about the father of her child leaves Joan unable to distinguish one 'gentleman' from another, so that she thinks even Uther ('Uter' in the play) Pendragon may have been responsible.

Uter, on the other hand, who calls Joan 'Witch, scullion, hag' (17) because of her sin and her accusation, is unable to perceive, at least initially, that another woman is far more wicked and dangerous. He is attracted to Artesia, sister of the Saxon general Ostorius. But Artesia, who is wed to Uter's brother *Aurelius, manipulates his affections to cause a breach between the brothers. Finally recognizing her evil, Uter says she is a 'witch by nature, devil by art' (44). Just as Joan was deceived by the devil, so the devilish Artesia deceives Uter, temporarily, and Aurelius, fatally. (Later it is revealed that Aurelius has been poisoned by Artesia and Ostorius.)

In both plots, Merlin helps to set things right. Through the familiar device of the red and white dragons that struggle beneath the site where Vortiger would build a castle, Merlin predicts the downfall of Vortiger and the victory of Uter as well as the birth of Uter's two children, one of whom will be Queen of Ireland, the other (Arthur) a great conqueror who will win thirteen crowns. In the comic plot, when the devil returns to take advantage of Joan a second time, Merlin—in an action that echoes his own fate in other stories—seals him in a rock where he will never touch a woman again. The play ends with another complex prediction by Merlin: that the Saxons will ultimately triumph, but first Arthur will win great fame, only to die 'in the middest of all his glories'. Uter, aware that Fate 'must be observ'd', seems content with the prediction of his son's glory (65).

In the eighteenth century, Merlin appeared in satires, burlesques, masques, and popular entertainments as a type of the magician or wizard and with little connection to traditional Arthurian material. Lewis Theobald's (1688–1744) *Merlin or The Devil of Stone-Henge*, an entertainment with dances and music by John Galliard (1687?–1749), for example, portrays Merlin as wicked. It declares him to be demon-born and therefore an agent of the devil in beguiling humans, including Faust. And it concludes with the moral: 'How sutilly Hell's Cunning silly Mortals beguiles, | Who tho' warned by Examples, still yield to our Wiles!' (22). A slight piece, the play is perhaps most interesting for the suggestion in its introduction that Merlin erected *Stonehenge as a monument to his mother.

Aaron Hill (1685–1750) called his *Merlin in Love or Youth against Magic* (published 1760 but written earlier) a 'pantomime opera'. Replete with songs and spectacular dramatic effects, the play presents Merlin 'dress'd like a conjurer, with his wand, long beard, and trailing robe' (321). Possibly in a faint echo of the Merlin and Vivian relationship, Hill's Merlin becomes enamoured of a young woman named Columbine. She accepts his love in order to save her lover Harlequin from Furies that Merlin has called upon to torment him. Later, when Merlin gives Columbine a magic wand to save Harlequin once again, she uses it to change the wizard into an ass. The play ends with the moral 'Let a *young* woman loose, at an *old* cunning man; | The conjurer proves but an ass' (342).

Karl Leberecht Immermann (1796–1840), who has been called the German 'Merlin poet "par excellence" ' (Weiss 104), wrote the philosophical poem 'Merlins Grab' ('Merlin's Grave', 1818) in which a young man seeks the wisdom of the entombed Merlin. But he is better known for his ambitious play about the mage,

Merlin: Eine Mythe (written in 1832 but not performed until 1918). The play enacts Satan's attempt to beget a child who will win back mankind from Christ. But the plan is frustrated, and Merlin undertakes to rescue the Grail from Titurel and his followers and entrust it to Arthur and his knights. As Merlin journeys to Mont-salvatsch, Titurel has the Grail taken to the Orient. Merlin meets Niniane in a forest and reveals to her a fatal word, which she carelessly though not maliciously repeats and traps Merlin forever. Arthur and his knights are therefore unable to recover the Grail and in fact perish in a desert as they seek it. Satan then tempts Merlin, but he is steadfast in his devotion to God and dies saying the Paternoster (cf. Weiss 104–26), his final words being 'Geheiliget werde dein Name!' (v. 679). Immermann's play was the basis for the opera *Merlin*, completed in 1905, by Felix Draeseke (1835–1913). It, along with a number of other Arthurian texts, also influenced a more recent Merlin play, *Merlin oder das wüste Land* (1981) by Tankerd Dorst and Ursula Ehler. Dorst and Ehler's play contains ninety-seven scenes that 'tell the story from Merlin's birth to the end of the Arthurian world' (Müller and Wunderlich 314).

Like their German counterparts, American and British authors of the nineteenth and twentieth centuries have drawn on tradition as needed for their dramatic purposes but added original elements to the story of Merlin. In *Merlin: A Drama in Three Acts*, a short play first published in the *Baltimore North American* in 1827, Lambert A. Wilmer (1805?–1863) uses Merlin as a character because his plot demands a readily recognizable figure of power, but he ignores most of the traditional associations since they were not suitable to his dramatic intentions. As Thomas Ollive Mabbott, the play's editor, has noted, *Merlin* was a response to Edgar Allan Poe's unhappy love for Sarah Elmira Royster. Their engagement had been broken off by Sarah's parents, who considered Poe an unpromising prospect (pp. v–vi). The relationship, treated poetically in Poe's *Tamerlane* (1827), apparently left the poet so despondent that his friends worried about the possibility of his suicide. Wilmer, an acquaintance of Poe's brother, wrote *Merlin* as a way of suggesting that Poe should avoid despair because the seemingly hopeless situation might eventually turn out for the best.

In the play, Alphonso loves a woman named Elmira, whose father demands that Alphonso seek his fortune before wooing his daughter. In his absence, Merlin overhears Elmira's complaint and, with the help of attendant spirits, acts as a *deus ex machina*: he frustrates the wrath of the Furies when they shipwreck Alphonso, has the treasure that would have been lost in the wreck restored to him, and ultimately reunites the lovers. The action of the play takes place on the banks of the Hudson River. Even stranger than the New World setting, however, is the choice of Merlin for the task of bringing together Alphonso and Elmira, since the wizard's traditional record in arranging happy love affairs is hardly exemplary. Wilmer's Cupid-playing Merlin is a Prospero figure who commands both the spirits and the elements and in whom the play's Arthurian, Shakespearian, and classical influences blend.

Another American author, Ethel Watts Mumford (1878–1940), wrote the text of *Merlin and Vivian*, a short play set to music by Henry Hadley. In the play, Morgan-le-Fay, who rules *Avalon, sends Vivian to deceive Merlin, who can be overcome only by love. The two women enchant a ring that Vivian gives to Merlin and that makes him love her. Despite Arthur's warnings, Merlin finds Vivian irresistible. He takes her to the forest of Arroy, has spirits build Joyousguard for them, and teaches her his magic. She reciprocates by enshrouding him in a 'spiderweb of Hate' (p. x), made of her own hair, and seals him in a tomb. With his final words, Merlin, still enamoured, forgives her.

British dramatist Gordon Bottomley (1874–1948) also took up the theme of Merlin's entombment in *Merlin's Grave* (1929). Set in the modern world, the play depicts the return of the Lady of the Lake to an ancient thorn tree in which Merlin is confined. She comes to renew the spell, despite Merlin's pleas that she 'make mercy' her 'one gift' to him. Driven by some force of fate, 'She does what she must' and 'dances with power' (70, 72) to weave the spell that will renew Merlin's imprisonment.

Christopher Fry's play *Thor, with Angels* (1948), set in Britain in 596 when Augustine arrives to spread Christianity, tells of Cymen, a Jute who has captured a British Christian prisoner and spared his life. Though his family urges him to sacrifice the prisoner to the gods, he cannot bring himself to do so. He seems controlled by a new literal and figurative spirit of mercy. Cymen's daughter has dug up an old man, Merlin, whom she 'found in the quarry where it caved in' and whose 'beard was twisted like mist in the roots of an oak-tree' (21). Merlin 'is not only the familiar figure of legend . . . ; he is also the seer who has experienced terrible defeat yet who is the harbinger of God's new kingdom in Britain' (Starr 140), the prophet of the new Christianity, just as in the Vulgate Cycle he is a prophet of the Grail. Cymen is summoned by Ethelbert, King of Kent, to hear Augustine; and, under the influence of Merlin's words and those of Augustine and inspired by divine grace, he accepts Christianity.

Merlin in Modern Poetry

With the many poems about Merlin as with the plays, some offer original interpretations of traditional material, and a few deviate considerably from the traditional accounts of his life and deeds. *Merlin's Youth* (1899) by British poet George Bidder (1863–1953), for example, tells of the young Merlin's love for a woman named Yberha. Skilled in magic, Yberha, who controls the wolves that Merlin thinks he must protect her from, advises him that she can only marry one who learns all the spells she knows; otherwise she would have to give up her magic, and her husband would 'wed me as a powerless maid'. Wanting 'no weakling for a bride', Merlin learns from her (27). When Yberha's father is killed in battle, she blames Merlin, even though he fought bravely in the vanguard and caused the enemy to flee; and she pledges herself to Merlin's cousin instead. Although subsequently Merlin becomes a powerful figure who controls kings and councils and who directs armies, he never forgets his love for Yberha. She in turn lives 'another woman's quiet life' as a faithful wife but knows that 'once I lived myself' (56).

A number of poems use Merlin's wisdom or his bardic vision as a source of theme or metaphor. In his poems 'Merlin I', 'Merlin II', and 'Merlin's Song', American Transcendentalist Ralph Waldo Emerson (1803–82), for example, presents Merlin as a type of bardic power and insight. Rather than a character in a story, Merlin becomes, in effect, a symbol for the visionary, self-reliant individual that Emerson sees as an ideal. In none of these poems is there a suggestion of or allusion to any specific incidents from Malory or other Arthurian romances. Instead, Emerson is concerned almost solely with Merlin's symbolic value as a poet and a prophet.

Several British poets take up the theme of Merlin's wisdom more directly. Wilfred Scawen Blunt (1840–1922) presents his own ideas about life as 'The Wisdom of Merlin' (1914). He proclaims that wisdom is learning 'the proportion of things' and that 'the knowledge of women the beginning of wisdom is' (ii. 454, 456). Blunt's 'To Nimue' (1914) describes Nimue's mature beauty, which makes Merlin 'a prophet no more, but a desolate voiceless man' (i. 390). In Alfred Noyes's (1880–1958) 'The Riddles of Merlin' (1920), Merlin's 'miracles' (62) are a metaphor for the beauties of nature which cannot be explained by science. And Edwin Muir's (1887–1959) poem 'Merlin' (1937), in which Mary Stewart found the title for her novel *The Crystal Cave*, also looks to Merlin for the answer to life's mysteries. But perhaps the best and best-known of such poems is Tennyson's 'Merlin and the Gleam' (1889), in which Merlin represents Tennyson himself, and the Gleam he follows is the artist's imagination.

Motifs borrowed from medieval chronicle and romance inform a number of the Merlin poems. The blank-verse poem *Merlin* (1930) by American poet Clyde B. Furst (1873–1931) depicts a Merlin whom the devil tries 'to make a son in deed, as well as might', but who rises above the conflict between 'the saint and fiend within his veins' (13–14) by devoting his life to serving Church and state, and by making health care, education, and art available to the people. 'The Throne of Merlin' (1937) by Robert Clark Schaller (b. 1905) tells of Merlin's creating a throne which men call the *Siege Perilous because they believe that it will consume anyone who sits in it. In fact, it transports a person beyond 'the realms of sense' to 'distant Avilion', where Merlin himself longs to go. But before he can use it, the Lady of the Lake, whose magic was 'subtler' than his, commands him to destroy it. After he does so, he 'blesses the stars for his escape' and lives 'for many years a godly man' (101–2).

The relationship between Merlin and Vivian, the most common theme in Merlin poems, is sometimes placed in the larger context of Arthur's reign and Merlin's life, though at other times, especially in the shorter poems, that larger context is merely alluded to, if considered at all. A Victorian version of the relationship is presented in *Merlin: A Dramatic Poem* (1890) by Ralph Macleod Fullarton, who follows Tennyson in making Vivien unredeemably evil. She steals from Merlin a ring which can induce sleep and uses it on him. Morgan the fay, who loves Merlin and who is uncharacteristically virtuous, wakes him by the power of the crucifix she wears. Vivien then manipulates Merlin into creating, as a sign of his love for her, a tomb in which she seals him and he dies. His 'spirit passes into light', while 'Vivien goes alone into the night' (146).

A more interesting dramatic poem is 'Time and the Witch Vivien' (1889) by noted Irish poet and playwright William Butler Yeats (1865–1939), in which Vivien encounters Time and wants to buy his hourglass, but Time refuses because without it he would be a 'sorry clown'. When she says he has a whiter beard than Merlin had, Time responds that he has no desire to 'slumber 'neath an oak' (515). They agree to gamble for the hourglass, but when Vivien loses, she asks for 'triumph in my many plots'. They then play chess to decide if she will get her wish. Time, who has warned her that 'Defeat is death', mates her and she dies. The triumph in her plot against Merlin is now hollow since she shares the same fate.

The influence of Tennyson is apparent not only in the depiction of Vivien in Fullarton's poem and the plotting character in Yeats' but also in what is perhaps the best extended modern interpretation of the Merlin and Vivian story since Tennyson's idyll, Edwin Arlington Robinson's (1869–1935) poem *Merlin* (1917). *Merlin* is the most effective of Robinson's Arthurian poems because it best adapts an aspect of the legend to the concerns of his own day. In the process, Robinson creates intriguing characters. Although Merlin alludes to the rumours that call him the son of a devil (65), he says he does not believe them; and there is no cause for the reader of the poem to do so either. Merlin is not the mystical figure, not the prophet or magician or shape-shifter that he is in earlier versions of the story. Even Merlin's confinement in *Broceliande is divested of its magical element. Of his own free will, Merlin remains with Vivian, who is a fascinating woman, neither controlling nor manipulative, whose natural charm, not any supernatural one, keeps them together. Despite the obvious influence of Tennyson on Robinson's poem, his Vivian is nothing like the wicked woman of the *Idylls*.

Robinson sets his poem at a time when Arthur's kingdom is crumbling, a clear echo of the world war being fought when the poem was written. Yet *Merlin* must be read in a larger context than that of a world ravaged by war. Broceliande, where Merlin and Vivian live happily for a while, is described as an 'elysian wilderness' (60), an obviously Edenic place. Later in the poem, Robinson makes that association explicit. As Merlin prepares to leave because of his concern for Arthur and *Camelot, Vivian says to him that Eden is a better name for their retreat because it has been inhabited by a man and a woman and now there is 'a Tree of Knowledge' (126–7). Merlin's departure from Broceliande is therefore prompted by his inability to ignore the concerns of the real world, represented by the fate of Camelot. But even though he returns to Camelot, he is unable to save the doomed kingdom.

Robinson's Arthur and Merlin consider Camelot an ideal. But what Merlin created at Camelot was no more important than Broceliande. Unfortunately, the pull between the political and the personal makes it impossible for Merlin to be totally happy in either realm. Thus, there is a double fall in Robinson's poem: Arthur's ideal kingdom collapses and Merlin's own happiness is destroyed because he cannot ignore the larger political situation that necessarily overrides, or at least overshadows, personal considerations. Though Merlin is not trapped as he is in medieval story, what he 'could never escape from was the "wilderness" of his dual obligations' (Starr 114). The historical and social forces that affect men's lives make both Broceliande and Camelot fallen worlds. Merlin imagines Vivian saying late in the poem that 'much is lost | Between Broceliande and Camelot' (163). Lost in the pull between the personal Eden and the ideal society is Merlin's ability to achieve perfect contentment in either sphere.

But *Merlin* is not just a lament that things pass or change; it, in fact, suggests an evolution that redeems change. Crucial to an understanding of this aspect of the poem is an explanation of the two lights that Robinson refers to as 'the torch | Of woman' and 'the light that *Galahad found', which 'Are some day to illuminate the world' (155). Asked the meaning of these symbols, Robinson commented that 'Galahad's "light" is simply the light of the Grail, interpreted universally as a spiritual realization of Things and their significance'. Less clear about the second part of the phrase, Robinson said merely that 'the "torch of women" is to be taken literally' (*Selected Letters* 113). In the poem, *Dagonet repeats the phrase and adds the fact that the torch of woman and the light that Galahad found 'Will some day save us all, as they saved Merlin' (158). What actually saves Merlin is the combination of attempting to create an ideal world where moral goals are paramount and at the same time finding some solace and personal happiness in the world that Vivian has created for him. She makes his personal life something of significance so that he is not wholly absorbed by the speckled machinations of politics and power. In *Merlin*, there is the hope that these two forces will become increasingly vital and will combine 'to light the world' (166). This hope explains why, although the last line of the poem is 'And there was darkness over Camelot', Robinson could say that the ending of *Merlin* was not sad. For him, the darkness will one day be dispelled by the two lights that Merlin predicts.

In *The Voice of Merlin* (1946), British poet Alec Craig tells the story of Merlin with 'such twists and turns to the old tale as his fancy suggests'. Much as Robinson sees in Arthur's reign a symbol of the world at war, Craig uses the reign of Uther as a metaphor for 'the chaos of nineteenth-century Europe' and Arthur as analogous to 'the politicians who imposed a seeming order on that chaos' (5). In a radical deviation from the traditional story, Craig has Merlin father Arthur, while Uther and *Ulfius are made by Merlin's magic to sleep and dream that Uther has intercourse with Igraine.

In Craig's poem, Merlin becomes enamoured of Nimue and teaches her his lore. But Nimue loves *Pelleas more than Merlin, whom she rejects and from whom she flees to a mountain retreat. In the course of his wanderings, Merlin comes to her retreat and stays with her a while, kept only by 'bands of love' and happy even though they are linked only by 'intellectual love' (61–2). Hearing of the trouble at Arthur's court, however, Merlin returns in disguise to witness Mordred's plotting, the condemnation and rescue of Guinevere, and Arthur's final battle. After Arthur's death, Merlin again seeks out Nimue's retreat but finds her gone. When *Constantine, who reigns after Arthur, charges him with treason and sorcery, Merlin defends himself and predicts that the learning and art that began to flourish under Arthur will return and warns that only one thing can 'defeat our country's destiny'; that is, if the people mistake 'the form of virtue for its substance' and 'curb and bridle the soul of man'. The 'sole true function' of force, he declares in his final didactic speech, is to protect 'each spiring spirit from the fear | Of violence and oppression' (76). Acquitted of the charges against him, he returns to Nimue's former retreat to await death.

The relationship between Merlin and Vivian is also the subject of several shorter lyrical poems. In 'Merlin Is Wise' (1925), American poet Margaret Widdemer (1884–1978) describes a Merlin who 'ruled demons and great kings' but whose wisdom had little room for his heart (104). The poem suggests that if he should 'Go with her to Broceliande', he would achieve the wisdom that 'was long in coming' (105). L. Sprague de Camp (1907–2000), best known as a writer of science fiction, has Merlin speak from an ancient oak tree to a modern tourist in 'Merlin' (1981). After enquiring about the tourist's camera, Merlin admits that he allowed that 'baggage Vivian' to imprison him in the oak because her 'never-ending speech' made it impossible for him to think. Since as 'a gentleman of Wales' he could not refuse her requests or coldly reject her, he taught her the spell that entrapped him, knowing full well what she would do. As a result, Merlin has spent 'fourteen centuries' in 'ecstasy of thought' (147–8).

While de Camp's poem is light and humorous, other poets use Merlin for more serious and symbolic purposes. Three poets in particular have written short modern masterpieces of Merlin literature. Thom Gunn's 'Merlin in the Cave: He Speculates without a Book' (1955) and Richard Wilbur's 'Merlin Enthralled' (1956) both treat the same incident from the legends: they show Merlin after he has been beguiled and trapped in the cave or the tree; but they treat this material in very different ways. Once he is sealed in a cave without a book, Gunn's Merlin sees that there is a real world of change, the world of the bee and the rook. In the cave, he watches 'the flux I never guessed' and realizes that the world of the absolute is 'very cold' (57). In the end, he determines that the meaning of life is 'in each movement that I take' and that the rook and the bee 'are the whole and not a part'. In short, he realizes that meaning must be found in each event, in each individual thing in the world, and not in some static theory of the absolute. Thus for Gunn's Merlin, entrapment is 'another start' (58).

Richard Wilbur's account of Merlin's entrapment in 'Merlin Enthralled', on the other hand, symbolizes a necessary end. In a poem that exemplifies Wilbur's brilliant use of language and imagery, he shows that, though 'Fate would be fated' and 'Dreams desire to sleep', the 'forsaken will not understand' their loss (18). So the king and the knights depart in quest of Merlin. They go out 'aimlessly riding', but not with the Providence-directed aimlessness of the traditional quest. And they leave 'their drained cups on the table round' (17), a phrase that suggests on the one hand a striking contrast to the ever-full cup of the Grail and on the other the lack of order that negates the wholeness and purpose of the Round Table. The body of the poem also develops a pattern of water imagery, which culminates when Niniane receives Merlin 'as the sea receives a stream'. The flow of the water is perfectly appropriate to the flow of events that result in the passing of the glory of Camelot. The poem concludes with an image that sums up and concretizes the passing: the mail of the questing knights 'grew quainter as they clopped along. | The sky became a still and woven blue' (18). The word 'clopped' turns the war-horses of the knights into tired nags; and as the sky becomes a 'still and woven blue', the heroes become figures in a tapestry.

An outstanding treatment of the Merlin and Nimue story even more recent than Wilbur's transports the legendary figures to modern America and shifts the focus and the voice from Merlin to Nimue. Valerie Nieman's 'The Naming of the Lost' (1989), a beautifully lyrical poem, infuses a West Virginia countryside with mythic resonance. A simple oak chair with a broken rung is transformed into a Siege Visionary in which a lost and nameless wanderer discovers her identity as Nimue and is reconciled with Merlin. Their reconciliation is presented in striking imagery and a blank verse that flows as smoothly as the river and 'water-flow' with which Nimue is associated. As Merlin, with a touch, lifts Nimue from the chair, he says, 'We'll sing together a song, and arches raise | of a new Camelot which shall not fall'. In a deft contrast of images, 'The chair crumbles, falls fine to ash and sifts | upon the flowered lawn' (343), just as the two mythic figures raise through their reunion the new Camelot of personal reconciliation, love, and happiness.

MERLIN IN MODERN FICTION

Merlin in Nineteenth- and Twentieth-Century Fiction

Although nineteenth-century writers were more likely to treat Merlin and other Arthurian themes in verse or drama than in novels, the wizard does make some appearances in fiction. For instance, in one of the earliest novels about Merlin, *Merlin l'enchanteur* (*Merlin the Enchanter*, 1860), French Romantic novelist Edgar Quinet (1803–75) depicts a Merlin who represents France in opposition to German intellectualism and English industrialization (Glencross 165). Other fiction writers, including several major nineteenth-century American authors, make equally interesting use of Merlin in their short stories and novels. In Herman Melville's (1819–91) *Billy Budd* (written just before the author's death and first published in 1924), the Old Dansker who advises Billy is compared to Merlin; like the adviser of Arthurian story, he is unable to prevent the tragic death of the protagonist. The short story 'The Antique Ring' (1876) by Nathaniel Hawthorne (1804–64) tells of a minor writer named Edward Caryl who gives an antique ring to Clara Pemberton, his fiancée. She asks Edward to create a legend to accompany the gift, a romantic story that need not be 'too scrupulous about facts' (107); and he obliges with a tale tracing the ring's provenance to Merlin. And Mark Twain makes Merlin a representative of superstition and undemocratic values, and thus a villain, in his *Connecticut Yankee in King Arthur's Court* (1889, discussed in detail in Chapter 3).

Merlin's role in twentieth-century fiction, however, is much larger. He is prominent in accounts of Arthur's reign such as those by T. H. White, Thomas Berger, and others (discussed in Chapter 3). But he is also the protagonist in works ranging from satirical and historical novels to science fiction and fantasy; and he figures not only in novels set in the Middle Ages but also in those set in the modern world or even in the future.

In American author James Branch Cabell's (1879–1958) episodic satiric novel *Something about Eve*, Gerald Musgrave, a young writer, allows a devil to take over his earthly body so he can seek Antan, a land where he believes he will find perfect happiness. Along the way, he has many experiences and meets many characters who make him question and ultimately abandon the journey. One of the most important is Merlin, who explains the notion of chivalry that he gave Arthur and his knights 'to play with'. This notion was 'very beautiful' and for a time 'created beauty everywhere'; and the knights 'discharged their moral and constabulary duties quite picturesquely'. But it was also 'a rather outrageous notion upon which all was founded' (230–1). After a while, his 'toys...began to break one another. Dissension and lust and hatred woke among them. They forgot the very pretty notion which I gave them in their turn to play with' (233). The knights fight one another, often unchivalrously. This fighting continues until Arthur dies and the Round Table is dissolved. Merlin, who had left behind his 'toys' so that he could dwell with Nimue, finds a measure of domestic bliss with her, but no variety. And so he leaves her to seek Antan.

Gerald's encounter with Merlin (and other characters in the book) convinces him of something that even wise Merlin did not learn from his own experiment with chivalry—that 'the one way for a poet to appreciate the true loveliness of a place is not ever to go to it' (339). Thus *Something about Eve* has a comic ending, but the tragic implications are clear: Cabell suggests that dreams and ideals remain beautiful only until they come in contact with reality. And he presents Merlin's chivalry as illusory because it maintains its perfection only as long as it is the toy of men's minds and only as long as there is no attempt to make the dream real.

Galician writer Alvaro Cunqueiro (1911–81) tells a series of tales about Merlin, who lives with Guinevere in a house named Miranda in Galicia in *Merlin e familia* (1955, translated as *Merlin and Company*). Its narrator Felipe, who served Merlin as a 'page-boy and factotum' (7), comments on some of those who came to Miranda to seek help from Merlin. The fanciful tales borrow little from the traditional accounts of Merlin but depict him as a figure of legend who interacts with Hamlet and studies lightning with Benjamin Franklin. He is involved in the creation of a mirror which reveals scenes of the future but which begins 'to weave things of its own invention in among the future truths' (54) because Merlin 'overdid one of the ingredients'. He is also able to teach a countess's Pekinese to whistle an aubade and to dye the tail of a mermaid black as a sign of mourning for her dead lover.

More traditional representations of Merlin are found in a number of novels by English and American authors. John Cowper Powys's (1872–1963) novel *Porius* was so long that Powys found a publisher in 1951 only by cutting about five hundred pages from the original typed manuscript. (The full text, with all of the excised pages restored, was edited by Wilbur T. Albrecht and published by Colgate University Press in 1994.) Set in the year 499, *Porius* is as much a depiction of an age and its political and religious conflicts as it is the story of the title character. Porius, a British prince whose mother is Arthur's cousin, is descended from the aboriginal giants who inhabited Britain and therefore is described as a 'Brythonic Samson' and as 'Herculean' (571, 660). In the novel, which Powys subtitled 'A Romance of the Dark Ages', Myrddin Wyllt (Merlin), a figure obviously influenced by Celtic traditions, is the counsellor both of the Emperor Arthur and of Uthyr Pendragon before him. His imagination confuses his mother, 'the proud, pure nun, loved by that celestial visitor' (282). Porius considers Myrddin a '*deus mortuus* or corpse-god' who is 'roused to any natural life at all by his weird mania for Nineue's satiny skin' and by 'his feeling for his animals' (115). Myrddin allows Nineue to think that he cannot break the spell she uses on him, and he lies 'for days without moving' but he is 'pretending all the time' (271).

Myrddin's philosophy epitomizes the theme of the novel. He claims that 'the Devil is every god that extracts obedience' and that 'the world wants... more common-sense, more kindness, more indulgence, more leaving people alone' (276). He believes that 'the hope of the world' is that the 'earth lasts and man lasts, and the animals and birds and fishes last, but gods and governments perish' (277). In the end, Myrddin wants 'to go under a stone for two thousand years', to await 'a second Golden Age wherein men and animals and birds and fishes will live in peace' (661).

Among the most popular of Merlin novels were those by Mary Stewart (b. 1916). Told from Merlin's point of view, Stewart's trilogy begins with *The Crystal Cave* (1970), which is based largely on Geoffrey of Monmouth's account. Merlin's mother tells a tale of his birth that suggests he is the son of the prince of darkness, but he is actually the son of Ambrosius, 'prince of light' (228), and brother to Uther. Merlin is instructed by a wise man named Galapas, who lives in a cave, in the recesses of which is a smaller crystal cave wherein Merlin sees visions of future events. By the time he is taken to Vortigern, Merlin has already met and allied himself with Ambrosius. Stewart attributes the vision of the fighting dragons beneath the foundation of the tower Vortigern tries to build to natural if timely events— Vortigern's white dragon banner falls in the pool beneath the foundation and a shooting star appears in the sky—just as Merlin's raising of the stones at Stone-henge is the result of engineering, not magic. Merlin is, nevertheless, gifted with special sight and prophecy. The novel culminates with his assisting Uther to reach Ygraine and the conception of Arthur, an act accomplished with Ygraine's collusion. (The novel was adapted by Steve Bescoby for a 1992 BBC movie called *Merlin of the Crystal Cave*, directed by Michael Darlow.)

The Hollow Hills (1973), the second book in Stewart's trilogy, recounts the birth of Arthur, who is protected by Merlin until he is old enough to rule. Merlin searches for the sword *Caliburn, said to be the sword of Macsen Wledig or the Emperor Maximus, as a symbol of Arthur's right to lead his people. Immediately before his death, Uther passes on his battle sword to Arthur and names him his successor, but the sword has been broken, which some see as an omen. Arthur's taking of the sword of Macsen from a stone altar, where it seems surrounded by flames, proves that he is the rightful heir to the throne.

In *The Last Enchantment* (1979), the final volume of the trilogy, *Morgause seduces the young king after his first battle. When their union produces a son, Morgause's husband Lot slaughters all the babies born on May Day in order to eliminate a child not his own; but Morgause places the blame for the slaughter on Arthur and hides her son, Mordred, from the vengeance. Morgause is also responsible for poisoning Merlin. He survives, albeit maddened by the poison; when his senses return, he is chronically ill and ultimately lapses into a coma. Believed to be dead, he is laid to rest in his cave, which is sealed with rock. Nimuë, whom he has been teaching and with whom he has developed a loving relationship, takes over his role as prophet and adviser to Arthur. When Merlin wakes in the cave, he keeps himself alive until he is finally released by Stilicho, a former servant; but soon he retires to his cave to live in seclusion with occasional visits from Arthur.

Sixth-century British history and Celtic literature and law form the basis for Nikolai Tolstoy's *The Coming of the King* (1989). Meant to be the first book of a trilogy (the other books of which have not appeared), the novel is, as Tolstoy said in an interview, 'an autobiography of Merlin; . . . it's supposed to have been discovered in a medieval manuscript transcribed by Christian priests from an oral recitation two generations after Merlin's own time. . . . The whole novel takes place around the year 556, when a battle [with the Saxons] is mentioned in *The Anglo-Saxon Chronicle*.' Since Tolstoy is writing about the Merlin of the late sixth century, Arthur is just a memory or, to some, a myth. Tolstoy's Merlin advises a different king, Maelgwn Gwynedd, in a relationship comparable to that which Merlin traditionally enjoys with Arthur, 'but otherwise the Merlin of Malory is entirely absent. He is replaced by Merlin the shaman who mediates between this world and the otherworld' (Thompson, 'Interview with Nikolai Tolstoy').

A number of sources influence *Merlin* (1978) by British novelist and poet Robert Nye. Geoffrey of Monmouth, the Vulgate *Merlin*, Tennyson, and Welsh poetry all contribute to Nye's frequently erotic account of Merlin's birth and exploits. As in the Welsh 'Yr Oianau' ('The Little Pig Stanzas'), Merlin often addresses his narrative to a 'little pig'; and his being sired by the devil, his revelation to Vortigern concerning the tower, his erecting the monument at Stonehenge, and his entrapment by Nimue are recounted. However, the retelling of Merlin's story is decidedly original in some details and in the sexual nature of many of the events described, such as *Blaise's lengthy questioning of Merlin's mother about the salacious details of her coupling with the devil. At the novel's conclusion one of the devils, who have been commenting on events throughout, directs Merlin to '[b]egin again' because, as he observes, ' "This is just the end of the story" '(215). As his comment suggests, part of the point of the novel is that such stories are endlessly malleable and therefore endlessly retold.

Merlin confronts forces of evil even more threatening than the devils of Nye's book in *That Hideous Strength* (1945) by C. S. (Clive Staples) Lewis (1898–1963). The novel, called by Lewis 'a modern fairy-tale for grown-ups', completes the trilogy begun with *Out of the Silent Planet* (1938) and continued in *Perelandra* (1943). *That Hideous Strength* brings Merlin back to assist Ransom, the hero of the two earlier books, who is now called both *Fisher-King and Pendragon, in combating the forces of evil as represented by the National Institute of Co-ordinated Experiments. NICE is led by a literal 'Head', the head of an executed criminal kept alive technologically. The goal of the Institute is to make a new type of man th⸱⸱ ʰ. 'sterilization of the unfit, liquidation of backward races . . . , selective breedⁱ ₍ (37), and ultimately to do away with all vegetation and animal life; but Ransom and a group of faithful followers oppose the efforts of NICE in order to protect the natural world and the natural order.

Both Ransom and the agents of NICE attempt to find Merlin, buried in Bragdon Wood, land originally owned by a local college before being sold to NICE. Though Ransom's followers fear that Merlin's sympathies might be with their enemies, he in fact becomes their ally and works to destroy the evil Institute. Combining elements of science fiction and fantasy, *That Hideous Strength* is indeed a modern fairy tale with all the realism and violence typical of that genre; but its philosophical exploration of natural order, good and evil, and the nature of man make it a fairy tale for adults.

The struggle between good and evil and the dangers of an over-reliance on technology, two important themes in Lewis's novel, are also found in a number of American works in which Merlin is a key figure. In K. W. Jeter's *Morlock Night* (1979), Merlin must overcome another threat to civilization, in this case, Victorian civilization. In the novel, a sequel to H. G. Wells's *The Time Machine*, Merlin must prevent the Morlocks, who have used the time machine to invade from the future, from taking over the world. Merlin himself becomes a threat to civilization in another science-fiction novel, Roger Zelazny's *The Last Defender of Camelot* (1980). *Launcelot, kept alive until the twentieth century by a spell of Merlin's, is still searching for the Grail. Morgan and Merlin have also survived, and Merlin plans to use Launcelot to start rebuilding a world like Camelot. But Morgan warns Launcelot that Merlin's 'was the most dangerous morality of all. He was a misguided idealist. In a more primitive time and place and with a willing tool like Arthur, he was able to create a legend. Today, in an age of monstrous weapons, with the right leader as his catspaw, he could unleash something totally devastating. He would see a wrong and force his man to try righting it. He would do it in the name of the same high ideal he always served, but he would not appreciate the results until it was too late' (279–80).

The dangers of technology in the hands of a truly evil force is a central theme in Rita Hildebrandt's *Merlin and the Dragons of Atlantis* (1983), in which Merlin is a scientist in Atlantis. His friend Zaran, another scientist who has bio-engineered dragons as a military weapon, is maddened by his own power; and when he kills the ruler of Atlantis and takes control, he becomes a cruel despot. Ultimately Merlin must kill him to end his reign of terror; but Zaran's last acts are to destroy Atlantis and to instruct his dragons to seek and kill Merlin. When Merlin awakens from one of his centuries-long sleeps caused by a serum he has developed, he is attacked by and slays the last of the dragons. Another sleep brings him to the time of Arthur and Camelot, which are alluded to only briefly at the end of the novel. The characters, places, dragons, and scientific achievements of Atlantis are depicted in illustrations by fantasy artist Tim Hildebrandt.

Atlantis figures in another novel, *Taliesin* (1987), the first volume of Stephen R. Lawhead's Pendragon Cycle. When Atlantis, the home of Charis, daughter of Avallach, is destroyed, its inhabitants flee to Britain and settle in *Glastonbury, where they are called the Faery or the Fair Folk. Charis, who is known as the Lady of the Lake, falls in love with Taliesin and they have a child, Merlin. The second novel in the sequence, *Merlin* (1988), depicts Merlin as a warrior-king, a seer, and a wise man who prepares the way for Arthur. Lawhead's third novel *Arthur* (1989) tells the story of Arthur's reign, from the pulling of the sword from the stone to his being taken to Avalon for healing. It includes his marriage to Gwenhyvar, an Irish warrior queen; the founding of the Round Table; and the plotting of Morgian, daughter of Avallach.

Lawhead's *Pendragon* (1994), narrated by Merlin, covers much of the same time period as *Arthur*, but is of interest for its reinterpretation of the Celtic story of the hunting of the giant boar *Twrch Trwyth. Lawhead rationalizes the legendary struggle: just as Arthur is called the Bear of Britain, Amilcar, the leader of an army of Vandals who attack Ireland and then Britain, is called 'Twrch Trwyth . . . Black Boar of the Vandali' (168). The slaying of the giant boar is transformed into a conflict with an enemy who ravages the British Isles, a conflict that ends in a single combat in which Arthur kills Amilcar. At the end of the novel, Arthur's grievous battle wounds can be cured only by the Grail, which is under the protection of Avallach, the Fisher King.

Lawhead's sequence concludes with the novel *Grail* (1997), which is narrated by Gwalchavad, twin brother of Gwalcmai. Gwalchavad's name is difficult for the Germanic people who have come to Britain, who pronounce it Galahad. The novel tells of the theft by Morgian of the Grail and of Arthur's sword Caledvwlch, made in Atlantis and given to him by Charis, the Lady of the Lake. Arthur's elite knights, the Dragon Flight, search for the lost treasures, which are ultimately recovered by Gwalchavad, *Bors, and *Gereint. The three knights defend the treasures against Morgian and the forces of evil and return the Grail to Avallach.

In addition to his appearances in Victorian and twentieth-century England and in the distant future, Merlin appears in other unusual settings. In H. Warner Munn's *Merlin's Godson* (1976), for example, Merlin reaches the new world after the fall of Arthur's realm and becomes a military leader of the Aztecs. And in *The Drawing of the Dark* (1979), Tim Powers brings him to sixteenth-century Vienna, where he helps an Irish adventurer named Brian Duffy realize that he is Arthur reincarnated and that he must save the West from the invading Turkish army.

The theme of the danger of technology without the wisdom needed to use it properly—a theme popular in science-fiction and fantasy novels about Merlin—is also found in *Merlin's Mirror* (1975) by Andre Norton, one of several novels which explores the relationship between Merlin and Vivian. Norton cleverly adapts traditional elements of Merlin's story to the science-fiction genre. The product of an advanced civilization from outer space, Merlin is fatherless because he is conceived not by the devil but by means of artificial insemination when a metal container travelling through space detects a beacon left by former alien visitors to earth, descends, and impregnates a British woman. As the novel progresses, Merlin comes into conflict with Nimue, descendant of an alien race hostile to Merlin's, as he tries to help Arthur establish a new order based on the superior knowledge to which Merlin has access. When Nimue seals him in his cave with a force field, he uses a suspended animation machine to survive until the field's power weakens.

Though the reader's sympathies throughout much of the book are with Merlin, in the end it is clear that Nimue acted responsibly in undermining the kingdom he wanted to create. As she says, 'Once before, men became the playthings of the Star Lords who used them carelessly, taught them what they were not yet ready to know, drew them into their own disputes with one another. Finally this world itself was riven and nearly destroyed' (202). Thus, Nimue suggests, men have not advanced far enough to deal wisely with the knowledge Merlin would bring to them; and the ideal world Merlin envisions would be even more dangerous than the one they live in.

Just as Nimue is given an authority greater than Merlin's in Norton's novel, so Niviene becomes the primary character in *Merlin's Harp* (1995) by Anne Eliot Crompton. Crompton's novel is concerned as much with the women as the men of Camelot. Fairy-born Niviene, the narrator, touches the lives of most of the main characters of the Arthurian story and is involved in most of the major events. She is the sister of Lancelot (called Lugh in their native realm of Avalon) and the friend of Elana (*Elaine), who dies of unrequited love for him. Niviene encounters Arthur and begets a son named Bran (later called Mordred), though she does not know Arthur's identity when she first meets him in the forest and spends the night with him. Later, she assists her brother in returning Gwenevere to Arthur when Mellias, who dwells in the fairy realm, kidnaps the queen. Niviene also becomes an apprentice to Merlin but is neither his lover nor his enemy. After supporting him as he assists Arthur, she accompanies Merlin to Counsel Oak, the largest tree in Avalon, to be sealed up, at his own request, as he dies from a wound received when he and Niviene participated in the rescue of the queen. After the battle of Camlann and the return of Caliburn, Niviene and Morgan take Arthur to be healed in Avalon; but his wounds are too severe and he dies.

In Ian McDowell's *Merlin's Gift* (1997), a sequel to *Mordred's Curse* (1996), Nimüe and Merlin, a decidedly wicked character, interact in an unusual manner. In *Mordred's Curse*, Mordred, the narrator of both books, declares that he is telling not 'Mordred's Life of Arthur, but Mordred's Life of Mordred' (3). He recounts his own heroic exploits, his saving of Arthur's life, and yet Arthur's rejection of him because of the guilt he feels. It is Mordred, not Lancelot, who rescues Guinevere from *Melwas, a fairy king. In the sequel, Merlin, who had assisted Morgawse in seducing Arthur, has been exiled. The king considers the sorcerer an irredeemable man (124), but he is the only one who can help Nimüe, Guinevere's half-sister. Born a girl, Nimüe grows a penis when she approaches puberty; and only Merlin's power to transform the nature of things can restore her feminine form. Yielding to Guinevere's plea, Arthur calls Merlin out of exile to effect the transformation; but when Merlin speaks of the affair of Mordred and Guinevere, Arthur beheads him. Later, when Arthur fulfils a plan to conquer Gaul and begin to restore the empire, the exiled Mordred invades, kills his brother Gawain in battle, and awaits an encounter with Arthur, even as he recognizes that Arthur will be remembered 'more fondly than me, for both his triumphs and his failures were on a much grander scale than mine, and that's the true stuff of legend' (251).

Merlin and Vivien also appear in several novels set in the modern world. In *The Elixir* (1971) by American novelist Robert Nathan (1894–1985), the narrator, an American history professor named Robert Irwin, falls in love with a young woman he meets at Stonehenge on Midsummer Night. Called Nimue, Niniane, and Anne in the novel, she creates strange stories about her past and leads Irwin on a series of adventures in which he meets Merlin, now a bookseller and apothecary in Cornwall. Irwin also encounters various Arthurian knights as well as Richard the Lionheart, Robin Hood and his band, and other characters from history and legend. Eventually, Niniane 'must leave the world of living men and women for the world of my childhood' which Merlin finds for her (171), and Irwin returns to his teaching with a new awareness that 'today and yesterday are equal parts of a tapestry' and that 'one can fall in love with a legend' (176).

Triad (1973), a horror novel by Mary Leader, is the story of a woman named Branwen who as a child accidentally killed her wicked cousin Rhiannon. The trauma causes Branwen to develop a split personality; she is also possessed by the spirit of Rhiannon, whose name is said 'to have been corrupted into "Niniane," another name for the Lady of the Lake' (118). Branwen is being treated for her problems by Dr Ambrose, Merlin in a modern guise, who is assisted by his colleague Dr Blehys. But soon Ambrose disappears, presumably sealed in a cistern by Rhiannon on one of those occasions when she takes over Branwen's consciousness. Branwen writes her story from the psychiatric institution to which she has been committed and where she is content in the knowledge that as long as she is imprisoned, Rhiannon can work no further evil.

Merlin in Juvenile Fiction

Merlin also figures in quite a few juvenile novels, some of which tell the story of the young Merlin. For example, The Lost Years of Merlin series by American novelist T. A. Barron, which includes *The Lost Years of Merlin* (1996), *The Seven Songs of Merlin* (1997), *The Fires of Merlin* (1998), and *The Mirror of Merlin* (1999), recounts adventures in which the young Merlin is blinded but develops second sight and other powers.

Another American author, Jane Yolen, creates a youth for Merlin in The Young Merlin Trilogy. The titles of the novels in this trilogy use the metaphor of a developing falcon to suggest the gradual maturing of Merlin. In *Passager* (1996), Merlin, as an 8-year-old boy, is abandoned in the woods; after a year of sleeping in the trees and foraging for food, he is captured by a falconer who tames him as he would a passager, an immature bird caught in the wild, and who helps the boy relearn the things that he has forgotten. Among the falconer's hawks and merlins, the boy finally remembers his own name and begins reclaiming his magical identity. After his adoptive family is destroyed by fire in *Hobby* (1996), Merlin is orphaned again. Assuming new identities as 'Hawk' and 'Hobby' (the name of a small falcon), the birds that recur in his dreams, he explores his new powers, especially the dreams that come true 'on the slant' (82). In *Merlin* (1997), the now 12-year-old boy falls into the hands of another band of outcasts, the *wodewose*, or wild folk, and begins to develop his powers. His dreaming, however, continues to mark him as an outsider; and his survival seems to depend on the 'Cub' he meets— Artus, or 'bear-man'—for whom some of Merlin's dreams, like that of a table round, eventually materialize.

In *The Dragon's Boy* (1990), an earlier juvenile novel independent of the character and story in the trilogy, Yolen presents a different Merlin, one known to most as Old Linn, the apothecary. He is revealed to be the dragon whom Artos (Arthur) encounters in a dark cave and who imparts the knowledge Artos needs to become a man and a warrior. Yolen is also the author of *Merlin's Booke* (1986), a collection of tales for both children and adults about Merlin as a boy, as a man, and as a legendary figure. In the final and best tale, 'Epitaph', Merlin's grave is discovered; and when a casket containing his heart is opened, it gives different observers visions of the past, the present, and an apocalyptic future.

Still other novels tell of adventures in which children interact with the older wizard. Merlin plays a key role in *The Boy Apprenticed to an Enchanter* (1920) by Irish author Padraic Colum (1881–1972). In the tale, the boy Eean is apprenticed to

Zabulun, a wicked magician. With the girl Bird-of-Gold, he escapes his master and seeks the help of the three greatest enchanters. Refused by two, Chiron the Centaur and Hermes Trismegistus, the youngsters seek the help of the third, Merlin. After Zabulun follows them to the island where Merlin and Vivien are living, Merlin engages in a contest with Zabulun in which he changes Eean into different forms to hide him from the wicked magician. But Zabulun counters by changing his own form to help him find the boy—an episode similar to the battle between Merlin and Madam Mim in T. H. White's *The Sword in the Stone*. After several transformations, Zabulun and Eean return to their own forms, fight, and wrestle. When Eean wins, he is released from his servitude.

Merlin interacts with children in a very different way in *The Weathermonger* (1968) by British novelist Peter Dickinson. This novel reverses the pattern of those books in which there is a suspicion of and danger from technology. In *The Weathermonger*, technology has become so hated in Britain that anyone who is at all interested in machinery is put to death. A young boy, Geoffrey Tinker, and his sister Sally are among those who resist this hatred. But since the 'Changes', the imposition of a medieval mentality on the people of Britain, Geoffrey has gained the power to control the weather, a power he uses first to escape death and flee to France, and then to return to England to learn the source of the problem. The children discover Merlin, whose resting place was uncovered by a man named Furbelow, who attempted to control Merlin by giving him morphine but who instead became a servant to Merlin, whose drug-clouded mind imposed the medieval mentality on England. The children are able to prevent further drugging of Merlin and explain to him what happened, and thus to restore normalcy, including a normal use of technology, to the country.

In *Merlin's Mistake* (1970), American author Robert Newman tells the story of a young boy named Tertius, to whom Merlin has mistakenly given 'all *future* knowledge' (15) but not the power to do simple spells. When Tertius goes on a quest to find a magician to teach him magic, he meets another boy, 16-year-old Brian, who has been kept at home *Perceval-like by his mother. Brian joins Tertius and undertakes a parallel quest, to find the Knight with the Red Shield, the only one who can defeat the Black Knight who plagues the people of Meliot. In the course of their quests, they come to the castle of Nimue and are imprisoned by her. Using his future knowledge to create gunpowder, Tertius blasts a hole which frees Merlin, who has allowed himself to be imprisoned under a stone by Nimue in order to escape her incessant chattering. The questers then learn that Brian, when knighted, is in fact the Knight with the Red Shield. He defeats the Black Knight, who is his own father, thought to have been killed in a Crusade. Merlin agrees to set right his mistake and teach Tertius magic, so both quests are successfully completed.

In *The Testing of Tertius* (1973), the sequel to *Merlin's Mistake*, Tertius must use the magic he has learned to release Merlin and Blaise from a spell put upon them by the wicked magician Urlik. Tertius is aided by Brian and several other characters from the first book, including Lianor, a young princess of Meliot to whom Brian is engaged. The youngsters must journey to France, where Urlik's tower is located. There, they meet Arthur and assist him in defeating Urlik's army. Ultimately they free Merlin and Blaise, who, though weakened by the spell from which they have just recovered, must engage in a magician's battle with Urlik and Nimue. Tertius ends Urlik's evil by calling down lightning to strike his iron throne and kill him.

Among the best of the books in which Merlin interacts with children are those of The Dark Is Rising series by British-born novelist Susan Cooper. The books describe the ongoing struggles between the forces of the Light and those of the Dark. The figure of Merriman Lyon, who is revealed to be Merlin, is a unifying character throughout the sequence. Of Merriman, Cooper has said, 'he's my character, not the Merlin of tradition. Merriman is an Old One in my books, a figure of the Light that opposes the Dark, which is my rather obvious classification of good and evil. He doesn't have the ambiguous dark qualities of Merlin in Arthurian legend. The sinister side of Merriman Lyon, and indeed all the Old Ones, is that absolute good, like absolute evil, is fanatical. As one of my characters points out, there is no room for human ambiguity' (Thompson, 'Interview with Susan Cooper').

Each of the five books involves a quest to find one of what are called in The Grey King (1975), the fourth book in the series, the 'weapons' needed to fight the attempts of the Dark to rise and take over the world: 'Six enchanted Signs of the Light, a golden grail, a wonderful harp, a crystal sword' (34). In Over Sea, Under Stone (1965), Merriman is assisted by the three Drew children—Simon, Jane, and Barney—in the finding of the Grail. In The Dark Is Rising (1973), the second book in the series, a different child undertakes a quest. Eleven-year-old Will Stanton, the last of the Old Ones, must gather the Six Signs of the Light to stave off an assault by the Dark. Greenwitch (1974) relates the adventures of the Drew children as they recover the Grail, stolen by those aligned with the Dark, and a manuscript that was lost at the end of the first book. The manuscript is needed to interpret an inscription on the Grail, which leads to the finding of the magical harp in The Grey King, a novel in which Bran, the son of Arthur and Guinevere and therefore the Pendragon, joins forces with Will Stanton and the Drew children. In the final book, Silver on the Tree (1977), Will, Bran, the Drew children, and Merriman form a group of six who recover the crystal sword, which must be used in repelling a final massive assault by the Dark in the present as Arthur overcomes the forces of the Dark at Mount *Badon in the past before coming to the future to assist in the struggle there. The events are connected because 'all times co-exist . . . and the future can sometimes affect the past, even though the past is a road that leads to the future' (28).

After preventing the Dark from rising, the Drew children forget the events in which they have participated. Only Will, as one of the Old Ones, retains the memory of them. And Merriman departs from the world of the present after imparting to the children some words of wisdom, the only thing they will remember: that since Arthur has returned for the confrontation with the Dark, he will not return again; thus 'the world is yours and it is up to you. Now especially since man has the strength to destroy this world, it is the responsibility of man to keep it alive, in all its beauty and marvellous joy' (267).

MERLIN IN POPULAR CULTURE

Even before the interest in medieval Arthurian literature was revived in the nineteenth century, Merlin was embraced by popular culture; and fascination with him has persisted to the present. In the Renaissance, Merlin figured in the prophetic tradition (discussed above) and in alchemical texts (cf. Goodrich). In the eighteenth century, the prophetic tradition continued and was parodied; and another phenomenon, the structure known as Merlin's Cave—built by William Kent (1685–1748) in 1735 for Queen Caroline, the wife of George II—inspired much comment, including political satire, dramatic presentations, and verse. Merlin's Cave was, in fact, not a cave but 'a thatched "Gothic" cottage'. Tended by minor poet Stephen Duck and his wife, the Cave contained statues of Merlin and other figures from British history and literature and implied that Caroline 'was the latest heiress in a single royal line leading ultimately back to Arthur' (Colton 5, 10–15).

Dramatic spectacles like *The Royal Chace or Merlin's Cave* (1736) by Edward Phillips (*fl.* 1730–40) document the popular interest in the site. In the course of this masque, Merlin calls up a pageant of Graces, Zephyrs, and other mythological beings to honour Diana, who represents the queen. *Merlin: A Poem* dedicated to Queen Caroline by Jane Brereton (1685–1740), writing under the pseudonym of Melissa, presents Merlin urging Melissa to bring fame to his 'honour'd Modern Cave' and to his 'Ancient Name' (3) and includes a prophecy that the queen's son Frederick will carry on the '*glorious Race*' of George and Caroline.

In more recent popular culture, Merlin appears frequently in film. He has a prominent role in many of the movies that recreate events from the romance tradition and in numerous *Connecticut Yankee* remakes (discussed in Chapter 3). He is also the central character in some movies, telefilms, and television shows. *Arthur the King* (CBS, 1985; dir. Clive Donner), also known as *Merlin and the Sword*, tells the story of Katherine Davidson (Dyan Cannon), a modern tourist to Stonehenge, who falls into the cave where Merlin and Niniane have been imprisoned since Arthur's day; from there, Katherine watches the happy love that develops between Gawain and *Ragnell, the doomed love between Guinevere and Lancelot, and other events at Camelot. Although at first Katherine cannot change what she observes, she persuades Niniane to explain why she betrayed Merlin and caused their mutual confinement and encourages the wizard to leave his 'physical self' and use his 'astral body' to save Lancelot from the dragon that Morgan has conjured to destroy him. After Merlin vanquishes the creature and impales Morgan with Excalibur (which Mordred had stolen after stabbing Arthur), he returns to the cave, where Katherine informs him that he has always possessed the power to end his confinement. 'Love', she says, 'cancels all curses; love breaks all spells.' As Merlin and

Niniane float magically away, Katherine falls on a rock and awakens back at Stonehenge, with only Merlin's fading voice and a piece of fabric from his robe to attest to her adventure.

Merlin, a four-hour television miniseries (NBC-TV, 1998; dir. Steve Barron), recounts most of the major events of Merlin's life, including the circumstances of his birth (a 'half-human' with no 'mortal father'); his enduring love for Nimue, whom he rescues from a patch of quicksand and from the scorching breath of the great dragon to whom she is to be sacrificed; his role as adviser and wizard to a succession of kings—Vortigern, Uther, Arthur—and his ongoing struggle with Queen Mab (Miranda Richardson), a practitioner of the 'old ways' who hopes to enlist him in her own battle against the new Christianity, which threatens to destroy her legacy. The miniseries incorporates many elements of the traditional legend: Merlin (Sam Neill), for instance, foresees the defeat of the red dragon (Vortigern) by the white dragon (Uther); assists Uther in satisfying his passion for Igraine; and recognizes Arthur's error in choosing Guinevere for his wife and queen. But the miniseries also takes liberties with the familiar story: it is Merlin, for instance, who, disappointed by Uther's unwise use of Excalibur, plunges the sword into a stone until Arthur can reclaim it; Uther, after fulfilling his desire for Igraine, eventually goes mad and kills himself; Elaine, here the wife of Lancelot, combines the roles of the two Elaines, as mother of Galahad and broken-hearted lily maid borne by barge to Camelot; and a new character, Mab's shape-shifting gnome Frik (Martin Short), tutors both Merlin and Morgan and eventually alters his allegiance from Mab to Merlin.

In the television series *Mr. Merlin* (1981–2), Barnard Hughes starred as Merlin in the modern world. A garage owner and mechanic in late twentieth-century San Francisco, Merlin takes on a teenaged apprentice, Zachary Rogers, after he pulls a crowbar from a block of concrete, and tries to teach Zachary to use magic wisely.

Merlin is also the most common Arthurian character in comic books. He appears in series like *Camelot 3000* and in single comics like *Last Defender of Camelot* (1993), based on the story by Roger Zelazny. The Marvel Preview comic *Merlin* (Summer 1980) by John Buscema and Doug Moench contains the story 'Quest of the King!' in which Merlin must help Arthur defeat the forces of evil in order to rescue Guinevere. A six-part *Merlin* series (Dec. 1990–July 1991), published by Adventure Comics, tells Merlin's story from his demon birth to his fathering of Uther Pendragon on a lady named Millicynthe. Merlin cannot acknowledge the child to be his son; instead, he must be raised as Aurelius' heir. In a comic called *Eerie* (67 (Aug. 1975)), 'Merlin: The Kingmaker' retells the Uther and Ygrain story; and another issue (116 (Nov. 1980)) contains a Merlin and Vivien story. Merlin also figures in numerous other comic books. For instance, he helps Spider-Woman prevent Morgan le Fay from using Excalibur for her wicked purposes (*Spider-Woman*, 2 (May 1978)); he assists Wonder Woman (*Wonder Woman*, 124 (Aug. 1997)) and Batman and Superman (*World's Finest*, 265 (Nov. 1980)) in their struggles against evil; and he, along with Arthur, meets Doctor Who in the future (*Doctor Who*, 60 (Jan. 1982)).

In recent years, Merlin has gained a wide popular following through the writings of contemporary spiritualist and best-selling author Deepak Chopra. In Chopra's novel *The Return of Merlin* (1995) as well as in his self-help book *The Way of the Wizard: Twenty Spiritual Lessons for Creating the Life You Want* (1995), Merlin has emerged as a New Age healer and a curative force for the ills of modern life. Chopra writes in his 'Key to Merlin', a preface to his novel, which moves from the Arthurian past to the present, that the story is 'a reminder that we are ancient souls from ancient places and ancient times', that 'life is an open-ended horizon, and that we are magical beings'. The notion that Merlin can be seen as a guide to conduct is also reflected in other New Age works and in *The Merlin Tarot* (1992), which is said to offer 'Images, Insight and Wisdom from the Age of Merlin'.

BIBLIOGRAPHY

The Origins of Merlin

Binyon, Laurence. *The Madness of Merlin*. London: Macmillan, 1947.

Buile Suibhne [*The Frenzy of Suibhne*], ed. J. G. O'Keeffe. Dublin: Dublin Institute for Advanced Studies, 1931 (repr. 1952).

Geoffrey of Monmouth. *History of the Kings of Britain*, trans. Sebastian Evans, rev. Charles W. Dunn. New York: E. P. Dutton, 1958.

—— *Life of Merlin: Vita Merlini*, ed. and trans. Basil Clarke. Cardiff: University of Wales Press, 1973.

Goodrich, Peter (ed.). *The Romance of Merlin: An Anthology*. New York: Garland, 1990.

Jarman, A. O. H. 'Early Stages in the Development of the Myrddin Legend', in Rachel Bromwich and R. Brinley Jones (eds.), *Astudiaethau ar yr Hengerdd: Studies in Old Welsh Poetry*. Caerdydd: Gwasg Prifysgol Cymru, 1978: 327–49.

—— 'The Merlin Legend and the Welsh Tradition of Prophecy', in Rachel Bromwich, A. O. H. Jarman, and Brynley F. Roberts (eds.), *The Arthur of the Welsh: The Arthurian Legend in Medieval Welsh Literature*. Cardiff: University of Wales Press, 1991: 117–45.

Kentigern and Lailoken, trans. Aubrey Galyon and Zacharias P. Thundy, in Peter Goodrich (ed.), *The Romance of Merlin: An Anthology*. New York: Garland, 1990: 5–8.

Meldred and Lailoken, trans. Zacharias P. Thundy, in Peter Goodrich (ed.), *The Romance of Merlin: An Anthology*. New York: Garland, 1990: 9–11.

Uhland, Ludwig. 'Merlin der Wilde', trans. Nicole Dentzien, www.lib.rochester.edu/camelot/LUMerlin.htm.

Veitch, John. 'Merlin', in *Merlin and Other Poems*. Edinburgh: William Blackwood and Sons, 1889: 4–36.

Weiss, Adelaide Marie. *Merlin in German Literature: A Study of the Merlin Legend in German Literature from Medieval Beginnings to the End of Romanticism*. 1933; repr. New York: AMS Press, 1970.

Prophecies of Merlin

D[arley], G[eorge]. 'Merlin's Last Prophecy', *Athenæum* (14 July 1838), 495–6.

Gunnlaugr Leifsson. *Merlinus spa*, in Finnur Jónsson (ed.), *Hauksbók*. Copenhagen: Thieles Bogtrykkeri, 1892–6: 277–84.

Heywood, Thomas. *The Life of Merlin, Surnamed Ambrosius; his Prophecies and Predictions Interpreted, and their Truth Made Good by our English Annals: Being a Chronological History of All the Kings and Memorable Passages of This Kingdom, from Brute to the Reign of King Charles.* London: J. Okes, 1641.

Jonson, Ben. *The Speeches at Prince Henries Barriers*, in *Ben Jonson*, vol. vii, ed. C. H. Herford and Percy and Evelyn Simpson. Oxford: Clarendon Press, 1952: 323–36. (Written for the investiture of Henry, eldest son of James, as Prince of Wales in 1610. First printed in the folio of 1616.)

Leigh, Joseph. *Illustrations of the Fulfilment of the Prediction of Merlin: Occasioned by the Late Outrageous Attack of the British Ship of War the Leopard on the American Frigate Chesapeake, and the Measures Taken by the President, Supported by the Citizens Thereon.* Portsmouth, NH: Printed for the Author, 1807.

Merriman, James Douglas. *The Flower of Kings: A Study of the Arthurian Legend in England between 1485 and 1835.* Lawrence: University of Kansas Press, 1973.

Peacock, John. 'Jonson and Jones Collaborate on *Prince Henry's Barriers*', *Word and Image*, 3.2 (Apr.–June 1987), 172–94.

Les Prophécies de Merlin: Edited from Ms. 593 in the Bibliothèque Municipale of Rennes, ed. Lucy Allen Paton. 2 vols. 1926; repr. New York: Kraus Reprint Corp., 1966.

The Prophetia Merlini of Geoffrey of Monmouth: A Fifteenth-Century English Commentary, ed. Caroline D. Eckhardt. Cambridge, Mass.: The Medieval Academy of America, 1982.

Reade, John. 'The Prophecy of Merlin', in *The Prophecy of Merlin and Other Poems*. Montreal: Dawson Brothers, 1870: 3–28.

Swift, Jonathan. 'A Famous Prediction of Merlin, the British Wizard, Written Above a Thousand Years Ago, and Relating to the Year 1709', repr. in Alan Lupack (ed.), *Modern Arthurian Literature*. New York: Garland, 1992: 81–4.

Merlin in Medieval Romance

[*Arthour and Merlin*.] *Of Arthoure and Merlin*, ed. O. D. Macrae-Gibson. 2 vols. EETS os 268, 279. London: Oxford University Press for the Early English Text Society, 1973, 1979.

Besamusca, Bart. 'The Medieval Dutch Arthurian Material', in W. H. Jackson and S. A. Ranawake (ed.), *The Arthur of the Germans: The Arthurian Legend in Medieval German and Dutch Literature.* Cardiff: University of Wales Press, 2000: 187–228.

[*Estoire de Merlin*.] *The Story of Merlin*, in *Lancelot–Grail: The Old French Arthurian Vulgate and Post-Vulgate in Translation*, gen. ed. Norris J. Lacy, vol. i. New York: Garland, 1993: 165–424. (*The Story of Merlin* is translated by Rupert T. Pickens.)

[Heldris de Cornuälle.] *Silence: A Thirteenth-Century French Romance*, ed. and trans. Sarah Roche-Mahdi. East Lansing, Mich.: Colleagues Press, 1992.

Lovelich, Henry. *Merlin: A Middle-English Metrical Version of a French Romance*, ed. Ernest A. Kock. 3 vols. EETS es 93, 112, os 185. London: Oxford University Press for the Early English Text Society, 1904, 1913, 1932.

A Lytel Treatyse of þe Byrth and Prophecye of Marlyn. [London]: Wynkyn de Worde, 1510.

Matthews, John. 'The Story of Grisandole', *Round Table*, 4 (1987), 6–9.

Merlin or The Early History of King Arthur: A Prose Romance, ed. Henry B. Wheatley. EETS os 10, 21, 36, 112. 1865–99; repr. in 2 vols. New York: Greenwood Press, 1969. [Complete edition of the Middle English *Prose Merlin*.]

Prose Merlin, ed. John Conlee. Kalamazoo, Mich.: Medieval Institute Publications for TEAMS, 1998. [Abridged, with omitted passages summarized.]

[*Suite du Merlin.*] *The Merlin Continuation*, in *Lancelot–Grail: The Old French Arthurian Vulgate and Post-Vulgate in Translation*, gen. ed. Norris J. Lacy, vols. iv–v. New York: Garland, 1995–6: iv. 161–277; v. 1–109. (*The Merlin Continuation* is translated by Martha Asher.)

Tom Thumb

[Craik, Dinah Maria Mulock.] *The Fairy Book: The Best Popular Fairy Stories Selected and Rendered Anew.* London: Macmillan, 1863.

Fielding, Henry. *Tom Thumb and the Tragedy of Tragedies*, ed. L. J. Morrissey. Berkeley and Los Angeles: University of California Press, 1970.

[Haywood, Eliza, and Hatchett, William.] *The Opera of Operas; or, Tom Thumb the Great. Alter'd from the Life and Death of Tom Thumb the Great and Set to Music after the Italian Manner.* London: William Rayner, 1733. (Reprinted in facsimile in *The Plays of Eliza Haywood*, ed. Valerie C. Rudolph. New York: Garland, 1983.)

Johnson, Richard [whose name appears only as R.I. in the 1621 edition]. *The History of Tom Thumbe, the Little, for his Small Stature Surnamed, King Arthurs Dwarfe.* London: Thomas Langley, 1621. Reprinted in *Merie Tales of the Mad Men of Gotam and The History of Tom Thumbe*, ed. Curt F. Bühler. Evanston, Ill.: Northwestern University Press for the Renaissance English Text Society, 1965.

O'Hara, Kane. *Tom Thumb: A Burletta: Altered from Henry Fielding, Esq. by Mr. O'Hara.* London: J. Barker, 1805.

Tom Thumbe, his Life and Death. London: For John Wright, 1630. (Reprinted as 'The Life and Death of Tom Thumb' in *The Legendary Ballads of England and Scotland*. London: Frederick Warne, n.d.)

Wagstaffe, William. *A Comment upon the History of Tom Thumb.* London: J. Morphew, 1711. (Reprinted by the Augustan Reprint Society in Publication 63: *Parodies of Ballad Criticism [1711–1787]*), ed. William K. Wimsatt, Jr. Los Angeles: William Andrews Clark Memorial Library, University of California, 1957.)

[Yonge, Charlotte]. *The History of Sir Thomas Thumb.* Edinburgh: Thomas Constable, 1855.

Merlin in Drama

Bottomley, Gordon. *Merlin's Grave*, in *Scenes and Plays.* London: Constable, 1929: 59–76.

Dorst, Tankred, and Ehler, Ursula. *Merlin oder das wüste Land.* Frankfurt am Main: Suhrkamp, 1981.

Fry, Christopher. *Thor, with Angels.* London: Oxford University Press, 1949.

Hill, Aaron. *Merlin in Love or Youth against Magic: A Pantomime Opera*, in *Dramatic Works of Aaron Hill, Esq.* 2 vols. London: T. Lownds, 1760: i. 319–42.

Immermann, Karl Leberecht. *Merlin: Eine Mythe. Werke in fünf Bänden*, ed. Benno von Wiese. Wiesbaden: Athenaion, 1971–7: v. 549–679.

—— 'Merlins Grab', in *Merlin: Eine Mythe. Werke in fünf Bänden*, ed. Benno von Wiese. Wiesbaden: Athenaion, 1971–7: v. 680–5.

Müller, Ulrich, and Wunderlich, Werner. 'The Modern Reception of the Arthurian Legend', in W. H. Jackson and S. A. Ranawake (eds.), *The Arthur of the Germans.* Cardiff: University of Wales Press, 2000: 303–23.

Mumford, Ethel Watts. *Merlin and Vivian: A Lyrical Drama for Chorus, Soli and Orchestra* (music by Henry Hadley, Op. 52, poem by Ethel Watts Mumford). New York: Schirmer, 1907.

Rowley, William. *The Birth of Merlin*, in Alan Lupack (ed.), *Arthurian Drama: An Anthology.* New York: Garland, 1991: 3–65. (The play was originally written *c.*1620 and first published in 1662.)

Starr, Nathan Comfort. *King Arthur Today: The Arthurian Legend in English and American Literature 1901–1953.* Gainesville: University of Florida Press, 1954.

Theobald, Lewis. *The Vocal Parts of an Entertainment Call'd Merlin, or, The Devil of Stone-Henge.* London: John Watts, 1734.

Tieck, Ludwig (trans.), *Die Geburt des Merlin, oder das Kind hat seinem Vater gefunden*, in *Shakspeare's Vorschule.* 2 vols. 1823; 2nd edn. Leipzig: F. A. Brockhaus, 1829: ii. 219–366.

Weiss, Adelaide Marie. *Merlin in German Literature.* 1933; repr. New York: AMS Press, 1970.

Wilmer, Lambert A. *Merlin: Baltimore, 1827: Together with Recollections of Edgar A. Poe*, ed. Thomas Ollive Mabbott. New York: Scholars' Facsimiles & Reprints, 1941.

Merlin in Modern Poetry

Bidder, George. *Merlin's Youth.* Westminster: Arnold Constable, 1899.

Blunt, Wilfred Scawen. 'To Nimue', in *The Poetical Works.* 2 vols. London: Macmillan, 1914: i. 388–90.

—— 'The Wisdom of Merlin', in *The Poetical Works.* 2 vols. London: Macmillan, 1914: ii. 451–71.

Craig, Alec. *The Voice of Merlin.* London: The Fortune Press, 1946.

de Camp, L. Sprague. 'Merlin', in *Heroes and Hobgoblins.* West Kingston, RI: Donald M. Grant, 1981: 147–8.

Emerson, Ralph Waldo. *Poems.* 1904; repr. New York: AMS Press, 1968.

Fullarton, Ralph Macleod. *Merlin: A Dramatic Poem.* Edinburgh: William Blackwood and Sons, 1890.

Furst, Clyde B. *Merlin.* New York: n.p., 1930.

Gunn, Thom. 'Merlin in the Cave: He Speculates without a Book', in *The Sense of Movement.* London: Faber and Faber, 1957: 56–8.

Muir, Edwin. 'Merlin', in *Collected Poems.* New York: The Grove Press, 1953: 51–2.

Nieman, Valerie. 'The Naming of the Lost', 1989; repr. in Alan Lupack and Barbara Tepa Lupack (eds.), *Arthurian Literature by Women.* New York: Garland, 1999: 337–43.

Noyes, Alfred. 'Riddles of Merlin', in *The Elfin Artist and Other Poems.* New York: Frederick A. Stokes, 1920: 60–2. (*Collected Poems*, vol. iv. Edinburgh: William Blackwood, 1927: 182–4, contains 'Riddles of Merlin' in a version expanded from that in *The Elfin Artist*.)

Robinson, Edwin Arlington. *Merlin: A Poem.* New York: Macmillan, 1917.

—— *Selected Letters of Edwin Arlington Robinson.* New York: Macmillan, 1940.

Schaller, Robert Clark. 'The Throne of Merlin', in *The Throne of Merlin.* Chicago: Argus Books, 1937: 98–102.

Starr, Nathan Comfort. 'The Transformation of Merlin', in Ellsworth Barnard (ed.), *Edwin Arlington Robinson Centenary Essays.* Athens: University of Georgia Press, 1969: 106–19.

Widdemer, Margaret. 'Merlin Is Wise', in *Ballads and Lyrics.* New York: Harcourt, Brace & Co., 1925: 104–5.

Wilbur, Richard. 'Merlin Enthralled', in *Things of This World.* New York: Harcourt, Brace and Co., 1956: 17–18.

Yeats, W[illiam] B[utler]. 'Time and the Witch Vivien', 1889; repr. in *The Poems*, ed. Richard J. Finneran. New York: Macmillan, 1983: 514–17.

Merlin in Modern Fiction

Barron, T. A. *The Fires of Merlin*. New York: Philomel Books, 1998.

—— *The Lost Years of Merlin*. New York: Philomel Books, 1996.

—— *The Mirror of Merlin*. New York: Philomel Books, 1999.

—— *The Seven Songs of Merlin*. New York: Philomel Books, 1997.

Cabell, James Branch. *Something about Eve*. New York: R. M. McBride, 1927.

Colum, Padraic. *The Boy Apprenticed to an Enchanter*. New York: Macmillan, 1920.

Cooper, Susan. *The Dark Is Rising*. New York: Atheneum, 1973.

—— *Greenwitch*. New York: Atheneum, 1974.

—— *The Grey King*. New York: Atheneum, 1975.

—— *Over Sea, Under Stone*. New York: Harcourt, Brace & World, 1965.

—— *Silver on the Tree*. New York: Atheneum, 1977.

Crompton, Anne Eliot. *Merlin's Harp*. New York: Donald I. Fine, 1995.

Cunqueiro, Alvaro. *Merlin and Company* (From the Spanish *Merlin e familia i outras historias*, 1955), trans. Colin Smith. London: Everyman, 1996.

Dickinson, Peter. *The Weathermonger*. New York: Delacorte Press, 1986.

Glencross, Michael. *Reconstructing Camelot: French Romantic Medievalism and the Arthurian Tradition*. Cambridge: D. S. Brewer, 1995.

Hawthorne, Nathaniel. 'The Antique Ring', in *The Dolliver Romance and Other Pieces*. Boston: James R. Osgood and Co., 1876: 107–24.

Hildebrandt, Rita. *Merlin and the Dragons of Atlantis*, ill. Tim Hildebrandt. Indianapolis: Bobbs-Merrill, 1983.

Jeter, K. W. *Morlock Night*. New York: DAW Books, 1979.

Lawhead, Stephen R. *Arthur*. The Pendragon Cycle, book 3. Westchester, Ill.: Crossway Books, 1989.

—— *Grail*. The Pendragon Cycle, book 5. New York: Avon Books, 1997.

—— *Merlin*. The Pendragon Cycle, book 2. Westchester, Ill.: Crossway Books, 1988.

—— *Pendragon*. The Pendragon Cycle, book 4. New York: Morrow/AvoNova, 1994.

—— *Taliesin*. The Pendragon Cycle, book 1. Westchester, Ill.: Crossway Books, 1987.

Leader, Mary. *Triad*. New York: Coward, McCann & Geoghegan, 1973.

Lewis, C. S. *That Hideous Strength: A Modern Fairy-Tale for Grown-Ups*. New York: Macmillan, 1946.

McDowell, Ian. *Merlin's Gift*. New York: Aron Books, 1997.

—— *Mordred's Curse*. New York: Aron Books, 1996.

Melville, Herman. *Billy Budd, Foretopman*. 1924; repr. in *The Shorter Novels of Herman Melville*, ed. Raymond Weaver. Greenwich, Conn.: Fawcett Premier, 1956: 198–272.

Munn, H. Warner. *Merlin's Godson*. New York: Ballantine, 1976.

Nathan, Robert. *The Elixir*. New York: Alfred A. Knopf, 1971.

Newman, Robert. *Merlin's Mistake*. New York: Atheneum, 1970.

—— *The Testing of Tertius*. New York: Atheneum, 1973.

Norton, Andre. *Merlin's Mirror*. New York: Delta, 1978.

Nye, Robert. *Merlin*. London: Hamish Hamilton, 1978.

Powers, Tim. *The Drawing of the Dark*. New York: Ballantine Books, 1979.

Powys, John Cowper. *Porius: A Romance of the Dark Ages*. London: Macdonald, 1951.

Quinet, Edgar. *Merlin l'enchanteur*. 1860; repr. Geneva: Slatkine Reprints, 1977.

Stewart, Mary. *The Crystal Cave*. New York: William Morrow, 1970.

—— *The Hollow Hills*. New York: William Morrow, 1973.

—— *The Last Enchantment*. New York: William Morrow, 1979.

Thompson, Raymond H. 'Interview with Nikolai Tolstoy', www.lib.rochester.edu/camelot/intrvws/tolstoy.htm.

—— 'Interview with Susan Cooper', www.lib.rochester.edu/camelot/intrvws/cooper.htm.

Tolstoy, Nikolai. *The Coming of the King*. New York: Bantam Books, 1989.

Yolen, Jane. *The Dragon's Boy*. New York: Harper & Row, 1990.

—— *Hobby*. New York: Harcourt Brace & Co., 1996.

—— *Merlin*. New York: Harcourt Brace & Co., 1997.

—— *Merlin's Booke*. Minneapolis: SteelDragon Press, 1986.

—— *Passager*. New York: Harcourt Brace & Co., 1996.

Zelazny, Roger. *The Last Defender of Camelot*. New York: Pocket Books, 1980.

Merlin in Popular Culture

[Brereton, Jane, writing under the pseudonym Melissa.] *Merlin: A Poem Humbly Inscrib'd to Her Majesty. To Which Is Added, The Royal Hermitage: A Poem. Both by a Lady*. London: Edward Cave, 1735.

Chopra, Deepak. *The Return of Merlin*. New York: Harmony Books, 1995.

—— *The Way of the Wizard: Twenty Spiritual Lessons in Creating the Life You Want*. New York: Harmony Books, 1995.

Colton, Judith. 'Merlin's Cave and Queen Caroline: Garden Art as Political Propaganda', *Eighteenth-Century Studies*, 10.1 (Fall 1976), 1–20.

Goodrich, Peter H. 'The Alchemical Merlin', in James Gollnick (ed.), *Comparative Studies in Merlin from the Vedas to C. G. Jung*. Lewiston, NY: Edwin Mellen, 1991: 91–110.

Phillips, Edward. *A New Dramatic Entertainment Called the Royal Chace or Merlin's Cave*. London: T. Wood, 1736.

Tristan and Isolt

Few stories have inspired more works of literature, art, and music than the tragic love of *Tristan and *Isolt. The survival in Cornwall of a megalith known as the *Tristan Stone suggests that this legendary romance may have had some basis in fact. The monument, dating from perhaps the sixth century and inscribed 'Drustanus hic jacit Cunomori filius' (Here lies Drustan, son of Cynvawr) is located near *Castle Dore, about which C. A. Ralegh Radford has said: 'evidence that Castle Dore was occupied as a chieftain's residence' from the fifth to the seventh century 'is conclusive and the identification as the court...of Cynvawr can hardly be avoided' (77). The Breton monk Wrmonoc's ninth-century *Life of St Paul Aurelian* (St Pol, a monk of Landevennec and patron saint of Paul in Cornwall) equates Cunomorus (Welsh Cynvawr), who ruled Cornwall in the early sixth century, with a King *Mark. Yet, while the Tristan Stone and the connection between Mark and Cynvawr raise the possibility that the Tristan legend has a historical basis, they are by no means proof of such historicity.

The question of origins is complicated by the fact that, though the Tristan story is generally associated with Cornwall, Drustan is a Pictish name and 'Drust, son of Tallorcan, is a Pictish king in the late eighth century' (Radford 72). Added to whatever historical kernel of the story there may be are literary influences. Scholars have pointed to analogues to some elements of the story in the Irish tale of Diarmaid and Grainne and the Persian tale of Vis and Ramin (cf. Gregory's introduction to Thomas's *Tristran* 6). No doubt a number of influences combined to produce the romances of the twelfth century.

Welsh literature refers to Tristan as the son of Tallwch—as in Triad 19, in which Drystan son of Tallwch is one of the 'Three Enemy-Subduers of the Island of Britain'; in Triad 21, in which he is one of the 'Three Battle-Diademed Men of the Island of Britain'; and in Triad 71, in which one of the 'Three Lovers of the Island of Britain' is said to be 'Drystan (son of Tallwch, for Essyllt, the wife of his uncle March)'. Triad 26, which contains a brief narrative expansion on the elements of its list, notes that Drystan son of Tallwch was one of the 'Three Powerful Swineherds of the Island of Britain' because he tended 'the swine of March son of Meirchyawn, while the swineherd went with a message to Essyllt'. *Arthur, March, *Cai, and *Bedwyr all apparently attempt to steal a pig but fail 'in getting so much as one pigling' while Drystan guards them.

In addition to the references to the lovers in the Triads and allusions in other Welsh poetry, a work called the *Trystan ac Esyllt* or the *Ystorya Trystan* (translated by R. L. Thomson under the title *The Welsh Fragment of Tristan*) survives in manuscripts from the sixteenth to the eighteenth century but almost surely contains material that is considerably older. *Trystan ac Esyllt* combines a prose narrative with conversations between characters in verse. Trystan ap Trallwch and Esyllt, the wife of March ap Meirchion, have run off 'as outlaws to the forest of Cylyddon' with a handmaiden and a page. March seeks help from Arthur to redress the wrong done him by Trystan. But Trystan has a special property by which anyone from whom he draws blood will die and anyone who draws blood from him will also die, a power that makes March and his men reluctant to fight him. After calming Trystan with music, Arthur sends his nephew *Gwalchmai, 'the chief of peace' (3), to speak to him. Gwalchmai convinces him to talk with Arthur, whose decision he ultimately accepts. Arthur 'adjudged her [Esyllt] to the one when the leaves were on the trees, and to the other when there were no leaves on the trees'. March, who is allowed to choose, prefers to have her when there are no leaves on the trees 'because the night would be longest at that time'. But Esyllt uses the trickery that her counterparts employ in later romances and says that three trees, holly, ivy, and yew, 'keep their leaves as long as they live. I am Trystan's as long as he lives' (4).

Perhaps the only Welsh Tristan material that pre-dates the twelfth-century French romances is a fragmentary poem in the Black Book of Carmarthen, to which Rachel Bromwich assigns 'a date of composition before 1100, perhaps a century or even more earlier' (55). The narrative background to the poem, which mentions Drystan and March as well as an unidentified character named Kyheic and a dwarf, is unclear, but it has a 'pervading atmosphere . . . of regret or repentance for some calamitous act which remains unexplained' (Bromwich 56).

Interesting and suggestive as the Welsh Tristan material is, it is not these works but the Anglo-Norman and French romances of the twelfth century that are the basis for the plethora of retellings of the tragic story over the centuries.

THE COMMON AND COURTLY VERSIONS OF THE TRISTAN STORY

The early medieval Tristan material may be divided into two traditions, the common or primitive and the courtly. These traditions are represented in French literature by the *Tristran* of Béroul (written in the last quarter of the twelfth century) and the *Tristran* (c.1170) of Thomas. Some scholars assume that both poems descend from an original *Ur-Tristan* that has not survived. The designations for these traditions are not meant to be value judgements but merely indications of the belief that the content of the 'primitive' tradition may be closer to the original version, the lost *Ur-Tristan*, that is assumed to have preceded the surviving versions.

Béroul

In Béroul's *Tristran*, composed in rhyming couplets in the Anglo-Norman dialect, there are references to Tristran's slaying *Morholt and to the drinking of the love potion; but these scenes are not extant since the one surviving manuscript of the poem lacks the beginning as well as the ending. The existing portion opens with the scene in which Tristran and Yseut have arranged a tryst but, recognizing that Mark is watching them from a tree, proclaim their innocence of the malicious charges brought against them and talk of their love for Mark. Tristran speaks of the service he has done for his uncle and Yseut declares that she loved Tristran only for the sake of her husband. Convinced that he has been misled, Mark vows to punish the dwarf Frocin, who accused the lovers. Frocin's ability to foresee the future allows him to escape Mark's wrath—although later in the narrative Mark kills him for revealing the secret that Mark has the ears of a horse.

Despite the lovers' good fortune in deceiving Mark, the continuing enmity of three of Mark's barons towards Tristran and the machinations of the wicked dwarf lead to the condemnation of the lovers. Frocin sprinkles flour between the beds of Tristran and Yseut; and though Tristran jumps across, blood from a wound received from a boar drops on the flour and stains the beds. Their love revealed, Tristran is condemned to death and Yseut is surrendered to a colony of lepers as their 'common property' (61). Leaping from the window of a chapel on the edge of a cliff overlooking the sea where he is allowed to pray on his way to execution, Tristran lands on a flat rock halfway down the cliff and then jumps down to the beach and escapes. With his tutor *Governal, he rescues Yseut; and the lovers flee to the Forest of Morrois.

In the forest, Tristran's skill as a hunter allows them to live a hard yet happy life. But one summer morning, tired from hunting, Tristran lies down next to Yseut and places his sword between them. Their bower is discovered by a wicked forester, who reveals it to Mark. The king, finding them clothed and with a sword separating them, thinks them innocent. After putting a glove in a hole to keep the sun from shining on Yseut's face, exchanging rings with her, and substituting his sword for Tristran's, Mark leaves them in peace.

In one of the motifs that distinguishes the common from the courtly tradition, the love potion loses its potency after three years and the lovers repent. On the advice of the hermit Brother Ogrin, Tristan writes to Mark asking that they be reconciled. Mark agrees to take back his wife but is convinced by his barons to exile Tristran. However, in order to satisfy the barons, Yseut must vindicate herself through an ordeal. She has Tristran pose as a begging leper and then demands that he carry her across a ford so she will not stain her clothes. Having mounted him 'like a horse' (177), she is then able to swear on all the relics to be found in Cornwall an equivocal oath: that 'no man has ever been between my thighs' except her husband and the leper who carried her (187). During the ordeal, Governal sees and slays the forester who betrayed the lovers. Tristan soon kills two of the barons, Denoalen and Godoine. The manuscript breaks off before he kills the third and worst of them, Ganelon, and before the inevitable account of the death of the lovers.

Béroul's poem is marked by wit, humour, brutality, and a narrator who becomes involved in his story—cursing the wicked barons, for example, and wishing they would burn in hell. Episodes like Mark's surrender of Yseut to the lepers and Tristran's feud with the barons as well as details like the limited duration of the love potion mark it as less controlled by the ethos of chivalry and courtly love than Thomas's version of the story.

Thomas of Britain

Thomas's *Tristran* survives only in nine fragments, the last of which, the Carlisle fragment, was discovered in 1995. Because of the fragmentary nature of Thomas's poem, much of it has been reconstructed from the German and Norse versions (discussed below). Thomas's poem, in rhyming couplets in the Anglo-Norman dialect, is unified around the theme of the pain and joy caused by a passionate, undying love. This theme is reflected even in the style: the poem contains long passages of introspection and internal debate about matters of love. Tristran, for example, muses on love. He thinks about and justifies taking *Yseut of the White Hands as a bride because he wants 'to discover what Yseut's life must be like' and whether her marriage to Mark could make her forget him and thus to 'share her experience' (trans. Gregory 23). He marries Yseut of the White Hands for her name as much as for her beauty; but on their wedding night, the ring Yseut gave him reminds him of his true love. Tristran again ponders his dilemma. His natural instincts vie with his reason, which 'told him to remain true to Yseut' (41). To avoid being unfaithful to Yseut of Ireland, he tells his wife that he has an ailment that has 'long afflicted' him (43), not revealing that his true ailment is his love of another woman.

Yseut, like Tristran, engages in long musings on love. One of the most striking occurs as she is caught in a storm while travelling to Brittany to cure the wounded Tristran. Fearing that she will die at sea and not in Tristran's arms as she hoped, she speculates that if she drowns, perhaps Tristran too will drown and 'a fish might devour the two of us!' Then, if the fish is caught and their bodies are recognized inside it, they might be given a common grave to honour their love (137). Yseut herself immediately realizes how unlikely this scenario is, and her thoughts turn to fears that Tristan will live and forget her or take another lover.

The wordplay found in the Carlisle fragment is yet another stylistic feature focusing attention on the joy and sorrow of love. On their journey from Ireland to Britain after they have drunk the love potion, the potency of which in this version is not limited in duration, Tristan does not know if Yseut is suffering 'because of the sea or because of love' ('de la mer ou de l'amur') or if when she speaks of 'loving' ('*amer*') she means 'the sea' ('*la mer*'); or if instead of love ('l'amur') she is referring to 'bitterness' ('*amer*') (trans. Short 178–9).

Tristan also has statues made of Yseut and *Brengain so that he might speak openly of 'the pain he felt, and the joy of love' (55). After falling in love with Brengain, *Kaherdin, brother of Yseut of the White Hands, joins Tristran in taking 'pleasure in the statues' of the women (105); and he demonstrates that love overcomes even family ties. As Yseut of the White Hands is riding her horse, water splashes upon her thigh and makes her laugh because, as she tells her brother, the water came higher up her thighs 'than where Tristan ever sought to touch me' (65). But rather than avenging the affront to his sister, Kaherdin travels to Britain with Tristran to see Yseut of Ireland.

When Tristran the Dwarf requests help to retrieve his love, who has been abducted by a knight named Estout l'Orgillus, he wins immediate support by appealing to Tristran as a lover and suggesting that one who knew the sorrow of losing his beloved would want to help without delay rather than prolonging another lover's grief. They succeed in killing Estout and his six brothers; but in the encounter, Tristran the Dwarf is killed and Tristran is wounded with a poisoned spear. Realizing that only Yseut of Ireland can cure him, Tristran sends Kaherdin to bring her to him with instructions that if he is successful he should fly a white sail on his return, but if Yseut is not with him he should fly a black sail. When Kaherdin is returning with Yseut, he raises the white sail; but Yseut of the White Hands, having overheard Tristran's instructions, tells her husband that the sail is black. Unable to live any longer without Yseut, Tristran dies calling her name. She arrives too late and, finding him dead, lies beside him, takes him in her arms, and dies 'out of the grief she felt for him' (145).

Shorter French Tristan Pieces

Two works, both with the title *La Folie Tristan* (*The Madness of Tristan*) but distinguished by the locations of the manuscripts in which they appear—Berne and Oxford—recount an episode of the legend in which Tristan goes to Mark's court disguised as a madman in order to gain access to Yseut. In each, he recounts their past adventures to convince her that he is really Tristan. The Berne *Folie* is clearly descended from the common version found in Béroul's poem since it includes characters and events from that version, such as Ogrin the Hermit and Yseut's being handed over to the lepers. The Oxford *Folie* includes events from the courtly version, such as Tristan's killing the dragon and putting its tongue in his boot.

Another meeting of the lovers is described in *Tristan rossignol* (*Tristan the Nightingale*), which appears in the *Donnei des amants* (*The Lovers's Conversation*), a didactic poem written in the late twelfth century. In the poem, a young man uses examples of famous lovers to win the love of a lady. One of those examples is Tristan, who imitates a nightingale, an oriole, and a parrot as a way of letting Iseult know that he is near. Seen leaving her room, Iseult is accosted by a 'vile dwarf' (209) whom she strikes, knocking out four of his teeth. In spite of the fact that he is used in the poem as an example of the jealous husband, Mark believes she would not have been so angry and so violent unless she was falsely accused and therefore allows her to go to amuse herself in her garden, where she meets Tristan.

Another work in the courtly tradition is *Chèvrefeuille* (*The Honeysuckle*), a short lay written by Marie de France in the latter half of the twelfth century, which begins by acknowledging the ultimate tragedy but focuses on a scene in the forest where Isolde and her exiled Tristan are enjoying a brief idyll. The passion of the lovers—and the entwining of their destinies—is evoked by the entwining of the honeysuckle on the hazel tree: together they can survive; but if they are torn apart, 'the hazel would quickly die | and the honeysuckle as well' (191). Yseut notices a message that Tristan carved on a hazel branch, and the two meet in the woods. After parting, Tristan composes a lay called *Honeysuckle*. (Marie's lay was translated into Norse prose as *Geitarlauf* in the collection of lays known as *Strengleikar*.)

The lay of the honeysuckle is referred to in *Tristan menestrel* (*Tristan the minstrel*), an episode in Gerbert de Montreuil's Continuation of Chrétien's *Perceval*, sometimes referred to as the Fourth Continuation (*c.*1230). In the episode, Tristan and a group of knights from Arthur's court disguise themselves as minstrels so that Tristan may gain access to Iseut. Tristan plays for her the *Lay of the Honeysuckle*, which, Iseut says, she and Tristan wrote together. The lay becomes the sign by which Iseut is able to see through Tristan's disguise.

Eilhart von Oberge

Both the common and the courtly versions of the Tristan story are represented in medieval German literature. Eilhart von Oberge's poem *Tristrant* (written between 1170 and 1190), which is the earliest Tristan poem to survive complete (in two manuscripts from the fifteenth century, in which the author's name is given, as well is in fragments from the late twelfth and thirteenth centuries). It is probable that Eilhart wrote at the Brunswick court under the patronage of Matilda, daughter of Henry II of England, who had married Henry the Lion, Duke of Saxony and Bavaria; and he may have based his tale on a French or Anglo-Norman source.

Eilhart's poem tells of *Rivalin of Lohenois's winning of *Blankeflur by aiding her brother Mark in battle. As the pair return to Lohenois, Blankeflur becomes so sick at sea that she dies and her child Tristrant must be cut from her womb. Raised under the tutelage of Kurvenal, Tristrant wishes to see foreign lands. He arrives in Cornwall to find it threatened by Morolt, brother of the Queen of Ireland, who demands as tribute every third child born in Cornwall for the last fifteen years. Tristrant offers to fight for Cornwall and kills Morolt, leaving a fragment of his sword in his opponent's head, but receiving a wound that festers from the poison with which Morolt had treated his spear. When 'the poison in the wound made him stink so that no one could come near him' (60), Tristrant sets out in a boat and arrives by chance in Ireland, where the king's daughter Isalde heals him.

After Tristrant's return, Mark's barons want him to take a wife to assure succession, but Mark considers Tristrant his heir and has no wish to marry. When two swallows fly into his castle fighting over a strand of hair, Mark, as a way of placating his barons without marrying, says that he will wed only the woman from whom the hair came. The barons see through the ruse and blame Tristrant, who, to help Mark, sets out to find the owner of the hair. Driven by chance to Ireland, a place he sought to avoid, he discovers that the hair was Isalde's and wins her for Mark by slaying a dragon that is ravaging the land. Though Mark's steward claims to have slain the dragon, Tristrant has cut out the beast's tongue, proof that he was the actual slayer. In curing him from the dragon's poison, Isalde discovers the notch in his sword but is convinced by Brangene not to insist on his death lest she be forced to marry the steward.

On the journey to Cornwall, where Isalde is to wed Mark, Tristrant and Isalde mistakenly drink the love potion entrusted to Brangene and intended for the betrothed couple by Isalde's mother; and they fall in love. As is typical of the common version of the story, the potion is of limited duration, in that any man and woman drinking it 'could by no means leave each other for four years'; they would in fact 'love each other with their whole being as long as they lived, but for four years the passion was so great that they could not part for half a day' without becoming sick (74). The power of the potion explains why Tristrant, who is loyal to Mark, betrays him; as the narrator notes when Brangene substitutes herself for Isalde on her wedding night: 'it was not disloyalty, for it was done against his will: the fatal potion was to blame' (80).

Tristrant is hated and slandered by some of Mark's dukes and counts; and a wicked dwarf named Aquitain becomes the lovers' nemesis, instructing Mark to spy on them from a tree and at one point putting flour on the floor between their beds. When the latter trick leads to the discovery of their love, Tristrant is condemned to be broken on the wheel and Isalde to be burned until 'a leprous duke' asks that she be given to the colony of lepers, who will rape her until she dies (96). Tristrant escapes by leaping from a chapel window into the sea; and he and Kurneval rescue Isalde. The lovers live a difficult but happy life in the forest, where Mark discovers them sleeping with a sword between them. When the potion wears off, Isalde is returned to Mark with the help of the hermit Ugrim.

At Arthur's court, Tristrant receives help from *Gawain and other knights to visit and sleep with Isalde. He in turn helps Kehenis, brother of the Isalde he marries, to sleep with Gariole, wife of Namptenis. Afterwards, Namptenis and eight knights attack Tristran and Kehenis. Although they kill seven of the knights and wound the eighth—Namptenis survives but knows he 'cannot escape the friends of these two' (152)—Kehenis is killed and Tristrant is given another wound with a poisoned weapon. He sends for Isalde to cure him; but when his wife lies and tells him the ship returning from Cornwall flies a black sail, a sign that Isalde is not on board, he dies. Isalde, finding him dead, lies down beside him and dies as well. When Mark learns of the power of the potion, he regrets his treatment of the lovers and buries them together with a rose bush planted over her and a grapevine over him. The two plants become so entwined that 'they could not be separated without being broken' (155).

Eilhart's poem is remarkable not only as an early version of the Tristan story, which has some interesting similarities to and variations from Béroul's *Tristran*. It also shows an awareness of an audience, addressed at the beginning of the poem, and of variant versions of the story, for Eilhart says 'we all know indeed that it [the story of Tristrant] is not always told the same way. But Eilhart has it right' (155). Eilhart's poem was also known through a prose adaptation, *Tristrant und Isalde*, published as a chapbook in 1484 and reprinted often in the next two centuries; it, along with Gottfried's *Tristan* and the continuation of Gottfried's incomplete romance by Heinrich von Freiberg, was a source for the late fourteenth-century Czech poem *Tristram a Izalda*. The chapbook served, in turn, as the source for the play *Tragedia mit 23 Personen von der strengen Lieb Herr Tristrant mit der schönen Königin Isalden* (*Tragedy with 23 Persons, of the Severe Love of Sir Tristrant for the Beautiful Queen Isalde*, 1553) by Hans Sachs (1494–1576).

Gottfried von Strassburg

Gottfried von Strassburg asserts that his verse romance *Tristan* (c.1210), one of the great masterpieces of medieval literature, is based on Thomas's poem; but it breaks off just before Tristan's wedding to Isolde of the White Hands. Two continuations of Gottfried's *Tristan* followed. Ulrich von Türheim's *Tristan* (c.1240) and Heinrich von Freiberg's *Tristan* (1285–90) tell of the events from Tristan's marriage to Isolde of Brittany until the death of the lovers. Some of the manuscripts of Gottfried's poem include one or the other of these later works to bring the story to its conclusion. Another poem, *Tristan als Mönch*, in which Tristan disguises himself as a monk in order to see Isolde, also appears in two manuscripts between Gottfried's and Ulrich's poems (cf. Chinca 126–30).

In a preface that is apparently Gottfried's own creation, he says that he is writing his poem to 'solace noble hearts' (42). Even though 'joy and sorrow ever went hand in hand' in love, 'Love is so blissful a thing, so blessed an endeavour, that apart from its teaching none attains worth or reputation' (44, 43). Gottfried's poem demonstrates the sorrow but also the surpassing bliss of true love. Paradoxically, the sorrow of love 'is so full of joy. . . that, having once been heartened by it, no noble heart will forgo it' (42).

Gottfried tells first of the love between Tristan's parents, Rivalin and Blancheflor, the sister of King Mark of Cornwall. Rivalin, lord of Parmenie, is a vassal of the Breton Duke Morgan. In a conflict with Morgan, Rivalin is killed. The grief Blancheflor feels causes her to die a few days after her husband and just after the birth of their son Tristan, who is raised by Rivalin's Marshal Rual li Foitenant and his wife Floraete. When Tristan and his tutor Curvenal are abducted by Norwegian merchants, they arrive at Cornwall, where Tristan's courtly accomplishments make him a favourite. He is able, for example, to flay a hart in a manner that surpasses anything known by Mark's huntsmen. Similarly, he plays the harp better than any of the local minstrels.

Gottfried is much more interested in such courtly achievements and the fate of the lovers than in the jousts and tournaments that make up so much of the narrative in some medieval romances. Of the bohort (or tournament) that is held after the knighting of Tristan, Gottfried says, 'I am no herald to cry all their jousting' (110). And even the vengeance that Tristan takes on his father's adversary Morgan, an event significant in establishing Tristan's position, is very briefly told. Tristan's combat with Morold receives more attention—undoubtedly because it leads to the fateful meeting between the lovers. Tristan must have the poisoned wound he received from Morold treated in Ireland. Later he returns to Ireland to win Isolde as a bride for Mark, though Gottfried scoffs at the notion of a swallow bringing one of her hairs from Ireland. Because Mark's advisers are jealous of Tristan's position as Mark's favourite and intended successor, they suggest that Tristan be sent to bring Isolde to the king; and he agrees to do this, in spite of Mark's concern for the danger his nephew would face by returning to Ireland. The Mark of Gottfried's poem is not the wicked king of the *Prose Tristan* or of Malory (see below for a discussion of Mark's character in these works). He is called 'good King Mark' and is said to be 'the best and most loyal of men' (99, 221).

After Tristan succeeds in winning Isolde for Mark by slaying a dragon that has been ravaging Ireland, he must be cured once again—this time of the dragon's poison. And even though Isolde discovers the notch from his sword that proves he slew Morold, she is convinced that it would be better to let Tristan live than to be forced to marry the cowardly steward who claims to have killed the dragon. Nevertheless, she tells Tristan that she hates him. It is not until they drink the potion intended for her and Mark that their love, with its joy and sorrow, blossoms. In translating the pun that is found in the Carlisle fragment of Thomas's poem, Gottfried must resort to keeping the French words for bitterness, love, and the sea, which are similar in French but not in German.

Having drunk the potion, the lovers are unable to remain apart. They must attempt to hide their love and to deceive Mark, as in the episode in which they realize that he and the wicked dwarf Melot are hiding in a tree and they speak in such a way as to convince the king of their innocence. When Melot sprinkles flour on the floor between the lovers's beds and the evidence suggests their guilt, Isolde must undergo an ordeal. By having Tristan pose as a pilgrim and fall as he carries her so that she lies with legs and arms around him, she is able to swear to the equivocal oath that no man has lain in her arms but her husband and the pilgrim. She is then able to hold the hot iron without being burnt.

Later, when his suspicions haunt him, Mark banishes the lovers. But their life in the woods is not full of hardship, as in the common version of the story. Rather, it is a time of bliss. Gottfried does not talk of their hunger and the rigours of surviving on only the meat Tristan can win through hunting; he says instead that they 'fed in their grotto on nothing but love and desire' and were nourished by 'pure devotion'.

They need no other company: 'Their company of two was so ample a crowd for this pair that good King Arthur never held a feast in any of his palaces that gave keener pleasure or delight' (262–3). This glorification of love is emphasized by the allegorical reading that is applied to every aspect of the cave in which the lovers dwell. To give one example from this extended allegory, the three windows in the cave represent Kindness, Humility, and Breeding; through these 'the sweet light, the blessed radiance, Honour... smiled in and lit up that cave of earthly bliss' (265).

Mark discovers the lovers sleeping in the cave with a sword between them, deliberately placed there to deceive anyone who might come upon them. Thinking them innocent, Mark does them no harm and later invites them back to court. 'Their need of one another', however, instead of lessening, 'was more painful and urgent than it had ever been' (276); and Mark soon finds them sleeping together. Tristan runs off to Brittany, where he meets and assists Kaedin, brother of Isolde of the White Hands. While the poem ends before Tristan's marriage to this second Isolde and before the deaths of the lovers, it is clear that for Gottfried their love was essential and their noble hearts could not survive without it. He retells their tale because 'wherever still today one hears the recital of their devotion, their perfect loyalty, their hearts' joy, their hearts' sorrow', it is 'like bread to all noble hearts' (44).

Tristan in Scandinavian Literature

The surviving portions of Thomas's *Tristran*, which preserves the end of the narrative, and of Gottfried's *Tristan*, which preserves the beginning, combine to give a complete picture of the courtly version of the Tristan story. The two overlap primarily in the scenes found in the Carlisle manuscript. Another work, *Tristrams saga ok Ísöndar (The Saga of Tristram and Ísönd)*, a Norse prose adaptation of Thomas's poem, is the earliest work in which a complete rendition of the courtly version survives. A prefatory comment notes that the saga was translated into Norse in 1226 by Brother Robert for King Hákon Hákonarson, who ruled Norway from 1217 to 1263 and sponsored a series of translations from Anglo-Norman and French.

Tristrams saga is a fairly faithful rendition of the narrative episodes of the Thomas version. It does, however, differ in style; and it shortens considerably the passages of introspection and musing on matters of love. Also, some details are changed or added, and some episodes abbreviated. When Mark spies from the tree, for example, both Tristram and Ísönd see him and leave without having the self-serving conversation in which they speak of their innocence. At the end of the saga, even after the death of the lovers, Tristram's wife Ísodd remains jealous and 'had them buried on separate sides of the church so that they couldn't be close to each other in the future'; but in time 'an oak tree or other large tree sprouted from each of their graves and grew so tall that their limbs intertwined above the gable of the church', a sign of the great love they shared (223).

Even more radical in its abridgement and in its variation in detail is the *Saga af Tristram ok Ísodd* (*The Saga of Tristram and Ísodd*, sometimes called *Tristrams saga ok Ísoddar*). The fourteenth-century Icelandic *Saga af Tristram* is based on the earlier saga but transforms it 'from tragic romance to irreverent parody' (Kalinke 211), or at least to a very different kind of tale from its source. Names and locales are changed: Tristram's parents are Kalegras and Blenzibly, and his uncle is Mórodd; he marries Ísodd the Dark and rules in Spain. Motifs from Arthurian romance—such as marrying the slayer of a husband/relative and the love trance—are parodied (cf. Kalinke 199), as are elements of the Tristan story: when Tristram leaps onto Ísodd's bed and cuts himself, she deliberately cuts herself with scissors and bleeds on the sheets 'so that the king would not know that it was man's blood' (279); the lovers go to live in a cave in the forest 'for a week without food' (281); and the tragic ending is undercut by the claim that Tristram's son by Ísodd the Dark, Kalegras Tristramsson, was made king of England by Mórodd, who goes to Jerusalem and becomes a hermit, and that 'the sons of Kalegras became very promising men' about whom 'a great saga' has been written (291).

The short Icelandic ballad 'Tristrams kvæði' ('Tristrams Poem', of uncertain date but perhaps written before 1400) retells the final events of *Tristrams saga* with the sparseness and the ominous tone of a ballad. The poem begins with the wounding of Tristram. He sends for his beloved fair Ísodd, with the instruction that the returning ship should fly a blue sail if she is aboard and a black one if not. Though she is coming to him, his wife, the dark Ísodd, says the sail is black, and his pain is so great 'that from five miles away | you could hear his heart burst' (235). Finding him dead, Ísodd dies; and the dark Ísodd has them buried in stone sepulchres so they 'shall not enjoy each other in death' (237). But despite her intentions and despite the refrain that follows each of the four-line stanzas in four of the five versions of this poem—'They had no other fate than to be parted' (the fifth version having the refrain 'He is happy who sleeps next to her' (cf. 229))—two trees grow from their tombs and join together over the church.

In addition to the Icelandic ballad, there are also Danish and Faeroese ballads of uncertain date. In the Danish 'Tistram og Isold', the lovers meet for an assignation; on her return, Isold is confronted by her husband but saved by her quick-thinking maid, who says they were attending a lady who gave birth. 'Tistram og Jomfru Isolt' ('Tistram and the Maiden Isolt') exists in various versions: in some, the lovers marry and are happy; but in others, they are brother and sister and are poisoned and die in each other's arms. The Faeroese 'Tístrams Táttur' ('Tístrams Tale') tells of the love of Tístram for the lady Ísin, a love to which his parents object so strongly that they send him to the King of France with a letter that says he should marry the king's daughter or be put to death. Refusing to renounce his love for Ísin, he is killed. When Ísin hears of his death, she journeys to France and burns down the king's palace 'with the women and children inside'. After taking the body of Tístram from the gallows, she dies of heartbreak. The poet observes that 'such things happen to no-one now' (157–8).

Sir Tristrem

The Middle English romance *Sir Tristrem*, written at the end of the thirteenth century and preserved only in the great anthology of Middle English literature known as the Auchinleck Manuscript, is the sole surviving medieval English version of the courtly form of the Tristan story. In fact, except for 'The Book of Sir Tristram' in Malory's *Morte d'Arthur*, no other Middle English Tristan story exists.

Sir Tristrem abbreviates the episodes found in the Thomas version, and much of the material has a less than courtly cast to it. There are also elements in the poem that seem intended to parody the traditional story. For example, in the crucial encounter with Duke Morgan, who has usurped Tristrem's patrimony, Morgan insults Tristrem's parents, accusing them of 'horedom'; and Tristrem slaps him and gives him a nosebleed (180). Although Tristrem goes on to slay Morgan, the initial response seems comically incongruous. Even the fight with the dragon loses some of the heroic quality it has in *Tristrams saga*. Later, when Tristrem and Ysonde drink the love potion, the tragically romantic moment is comically undercut by having the hound *Hodain lap the cup. After describing Tristrem's delight in being able to spend his time making love with Ysonde night and day, the author notes that 'Thai loved with al her [their] might | And Hodain dede also' (203–4). In these and other scenes, the poet seems to be playing with romance conventions.

Sir Tristrem is noteworthy, nevertheless, as a popular response to the courtly material. It is also significant because of the first printed edition of the poem, which was prepared by Sir Walter Scott. Scott believed that *Sir Tristrem* was a Scottish poem written by Thomas of Erceldoune, also called Thomas the Rhymer, a thirteenth-century Scottish poet and prophet. Though Scott's theories about the dialect of the poem and about its authorship have been rejected by modern scholarship, his was nonetheless one of the first great editions of a Middle English work. It virtually set the standard for future editions with its lengthy introduction, elaborate notes, and glossary. And Scott was determined to present the Middle English text faithfully, though with those editorial aids that have become standard in modern editions. When he added to the text by writing a pseudo-Middle English ending for it, he acknowledged that fact and made it clear where the Middle English text ended and his reconstruction began, something that was not common practice in his day. Thus, more than his one original Arthurian poem, 'The Bridal of Triermain', Scott's edition of *Sir Tristrem* made a contribution to the popular and the scholarly reception of Arthurian material.

The Chertsey Abbey Tiles

Often treated in medieval decorative arts, the Tristan legend appears on ivory carvings, embroideries, murals (including those at Castle Runkelstein near Bolzano), and manuscript illuminations. One early use of the legend in the decorative arts is found on a series of tiles (created *c*.1270) at Chertsey Abbey in Surrey. More than thirty tiles or fragments of tiles depict such scenes from

Thomas's version of the story as Tristan playing chess on the Norse ship, Tristan harping, Tristan slaying Duke Morgan, Morholt wounding Tristan and Tristan slaying Morholt, Mark visiting the wounded Tristan and holding his nose because of the stench, Tristan slaying the dragon, and Tristan presenting the love potion to Isolt.

THE *PROSE TRISTAN* AND ITS INFLUENCE

The *Prose Tristan*

The most important development in the Tristan story in the thirteenth-century was the writing of the *Prose Tristan*, a very long prose romance that was both popular, surviving in more than eighty manuscripts, and influential. The romance exists in two versions, a shorter and earlier one, and a somewhat later, expanded version. The writer who concludes the romance names two authors, 'Master Luce de Gat who first began to translate . . . and myself, called Helie de Boron' (325). Contemporary scholars generally feel, however, that neither name is actually that of one of the authors. The *Prose Tristan* is a biography of Tristan from his birth to his death; but, in addition to adapting the tale to prose, it introduces a number of innovations.

The *Prose Tristan* tells of Tristan's sad birth to *Meliadus and *Elyabel—sad because his mother dies just after giving birth. Merlin entrusts the baby to Gorvenal to raise and instruct. After a number of years, Meliadus remarries and Tristan's stepmother, fearing that her own child will not inherit, attempts to poison Tristan; but instead her own son is mistakenly given the poisoned drink and dies. A second attempt on Tristan's life is thwarted when Meliadus is about to drink another poisoned draught but is stopped by his wife who, in so doing, reveals her own guilt. Only Tristan's intervention, which is an early sign of his nobility, prevents Meliadus from putting her to death.

Tristan gains fame when he travels to the court of his uncle Mark and defends Cornwall against Morholt, the brother of the Queen of Ireland, who has come as a champion to demand tribute. The wound Tristan receives from Morholt's poisoned lance causes him to set out in a boat to seek a cure. Arriving by chance in Ireland, he is cured by Iseut. In Ireland, he participates in a tournament and defeats the Saracen knight *Palamedes, a major character in the *Prose Tristan*, where he is used by the author to complicate the love triangle. Tristan must contend not only with Mark for the love of Iseut but also with Palamedes. At one point in the story, Palamedes elicits a rash promise from Iseut. After ordering the death of her devoted attendant Brangain, who is discovered tied to a tree in a forest and is saved by Palamedes, Iseut regrets her deed. Palamedes offers to restore Brangain to her in return for a boon. Iseut agrees, and he asks that she (Iseut) be given to him. Ultimately Tristan arrives to fight Palamedes for her freedom, but she stops the contest between them and sends Palamedes with a message to *Guinevere proclaiming her love for Tristan and declaring that 'there are only two ladies and two knights in the world' (123), that is, Iseut and Guinevere and Tristan and *Lancelot.

The love triangle is complicated yet again when Kahedin, brother of Iseut of Brittany, falls in love with Iseut of Ireland. Tristan has married this second Iseut largely because her name reminds him of his true love; but he never consummates his marriage. When Tristan admits to his brother-in-law that he loves a woman other than his wife, Tristan and Kahedin travel to Cornwall to see her; and Kahedin is overcome by her beauty. For a time, Tristan is led to believe that Iseut loves Kahedin, and the thought drives him mad. But the mistake, caused by a letter Iseut wrote to Kahedin encouraging him so he would not languish and die, is eventually revealed. Like this and other letters, lays written by the characters play an interesting part in the romance. Kahedin writes a last lay to Iseut proclaiming his love and she responds with a lay of her own. Upon hearing it, Kahedin realizes that she feels 'total animosity' towards him and so 'his fate was sealed' (280). He suffers just the fate Iseut had hoped to prevent with her first letter—he languishes and dies.

Another striking feature of the Prose Tristan is the character of Mark. His squire knows him to be 'extremely cruel and treacherous' (61); and Mark's actions prove this assessment to be true. He hates Tristan and wishes for his death because he fears that his nephew will 'one day dispossess him of all his lands' (70), thus making him analogous to the wicked stepmother who sought Tristan's death because she feared he would inherit instead of her sons. Mark sends his nephew to Ireland to seek the hand of Iseut in the hope that he will be killed there. When he hears that Tristan has returned with Iseut, he is 'furious, for he had hoped never to see Tristan again' (93). Having mistakenly drunk the love potion intended for Mark and Iseut, Tristan and Iseut fall hopelessly in love, and their affair renews the contention between nephew and uncle that began when they were rivals for the love of the wife of *Segurades. Although Mark had not hoped for Tristan to be successful in bringing Iseut from Ireland, he comes to love her and does not wish to dishonour her (237). Yet when the lovers are taken together, Mark does not hesitate to condemn them both to death and then to follow the advice of his barons that he turn Iseut over to the lepers to 'let them do what they like with her' (156).

Given his animosity towards Tristan, it is fitting that Mark is the one who gives him his fatal wound. Striking him with a poisoned lance, Mark is delighted that his nephew will die—though he does have some regrets when Tristan is near death, and even grants his request that Iseut be at his bedside in his last moments. Not wishing to live without him, she dies in his arms at the instant that he passes away. The fact that the poisoned lance with which Mark slays Tristan was given to him by *Morgan le Fay (cf. 315) suggests another significant feature of the Prose Tristan. The romance incorporates Tristan into the Round Table fellowship and recounts many adventures, some taken from the *Vulgate Cycle, of knights such as Lancelot, Lamorat (*Lamorak), and *Dinadan. So integrated into the Arthurian world is Tristan that he even takes part in the quest for the *Grail.

Italian Tristan Romances

In the English-speaking world, the *Prose Tristan* is perhaps best known as the source for Malory's 'Book of Sir Tristram' (discussed in Chapter 3); but it was also a source for other medieval romances. The *Prose Tristan* was translated, adapted, and expanded in Spanish, and several Italian works also derive from it. A group of six short Italian poems known collectively as the *Cantari di Tristano* are based on themes from the prose tradition. In addition, several Italian romances rework the *Prose Tristan*. Following a pattern developed in the first Italian prose romance about Tristan, the *Tristano riccardiano* (written in the last quarter of the thirteenth century), the early fourteenth-century *Tristano panciatichiano* emphasizes chivalry over love. As Tristano says, 'he cannot attain honor who does not move his heart in loving' (421). The romance also incorporates material from the Vulgate *Queste* and *Mort Artu*. From the latter, for example, the author borrows the story of the tournament at *Winchester and the love of the damsel of *Escalot for Lancelot. The climax of the romance is another tournament, the one held at Loverzep (Malory's Lonezep). The deaths of the lovers seem anticlimactic, and even the description of the death scene emphasizes chivalric bonds. On his deathbed, Tristano asks *Sagremor to bring him his sword and shield, both of which he kisses. Aware that he is dying, Tristano speaks of his encounter with Death as if it were a chivalric contest: he declares, 'I am defeated,' and comments that never before did he say such a 'villainous word' (721). Before speaking to Ysotta, he addresses his principal adversary Palamedes, as well as Dinadan, and even King Mark, who treacherously struck him with a poisoned lance. When the lovers die, they are richly entombed by Mark; but there is no mention of the trees that grow from their graves in most versions of the story. Rather, the symbolism that provides a final comment on Tristano's history is the bringing of his sword and shield to *Camelot by Sagremor, an act that once again gives primacy to the chivalric over the amorous.

Of the Italian adaptations that owe a debt to the *Prose Tristan*, the most significant is the fourteenth-century Italian *La Tavola Ritonda* (*The Round Table*), which borrows from a number of sources to form an Arthurian cycle in which Tristano (Tristan) is the greatest knight. The author makes a distinction between the Old Table of *Uther and the New Table of Arthur. At the latter, Tristano is 'the source and foundation of all chivalry' (8). Clearly the boldest and most valiant knight, he accomplishes tasks that others shun.

Tristano's father Meliadus is the brother of Marco (Mark), who is 'the handsomest, but the least wise and the most despicable' (11) of three brothers. As in the *Prose Tristan*, Marco lacks virtue or courage. He kills his brother Perna for criticizing him for being willing to pay tribute to Ireland. As is usual, Tristano fights the Irish champion, Amoroldo, to end the custom, receives a poisoned wound in the combat, and must be healed by Isotta of Ireland. While there, he meets Palamidesso (Palamedes) and defeats him in a tournament. After his identity is discovered by the piece of his sword that he left in Amoroldo's head, Tristano is protected by Isotta and allowed to return to Cornwall.

Hoping for Tristano's death, Marco sends him back to Ireland to ask for Isotta's hand; and, as he returns with her, the two mistakenly drink the love potion prepared for her and Marco by her mother. The power of the potion excuses whatever offence might be found in their love: it is so strong that it can 'compel nature' and 'set the reason under the will' and make 'a hundred diverse creatures all of diverse natures, such as Christians, Saracens, lions, and serpents...into one thing and never would they abandon each other' (80). After Isotta's dog *Idonia licks the potion from the bottle, which was broken by Governale when he realized the mistake, he remains forever a companion of the lovers (though he does not, like the dog in the Middle English *Sir Tristrem*, join them in their love play). And Governale and Brandine (Brangwen) are forever loyal to the lovers merely because they smelled the potion. The author embellishes other conventional motifs. In the forest, the lovers sleep with the sword between them, for example, 'as a sign of the cross, because the place was wild and uncivilized' (158). And at the tournament at Verzeppe, Tristano fights first on one side and then on the other and thus defeats all the champions in both parties.

As in the prose tradition generally, jousts and tournaments seem more important than the lovers's trysts, and the adventures of Tristano and other knights are prominent in the story. Lancilotto (Lancelot), though clearly inferior to Tristano, is a central character. His sojourn with the *Lady of the Lake, his winning of *Dolorous Guard and changing of its name to *Joyous Guard, his love for Ginevara (Guinevere), his fathering of Galasso (*Galahad), his quest for the Grail, the enmity of Calvano (Gawain), which here exists long before Lancilotto has slain his brothers, and his various battles with Tristano are all briefly recounted. So too are other adventures from the Grail quest and the end of the Round Table. Mordarette (*Mordred) slays Artù (Arthur) and then returns to besiege Ginevara. Lanciletto must defeat Mordarette's forces and kill him. Ginevara, hearing the news of Artù's death, dies of grief; and Lancilotto enters an abbey, becomes a priest, and lives a holy life until his death.

Therefore, Lancilotto and Ginevara have a very different end from that of Tristano and Isotta, who die together after he has been wounded with a poisoned spear by Marco. The grapevine that grows from their graves shows that 'as vines bear fruit that bring rapture to all mankind, so the life of Tristano and Isotta was a tree of love which long afterward comforted and inspired all courtly lovers' (324). They become the epitome of lovers. In contrast to the pattern in Malory's *Morte*, Lancilotto and Ginevara's love is less perfect than theirs; for 'love never again lasted so nobly and so loyally between two lovers as it did between those two [Tristano and Isotta], for they had in themselves the seven qualities that make the perfect lover' (323).

Moreover, the author notes as one of the 'principal matters' of the story of Tristano 'the very great vengeance that was taken on his behalf' (9). The romance recounts the attack on Marco's castle by King Amoroldo of Ireland, Governale, now king of Liones, and Artù. When Marco tries to flee, Governale captures and imprisons him in an iron cage on top of a tower overlooking Tristano's tomb so that he, who 'had not protected Tristano' while he was alive, 'could watch over him now that he was dead'. Marco lives in the cage for thirty-two months before he dies; and since he was sentenced to remain there even after his death, his 'bones are still in the cage' (333). Although the addition of this punishment might seem to dilute the tragic effect of the deaths of the lovers, it is, rather, a means of reinforcing the significance of Tristano to the chivalric order of which he was the epitome.

Povest' o Tryshchane (The Romance of Tristan)

The influence of the Prose Tristan extends even to the Povest' o Tryshchane (The Romance of Tristan), or the Byelorussian Tristan (c.1580), a romance derived in large part from the Italian translation of the Prose Tristan known as the Tristano Veneto. The Byelorussian romance, however, contains episodes which derive from neither the Italian nor the French precursors. It downplays the love interest and uses only a couple of the prominent motifs found in most Tristan stories, such as the love potion and the episode in which Mark spies from a tree—here an apple tree. But most of the romance is devoted to the combats of Tryshchane (Tristan), which seem of much greater consequence than the love affair. In fact, the series of combats leads to a battle with Erdin (Kahedin) in which Tristan is seriously wounded. The romance ends rather anticlimactically when Marko (Mark) allows Izhota (Isolt) to try to heal Tristan and the author comments: 'I do not know whether he recovered from those wounds or died. This is all that is written about him' (146).

PALAMEDES

Palamedes in Medieval Literature

Palamedes, a fascinating figure in the Tristan story, is a Saracen who loves Isolt without hope of requital and who, in the end, gives up that love and adopts Christianity. He is a great knight, but his desire to overcome Tristan causes him to do some unchivalrous deeds. In the popular French Prose Tristan of the thirteenth century, which was considered by Eugène Vinaver 'to all intents and purposes, a sequel to, and an elaboration of, the French Vulgate cycle' (338), Palamedes is a rival to Tristan for the love of Iseut. In the Prose Tristan, Palamède is Iseult's faithful knight, doomed never to be loved in return, and yet invariably generous and loyal to his successful rival, Tristan (cf. Vinaver 340–4).

The Post-Vulgate Queste del Saint Graal borrows material from the Prose Tristan, including the account of Palamède's slaying of the *Questing Beast and his love for Iseut. When forced to fight Galahad, he promises to convert if he survives the battle, a promise he lives to fulfil. He meets his death later in the romance at the hands of *Agravain and Gawain, who fight him even though he is tired and wounded. When he is defeated, Gawain stabs him to assure his death.

Written after the first version of the *Prose Tristan* was the French romance *Palamedes*, which includes an account not only of the parents of Palamedes but also of Tristan's father Meliadus and his ally Guiron le Courtois. The romance was included in the *Compilation* of Rusticiano de Pisa (a work written in French by an Italian author in the late thirteenth century), along with other narratives from various sources. In the sixteenth century, the two parts of *Palamedes*, in which Meliadus and Guiron, respectively, are prominent, were published separately as *Meliadus de Leonnoys* and *Gyron le Courtoys*. An episode from Rusticiano's *Compilation* was the source of the fourteenth-century Greek poem 'Ho Presbys Hippotes' ('The Old Knight'), in which Palamedes, along with Gawain, Lancelot, and Tristan, is defeated by an old knight.

Thomas Malory draws his depiction of the Saracen knight who pursues the Questing Beast and loves, without hope of success, La Beale Isode, from the French *Prose Tristan* and, in the process, creates 'without question the most complex and interesting of any literary Saracen of the period' (Dulin-Mallory 165). But his Palomydes is subordinated to the larger goals of the 'Book of Sir Tristram' and ultimately to the *Morte* as a whole. He is, as Andrew Lynch has observed, 'a foil to Tristram, as an unsuccessful rival in arms and love' (108) and, as Terrence McCarthy has noted, also a foil 'even to Lancelot, whose understanding of Palomydes' situation shows how close his own experience is' (McCarthy 35). Although McCarthy does not elaborate on this connection, it is a critical one. For Palomydes is the only other knight in the *Morte* besides Lancelot who is concerned with perfecting himself in the three areas of chivalric valour, religion, and love.

In fact, Palomydes is perhaps the closest Malory comes to presenting a courtly lover of the sort described by Andreas Capellanus. When Palomydes sees Isode, 'he was so ravysshed that he myght unnethe speke. So they wente unto mete, but sir Palomydes myght not ete' (440). And because of his unrequited love, 'ever sir Palomydes faded and mourned, that all men had merveyle wherefore he faded so away' (473). He remains 'her knyght' even though he has been unrewarded, 'long gwardonles', and has 'had never reward nother bounté of her dayes of my lyff'. Despite the fact that he knows that, unlike Tristram, 'had I nevir, nor never [am] like to have' his 'desyre of her', still he will 'love her to the uttermuste dayes of my lyff' (474). Love crazes him and leads him to perform some unchivalrous acts, but it also inspires him to great deeds. At the tournament at Lonezep, he sees Isode looking down from a window and 'therewyth he toke suche a rejoysynge that he smote downe, what wyth his speare and wyth hys swerde, all that ever he mette, for thorow the syght of her he was so enamered in her love that he semed at that tyme that and bothe sir Trystram and sir Launcelot had bene bothe ayenste hym they sholde have wonne no worshyp of hym' (448).

But Palomydes, who yearns for success in knightly combat as a means of displaying his worth to Isode, is never able to get the better of Tristram. 'I may never', he complains, 'wyn worship where sir Trystram ys' (325). And in the hierarchy of knights, he is always below Lancelot and Tristram. In both love and chivalry, he is dishonoured. After defeating Palomydes in one of their encounters, Tristram makes him swear not only to forsake Isode but also for a year and a day 'that ye bere none armys nother harneys of were' (241), in effect un-knighting him for the specified time. After another defeat by Tristram, one in which he might have been killed had Isode not been reluctant to have him die a Saracen, she inflicts an even greater indignity on him by making him deliver a message to Guinevere proclaiming that 'there be within this londe but four lovers, and that is sir Launcelot and dame Gwenyver, and sir Trystrames and quene Isode' (267).

Although not a successful lover, Palomydes is truer than anyone but Lancelot. Even Tristram dallies with the wife of Sir Segwarydes and marries a woman other than his beloved. But Palomydes never thinks of another woman. In the end, however, despite the hopelessness of his situation, he is brought into the fellowship of the Round Table through religion. Tristram stands as one of his godfathers at his christening, which is followed by a feast at Arthur's court, the same feast at which Galahad takes his place at the *Siege Perilous. Thus, while not a Grail knight himself, Palomydes bears fellowship to those who achieve the Grail. And, like Lancelot, he finds little ultimate happiness in love or chivalry but takes some comfort in being saved from a life that would have led to damnation.

Palamedes in Modern Verse

Modern authors, who get their knowledge of Palamedes almost totally from Malory, rarely recognize the potential of the character; but when they do, his status as someone who is on the fringes of Arthurian society, if not totally alien to it, allows for a great variety of reinterpretations. Some of these offer little in the way of depth or insight; but in other works, Palamedes plays an interesting role. As they focus on two traditional elements of the story of Palamedes, his pursuit of the Questing Beast and his undying but hopelessly unrequited love of Isolt, modern writers give a traditional context to what are often radical reconstructions of the medieval character.

Palamedes is a key figure in two long poems by Francis Carr, who wrote under the pseudonym of Ælian Prince. Prince's poems *Of Palomide* and *Of Joyous Gard* (both published in 1890) present, in overwritten verse, a good bit of standard Tristan material derived primarily from Malory (including the love potion, the two Isolts, and the recognition of Tristram by his faithful hound). But in a rather bizarre reinterpretation of his background, Palomide becomes a black knight descended from the Scandinavian gods. When he is yet again defeated by Tristram, who refuses to slay him, he adopts Christianity almost as an act of despair because of his unrequited love rather than as an act of faith. However, changing his religion is not the triumph that it is in Malory's tale. For Palomide remains irredeemably other. When Galahad and his companions seek the Grail, Palomide seeks instead the Questing Beast. And in the end, when Mark, provoked by Mordred, kills Tristram with Palomide's spear, Palomide, who has come to delight in Tristram's reputation, kills Mark and resumes his quest for the Beast, declaring, 'I've slain the whelp! | Now for the sire!' (*Of Joyous Gard* 189).

The Questing Beast is central to another strange work about the Saracen knight, *The High History of Good Sir Palamedes the Saracen Knight and of his Following of the Questing Beast* (1912) by Aleister Crowley (1875–1947), who was known as the wickedest man in the world. For a time, Crowley was a member of the Hermetic Order of the Golden Dawn, an organization designed for the study of magic and the occult, and called himself the Beast and later the Beast 666, the designation of the Antichrist in the Book of Revelations. In his poem, Crowley uses the quest of Palamedes as a metaphor for his own quest for self-knowledge and a kind of mystical wisdom.

A more traditional version of the story was presented by William Morris, who combined the Questing Beast motif with the notion of unrequited love in his unfinished poem 'Palomydes' Quest'. Morris depicts Palomydes imagining the successful completion of that quest and envisioning the rejoicing of the people when he leads the beast Glatysaunt home. Although he sees himself being hailed as 'the best knight living' (70) by Launcelot, Palomydes asks rhetorically, 'When all this noble fame has been compassed | Shall Iseult's love be nearer to me brought?' (71). The poem therefore proclaims both the power and the limitations of imagination and the conflict between hope and despair.

Another Victorian focused on Palamedes' love for Isolt without mentioning the Questing Beast. Austin Dobson's short twenty-five-line poem 'Palomydes', which appeared in his collection called *At the Sign of the Lyre* (1885), compares the narrator's undying love for the woman to whom the poem is addressed with that of Palomydes, who 'unloved ever, still must love the same'. The poem ends by asking whether his beloved will 'deny me still in Heaven' (44–5).

A similar emphasis on unrequited love occurs in a poem by noted medieval scholar Derek Brewer, who composed an Arthurian sequence that appears in his *Seatonian Exercises and Other Verses* (2000). One of the poems in the sequence, 'Palomides to Isolde', is a fine expression of Palomides' realization of the hopelessness of his love. Autumn birches that are 'Green-gowned' and 'touched with gold against the blue' gracefully 'sway without concern' until 'the storm lashes them into | Distress and wildness, and the sky rains tears' (221), an image that suggests the passion with which Isolde loves another. As the final simile makes evident, Palomides is painfully aware that her affection is unchangeable: 'And like you they are rooted firm elsewhere | In grounded love where I cannot approach'. (221)

Brewer was preceded in the symbolic use of Palamides by another British scholar-poet, Charles Williams, author of two collections of Arthurian verse, *Taliessin through Logres* (1938) and *The Region of the Summer Stars* (1944) (discussed also in Chapter 4), in which the Grail quest is central. Palomides is, however, the focus of three poems in the cycle Williams developed in these books: 'The Coming of Palomides', 'Palomides before his Christening', and 'The Death of Palomides', all of which appear in *Taliessin through Logres*.

'The Coming of Palomides' is a crucial poem in the cycle because it is one of the clearest expressions of Williams's idea of the goodness of matter, the awareness of which was lost with the Fall of Man. When Palomides first sees Iseult, he is awestruck: 'down her arm a ruddy bolt | fired the tinder of my brain', he says. Mesmerized by her arm, he sees it become 'a rigid bar of golden flame' and then is led by 'the queen's arm's blissful nakedness' to 'unions metaphysical' (47–8). As Elisabeth Brewer has observed, Iseult 'provides the hint of beauty, of divine perfection. It is her loveliness and what it represents that is significant' (106). Of this 'Beatrician experience', C. S. Lewis says, 'There is no mistake about its Beatrician quality; indeed nowhere, in my opinion, has the poet expressed so perfectly what he had to say about the human body' (Lewis in *Arthurian Torso* 125), that is, that the human body is part of the creation that God declared good. But Palomides does not learn a lasting lesson from this vision. As Palomides sees Iseult's arm lying 'there destitute, | empty of glory' (49), the vision turns into 'a Beatrician experience going wrong' (Lewis in *Arthurian Torso* 125). The failure to realize in any permanent sense the meaning of his experience is a direct cause of the pursuit of the Questing Beast, which Palomides hears at the end of the poem (49). As John Heath-Stubbs, himself the author of a volume of Arthurian poetry, explains, Palomides 'is in pursuit of the questing beast, one of Williams's subtle images of Evil. The beast appears at the moment when Palomides becomes conscious of the discrepancy between his ideal image of Iseult and her human imperfection' (37)—or perhaps, to put it more precisely, when he lets the awareness of her human imperfection and her unattainability overshadow the goodness of her beauty.

In 'Palomides before his Christening', it is revealed that the Saracen knight has been attempting to capture the Questing Beast in order to gain praise as one 'who had done what neither Tristram nor Lancelot did' (72). This pursuit, like his love for Iseult, inevitably leads to failure and a kind of dark night of the soul. Palomides enters a cave where he lies listless and purposeless, unwilling to move even though 'the beast | lay at the cave's mouth' (72), and remains there until bats frighten him and he determines to ride to his friend Dinadan, who sees joy in life despite the fact that he is neither a great knight nor a great lover. Dinadan has offered to be godfather, should Palomides choose to be christened, as he does now that he has lost interest even in the vanities that have occupied him. Palomides knows that he will 'look a fool before everyone' but does not care (73).

In 'The Death of Palomides', the Saracen turned Christian looks back on his life: 'I left the Prophet; I lost Iseult; I failed | To catch the beast out of *Broceliande; | Lancelot forgave me' (83). C. S. Lewis comments on these lines: 'All those things which had agitated, for good or evil, the soul of the Saracen Knight, have fallen away from him. Iseult, fame, the Questing Beast, Dinadan—all that is over. These things had once appeared to him as "stations", places at which the soul could stop or in which she could even live. Now he knows that they were only paths' (Lewis in *Arthurian Torso* 173). As Palomides sits in a hut with old men and reviews his life, he can sing with them '*The Lord created all things by means of his Blessing*' (83). Thus he is finally aware of the goodness of the world. Lewis has suggested that the 'anachronism whereby Islam is made contemporary with Arthur is deliberate: Islam was for Williams the symbol . . . of something which is eternally opposite of *Sarras and *Carbonek. Islam denies the Incarnation' (Lewis in *Arthurian Torso* 124). Lewis is correct about the symbolism. Palomides' final realization is of the goodness of the world, of which the Incarnation and the Grail are indicators.

Palamedes in Modern Fiction

In fiction, Palamedes is not one of the more popular Arthurian figures; but even in this genre, a few authors make fascinating use of the character. John Erskine's novel *Tristan and Isolde: Restoring Palamede* (1932) ignores the Questing Beast and focuses solely on Palamede's courtly love for Isolde. 'Courtly love' is the right descriptor for Palamede's devotion to Isolde, for Erskine is deliberately presenting, through the Saracen knight, an idealized and exaggerated view of love, a view that Palamede has adopted based on the stories he has heard from a Christian slave, a captured Crusader named Jaafar, in which, as in some of the medieval romances, 'all the women became beautiful, and their admirers beyond reproach' (20). Since Palamede is 'a dreamer, but of the dangerous kind' for whom 'the world had to be as he saw it, not as God made it' (22), his homeland seems bland and pedestrian compared to the country of Jaafar's stories, and so he sets out to find such a place and, in turn, a woman worthy of the fabled devotion of the tales. But as in Erskine's novel *Galahad*, 'much of the book's irony and humour arises from the conflict between a naïve young man's conception of chivalry and the realities of men and women' (Taylor and Brewer 201).

Palamede's encounters with knights and ladies in Cornwall would be disillusioning to a less romantic person. Mark, who was mentioned in Jaafar's stories, is neither courtly nor gracious; and Tristan is crude and boorish and is attracted to other women besides Isolde. But when Palamede sees Isolde, he knows instantly that she is 'the woman he was born to worship' (171) and offers his love even if there is no hope that it will be requited. Palamede's ideal view of love is tested repeatedly. He learns that Isolde does not love her husband, as he believes a woman should; but he accepts this because he considers Mark unworthy. Realizing that Tristan is also unworthy of her love, Palamede has himself baptized so that Isolde can love him without risking her soul—and not, as in Malory and Charles Williams, because he realizes the futility and vanity of earthly pursuits. Palamede then goes to Tristan in Brittany and tells him that he will take Isolde from her husband. As a counter to Tristan's argument that Isolde loves him and not Palamede, he suggests that he will inform her that Tristan has wed the other Isolde, a betrayal that will offend her 'maiden soul' (319). But Tristan says Isolde is a maiden soul who is 'at home in the world' (320). As proof, he tells of her asking Brangain to sleep with Mark on the night of Isolde and Mark's wedding, a charge that Palamede finds so offensive that he calls Tristan a liar. In the ensuing fight, Palamede gives Tristan a fatal wound but then agrees to return to Cornwall and to bring Isolde to her dying lover.

When Palamede learns from Brangain that Tristan's account of Isolde's wedding night is true, his faith in himself and in the world of Jaafar's stories is undermined. Yet he can still say, 'I did not come in vain! I have seen one woman, noble beyond hope, one flawless love, not for me!' (344). In the end, it is not his love for Isolde that supports his faith in an ideal love; rather, it is Isolde's love for Tristan. Her willingness to sacrifice anything and anyone because of her single-minded devotion to Tristan is what allows Palamede to remain a dreamer and an idealist who can believe in courtly love.

The other major use of the Saracen knight in modern fiction is in T. H. White's *The Once and Future King* (1958), in which Palomides becomes, uniquely in the Arthurian tradition, a comic figure. White is also one of the few interpreters of Palamedes who virtually divorces him from the story of Tristan and Isolt. Perhaps this is because White did not think much of Tristan or of the way Tristan treated Palomides. In manuscript notes that he made before writing *The Once and Future King*, White observed, 'Tristram bears malice. Then there is the unfortunate Saracen Palomides, who is always just failing to be the hit of the party on account of T. turning up and going one better. T.'s malice towards Palomides is incomprehensible, except on the grounds that T. himself is a little mad. He is a kind of British Israelite or crank, all mixed up about moral values and going for Palomides' because he is black.

White introduces Palomides in the second instalment of his sequence, the book originally called *The Witch in the Wood* and then renamed 'The Queen of Air and Darkness' when it was published as part of *The Once and Future King*. In this instalment, which bridges the divide between 'The Sword in the Stone', the children's story that forms the first part of White's Arthuriad, and the more mature concerns of the third part, 'The Ill-Made Knight', White uses Palomides and *Pellinore, who was already established as a comic figure in 'The Sword in the Stone', to continue the comedy but to point it towards the more serious and ultimately tragic theme of love. While he makes a passing reference to the fact that Palomides is 'supposed to be in love with La Beale Isoud' (202), White otherwise ignores this aspect of the tradition, though he does introduce, for comic purposes, the Questing Beast. Initially, Pellinore, who pines for the daughter of the Queen of Flanders, affectionately known as Piggy, is pursuing the Questing Beast. When the Beast takes to the sea, Pellinore flags down a boat in which Grummore and Palomides are sailing. They all follow the Beast to the realm of *Lot and *Morgause, where the wicked queen, modelled after the mother White hated, tries to seduce her guests. But they are too worldly-unwise even to realize what is happening.

To distract Pellinore from his love-sickness, his two companions create a costume in which they dress themselves as the Beast so he will be able to resume his quest; but the real Beast reappears and falls in love with the mock one. When the Beast besieges the castle to which Palomides and Grummore have retreated, Merlin suggests psychoanalysing her. Palomides undertakes the task and makes her see reason; but she transfers her affection, 'as so often happens in psycho-analysis' (307), to the successful analyst. As a result, Pellinore must resign the quest to Palomides. This instance of love gone awry foreshadows comically the tragic love of the book. As Sir Grummore says of the situation, 'Love . . . is a pretty strong passion, when you come to think of it' (202). Palomides and the Questing Beast provide a comic example of this principle that plays such an integral part in the tale of Arthur, Lancelot, and Guinevere.

Tristan and Isolt in the Victorian Age

Like Arthurian literature in general, the Tristan story saw a revival in the Victorian age. Matthew Arnold (1822–88) offered one significant version in his poem 'Tristram and Iseult' (1852). Arnold's plot begins with a dying Tristram awaiting a last visit from Iseult of Ireland. The lovers spend a final moment together, but then both die. Arnold's Iseult has not come with the power to cure, merely to join him in death, which cools the heat of their passion. Very soon they are 'cold as those who lived and loved | A thousand years ago' (212). In a nice play of imagery of heat and cold, the 'air of the December night | Steals coldly' around the chamber where the lifeless lovers lie and flaps the tapestry on which is depicted a huntsman in 'a fresh forest scene', who seems to stare at the pitiful lovers 'with heated cheeks and flurried air' as he wonders who they might be (211). The hunter in the tapestry is a variation on the 'cold pastoral' of Keats's 'Ode on a Grecian Urn'; he is warmer than the real lovers because he represents life. And the confusion ascribed to him as he seems to ponder the scene before him suggests that art, like life, is not an escape from reality.

In the last section of the poem, 'Iseult of Brittany', Arnold portrays a saddened Iseult of Brittany who 'seems one dying in a mask of youth' (214). The picture of a woman who has grown old before her time is heightened by the fact that she watches over her own children, whose vitality has not yet been dried up by the world's sorrow. And yet their very warmth (their cheeks were 'flush'd' and their brows 'hot' (213)) implies that they too are subject to 'the gradual furnace of the world' (215) that has already robbed Iseult of joy.

Another original touch that Arnold adds to his plot is its ending: Iseult tells her children the story of Merlin and *Vivian, an ironically appropriate tale. It underscores the plight of Iseult, who wanted her lover beside her, by describing a Vivian who 'grew passing weary of her love'. Iseult is actually more like Merlin than Vivian: she is trapped in a life that holds little joy for her and that is very limited, trapped because she was rejected by a lover who did not desire her attentions.

Alfred, Lord Tennyson's version of the Tristan story is told in 'The Last Tournament' idyll in the *Idylls of the King* (discussed in Chapter 3). First published in 1872, 'The Last Tournament' presents the love affair as sordid and subordinates passionate love to Victorian morality. Reacting to Tennyson's treatment of the Arthurian material and wishing to restore something of the spirit of the medieval romances, Algernon Charles Swinburne (1837–1909) published *Tristram of Lyonesse* in 1882 (though he began writing it in 1869). But Swinburne was already interested in the Tristan story as early as 1857–8, when he began writing *Queen Yseult*, a poem which he never completed. Influenced by *Sir Tristrem*, *Queen Yseult* tells of Tristram's life from his birth to his marriage to Yseult of Brittany and ends with a depiction of Yseult of Ireland alone in Cornwall and hated by Mark. Swinburne also wrote the short poem 'Joyeuse Garde' (1859), which alludes to Mark's hatred and Palomydes' love for Yseult and which is rich in natural imagery.

Tristram of Lyonesse, Swinburne's best and most fully developed treatment of the story, opens with a 'Prelude' that defines and glorifies love as a powerful and essential force which not only orders the world and 'is the root and fruit of terrene things' but which also defines heaven by its presence and hell by its absence (14). The irresistible power of love is symbolized by the love potion. After unwittingly drinking the potion, the lovers kiss: 'And their four lips became one burning mouth' (46). This image, which closes the first of the poem's nine sections, is part of a pattern of images of fire and heat that suggest the burning passion and the elemental nature of their love. The passion exists until their deaths when, in a line that echoes the description of their first kiss, Iseult finds Tristram dead and dies herself as she kisses him one last time, a kiss in which 'their four lips became one silent mouth' (156).

Although *Tristram of Lyonesse* includes a number of the motifs from the traditional story—the love potion, the substitution of Brangwain for Iseult in Mark's bed on the wedding night, Palamede's love for Iseult, Tristram's marriage to Iseult of Brittany, the slaying of the giant Urgan, the black and white sails, and the slaying of Tristram by Mark—it is less a narrative of the life of Tristan than a philosophical poem which, as Swinburne observed in his 'Dedicatory Epistle' to the 1904 edition of his poems, contains 'meditations on man and nature, life and death, chance and destiny'. He recognized that some might object to such meditations by 'a typical hero of chivalrous romance'; but he thought this objection valid only if 'the slightest attempt had been made to treat the legend as in any possible sense historical' (p. xix).

While Victorian fiction virtually ignored the Arthurian legends, one relatively unknown work is nevertheless a fascinating Arthurian document. *The Feasts of Camelot*, written in 1863 by Mrs T. K. Hervey (Eleanora Louisa Montagu Hervey (1811–1903)), is a series of tales told by various members of Arthur's court. Influenced by Chaucer's *Canterbury Tales*, the Gothic novel, and Malory's *Morte d'Arthur*, *The Feasts of Camelot* is among the earliest works of Arthurian fiction. And, despite the fact that the form seems well suited to the Matter of Britain, Hervey's book remains one of the very few unified collections of short Arthurian tales to be written in the modern period.

Perhaps the most interesting aspect of *Feasts* is what Hervey does with the legend of Tristram, Isond, and Mark. Their stories are told in three tales that seem designed to redeem not only the lovers but even King Mark. Though Hervey clearly draws on traditional material, her account is unconventional in many ways. In Chapter 3, Tristram's tale of 'Mad King Mark' presents an evil Mark and a Tristram who, in a bizarre plot devised by Isond, goes to her namesake (who resides not in Brittany but in Wales) to heal an old wound that has reopened. Tristram marries Isond of Wales, and she is still his wife as the tales are being told at Camelot.

Later in the book, Isond relates Mark's 'One Good Deed'. Most of her account does not concern Mark at all, but rather the deeds and misdeeds of two brothers, elements of whose tale are reminiscent of Malory's treatment of *Balin and *Balan. One brother, Bertrand, is responsible for the death of the other, Walter, and, at least in part because of the guilt he feels, dies shortly thereafter. Mark's good deed is to have the body of Walter brought back to his castle to be buried beside the woman he loved and to have prayers said for both of them. Of course, as Arthur says, 'It could be wished that the living rather than the dead had been so humanely dealt with' (222). The redemption of Mark is not completed until the last chapter in the *Feasts*, which contains a tale told by Alisaunder, the *Alysaundire the Orphelyn who is treasonously slain by Mark in Malory's *Morte*. But here he is not slain. In fact, he responds to Arthur's requests for a tale revealing that someone of Mark's 'blood and race' has done 'acts of nobleness and generosity, whence we may infer that nature is not all in fault, but that circumstance has wrought in him some of the ill that he has done' (222).

Alisaunder tells of the young Tristram's forgiveness of his stepmother, who twice tried to poison him. Tristram's plea saved her from death to which his father, Meliodus, had condemned her; and this act of mercy even transformed her from a wicked to a devoted stepmother who 'loved him tenderly ever after' and a penitent who 'scourged herself and wore sackcloth for her sin'. As a result of the story, Arthur is forced to admit that Tristram, Alisaunder's father (Mark's brother), and Alisaunder himself show that there are 'traits of nobleness and self-denial in the blood of King Mark's line' (230).

Since Mark's misdeeds are not a fault of nature, the explanation for them can be found in the realm of nurture. Merlin recounts a rumour that he had prophesized that 'one near akin' to Mark would 'usurp his power, and hold him captive till his death-day'. The prophecy kept Mark 'ever in dread' and caused him to wage 'unnatural war with all his race'. Even his wife asserts that 'King Mark has ever been kind and tender to me' and cruel or unjust only when 'led to suspect treachery through a foolish rumour' (231). Mark, now rightly understood, is led in and allowed to join in the feasting and fellowship.

Another eccentric Victorian use of Tristan occurs in the didactic prose tale *Sir Tristram's Axe* (1892) by an author identified as The Wanderer (pseudonym of Elim

Henry d'Avigdor (1841–95)). The tale tells of a man named Simon Hardheart, who is mean to his daughter: he kicks her kitten and stops her from feeding birds. The queen of the fairies sends the spirit of Sir Tristram to teach him a lesson. In the process of learning this lesson, Simon is transformed first into a kitten, then into a black man who finds himself in a jungle where he is threatened by a symbolically evil serpent, and ultimately into a knight in Arthurian England. In this final transformation, Simon proves himself worthy, and he and Sir Tristram become 'sworn companions' (50). Just before his death, Simon has a vision in which he sees not only his daughter but also Tristram and Galahad waiting to lead him to his final reward.

The story of Tristan and Isolt was also depicted by a few major Victorian artists. William Dyce used Tristram in two of the decorations for the Queen's Robing Room in the New Palace at Westminster—Courtesy (*Sir Tristram Harping to la Beale Isoud*) and Hospitality (*The Admission of Sir Tristram to the Fellowship of the Round Table*)—and Dante Gabriel Rossetti painted *Sir Tristram and La Belle Yseult Drinking the Love Potion* (1867). Perhaps the most significant representations of the Tristan story were undertaken by William Morris and the group of artists (Val Prinseps, Arthur Hughes, Dante Gabriel Rossetti, Edward Burne-Jones, and Ford Madox Brown) he enlisted when, in 1862, his company was commissioned to create stained-glass panels for Harden Grange, the Yorkshire home of Walter Dunlop, a wealthy merchant from Bradford. Morris designed a series depicting scenes from the Tristan legend, generally following Malory's version of the story: Tristram's birth, his combat with Marhaus, his departure with Isoude from Ireland, the drinking of the love potion, Tristram's marriage to Isoude of Brittany, Isoude's attempt at suicide, the madness of Tristram, Tristram recognized by his dog, the lovers at Arthur's court, the death of Tristram, the tomb of the lovers, Queen Guinevere and Isoude of the White Hands, and King Arthur and Lancelot (cf. Sewter ii. 26–7). The panels now reside at the Bradford City Art Gallery. Earlier, in 1857, Morris began a painting of the recognition of Tristram by the dog he had given Iseult. This work was never completed, but Morris's one surviving painting is called *La Belle Iseult* (1858, formerly and still identified by some as a depiction of Guinevere).

TRISTAN PLAYS

A surprising number of twentieth-century authors have turned their attention to the Tristan legend in plays, poems, and novels. The popularity of the Tristan legend in the twentieth century was no doubt due in large part to the brilliant artistry of Wagner's dramatic/operatic interpretation of the legend coupled with Joseph Bédier's popular retelling of the Tristan story.

The opera *Tristan und Isolde* (completed 1859, premièred 1865) by Richard Wagner (1813–1883) was influenced by Gottfried von Strassburg's *Tristan*. As he did with Wolfram's *Parzival* in his opera *Parsifal*, Wagner greatly simplified the plot of his source, so greatly in fact that it might be more accurate to say that Gottfried's poem was the inspiration for the opera rather than its source. Wagner's first act presents Tristan and Isolde on the ship that is bringing her to marry Marke. Isolde has cured Tristan, the slayer of her fiancé Morold. Her anger at Tristan, whom she has begun to love, is intensified because he is delivering her to Marke, so she tells her handmaiden Brangäne to prepare a poisoned drink for her and for Tristan. But Brangäne prepares a love potion instead. Believing it will kill them, Tristan and Isolde drink the potion and then declare their love for each other. In the second act, the lovers meet when Marke leaves to go hunting. But the king and his party return to find them together. Melot, one of Marke's knights, denounces the lovers and mortally wounds Tristan. In the third act, Tristan, tended by his faithful companion Kurwenal, lies dying in his castle in Brittany. When a ship bearing Isolde approaches, Tristan rushes to meet her so that he can be healed by being united with her in death, and he dies in her arms. Marke and Melot arrive on another ship; Kurwenal slays Melot and is himself killed by Marke's retainers. Though Marke has come to pardon the lovers, Isolde also dies and is united with Tristan, as is symbolized by the beautiful music of the *Liebestod*, Isolde's song in which love and death are thematically linked.

The general interest in the tragic tale of the lovers was also greatly amplified by the publication of *Le Roman de Tristan et Iseut* (1900) by French scholar Joseph Bédier (1864–1938), a reconstruction of the legend, which drew on a variety of medieval sources, including, but not limited to, Thomas, Béroul, Eilhart, and Gottfried. Bédier's book became known to the English-speaking world through the translation done by English poet Hilaire Belloc (1870–1953) in 1903—though with some chapters and passages omitted. (These omissions were supplied in the 1945 revision of Belloc's translation by Paul Rosenfield.) Bédier himself later co-authored a play, *Tristan et Iseut* (1929), with Louis Artus (b. 1870), which reworked many of the classic scenes described in his retelling and which culminated in the deaths of the lovers: after Iseut aux Blanches Mains lies about the colour of the sail on the ship bringing Iseut la Blonde, Tristan dies; and his lover expires when she finds him dead. In the wake of Bédier's retelling and Belloc's translation, many other writers, including quite a few dramatists, undertook reworkings of the legend.

German dramatist Ernst Hardt's (1876–1947) play *Tantris der Narr* (1909), translated as *Tristram the Jester* (1913) by John Heard, Jr. (b. 1889), begins after the drinking of the potion and ends without enacting the tragic deaths of the lovers. After Iseult has been in Mark's court for ten years without Tristram, Mark learns that Tristram has returned and he decrees that Iseult be given to the lepers for their pleasure. Tristram, disguised as a leper, rescues her in a manner that leads Mark and his barons to believe that it was God's doing. Later, after Iseult has returned to Mark, Tristram, in another disguise, comes to court as a jester. It is only when Tristram's hound *Husdent, called 'savage' and 'wolflike' (41), recognizes his master and runs off with him that Iseult realizes she has been visited by Tristram; and her love, turned to anger by his marriage to Isot of the Fair White Hands, is rekindled.

Among the many English and American plays based on the legend, some are overly dependent on the traditional story, while others attempt, occasionally successfully, to take an original approach to the material. In *Tristram and Iseult: A Play in Five Acts* (1911), Maurice Baring (1874–1945) tries so hard to retell the medieval story that his play lacks any sense of originality. In a note to his play, Baring says that the subject matter is taken almost entirely from Bédier's retelling of the legends (89). He includes numerous motifs and elements of plot from his source but pays little attention to dramatic development, motivation, or even plausibility. Almost all the scenes in the play are brief, and the action leaps from one traditional event or motif to another with little regard for dramatic structure. A similar flaw mars *Tristram and Iseult* (1930) by Amory Hare (pseudonym of [Mary] Amory Hare Hutchinson (b. 1885)). In an author's note, Hare suggests that Masefield (and Edwin Arlington Robinson, whose poem *Tristram* appeared in 1927, the same year as Masefield's play) 'departed considerably from the traditions of the old manuscripts' and that she owes 'the greater portion' of her play to Bédier's rendition and to other medieval sources—except that she has omitted 'the supernatural elements' (8–9). Like Baring's play, Hare's is derivative and unfocused. Her notion of character creating destiny seems to be an afterthought rather than a determining force or an essential element in the development of the play. As a result, her creation is not nearly so interesting as those she criticizes.

Other dramatists, however, achieve a better balance between authority and imagination. Louis Anspacher (1878–1947), for example, in *Tristan and Isolde: A Tragedy* (1904) tries to present the elements of the tragedy in the space of a single day. The first act begins in the late afternoon of one day, and the fifth and last act takes place at twilight on the next day. This structure, of course, demands a good deal of exposition to reveal the generally familiar events that lead up to the tragic moment. Anspacher also creates a subplot in which Isabel, Isolde's maid, is wooed by two lovers. Neither of these devices is totally successful; the attempt at a unity of time leads to much more talk than action and the subplot lacks the relevance that those of Shakespeare achieve. But Anspacher presents an interesting picture of Mark, who is a good person and is not the agent of Tristan's death. In fact, he becomes the tragic hero.

The treatment of the tragedy is much different in the *Tristram and Isoult* (1905) of Martha W. Austin, who writes in her foreword that she saw a notice of the publication of Anspacher's work when hers was already finished and that she delayed reading his play for six months because she feared it would make her own treatment 'superfluous'. But upon reading it, she found that 'there was still a place for my own version, as the two differed almost as much as it was possible for any two treatments of the same theme to differ' (5). She further observes that while Anspacher based his play on the German tradition that Wagner followed, her source was Malory, especially in the crucial instance of Mark's character and in the contrast of the Tristram–Isoult–Mark triangle with that of Lancelot, Guinevere, and Arthur. Austin is, however, most successful when she avails herself of the poetic licence she claims, 'the privilege of each to draw the thing as he sees it' (6). Particularly noteworthy is the general lack of guilt that Tristram feels. In a blending of legends, he goes so far as to compare the cup from which he drank the love potion to the Grail (18). But though Tristram is the best-drawn character in the play, even he is not developed fully enough to make an audience experience the tragedy as something personal yet legendary.

J. Comyns Carr's (1849–1916) *Tristram and Iseult* (1906) attempts to cover too much dramatic ground in too short a space. For example, Carr introduces Palomide, the Saracen knight who fights for and nearly wins the hand of Iseult, only to be bested by Tristram. But instead of the traditional continuing conflict between the Saracen and Tristram, Palomide, having served as a means of forwarding the plot, is not heard from again. Nevertheless, Carr finds an original and dramatically effective means of abridgement of other elements of his sources. For instance, instead of trying to incorporate Tristram's marriage to Iseult of the White Hands, he presents her as a spectral figure who utters an ominous prediction about the future of the lovers. In the last scene, the vision appears again, stretching her white hands over the dying lovers. The audience realizes with Iseult that the white hands represent death and yet they bring healing too, since, as Tristram says in his final words, 'For all Love's wounds there is no cure but Death' (71).

Reacting to what he considered the classical tragedy of Carr in which 'dramatic situation' (p. x) is paramount, Thomas Herbert Lee intended his romantic tragedy *The Marriage of Iseult* (1909) to focus more on character. In the two scenes of his short play, the lovers drink the love potion and then drink poison and die together. The characters are not, in fact, well developed; but Iseult does attain some definition by declaring her forced marriage to Mark a rape and by asserting that her soul is her own.

Isolt (1915) by Antonia R. Williams is, as its subtitle *A New Telling* implies, an obvious and deliberate departure from the medieval traditions. Williams' attempt at innovation takes the form of turning the play into a rather heavy-handed allegory of 'Two Ideas in Conflict: Love and Fear' and of giving the tragic story a happy ending. This ending seems artificial—a distortion of the tradition rather than an addition to it. Led astray by her allegory, Williams undervalues the story and even the characters in her attempt to make something new of the old tale.

The Tragedy of Pardon (1911) by Michael Field (a pseudonym for British authors Katherine Harris Bradley (1846–1914) and Edith Emma Cooper (1862–1913)) begins on a promising note, with a prologue that is one of the most original scenes in all the Tristan plays. It presents Queen Iseult of Ireland in a laboratory preparing the love potion, which is empowered by 'star-rays' that 'fall on the alembic and ignite it' (3). This visual symbol of the power of the potion and, by extension, the love it produces could, with proper staging, provide a dramatically compelling opening.

Unfortunately, the promise of the prologue is unfulfilled by the play itself. There is a good deal of action throughout: Tristan shoots the spying Marjodo with an arrow and Melot buries the body; Iseult undergoes the ordeal of the hot iron to prove her innocence; Tristan and Iseult are discovered by Mark in their forest cave. But the episodes lack unity, especially the kind that could be imparted by the consistent development of character.

Tristan and Iseult (1917) by British poet and dramatist Arthur Symons (1865–1945) is structurally flawed in a manner that undermines the effectiveness of the drama. Trying to include all the elements of the traditional story, Symons employs a large cast of characters in action that is at times so diffuse that it does not allow for real development of either plot or characters. Mark, for example, does very little in the play except to banish Tristan after learning of his love for Iseult and to arrive in Brittany in time only to forgive the dead lovers and command a royal funeral for them. Meriadoc, who himself loves Iseult and who ultimately gives Tristan his fatal wound, is almost as weakly drawn as Mark. He begins by hating Tristan, the slayer of his father Morholt; but then he is reconciled with him for no particular reason except that Iseult now looks with favour on Tristan. Finally, but without any real explanation of the reversion to hatred, Meriadoc stabs Tristan with a poisoned knife. In Gottfried's *Tristan*, the shift in Marjodoc's feelings from friendshi hatred for Tristan is explained in some detail. Marjodoc is upset to learn that his friend has been having an affair without telling him—and this disgruntlement intensifies to hatred when he discovers that Tristan's beloved is Isolde whom he (Marjodoc) also loves. Thus the motivation is clear; but Symons, who asks his audience to accept two changes in affection, gives virtually no reasons for them. Such superficial treatment of characters results from an over-reliance on the traditional elements of the story to support the action of the play. Where Symons is original, however, is in his use of the theme of honour as a focus for the events of the play. The main characters experience a conflict between honour and the real emotions of love and hatred.

Thomas Hardy's *The Famous Tragedy of the Queen of Cornwall at Tintagel in Lyonnesse* (1923) extends the action beyond the point at which it usually ends. Typically, when Iseult of Brittany lies about the colour of the sail, Tristram dies, as does Iseult of Ireland upon learning of his death. But Hardy arranges the action so that Tristram and Iseult do not die so soon. Iseult of Brittany rushes to the pier before the Queen of Cornwall can disembark and tells her rival, falsely, that Tristram is dead. After Iseult has returned to Cornwall, Tristram, followed shortly by his wife, arrives at Mark's court, where Mark kills him in jealous rage and then is slain by his queen. After stabbing Mark with the same knife he used to kill Tristram, she leaps to her death. The inevitable tragedy coupled with the twist that Hardy gives to the traditional story emphasizes his theme, which is made specific in the words of Iseult the Whitehanded. When she learns of the deaths of Tristram, Iseult, and Mark, she observes that 'even had I not come | Across the southern water recklessly | This would have shaped the same' (74–5). The significant word 'shaped' is used to suggest that the deaths were fated. Iseult realizes that there is a force working to shape her destiny and the destinies of the others and that her actions have little effect on the ultimate outcome.

The short play *Tristram and Iseult: A Dramatic Poem* (1924) by Irish playwright An Pilibin (pseudonym of John Hackett Pollock) is a masterpiece of mood. A stage direction at the beginning of the piece indicates that 'The players throughout, move and speak with marked slowness and precision' (7). The motion matches the setting: high summer on a ship becalmed at sea. But the calm is about to be broken by a fierce storm. Myriads of swallows, sensing the coming tempest, roost on 'every spar and shroud' of the ship. Iseult, young and innocent, asks about one white bird that used to 'house above | My casement' (28–9). After the storm, a symbol that foreshadows the coming tempest in the lives of Tristram and Iseult, Tristram is seen holding the white bird—now dead. Tristram's apostrophe to the dead bird is the thematic centre of the play. He calls the bird a poor thing for Death to 'prey upon'; but that very fact gives dignity to the bird even in death 'Since men, and gods, and planets likewise die' (37). The dead bird also represents Iseult's dead innocence—moments later she and Tristram drink the love potion—as well as the tragic nobility of the death that will come to them. But that death is not portrayed in Pilibin's play. After the lovers drink the potion, they 'speak and move in a sonambulistic [sic] fashion' which reflects the calm that they attain when they realize their place and purpose in the universe. They achieve a cosmic perspective that links them, like the dead bird, to a larger scheme in which the impending tragedy is overshadowed by their triumph, a triumph reflected in the 'Recitative' which closes the play, wherein their names are said to be made immortal by the gods (47).

Martha Kinross's *Tristram and Isoult* (1913) is one of the most fascinating of the Tristan plays, largely because of its focus on and depiction of Isoult. Whereas Malory highlighted the tragedy of Arthur by contrasting his nobility to Mark's mean-spiritedness and cowardice, Kinross makes Guinevere a foil by means of which Isoult's independence, courage, and strength can be clearly seen. Early in the play, Guinevere calls Isoult 'fearless' and says that she envied her living openly with Tristram at Joyous Gard (6). This openness, coupled with a strength rare in the typical portrayal of Isoult, makes Kinross's heroine a compelling character. Isoult's fearlessness, from which her strength derives, is dramatically depicted when Mark confronts her in a tower at Tintagil. Isoult's open defiance of him extends to an admission of her love for Tristram and even to contemptuous insult. She compares Mark to a dog that sniffs 'at the thresholds | Of doors are shut to thee' (38). Her passion and her strength last to the end of the play when, with Tristram dead, she drinks a poisoned cup, which she compares to the Grail, an image that demonstrates her independence from conventional moral standards. Her inversion of the traditional life-giving and religious associations of the Grail suggests that Isoult will decide her own faith and her own fate. The prominence of Isoult and her strength of character give the play fairly obvious feminist overtones that are unusual for its time and that make it a forerunner of the tendency in recent Arthurian literature towards giving female characters central roles.

Four Tristan plays appeared in 1927. John Todhunter's (1839–1916) *Isolt of Ireland* is close to the spirit of medieval romance, but it also uses complex relationships to explore the theme of trust and betrayal. D. M. Mitchell's *Sir Tristram* depicts Mark as a basically good man with a tragic flaw. While both are of passing interest, two other plays published in that year, one by John Masefield (1878–1967) and the other by American author Don Marquis (1878–1937), are exceptional. In *Tristan and Isolt*, Masefield uses as one of his sources the Welsh Triad of 'Three Powerful Swine-herds of the Island of Britain', the first of whom is 'Drystan son of Tallwch, who guarded the swine of March son of Meirchiawn, while the swineherd went to ask Essyllt to come to a meeting with him. And Arthur was seeking (to obtain) one pig from among them, either by deceit or by force, but he did not get it' (*Trioedd Ynys Prydein* 45). Masefield's Tristan similarly guards the swine while the swineherd Hog goes to warn Isolt not to meet him because of a trap set by Kai. Kai, in turn, wants to punish Hog and Tristan by stealing a pig while the latter is on guard. Arthur, who in this play is a 'Captain of the Host' subordinate to Marc, goes along with Kai but is actually sympathetic to Tristan and Isolt. The plot to steal the hog is frustrated by Tristan and Hog, but the comic castigation of Kai and his accomplice Bedwyr cannot prevent the ultimate tragic ending. In fact, the comic subplot, in which the transgressions of Kai and Bedwyr are punished, is a way of highlighting the inevitability of the tragic ending, an inevitability suggested at the very beginning of the play by the opening speech of a character called Destiny (1).

But Masefield's most innovative plot twist is in the working out of the foreordained tragedy. It is not a vengeful Marc who slays Tristan. Marc is himself killed by 'the heathen' at the Battle of *Badon Hill (132). During his absence, Tristan, maddened by his separation from Isolt, returns to court seeking her. Since she has come to believe that 'This love, that I thought was great, is blindness and greed' (117), she rejects him and has him flogged as a felon. Tristan, who has been living 'upon leaves and grass', dies from the punishment. But Isolt, who is freed from her duty to Marc by news of his death, rushes to Tristan; and they have a final moment to express their love before he dies and she stabs herself. Thus Masefield's Isolt is a tragic figure who is caught between her love and her sense of duty. It is precisely the blend of this pre-romantic material from the Welsh *Triads* with the later romantic elements that creates the tragic dilemma for Isolt. The duty she feels and the harsh justice she administers, both consistent with the heroic world of early Celtic literature, are at odds, in her character and in the action of the play, with her romantic love for Tristan. By allowing the two worlds to meet, Masefield creates the tragedy of Isolt.

Like Masefield's *Tristan and Isolt*, Don Marquis's play *Out of the Sea* offers an outstanding dramatic version of the Tristan story. Marquis recasts the legend in a modern setting, in which his characters, rather than seeming diminished versions of their medieval originals, gain a mythic dimension. The setting of the play is on the Cornish coast, near where the ancient land of *Lyonnesse sank into the sea. Strange sounds of Tristram's ghostly hunt echo throughout the play. The modern counterpart of Tristram is John Harding, an American poet, who is taken with the romance of Cornwall, where, he says, the ghosts from Lyonnesse speak to him *out of the sea*. The Isolt character is Isobel Tregesal, who was found in an open boat as a child with an ancient bronze bodkin beside her. Her husband Mark is jealous and cruel, crueller 'than the old king was to them other lovers', as one of the characters says (62). As Mark begins to suspect that his wife and Harding are lovers, his deliberate cruelty to her convinces Harding and Isobel that they must run away together, a decision that is supported by her foster-father and by Arthur Logris, the owner of the house in Cornwall in which much of the action takes place.

When Mark discovers Isobel in a cave where the lovers have met before, he attempts to force her to remain with him. She is defiant, but he, like her, is 'elemental' (112). Not only does he try to stop her, but he proclaims his desire for a son and attempts to rape her in the cave. Isobel resists and finally stabs him with the bronze bodkin. Confronted with the violent deed, the American poet reveals that he has none of the elemental force of the other characters. He says, 'I never thought . . . that it would come . . . to bloodshed' (130). When Isobel, now 'free even of love' (131), leaps into the sea, Harding says that he should follow her. But Logris, recognizing that Harding lacks the ancient passion that is bred into those who have lived on the coast of Cornwall and in the presence of the legend of Lyonnesse, says, 'You won't, though. You'll write a poem about it' (133). *Out of the Sea* is the tragedy not of Mark, who is too cruel to be a tragic hero, or of Harding, who is not noble enough, but of Isobel, whose return to the sea is a tragic victory over both the cruelty of Mark and the pusillanimity of Harding.

In addition to his Arthurian novels (discussed in Chapter 1), Henry Treece wrote the short play *The Tragedy of Tristram* (performed as a radio play in 1950 and published in 1952). The only characters are the ghosts of Tristram, Mark, and Yseult Blanchemain, all of whom 'must walk up and down | The restless world and play [their] parts again | And yet again' (39). The characters meet and act as if they were alive, with Mark wanting to kill Tristram and Yseult Blanchemain protecting him. Tristram recognizes that he betrayed Mark but says that he 'held fast to Arthur' and even shed his blood 'to fetch the Grail | Out of the heathens' land' (17). Yet the betrayal of his wife and his uncle as well as his only partially fulfilled desire for Yseult of Ireland prevent him from achieving peace and therefore rest. Tristram's tragedy is that he and those affected by his actions must play their parts over and over again (39).

The play *The Fair Eselt* (1969) by George Brandon Saul (1901–86) tries to capture the spirit of the story as it appeared in the 'pre-*Ur-Tristan*', a process that 'substitutes rational for faery motivation' (219). This is evidenced primarily in the omission of the potion as the cause of the love. Despite the love between Tristan and Eselt, Marc is not presented as a wicked or even a jealous husband but as a 'kindly man' (232) who accepts the return of Eselt as queen but renounces 'all rights | Unto her private person' (248) on the chance that the lovers might be reunited sometime in the future.

THE TRISTAN LEGEND IN TWENTIETH-CENTURY VERSE

Of the many poets who have treated the Tristan legend, some have retold the entire story; others have focused on a single episode or event; and some have created sequences of poems to emphasize themes of particular interest to them. Among those who retold the entire story was folklorist William Wells Newell (1839–1907). In his poem *Isolt's Return*, a minstrel tells the tale of Tristran and Isolt for a romantic young woman, who is disappointed in his narrative, which is based on Béroul's version but which ends when Tristran returns Isolt to Mark and goes off to win fame as a knight, with no further meeting of the lovers and no account of their tragic deaths. In an essay accompanying the poem, Newell explains that he believed the original story ended with the final separation of the lovers, either because it was unfinished or because it was episodic and deliberately did not take the story to the conclusion that it has in later versions (94).

Tristram (1927) won for Edwin Arlington Robinson (1869–1935) the Pulitzer Prize. In the poem, Robinson rejects the traditional endings of the story. Although, like Matthew Arnold's 'Tristram and Iseult', *Tristram* opens with a view of Isolt of Brittany, it is not she who brings about Tristram's death by lying about the colour of the sail (a device Robinson shuns). In fact, although Robinson's poem ends as it begins, with Isolt of Brittany looking out to sea, she seems too resigned to her fate. Clutching melodramatically an agate that Tristram had given her years before, an agate that is worth more to her than a fleet of ships with a 'golden cargo' (209), she muses that 'He had been all, | And would be always all there was for her'; and although 'he had not come back to her alive', she believes 'It was like that | For women, sometimes' (209). Having little of the passion needed for great tragedy, Isolt of Brittany becomes at best a pathetic figure who does not even elicit the sympathy that her counterpart in Arnold's poem does.

Nor does Robinson allow Mark's jealousy to be the cause of Tristram's death, as happens in Malory's *Morte d'Arthur*, which is the major source of Robinson's poem. Robinson's Mark appears to be of a villainous and passionate enough nature to do the deed: he is arrested and imprisoned for forging the pope's name on a document instructing Tristram to go 'to fight the Saracens | And by safe inference to find a grave' (107), a device that seems as 'clumsy beyond credence' in the plot as Gawain claims it to be (108). Nevertheless, the imprisonment removes Mark long enough for Tristram and his beloved Isolt of Ireland to enjoy an Edenic retreat at Joyous Gard. As soon as Mark is free—with no explanation of how or why he is freed—he sends his men in a small boat to capture Isolt as she walks on the coast near Lancelot's castle and to carry her off to Cornwall. Once he has her, he experiences a sudden and unexplained change of heart, shows Isolt kindness, and even allows her to see Tristram.

Tristram is prompted to travel to Cornwall by a letter he receives from Morgan (who is not called 'le Fay' because of the general demystification of the story that Robinson intends). The letter urges him to go to Isolt of Ireland, who is 'alone and sore bestead' (174); but when he arrives, he is killed by *Andred. Mark wonders 'How much there was of Morgan in this last | Unhappy work of Andred's' (199), and it is clear from her letter to Tristram that she has plotted his death. A minor figure in the poem, Andred is compared to a 'reptile', a 'lizard', and a 'serpent' (60, 63, 81). Earlier, he had his skull cracked against the castle wall by Tristram, on whom he had been spying. That incident presumably provides Andred's motivation for slaying Tristram. But the roles of Morgan and Andred seem removed from the love triangle that is central to the action of the poem. For Robinson, the tragic force is not the great love between Tristram and Isolt; in fact, that love is diminished all the more by Andred's 'worse than insane love' for Isolt (179).

Even granting that it is meant to be dramatic rather than narrative, *Tristram* suffers from excessive use of dialogue. There are, to be sure, moments of lyric beauty in the poem. The sea and things related to the sea, such as seabirds and ships, provide a pattern of imagery that Robinson skilfully uses as a unifying device. Many of the dramatic moments, such as Isolt of Brittany's looking to the ocean and Isolt of Ireland's abduction on the shore, are set near the sea; some of the finest metaphors and similes relate to the sea; and the 'changefulness and irrationality' of the medieval versions of the legend 'are at every turn symbolized by the sea—unpredictable, uncontrollable, calm or frenzied on its surface, mysterious in its depths' (Barnard 86). Therefore, even though *Tristram* has some serious flaws, it also contains a good deal of powerful and evocative imagery and dramatic confrontation, along with some of the mystery and intensity of the original stories.

Like Robinson, British poet Florence M. Pomeroy wrote a book-length version of the Tristan story. In her *Tristan and Iseult* (1958), subtitled *An Epic Poem in Twelve Books*, she sees Tristan as an epic hero and claims that treating the romance as an epic will result in a 'fuller and less remote' narration 'than excerpting dramatisations and *a fortiori* Wagnerian music-drama' (11–12). Yet the twelve books comprise little more than a recounting of the various episodes of the romance. Pomeroy's epic similes, often comparisons between events in the story and classical myths, and her allusions to classical figures and stories seem strange and sometimes inappropriate. Calling the giant Urgan a 'Cambrian Polypheme' and saying his den was 'like the Cyclops' cave' (175) adds little to the scene in which Tristan slays him in a contest. And little in the narrative distinguishes Tristan from the traditional romance hero.

In their retellings, two earlier British poets abbreviate the story in order to emphasize the emotions it embodies. *Tristram and Iseult* (1930) by Ernest Reynolds (b. 1910) is, as the author says in a note to the poem, 'pictorial poetry' and not a narrative. He acknowledges Wagner as a source for the sequence of events, but Reynold's poem assumes the story rather than tells it; and his highly imagistic verse uses recurring motifs, especially images of flowers, birds, and music, to convey mood and feeling. Frank Kendon's *Tristram* (1934) focuses on the places of the legend in its nine parts. These parts, which follow but abbreviate the events of the traditional story, are interspersed with lyric poems that further emphasize the emotions evoked by the narrative.

In contrast to those poems that attempt to retell the entire story are those based on a single episode or event from the legend. Grace Constant Lounsbery, for example, captures a moment of love between Tristram and Iseult in 'An Iseult Idyll' (1901), which describes the instant when the lovers first utter each other's names after drinking the love potion. Iseult's whispered 'Tristram', in reply to his 'Iseult', is followed only by 'the sea's reverberate monotone, | With Love's own voice in unison'. This interplay of soft sounds and silence ends the poem on exactly the right note of awe. But what is most interesting is that Lounsbery—as her title suggests—highlights Iseult's moment of awareness and not Tristram's. In 'At Tintagil' (1926), Sara Teasdale (1884–1933) depicts the loneliness and sadness of Iseult and yet concludes that 'with no woman born would you have changed your lot', even with queens who had more happiness (20). Joseph Auslander's (1897–1970) sonnet 'Yseult' (1924) describes the beauty, love, and lasting sorrow of Yseult. In her brief poem 'Iseult of Brittany' (1931), Dorothy Parker (1893–1967) portrays a character more neglected than her namesake from Ireland. Known as Iseult of the White Hands, Iseult of Brittany sees 'a bitterness' in her hands, the physical feature that 'might have been my pride' but which are 'Too frail to cup a heart within, | Too soft to hold the free' (39). Although Parker uses the word 'cup' as a verb and not as a noun, she nevertheless evokes the image of the inevitable drinking of the love potion by Tristram and Iseult of Ireland; and she heightens the reader's awareness of the sadness that Iseult of Brittany's white hands, emblematic of her failure to 'cup [Tristan's] heart within', represent to her. British poet Cyril Emra also focuses on the love potion in 'The Love-Song of Tristram and Iseult' (1905). On the ship, with everyone but the lovers lulled into sleep by Tristram's music, Iseult deliberately shares with Tristram the drink that shackles him with the 'fetters of a fate | He might not guide nor shun' (23). American poet William Alexander Percy (1885–1942), a cousin of novelist Walker Percy (author of the novel *Lancelot*), also writes about the drinking of the love potion, from the perspective of a bird flying over the ship on which the lovers sail to Cornwall, in 'The Green Bird Seeth Iseult' (1924).

In 'Tristram's Journey' (1937, originally published in *Six Poems* as 'Tristram Crazed' (1932)), Edwin Muir (1887–1959) tells of the madness of Tristram that results from his thinking that Isolt no longer loves him. John Masefield (1878–1967) also describes Tristan's madness in 'Tristan's Singing' (1931). When he and Isolt quarrel and she returns to Marc, Tristan runs off mad to the forest where he learns from nature wisdom that he puts into song. The process cures him of his madness; and his song reunites him with Isolt. In Masefield's 'The Love Gift' (1931), Marc receives as a reward from a forest goddess a quince that grants immortality. He gives it to Isolt, who passes it on to Tristan. But Tristan does not want immortality without Isolt, so they give it to Brangwen, who returns it to Marc. Realizing that Isolt has betrayed him, Marc bestows it upon a boy whose mother is dying. In 'Tristan and Isolt' (1949), Masefield recounts Isolt's feigning of death so that she can avoid marrying Marc and can run off with Tristan.

In 'Tristram's Tomb' (1928), James Ormerod portrays Mark's grief at the death of the lovers. Mark brings their bodies back to Cornwall, where a briar-tree grows from Tristram's tomb to Iseut's, a sign that they are now wed 'in Death's orat'ry' (13). Laurence Binyon (1869–1943) also describes the deaths of the lovers in 'Tristram's End' (1913). Despite his wife's lie about the colour of the sail, Tristram lives to see Isoult and realizes that, by being true to his word to bring her to Mark as a bride, he 'Yielded my life to a lie, | To save the truth of a word' (18). Both Isoult of Brittany and Mark are left to live alone, while Tristram and Isoult are joined in death.

American poet Edith Tatum (1877–1955) looks to the beginning rather than the end of the tragic love in *The Awakening of Iseult* (1933). She tells of Tristram's journey to Ireland to be cured after he has slain Marhaus. There he and Iseult, who nurses him, fall in love. Annoyed by the attention of Palamides, Iseult has promised her hand to the one who can defeat him in a tournament. When Tristram defeats Palamides, she is surprised that he does not ask to marry her—until she learns that he is the slayer of Marhaus. He vows to return for her, but as he leaves, Iseult hears 'the echo of a closing door' (44), a symbol of the loss of the opportunity for the lovers to wed and live happily together.

Some of the most interesting verse based on the Tristan legend is found in sequences of poems. British poet and dramatist Henry Reed (1914–1986) devotes one poem to each of the four major characters of the legend in his 'Tintagel' sequence (1946). The poems suggest that the pattern of the tale is often repeated, the story of the lovers is 'perpetually recurring', and Iseult is 'eternally-reappearing' (55, 61). Reed's poems also comment on the nature of love. When Mark finds the lovers with the sword between them, the narrator observes that no sword can part them and says that Mark has 'fallen upon a grotto of sudden light | And it is so bright you cannot call it darkness' (60). Another British poet, Ken Smith (b. 1938), in his ten-poem sequence *Tristan Crazy* (1978), alludes to traditional events and motifs, such as Mark's turning Isolde over to the lepers, Tristan's harping, and the black and white sails; but the poems are more lyric than narrative and nicely convey both the maddening sorrow and the beauty of love. Another British poet, Edward Lucie-Smith, includes the sequence 'Fragments of a "Tristan" ' in 'Adam and Tristan', a section of his book *Towards Silence* (1968). The four poems of the sequence conclude with 'Tristan's Madness', in which Tristan comes disguised as a madman to Mark's court, his disguise symbolizing the madness of love. The sequence is followed by a poem called 'Adam and Tristan', which suggests that the 'voice of legend' 'echoes' and 'repeats itself' throughout the ages (12).

The sequence 'Tristan & Isoldes' (1968) by Australian poet Norman Talbot merges modern characters with the medieval legend to imply that ancient patterns of love, tragedy, and strife recur from age to age. To suggest the eternal nature of the story, the poet has Tristan and Isolde drink the love potion on an ocean liner and notes that one of the poems is 'Written while the Americans are invading Viet Nam' (51). Another sequence by Talbot, 'Tristan in the Distance' (1971), speaks of the medieval characters in poems devoted to the healing of Tristan, the love triangle, and Isolde's jealousy. In the third of three poems on her jealousy, Isolde says of her rival, 'I like to think of her dead | —or almost' (42).

'Iseult, We Are Barren' (1987), a sequence of soliloquies by Canadian poet Maria Jacobs, captures the sometimes ambivalent feelings of Mark, Iseult, and Tristan. Mark, for example, decrees that Tristan be put to death and Iseult be given to the lepers, but hopes that they may 'save themselves' (60). And Iseult wishes her love for Tristan were not so consuming that it prevented her from enjoying other things. She concludes a series of images suggesting that her senses can detect nothing else by saying, 'your face etched | on my retina leaves me blind' (53). The short lyric poems use allusions to the traditional story to give a sense of character as well as emotion. When the dwarf Frocin reveals to Mark 'the hateful truth | that is a lie', Tristan realizes that he and Iseult will have only as much time for their affair as it takes 'a giant to grow | into a dwarf' (54), that is, for Mark to become petty and mean-spirited because of their betrayal of him.

In a sequence of poems called *Tristram's Book*, another Canadian, Brian Fawcett, merges the voice of the poet with that of Tristram; and the love of Tristram for Isolde becomes a means of exploring the poet's own love. Fawcett uses elements of the Tristan legend borrowed from Malory, Gottfried, and the film *L'Éternel Retour* as well as images from the modern world to suggest 'the tension between sexual passion and public duty' (3), which he sees as the essence of the story.

American poet David Mus (b. 1936) focuses his four-poem sequence 'Before the Hill' on Marie de France's *Chèvrefeuille*, which is retold in the second poem. In the first poem, 'Hillside', the image of a hill, a tree, and a forest allows the poet to 'enter the past' through 'an effort of the imagination' (81). This leads, in the poem 'Terrain', to the poetic experience of 'High love, which we have no words for, | but images, images of' (95). The image central to Marie's poem becomes 'the ground-work of a tale' (101). 'Tree', the final poem of the sequence, suggests the multiplicity of meanings a tree can evoke and therefore the multiplicity of tales it could inspire.

TRISTAN AND ISOLT IN FICTION

The many retellings of the Tristan legend in fiction include historical and romantic novels set in the Middle Ages as well as reworkings of the story in a modern setting. Authors draw on early romances and on Malory's *Morte d'Arthur* to create quite a variety in a story whose outlines and ending are determined by the authority of the traditional tales. A surprising number of these retellings are by women, whose narratives often create interesting portrayals of the two Isolts and Brangwain and even depict the ill-fated love from the perspectives of the female characters.

Though Sir Tristram is barely mentioned in *The Clutch of Circumstance* (1908) by Dorothy Senior (b. 1884), the novel transfers many of the motifs of the Tristan story to other, non-Arthurian characters. Sir Arnold of Abblasoure fights and kills the champion of the Irish king Cormac, leaving a piece of his sword in the knight's skull. In Ireland, where he goes to be cured of the wound he received from his opponent's poisoned sword, Arnold falls in love with Finola, Cormac's daughter; but his identity is revealed by the notch in his sword. A Saracen knight, Sir Persides, also loves Finola and intends to punish Arnold but is unable to defeat him. Arnold must then win Finola's hand for his wicked uncle Baradine, who recognizes the love between them, imprisons Arnold, and sends Finola to a community of lepers. Arnold escapes by leaping from a window down a rocky cliff. Clearly, Senior rewrites the Tristan story while changing the names of the principal characters. Perhaps her desire for the joyous reunion and marriage of the lovers and the death of Baradine prevented her from calling her main characters Tristan, Isolt, and Mark.

Other modern authors have retold the story of the tragic lovers in various ways in novels and short fiction. Maurice Baring, author of the play *Tristram and Iseult* (discussed above), wrote a short prose piece called 'From the Diary of Iseult of Brittany' (1913), which purports to be a series of entries from the scatterbrained Iseult of Brittany's diary during the time of Tristram's visit. The diary recounts her engagement to him less than a week after they meet; their marriage a few days later; Tristram's almost immediate departure for a tournament, at which he is wounded; and her own announcement to Tristram that the sail on the ship bearing the Queen of Cornwall for a visit is black (not out of malice, but because Tristram asked if it was black and the doctors had told her to humour him). The last entry announces that the Queen of Cornwall has arrived and that Tristram is unconscious and closes with: 'Too busy to write' (20). The matter-of-fact tone of the diary and the mundane details intentionally take much of the romance out of the legend.

A similarly whimsical short piece is 'Mark vs. Tristram', a series of letters written by C. S. Lewis (1898–1963) and Owen Barfield (1898–1997) purporting to be an exchange of correspondence between the lawyers of Mark and Tristram. These letters, written in 1947 but first published in 1967, began when Barfield, reacting to a line in Lewis's critical writing, wrote a letter from Mark's solicitors announcing Mark's intention to divorce his wife and putting Tristan on notice that they are considering legal action against him. They ask to be notified if Tristan has a proposal for compensating Mark for the wrongs done to him. A response, written by Lewis as if from the firm of '*Blaise & Merlin', suggests that two witnesses, Gouvernail and Brangwen, will testify that there was no misconduct. Further letters by Barfield are full of legal jargon; Lewis replies with a letter from 'Maistre Bleyse' written in pseudo-Middle English.

A more realistic novel about Tristan and Isolt is *Tristan* (1940) by British author Hannah Closs (1905–53), who rationalizes some of the traditional events of the story. For example, there is no love potion; but when Tristan and Iseult are on the ship to Cornwall, the beginning of their love is marked by a moment in which Iseult 'caught the spray in her hands and held them up, cupped and translucent in the tremulous air—like some holy chalice shining with its own light' (185). Closs describes Tristan's youth, including his imagination, his 'ungovernable passions' (48), and his desire for revenge against Morgan, the slayer of his father Rivalin. Throughout the novel, Closs also presents the thoughts of the main characters, particularly Tristan and Iseult, about their situation. Through this device, Tristan's internal struggle becomes more important than the battles he fights.

A later work, *Drustan the Wanderer* (1971) by British author Anna Taylor (b. 1944), strives for the realism of a historical novel by drawing on the early sources of the legend and 'archaeological evidence' (p. vi). Taylor retains features such as the love potion made by Iseult's mother, who was trained in Druid lore, and incorporates Arthurian elements such as the figure of Myrddin and the death of Arthur in battle against Modred into her story. After Drustan and Essylt live together in the forest, he returns her to Mark and then wanders the earth before marrying Essylt of Armorica. He is finally reunited with Essylt of Ireland just before his death.

More common than realistic approaches to the legend are romantic ones. Ruth Collier Sharpe's *Tristram of Lyonesse* (1949) incorporates elements from popular romance into her strange, sometimes anachronistic retelling. So intent are some of the characters on acting properly that Morholt allows himself to be struck by Tristan so that Cornwall will be free. And Tristan, who is challenged to a duel by Sir Gerald, the man who loves Ysolt of Brittany and who has discovered that she loves Tristan, forgoes the chance to slay his challenger and in the process is wounded with a poisoned sword. Tristan does not, however, die before the arrival of Ysolt of Ireland, to whom he has been legally married.

The Enchanted Cup (1953) by Dorothy James Roberts (1903–90) is a better novel than Sharpe's. Basing her story largely on Malory, Roberts nevertheless creates original characters. Yseut of Brittany loves Tristan from her childhood, when he was raised at the court of her father Hoël, and becomes jealous after her marriage to Tristan when she discovers that his love for Isoud of Ireland has not died. Isoud, a strong-willed woman who deliberately drinks the love potion with Tristan, is unwavering in her love and her courage in following her heart. When Mark, who is ruined by his jealousy, kills Tristan as he harps and sings for Isoud, she laments her lover and then 'stretched herself beside him and died as he died' (368). Roberts also makes Palomides an intriguing figure whose love for Isoud drives him to mad, unchivalrous acts even as he strives to be a knight worthy of her. Tristan himself is sometimes torn between his duty and his love, but his love always triumphs. Roberts's ability to create interesting characters is seen even in minor figures like Meliodas, who has little fatherly love for Tristan, and Dinadan, who, as in the medieval sources, is not eager to engage in knightly activities but who is bravely loyal to Tristan.

Other women novelists place even more emphasis on the women of the story. In *Iseult: Dreams That Are Done* (1985), Dee Morrison Meaney filters the events of the legend through Iseult's perception. Many of Tristan's traditional exploits are related to Iseult so that the focus of the novel is on her reaction to the deeds rather than on the deeds themselves. Diana L. Paxson's novel *The White Raven* (1988) is told by Branwen, whose name means 'white raven'. Branwen's experiences, rather than those of Drustan and Esseilte, are central to Paxson's story. Not only does Branwen take Esseilte's place on her wedding night, but she falls in love with Marc'h (Mark) and feels the responsibility of a queen to protect him and the land. Her loyalties are divided between Marc'h and Esseilte; and her struggle to be true to both of them forms the major conflict of the book. *The Lovers: The Legend of Trystan and Yseult* (1999) by Kate Hawks (pseudonym of Parke Godwin) is narrated by a male character, Gareth mac Diarmuid, an Irishman who, because of a curse put upon him, is sent from his homeland to serve Trystan in Cornwall. Gareth's skill with horses eventually allows him to become one of Arthur's trusted companions. Trystan, whose love for Yseult causes him to drink and become foolish and even violent, is banished and marries Isolt of the White Hands. He sends for Gareth to help him train troops, and, although Gareth falls in love with Isolt, he remains true to his wife of many years. When Trystan is fatally wounded and sends for Yseult, she arrives before he dies despite his wife's lie about the colour of the sail on the ship bearing her. Yseult lives on after Trystan's death; and Gareth, having returned to his former life, is troubled when he hears a harper romanticize the story by having Yseult die with Trystan. In her Tristan and Isolde Novels as in her Guenevere Novels, Rosalind Miles gives prominence to the legend's women. Isolde of Ireland is the central character in *Isolde, Queen of the Western Isle* (2002), and Isolde of the White Hands in *The Maid of the White Hands* (2003). *The Lady of the Sea* (2004), which concludes the trilogy, again features Isolde of Ireland.

A very different approach is taken by British novelist Paul Griffiths in *The Lay of Sir Tristram* (1991). His postmodern reworking of the Tristan story displays a consciousness of the multiple versions of the narrative, many of which are referred to specifically, and suggests multiple possibilities for development of parts of the story based on those multiple versions. Griffiths treats most of the standard motifs, including Tristram's fight with Marhalt, the love philtre, Mark's observation of the lovers from the tree, the wicked dwarf Frocin, and the two Isolts, as he creates a story recognizing and reflecting that the medieval tale is one of 'inversion in inversion' and, like the hall of mirrors referred to in the novel, 'reflections of reflections of reflections' (19, 103). This multiplication of narratives is demonstrated by the fact that in *The Lay of Sir Tristram*, the tale of the medieval lovers is reflected in the story of Richard Wagner composing an opera about them and of the narrator re-enacting elements of the story in his own love life.

The universal appeal of the tragic love of Tristan and Isolt is confirmed by the number of novelists from various countries who have reworked the story in a modern setting. In his novella *Tristan* (1903), Thomas Mann (1875–1955) tells of a writer named Spinell who forms a romantic image of Gabriele Klöterjahn, a married woman and a fellow patient in a sanatorium. After she plays music from Wagner's *Tristan und Isolde*, Spinell is moved to write a letter to her husband telling of his vision of her and his contempt for him. Herr Klöterjahn responds with a tirade against Spinell, which is interrupted by a report that Gabriele is coughing up blood. Spinell does not rush to her but rather goes for a stroll during which he encounters the Klöterjahns' son, who laughs at him. Spinell can only walk off like a man who is 'trying to hide the fact that he is mentally running away' (149). None of the characters has the passion or the tragic grandeur of the legend to which the tale alludes.

Polish novelist Maria Kuncewicz (1899–1989) translates the legendary characters to post-war Europe and America in *Tristan 1946* (1967; translated into English as *Tristan* in 1974). Michael Gaszynski, who fought against the Nazis during the war and even refers to a Nazi as the dragon he slew, is the Tristan figure in the novel; and Kathleen McDougall, a beautiful Irishwoman who works as a model and an actress, is his Yseult. Despite her marriage to someone else, they engage in a passionate affair; but when Michael goes to America, he marries an American woman whose hands are 'very white' (239) and who, like Yseult of the White Hands, lies about a message involving black and white—here, words sent in a cable rather than the colours of sails. Michael and Kathleen do not die, however, as a result of the misrepresentation. She arrives to find him still alive; but 'something had come to an end which had been expected to last forever' (262). The passion has gone from their love and thus the novel lacks the truly tragic ending of so many of the versions of the Tristan story.

Sir Arthur Quiller-Couch (1863–1944) left the novel *Castle Dor* unfinished. Completed in 1961 by Daphne du Maurier (1907–1989), it presents characters who act out the ancient tragedy in nineteenth-century Cornwall. A Breton peasant named Amyot Trestane comes to Cornwall and falls in love with Linnet, the wife of Mark Lewarne. Some of the characters in the novel are conscious that the earlier tragedy is being re-enacted by Linnet and Amyot and make specific references to versions of the tale. Elements of the medieval stories, such as the love potion, the dog 'Pettigrew', the equivocal oath, Tristan's disguise, Tristan's leap, the wounding with a poisoned weapon, the jealousy of the second Isolt (represented here by a young girl named Mary) and her lie about the black sail are worked skilfully into the nineteenth-century setting.

Using Gottfried von Strassburg's *Tristan* and Thomas's *Tristran* as her primary sources, British novelist Jean MacVean also retells the story of the tragic love in a modern setting in *The Intermediaries* (1965). When Mark marries Isobel, his nephew Charles falls in love with her; and Mark discovers that they are lovers. Charles leaves and, after marrying another woman named Isobel, is mortally wounded in

Hungary on a secret mission for the British government. The first Isobel, who arrives too late to see Charles before his death, kills herself. The novel explores the psychology of the characters but condenses the events after Charles's departure into a series of short letters.

One of several American novelists who incorporated aspects of the Tristan legend into their work was Mary Ellen Chase (1887–1973). In *Dawn in Lyonesse* (1938), Chase's protagonist Ellen Pascoe, a poor Cornishwoman, reads the story of Tristan and Iseult. When her fiancé Derek kills himself after an affair with her best friend Susan, Ellen's understanding of that story transforms her so that she forgives Susan and takes joy in the fact that she (Ellen) and Derek were happy 'for even a little' (111).

Joyce Carol Oates (writing under the pseudonym Rosamond Smith) also uses elements of the Tristan story in *You Can't Catch Me* (1995), a tale of serial murder and betrayal. Tristram Heade falls in love with a woman named Fleur, whose two personalities may reflect the two Isolts. Tristram, who is confused with and takes on the personality of a man named Markham, is ultimately betrayed by Fleur, whom he sees at an opening of Wagner's *Tristan* with her lover. Therefore, Tristram becomes a Mark figure, as the name of his alternative persona implies. The revelation that Tristram/Markham is a serial killer suggests how far the characters and themes of the book depart from the traditional story.

An equally unusual use of the legend is found in John Updike's story 'Tristan and Iseult' (1994), in which Tristan is a dental patient and Iseult is his new hygienist. The patient's immediate recognition of the hygienist as 'a rare one, one he could trust not to hurt him more than necessary' (148), lampoons the romantic notion of instant, undying love. The threat of pain that adds 'mystical spice to these liaisons' (148) heightens the intimacy of their encounter. Like a courtly lover, 'Tristan' dares not glance directly at the eyes of 'Iseult' but rather gathers their 'spiritual, starlike afterimage' (150) in her safety goggles. Once Tristan's teeth have been cleaned and polished, the relationship changes: 'without the threat of pain, their encounter became small' (152). Iseult, however, recommends an additional procedure, a bleaching process to retard staining. Tristan believes that this is her way of trying to extend their encounter; yet he is aware that she will not be witness to the shining result. Since she is a stranger to him and since he knows it is unlikely that he will find himself in her chair again, Tristan concludes that this 'principle lay between them like a sword. Otherwise, it wouldn't be sublime' (153).

Updike first reworked the Tristan legend in an epistolary short story, 'Four Sides of One Story', originally published in the *New Yorker* and collected in *The Music School* (1966). As the title indicates, the story consists of four letters, one from each of the protagonists of the tale: Tristan, the two Iseults, and Mark. The first and longest letter, from Tristan, is addressed to his beloved, Iseult the Fair. To escape his obsession with her and to avoid the divorce suit her husband has initiated, Tristan has booked passage on an ocean liner to some unknown destination; from on board, he attempts to rationalize his conduct. Tristan's wife, Iseult of the White Hands, apparently possesses a sensibility as modern as her husband's. In her letter to her brother Kaherdin, she complains about her three bratty children, bemoans her own lack of dignity in Tristan's ongoing affair, and explains her conflicting emotions about the other Iseult. She observes that it was the ordinariness of married life that terrified Tristan the most. Iseult the Fair, on the other hand, has more pressing concerns: a husband who is ready to divorce or commit her. The final letter, 'dictated but not signed' (100), is from King Mark to his retainer Denoalen. The legal proceedings against Tristan and Iseult, Mark advises, should be temporarily halted: 'confronted with the actuality of marriage, the young man bolted even sooner than we had anticipated', leaving Iseult 'accordingly disillusioned and satisfactorily tractable' (99). At the moment, though, the queen is a political asset; should her therapy fail, there is always commitment. Either way, Mark believes that he is 'fully in control of matters at last' (100).

Updike's most extended reworking of the Tristan theme occurs in the novel *Brazil* (1994), for which, he acknowledges in an afterword, Bédier's *The Romance of Tristan and Iseult* 'gave me my tone and basic situation'. Set in Brazil, the novel tells the story of the love of Tristão Raposo, a dark-skinned slum dweller, for Isabel Leme, a light-skinned daughter of wealthy parents. They meet on the beach at Copacabana, where he approaches her with tremendous 'courtliness' (7) and offers her a stolen ring, a gift that instantly binds them as husband and wife. Afterwards, in the nearby apartment of Isabel's affluent Uncle Donaciano, they make love, Isabel's virginal blood leaving on the sheets a chalice-shaped stain as symbolic testament to the sanctity of their union. Both families, however, disapprove of the relationship and force them to take flight and undergo a series of trials and hardships.

As in the best tradition of South American magical realism, which is an obvious influence on Updike's novel, the story at times assumes an almost fairy-tale quality. Isabel journeys for seventeen days to find a shaman, to whom she offers a bejewelled cross stolen from her uncle. He asks instead for the ring with which Tristão had originally pledged his love and then makes clear that 'for every gain, there is a sacrifice, somewhere else' (186). After Isabel agrees 'to change [her]self, to sacrifice', for Tristão, the shaman's magic transforms her from a pale beauty into an ebony-skinned warrior woman, while in a simultaneous transformation, Tristão sheds his handsome blackness for a blond whiteness.

Brazil combines elements of the realistic novel and of South American magical realism with the tone and occasional motifs from medieval romance, such as Tristão and Isabel's ill-fated love at first sight which survives almost overwhelming trials, their sleeping with a sword between them, and occasional references to Tristão as a knight. The novel ends with Tristão's death at the hands of robbers from the slums, young men such as he himself once was. Although Isabel remembers the story of a woman who willed herself to die beside her dead lover, when she lies next to Tristão she does not die because 'the spirit is strong, but blind matter is stronger'. Thus in the end, realism is dominant over the romance and magic in the novel.

TRISTAN AND ISOLT IN FILM

Early in the twentieth century, as the Tristan legend was becoming increasingly popular on the stage, it was also being adapted to the new medium of film. In little more than a decade, three silent films based on the legend were produced in Europe: *Tristan et Yseult* (Pathés Frères, 1909; dir. Albert Capellani), *Tristan et Yseult* (Il Film d'arte Italiana, 1911; dir. Ugo Falena), and *Tristan et Yseut* (Nalpas, 1920; dir. Maurice Mariaud) (cf. Harty 512–13 for further information on these films). Surprisingly, five decades passed before the Tristan story was again adapted to the screen. In 1972, the French film *Tristan et Iseult* (Film du Soir, 1972) was directed by Yvan Lagrange, who produced an experimental cinematic 'opera' using almost no dialogue in order to convey 'impressions of the themes of the myth'. To convey these impressions, Lagrange repeats sequences to create the effect of 'a leit motiv in music' (Selcer 45, 48). He also uses striking, almost outrageous, images such as Iseult wrapped in cellophane or the dead lovers in the final scene lying together 'in a large, bloody beef carcass' with white roses in their mouths (McMunn 214).

Other films, however, take a more conventional approach to the narrative. The Irish film *Lovespell* (also called *Tristan and Isolt*) (Clar Productions, 1979; dir. Tom Donovan), starring Richard Burton as Mark and Nicholas Clay and Kate Mulgrew as the lovers, is as traditional a narrative as Lagrange's film is avant-garde. Yet while *Lovespell* employs such standard motifs as the love potion and the black and white sails, it alters the plot in ways that make Mark a central character (and thus give Richard Burton more screen time). It is Mark who first visits Ireland and meets and befriends Isolt. He then sends Tristan to have healed the wound received from Morholt and to ask Isolt to be his bride. When the lovers are discovered, escape, and are eventually caught by Mark (with a sword between them as they sleep), Tristan is exiled to Brittany, where he is grievously wounded. Isolt too languishes because of her spiritual union with Tristan and wishes to go to him to save his life. Because she is too weak to travel, Mark agrees to bring Tristan to her. As the ship transporting them approaches Cornwall, Tristan tells Mark of the love potion and the unbreakable bond between himself and Isolt. In response to Mark's anger, Tristan leaps into the sea and must be saved from drowning by Mark, who brings him to shore just as Isolt, who has left her sickbed, climbs down a cliff towards him. She falls, and Tristan crawls to her. As the lovers link hands, they die.

Feuer und Schwert (*Fire and Sword*) (Genée and von Fürstenberg Filmproduktion, 1981; dir. Veith von Fürstenberg), a German film, also presents a narrative built around motifs from medieval romance, from Tristan's encounter with Morholt to the deaths of the lovers. It includes the love potion, Tristan's leap, Isolde's ordeal, the handing over of Isolde to the lepers, the white and black sails, the second Isolde (not the daughter of a nobleman but a peasant woman whom Tristan rescues), and the death of Isolde when she arrives too late to save Tristan. It even offers an account of the fates of Tristan's parents Rivalin and Blanchefleur, though this is narrated and not enacted. But the film departs from the traditional story in a number of ways. When Tristan first arrives in Ireland, Isolde is working in a convent and therefore seems merely a woman with the same name as the princess whose hand Mark has sent Tristan to request; and Isolde returns to Mark because civil war has broken out when Andret rebels against Mark. In the final scene, Governal burns the bodies of the lovers on one pyre, uniting them in death.

The Icelandic *I Skugga Hrafnsina* (*In the Shadow of the Raven*; also called *The Shadow of the Raven*) (Sandrews, 1988; dir. Hrafn Gunnlaugsson) resets the story in Iceland in 1077. A feud between two families begins when they fight over possession of a beached whale. Erikur, the father of Isold, is killed in the feud with the family of the hero Trausti, who is returning from theological studies. Though Isold is promised to the son of the local bishop, she falls in love with Trausti and seals their bond with a love potion. The lovers marry, but the families of Erikur and of the bishop plot to destroy Trausti. As they burn the building in which the lovers are spending their wedding night, Isold is killed but Trausti escapes and eventually avenges her murder. Left with Isold's daughter by another man and inspired by his love of Isold and his training in theology, Trausti advises the young girl to let the 'dream of love become a light in the darkness'. Despite this concluding comment on love and the use of a love potion, Gunnlaugsson's film has a gritty realism and a feel for medieval life that distinguishes it from other versions of the Tristan story.

Other films reinterpret the legend in a modern setting. The best of these is *L'Éternel Retour* (*The Eternal Return*) (Discina International, 1943; dir. Jean Delannoy), the screenplay for which was written by Jean Cocteau (1889–1963). Made in occupied France, the film's glorification of the blond Patrice (Jean Marais) and Nathalie (Madeleine Solonge) and the cruelty and pettiness of the dwarf Achille (Piéral) and his dark-haired relatives have overtones of the sort of racial stereotyping that would have appealed to the Nazi occupiers. Nevertheless, these characteristics also function as visual symbols of both the link between Patrice and Nathalie and their difference from everyone else in the film.

Cocteau's title emphasizes the film's dependence on the Tristan story by suggesting that some legends recur throughout time. Patrice, the Tristan figure in the film, sets out to find a wife for his uncle. On an island, he encounters the beautiful Nathalie, who is being humiliated by the drunken Morholt. After receiving a knife wound in the ensuing fight, Patrice is healed by Nathalie and her foster-mother Anne, a Brangwen figure, and asks Nathalie to return with him as a bride for his uncle. Anne prepares a love potion, labelled 'poison' so no one but Marc and Nathalie will drink it. The dwarf Achille, the evil son of Marc's sister Gertrude Frossin, uses the potion to try to poison the lovers but succeeds only in making their love irresistible. However, as in Wagner's opera, love and death are inextricably linked and the potion is, in the end, the cause of their deaths.

In addition to the potion and the wicked dwarf, Cocteau borrows other motifs from the traditional legend. As Tristan does in *Tristan rossignol*, Patrice uses bird calls to signal his beloved. When Patrice and Nathalie are meeting by a stream, he sees the reflection of a spying Marc, signals Nathalie, and initiates a conversation designed to suggest their innocence. The lovers are discovered, however, when Marc feigns a trip but returns that same night. Rescued by Patrice, Nathalie joins him in an idyllic existence in a cottage until Marc finds them and forces her to return to his home.

To earn money, Patrice must work in a garage. There, he meets another Nathalie, the sister of the owner, Lionel. Patrice and Nathalie plan to marry on the island where he met his true love, but the wedding never takes place because the second Nathalie, like Isolt of Brittany in the traditional story, realizes that he does not love her. When Patrice returns to see his beloved Nathalie one last time, Achille shoots him. After making his way back to the island, Patrice asks Lionel to bring his love to him. As the boat returns, the second Nathalie tells Patrice that it flies its red pennant and not the white scarf that was to signal that Lionel was successful; so he dies, just before the Nathalie he loves makes her way to him. As she expires on his deathbed, the final image of the two lovers joined in death with light streaming into the boathouse where they lie together suggests the tragic transcendence of their love.

Another French film, *La Femme d'à côté* (*The Woman Next Door*) (Les Films di Carrosse-TFI/UA, 1981; dir. François Truffaut), is considered by some (though not all) critics a modern version of the Tristan story. Truffaut's film, an account of an irresistible attraction between Bernard and Mathilde, both of whom are now married to others, has little to link it to the legend except the tragic love and the final comments of Madame Jouve, who says that they are not likely to be buried together and that the epitaph she would choose for them is 'Neither with you nor without you'. That line loosely and pessimistically echoes one found in Marie de France's *Chèvrefeuille*: 'Ne vus sanz mei, ne mei sanz vus' (Neither you without me nor me without you).

A clearer use of the legend occurs in *Tristana* (Epoca Film, 1970; dir. Luis Buñuel), a film based on the novel *Tristana* (1892) by Spanish novelist Benito Pérez Galdós (1843–1920), which 'contains numerous elements that recall the Tristan legend, yet always in a way that is somehow twisted: inverted, subverted, even perverted' (Grimbert 110). The most interesting example of this subversion of the legend is found in the fact that the heroine functions at different times as both the Isolt and the Tristan figure. It is she who has an aptitude for music and she who is 'wounded' and in need of the love more than the care of her lover Horacio, who visits her only after her leg is amputated and who provides little help in her healing. Buñuel's cinematic adaptation maintains the motifs of music and the wound that make Tristana like the Tristan of legend but also emphasizes her resentment of her husband Don Lope. In a final scene that departs from the legend and from the novel that is the film's source, she fails to call a doctor when her husband has a heart attack, thus ensuring his death.

BIBLIOGRAPHY

Tristan in Welsh Literature

Bromwich, Rachel. 'The "'Tristan"' Poem in the Black Book of Carmarthen', *Studia Celtica*, 14/15 (1979/80), 54–65.

Radford, C. A. Ralegh. 'Romance and Reality in Cornwall', in Geoffrey Ashe et al., *The Quest for Arthur's Britain*. 1968; repr. St Albans: Paladin, 1976: 59–77.

Thomas. *Tristran*, ed. and trans. Stewart Gregory, in Norris J. Lacy (ed.), *Early French Tristan Poems*, vol. ii. Cambridge: D. S. Brewer, 1998: 1–172.

Trioedd ynys Prydein: The Welsh Triads, ed. Rachel Bromwich. Cardiff: University of Wales Press, 1978.

The Welsh Fragment of Tristan (Trystan ac Esyllt), trans. R. L. Thomson, in Joyce Hill (ed.), *The Tristan Legend: Texts from Northern and Eastern Europe in Modern English Translation*. Leeds: The University of Leeds Graduate Centre for Medieval Studies, 1977: 1–5.

The Common and Courtly Versions of the Tristan Story

Béroul. *Tristran*, ed. and trans. Norris J. Lacy, in Norris J. Lacy (ed.), *Early French Tristan Poems*, vol. i. Cambridge: D. S. Brewer, 1998: 1–216.

Chinca, Mark. 'Tristran Narratives from the High to the Late Middle Ages', in W. H. Jackson and S. A. Ranawake (eds.), *The Arthur of the Germans: The Arthurian Legend in Medieval German and Dutch Literature*. Cardiff: University of Wales, 2000: 117–34.

Eilhart von Oberg[e]. *Tristrant: Édition diplomatique des manuscrits et traduction en Français moderne*, ed. Danielle Buschinger. Göppingen: Kümmerle, 1976.

—— *Tristrant*, trans. J. W. Thomas. Lincoln: University of Nebraska, 1978.

Les Folies Tristan [La Folie Tristan (Berne) and *La Folie Tristan* (Oxford)], ed. and trans. Samuel N. Rosenberg, in Norris J. Lacy (ed.), *Early French Tristan Poems*, vol. i. Cambridge: D. S. Brewer, 1998: 217–315.

Geitarlauf, in *Strengleikar: An Old Norse Translation of Twenty-One French Lais*, ed. and trans. Robert Cook and Mattias Tveitane. Oslo: Norsk Historisk Kjeldeskrift-Institutt, 1979: 195–9.

Gottfried von Strassburg. *Tristan*, ed. Peter Ganz from the edition of Reinhold Bechstein. 2 vols. Wiesbaden: F. A. Brockhaus, 1978.

—— *Tristan. With the Surviving Fragments of the Tristan of Thomas*, trans. A. T. Hatto. Baltimore: Penguin Books, 1967.

Heinrich von Freiberg. *Tristan*, ed. Danielle Buschinger. Göppingen: Kümmerle, 1982.

Kalinke, Marianne E. *King Arthur North-by-Northwest: The Matière de Bretagne in Old Norse-Icelandic Romances*. Copenhagen: C. A. Reitzels, 1981.

Loomis, Roger Sherman. *Illustrations of Medieval Romance on Tiles from Chertsey Abbey*. Urbana: University of Illinois, 1916.

Marie de France. *Chèvrefeuille/The Lay of the Honeysuckle*, ed. and trans. Richard O'Gorman, in Norris J. Lacy (ed.), *Early French Tristan Poems*, vol. ii. Cambridge: D. S. Brewer, 1998: 185–97.

Sachs, Hans. *Tragedia mit 23 Personen von der strengen Lieb Herr Tristrant mit der schönen Königin Isalden*. Greifswald: Reineke-Verlag, 1993.

Saga af Tristan ok Ísodd, ed. Peter Jorgensen, trans. Joyce M. Hill, in Marianne E. Kalinke (ed.), *Norse Romance*, i: *The Tristan Legend*. Arthurian Archives 3. Cambridge: D. S. Brewer, 1999: 241–92.

Sir Tristrem, in Alan Lupack (ed.), *Lancelot of the Laik and Sir Tristrem*. Kalamazoo, Mich.: Medieval Institute Publications for TEAMS, 1994: 143–277.

Thomas. *The Carlisle Fragment of Thomas's Tristran*, ed. and trans. Ian Short, in Norris J. Lacy (ed.), *Early French Tristan Poems*, vol. ii. Cambridge: D. S. Brewer, 1998: 173–83.

—— *Tristran*, ed. and trans. Stewart Gregory, in Norris J. Lacy (ed.), *Early French Tristan Poems*, vol. ii. Cambridge: D. S. Brewer, 1998: 1–172.

'Tistram og Isold' and 'Tistram og Jomfru Isolt', trans. S. A. J. Bradley, in Joyce Hill (ed.), *The Tristan Legend: Texts from Northern and Eastern Europe in Modern English Translation*. Leeds: The University of Leeds Graduate Centre for Medieval Studies, 1977: 144–55.

'Tístrams Táttur', trans. W. B. Lockwood, in Joyce Hill (ed.), *The Tristan Legend: Texts from Northern and Eastern Europe in Modern English Translation*. Leeds: The University of Leeds Graduate Centre for Medieval Studies, 1977: 156–8.

Tristan als Mönch, ed. Betty C. Bushey. Göppingen: Kümmerle, 1974.

Tristan rossignol and *Tristan menestrel*, ed. and trans. Karen Fresco, in Norris J. Lacy (ed.), *Early French Tristan Poems*, vol. ii. Cambridge: D. S. Brewer, 1998: 199–281.

[*Tristram a Izalda*.] *Das altčechisce Tristan-Epos*, ed. Ulrich Bamborschke. 2 vols. Wiesbaden: Otto Harassowitz, 1968, 1969.

Tristrams kvœði, ed. and trans. Robert Cook, in Marianne E. Kalinke (ed.), *Norse Romance*, i: *The Tristan Legend*. Arthurian Archives 3. Cambridge: D. S. Brewer, 1999: 227–39.

Tristrams saga ok Ísöndar, ed. and trans. Peter Jorgensen, in Marianne E. Kalinke (ed.), *Norse Romance*, i: *The Tristan Legend*. Arthurian Archives 3. Cambridge: D. S. Brewer, 1999: 23–226.

Tristrant und Isalde: Prosaroman, ed. Alois Brandstetter. Tübingen: Max Niemeyer, 1966.

Ulrich von Türheim. *Tristan*, ed. Thomas Kerth. Tübingen: Max Niemeyer, 1979.

The Prose Tristan and its Influence

Cantari di Tristano, ed. Giulio Bertoni. Modena: Società Tipografica Modense, 1937.

[*Povest' o Tryshchane (The Romance of Tristan)*.] *The Byelorussian Tristan*, trans. Zora Kipel. New York: Garland, 1988.

[*Prose Tristan*.] *The Romance of Tristan: The Thirteenth-Century Old French 'Prose Tristan'*, trans. Renée L. Curtis. Oxford: Oxford University Press, 1994.

[*Prose Tristan*.] *Le Roman de Tristan en Prose*, ed. Philippe Ménard et al. 9 vols. Geneva: Droz, 1987–97.

[*La Tavola Ritonda*.] *Tristan and the Round Table: A Translation of La Tavola Ritonda*, trans. Anne Shaver. Binghamton, NY: Medieval & Renaissance Texts & Studies, 1983.

La Tavola Ritonda o l'istoria di Tristano, ed. Filippo-Luigi Polidori. 2 vols. Bologna: Gaetano Romagnoli, 1864–5.

Il Tristano panciatichiano, ed. and trans. Gloria Allaire. Arthurian Archives 8. Cambridge: D. S. Brewer, 2002.

Il Tristano riccardiano: Testo critico di E. G. Parodi, ed. Marie-José Heijkant. Parma: Pratiche Editrice, 1991.

[*Tristano Veneto*.] *Il libro di messer Tristano ('Tristano Veneto')*, ed. Aulo Donadello. Venice: Marsilio, 1994.

Palamedes

Arthurian Torso: Containing the Posthumous Fragment of The Figure of Arthur by Charles Williams and a Commentary on the Arthurian Poems of Charles Williams by C. S. Lewis. London: Oxford University Press, 1948.

Asher, Martha. *The Post-Vulgate Quest for the Holy Grail*, in *Lancelot–Grail: The Old French Arthurian Vulgate and Post-Vulgate in Translation*, gen. ed. Norris J. Lacy. 5 vols. New York: Garland, 1993–6: v. 111–289.

Brewer, Derek. *Seatonian Exercises and Other Verses*. London: Unicorn Press, 2000.

Brewer, Elisabeth. 'Women in the Arthurian Poems of Charles Williams', in Brian Horne (ed.), *Charles Williams: A Celebration*. Leominster: Gracewing, 1995: 98–115.

Crowley, Aleister. *The High History of Good Sir Palamedes the Saracen Knight and of his Following of the Questing Beast: Rightly Set Forth in Rime*. London: Wieland & Co., 1912.

Dobson, Austin. 'Palomydes', in *At the Sign of the Lyre*. New York: H. Holt, 1885: 44–5.

Dulin-Mallory, Nina. ' "Seven trewe bataylis for Jesus sake": The Long-Suffering Saracen Palomides', in David R. Blanks and Michael Frassetto (eds.), *Western Views of Islam in Medieval and Early Modern Europe: Perception of Other*. New York: St Martin's, 1999: 165–72.

Erskine, John. *Tristan and Isolde: Restoring Palamede*. Indianapolis: Bobbs-Merrill, 1932.

Gyron le Courtoys c.1501, introd. C. E. Pickford. London: Scolar Press, 1977. (A facsimile of the 1501 edn.)

Heath-Stubbs, John A. *Charles Williams*. Writers and their Work 63. London: Longmans, Green & Co. for The British Council and the National Book League, 1955.

Lynch, Andrew. *Malory's Book of Arms: The Narrative of Combat in Le Morte Darthur*. Cambridge: D. S. Brewer, 1997.

McCarthy, Terence. *An Introduction to Malory*. Cambridge: D. S. Brewer, 1991.

Malory, Sir Thomas. *Works*, ed. Eugène Vinaver, 2nd edn. London: Oxford University Press, 1971.

Meliadus de Leonnoys 1532, introd. C. E. Pickford. London: Scolar Press, 1980. (A facsimile of the 1532 edn.)

Morris, William. 'Palomydes' Quest', in *The Collected Works of William Morris: With Introductions by his Daughter May Morris*, vol. xxiv. London: Longmans Green and Co., 1915: 70–1.

['Ho Presbys Hippotes' ('The Old Knight').] 'A Greek Poem about the Deeds of King Arthur, Tristan, Lancelot, Gawain, Palamedes, and Other Knights of the Round Table', trans. R. H. Martin, in Joyce Hill (ed.), *The Tristan Legend: Texts from Northern and Eastern Europe in Modern English Translation*. Leeds: The University of Leeds Graduate Centre for Medieval Studies, 1977: 41–6.

Prince, Ælian [pseudonym of Francis Carr]. *Of Joyous Gard*. London: E. W. Allen, 1890.

—— *Of Palomide: Famous Knight of King Arthur's Round Table*. London: E. W. Allen, 1890.

Taylor, Beverly, and Brewer, Elisabeth. *The Return of King Arthur: British and American Literature since 1900 [i.e. 1800]*. Cambridge: D. S. Brewer, 1983.

Vinaver, Eugène. 'The Prose *Tristan*', in Roger Sherman Loomis (ed.), *Arthurian Literature in the Middle Ages: A Collaborative History*. Oxford: Clarendon Press, 1959: 339–47.

White, T. H. *The Once and Future King*. New York: Berkley Medallion, 1967.

Williams, Charles. *Arthurian Poets: Charles Williams*, ed. David Llewellyn Dodds. Woodbridge: The Boydell Press, 1991. (Contains *Taliessin through Logres*, originally published in 1938, and *The Region of the Summer Stars*, originally published in 1944, and other published and previously unpublished poems by Williams.)

Tristan and Isolt in the Victorian Age

Arnold, Matthew. 'Tristram and Iseult'. 1852; repr. in Alan Lupack (ed.), *Modern Arthurian Literature: An Anthology of English and American Arthuriana from the Renaissance to the Present*. New York: Garland, 1992: 196–218.

Hervey, Mrs. T. K. *The Feasts of Camelot, with the Tales That Were Told There*. London: Bell and Daldy, 1863.

Sewter, A. Charles. *The Stained Glass of William Morris and his Circle: A Catalogue*. 2 vols. New Haven: Yale University Press for the Paul Mellon Centre for Studies in British Art (London), 1975.

Swinburne, Algernon Charles. *Arthurian Poets: Algernon Charles Swinburne*, ed. James P. Carley. Woodbridge: The Boydell Press, 1990.

—— 'Dedicatory Epistle', in *The Poems of Algernon Charles Swinburne*, vol. i of 6. New York: Harper & Brothers, 1904.

Tennyson, Alfred, Lord. *Idylls of the King and a Selection of Poems*. New York: Signet/New American Library, 1961.

The Wanderer (pseudonym of Elim Henry d'Avigdor). *Sir Tristram's Axe: An Allegorical Fairy Tale*. London: Simpkin, Marshall, Hamilton, Kent, [1892].

Tristan Plays

Anspacher, Louis K. *Tristan and Isolde: A Tragedy*. New York: Brentano's, 1904.

Austin, Martha. *Tristram and Isoult*. Boston: The Poet Lore Co., 1905.

Baring, Maurice. *Tristram and Iseult: A Play in Five Acts*, in *The Collected Poems of Maurice Baring*. London: John Lane, 1911, 89–176.

Bédier, Joseph. *Le Roman de Tristan et Iseut: Renouvelé par Joseph Bédier*. Paris: H. Piazza, 1900.

—— *The Romance of Tristan and Iseult: Drawn from the Best French Sources and Re-told by J. Bédier*, trans. Hilaire Belloc. London: George Allen, 1903.

—— *The Romance of Tristan and Iseult*, trans. Hilaire Belloc, completed by Paul Rosenfield. New York: Pantheon Books, 1945.

—— and Artus, Louis. *Tristan et Iseut: Pièce en trois actes, un prologue et huit tableaux*. Paris: L'Illustration, 1929.

Carr, J. Comyns. *Tristram and Iseult: A Drama in Four Acts*. London: Duckworth and Co., 1906.

Field, Michael (pseudonym of Katherine Harris Bradley and Edith Emma Cooper). *The Tragedy of Pardon*. London: Sidgwick and Jackson, 1911.

Hardt, Ernst. *Tristram the Jester*, trans. John Heard, Jr. Boston: The Gorham Press, 1913.

Hardy, Thomas. *The Famous Tragedy of the Queen of Cornwall at Tintagel in Lyonnesse: A New Version of an Old Story Arranged as a Play for Mummers in One Act Requiring No Theatre or Scenery*. London: Macmillan, 1923.

Hare, Amory (pseudonym of [Mary] Amory Hare Hutchinson). *Tristram and Iseult*. Gaylordsville, Conn.: The Slide Mountain Press, 1930.

Kinross, Martha. *Tristram and Isoult*. London: Macmillan, 1913.

Lee, Thomas Herbert. *The Marriage of Iseult. A Tragedy in Two Scenes*, in *The Marriage of Iseult and Other Plays*. London: Elkin Mathews, 1909: 1–19.

Marquis, Don. *Out of the Sea: A Play in Four Acts*. Garden City, NY: Doubleday, Page and Co., 1927.

Masefield, John. *Tristan and Isolt: A Play in Verse*. London: Macmillan, 1927.

Mitchell, D. M. *Sir Tristram: A Tragedy in Four Acts*. London: Fowler Wright, 1927.

Pilibin, An (pseudonym of John Hackett Pollock). *Tristram and Iseult: A Dramatic Poem*. Dublin: Talbot, 1924.

Saul, George Brandon. *The Fair Eselt: A Play*, in *Hound and Unicorn: Collected Verse, Lyrical, Narrative, and Dramatic*. Philadelphia: The Walton Press, 1969: 217–53.

Symons, Arthur. *Tristan and Iseult: A Play in Four Acts*. London: William Heinemann, 1917.

Todhunter, John. *Isolt of Ireland*, in *Isolt of Ireland: A Legend in a Prologue and Three Acts and The Poison Flower*. London: J. M. Dent, 1927: 1–89.

Treece, Henry. *The Tragedy of Tristram*, in *The Exiles*. London: Faber and Faber, 1952: 13–39.

Trioedd ynys Prydein: The Welsh Triads, 2nd edn., ed. and trans. Rachel Bromwich. Cardiff: University of Wales Press, 1978.

Williams, Antonia R. *Isolt: A New Telling*. London: Published by the Author, [1900].

The Tristan Legend in Twentieth-Century Verse

Auslander, Joseph. 'Yseult', in *Sunrise Trumpets*. New York: Harper & Brothers, 1924: 64.

Barnard, Ellsworth. *Edwin Arlington Robinson: A Critical Study*. New York: Macmillan, 1952.

Binyon, Laurence. 'Tristram's End', in *Odes*. London: Elkin Mathews, 1913: 9–28.

Emra, Cyril. 'The Love-Song of Tristram and Iseult', in *The Love-Song of Tristram and Iseult and Other Poems*. London: Elliot Stock, 1905: 1–23.

Fawcett, Brian. *Tristram's Book*, *Capilano Review*, 19 (1981).

Jacobs, Maria. 'Iseult, We Are Barren', in *Iseult, We Are Barren*. Windsor, Ont.: Netherlandic Press, 1987: 49–70.

Kendon, Frank. *Tristram*. London: J. M. Dent & Sons, 1934.

Lounsbery, G[race] Constant. 'An Iseult Idyll', in *An Iseult Idyll and Other Poems*. London: John Lane, 1901: 1–8.

Lucie-Smith, Edward. 'Fragments of a "Tristan"' and 'Adam and Tristan', in *Towards Silence*. London: Oxford University Press, 1968: 7–11, 12.

Masefield, John. 'The Love Gift', in *Minnie Maylow's Story and Other Tales and Scenes*. London: William Heinemann, 1931: 32–43.

—— 'Tristan and Isolt', in *On the Hill*. London: William Heinemann, 1949: 77–88.

—— 'Tristan's Singing', in *Minnie Maylow's Story and Other Tales and Scenes*. London: William Heinemann, 1931: 44–61.

Muir, Edwin. 'Tristram's Journey', in *Collected Poems*. London: Faber and Faber, 1960: 64–6.

Mus, David. 'Before the Hill', in *Wall to Wall Speaks*. Princeton: Princeton University Press, 1988: 75–107.

Newell, William Wells. *Isolt's Return*. Wayland, Mass.: Hazlebrook, n.d.

Ormerod, James. 'Tristram's Tomb', in *Tristram's Tomb and Other Poems*. London: Elkin Mathews & Marrot, 1928.

Parker, Dorothy. 'Iseult of Brittany', in *Death and Taxes*. New York: Viking, 1931: 39.

Percy, William Alexander. 'The Green Bird Seeth Iseult', in *Enzio's Kingdom and Other Poems*. New Haven: Yale University Press, 1924: 40–1.

Pomeroy, Florence M. *Tristan and Iseult: An Epic Poem in Twelve Books*. London: The Bodley Head, 1958.

Reed, Henry. 'Tintagel', in *A Map of Verona and Other Poems*. New York: Reynal & Hitchcock, 1947: 53–63.

Reynolds, Ernest. *Tristram and Iseult*. Nottingham: John Clough and Son, 1930.

Robinson, Edwin Arlington. *Tristram*. New York: Macmillan, 1927.

Smith, Ken. *Tristan Crazy*. Newcastle upon Tyne: Bloodaxe, 1978.

Talbot, Norman. 'Tristan & Isoldes', in *Poems for a Female Universe*. Sydney: South Head Press, 1968: 45–60.

—— 'Tristan in the Distance', in *Son of a Female Universe*. Sydney: South Head Press, 1971: 33–42.

Tatum, Edith. *The Awakening of Iseult*. Oglethorpe, Ga.: Oglethorpe University Press, 1933.

Teasdale, Sara. 'At Tintagil', in *Dark of the Moon*. New York: Macmillan, 1926: 20.

Tristan and Isolt in Fiction

Baring, Maurice. 'From the Diary of Iseult of Brittany', in *Lost Diaries*. London: Duckworth, 1913: 10–20.

Batts, Michael S. 'Tristan and Isolde in Modern Literature: L'Éternel retour', in Joan Tasker Grimbert (ed.), *Tristan and Isolde: A Casebook*. New York: Garland, 1995: 505–20.

Chase, Mary Ellen. *Dawn in Lyonesse*. New York: Macmillan, 1938.

Closs, Hannah. *Tristan*. London: Andrew Dakers, 1940.

Griffiths, Paul. *The Lay of Sir Tristram*. London: Chatto and Windus, 1991.

Hawks, Kate (pseudonym of Parke Godwin). *The Lovers: The Legend of Trystan and Yseult*. New York: Avon Books, 1999.

Kuncewicz, Maria. *Tristan*. New York: George Braziller, 1974. (English translation of the Polish *Tristan 1946* by Maria Kuncewiczowa.)

Lewis, C. S., and Barfield, Owen. *Mark vs. Tristram: Correspondence between C. S. Lewis & Owen Barfield*, ed. Walter Hooper, ill. Pauline Baynes. 1967; repr. Oxford: Oxford University C. S. Lewis Society, 1990.

MacVean, Jean. *The Intermediaries*. London: Victor Gollancz, 1965.

Mann, Thomas. *Tristan*, in *Death in Venice and Other Tales*, trans. Joachim Neugroschel. New York: Viking, 1998: 103–49.

Meaney, Dee Morrison. *Iseult*. New York: Ace, 1985.

Miles, Rosalind. *Isolde: Queen of the Western Isle*. New York: Crown, 2002.

—— *The Lady of the Sea*. New York: Crown, 2004.

—— *The Maid of the White Hands*. New York: Crown, 2003.

Paxson, Diana L. *The White Raven*. New York: William Morrow, 1988.

Quiller-Couch, Sir Arthur, and du Maurier, Daphne. *Castle Dor*. London: J. M. Dent, 1962.

Roberts, Dorothy James. *The Enchanted Cup*. New York: Appleton-Century-Crofts, 1953.

Sharpe, Ruth Collier. *Tristram of Lyonesse: The Story of an Immortal Love*. New York: Greenberg, 1949.

Senior, Dorothy. *The Clutch of Circumstance or The Gates of Dawn*. London: Adam and Charles Black, 1908.

Smith, Rosamond (pseudonym of Joyce Carol Oates). *You Can't Catch Me*. New York: Dutton, 1995.

Taylor, Anna. *Drustan the Wanderer: A Historical Novel Based on the Legend of Tristan and Isolde*. London: Longman, 1971.

Updike, John. *Brazil*. New York: Alfred A. Knopf, 1994.

—— 'Four Sides of One Story', in *The Music School: Short Stories*. New York: Alfred A. Knopf, 1966: 87–100.

—— 'Tristan and Iseult', in *The Afterlife and Other Stories*. New York: Alfred A. Knopf, 1994: 148–53.

Tristan and Isolt in Film

Grimbert, Joan. 'Galdós's *Tristana* as a Subversion of the Tristan Legend', *Anales Galdosianos*, 27–8 (1992–3), 109–23.

Harty, Kevin J. *The Reel Middle Ages: American, Western and Eastern European, Middle Eastern and Asian Films about Medieval Europe*. Jefferson, NC: McFarland, 1999.

McMunn, Meradith T. 'Filming the Tristan Myth', in Kevin J. Harty (ed.), *Cinema Arthuriana: Twenty Essays*, rev. edn. Jefferson, NC: McFarland, 2002: 211–19.

Pérez Galdós, Benito. *Tristana*. Madrid: Alianza Editorial, 1996.

—— *Tristana*, trans. R. Selden Rose. Peterborough, NH: Richard R. Smith, 1961.

Selcer, Robert W. 'Yvan Lagrange: Impressions of a Filmmaker (Interview)', *Tristania*, 4.2 (May 1979), 44–50.

Afterword

FOR centuries, authors have found ways to adapt the wealth of tales and characters that make up the Arthurian legend to new artistic forms and new cultural concerns: the political, religious, and social issues of the Middle Ages are reflected in many of the chronicles and romances that tell of Arthur; Renaissance historical drama, political prophecy, and romance indicate the concerns of that era with political stability and succession; the eighteenth century's more rational approach is reflected in satire and parody; the uncertainties of the Victorians about faith and doubt are echoed in the best Arthurian poetry of that age; anxiety over war, technology, and a decline of values is apparent in some of the fiction, drama, and film of the twentieth century. Of course such a survey is reductive and overly simplified; nevertheless, it demonstrates that each succeeding age continues to discover innovative ways of interpreting the legend and drawing on its remarkable diversity to comment on contemporary fears and values.

Even in the twenty-first century the Arthurian legend remains vital. A number of trilogies and sequences of novels are in progress, a new film about King Arthur has recently been released, and plays are being produced; and undoubtedly other poems, plays, novels, comic books, illustrated retellings, and films with Arthurian themes are being planned or executed. Perhaps none of these contemporary works is the masterpiece that Geoffrey's chronicle or Chrétien's romances were in the twelfth century, or that the Vulgate Cycle and the *Prose Tristan* were in the thirteenth, or that *Sir Gawain and the Green Knight* was in the fourteenth, or Malory's *Morte d'Arthur* in the fifteenth, or Tennyson's *Idylls of the King* in the nineteenth, or T. H. White's *Once and Future King* in the twentieth century—to name just a few of the highest of high points of Arthurian literature over the years. But even lesser or more popular reworkings of the Arthurian story keep the legend alive until the next great Arthurian work—be it in fiction, drama, poetry, film, art, or music—captures the spirit of the times and embodies it in a significant and lasting form.

The stories of Arthur and the knights and ladies of his court are so enduring because their themes are universal and therefore remain important, even in this century. The essence of the legend involves love and hate; honour and duty; religion and repentance; friendship and betrayal; war and peace; leadership; the relationship between weak and powerful individuals or nations; values and ideals, and codes by which to live; the struggle to overcome baser instincts and to do what is right despite the cost; the choice between conflicting ideals.

In its great variety of tales and characters, the Arthurian legend seems a perfect medium for expressing concerns that are both personal and global, ideals as well as fears, aspirations as well as anxieties. As timely as they are timeless, the stories of Arthur, Lancelot and Guinevere, Tristan and Isolt, Merlin, Gawain, and the quest for the Grail continue to entertain, to edify, and to fascinate. No doubt, through the creations of high and popular culture, Arthur will return again, as he so often has in the past, for centuries to come.

Arthurian People, Places, and Things

Accolon In Thomas Malory's *Morte d'Arthur,* Accolon is *Morgan le Fay's lover. She gives him *Excalibur, which *Arthur has entrusted to her, to use against Arthur in a battle between the champions of Damas and his brother Ontzlake. Damas has usurped his brother's land, but Arthur fights for him in order to escape imprisonment. With the aid of *Nenyve, Arthur recovers Excalibur during the battle and kills Ontzlake's champion Accolon, who did not realize he was fighting the king. Arthur then has Accolon's body sent to Morgan. Malory based his story of Accolon on the thirteenth-century Old French *Merlin Continuation (Suite du Merlin),* the source for much of the early material in his *Morte d'Arthur.*

Accolon's story is retold in verse by American poet Madison Cawein. His *Accolon of Gaul* (1889) is based on Malory's version but presents Morgane as desirous of a passionate love affair and eager to have Accolon crowned in place of Arthur so that the emphasis in the kingdom will shift from war to love.

Aglovale (Agloval, Acglavael) Aglovale is one of the sons of *Pellinore and a brother of *Perceval. In the Middle Dutch romance *Moriaen,* Aglovale (Acglavael in the Dutch) is the father of Moriaen, a Moor whose mother is left by Aglovale, who does not know she is pregnant. In the Vulgate *Lancelot,* Agloval encourages Perceval to come with him to Arthur's court to be made a knight, despite their mother's wish to keep Perceval with her. In Malory's *Morte d'Arthur,* Aglovale is one of the knights slain by Lancelot and his followers in the rescue of the queen.

Aglovale's story is central to *The Life of Sir Aglovale de Galis* (1905) by Clemence Housman, in which he rises above the feuds that consume other knights. He saves *Agravaine and *Gaheris even though they tried to kill him because his father Pellinore killed their father *Lot.

Agravain(e) (Agravayne) Agravain is the son of *Lot and *Morgause and brother of *Gawain. In the thirteenth-century Vulgate *Lancelot,* Agravain is said to be arrogant and jealous and ready to speak evil words. Although he shows no pity or love, he is a bold knight. In the Vulgate *Mort Artu,* he tells *Arthur that *Lancelot loves *Guinevere and then traps the lovers in the queen's room. He is killed by Lancelot in the rescue of the queen from the pyre. In Malory's *Morte d'Arthur,* Agravayne plots with *Mordred to trap Lancelot and Guinevere and is killed in the fight at the door of the queen's chamber. The death of Agravayne does not cause Gawain to seek vengeance because he had warned his brother of the dangers of plotting against Lancelot; Gawain feels that Agravayne was responsible for his own death.

In T. H. White's *Once and Future King* (1958), Agravaine is given a prominent role. It is Agravaine who is most affected by his mother Morgause's coldness towards her sons. He kills a unicorn to please her, but she does not even recognize the gesture. Later when he finds her in bed with *Lamorak, he (not *Gaheris, as in Malory) slays her. Agravaine is the first knight to be slain by Lancelot when he is trapped in the queen's chamber and thus it is his armour that Lancelot uses as he fights off the attackers.

Alain le Gros Alain is a *Fisher King. According to Robert de Boron and the *Perlesvaus,* he is the father of Perceval.

Alexander the Orphan (Alysaundir le Orphelin) Alexander is the son of Bodwyne, brother of King *Mark. In Thomas Malory's *Morte d'Arthur,* Bodwyne defends Mark's lands; but Mark is angry at his brother's success and kills him. Bodwyne's wife Anglydes flees with her son Alexander and is allowed to live by Sadoke, the knight Mark sends after them, on the condition that Anglydes raise her son to avenge his father. Alexander later marries Alys le Beall Pylgryme, daughter of Aunserus the Pylgryme, and they have a son named Bellengerus, to whom is left the task of avenging Bodwyne when Mark treacherously kills Alexander.

Mary Stewart retells the story of Alexander and Alice in her novel *The Prince and the Pilgrim* (1995), in which Alexander does not avenge his father because he hears that March (Mark) is ill and will die within a year. He and Alice live happily together, and though he never reaches Camelot, he finds what it represents in his love for her.

Alliterative Revival   The Alliterative Revival was a literary movement of the late fourteenth and fifteenth centuries, predominantly in the north and west of England. Poets used an alliterative line as the controlling metrical device. The movement is perhaps a development of a continuing tradition dating back to Old English verse and reflected in Layamon's *Brut*. A number of the poems of the Alliterative Revival are romances in which *Gawain is the epitome of courtesy and chivalry.

Alys le Beall Pylgryme   See ALEXANDER THE ORPHAN.

Ambrosius Aurelianus (Aurelius Ambrosius, Emrys)   Ambrosius Aurelianus is said by Gildas and by Bede to be the leader of resistance against the Saxons. Gildas's account has been read as suggesting that he was the British leader at *Badon. For Nennius, Ambrosius is the child without a father who reveals to *Vortigern the reason why his tower will not stand (the role assigned to *Merlin by Geoffrey of Monmouth, who says that his name is Merlin Ambrosius). Geoffrey calls the Ambrosius Aurelianus of earlier writers Aurelius Ambrosius. After his older brother *Constans is assassinated, Aurelius and his other brother *Uther are taken to the continent for their safety. When Aurelius returns to Britain, he is declared king and he burns Vortigern in his stronghold. Wishing to build a monument to the British nobles treacherously slain by the Saxons, he sends Merlin to Ireland to retrieve the Giant's Dance, which is reconstructed on Salisbury Plain as *Stonehenge. Poisoned by the treacherous Saxon Eopa, Aurelius is himself buried within the circle of Stonehenge. The meteor in the shape of a dragon which marked the death of Aurelius is reflected in the dragon standards that Uther has made and leads to his being called Uther Pendragon.

Amesbury (Almesbury)   Amesbury is a town in Wiltshire, near Salisbury Plain. In various sources, Amesbury is said to be the site of the convent to which *Guinevere flees after *Arthur and *Mordred have killed each other. In time, she becomes the abbess of the convent; and it is there that she dies a holy death. Geoffrey of Monmouth calls the place the Cloister of Ambrius, because it was founded by an abbot named Ambrius, and says that it is the site of the meeting at which the Saxons treacherously slew the British nobles. According to the *Prose Brut*, Amesbury was founded by a knight named Anbry, was destroyed by the Saxons, and was rebuilt by Aurilambros (*Aurelius Ambrosius).

Amhar   See ARTHUR'S CHILDREN.

Amite   See ELAINE OF CORBENIC.

Amr   See ARTHUR'S CHILDREN.

Andred (Andret)   In Béroul's *Tristran* (last quarter of the twelfth century), Andret is a noble from Lincoln who advises *Mark not to banish *Tristan. In the *Prose Tristan* (thirteenth century) and in Malory's *Morte d'Arthur*, Andred is Tristram's cousin and his enemy who spies on the lovers and tries to destroy them. Malory names Andred as an accomplice of Mark in the death of Tristram. In Edwin Arlington Robinson's *Tristram* (1927), Andred has an insane love for *Isolt and ultimately kills Tristram at the instigation of *Morgan.

Anfortas   In Wolfram von Eschenbach's *Parzival*, Anfortas, *Parzival's uncle, is the wounded king who must be healed by the Grail knight. His story is told by his brother Trevrizent to Parzival. When his father Frimutel died, Anfortas was chosen to succeed him as Grail king. Fighting for love of a lady (and not in service of the *Grail), Anfortas was wounded in the genitals by a heathen's poisoned spear. No physician or medicine was able to cure him; but since he was brought into the presence of the Grail, he was not able to die. And so he is doomed to live in agonizing pain until a knight should come and ask the appropriate question: 'Sir, why is it you suffer so?' On his first visit to the Grail castle at *Munsalvaesche, Parzival does not ask this question, and Anfortas's agony continues. Finally, Parzival returns, asks the question, and frees Anfortas from his pain.

In Richard Wagner's opera *Parsifal*, Amfortas is the wounded king who can be healed only by the Grail knight; but his wound, like that of Christ who was pierced by the same spear, is in the side. Influenced by Wagner, Australian playwright T. Hilhouse Taylor retold the story of the Grail, including the story of the wounding and curing of Amfortas, in his play *Parsifal* (1906). In the battle with *Klingsor's wicked knights, Amfortas loses the Sacred Spear, which the Grail knight must retrieve. When the spear is returned, Parsifal is named Grail king and Amfortas promises to free *Kundry from Klingsor; but Amfortas soon learns that Parsifal has freed her and brought her with him. Parsifal unites them so that together they may fulfil their quest to lead men from darkness to light.

Anglydes See ALEXANDER THE ORPHAN.

Anguysh, Angwysaunce, Anguin See ISOLT OF IRELAND.

animals See BEL JOEOR, CABAL, GRINGALET, HUSDENT, LLAMREI, PASSELANDE, PETIT-CREU, QUESTING BEAST, TWRCH TRWYTH.

Anna Geoffrey of Monmouth and other chroniclers identify Anna as the daughter of *Uther and *Igraine (and thus *Arthur's sister) and the wife of *Lot and mother of *Gawain and *Mordred (a role taken on by *Morgause in later literature). At one point, Geoffrey says that she is the sister of Aurelius (*Ambrosius Aurelianus) and Uther. Some Scottish chroniclers use this statement to suggest that she was indeed Aurelius' sister, in which case her son Mordred would have a better claim to the throne than Arthur, and so Mordred's rebellion would be justified. In his history of Scotland, George Buchanan explains the confusion by suggesting that Uther had both a sister and, by a concubine, a daughter named Anna and that it was the sister who married Lot.

Antor See ECTOR.

Arfderydd, battle of See MERLIN.

Argante According to Layamon, Argante is the elf queen of *Avalon who would heal *Arthur's wounds. J. D. Bruce ('Some Proper Names in Layamon's *Brut* Not Represented in Wace or Geoffrey of Monmouth', *Modern Language Notes*, 26.3 (Mar. 1911), 65–9) argues that Argante is a corruption of *'Morgan'.

Arthur Arthur is the central figure of the Arthurian legends, though he is only occasionally the protagonist of medieval Arthurian tales. Traditionally called King Arthur, Nennius refers to him as '*dux bellorum*', a term designating a military leader rather than a king. Nennius also names Arthur as the victor in a series of *twelve battles against the Saxons, which culminate in a decisive victory at Mount *Badon. Early Welsh tales like *Culhwch and Olwen* depict him as the leader of a group of semi-mythological warriors with super powers. Welsh saints' lives sometimes portray him as an enemy of the Church, who commandeers its treasures to support his wars. How much, if any, historicity can be assigned to Arthur is a matter of debate. Some have suggested that an earlier or contemporary historical figure performed deeds that became attached to a fictional 'Arthur'. One theory is that Arthur is based on Lucius Artorius Castus, a second-century Roman officer. Castus led a troop of Sarmatian cavalry stationed in Britain. Analogues between the folklore of the descendants of the Sarmatians and the Matter of Britain have led some to posit a Sarmatian connection, a link between Sarmatian culture and elements of the Arthurian legends. Geoffrey Ashe, on the other hand, has called attention to a figure referred to as 'Riothamus', a title meaning 'high king', who led an army to the continent and who, Ashe speculates, may have been associated by Geoffrey of Monmouth with Arthur (a theory put forth in *The Discovery of King Arthur* (Garden City, NY: Anchor Press/Doubleday, 1985)). If someone did inspire the legend of King Arthur by resisting the Germanic invaders, he would have been a warrior of the late fifth and/or early sixth centuries and not the sort of person often depicted in literature, a king living in a castle with knights in shining armour serving him.

Geoffrey of Monmouth is a seminal figure in the development of the character and the medieval and modern image of Arthur. Geoffrey gives Arthur a place in the line of British kings and establishes him anachronistically but indelibly as a king and emperor in the medieval sense. Geoffrey also incorporates into the legend the role of Merlin and his magic in Arthur's birth to *Uther Pendragon and *Igerne and makes the betrayal by *Mordred, Arthur's nephew but in later accounts his son, a staple of the king's history. Mordred marries *Guinevere in spite of her marriage to

Arthur. (Mordred is one of a number of characters named as children of Arthur in various works—see ARTHUR'S CHILDREN.)

The betrayal of Arthur by his wife is generally attributed in the romance tradition to her love for *Lancelot rather than Mordred. But even when the queen is not enamoured of Mordred, he betrays Arthur by declaring himself king and trying to wed her, a union she escapes by fleeing to a nunnery. Arthur must return from conquests on the continent or from besieging Lancelot after his affair with the queen has come to light, to fight the traitorous Mordred in a final battle, said in early tradition to take place at *Camlann. In the battle, Arthur slays Mordred but is himself grievously wounded and must be taken to *Avalon for his wounds to be healed. In some works, Arthur dies of his wounds; other accounts suggest that he will be restored to health and will return to rule again. Before he is taken to Avalon, the sword *Excalibur, which he received from the *Lady of the Lake, must be returned to the water. Arthur names as his successor his relative *Constantine, son of *Cador, Duke of Cornwall.

Arthur's fame rests largely on the *Round Table, a physical object but also an order of knights devoted to Arthur and, in many works, to a code that involves championing women and the weak and punishing evildoers. The knights of Arthur's court undertake quests, many of which the king himself has little part in except at times to choose the knight for the task. Much of Arthur's fame in medieval romance rests on the accomplishments of the knights of the Round Table. He himself does, however, occasionally perform great deeds, such as the slaying of the *Giant of St Michael's Mount. He is also the leader in the continental wars that in some works make him an emperor and not just King of Britain.

Modern authors borrow much from the medieval sources of the story of Arthur. But he also undergoes some radical transformations. Tennyson, for example, makes him faultless, a man so perfect that he has risen almost to the level of the angels. T. H. White makes his great accomplishment learning to think so that he can arrive on his own at the conclusion that might is not an end unto itself but must be used for right and then ruling his kingdom according to this belief.

Arthur's children The children *Arthur fathers differ in various texts. Two poems in the Black Book of Carmarthen refer to Llachau as Arthur's son, though they give few details about him except that he was a warrior and that he died, presumably in a battle of some sort.

Loholt is said in a number of texts to be Arthur's son. In Perlesvaus (probably written in the first decade of the thirteenth century), he kills a giant and then is slain by Kay, who wants the glory of the deed for himself. Kay's killing of Loholt is also recounted in Dorothy James Roberts's Kinsmen of the Grail (1963), which has its source in Perlesvaus. In Ulrich von Zatzikhoven's Lanzelet (c.1200–4), when Ginover (*Guinevere), Arthur's queen, is abducted, their son Loüt or Lont (? Loholt) rides to the siege of the castle of her abductor Valerin. Ulrich notes that finally Loüt rode off with his father and that the Bretons 'expect both of them evermore'.

Nennius lists as one of the wonders of Britain the tomb of Amr, Arthur's son, which is a different size each time it is measured. Amr was killed by Arthur and then buried in this tomb. In the thirteenth-century Welsh tale Gereint Son of Erbin, Amhar son of Arthur is named as one of the four chamberlains who guarded Arthur's bed. (It is unclear whether Amr and Amhar are the same person.) According to the Post-Vulgate Queste del Saint Graal, Arthur rapes the daughter of a lord named Tanas and she bears a son who Arthur says should be named Arthur the Less.

According to Malory, Arthur has an illegitimate son with *Lyonors, the daughter of Earl Sanam. The son, named Borre, eventually becomes a knight of the Round Table. In the novel Lionors (1975) by Barbara Ferry Johnson, which is based on this episode, the child is a daughter named Elise. Arthur's most famous child is, of course, his illegitimate son *Mordred, who, in the *Vulgate Cycle, in Malory's Morte d'Arthur, and in many works based on these sources, betrays and then slays his father.

In the seventeenth-century romance The Most Pleasant History of Tom a Lincolne (part 1, 1599; part 2, 1607) by Richard Johnson (R.I. in the original publication) (1573–1659), Arthur has an affair with Angellica, daughter of the Earl of London, and they have an illegitimate son called Tom. Arthur leaves him to be raised by a shepherd from Lincoln named Antonio. To exercise his martial skills, Tom forms an outlaw band and gives each of his followers a red rose and thus comes to be known as the Red-Rose Knight. Arthur hears of Tom's deeds, believes him to be his son, and has him brought to court, where he is made a knight of the Round Table. The Red-Rose Knight has an affair with Caelia, the Queen of Fayrie-land, and they have a son called the Fayrie Knight. Later in his travels, the Red-Rose Knight falls in love with and marries Anglitora, the daughter of *Prester John. They have a son known as the Black Knight. When Arthur, near death, reveals his affair with Angellica, Anglitora leaves her husband because of his illegitimate birth—though she has an affair with another knight as she journeys home to Prester John's realm; and when the Red-Rose Knight finds her, she kills him and buries him in a dunghill. His son, the Black Knight, subsequently avenges him.

In the film *Siege of the Saxons* (1963), Arthur is assassinated, and his daughter Katherine, with the assistance of *Merlin and a Robin Hood-like outlaw named Robert Marshall, must struggle to regain the throne. Similarly, in the novel *King Arthur's Daughter* (1976) by Vera Chapman, Ursulet, the daughter of Arthur and Guinevere, struggles for control of the kingdom against Mordred after Arthur's death. In Henry Fielding's plays about Tom Thumb, Arthur has a daughter named Huncamunca by his queen Dollalolla. In the novel *The Winter Prince* (1993) by Elizabeth E. Wein, Artos names his legitimate son Lleu as his heir. The illegitimate Medraut initially opposes but ultimately recognizes his half-brother.

Arthur's weapons and armour See CARN-WENNAN, CLARENT, EXCALIBUR, GOSWHIT, PRIDWEN, RON, WYNEBGWRTHUCHER.

Arthur the Less See ARTHUR'S CHILDREN.

Astolat (Ascolat, Escolat) See ELAINE OF ASTOLAT.

Aurelius Ambrosius See AMBROSIUS AURELIANUS.

Avalon (Afallach, Avilion) Avalon, which is sometimes equated with *Glastonbury, is generally said to be the island to which Arthur is brought after his final battle. Occasionally, as in *The Mists of Avalon* (1982) by Marion Zimmer Bradley, Avalon and Glastonbury are seen as different manifestations of the same place.

In the *Historia regum Britanniae* (1138), Geoffrey of Monmouth identifies Avalon as the place where

Arthur's sword Caliburn was forged and the place to which he was taken after the battle of *Camlann so that his wounds might be healed. In his *Vita Merlini* (c.1150), Geoffrey speaks of the Island of Apples and equates it with The Fortunate Isle, which is ruled by nine sisters, of whom the fairest and most skilled in healing arts is *Morgan. It is to her that Arthur was taken after the battle at Camlann. The two accounts suggest that Geoffrey sees Avalon and the Island of Apples as equivalent. In *The Antiquities of Glastonbury* (c.1135), William of Malmesbury translates 'Insula Avallonia' as 'Apple Island' ('avalla' meaning 'apple') and also equates the two names with Glastonbury.

Numerous authors refer to the belief that Arthur will return from Avalon. The *Vera historia de morte Arthuri* (c.1200), which locates Avalon in Gwynedd, suggests that there is mystery about Arthur's death and that some believe he still lives. Both Wace and Layamon mention the belief in Arthur's return. Malory writes that so   .n think that Arthur is not dead and th' ne will come again; he also writes that Arthur was taken to the Vale of Avalon in a barge by three queens (Morgan le Fay, the Queen of North Galis, the Queen of the Waste Lands) and *Nyneve, the chief Lady of the Lake. (See also GLASTONBURY.)

Bademagu (Bademagus, Bagdemagus) In Chrétien's *Lancelot*, Bademagu is the King of Gorre and the father of *Meleagant. Unlike his son, he is courteous and considerate; and he treats *Guinevere with honour while she is held captive by Meleagant. The thirteenth-century Vulgate *Lancelot* tells the history of Bademagu's kingdom of Gorre, which no inhabitant of Arthur's realm could leave once he or she entered. Gorre was formerly the kingdom of *Urien, who refused to swear allegiance to *Uther. When Urien was captured, Uther threatened to hang him if he would not swear fealty. Urien's nephew and heir Bademagu yielded the land to Uther to save his uncle's life. Later, Urien retook Gorre and gave it to his nephew, who decided to repopulate his devastated land with the people of Uther's kingdom. He had two bridges built, the only means of access to his realm, and arrested anyone from Uther's kingdom who entered and made them swear never to return to their homeland until a knight would win them back. When Gorre was repopulated, Bademagu tore down the bridges and built two new ones, one an underwater bridge and an even more treacherous Sword Bridge, a steel beam made as sharp as a sword and only one foot wide. When Guinevere is kidnapped by Meleagant, *Lancelot crosses the Sword Bridge and ultimately frees the queen and all of Arthur's subjects held captive in Gorre.

According to the Vulgate *Queste*, Bademagu wears the shield intended for *Galahad, for which he is grievously wounded by a knight in white armour. In the Post-Vulgate *Queste*, Bademagu intervenes when *Mordred is about to rape a maiden. After Mordred beheads the woman, Bademagu wounds him. *Gawain, hearing from Mordred that a knight wounded him treacherously, seeks to avenge him. Without knowing his identity, Gawain gives Bademagu a mortal wound. When the two knights recognize each other, Gawain asks for forgiveness, and Bademagu grants it just before he dies.

Badon See TWELVE BATTLES OF ARTHUR.

Balan See BALIN.

Balin The story of Balin is recounted in the Old French *Suite du Merlin* and in Thomas Malory's *Morte d'Arthur*. Balin and Balan are the tragic brothers who, despite their nobility, unwittingly kill each other. Balin in particular seems cursed by fate. For example, when he offers protection to a knight, he is unable to foresee—or even see—that the knight will be treacherously slain by Garlon, who rides invisible. Balin goes to the castle of *Pellam, Garlon's brother, to avenge the treacherous act. When he plunges his sword into Garlon and kills him, Pellam pursues him through the castle to take vengeance. Needing a weapon, Balin finds *Longinus' spear, which was used to pierce the side of Christ as he hung on the cross. When he uses it to wound Pellam, Balin strikes the *Dolorous Stroke, which destroys not only Pellam's castle but also three surrounding countries. These lands will not be restored nor will Pellam's wound be healed until the *Grail is achieved. Balin's misfortune lasts to his final act, combat with his brother Balan, whom he does not recognize. In the battle, both are fatally wounded. Ironically, this battle was fated from the first appearance of Balin in Malory's version of the story, when he proves himself to be 'a passynge good man' by removing a sword that a lady has been forced to wear and thus, by winning a second

sword, becoming known as The Knight with Two Swords. After succeeding in this test, Balin decides to keep the sword even when warned that if he does so he will slay the man he loves most in the world and bring about his own destruction. Unwilling to believe this prophecy, he keeps the sword and seals his brother's doom as well as his own.

Tennyson's Balin is known as 'the Savage' (Malory called him 'Balin Le Savage') and figures in the struggle of Arthur to destroy the bestial both in his realm and in his subjects. Swinburne retold the story of Balin in his *The Tale of Balen* (1896), which follows Malory much more closely than Tennyson's version does. The story of Balin and Balan is also central to the first of the three parts of John Arden and Margaretta D'Arcy's play *The Island of the Mighty* (1972), in which the brothers separate when Balin joins *Arthur's band, only to be banished from it because he kills an ambassador from the Picts in Arthur's presence. *Merlin instructs Balin to keep the ambassador's sword, which is now cursed; and so he becomes a knight with two swords. Balan is captured by and then joins the Picts as a warrior. After marrying the princess of the Picts, he meets Balin in a ritual battle. The brothers fight, both in masks, and kill each other unwittingly. Persia Woolley, in one of the most interesting parts of the first novel in her Guinevere trilogy, presents Balin and Balan as two sides of the same personality. Douglas Carmichael's story 'The Grievous Stroke' (*The Round Table* 5 (1989), 25–34) places Balin's wounding of Pellam in a Celtic rather than a Christian context. And British artist Graham Clark tells a simplified version of Malory's tale of Balin and Balan in an elaborately illustrated edition (*Balyn and Balan* (Boughton Monchelsea: Ebenezer Press, n.d.)).

Ban (Pant) King Ban of Benoic or Benwick is the father of *Lancelot and of an illegitimate son, *Hector de Marys, who is born when Merlin casts a spell on Ban and the beautiful daughter of Agravadain the Black, which causes them to spend the night together. Ban is the brother of King *Bors of Gaunes. In Ulrich von Zatzikhoven's *Lanzelet* (c.1200–4), he is called Pant and is said to be a cruel overlord who drives his vassals to rebellion. In the Vulgate *Lancelot*, however, Ban is a noble lord who is attacked by his treacherous neighbour *Claudas and betrayed by his own seneschal. He dies of grief when he sees his castle burning. According to Malory, Ban and Bors assist Arthur in his war against the rebellious kings.

Beaumains See GARETH.

Bedivere (Bedevere, Bedwyr) Bedwyr and Cai (*Kay) are among the warriors earliest associated with *Arthur. Bedwyr son of Bedrawc is said in Triad 21 to be 'diademed above' the three battle-diademed men of Britain (that is, Drystan, Hueil, and Cai). The author of *Culhwch and Olwen* (c.1100) says of Bedwyr that he never shrank from any enterprise on which Cai was bound. In that tale, the two are instrumental in one of the tasks that must be achieved in order for Culhwch to marry Olwen, the rescue of Mabon, who was taken from his mother when he was only three days old. In the late fourteenth-century *Alliterative Morte Arthure* and other works that tell the story of the *Giant of St Michael's Mount, Kay and Bedivere accompany Arthur as he sets out to confront the giant.

According to Geoffrey of Monmouth, Arthur gives Bedevere the province of Normandy for his service in the war in Gaul; later, Bedevere is slain in Arthur's continental war against *Lucius. Wace says Bedivere is one of Arthur's privy counsellors and that he and Kay are Arthur's two most loyal subjects. In Malory's *Morte d'Arthur*, Bedivere survives the continental wars and is with Arthur at the end of his final battle. Arthur orders him to return Excalibur to the lake (a task entrusted to *Girflet in the Vulgate *Mort Artu*). Tennyson adds to Malory's account a depiction of Bedivere watching the barge bearing Arthur as it grows smaller and smaller and finally disappears.

In Rosemary Sutcliff's *Sword at Sunset* and in Mary Stewart's *The Wicked Day*, Bedwyr takes on the role of lover of Arthur's queen. Bedivere is the narrator of George Finkel's *Twilight Province* (1967, published in the United States as *Watch Fires to the North*) and of Catherine Christian's *The Sword and the Flame* (1978, published in the United States as *The Pendragon*).

Bel Inconnu, Le (Lybeaus Desconus) See FAIR UNKNOWN.

Bel Joeor Bel Joeor is the name Béroul gives to Tristan's horse.

Bellengerus See ALEXANDER THE ORPHAN.

Bellicent (Belisent) See MORGAUSE.

Bendigeidfran See BRAN THE BLESSED.

Bernard of Astolat See ELAINE OF ASTOLAT.

Beste Glatissant See QUESTING BEAST.

Blaise (Bleyse) In the prose version of Robert de Boron's *Merlin*, Blaise is *Merlin's mother's confessor who saves her from being put to death after she is impregnated by a devil. At Merlin's request, Blaise records the story of *Joseph of Arimathea and of Merlin himself as well as the story of *Perceval's achieving of the *Grail, after which Merlin brings Blaise to the house of the new *Fisher King, Perceval, where he remains. Blaise plays a similar role in relation to Merlin's mother and the recording of the events told to him by Merlin in a number of subsequent works. The text of the thirteenth-century Vulgate *Merlin* claims it is the account which Merlin instructed him to write. In Tennyson's idyll 'The Coming of Arthur' (1869), Bleyse is said to be the source of the alternative account of the coming of *Arthur, that is, Arthur's coming onto the shore below *Tintagel on the ninth wave.

Blanchefleur (Blancheflor) In Chrétien's *Perceval*, Blanchefleur is the maiden who is besieged by the forces of Clamadeu and whom *Perceval rescues by defeating both Clamadeu and his seneschal in single combat. Ultimately Perceval and Blanchefleur are married. In Edwin Austin Abbey's Grail murals, because of the conflation of the stories of Galahad and Perceval, Blanchefleur is depicted as the bride of Galahad.

Blankeflur See TRISTAN'S PARENTS.

Blaunchefleur See TRISTAN'S PARENTS.

Bleyse See BLAISE.

Bodwyne See ALEXANDER THE ORPHAN.

Bohort See BORS.

Borre See ARTHUR'S CHILDREN.

Bors (Bohort) In the thirteenth-century *Vulgate Cycle, Bors is the son of King *Bors of Gaunes and the cousin of *Lancelot. Along with his brother Lionel, Bors is protected as a child by the Lady of the Lake. He is made to love the daughter of King Brandegorre by means of a magic ring that her governess gets him to wear. They sleep together once and conceive a son, Helaine the White. Despite the fact that he slept with a woman, Bors is one of the three knights who achieve the quest for the Holy *Grail. He accompanies *Galahad and *Perceval on the ship that brings the Grail from Britain to *Sarras and remains there with them until both are dead. He then returns to *Camelot and becomes an ally of Lancelot when he is caught in the queen's chamber. After *Arthur's final battle with *Mordred, Bors joins Lancelot in leading a holy life. When Lancelot dies, Bors and other of Lancelot's kin go to the Holy Land to fight infidels. There, he dies on a Good Friday.

In the novel *Launcelot, my Brother* (1954) by Dorothy James Roberts, Bors, the narrator, is said to be Launcelot's brother.

Bors (Bohort) of Gaunes King Bors is the brother of *Ban of Benwick and the father of *Bors and *Lionel. According to Malory, he, along with his brother, assists Arthur in his struggle against the rebellious kings.

Brangwain (Brengain, Brangene, Brangwayne, Branwen, Bringvet) Brangwain is *Isolt's maid or nurse. Isolt's mother entrusts to Brangwain a love potion intended for Isolt and *Mark on their wedding night; but *Tristan and Isolt mistakenly drink it and fall in love. In several versions of the story, Brangwain substitutes for Isolt in Mark's bed on his wedding night so that he remains unaware that Isolt is not a virgin. Fearing that Brangwain may reveal her secret, Isolt orders Brangwain killed but soon repents. Fortunately, since those charged with slaying Brangwain had not yet killed her, she is returned to Isolt, and the two are reconciled. Brangwain again helps the lovers to conceal their affection and their assignations. In Thomas's version of the story, *Kaherdin, the brother of Yseut of Brittany, falls in love with Brengain when he sees her statue in Tristan's Hall of Statues. In the novel *The White Raven* (1988), Diana L. Paxson makes Branwen, whose name is said to mean 'white raven', the narrator and the central character. She is torn between her loyalty to Esseilte (Isolt) and her genuine love for Marc'h (Mark).

Bran the Blessed (Bendigeidfran) Bran is the son of Llyr, a Celtic sea god. In the *Mabinogion* tale

of *Branwen, Daughter of Llyr*, Bran (Bendigeidfran) is said to be the King of Britain. Because of an insult to his sister Branwen, he invades Ireland and is wounded by a poisoned spear (a detail that, along with a life-restoring cauldron in *Branwen*, leads some to see in Bran the source of *Bron from the Grail legends). Because of the wound, Bran instructs that his head be cut off and buried on the White Mount in London facing France. Triad 37 speaks of the burying of Bran's head as one of the three fortunate concealments of Britain because 'as long as it was in the position in which it was put there, no Saxon oppression would ever come to this Island'. The triad also says that one of the three unfortunate disclosures occurred when *Arthur disclosed the head of Bran because he did not think it right 'that this island be defended by the strength of anyone but by his own'.

Breuse (Bruns, Breunys, Brehu) sans Pity (The Brown Knight without Pity) Breuse sans Pity, an anti-chivalric figure, is a treacherous knight who mistreats ladies and breaks the rules of knightly combat and behaviour. He is cowardly and runs from better knights like *Tristram and *Palomides. Malory calls him 'the moste myschevuste knyght lyvynge' and says that *Gareth killed him.

Brewnor (Brunor) le Noyre See COTE MAL TAYLE, LA.

Bringvet See BRANGWAIN.

Brisen (Brisane, Brysen, Brusen) In the thirteenth-century Vulgate *Lancelot* and in Malory's *Morte d'Arthur*, Brisen is the handmaiden of *Elaine of Corbenic, daughter of *Pelles. Malory calls her one of the greatest enchanters in the world. She uses her craft to drug *Lancelot so that he does not realize that he is sleeping with Elaine instead of *Guinevere. As a result, Galahad is conceived. Brisen later deceives Lancelot again by pretending to lead him to Guinevere's bed but actually taking him to Elaine's. When Guinevere discovers that Lancelot has slept with Elaine a second time, she rejects him and he goes mad. Later, when he is discovered in his madness, Brusen enchants him so that he will sleep while he is brought to Pelles' castle where he is cured by the *Grail.

Broceliande Broceliande is the forest in which Chrétien's *Yvain begins his adventures by pouring water from a spring on a stone and thus causing a great storm which brings forth the knight Esclados le Ros to defend his land. In the *Roman de Rou* (begun in 1160), Wace speaks of a similar fountain in Broceliande, a place 'about which the Bretons often tell stories'. He says that hunters scoop water from the fountain of Barenton in Broceliande and moisten the top of an adjacent stone in order to cause rain to fall. Wace also says that people saw fairies and many other marvels there; but although he travelled to the forest in search of such marvels, he saw none. He adds that he went there as a fool and returned as a fool. (Cf. *The Roman de Rou*, trans. Glyn S. Burgess (St Helier: Société Jersiaise, 2002), 237.)

In various works, from the thirteenth-century Vulgate *Estoire de Merlin* to Tennyson's 'Merlin and Vivien' idyll (1859), Broceliande is the forest in which *Vivien entraps *Merlin. In Edwin Arlington Robinson's *Merlin* (1917), Merlin lives willingly for a time with Vivien in Broceliande, which is described as an 'elysian wilderness'. In his short poem 'Broceliande' (1916), American poet Alan Seeger (1888–1916) tries to capture the mood suggested by the forest of romance.

Bron According to Robert de Boron, Bron is the brother-in-law of *Joseph of Arimathea and the father of Alain le Gros, the father of *Perceval. He is also called the *Fisher King. When Perceval returns to the *Grail castle and asks the appropriate question, Bron's wound is healed; Bron lives for three days and then dies, his soul being greeted by David with his harp and a host of angels. Perceval then becomes the new Fisher King and guardian of the Grail.

Brunor le Noyre See BREWNOR LE NOYRE.

Brusen See BRISEN.

Brutus (Brute) Brutus, the great-grandson of Aeneas, led a group of Trojan exiles ultimately to the island that is named Britain after him. A number of chronicles and historical romances telling the history of Britain are called 'Brute' from the practice of beginning such histories with Brutus' founding of the kingdom.

Cabal (Cafal, Cavall) Nennius' *Historia Brittonum* (c.800) tells the story of the hunting of the giant boar Troynt, during which *Arthur's dog Cafal impressed his footprint into a stone. Arthur built a commemorative mound with this stone on top. Men try to carry it off; but even after being carried for a day and a night, the next day it appears back atop Carn Cafal. Nennius' story of the hunting of Troynt is almost certainly the equivalent of the hunting of the giant boar *Twrch Trwyth in *Culhwch and Olwen* (c.1100), in which Cafal also participates. In the Welsh romance *Gereint Son of Erbin*, Cafal plays a part in the hunting of the stag.

Modern novelists sometimes introduce Arthur's dog into their stories. In Guy Gavriel Kay's *The Wandering Fire* (1986), Cavall fights alongside Arthur and accompanies him on his quest to Cader Sedat (the equivalent of Caer Sidi). Rosemary Sutcliff gives Arthur several dogs named Cabal in *Sword at Sunset* (1963).

Cadbury Castle See CAMELOT.

Cador of Cornwall Geoffrey of Monmouth and others who are influenced directly or indirectly by him depict Cador as a fierce warrior in *Arthur's battles against the Saxons and his wars on the continent and as an adviser to the king. Cador's son *Constantine succeeds to the throne upon Arthur's death. In William Hilton's *Arthur, Monarch of the Britons* (completed in 1759; first published in 1776), Cador dies in battle as an ally of Arthur's.

Cafal See CABAL.

Cai See KAY.

Caliburn (Caliburnus) See EXCALIBUR.

Camelot Although Camelot is, for most modern readers, the legendary centre of King *Arthur's realm, in many medieval texts Arthur holds court at Caerleon or some other city. Camelot is first mentioned in line 34 of Chrétien de Troyes's *Lancelot* (though the name does not appear in all manuscripts of that romance). In the thirteenth-century *Vulgate Cycle, Camelot is said to have been converted by the son of *Joseph of Arimathea, *Josephus, who had built there the Church of St Stephen, in which some texts say Arthur and *Guinevere were married. Camelot becomes the principal city of Arthur's realm and remains so in many, though not all, later texts. Malory identifies Camelot as Winchester.

The image most modern readers have of Camelot coincides with Tennyson's description of it in 'The Lady of Shalott' (1833; revised in 1842) as 'many-tower'd Camelot'. Tennyson's image of Camelot is much more complex, however, in the idyll 'Gareth and Lynette' (1872), where it is described as a city built to music and where it is suggestive of Tennyson's theme of appearance and reality 'For there is nothing in it as it seems | Saving the King.'

Since Camelot is a legendary place, it is perhaps futile to speak of its location. John Leland, however, identified it with Cadbury Castle, a hill fort in Somerset. Excavations carried out at the site in 1966–70 confirmed that this large hill fort (with 1,200 yards of perimeter surrounding an eighteen-acre enclosure and rising about 250 feet above the surrounding countryside) was refortified in the Arthurian era and was occupied by a powerful leader and his followers. More recently, largely through the influence of T. H. White, Camelot has come to be associated with the values that Arthur and his realm are believed to have represented (White's 'Might for Right'). The moral overtones still often remain, but sometimes 'Camelot' is used only to represent an ideal place.

Camlann (Camlan) The battle of Camlann is first referred to in the *Annales Cambriae* (*Welsh Annals*), where, for the year 539 (given as 537 in most editions), it is described as a battle in which *Arthur and Medraut (*Mordred) fell; but there is no indication that they were fighting against each other or killed each other. The battle is alluded to in the Welsh tales *Culhwch and Olwen* (c.1100) and *The Dream of Rhonabwy*, in which Iddawg the Embroiler of Britain is said to have been sent by Arthur on a mission of peace to Medrawd; but by being deliberately provocative rather than conciliatory, he caused the battle instead of averting it. Triad 51 recounts Medrawd's (Mordred's) treachery (he is one of the three dishonoured men of Britain and worse than *Vortigern) and the battle at Camlan in which Medrawd and Arthur died. Triad 53 assigns the cause of the battle at Camlan to the blow with which *Gwenhwyfar was struck by Gwenhwyfach, said in *Culhwch and Olwen* to be her sister (an event also alluded to in Triad 84, where Camlan is called the most futile battle of the Island of Britain because it was instigated by

such a barren cause as the quarrel between Gwenhwyfach and Gwenhwyfar).

Geoffrey of Monmouth places Arthur's final battle with Mordred at the River Camblan in 542. In the battle Mordred dies, and Arthur is carried off to the Isle of *Avalon to have his wounds treated. Wace locates the battle by the River Camel near the entrance to Cornwall; and Layamon places it at Camelford on the River Tamar in Cornwall. Malory, following the Vulgate, locates the battle on Salisbury Plain.

Carbonek See CORBENIC.

Carnwennan Carnwennan is the name given to Arthur's dagger in *Culhwch and Olwen* (c.1100).

Castle Dore Castle Dore, a hill fort in Cornwall, is said to be the residence of Cunomorus, who has been identified with *Mark from the *Tristan legend. Castle Dore is the geographic and symbolic centre of the novel *Castle Dor* (1961) by Sir Arthur Quiller-Couch and Daphne du Maurier.

Cei See KAY.

Cerdic Cerdic is a king of the Saxons (though his name is Welsh) and the reputed founder of the kingdom of Wessex. The *Anglo-Saxon Chronicle* records that he and his son Cynric came to Britain in 495 and immediately began fighting the Welsh. Later chroniclers (like John of Glastonbury, Henry of Huntingdon, and Ranulf Higden) make him a contemporary and an adversary of *Arthur's. According to one tradition, Cerdic was the Saxon leader at the battle of Mount *Badon.

The fact that Cerdic's name seems to be Celtic rather than Germanic inspired the novel *Conscience of a King* (1951) by Alfred Duggan. Cerdic, originally the Roman-British Coroticus, offers his service to *Hengist's son Oisc, who renames him Cerdic Elesing. Unscrupulous both before and after his service to Oisc, Cerdic is ultimately defeated by Arthur at Mount Badon. In John Lesslie Hall's poem 'Cerdic and Arthur' (1899), which tells the story of the invasions from an Anglo-Saxon perspective, Cerdic is praised as the 'Father of England' and as the 'founder of freedom'.

Clarent *Arthur's ceremonial sword is named Clarent. In the *Alliterative Morte Arthure* (late fourteenth century), *Mordred uses this sword against Arthur, who wields *Caliburn, in their final battle.

Clarisant (Clarissant, Klarisanz) In the First Continuation to Chrétien's *Perceval* (c.1200), Clarisant is the daughter of *Lot and Morcadés (*Morgause) and the sister of *Gawain. She is in love with Guiromelant, who accuses Gawain of treachery. Clarisant postpones a duel between her lover and her brother and then ends it by marrying Guiromelant. A similar story of the love of Klarisanz for Giremelanz is told in Heinrich von dem Türlin's *Diu Crône* (c.1225).

Claudas Claudas is the lord of Bourges. His lands are adjacent to those of *Lancelot's father *Ban. Claudas's kingdom is called the Land Laid Waste because it was devastated by Aramont of Brittany, overlord of Ban, and *Uther Pendragon, whose liegeman Aramont became. When Aramont and Uther die and Arthur is occupied with the rebellion in his own land, Claudas regains the lands he lost. Claudas captures Ban's city of Benoic, and Ban must flee with his wife and child; when Ban sees that Claudas has burned his castle, he dies. Ultimately, Arthur fights and defeats Claudas.

Cligés The protagonist of Chrétien's romance *Cligés* (c.1176), Cligés is the nephew of *Gawain and the heir to the throne of Greece. His father's younger brother Alis breaks an agreement that allowed him to rule instead of his elder brother, provided he would not marry and have heirs, thus allowing Cligés to rule after him. Alis's bride Fenice and Cligés are in love and use magic first to make Alis think he has consummated the marriage when he has not and then to make Fenice appear dead so she can live in seclusion with Cligés. When they are discovered, Cligés goes to Britain and raises an army to force Alis to give Cligés his due; but Alis dies and Arthur's army is disbanded. Cligés marries Fenice and reigns, as is his right.

Clinschor (Klingsor) Clinschor is a wicked magician in Wolfram's *Parzival* (first decade of the thirteenth century). Formerly a knight, he loved Iblis, the wife of Ibert, King of Sicily. When Ibert discovered their love, he castrated Clinschor. Consequently, Clinschor bears ill will to all, and he especially tries to rob of their joy those who are honoured.

In Wagner's *Parsifal* (first produced 1882), Klingsor is an evil magician who has wounded *Amfortas with the holy spear and who seeks to possess the *Grail, as he does the spear. Failing to become a knight of the Grail because of his lust, he castrates himself so he can suppress his desires and he turns to magic. When *Kundry fails in her attempt to seduce *Parsifal and thus frustrate his quest, Klingsor hurls the sacred spear at him; but it stops in midair, allowing Parsifal to seize it and use it to make the sign of the cross. This act dispels the enchantment of Klingsor, whose magic castle and garden then disappear.

Condwiramurs In Wolfram von Eschenbach's *Parzival* (written in the first decade of the thirteenth century), Condwiramurs is *Parzival's wife and the niece of *Gornemant, the knight who tutors him. She is also the mother of Parzival's two sons, Loherangrin (*Lohengrin) and Kardeiz.

Constans See VORTIGERN.

Constantine (Arthur's successor) Constantine, the son of Duke Cador of Cornwall and a relative of *Arthur, is Arthur's successor as ruler of Britain, according to numerous chronicles, Malory, and other sources. Wace says that Constantine reigned for three years and then died and was buried at Stonehenge. Geoffrey records that the Saxons and the two sons of *Mordred rebelled against Constantine; but Constantine defeated the Saxons and slew Mordred's sons, each of them in a different church, sacrilegious acts for which he himself was killed by the vengeance of God. He was buried next to *Uther at *Stonehenge. In some Scottish chronicles, Arthur's naming of Constantine as his successor is cited as justification for Mordred's rebellion since Arthur had previously promised that the sons of *Lot would reign after Arthur's death.

Constantine is the reigning king in the poems that comprise the volume *Under King Constantine* (1893) by Katrina Trask, poems which seem to reflect none of the chaos of civil war that led to Arthur's death and Constantine's assuming the throne.

Constantine (Uther's father) Constantine is the father of *Constans, *Aurelius Ambrosius, and *Uther Pendragon. According to Geoffrey, he is the brother of Aldroenus, the King of Brittany. Constantine comes to Britain to fight its invaders, rallies the people, is victorious, and is named king. A Pict in his service assassinates him. After the death of Constantine, *Vortigern convinces *Constans that he should accept the crown and then manipulates him and becomes the power behind the throne.

Corbenic (Carbonek, Carbonic) In the thirteenth-century *Estoire del Saint Graal*, *Alain le Gros, one of the keepers of the *Grail, journeys to the Land Beyond, whose leprous king Calafes is cured by the Grail after he converts to Christianity. Calafes asks Alain to let the Grail remain in his kingdom and promises to build a castle for it and to marry his daughter to Alain's brother Joshua, to whom the Grail is to be entrusted after Alain's stewardship. When the stronghold is built, an inscription appears in Chaldean saying the castle should be called Corbenic, which in that language means 'Holy Vessel'.

The Post-Vulgate *Queste del Saint Graal* says that Tanabos the Enchanter, who lived before Uther Pendragon and who was the wisest magician ever in *Logres except for *Merlin, made it so that no knight could find the castle except by chance, even if he had been there a hundred times before. Tanabos did this to keep his wife hidden from a knight who loved her. The spell remained in effect until Charlemagne destroyed the castle.

At Carbonic, *Lancelot frees *Elaine, the daughter of *Pelles, from a tub of burning water. It is also at Carbonek that Lancelot fails to achieve the Grail and *Galahad, *Perceval, and *Bors succeed.

Cote Mal Tayle, La (Vallet à la Cote Mautaill-liée) La Cote Mal Tayle is the name that *Kay gives to Brewnor le Noyr, who arrives at *Arthur's court wearing an ill-fitting garment. While Brewnor's father slept, he was killed by a knight. Brewnor vows to wear his father's tunic until he has avenged him. He is knighted by Arthur when he saves *Guinevere from a lion and then undertakes a quest with the lady Maledysaunte, who frequently rebukes him; but *Lancelot convinces her to forbear her insults. She explains that she acted out of love for Brewnor since she thought him too young and wished to discourage him from embarking on such a dangerous quest. She is then called Beau-Pensaunte by Lancelot. Brewnor marries her and eventually avenges his father.

In the French *Prose Tristan* (thirteenth century) and the Italian *Tavola Ritonda* (second quarter of the fourteenth century), Brunor/Brunoro is said to be the brother of *Dinadan.

Cundrie (Kundry) In Wolfram's *Parzival* (first decade of the thirteenth century), Cundrie is the messenger of the *Grail. Very learned, she speaks several languages and has knowledge of dialectic, geometry, and astronomy. Although she is richly dressed, her appearance is that of a hag. Her hair is dark, hard, and overly long; her nose is like a dog's; and she has teeth like a boar's tusks, ears like a bear's, and fingernails like a lion's claws. She berates *Parzival after he has failed to ask the question that would cure the wounded king; but later when Parzival's name appears on the Grail, indicating that he is the next Grail King, she praises him and leads him to the Grail castle. In Wagner's *Parsifal* (first produced 1882), because she laughed at Christ on the cross, Kundry is cursed to live until someone resists her temptations. When Parsifal does so, he baptizes her and frees her from her curse (and from life).

Curvenal See GOVERNAL.

Dagonet (Daguenet) Dagonet is a knight who serves as *Arthur's jester. In Malory's *Morte d'Arthur*, *Dinadan frightens *Mark by telling him that Dagonet is *Lancelot; rather than jousting with the knight, Mark flees. In Tennyson's idyll 'The Last Tournament' (1872), Dagonet recognizes the immorality of the relationship between *Tristram and *Isolt and refuses to dance to what he calls Tristram's 'broken music', symbolic of the breaking of the moral order. Similarly, in Edwin Arlington Robinson's *Merlin* (1917), Dagonet is unable to sing at Arthur's request because of the disorder brought about by the love of *Lancelot and *Guinevere. At the end of Robinson's poem, he says that now he is Merlin's fool, and the seer and the fool leave Camelot together. In Edgar Fawcett's burlesque play *The New King Arthur* (1885), Dagonet is the one character who is true to Arthur. Since virtually all the other characters, who have been attempting to steal *Excalibur, blame him for the theft, he is declared insane and confined in a monastery. In her poem 'The Dwarf's Quest' (1905), Sophie Jewett makes the physically deformed and sharp-tongued Dagonet a knight who achieves the *Grail because of his moral character.

Degrevant (Degravant, Degrevaunt) In the Middle English romance *Sir Degrevant*, Degrevant is said to be both a knight of the Round Table (though there is no other Arthurian content to the romance) and a Crusader. In Malory's *Morte d'Arthur*, Degrevaunt is listed as one of the knights of the Round Table who try to heal Sir *Urre.

Dinabuc (Dinabroke) See GIANT OF ST MICHAEL'S MOUNT.

Dinadan Dinadan comes to prominence in the French *Prose Tristan* (thirteenth century), where he is a foil to those knights who unquestioningly accept the assumptions of chivalry and courtly love. In the Italian *Tavola Ritonda* (second quarter of the fourteenth century), Dindano is the cousin of Breus sanz Pietà. He comments on the folly of love but becomes devoted to *Tristano. When Marco (*Mark) is captured after killing Tristano, Dindano tries to kill him, an act for which he himself would have been put to death—since Artù (*Arthur) will not allow the slaying of a prisoner—had Marco himself not pardoned him for the offence.

In Malory's *Morte d'Arthur*, Dinadan remains a mocker of chivalry but, as in earlier sources, he is brave when called upon to fight. He admires good knights like Tristram and *Lamorak and says self-deprecatingly that although he is not 'of worship' himself, he loves those who are. Hated only by 'murtherers', according to Malory, Dinadan has great affection for Lamorak, which wins him the enmity of *Gawain and *Agravaine, who ultimately slay him. Contemptuous of Mark, Dinadan writes a scathing lay about him, which he teaches to the harper Eliot so he can perform it before Mark. (Ernest Rhys constructs the mocking lay supposed to have been made by Dinadan in his poem 'The Lay of King Mark' (1905).)

Dinas Emrys Dinas Emrys or the Fort of *Ambrosius is the site at which *Vortigern attempted to build a tower, which repeatedly collapsed. In Nennius' account, it is Ambrosius (Emrys), and in Geoffrey, it is *Merlin, who tells Vortigern that the tower falls because of a pool with two dragons fighting in it beneath the foundation. According to Nennius, Ambrosius advises Vortigern to seek another site for his tower, but he does not. This tale draws on Celtic lore such as that found in *Lludd and Llefelys* in the *Mabinogion*, which speaks of three plagues that

befell Britain, the second of which is a scream on every May Eve that makes men lose their strength and women their fertility. Lludd explains that the scream is caused by a dragon which represents Britain fighting with a dragon which represents foreigners. He advises that the plague can be lifted by digging up the dragons in the exact centre of Britain, said to be at Oxford, and reburying them at Dinas Emrys. It is presumably these dragons which Ambrosius or Merlin reveals to Vortigern.

The story of Vortigern's tower is the central symbol in the novel *The Collapsing Castle* (1990) by Haydn Middleton. Set in the twentieth century, the novel has a protagonist who re-enacts Vortigern's lust and disastrous downfall.

Dolorous Guard See JOYOUS GUARD.

Dolorous Stroke In the *Estoire* and the *Queste del Saint Graal* (thirteenth century), the sword left by Solomon on the ship for *Galahad is said to have been taken and used by King Varlan against King Lambor. Lambor was killed by the blow, but as a result, both their kingdoms were laid waste. When Varlan returned to the ship to retrieve the scabbard, he placed the sword inside it and fell dead. In Thomas Malory's *Morte d'Arthur*, which follows its source in the *Suite du Merlin*, *Balin strikes the Dolorous Stroke when he uses *Longinus' spear to wound King *Pellam. The Dolorous Stroke not only gives to the king a wound that must be healed by the Grail knight but also causes his realm to become a *wasteland.

In Charles Williams' poems, the 'Dolorous Blow' becomes a symbol for original sin, which caused the good natural world created by God to be perceived as evil.

Drystan See TRISTAN.

Ector (Antor, Entor) Ector (called Antor in the French *Vulgate Cycle and in English works descended from it, such as the fifteenth-century Middle English *Prose Merlin*) is, according to Malory, the good knight to whom *Merlin entrusts the raising of *Arthur. He is also the father of *Kay. When Arthur draws the sword from the stone and gives it to Kay, Ector forces his son to tell the truth about how he obtained it. When it is clear that Arthur pulled out the sword and is the rightful king, Ector asks him to make Kay his seneschal, a request that Arthur, saddened to learn that Ector is not his real father, grants.

Ector de Maris See HECTOR DE MARIS.

Elaine of Astolat (The Lady of Shalott) Sometimes called 'the Lily Maid', Elaine is Malory's name for the dame of Astolat (Escalot) who falls in love with *Lancelot when he stays at the castle of her father Bernard at Astolat on his way to a tournament at *Winchester. When the great knight agrees to wear her token in the tournament, Elaine believes that he returns the love that she feels for him; but he wears the token merely to help disguise his identity, just as he wears the shield of Bernard's elder son Tirry so he will not be recognized. His own shield he leaves in Elaine's care. When Lancelot is seriously wounded in the tournament, Elaine, still believing he loves her, nurses him back to health. When he recovers and disabuses her of this notion, she pines away and, realizing that she will soon die from unrequited love, has her body put into a barge covered with black samite. With a letter to Lancelot clutched in her hand, she floats down to Westminster. When her letter is read, even *Guinevere, formerly jealous of Lancelot's relationship with Elaine, pities the dead young woman and asks Lancelot if he could not have shown her a little kindness. The story of the maiden known as the demoiselle d'Ascalot is told in the *Mort Artu* (thirteenth century) and in the *Stanzaic Morte Arthur* (fourteenth century), where she is called the Maid of Ascalot.

Using Malory's tale as his source, Alfred Tennyson recounts the story of Elaine in his 'Lancelot and Elaine' idyll (formerly called 'Elaine', 1859). Tennyson makes Elaine an image of true, devoted, but unrealistic love. He tells an alternative version of her story in his poem 'The Lady of Shalott' (1833, revised and reprinted in 1842). Tennyson's Lady of Shalott devotes her time to weaving and views the world through a mirror. Content in her world of shadows until she sees the image of Lancelot and her safe, vicarious world is disrupted, she, like Elaine, is unable to live any longer and dies as she floats down to *Camelot in a barge.

Largely because of the popularity of Tennyson's poems, the image of the lady who died for love of Lancelot and had her body put into a barge became extremely popular and was often depicted in art. But the romantic notion of the death of Elaine was challenged by Elizabeth Stuart Phelps in her short story 'The Lady of Shalott' (1879), in which the Lady is a young woman of the nineteenth century, crippled and living in poverty and ultimately suffering a pathetic rather than romantic death. T. H. White combines the two Elaines from Malory into one character. His Elaine is the mother of Galahad but also the woman who dies for love of Lancelot, though she is not the lily maid of other versions but a middle-aged woman clutching rosary beads instead of a letter.

Elaine of Corbenic Elaine is the daughter of King *Pelles and the mother of *Galahad. (The *Vulgate Cycle says 'she was called Amite though her true name was Helizabel'.) Because she was considered the fairest lady in that country, Elaine was put into a tub of boiling water by *Morgan le Fay and the Queen of Northgales and could be freed only by the best knight. After Elaine spends five years in the tub, *Lancelot arrives at *Corbenic and frees her from her torment. With the assistance of her handmaiden, the sorceress *Brisen, Elaine tricks Lancelot into sleeping with her, and she conceives Galahad. Later, Elaine visits Camelot and tricks Lancelot into her bed once again. *Guinevere's subsequent rejection of Lancelot drives him mad. Eventually, Lancelot comes to the castle of Pelles, who intends to make him a fool at the knighting of his nephew Castor. Elaine recognizes him and has him carried to the tower where the *Grail resides; there, he is cured by its power.

T. H. White conflates Elaine of Corbenic with *Elaine of Astolat. In John Erskine's novel *Galahad* (1926), Elaine, a free-thinking 'new woman', resists a traditional role and determines to have a child with Lancelot—an act that later causes her own son Galahad to reject her because he sees it as sinful.

Eldol See HENGIST.

Elyabel See TRISTAN'S PARENTS.

Elyzabeth See TRISTAN'S PARENTS.

Emrys See AMBROSIUS AURELIANUS.

Enid (Enide) See GERAINT.

Enite See GERAINT.

Entor See ECTOR.

Erec See GERAINT.

Erex See GERAINT.

Escalot See ELAINE OF ASTOLAT.

Esclabor See PALAMEDES.

Ettarde (Ettarre) See PELLEAS.

Evalach (Evelake) In the thirteenth-century Vulgate *Estoire del Saint Graal*, Evalach is the king of *Sarras. Converted by *Josephus, he takes the Christian name Mordrain, said to mean 'late to believe'. His wife Sarrasinte, whose name is said to mean 'full of faith', was secretly a Christian before his conversion. When Mordrain approaches too closely to the *Grail, a cloud descends upon him and takes away his sight and strength. He asks God that he might live until the good knight who is the last of *Nascien's line (i.e. *Galahad) achieves the Grail. Before his death, *Joseph of Arimathea's son Josephus makes a cross with blood from his bleeding nose on Mordrain's shield, the shield with the red cross that is destined for Galahad in the *Queste del Saint Graal* (thirteenth century). The Middle English poem *Joseph of Arimathea* (latter half of the fourteenth century) draws from the French romances the story of Evelake.

Evida See GERAINT.

Excalibur (Caliburn, Chaliburne, Kaletvwlch)
Geoffrey of Monmouth, Wace, and Layamon all observe that *Arthur's sword Caliburn was forged on the Isle of *Avalon. In his *Chronicle* (1338), Robert Mannyng of Brunne writes that the blade of Caliburn was ten feet long. Mannyng also records that when Richard I was reconciled with Tancred, he gave his former adversary 'the gude swerd Caliburne þat Arthur luffed so welle' (part 2, line 3804). Malory, following his French source, explains the name Excalibur as meaning 'Kutte [Cut] Steele'.

In Malory's *Morte d'Arthur*, Excalibur is the name given to the sword Arthur receives from the Lady of the Lake and entrusts to Bedivere to return to the water after his final battle. (There is only one place in the *Morte* where the sword drawn from the stone is referred to as Excalibur: in his battle with the kings who will not accept him, Arthur draws the sword from the stone, on

*Merlin's advice, only when he is losing the battle. When he draws 'his swerd Excalibur', it gives the light of thirty torches and helps him to put his enemies to flight.) When this sword from the stone breaks in two as Arthur fights *Pellinore, Merlin saves Arthur by casting an enchantment over Pellinore and then takes the king to receive another sword, Excalibur, from the *Lady of the Lake. Merlin tells Arthur that Excalibur's scabbard is even more valuable than the sword itself because while he wears it he will not lose any blood or be severely wounded. *Morgan le Fay, to whom Arthur has entrusted the care of Excalibur, gives the sword to her lover *Accolon to use against Arthur. Provided with a counterfeit Excalibur, Arthur is saved by *Nyneve. Morgan then steals the scabbard and throws it into a lake so it can no longer protect Arthur. Excalibur must be returned to the water at the end of Arthur's life, a task assigned to *Bedivere in Malory's account—but to *Girflet in the Vulgate *Mort Artu*; to his squire in the *Tavola Ritonda*; to Gawain, according to the fourteenth-century poem *The Parlement of the Thre Ages*; and to *Perceval in the film *Excalibur* (1981).

A number of modern playwrights, novelists, and film-makers have used Excalibur as an important symbol. Arthur's loss of Excalibur as a sign of weakness or trouble in his reign is a motif in the plays *The Fairy of the Lake* (1801) by John Thelwall, *Excalibur* (1893) by Ralph Adams Cram, and *The New King Arthur* (1885) by Edgar Fawcett; it has a similar function in the film *Excalibur* and even, in a less serious way, in the fifteen-part cliffhanger *The Adventures of Sir Galahad* (1950).

In the novel *Any Old Iron* (1989) by British novelist Anthony Burgess, the sword becomes a symbol of the Welsh past. In Mary Stewart's *The Hollow Hills* (1973), Caliburn is said to be the sword of Macsen Wledig (the Emperor Maximus).

Fair Unknown The Fair Unknown—or Le Bel Inconnu or Lybeaus Desconus—is a motif that appears in a number of medieval romances in which an unknown youth comes to *Arthur's court and proves himself to be a great knight. In several of them, the Fair Unknown is *Gawain's son, named Ginglain, Gyngolyn, Gyngelayne, or Guingalin (in various French and English romances) or Wigalois (in Wirnt von Grafenberg's early thirteenth-century romance *Wigalois*). The motif also appears in works about figures other than Gawain's son, such as Malory's Gareth.

False Guinevere See GUINEVERE, THE FALSE.

Famurgan See MORGAN LE FEY.

Feirefiz In Wolfram's *Parzival* (first decade of the thirteenth century), Feirefiz is *Parzival's half-brother, fathered by Parzival's father Gahmuret on Queen Belacane. Since one of Feirefiz's parents is white and one black, he is depicted as piebald or parti-coloured. Ultimately he is baptized and marries Repanse de Schoye, the *Grail maiden. They are the parents of *Prester John.

Felelolye See URRE.

Fisher King (Rich Fisherman, Roi Pescheor) The Fisher King is the guardian of the *Grail and is often but not always identified with the Maimed King who is wounded in the thigh or the genitals, whose wound is related to the fertility of his kingdom, and who can be healed only by the Grail knight. In Chrétien's *Perceval*, *Perceval meets a man fishing who offers him lodging. There he finds a king (the same man he met fishing) who has been wounded in battle in the thighs (or, in some manuscripts, between the legs). Perceval's failure to ask who is served by the *Grail and what is the meaning of the bleeding lance, the Grail, and the platter in the Grail procession dooms the Fisher King to continued suffering. Robert de Boron calls *Bron, brother-in-law of *Joseph of Arimathea and grandfather to Perceval, the Fisher King. Bron is succeeded as guardian of the Grail by Perceval. In *Estoire del Saint Graal*, *Josephus grants guardianship of the Grail to *Alain le Gros, Bron's twelfth son, and tells him to catch fish for the people. Alain catches only one fish, but it is multiplied. In honour of the miracle, he and all future guardians of the Grail are called the Rich Fishermen. In the French romance *Sone de Nausay*, Joseph of Arimathea is said to be the Fisher King. And Wolfram von Eschenbach names the Fisher King *Anfortas.

Novels set in the modern world sometimes feature Fisher King figures, such as Saul Henchman in Anthony Powell's *Fisher King* (1986), Pop Fisher in Bernard Malamud's *The Natural* (1952), and Emmett Smith in Bobbie Ann Mason's *In Country* (1985).

Gaheriet See GARETH.

Gaheris (Guerrehet) Gaheris is one of *Gawain's brothers, a son of *Lot and *Morgause. According to the Post-Vulgate Cycle and Malory, Gaheris kills his mother when he finds her in bed with *Lamorak. (In T. H. White's *The Once and Future King* (1958), it is not Gaheris but rather *Agravaine who kills his mother.) Gaheris, along with his brother *Gareth, is ordered by Arthur to form part of the guard that takes *Guinevere to the stake. The brothers are unable to refuse Arthur's command but insist on going 'in pesyble wyse' (that is, without armour). In the confusion of the rescue, *Lancelot kills both Gareth and Gaheris.

Galahad (Galaad) Although *Perceval was originally the *Grail knight, Galahad becomes the primary achiever of the Grail in the thirteenth-century French *Vulgate Cycle and in Malory's *Morte d'Arthur*. He is conceived by Amite or *Elaine of Corbenic, daughter of *Pelles, when *Lancelot is tricked into sleeping with her, under the influence of *Brisen's magic. A descendant of *Nascien and of the biblical David, Galahad is chaste and sinless and thus replaces his father as the best knight of the world. As the knight destined to achieve the Grail, he is able to sit in the *Siege Perilous. Galahad is the only knight who can wear with impunity the shield of *Evalach; and the sword of David on the ship of Solomon is destined for him as well. Solomon's wife originally made a girdle for that sword, which is replaced by the girdle *Perceval's sister weaves using her own hair. Along with Perceval and *Bors, Galahad achieves the Grail; and he heals the maimed king. The three knights accompany the holy cup to *Sarras, where Galahad becomes king and, after ruling a year, has a spiritual vision of the Grail and prays to leave the world. As he dies, a host of angels bear his soul to heaven.

In the nineteenth century, Tennyson's poem 'Sir Galahad' (published 1842, but written in 1834) created an idealized image of Galahad as one whose 'strength is as the strength of ten, | Because [his] heart is pure', which in turn influenced a notion of moral knighthood that had wide ramifications. Since Galahad is a knight of stainless purity, without the moral and ethical conflicts of someone like Lancelot, he is rarely the protagonist in modern fiction. An interesting exception is the novel *Galahad* (1926) by John Erskine, which presents Lancelot's son not as the achiever of the Grail but as someone trained by *Guinevere to seek perfection. His single-minded and inflexible moral code, which causes him to reject his father and even Guinevere herself, inspires tales that grow into the legend of the Grail.

Galahad, son of Joseph of Arimathea The thirteenth-century Vulgate *Estoire del Saint Graal* and *Lancelot* say that the younger son of *Joseph of Arimathea was named Galahad and that Wales, originally called Hoselice, was named after him (*Galles*, Old French for Wales, coming from the first syllable of his name).

Galatyn (Galantyne, Galuth) Malory calls *Gawain's sword Galatyn or Galantyne. In the *Alliterative Morte Arthure*, it is called Galuth.

Galehaut In the thirteenth-century Vulgate *Lancelot*, Galehaut attacks *Arthur's land, but when victory is in his grasp, he yields to Arthur at the request of *Lancelot, whose nobility has impressed him. Galehaut and Lancelot become close friends, and Galehaut arranges the first private meeting between Lancelot and *Guinevere. With Guinevere's help, Galehaut and the Lady of Malehaut become lovers. Galehaut's friendship and love for Lancelot are so great that when he hears a rumour of Lancelot's death, he stops eating and drinking; while he is in this weakened state, a wound he had received festers, and he dies.

Galuth See GALATYN.

Ganhardin See KAHEDIN.

Gareth (Gaheriet, Karyet) Gareth is the youngest brother of *Gawain and the son of *Lot and *Morgause of Orkney. As 'Karyet', he is one of the great heroes of *Arthur's court in Ulrich von Zatzikhoven's *Lanzelet* (c.1200–4).

In the thirteenth-century Vulgate *Lancelot*, Gaheriet is the most charming of all the brothers of Gawain and is described as valiant, handsome, and noble. (But he is also the least well spoken, and *Guerrehet is said to be Gawain's favorite brother—although in the *Mort Artu*, Gaheriet is the favourite. Thus there seems to be a discrepancy between the two texts.) In the *Mort Artu*, Gaheriet is tragically slain by Lancelot in the rescue of the queen; his death causes Arthur and Gawain great grief and inspires them to attack Lancelot.

Gareth plays a significant role in Malory's *Morte d'Arthur*. In Malory's 'Tale of Sir Gareth', Gareth initially works in the kitchen and is mockingly called Beaumains by *Kay. But he proves himself to be an exemplar of chivalry who is knighted by and devoted to *Lancelot and who acts chivalrously towards *Lynette despite her abuse of him. After Lancelot blindly slays Gareth in his rescue of Guinevere from the stake, Gawain turns against his former friend and demands that Arthur pursue him to punish him, thereby setting the stage for Mordred's usurpation of the throne.

In Tennyson's idyll of 'Gareth and Lynette' (1872), although Gareth, like almost everyone in Camelot, is not what he seems, he proves himself better than he initially appears to the sharp-tongued Lynette and the misjudging Kay when he defeats a series of knightly opponents and rescues *Lyonors. Gareth also figures in modern works such as E. M. R. Ditmas's *Gareth of Orkney* (1956) and T. H. White's *The Once and Future King* (1958).

Garlon See BALIN.

Gawain (Gauvain, Walewein, Gwalchmai) The character known as Gwalchmai in Welsh literature possesses some of the traits of the later character Gawain, with whom he is eventually equated. Triad 75 lists him as one of the three men most courteous to guests and strangers; and Triad 91 calls him one of the three most fearless men of the Island of Britain. The name 'Gwalchmai' is sometimes explained as meaning 'hawk of May', a phrase used as the title of Gillian Bradshaw's 1980 novel about the young hero.

Gawain is *Arthur's nephew, and in much Arthurian literature he is presented as the best of Arthur's knights. In a number of sources, his strength is said to increase until noon, at which point it begins to wane. According to the *Mort Artu*, his strength increases around noon because the priest who baptized him prayed that his strength would increase at noon, the hour he was baptized, and that no matter how oppressed he might be, he would be strengthened and refreshed at that time. Malory says that a holy man gave Gawain the gift of increasing strength from 'undern' (9 a.m.) until noon every day of the year.

In Geoffrey of Monmouth's history, Gawain is one of Arthur's most valorous knights in his continental wars, and he dies in the struggle against *Modred when Arthur returns to Britain. The author of *The Rise of Gawain* (twelfth century) tells of Gawain's being brought to Rome by Viamundus, the fisherman who stole the boy from the merchants, to whom *Anna, his mother, had entrusted him because he was born before she was married to Loth (*Lot). There, he is knighted by and serves the emperor. Gawain is said by Chrétien in his *Perceval* (1180s) to be the most courteous knight in the world. In this work, and in numerous others by various authors, Gawain is contrasted to Kay, whose boorishness is a foil to Gawain's courtliness. In several Dutch romances, Gawain is called the Father of Adventure, and he has great skill in healing as well as in fighting and diplomacy. In many of the French romances of the twelfth to the fourteenth centuries, Gawain is the most important hero; but *Lancelot eventually replaces him in this role.

In the thirteenth-century *Vulgate Cycle, Gawain is presented as the second-best worldly knight after Lancelot. According to the *Estoire del Saint Graal*, Gawain is a descendant of Peter, a relative of *Joseph of Arimathea. Known for his kindness to the poor, he is the most courteous knight, which causes many ladies to love him. In the *Queste del Saint Graal*, he is described as being 'of all the world's men . . . the best-liked by strangers'; but he does not have the spiritual qualities to achieve the quest for the *Grail. In the *Mort Artu*, Gawain admits that his killing of eighteen knights while on the quest was not a demonstration of his prowess but a consequence of his sin. He loves the *Maiden of Escalot, but his love is not returned because of her love for Lancelot. He refuses to join in *Agravain's accusation against Lancelot and *Guinevere; later, out of grief for his brothers—particularly his favourite *Gaheriet—who are slain in the rescue of the queen, he insists on pursuing and fighting with Lancelot. Although Lancelot refuses to slay him when he has the opportunity, Gawain ultimately dies from a head wound received in their fight. Nevertheless, before his death Gawain realizes that Lancelot was the best and most generous knight, wishes he could ask his forgiveness before his death, and advises Arthur to ask him for help.

In Malory's *Morte d'Arthur*, Gawain is at times brave and noble and at times vengeful and treacherous. He keeps alive the feud between the house of Lot and the house of *Pellinore by treacherously killing Pellinore and then *Lamorak. He is also unforgiving when Lancelot accidentally kills Gareth, and he refuses to allow Arthur to make peace with him. He does, however, try to dissuade *Mordred and *Agravain from accusing Lancelot; and he finally realizes that Lancelot is noble and Mordred wicked.

Gaynor See GUINEVERE.

Geraint (Gereint, Erec, Erex) Geraint may develop from a historical king of Dumnonia, who ruled in the sixth century. In Triad 88, Enid is said to be one of the three splendid maidens of Arthur's court. She and Geraint are the principal figures in the Welsh tale *Geraint the Son of Erbin*, to use Lady Charlotte Guest's title, or *Geraint and Enid*, a Welsh story analogous to Chrétien's *Erec et Enide* (c.1170). The Welsh version dates from the thirteenth century and so is later than Chrétien's. In both versions, the hero—called Erec by Chrétien—fights in and wins a tournament in which each knight defends the assertion that his beloved is the most beautiful and in which the prize is a sparrowhawk. When Enid and Geraint (or Erec) marry, the hero, delighting in marital bliss, forgets his knightly duties. In the Welsh tale, Enid laments that she is the cause of her husband's dishonour. Geraint, hearing only the last part of her lament in which she fears she is not a true wife because of the shame their marriage has brought to his knightly reputation, believes his wife to have been unfaithful and takes her with him on a quest in which he proves his prowess and she her fidelity. In Chrétien's version, Enide tells Erec directly of the talk of the court about his failure to act in a knightly manner, and a similar quest ensues. In both versions, after a series of adventures, the couple prove to each other their noble qualities and their love.

Chrétien's romance is the source for Hartmann von Aue's *Erec* (c.1180) and the thirteenth-century Icelandic *Erex saga*, in which the lovers are named Erex and Evida. But it was from the Welsh tale, known to him from its translation in Guest's *Mabinogion*, that Tennyson took his idylls about the two characters. Tennyson constructs the poems so that they support the theme of appearance and reality that runs through the *Idylls*, and he makes their story a tribute to faithful married love. Though not common figures in modern Arthurian literature other than Tennyson's *Idylls*, Geraint and Enid are the focus of two plays: Ernest Rhys's *Enid: A Lyric Play* (1918) and Donald R. Rawe's *Geraint: Last of the Arthurians* (1972). They also have a minor role in Edgar Fawcett's play *The New King Arthur* (1885) and are the subject of the book-length poem *Geraint of Devon* by Marion Lee Reynolds (1916).

Giant of St Michael's Mount The Giant of St Michael's Mount ravishes and kills maidens and plunders Brittany. Wace says the giant is named Dinabuc; in his *Chronicle*, Robert Mannyng of Brunne names him Dinabroke. In the *Alliterative Morte Arthure*, he lives outside the law and eats the flesh not only of animals but also of human children. In the various versions, he is killed by *Arthur just before he begins his Roman campaigns. Arthur's victory against the giant is generally prefigured by a dream in which a dragon overcomes a huge bear. The story of the Giant of St Michael's Mount is briefly recounted in *Tristrams saga* (1226) even though, as the author admits, it has nothing to do with the story, except that this giant came from Africa to Brittany, where he built the vaulted chamber in which *Tristram has craftsmen construct statues of *Ísönd and *Bringvet.

Giglain (Ginglain) See FAIR UNKNOWN.

Girflet (Gryfflet) In the thirteenth-century Vulgate *Mort Artu*, Girflet is the last survivor of the final battle between *Arthur and *Mordred, and it is to him that Arthur entrusts the task of returning *Excalibur to the lake (the task that Malory assigns to *Bedivere, since in the *Morte d'Arthur* Gryfflet is slain by *Lancelot's followers in the rescue of *Guinevere). Eighteen days after Arthur's death, Girflet dies.

Glastonbury Located in Somerset, Glastonbury is the focal point for a number of legends and stories relating to *Arthur and the *Grail and is sometimes equated with the Island of *Avalon, an association that is bolstered by the fact that the marshy lands of the region made Glastonbury virtually an island in its early history. The site of a medieval abbey and perhaps a sacred site even before the coming of Christianity to Britain, Glastonbury was, according to tradition, the first Christian settlement in Britain. By some legendary accounts, Christianity at Glastonbury can be traced back to *Joseph of Arimathea. In his fifteenth-century translation of the Vulgate *Estoire del Saint Graal*, Henry Lovelich asserts that Joseph of Arimathea was buried at Glastonbury.

In *The Antiquities of Glastonbury* (*c*.1135), William of Malmesbury explains that the name of Glastonbury came from a British king named Glasteing, who followed a sow until he found her under an apple tree; hence he called the place 'Insula Avallonia' or 'Apple Island' ('avalla' meaning 'apple'). William also offers the alternative explanation that Avallonia derives from Avalloc, a man who lived there with his daughters. According to William, the island was first called Ynyswitrin by the British and then Glastinbiry by the Angles, which he considers either the translation of Ynyswitrin or a name derived from Glasteing.

In his *Life of Gildas* (*c*.1130), Caradoc of Llancarfan reports that Glastonbury was called Ynisgutrin, Island of Glass, by its original British inhabitants but that the English renamed it Glastigberi, the City of Glass. Caradoc identifies it as the place where *Melvas, king of the summer country, had his stronghold, to which he brought Arthur's queen after abducting her.

In 1190 or 1191, Arthur's grave was said to have been found at Glastonbury. Giraldus Cambrensis records in his *De principis instructione* (1193) that Arthur was buried deep in the earth in a hollowed oak tree between two stone pyramids. A lead cross in the tomb contained an inscription declaring that the famous King Arthur and his wife *Guinevere were buried here on the Island of *Avalon. Other accounts of the lead cross—that, for example, by John Leland, who claims to have seen the cross—do not add Guinevere to the transcription (though Leland's report, like that of Giraldus, does record that her body was discovered in the tomb and that a lock of her golden hair crumbled to dust when touched by a monk). In literary accounts of Arthur's death, he is often buried at Glastonbury.

Glastonbury is also known for its connection to the Holy Grail, fostered by the link to Joseph of Arimathea, who in some accounts led the expedition that brought the Grail to Britain. The association with the Grail and with ancient spirituality has made Glastonbury a centre for people with traditional and non-traditional spiritual views. Dion Fortune, author of *Avalon of the Heart* (1934), suggested that Glastonbury can be approached not only through history and through legend but also through 'the Mystic Way', which leads to the 'Avalon of the Heart'; and she spoke of Glastonbury as 'a gateway to the Unseen'. In her book *The Mists of Avalon* (1982), Marion Zimmer Bradley uses a similar scheme of a historical Glastonbury coexisting with another realm called Avalon. (See also AVALON.)

Glastonbury Thorn An eighteenth-century chapbook, *The History of That Holy Disciple Joseph of Arimathea*, tells the legend of the Glastonbury Thorn: when Joseph planted his staff on a hill at Glastonbury, it sprouted into a thorn tree which continues to bloom each year on Christmas Day. In his play *Merlin* (1907), Francis Coutts says that *Merlin's wand is a branch from the Holy Thorn at Glastonbury. Niviane (*Vivien) is advised by *Morgan le Fay to steal the wand, which, in combination with a charm that Morgan teaches her, will allow Niviane to seal Merlin in a cave and gain her freedom from him.

Glatysaunt Beast See QUESTING BEAST.

Gorlois In the chronicles Gorlois, Duke of Cornwall, is generally a faithful ally to *Uther Pendragon and is valiant in the struggle against Uther's enemies; but Uther's desire for Gorlois's wife *Igraine or Ygerna causes a breach between them. Since Gorlois has placed Igraine in his impregnable castle at *Tintagel, Uther prevails upon *Merlin to help him satisfy his lust. Merlin changes him into the shape of Gorlois so he can gain access to Tintagel. As a result, *Arthur is conceived. When Gorlois is slain in combat, Uther is able to marry Igraine.

In the revenge tragedy *The Misfortunes of Arthur* (1587) by Thomas Hughes, the ghost of Gorlois calls for revenge on the house of Uther. In Warwick Deeping's novel *Uther and Igraine* (1902), Gorlois is not the noble and wronged figure of the chronicles. Instead, he uses Merlin's sorcery to trick Igraine into marrying him and then does all he can to break her spirit.

Gornemant (Gurnemanz) Gornemant is the knight who trains *Perceval in knighthood and instructs him in courtly behaviour. Gornemant advises the young man not to keep referring to his mother and not to talk too much. The latter admonition prevents Perceval from asking the crucial question when he first visits the *Grail castle.

Gorre (Gore) See BADEMAGU.

Goswhit Layamon writes that *Arthur's helmet of steel, which had belonged to *Uther and on which were numerous jewels set in gold, was named Goswhit.

Governal (Governale, Governail, Curvenal, Kurvenal, Kurwenal) Governal is *Tristan's tutor and protector. In Béroul's *Tristran* (last quarter of the twelfth century), he helps Tristran free *Yseut when *Mark delivers her to the lepers. Governal also kills the forester who betrayed Tristran when he and Yseut were hiding in the woods. In the thirteenth-century *Prose Tristan*, *Merlin entrusts Tristan to the care of Governal. In the prose tradition, Tristan makes Governal King of Lyonesse. The fourteenth-century Italian *Tavola Ritonda* says that Artù (*Arthur), with the help of other kings, including King Governale, besieges Marco (Mark) in order to punish him for Tristano's death. When Marco tries to escape, Governale captures him.

Grail The Holy Grail is generally considered to be the cup from which Christ drank at the Last Supper and the vessel used by *Joseph of Arimathea to catch his blood as he hung on the cross. This significance, however, was introduced into the Arthurian legends by Robert de Boron in his verse romance *Joseph d'Arimathie* (sometimes also called *Le Roman de l'estoire dou Graal*), which was probably written in the last decade of the twelfth century or the first few years of the thirteenth. In earlier sources as well as in some later ones, the Grail is something quite different. The term 'grail' comes from the Latin *gradale*, which means a dish brought to the table during various stages (Latin 'gradus') or courses of a meal. In Chrétien and other early writers, the term 'grail' suggests such a plate. Chrétien, for example, speaks of 'un graal', a grail or platter and thus not a unique item. Wolfram von Eschenbach's *Parzival* (first decade of the thirteenth century) presents the Grail as a stone which provides sustenance and prevents anyone who beholds it from dying within that week. In medieval romance, the Grail was said to have been brought to *Glastonbury in Britain by Joseph of Arimathea and his followers. In the time of *Arthur, the quest for the Grail was the highest spiritual pursuit. For Chrétien, author of *Perceval*, and his continuators, *Perceval is the knight who must achieve the Grail. For some other French authors, as for Malory, *Galahad is the chief Grail knight, though others (Perceval and *Bors in Malory's *Morte d'Arthur*) also achieve the quest.

Tennyson is perhaps the author who has had the greatest influence on the conception of the Grail quest for the modern English-speaking world through his *Idylls* and especially through his short poem 'Sir Galahad' (published 1842, but written in 1834). However, James Russell Lowell's *The Vision of Sir Launfal* (1848), one of the most popular of nineteenth-century American poems, gave to generations a democratized notion of the Grail quest as something achievable by anyone who is truly charitable. T. S. Eliot, who wrote another very influential poem based on the Grail stories, *The Waste Land* (1922), made use of the notion that the Grail story originated in fertility myths, a theory proposed by Jessie Weston in her book *From Ritual to Romance* (1920) but now no longer accepted.

Gringalet In Chrétien's *Erec* (c.1165), *Gawain's horse is named Gringalet; in Hartmann's *Erec* (c.1180), the name is Wintwalite; in the fourteenth-century *Sir Gawain and the Green Knight*, Gryngolet; and in the late fourteenth-century *Awntyrs off Arthur*, the horse is called Grissell and is killed in Gawain's fight with Galeron.

Grissell See GRINGALET.

Gryfflet See GIRFLET.

Guerrehet See GAHERIS.

Guinevere (Guenevere, Guenever, Guenver, Ginover, Gwendoloena, Gwenhwyfar, Gaynor, Waynor) Guinevere is *Arthur's wife and queen; according to the *Vulgate Cycle and Malory, she is the daughter of *Leodegrance of Carmelide. Geoffrey of Monmouth introduces the notion of Guinevere's infidelity (with *Modred) while Arthur is fighting on the continent. In the twelfth-century *Rise of Gawain*, Arthur's wife is called Gwendoloena and is said to have been initiated into sorcery and to be able to divine the future.

In Chrétien's *Lancelot*, Guinevere becomes *Lancelot's lover after he rescues her from *Meleagant. She is a demanding courtly lover; for example, she refuses to see Lancelot after he has suffered greatly in saving her because he hesitated two steps before leaping into a cart on his quest to rescue her, thus suggesting that his love was not absolute. But she loves deeply and contemplates suicide when she hears rumours of Lancelot's death.

Although generally in the romance tradition Guinevere is portrayed as Lancelot's lover, that is not the case in Ulrich von Zatzikhoven's *Lanzelet*. Ginover, who fails the chastity test of the mantle, is said to have erred only in thought. The nature of those thoughts is not revealed, but she and Arthur have a son and seem to be happily married. And she is an intimate friend of Lanzelet's beloved Yblis. Lanzelet does champion Ginover, but when she is abducted by Valerin, Arthur leads the expedition to rescue her and Lanzelet plays only a minor role.

In the Vulgate Cycle, the first meeting between Guinevere and Lancelot is arranged by *Galehaut, and Guinevere subsequently arranges for Galehaut and the Lady of Malehaut to become lovers. She is later accused of not being the true Guinevere by the illegitimate daughter of her father Leodagan and the wife of his seneschal. When Arthur falls in love with the False *Guinevere and accepts her as his queen, Guinevere is protected by Lancelot and Galehaut until the truth is revealed. Lancelot assists Guinevere again by rescuing her when she is abducted by Meleagant. In the *Mort Artu*, after Guinevere is found to be Lancelot's lover and condemned to be burned to death, Lancelot rescues her again and takes her to *Joyous Guard, but the pope demands that Arthur be reconciled with her. When Arthur leaves for France to attack Lancelot, Mordred tries to claim the throne and to marry Guinevere. She flees to the Tower of London and then, when Arthur returns, to a convent, where she later dies.

Malory's Guinevere is jealous and demanding but also a true lover. Her jealousy and anger drive Lancelot mad and lead her to say she wishes he were dead. Nevertheless, she remains true to him. She is accused several times of crimes—infidelity and the murder of *Mador's relative—and must be saved by Lancelot, as she is once again when their love is discovered and she is sentenced to be burned at the stake. When Mordred rebels against

Arthur and attempts to marry her, she flees first to the Tower of London and then to the nunnery at *Amesbury, where she becomes abbess. Lancelot visits her there after the death of Arthur, but she asks him to leave and never to return and refuses even to give him a final kiss. She dies a holy death, of which Lancelot learns in a vision that instructs him to have her buried next to Arthur.

While Malory is understanding of the true love of Guinevere, Tennyson makes her an example of an unfaithful wife. His Guinevere believes that 'He is all fault who hath no fault at all' and wants her lover to 'have a touch of earth'. Arthur, before whom she grovels with guilt when he visits her in the nunnery, says that she has 'spoilt the purpose of my life'.

Modern Arthurian fiction often gives prominence to Guinevere. In Parke Godwin's *Firelord* (1980) and *Beloved Exile* (1984), the latter of which she narrates, Guenevere is a strong and decisive woman who endures much hardship, including being enslaved by Saxons, but still manages to help shape events and the future of Britain. Marion Zimmer Bradley's *The Mists of Avalon* (1982) gives a less sympathetic picture of Gwenhwyfar, who supports and promotes a patriarchal Christianity throughout most of the book, though she and Morgaine, the representative of a more matriarchal and tolerant philosophy, achieve greater understanding of each other late in their lives. Guinevere is also the subject of a number of late twentieth-century and early twenty-first-century trilogies.

Guinevere, the False According to the Vulgate *Merlin*, the False Guinevere is the child of the wife of Cleodalis, seneschal to *Leodagan. On the same night that he fathered Guinevere, Leodagan raped Cleodalis's wife. The two children conceived on this night, born at virtually the same time and identical in appearance except for a crown-shaped birthmark on the back of Leodagan's legitimate daughter, were given the same name. In the Vulgate *Lancelot*, the False Guinevere claims to be *Arthur's true queen and Arthur accepts her claim, causing a break with *Lancelot. When the False Guinevere becomes ill and her flesh rots as punishment for her sin, she confesses the imposture before she dies.

Guingalin See FAIR UNKNOWN.

Gurmun See ISOLT OF IRELAND.

Gurnemanz See GORNEMANT.

Guyomar See MORGAN LE FAY.

Gwalchmai See GAWAIN.

Gwenhwyfar See GUINEVERE.

Gwretheyrn See VORTIGERN.

Gyngolyn (Gyngelayne) See FAIR UNKNOWN.

Hallewes According to Malory, Hallewes is a sorceress who creates the Chapel Perilous and its trials to try to trap *Gawain or *Lancelot. When Lancelot visits the chapel to retrieve the cloth and sword he needs to cure Sir Melyot of Logres, she tries to convince him to leave the sword. He refuses; and she informs him that if he had complied, he would never have seen the queen again. She then asks Lancelot for a kiss. After he refuses again, she tells him that the kiss would have resulted in his death, which she sought because she loves him but knows that only *Guinevere can have his devotion. Had he died, she would have preserved his body and hugged it and kissed it every day.

Hector (Ector) de Maris Hector de Maris (i.e. Hector of the marshes or fens), the half-brother of *Lancelot, is the illegitimate son of King *Ban of Benoic and the daughter of Agravadain, lord of the Castle of the Fens. According to Malory, after Arthur's final battle, Hector spends seven years seeking Lancelot, only to find him dead at *Joyous Guard. In his eulogy, Hector calls Lancelot the truest lover, the most courteous knight, the most meek and gentle among ladies, but the fiercest foe in battle. Hector goes with *Bors and other of Lancelot's kin to fight the infidels in the Holy Land, where he dies.

Helaine the White See BORS (BOHORT).

Helizabel See ELAINE OF CORBENIC.

Hengist (Hengest) Hengist is the Saxon leader who, along with his brother Horsa, was invited into Britain by *Vortigern as a mercenary to protect Britain from invaders. Hengist and Horsa and their followers began acquiring land for themselves and thus initiated the Anglo-Saxon invasion of Britain. Geoffrey and others recount how Hengist first received land in Kent from Vortigern in exchange for the hand of his daughter Renwein (*Rowena) in marriage. Hengist is forced from Britain by Vortigern's son *Vortimer, whom British nobles choose as ruler in place of his father; but after Renwein poisons Vortimer, Vortigern again becomes king and permits Hengist to return to Britain. When Hengist calls for a meeting with the British nobles to discuss peace, he betrays them by ordering his men to conceal weapons and, at the command 'Nimet oure saxes' (draw your short swords), slay the assembled British leaders. Eldol, Earl of Gloucester, escapes and later, after the return of *Ambrosius to Britain, captures Hengist and is allowed to behead him. A number of chronicles suggest that England takes its name from Hengist (or Engest), Engest-land becoming England.

Hoel Hoel, the King of Brittany, is said by Wace, following Geoffrey of Monmouth, to be *Arthur's sister's son. He assists Arthur in his wars in England and on the continent. In some versions of the *Tristan story, Hoel is the father of *Isolt of Brittany.

Holy Grail See GRAIL.

Horsa See HENGIST.

Houdain See HUSDENT.

Huncamunca See TOM THUMB.

Husdent (Houdain, Idonia, Utant) Husdent is *Tristan's hunting hound. Béroul says that Husdent tracked Tristran and *Iseut into the forest, making the same treacherous leap that his master did as he followed his trail. Fearing that the dog's barking will lead to their capture, Tristran is advised by Iseut to train him to hunt silently, so he strikes Husdent whenever he barks until he learns to be quiet. When Iseut is returned to Mark, Tristran leaves the hound with her. In several Tristan romances, it is Husdent who recognizes Tristan, even though Isolt does not, when he returns disguised to Cornwall. In Eilhart von Oberge's Tristrant (between 1170 and 1190), after Tristrant escapes, *Mark is so angry that he orders his dog Utant hung. The squire charged with this task frees the dog in the countryside, and he finds his master in the forest.

In the thirteenth-century English poem Sir Tristrem, Houdain licks the cup from which the lovers drank the love potion; he is faithful to them ever after. A similar incident occurs in the fourteenth-century Italian Tavola Ritonda, in which the hound Idonia licks the potion from the bottle broken by *Governale after Tristano and Isotta have drunk from it; because of the power of the potion, the dog remains forever a companion of the lovers.

Idonia See HUSDENT.

Igraine (Ygrain, Igerne, Ygerne) Igraine is the wife of *Uther Pendragon and the mother of *Arthur. Uther falls in love with her when she is married to the Duke of Cornwall, who in some sources is named *Gorlois. Uther's attention to Igraine causes a rift between him and her husband, who secures her in his impregnable castle at *Tintagel. Enlisted by Uther to help satisfy his lust, *Merlin transforms Uther into the shape of the duke so that he is able to enter the castle and spend the night with Igraine. From this union, Igraine conceives Arthur. After the duke dies in battle, Uther and Igraine marry; but when Arthur is born, he is given to Merlin, a condition to which Uther agreed when he first sought Merlin's assistance. According to Geoffrey of Monmouth and other chroniclers, Igraine and Uther are also the parents of a daughter named *Anna. In Malory's Morte d'Arthur, Igraine has three daughters before she marries Uther: *Morgause, *Morgan le Fay, and Elaine. In Arthour and Merlin (thirteenth century), Ygerne is said to have been married to King Harinan of Gascony, then to Duke Hoel of Cornwall, and then to his successor (called Tintagel and not Gorlois) in Cornwall before marrying Uther.

In Tennyson's account of Arthur's birth, Uther and Igraine conceive Arthur in lawful marriage after the death of Gorlois (though there is an alternative tale in which Arthur is washed ashore at Merlin's feet on a ninth wave and thus is not related to Uther and Igraine). T. H. White has *Gawain and his brothers recount the tale of the affront to their grandmother Igraine by Uther, 'the bloody King of England'. The story of 'the enormous English wickedness' is their mother Morgause's favourite tale and one of the few that she tells her children. In his novel Uther and Igraine (1902), Warwick Deeping creates a courageous, decisive, independent Igraine who defies powerful men in pursuing her love for Uther.

Isolt (Isolde, Isode, Ísönd, Yseult, Ysolt, Ysolde, Essyllt) of Ireland

Isolt of Ireland or Yseult la Blonde is the daughter of the king of Ireland (called Gurmun by Gottfried von Strassburg and Anguysh, Angwysaunce, or Anguin in English and French tales). Her uncle *Morholt (Marhaus) is slain by *Tristan, who then journeys to Ireland to be healed by Isolt. He later returns and wins her hand in marriage for his uncle *Mark. On the voyage to Cornwall, Tristan and Isolt drink a love potion (which is effective for three years in Béroul's version of the story but eternally in some other versions) prepared by her mother for her to drink with Mark on the night they are married. Isolt's love for Tristan forces her to deceive her husband. The deception begins with the substitution of *Brangwain for Isolt in Mark's bed on their wedding night so that he will believe that Isolt is still a virgin. In the prose romances, Isolt is also loved by the Saracen knight *Palamedes, a love which causes her more agitation than joy.

In several versions of the tale, Isolt must undergo an ordeal in which she swears an equivocal oath to convince Mark of her innocence. After many trials and following a period in which the lovers live together in the woods, Tristan is banished from court while Isolt remains. She returns to Tristan after his marriage to *Isolt of Brittany when she learns that he is grievously wounded. Arriving too late to heal him, she dies of grief and is buried with him. In the prose tradition, Tristan is mortally wounded by Mark; and Isolt and Tristan die together, hugging and kissing each other.

Isolt (Isolde, Isode, Ísönd, Ysolt, Ysolde) of Brittany or of the White Hands

Isolt of Brittany is sometimes said to be the daughter of *Hoel and the sister of *Kahedin. She is the woman whom *Tristan marries merely because her name reminds him of his true love, *Isolt of Ireland. Tristan, however, never consummates his marriage to Isolt of Brittany. In some versions of the story, when Tristan is wounded and sends for Isolt of Ireland, his jealous wife lies to him by saying that the sail on the returning ship is black when it is actually white, the sign that his beloved is coming to him. Overcome by his sorrow and his injury, Tristan dies before Isolt of Ireland can reach him.

Matthew Arnold's poem 'Tristram and Iseult' (1852) depicts an Iseult of Brittany who has children to care for after Tristram's death but who has been drained of all joy by her grief. Isolt of Brittany is also a prominent but pathetic figure in Edwin Arlington Robinson's *Tristram* (1927).

Ísönd See ISOLT.

Joseph of Arimathea

Joseph of Arimathea is the rich disciple of Jesus who, according to the Gospels (cf. Matthew 27: 57–60; Mark 15: 43–6; Luke 23: 50–3; John 19: 38), asked Pontius Pilate for the body of Jesus and provided a tomb for it. The Apocryphal Gospels expand on these brief references to tell of his imprisonment because of this service to Christ. According to legend, Joseph was the founder of Christianity in Britain and even brought the child Christ with him to Britain, where Joseph, as a tin merchant, would have conducted business (a legend reflected in William Blake's poem 'Jerusalem', which asks: 'And did those feet [of Christ] in ancient time | Walk upon England's mountains green?'). Triad 81 says that Joseph of Arimathea's is one of the three saintly lineages of the island of Britain. In the romances, most of the *Fisher Kings and *Grail knights are descended from him.

In Robert de Boron's *Joseph of Arimathea* and in the *Perlesvaus*, Joseph is said to have been a soldier of Pilate who asked as the only reward for his service to be allowed to take the body of Christ from the cross. Joseph preserved the Grail, the vessel in which he caught the blood of the crucified Christ, and *Longinus' spear, which was used to pierce Christ's side. According to the thirteenth-century Vulgate *Estoire del Saint Graal*, Joseph was imprisoned by the Jews but sustained by the Grail until the Emperor Vespasian, who had been cured of leprosy by the veil of Veronica, freed him. Afterwards, Joseph led the party that brought the Grail to Britain and was buried in Scotland at an abbey called the Abbey of the Cross. The Middle English alliterative poem *Joseph of Arimathea* makes Joseph a proselytizer spreading the word of God and converting pagans. According to the verse *Lyfe of Joseph of Armathia*, after his death and burial at Glastonbury, Joseph is responsible for numerous miracles.

Josephus (Josephe)

Josephus is the son of *Joseph of Arimathea and his wife Elyab. According to the thirteenth-century Vulgate *Estoire del*

Saint Graal, Josephus is consecrated by God as the first bishop. When he and his followers come to the coast, his 'under-tunic' miraculously expands and carries 150 servants of the *Grail over the sea to Britain. Before his death, Josephus makes a cross with blood from his bleeding nose on the shield originally given to *Mordrain (*Evalach) before his battle with Tholomer. This shield with the red cross is destined for *Galahad in the *Queste del Saint Graal* (thirteenth century). (The story of the shield is also told by Malory.) Before his death, Josephus entrusts the Grail to his cousin *Alain le Gros, the twelfth son of *Bron. Malory says that God sent Josephe to bear *Galahad fellowship as he prepared to die. Josephe tells Galahad that he was sent because Galahad resembled him in two ways: they both saw the marvels of the Grail and they were both pure virgins.

Joyous Guard In the Vulgate *Lancelot*, *Lancelot comes to a castle known as Dolorous Guard, where he must defeat ten knights at each of two walls of the castle and where he learns his identity by lifting a great metal slab from a tomb. By undergoing a series of trials, he obtains two keys that allow him to open a pillar and a chest contained therein which emits the sound of horrible voices that are the cause of all the spells and wonders of the castle. By opening the chest, he releases a whirlwind and a great noise, produced by 'all the devils'. With the spells broken, the castle comes to be called Joyous Guard. It is to Joyous Guard that Lancelot takes Guinevere when he rescues her from the pyre. In Malory's *Morte d'Arthur*, after Lancelot returns Guinevere to Arthur, he renames the castle 'Dolorous Garde'.

Kahedin (Kaherdin, Kehydyns, Caerdin, Ganhardin) In the thirteenth-century *Prose Tristan*, Kahedin, the brother of *Iseut of the White Hands, goes to Cornwall with *Tristan, who has told him of his love for *Iseut of Ireland. Kahedin is struck by the beauty of the Irish Iseut and falls in love with her. As a result, Tristan becomes his enemy and tries to kill him. Because his love is unrequited, Kahedin ultimately languishes and dies.

In the version of Thomas and of those who are influenced by him, Kaherdin does not fall in love with Yseut. Instead, he is so impressed with her beauty that he understands why Tristan has not consummated the marriage to his sister. Accompanying Tristan to Cornwall, he becomes enamoured of *Brangwain. Kahedin remains Tristan's friend, and goes to Cornwall to bring Yseut to her dying lover.

Karyet See GARETH.

Kay (Cei, Cai, Keie) Kay is depicted in *Culhwch and Olwen* (c.1100) as a character with exceptional powers: he is able to hold his breath under water for nine days, to make himself as tall as the tallest tree, to produce great heat that keeps things dry around him in the rain, and to wield a sword that gives a wound no physician can heal. He also has traits, such as being inhospitable to strangers and stubborn and quick to take offence, that are consistent with his character in later tales.

According to Geoffrey of Monmouth, *Arthur gives Kay the province of Anjou for his service in the war in Gaul; later, Kay is slain in Arthur's continental war against *Lucius. Wace calls Kay a brave and loyal knight, and he and *Bedivere are said to be Arthur's most faithful subjects. When Kay is killed, he is buried in his castle at Chinon, which Wace derives from Kay's name (in the French, 'Kynon' from 'Key').

Chrétien de Troyes says of Kay in his *Perceval* (written in the 1180s) that he 'was, is still, and always will be insulting, never wishing to say a good word'. Chrétien also claims that there is no man more handsome than Kay but that his 'malicious jests marred his beauty and his valor'. In his *Yvain*, Chrétien calls Kay 'quarrelsome and mean, sarcastic and spiteful'. In the *Lancelot* (1179–80), Kay believes his abilities to be greater than they are. He wants to defend the queen against *Meleagant but loses her to him. When *Lancelot rescues her, Kay accuses Lancelot of having shamed him by accomplishing what he could not. The author of the First Continuation to *Perceval* (c.1200) considers Kay abrasive but valiant and portrays him as always willing to undertake an adventure, though he sometimes overestimates his own abilities.

Hartmann von Aue outlines four sides to Kay's nature: sometimes he avoids evil deeds and words, but then his mood changes and he is deceitful in word and deed; sometimes he is brave but at other times cowardly. Wolfram von Eschenbach attempts to resolve the contradiction in Kay's personality; he maintains that though Kay was a carper, he behaved this way to protect his lord, that is, so he could separate the worthy from the unworthy who sought the king's attention or favours.

There is an ominous suggestion about Kay's character in the prose rendition of Robert de Boron's *Merlin*, where Entor asks Arthur to make Kay seneschal and to keep him in that office despite any wrong he might do. He explains that Kay's faults came to him from the woman who nursed him while his own mother nursed Arthur. In *Perlesvaus*, Kay is not only a boaster but also the slayer of *Loholt, the son of Arthur. He kills Loholt so that he can take to court the head of a giant that Loholt has slain and claim credit for the great deed. He then joins Arthur's enemy Brien of the Isles in attacking the king's lands. Kay is almost as wicked in the romance *Yder* (*c*.1215), in which he treacherously wounds *Yder, nearly fatally, and then gives him poisoned water, from which only the chance arrival of two knights with a cure saves him.

Kay has a penchant for mocking young men who will become much better knights than he. Such is the case with Chrétien's *Perceval, Malory's *Gareth, Guillaume le Clerc's Fergus of Galloway, and Miraudijs, known as the Knight of the Sleeve in the thirteenth-century Dutch romance *Riddere metter mouwen* (*The Knight with the Sleeve*). In English alliterative romances, Kay is generally portrayed as rash and discourteous, a foil to *Gawain, who is the exemplar of courtesy. In Malory, Kay is Arthur's foster-brother who, at the request of *Ector, is made seneschal when Arthur becomes king. Kay fights bravely in Arthur's domestic and foreign wars and accompanies him when he goes to kill the *Giant of St Michael's Mount. But he is also a poor judge of character and a knight who overestimates his own ability.

In modern literature, Kay is presented in both traditional and non-traditional ways. In John Gloag's novel *Artorius Rex* (1977), he is Caius Geladius, tutor to Arthur in Constantinople and chronicler of his deeds in a report to the emperor. In *The Idylls of the Queen* (1982) by Phyllis Ann Karr, Kay is the detective who solves the mystery of the murder of Sir *Patrise. *Sir Kay: A Poem in the Old Style* (1923) by American poet James Juvenal Hayes attributes Kay's cynicism to an incident in which the knight, while still young and exuberant, loves and loses a beautiful woman in a fairy realm. In his *Acts of King Arthur* (1976), John Steinbeck explains the change in Kay from a brave to a petty knight by suggesting that his job as seneschal

forced him to be so concerned with petty day-to-day details that 'all greatness [was] eaten away by little numbers as marching ants nibble a dragon and leave picked bones'.

Kehydyns See KAHEDIN.

Klarisanz See CLARISANT.

Klingsor See CLINSCHOR.

Kundry See CUNDRIE.

Kurvenal See GOVERNAL.

Lady of Shalott See ELAINE OF ASTOLAT.

Lady of the Lake The Lady of the Lake or Dame du Lac is generally the woman who raises *Lancelot and who gives *Arthur the sword *Excalibur. Chrétien de Troyes says that Lancelot was reared by a fairy. Ulrich von Zatzikhoven describes the enchanted realm in the sea where the fairy or 'mermaid', as Ulrich calls her, takes Lancelot to raise him. It is a land inhabited by 10,000 ladies and no men, and anyone dwelling there for even a day would never feel sorrow. In the *Vulgate Cycle, the Lady of the Lake is the woman who rears Lancelot as well as *Lionel and *Bohort. *Niniane, who entraps *Merlin, is a Lady of the Lake, a title held by more than one woman.

In Malory's account, the Lady of the Lake who gave Arthur Excalibur is killed by *Balin. *Nenyve, who beguiles Merlin, is another of the Ladies of the Lake. She assists Arthur, saving him from *Morgan's attempt to have her lover *Accolon slay him. After Arthur's final battle, she is in the barge that takes the king to *Avalon, at which time she is said to be the chief Lady of the Lake.

In John Thelwall's play *The Fairy of the Lake* (1801), the Lady or Fairy of the Lake not only gives Arthur Excalibur but also retrieves it for him when his pining for *Guenever causes him to lose it. She also saves Guenever from a burning tower.

Lailoken See MERLIN.

Lamorak (Lamorat) Lamorak is the son of *Pellinore and the brother of *Perceval and *Aglovale. According to Malory, he is one of the greatest knights, only *Lancelot and *Tristram being superior. Initially, Lamorak is hostile towards Tristram because, on *Mark's orders, he jousted with Lamorak, who was weary from fighting thirty other knights. To repay Tristram for his unchivalrous deed, Lamorak redirects to Mark's court a horn designed to test chastity and originally sent by *Morgan le Fay to Arthur's court.

Since Pellinore killed *Lot, *Gawain and his brothers bear enmity to his family. When Gawain kills Pellinore, Lamorak does not avenge his father out of reverence for *Arthur. Later, *Gaheris discovers his mother *Morgause in bed with Lamorak and slays her but not the offending knight. (In T. H. White's *The Once and Future King* (1958), it is Agravayne and not Gaheris who slays his mother.) Later, Gawain and his brothers (except for *Gareth, who dissociates himself from their villainy) kill Lamorak in an unfair fight. It is in revenge for the slaying of Lamorak that his cousin Sir Pynell tries to murder Gawain with a poisoned apple but kills instead Sir Patryse, cousin of *Mador, a deed for which *Guinevere is initially blamed.

Lancelot (Lanzelet, Lancilotto) In Chrétien's *Erec* (*c.*1165), Lancelot is said to be the third best knight after *Gawain and *Erec, but in Chrétien's *Lancelot* (1179–80), Lancelot becomes the central figure and the lover of *Guinevere who is willing to take any risk or to suffer any indignity in service of the queen. According to both Chrétien and Ulrich von Zatzikhoven, Lancelot was raised by a fairy. Ulrich tells how this woman who lives in an enchanted realm in the sea raises Lancelot until he is 15, at which point he asks to be allowed to go into the world to earn honour. In Ulrich's *Lanzelet*, Lanzelet never becomes the queen's lover; although he is a lover of several ladies, his true love is Yblis, whom he ultimately marries and with whom he has a daughter and three sons.

In *Tavola Ritonda* (second quarter of the fourteenth century), Lancilotto is taken and raised by the *Lady of the Lake when his mother Gostanza dies in childbirth. The Lady of the Lake names him Lancilotto, which is said to mean 'very wise and skilled knight of the lance and sword'.

In the thirteenth-century Vulgate *Lancelot*, Lancelot is raised by the Lady of the Lake when his father dies due to the treachery of *Claudas. It is from this upbringing that he is called 'du Lac' or 'of the Lake'. His baptismal name is Galahad in memory of *Galahad, the younger son of *Joseph of Arimathea and the first Christian King of Wales, whose tomb Lancelot opens. (This event was foreseen in a vision by monks from Wales, who are present at the time of the opening of the tomb and who take the body to Wales.) Lancelot is called Lancelot, however, after his grandfather. The text also says that 'just as the name Galahad had been lost to Lancelot by the flame of desire, so too was it restored to [his] offspring by mortification of the flesh'. Lancelot loves Guinevere from the first time he sees her. His friend *Galehaut arranges the first meeting between them. Later, as in Chrétien's *Lancelot*, he rescues the queen from *Meleagant. In order to do so, he must ride in a cart, something that was considered a shameful act, cross a sword bridge, and defeat Meleagant. After breaking iron bars so he can spend the night with Guinevere, he must defend her when blood that drips from his cuts onto the queen's sheets prompts Meleagant to accuse her of having slept with *Kay. Lancelot's accomplishments include not only deeds of valour but also, under the inspiration of love, the painting of beautiful murals in the room in which he is imprisoned by Morgan le Fay.

Tricked into thinking he is sleeping with the queen, Lancelot fathers *Galahad on the daughter of King *Pelles of *Corbenic. Guinevere's anger drives him mad, but he is ultimately cured by the *Grail. Lancelot's love for the queen keeps him from success in the quest for the Grail. In the *Mort Artu*, Lancelot resumes his affair with the queen shortly after his return from the quest. For love of her, he rejects the love of the *Maid of Escalot. When he and Guinevere are trapped by *Agravain, he flees but returns to save her from execution. In the course of the rescue, he tragically slays Gaheriet (Malory's *Gareth), Gawain's favourite brother, and thus causes the war which gives *Mordred the opportunity to seize the throne. After Arthur's death, Lancelot returns to *Logres to punish the sons of Mordred; then he becomes a hermit until his death, at which time he is buried in the same tomb as Galehaut.

In Malory's *Morte d'Arthur*, Lancelot is the central figure. (John Steinbeck called him Malory's 'self-character', the one who reflected the author's highest aspirations as well as his failings.) Malory's Lancelot also fails in the Grail quest—though he comes closer to success than any but the three who actually achieve it, one of whom is his own son Galahad. Lancelot strives for the highest achievement not only in this religious quest but also as a lover and as a knight. His devotion to the queen is unfailing. He has no other lover, rejecting even the beautiful *Elaine of Astalot, who dies because her love for Lancelot is unrequited. Although he sleeps with *Elaine of Corbenic, he does so thinking he is with Guinevere. While the Grail quest proves that Galahad, not Lancelot, is the best knight because of his spiritual qualities, Lancelot's healing of the Hungarian knight *Urre, a feat that can be accomplished only by the best knight, confirms that after the departure of Galahad from the world Lancelot is once again without peer. However, his love, which kept him from achieving the Grail, also allows Mordred to undermine Arthur's realm and his order of the *Round Table. When Lancelot is discovered by Mordred and his followers in the queen's chamber, he flees but returns to save her from the pyre (as he had rescued her on two earlier occasions). In the rescue, he tragically slays Gareth and *Gaheris. Since Gareth was particularly devoted to Lancelot, Gawain is unable to forgive the slaying and forces Arthur to besiege Lancelot. In the course of the siege, Lancelot reluctantly fights Gawain and gives him a serious wound. When Arthur returns to Britain and attacks Mordred because of his usurpation of the throne, the siege is lifted. After Arthur's final battle, Lancelot returns to Britain for a last meeting with Guinevere. When she refuses even to kiss him, he leaves and leads a holy life until his death.

Following Malory, who says that after Lancelot went mad and was cured by the Grail, he called himself 'ly Shyvalere Ill Mafeete, that ys to sey "the knyght that hath trespassed" ', T. H. White calls the third book of *The Once and Future King* (1958) *The Ill-Made Knight*. Lancelot sees himself as 'Mal Fet', ill-made or ugly—although he does recognize the alternative meaning of a knight who has done wrong. White presents a Lancelot who strives for perfection and who desires to work a miracle, which he believes his sin with Guinevere prohibits him from doing. Thus he is particularly moved when he is allowed to heal Sir Urre and, as in Malory's text, he 'wept, as he had been a child that had been beaten' because he feels that he is unworthy.

The love between Lancelot and Guinevere remains one of the most common and most often reinterpreted elements of the Arthurian story. It is a frequent and enduring theme in poetry, drama, fiction, and film.

Lancelot Compilation (Lancelot-Compilatie) The *Lancelot Compilation* is the great Dutch manuscript of Arthurian romances (*c*.1320), now in the Royal Library of the Hague (MS 129 A 10). It contains translations of the French Vulgate *Lancelot* (the first part of which has been lost), *Queste*, and *Mort Artu*, as well as seven other romances: *Perchevael, Moriaen, Wrake van Ragisel, Ridder metter mouwen (The Knight with the Sleeve), Walwein ende Keye, Lanceloet en het hert met de witte voet (Lancelot and the Hart with the White Foot)*, and *Torec*.

Lancelot–Grail Cycle See VULGATE CYCLE.

Lanval (Launfal) In Marie de France's lay *Lanval* (written in the latter half of the twelfth century) and in several Middle English renditions, Lanval is a knight who becomes impoverished. He encounters a fairy maiden who becomes his lover, but he is warned never to reveal that love. However, in response to a charge by the queen that he does not like women, he speaks of the beauty of his beloved, who then abandons him for violating the condition she imposed. Fortunately, she arrives at *Arthur's court in time to save Lanval from condemnation, her beauty being proof of his claim. The two then ride off together to *Avalon. In the various medieval retellings of his story, Lanval is generous, giving to all who are in need.

In James Russell Lowell's poem *The Vision of Sir Launfal*, Launfal is a knight from a time other than that of Arthur, but he also seeks the *Grail. Although initially a haughty man who only gives scornfully to beggars, he is taught by a dream vision that charity is the true meaning of the Grail. He then acquires the traditional trait of generosity, opening up his castle and sharing his wealth with all.

Lavayne (Lavaine) Lavayne is the brother of *Elaine of Astolat. He accompanies *Lancelot to the tournament at *Winchester, where he fights well with the encouragement of Lancelot. Lavayne develops a knightly love for his mentor that parallels his sister's romantic love. Eventually, Lavayne marries *Felelolye, sister of Sir *Urre. Because of his devotion to Lancelot, Lavayne is one of those who support him after he is discovered with the queen.

Leodegrance (Leodagan) In various sources, Leodegrance is the father of *Guinevere and the lord of Carmelide or Cameliard. *Uther gives him the *Round Table; and he passes it to *Arthur when he marries Guinevere. In the *Vulgate Cycle, Leodagan is also the father of an illegitimate daughter known as the *False Guinevere.

Lionel (Lyonel) According to the thirteenth-century Vulgate *Lancelot*, Lionel is the son of King *Bors of Gaunes, brother to King *Ban of Benwick, *Lancelot's father; thus Lionel is Lancelot's cousin. He is called Lionel because at his birth a red spot in the shape of a lion appeared on his chest and the baby Lionel seized the image as if to strangle it. The spot remained until he killed the crowned lion of Libya at *Arthur's court and gave the skin to *Yvain to wear on his shield. Lionel and his brother *Bors are protected from *Claudas by the *Lady of the Lake. One of her messengers gives them clasps of gold with precious stones that keep them from harm, and she makes them appear to be two greyhounds when they are pursued after killing Claudas's son Dorin; then she takes them to the realm of the Lady of the Lake. In the *Mort Artu*, Lionel is an ally of Lancelot's. When Lancelot and his forces return to England after Arthur's death to punish *Mordred's two sons, Lionel is killed by Melehan, the elder of those sons. His death is avenged when Bors slays Melehan.

Malory, reworking a story from the Vulgate *Queste del Saint Graal*, tells of an incident on the Grail quest in which two knights capture Lionel and beat him with thorns. His brother Bors sees his plight, prays for him, but leaves him to his fate, choosing to rescue a lady in distress instead. Even though the lady reveals that 500 men would have died if she had lost her virginity, Lionel is furious and, when he and Bors meet again, tries to kill his brother, who is reluctant to fight. After beheading a hermit who intercedes, Lionel is about to slay Bors when Sir Colgrevaunce intervenes and is slain by Lionel. A flaming cloud comes between the brothers, and a voice advises Bors to flee.

In his *Acts of King Arthur* (1976), John Steinbeck depicts Lyonel as one of a group of young knights who think that Lancelot is ridiculously old-fashioned. On a quest with Lancelot, however, Lyonel comes to appreciate those qualities that make Lancelot great.

Llachau See ARTHUR'S CHILDREN.

Llamrei Llamrei is the name given to Arthur's horse in *Culhwch and Olwen* (c.1100).

Loathly Lady See RAGNELLE.

Logres Logres is a name sometimes applied to Britain in Arthurian romance. The name is derived from Locrine, the first son of *Brutus. Locrine inherited the middle portion of Britain, which, according to Geoffrey of Monmouth, came to be called Loegria after him. In his *Chronicle* (written in the latter half of the fifteenth century), John Hardyng says that *Hengest changed the name of Logres to Engestes lande, which was shortened in the common speech to England.

Lohengrin (Loherangrin) Lohengrin is *Parzival's son, called Loherangrin in Wolfram von Eschenbach's *Parzival* (first decade of the thirteenth century). Wolfram says that Loherangrin was brought to the Princess of Brabant in a boat pulled by a swan. He marries her but insists that she never ask his identity. When she breaks her pledge, the swan brings the boat again and he returns to tend the *Grail. Lohengrin's story is also told in the thirteenth-century German poem *Lohengrin*, in which he leaves his wife Elsam of Brabant when she asks him to reveal his identity and is brought by the swan back to the realm of the Grail. He is the protagonist in Richard Wagner's opera *Lohengrin* (completed 1848, first produced 1850), in which Lohengrin acquits Elsa of Brabant of the charge of killing her brother Gottfried, who has been turned into the swan that pulls Lohengrin's boat. In answer to Lohengrin's prayer, the dove of the Grail descends, and Gottfried is restored to his own form. But because Elsa has insisted that Lohengrin reveal his identity, he must return to *Monsalvat.

Loholt See ARTHUR'S CHILDREN.

Longinus' spear Longinus is the Roman soldier said to have pierced the side of the crucified Christ with his spear. In the First Continuation (c.1200) to Chrétien's *Perceval*, the bleeding lance of the Grail procession is identified with Longinus' spear. Longinus' spear, called the Spear of Destiny, figures as a symbol of power in a number of occult and New Age books.

Lot (Loth) Lot is the King of Lothian. Geoffrey of Monmouth and other chroniclers say that he marries *Arthur's sister *Anna and has two sons, *Gawain and *Mordred, and that he assists Arthur in his struggles against the Saxon invaders. Later romances make him the husband of *Morgause and the father of Gawain, *Agravaine, *Gareth, and *Gaheris (but not of Mordred), all four being his children by Morgause. In the romances, Lot is presented not as an ally but as a rebellious king who is killed in battle by *Pellinore, an event which haunts his sons and which ultimately leads to revenge on Pellinore's family and contributes to the downfall of the Round Table. In his poem 'The Taking of Morgause', John Masefield presents Lot as an Orkney pirate who kidnaps Morgause as a child and later marries her.

Loüt See ARTHUR'S CHILDREN.

Lucan the butler Lucan is the knight who serves as *Arthur's 'butler' or wine-steward. In Malory's Morte d'Arthur, he is the son of Duke Corneus and brother of *Bedivere. According to Malory, Lucan and Bedivere are the last surviving knights in the final battle with *Mordred. Lucan, speaking of 'thys wycked day of Desteny', tries to discourage Arthur from a final encounter with his illegitimate son. After Arthur slays Mordred and is himself fatally wounded, Lucan and Bedivere bear him to a chapel. As he lifts the king to try to take him to a nearby town for healing, Lucan's guts spill out from a grievous wound he has received and he dies. In the thirteenth-century Mort Artu, Lucan and his cousin *Girflet are the last two knights alive. Arthur embraces Lucan so tightly that 'he crushed the heart within his chest' and Lucan dies.

Lucius In Geoffrey's Historia, Lucius Hiberius is the Roman procurator who, during the reign of Emperor Leo, demands tribute from *Arthur. This demand prompts Arthur's continental expedition, during which Lucius is killed in battle. Wace writes that Lucius was made emperor before his battle with Arthur's forces, in which he is slain by an unknown soldier's lance. Similarly, Layamon writes that no one could say who killed Lucius when he was found pierced by a spear at the end of a battle. Arthur sends Lucius' body to Rome as the tribute that had been demanded of him. In the late fourteenth-century Alliterative Morte Arthure

and in Malory's Morte d'Arthur, Arthur himself slays Lucius.

Lynet (Lynette, Lyonet) Lynet is a lady who comes to *Arthur's court seeking a knight to free her sister Lyones from Ironside, the Red Knight of the Red Lands, who is destroying her lands and besieging her castle. When the king grants *Gareth's request to be given the quest, Lynet insults Gareth because he has been working in the kitchen. But, as he defeats knight after knight, her opinion of him ultimately changes. When Gareth overcomes Ironside and falls in love with Lyones, Lynet prevents them from consummating their love before marriage. Gareth and Lyones marry on Michaelmas Day (29 Sept.); at the same time, *Gaheris weds Lynet and *Agravain marries Lyones's niece Lawrel. Tennyson's 'Gareth and Lynette' (1872) idyll is based on Malory but adapted to the larger themes of the Idylls of the King. Tennyson notes that the earlier version of the story (i.e. Malory's) claims that Gareth married 'Lyonors' (his name for Lyones) but that his later version says Gareth married Lynette.

Lyones (Lyonesse, Lyonors) (person) See LYNETTE.

Lyonesse (Lyonnesse, Lyones, Leones) (place) Lyonesse, the land ruled by *Tristan's father, has been associated with Lothian in Scotland (Layamon says that *Lot ruled 'Leones') and Leonais in Brittany. It is, however, generally considered to be a region to the west of Cornwall that was inundated and submerged.

In Tennyson's 'Passing of Arthur' idyll (1869), Lyonnesse—'A land of old upheaven from the abyss | By fire, to sink into the abyss again'—is said to be the site of the last battle between *Arthur and *Mordred. In his poem 'When I Set out for Lyonnesse' (1870), Thomas Hardy writes of Lyonnesse as a magical and transforming realm. In The Marvellous History of King Arthur in Avalon by Geoffrey Junior (1904), the sunken land of Lyonnesse is raised by Merlin after he revives the sleeping king so that Arthur can reign there and re-establish a kingdom devoted to the ideals of chivalry. Farnham Bishop and Arthur Gilchrist Brodeur's historical novel The Altar of the Legion (1926) is set in Lyonesse, which the authors say derives from the Latin legionis asa (altar of the legion). At the end of the novel, an earthquake and the resultant tidal wave devastate the Romanized Celtic city on the Cornish coast; and Legionis Asa, with all its Roman splendour, sinks into the sea to be remembered as the legendary land of Lyonesse.

Lyonors Lyonors is said by Malory to be the daughter of Earl Sanam. *Arthur has an affair with her, and she bears him a son named Borre, who later becomes a knight of the Round Table. Lyonors's tale, told in a short passage in Thomas Malory's *Morte d'Arthur*, is also told briefly in *Arthour and Merlin* (thirteenth century) and is the basis for the novel *Lionors* (1975) by Barbara Ferry Johnson.

Mador de la Porte Mador is a knight of the Round Table who accuses *Guinevere of poisoning his relative: in the thirteenth-century *Mort Artu*, it is Mador's brother Gaheris of Carahew who dies; in Malory's *Morte d'Arthur*, it is Mador's cousin Patryse. Mador's relative dies when he eats a poisoned apple at a dinner given by the queen for a group of knights. In the *Mort Artu*, a knight named Avarlan actually poisons the apple hoping that *Gawain, whom he hates, will eat it. In *Le Morte d'Arthur*, *Lamorak's cousin Pynell poisons the apple in order to avenge the death of Lamorak at the hands of Gawain and his brothers. In both accounts, *Lancelot defeats Mador in a trial by combat and forces him to withdraw his accusation of the queen. *Nyneve then reveals that Pynell is the murderer. Mador is one of the knights who later join *Mordred in attempting to trap Lancelot with Guinevere. He is killed in the fight at the door to the queen's chamber.

The murder of Sir Patrise becomes the subject of a medieval mystery story in *The Idylls of the Queen* (1982) by Phyllis Ann Karr. *Kay is the detective who solves the mystery.

Maid(en) of Ascalot See ELAINE OF ASTOLAT.

Maimed King See FISHER KING, PELLAM, PELLES, AND PELLINORE.

Marhaus See MORHOLT.

Mark Mark is King of Cornwall and, as brother of *Tristan's mother (named Elyzabeth in Malory; Blanscheflur in Gottfried; Blauncheflour in *Sir Tristrem*), uncle to Tristan. Mark appears in Celtic literature such as Triad 26, about the three powerful swineherds of Britain, in which 'Drystan son of Tallwch' watches over the swine of 'March' (Mark) while the swineherd delivers a message from Drystan to *Essylt. The Welsh work was the source for an episode in John Masefield's play *Tristan and Isolt* (1927), in which *Arthur appears as a 'Captain of the Host' and is subordinate to Mark. There is some evidence for an actual Welsh nobleman, March son of Meirchyawn, behind the figure of Mark. In the ninth-century life of Paul Aurelian (St Pol, a monk of Landevennec and patron saint of Paul in Cornwall) by Wrmonoc, Mark is identified with Cunomorus (Welsh Cynvawr), who ruled Cornwall in the early sixth century and who probably had his seat at *Castle Dore, a hillfort near Fowey. Wrmonoc says of St Paul: 'fama ejus regis Marci pervolat ad aures quem alio nomine Quonomorium vocant' (see *Revue celtique*, 5 (1881–3), 431) (his fame flew to the ears of King Marc, known also as Cunomorus). Cunomorus is associated with Tristan on the famous *Tristan Stone (also located in Fowey), a memorial stone commemorating Drustanus, son of Cunomorus. The *Prose Tristan* (thirteenth century) and *Tavola Ritonda* (second quarter of the fourteenth century) say that Mark was given his name because he was born on Tuesday (*mardi*) in the month of March (*Marz*). In the *Tavola Ritonda*, after Tristan's death, Mark is besieged, captured, and imprisoned in a tower in front of Tristan's sepulchre so that having failed to protect Tristan when he was alive, he should watch over him now that he is dead. Mark is condemned never to leave the tower, even after his own death.

Mark figures in the medieval Tristan and Isolt tales as the rival to Tristan, originally as a basically noble man caught up in the tragic circumstances, but increasingly as a figure who exhibits traits inconsistent with chivalrous conduct. The *Prose Tristan* emphasizes his hatred of Tristan. Malory describes Mark as a treacherous murderer, who breaks oaths and counterfeits letters, and ultimately as the slayer of Tristram. Lancelot calls him 'King Fox' because of his trickery and treachery. Mark, or a modern analogue to his character, also appears in reworkings of the legend, including those by Thomas Hardy, John Masefield, Martha Kinross, Don Marquis, Edwin Arlington Robinson, Sir Arthur Quiller-Couch, John Erskine, John Updike, and many others.

Medraut (Medrawd) See MORDRED.

Meleagant (Mellyagaunt, Melyagaunce, Melyagraunce, Melvas, Melwas) Meleagant is best known as the wicked knight who abducts *Guinevere and is ultimately slain by *Lancelot. The earliest form of the name, Melwas or Melvas, has been interpreted as meaning 'prince of death' or 'princely youth'. The classic account of the abduction story occurs in Chrétien de Troyes's *Lancelot* (1179–80), in which Lancelot, because of his great love for Guinevere, suffers the ignominy of riding in a cart, a form of transportation reserved for criminals, so that he can continue his quest to free her. The story of Guinevere's abduction is, however, told by others both before and after Chrétien. It can be found in *The Life of St Gildas* (c.1130) by Caradoc of Llancarfan, who says that Melwas, ruler in the summer region ('in aestiva regione'), is attacked by *Arthur because he carried off Guinevere. In this version, peace is restored with the help of Gildas. And a Welsh poem, formerly thought to be a dialogue between Arthur and Guinevere, is now titled the 'Dialogue of Melwas and Gwenhwyfar'. In addition to Chrétien's version, the abduction is found in French medieval literature in the thirteenth-century Vulgate *Lancelot*, which is the source for Malory's 'Knight of the Cart' episode.

In the modern period, the story of Guinevere's abduction by 'Melvas' is told by Thomas Peacock in *The Misfortunes of Elphin* (1829), in which the rescue is effected with the help of Taliessin. The slaying of 'Mellyagraunce' by Lancelot is alluded to in Morris's 'The Defence of Guenevere' (1858). In Catherine Christian's *The Sword and the Flame* (1978), Meliagrance, an outlaw, abducts Guinevere but is pursued and slain by *Bedivere. In Philip Lindsay's *The Little Wench* (1935), Mellygraunce is the son of *Morgain and the brother of *Mordred. In Ian McDowell's *Mordred's Curse* (1996), it is Mordred, not Lancelot, who rescues Guinevere from the fairy king Melwas and becomes her lover. Other versions of the story appear in the novels *Galahad* (1926) by John Erskine, *The Once and Future King* (1958) by T. H. White, and *Arthur Rex* (1978) by Thomas Berger; in James Ormerod's short play 'Meliagrance and Guenevere' (1913, published 1928); and in the film *First Knight* (1995).

Melehan See MORDRED.

Meliadus (Melyodas) See TRISTAN'S PARENTS.

Meliot (Melyot) of Logres In *Perlesvaus* (written in the first decade of the thirteenth century), Meliot is cured by *Lancelot, who retrieves from a chapel, at great personal risk, the sword and a piece of the shroud of Anurez, the knight who wounded him. Malory tells a similar tale of Lancelot's retrieving a cloth and sword from the Chapel Perilous to cure Melyot, whom he earlier identified as a cousin of *Nyneve. Despite this service, Melyot is one of those knights who attempt to trap Lancelot in *Guinevere's chamber and who is killed in the fight there.

Melwas (Melvas) See MELEAGANT.

Merlin Merlin plays many roles in Arthurian literature, including bard, prophet, magician, adviser, and warrior. Though usually a figure who supports Arthur and his vision of Camelot, Merlin is, because of the stories in which he is said to be the son of a devil, sometimes presented as a villain.

Celtic tradition contains a number of related figures—the Welsh Myrddin, the Scottish Lailoken, and the Irish Suibhne—who have characteristics similar to those of Merlin. These characters all go mad and become wild men of the woods. Myrddin, who appears in the Welsh poems 'Yr Afallennau' ('The Apple Tree Stanzas') and 'Yr Oianau' ('The Little Pig Stanzas'), is driven mad because of the death of his lord Gwenddolau at the hands of Rhydderch in the battle of Arfderydd (c.575). After the battle, Merlin lives in exile in the forest, where he utters prophecies. Geoffrey of Monmouth combines this historical figure, who lived at a time later than that in which a historical *Arthur could have lived, with the figure of the youth *Ambrosius Aurelianus from Nennius (Geoffrey says that Merlin's second name was Ambrosius); in so doing, he virtually creates the now-traditional Merlin. Gaston Paris postulated (*Romania*, 12 (1883), 375)—and most later critics have accepted—that the Welsh 'Myrddin' would have yielded the name 'Merdinus' but that Geoffrey avoided this form because of its similarity to the French word *merde*. (This scholarly theory is incorporated into Robert Nye's novel *Merlin* (1978), in which the devils want him to have the name Merdin as a vulgar joke, and in Steve Sneyd's poem 'A Time of Buried Questioning' (in Barbara Tepa Lupack and Alan Lupack (eds.), *A Round Table of Contemporary Arthurian Poetry* (Rochester,

NY: Round Table Publications, 1993), 35–42), where it is said to be an 'ironic name perhaps to deflate the terrifying'.) Geoffrey's Merlin, who is fathered by an incubus, explains why Vortigern's tower will not stand and utters a long series of prophecies. He then serves both *Aurelius and *Uther. After transporting the Giant's Dance from Ireland to Britain and setting it up as *Stonehenge, he assists Uther in satisfying his lust for *Ygerna. In Geoffrey's account, Merlin does not serve as an adviser to Arthur; but later writers expand his role to include helping Arthur become king and establish his authority.

In the works of Robert de Boron and in the *Vulgate Cycle, Merlin's birth is engineered by the devils in hell. They hope to bring into the world an Antichrist who will undo the good (or, as they see it, the harm) done by Christ in redeeming mankind. Merlin's mother is impregnated by an incubus; but upon the advice of her confessor *Blaise she baptizes her son; and he becomes a force for good, not evil. Since he is the son of a devil, he is endowed with the knowledge of all things past, and God bestows on him the gift of knowing the future. In the Vulgate Cycle, Merlin becomes a prophet of the *Grail. He is also instrumental in establishing Arthur's realm and the *Round Table, which is a reflection of the Table of the Grail. Merlin's service to Arthur ends when he is infatuated with *Niniane and allows her to seal him up with a charm that he himself has taught her.

Merlin undergoes a number of changes in modern fiction. In Twain's *Connecticut Yankee in King Arthur's Court* (1889), he represents the forces of superstition against which Hank *Morgan battles. In Godfrey Turton's *The Emperor Arthur* (1967), Merlin plots against Arthur and even allies himself with the Saxons and Mordred in the final battle. The Merlin of Parke Godwin's *Firelord* (1980) is a spirit depicted as a young boy whom Arthur calls his 'genius'. In Marion Zimmer Bradley's *The Mists of Avalon* (1982), Merlin is not the name of one person but rather a title passed to different people. Perhaps the most influential recasting of Merlin is in T. H. White's *The Once and Future King* (1958). White's Merlin, who is both a comic and a philosophical figure, is a tutor who encourages Arthur to think for himself and who is gratified when Arthur arrives at the notion that might should be used for right. White's Merlin knows the future because he lives backwards in time.

Monsalvat See MUNSALVAESCHE.

Morcadés See MORGAUSE.

Mordrain See EVALACH.

Mordred (Modred, Medraut, Medrawd) The *Annales Cambriae* (*Welsh Annals*) mentions Medraut as a participant in the battle of *Camlann but does not make clear whether he is an enemy or an ally of *Arthur. Triad 59 lists as one of the three unfortunate counsels of Britain Arthur's threefold dividing of his men with Medrawd at Camlann, a statement which adds little to the knowledge of traditions about the battle. Another Triad (54) speaks of the unrestrained ravagings of the Island of Britain, one of which occurred when Medrawd came to Arthur's court at Celliwig, consumed all the food and drink there, and dragged *Guinevere from her throne and struck her; another was when Arthur went to Medrawd's court and left no food or drink there.

Geoffrey of Monmouth introduces the notion of Mordred's usurpation of the throne and his adulterous relationship with Guinevere while Arthur is fighting his continental wars. Geoffrey names Mordred as one of two sons of *Lot and *Anna (the other being *Gawain). Mordred in turn has two sons who survive him but are killed by *Constantine, Arthur's successor.

In the thirteenth-century *Vulgate Cycle, Mordred is the son of Arthur by his half-sister, who is Lot's wife. In the Vulgate *Lancelot*, Mordred is said to be the worst knight of the brothers of Gawain; and though he is tall, blond, handsome, and strong, he is envious and deceitful and is 'truly the devil' because of his evil deeds. Although, in the Vulgate *Mort Artu*, it is *Agravain who accuses *Lancelot and Guinevere of adultery and leads the knights who trap them in the queen's chamber, Mordred betrays Arthur's trust when he is left in charge of the kingdom and the queen by forging a letter said to be from a dying Arthur declaring Mordred king and urging him to marry Guinevere. In the final battle of Salisbury Plain, Arthur kills Mordred but is fatally wounded by him. Mordred leaves behind two sons, the elder called Melehan and the younger unnamed. *Bors kills Melehan, who has slain *Lionel; and Lancelot kills the younger son.

In Malory's *Morte d'Arthur*, Mordred is the illegitimate son of Arthur and *Morgause. When

Arthur, who is unaware that she is related to him when they sleep together, learns that he has had a child by his half-sister, he attempts to kill Mordred by condemning all the children born on May Day to be set adrift on the sea. But his son survives when the ship he is in breaks up and he is cast up on the shore and found by a good man, who raises him until he is 14. Even before Mordred accuses Lancelot and Guinevere and plans to trap them, his villainy is clear. When Gawain and his brothers treacherously attack and slay *Lamorak, it is Mordred who gives him a fatal wound in the back. While Arthur is besieging Lancelot's castle in France, Mordred forges letters saying that Arthur is dead, claims the throne, and intends to marry Guinevere. In the final battle, Arthur gives Mordred a fatal wound; but Mordred thrusts himself up the length of Arthur's spear so he can strike his father. Although Mordred is generally presented as a villain in medieval and modern literature, a number of Scottish chronicles suggest that because of Arthur's illegitimate birth he had no right to the throne and that Mordred, in rebelling against him, only claimed what was rightfully his.

T. H. White's Mordred is a figure who is much like Hitler. He is the mad leader of a popular party whose members wear badges; he makes speeches about nationalism and Gaelic autonomy; and he promotes hatred of the Jews. In her novel The Wicked Day (1983), Mary Stewart presents a Mordred who is neither wicked nor traitorous, though he is destined to bring about Arthur's downfall.

Morgan, Hank Hank Morgan is the protagonist in Mark Twain's Connecticut Yankee in King Arthur's Court (1889) and a number of the retellings of that tale in film (where sometimes his name changes or he even metamorphoses into another character, such as a child or a woman). He is a practical man, but also one who has an almost mythic talent for making things. Hank is at one level a representative of American values; but he reveals a less than democratic side as power corrupts him, and he becomes in some ways as bad as or worse than those whom he opposes.

Morgan le Fay (Morgana, Morgen, Famurgan) Morgan le Fay is, in Malory's Morte d'Arthur, *Arthur's half-sister, the daughter of Arthur's mother *Igraine and her first husband, the Duke of Cornwall. She is also an adversary of Arthur:

she gives *Excalibur to her lover *Accolon so he can use it against Arthur (a story retold in Madison J. Cawein's poem 'Accolon of Gaul' (1889)) and, when that plot fails, she steals the scabbard of Excalibur which protects Arthur and throws it into a lake. In Sir Gawain and the Green Knight (late fourteenth century), she is the instigator of the Green Knight's visit to Arthur's court, partly motivated by her desire to frighten *Guinevere. Her enmity towards Guinevere has its origin in the thirteenth-century Vulgate Lancelot, where Guinevere puts an end to the affair Morgan is having with her (Guinevere's) cousin Guyomar. Despite the motif of Morgan's enmity towards Arthur and Guinevere, she is one of the women who takes Arthur in a barge to Avalon to be healed.

This view of Morgan as healer has its roots in the earliest accounts of her activities and perhaps in her origin in Celtic mythology. In the Vita Merlini (c.1150), Morgan is the first of nine sisters who rule the Fortunate Isle or the Isle of Apples and is a healer as well as a shape-changer. It is to this island that the wounded Arthur is brought (although Morgan awaits him rather than actually fetching him herself). Morgan proclaims that she can heal Arthur if he stays with her for a long time. In Hartmann von Aue's Erec (c.1180), Morgan is called Famurgan and is said to have left a wondrous healing plaster with Arthur when she died. She has other magic powers, including the ability to go around the world in an instant, to hover in the air, to dwell on or beneath the water, to be at home in fire, and to change a man into a bird or an animal. She can also control birds and beasts and evil spirits and can enlist dragons and fish to aid her. She was, Hartmann adds, a friend of the devil, who helped her; and she knew the properties of every herb that grows on the earth.

Morgan is also sometimes presented as the wife of King Uriens and the mother of *Yvain or Ywayne. In the Tavola Ritonda (second quarter of the fourteenth century), she has a daughter named Gaia Pulcella. In the French romance Ysaÿe le Triste, written in the late fourteenth or early fifteenth century, Morgan and Julius Caesar are the parents of the dwarf Tronc who, after finding a knight to accomplish a series of tasks, is released from a curse that has made him ugly and is transformed into the handsome fairy king Auberon.

Morgan appears in only a few post-medieval works—until the twentieth century, when there is a renewed interest in her character. In C. J. Riethmüller's *Launcelot of the Lake* (1848) and Francis Coutts's *The Romance of King Arthur* (1907), Morgan is said to be the mother of *Mordred, as is the case in John Boorman's movie *Excalibur* (1981) and a number of modern novels, where she is sometimes conflated with *Morgause. Fay Sampson makes her the central figure in five novels. One of the most interesting modern portrayals of Morgan occurs in Thomas Berger's *Arthur Rex* (1978) where, after a life devoted to evil, she decides to become a nun because of her belief that 'corruption were sooner brought amongst humankind by the forces of virtue'. In Parke Godwin's *Firelord* (1980), Morgan is the leader of the Prydn, called Faerie-folk. She bears Arthur's son Modred and is killed on Guenevere's orders. Morgan actually does become a defender of the good in modern stories like Roger Zelazny's 'The Last Defender of Camelot' (1980) and Sanders Anne Laubenthal's *Excalibur* (1973). In *The Mists of Avalon* (1982), Marion Zimmer Bradley makes Morgaine, a proponent of tolerant Goddess worship, the central figure in the Arthurian story.

Morgause (Morgawse, Morcadés, Orcades) Morgause, called Orcades or Morcadés in some early romances, is in many sources the daughter of *Igraine and *Gorlois, the wife of *Lot, and the mother of *Gawain and his brothers (replacing the *Anna of earlier stories as the mother of Gawain and *Mordred). In Malory's *Morte d'Arthur*, Morgause spies on Arthur and sleeps with him, without his knowing that she is his half-sister, and they conceive Mordred. Later, she has an affair with *Lamorak and is slain by her own son *Gaheris when he finds them sleeping together.

In *The Once and Future King* (1958), T. H. White depicts Morgause as a self-centred witch who causes her sons to develop deep psychological problems and is slain by *Agravain, the most disturbed of her sons. Morgause appears as a witch and a cruel mother in Gillian Bradshaw's *Hawk of May*, in which she attempts to teach her sons *Gwalchmai and Medraut (Mordred) sorcery and encourages them to serve the Darkness.

In *Arthour and Merlin* (thirteenth century), Lot's wife is called Belisent. Tennyson names her Bellicent, perhaps to avoid the suggestion of incest associated with Morgause in Malory's version of

the story and therefore to allow Arthur to be the blameless king.

Morholt (Morolt, Marhaus) Morholt is the brother of the Queen of Ireland and thus *Isolt's uncle. He is a great warrior: Eilhart von Oberge says that he has the strength of four men. In many versions of the Tristan story, Morholt is sent as a champion to Cornwall to collect tribute. *Tristan, as *Mark's champion, fights and kills him, leaving a chip from his sword in Morholt's skull. It is through this chip that Tristan is identified as Morholt's slayer when he visits Ireland. Tristan's fight with Morholt is a recurring motif in the Tristan story and occurs in several modern novels and even in films such as *Lovespell* (1979) and *L'Éternel Retour* (1943).

In Malory's *Morte d'Arthur*, Marhaus is a knight of the Round Table. *Gawain and *Uwaine come upon him as his shield is being dishonoured by a group of women who accuse him of hating ladies, but he says that those he hates are sorceresses who turn good knights into cowards. Marhaus, Gawain, and Uwaine meet three ladies, and each sets off on a quest with one of them. Later, Marhaus serves as the Irish champion and is slain by Tristan, as in the earlier Tristan tales.

Munsalvaesche (Monsalvat) In Wolfram's *Parzival* (first decade of the thirteenth century), Munsalvaesche is the *Grail castle where *Parzival fails to ask the question that would heal the wounded *Anfortas. In the end he returns, asks the appropriate question, and becomes the Grail king. In *Perlesvaus*, the Grail castle has three different names: Eden, the Castle of Joy, and the Castle of Souls.

Myrddin See MERLIN.

Nascien See SERAPHE.

Nenyve See VIVIEN.

Nimue See VIVIEN.

Nine Worthies The Nine Worthies (or *les neufs preux* in French) were a group of nine famous men notable for their valour and their worldly accomplishments. They included three classical pagan heroes (Hector, Alexander the Great, and Julius Caesar), three Jews (Joshua, David, and Judas Maccabeus), and three Christians (*Arthur,

Charlemagne, and Godfrey de Boulogne). The first extant reference to the group appears in the early fourteenth-century French romance *Vœux du paon* by Jacques de Longuyon. The Worthies were often used as an exemplum, as they are in two fourteenth-century alliterative poems, the *Alliterative Morte Arthure* and *The Parlement of the Thre Ages*, to demonstrate the folly of finding joy in earthly achievements since even the most powerful will ultimately have a downfall. In his preface to Malory's *Morte d'Arthur*, Caxton says the book will recount the deeds of the first of the Christian Worthies. In Act V, Scene ii of Shakespeare's *Love's Labour's Lost*, a pageant of the Nine Worthies is presented before King Ferdinand, but it is interrupted before Arthur is portrayed, perhaps as a parody of actual performances of the topos.

The Nine Worthies motif is also popular in art, architecture, tapestries, murals, and illuminations. Arthur appears prominently on a French tapestry (*c.*1400, now in the Cloisters in New York) that is one of what was originally a series of perhaps three tapestries depicting the Worthies. Murals in Runkelstein Castle outside Bolzano, Italy, depict the classical and Christian Worthies (as well as other Arthurian figures).

Niniane, Nimiane See VIVIEN.

Nyneve (Nineve) See VIVIEN.

Orcades See MORGAUSE.

Owain See YVAIN.

Palamedes (Palomides, Palamede, Palomydes) Palamedes is a Saracen knight who first appears in the French *Prose Tristan*. He is the son of the Saracen Esclabor and his wife, a shipwrecked Irishwoman, and is brother to Sir *Segwarydes and Sir Saphir. In the Post-Vulgate *Queste del Saint Graal*, Palamedes kills the *Questing Beast. When he is forced to fight *Galahad, he promises that if he survives the battle he will be baptized. Later, he is treacherously killed by *Gawain. In Malory's *Morte d'Arthur*, Palomydes, driven by his love for *Isode to do some great deeds but also some ignoble ones, is a foil to *Tristram. Repeatedly bested in his encounters with Tristram, he ultimately asks Tristram's forgiveness for the offences he has done to him and is baptized, with Tristram and another knight named Gal-

leron of Galoweye serving as his godfathers. After his baptism, Palomydes pursues the Questing Beast. He is also an ally of Lancelot after he and the queen have been caught together; for his service, Lancelot makes Palomydes Duke of Provence.

In *Taliessin through Logres* (1938), Charles Williams uses Palomides to examine the results of failing to see the goodness in the natural world. John Erskine's novel *Tristan and Isolde: Restoring Palamede* (1932) explores courtly love by focusing on Palamede's idealization of Isolde. In *The Once and Future King* (1958), Palomides' pursuit of the Questing Beast receives comic treatment. In the 1954 film *The Black Knight*, Palamides is divorced from the Tristan legend (except that he is in league with Mark) and becomes a villain who tries to undermine Arthur's reign and take control of Camelot.

Pant See BAN.

Parsifal See PERCEVAL.

Parzival See PERCEVAL.

Passelande Passelande is the name given to Arthur's horse in Béroul's *Tristran* (last quarter of the twelfth century).

Patryse (Patrise) See MADOR DE LA PORTE.

Pellam (Pellehan) Pellam is a wounded king who must be healed by the Grail knight. The thirteenth-century Vulgate *Estoire del Saint Graal* says that Pellehan was injured in a battle in Rome. Since the wound would not heal until *Galahad came to cure him, he was called the Maimed King. According to Malory, he received his wound from *Balin, who came to his castle seeking to avenge a treacherous act by Pellam's brother *Garlon. After he had slain Garlon, Balin searched for a weapon with which to defend himself and found *Longinus' spear in a room in the castle. When he used the spear to wound Pellam, he struck a *Dolorous Stroke and gave Pellam a wound from which he would be healed only by Galahad.

Pelleas In Malory's *Morte d'Arthur*, Pelleas is a knight who loves *Ettarde. After he wins a tournament and declares her the fairest woman, she scorns him. Just so he can see her, Pelleas lets himself be taken prisoner by her knights even though he has defeated them. *Gawain offers to help Pelleas by pretending to have killed him and thereby, presumably, forcing Ettarde to realize that she cares for him. Instead, she is glad to hear he is dead; and Gawain betrays his comrade by sleeping with Ettarde. When Pelleas discovers them together, he places his sword across their throats. *Nyneve helps Pelleas by curing his love for Ettarde and at the same time enchanting Ettarde so that she loves him. Eventually, Ettarde dies because of that love, and Pelleas and Nyneve become lovers. Malory writes that Pelleas was one of the four knights who achieved the *Grail, a strange statement since in his account and in his source only three of *Arthur's knights succeed in the quest and Pelleas is not one of them. Perhaps this statement indicates an early intention to give Pelleas a wider role in the *Morte*.

In his 'Pelleas and Ettarre' idyll (1869), Tennyson recounts Pelleas's love and Gawain's betrayal, which becomes one of several signs of the moral decline of Camelot. Without the assistance and love of Vivien, who is herself a wicked and deceitful figure in Tennyson's poems, Pelleas is driven mad by the betrayal.

Pelleas is the narrator of Godfrey Turton's *The Emperor Arthur*, in which he has a brief affair with Ettard before finding true love with Vivian. He is one of Arthur's knights and fights with him at *Badon and at *Camlan, where he slays *Mordred just as Mordred is wounding Arthur.

Pelles Pelles is the lord of *Corbenic, the father of *Elaine of Corbenic, and the grandfather of *Galahad. Malory says that he was called the Maimed King because when he found a sword on Solomon's ship and tried to draw it from its scabbard, a spear pierced him through both thighs.

Pellinore In the Post-Vulgate *Queste del Saint Graal*, Pellinore is said to follow the *Questing Beast and to be the father of *Aglovale, *Lamorak, *Perceval, *Perceval's sister, and other children. The thirteenth-century Vulgate *Merlin* says that he is the Maimed King and the brother of Alan the *Fisher King and of *Pelles. He is also, according to Malory, the father of an illegitimate son named Torre, whose mother is the wife of Aryes the cowherd and who is knighted when it is revealed that Pellinore is his father. In Malory's *Morte d'Arthur*, the sword Arthur drew from the stone breaks as he fights Pellinore. To save the king, *Merlin casts a spell on Pellinore and then takes Arthur to receive a new sword, *Excalibur, from the *Lady of the Lake. Subsequently, Pellinore becomes an ally of Arthur's and slays the rebellious *Lot, an act that leads to a feud between their families. Years later, *Gawain and his brothers kill Pellinore and Lamorak. In the first two books of T. H. White's *The Once and Future King* (1958), Pellinore becomes a comic figure.

Perceval (Percivale, Parzival, Parsifal, Perlesvaus) Perceval is the first *Grail knight and the hero of numerous medieval and modern stories of the Grail quest. In Chrétien's *Perceval* (written in the 1180s), he is sheltered by his mother but, upon seeing a group of knights, determines to be knighted himself. When he visits the castle of the *Fisher King and fails to ask the question that would heal him, Perceval must begin a journey and a process of maturation to correct his oversight. Chrétien's incomplete work prompted a series of 'continuations', in the third of which (c.1230), by an author named Manessier, Perceval achieves the Grail. Chrétien's story was also the inspiration for one of the greatest romances of the Middle Ages, Wolfram von Eschenbach's *Parzival* (first decade of the thirteenth century). Like Chrétien's Perceval, Wolfram's Parzival is initially naive and foolish, having been protected from the dangers of the chivalric world by his mother. In both versions, Perceval/Parzival is the guest of the wounded Fisher King (called *Anfortas by Wolfram but unnamed by Chrétien), at whose castle he witnesses the Grail procession, and—because he has been advised of the impoliteness of asking too many questions—fails to ask the significance of what he sees and, in Wolfram's romance, what causes Anfortas's pain. This failure is calamitous because asking the question would have cured the king. Other medieval versions of the story of Perceval can be found in the French texts known as the Didot *Perceval* (c.1220–1230) and the early thirteenth-century *Perlesvaus* (also called *The High Book of the Grail* or *Le Haut Livre du Graal*).

Perceval is the central character in the fourteenth-century Middle English romance *Sir Perceval of Galles*, which is apparently based on Chrétien's tale but which omits the Grail motif entirely. In Malory's *Le Morte d'Arthur*, Perceval is one of three Grail knights (the others being *Galahad and *Bors). Perceval functions as the narrator of the dramatic monologue which comprises most of Tennyson's idyll 'The Holy Grail', but much of what he relates focuses on Galahad as the primary Grail knight. In the opera *Parsifal* (1882), Richard Wagner draws his inspiration primarily from Wolfram von Eschenbach, though he greatly simplifies Wolfram's plot. As in the medieval stories, Parsifal is initially presented as a fool, but is pure enough to heal the wounded Anfortas and to become himself the keeper of the Grail.

Among the twentieth-century works to treat Perceval/Parsifal are the poem 'Parsifal' by Arthur Symons, several of Charles Williams' Arthurian poems, Robert Trevelyan's *The Birth of Parsival* (1905) and *The New Parsifal: An Operatic Fable* (1914), and the novels *Percival and the Presence of God* (1978) by Jim Hunter, *Parsifal* (1988) by Peter Vansittart, and Richard Monaco's Grail tetralogy. Eric Rohmer's *Perceval le Gallois* (1978), one of the most interesting Arthurian films, is a fairly faithful rendition of Chrétien's *Conte del Graal*. The story of Perceval is recast in a modern setting in another film, *The Fisher King* (1990).

Perceval's (Percival's) sister In the Vulgate *Queste del Saint Graal* (thirteenth century), *Perceval's sister leads *Galahad to Solomon's ship. From her own hair and from gold and silk, she makes a belt for the sword that Solomon left for Galahad. After agreeing to give her blood to cure a leprous woman even though she knows she will die as a result, Perceval's sister asks to be buried in the city of *Sarras because that is where Galahad will be buried. Malory gives a similar account. In Tennyson's 'Holy Grail' idyll, Percivale's sister has the 'vision'—probably a delusion inspired by her frustration in a love affair which led to her entering a convent—that begins the quest for the *Holy Grail.

Peredur Peredur is the hero of a Welsh romance that bears his name. He is analogous to *Perceval in many ways: he is raised in seclusion by his mother; he encounters knights and goes to Arthur's court; he follows advice without understanding it; and he has many adventures similar to Perceval's, including a visit to his wounded uncle's castle, where he fails to ask the healing question. But Peredur is not a *Grail knight. His most important task is not finding the sacred object or

comprehending its meaning but rather avenging his relatives by killing the witches who harmed them.

In Catherine Christian's *The Sword and the Flame* (1978), Lancelot's son is named Peredur. *Arthur declares Peredur his successor as Pendragon. Peredur claims to have seen a holy cup or Grail at a Pentecost feast at Arthur's court, a vision which seems to be inspired by his sister's account of the message of her grandfather Pelles. (The account of Peredur's vision and the subsequent swearing to seek the Grail is very much influenced by Tennyson.) Because of Peredur's interest in the Grail, Arthur realizes he is not a fit ruler and designates another in his place.

Perlesvaus See PERCEVAL.

Petitcreu (Petitcreiu, Peticrewe) According to Gottfried von Strassburg, the dog Petitcreiu was given to Duke Gilan of Swales by a fairy goddess from *Avalon as a sign of her love for him. The dog is multicoloured—a blend of so many colours that no one can say exactly what colour it is—and wears around its neck a chain of gold, on which hangs a bell that makes a music which banishes all care. In order to win Petitcreiu for *Isolde, *Tristan kills the giant Urgan who has been demanding tribute from Gilan. When she receives this gift from Tristan, Isolde breaks the bell so that she will not be happy while her lover is tormented by grief. In the Middle English *Sir Tristrem*, Tristrem wins the dog Peticrewe (said to be red, green, and blue) for Ysonde from a lord named Triamour by killing the giant Urgan.

In his poem ' "It Is a Shame"—with Apologies to the Modern Celtic School or P'ti'cru—A Ballad' (*Collected Early Poems of Ezra Pound*, ed. Michael John King (New York: New Directions, 1976), 273), Ezra Pound uses the dog to satirize 'the impassioned rehash of the mystically beautiful celtic mythology'.

Prester John Prester John was believed to be a priest-king who ruled an idyllic kingdom somewhere in Asia (or, in some versions of the legend, in Africa). The earliest recorded account of Prester John is in the *Chronicle* (c.1145) by Otto of Freising (1115–58), where he is said to be a descendant of the Magi, whose example inspired him to go to Jerusalem; but his plan was frustrated by the failure of the Tigris River to freeze and thus to allow him to cross (cf. *The Two Cities: A Chronicle* of *Universal History to the Year 1146 A. D.*, trans. Charles Christopher Mierow, ed. Austin P. Evans and Charles Knapp (New York: Columbia University Press, 2002), 443–4). A letter (*c.*1165) purportedly from Prester John described the exotic wonders of his domain. The realm of Prester John is also described in detail in the fourteenth-century *Mandeville's Travels*.

In Wolfram's *Parzival* (first decade of the thirteenth century), Prester John is the son of *Parzival's half-brother *Feirefiz and Repanse de Schoye. In *Der jüngere Titurel* (*c.*1270), the Grail is taken to his realm for safekeeping. In Richard Johnson's *Tom a Lincolne* (part 1, 1599; part 2, 1607), Arthur's illegitimate son, the Red-Rose Knight, visits Prester John's realm and persuades his daughter Anglitora to run off with and ultimately to marry him. In *Tom a Lincoln*, a play based on Johnson's romance and written sometime between 1607 and 1616, perhaps by Thomas Heywood, Bellamy, the wife of Prester John, is maddened by sorrow and kills herself when her daughter Anglitora runs off with the Red Rose-Knight. Subsequently, Prester John himself dies of grief. In Charles Williams' novel *War in Heaven* (1949), Prester John appears in modern Britain and assists in protecting the Grail from the forces of evil. And in Umberto Eco's novel *Baudolino* (2000), the title character writes a letter purportedly from Prester John, whose realm he seeks, to Frederick Barbarossa, with the help of 'Kyot' and 'Boron', who supply information about the Grail.

Priamus Priamus is a knight with whom *Gawain, according to the fourteenth-century *Alliterative Morte Arthure* and Malory, has a fierce battle during Arthur's Roman wars. He then joins Arthur's forces and fights valiantly. Priamus is descended from four of the *Nine Worthies: Alexander the Great, Hector of Troy, Judas Maccabeus, and Joshua. He is said by Malory to be one of those slain by Lancelot and his followers in the rescue of the queen.

Pridwen (Prydwen) In *Culhwch and Olwen* (*c.*1100) and 'The Spoils of Annwn', Prydwen is the name of *Arthur's ship. In Guy Gavriel Kay's *The Wandering Fire* (1986), Arthur and other characters sail in the *Prydwen* to the equivalent of the Celtic underworld to find and destroy a cauldron with magical powers. John Masefield calls the ship the *Britain* in 'The Sailing of Hell Race' (1928)

(perhaps punning on 'Prydain', the Welsh name for Britain).

Geoffrey of Monmouth and Layamon say that Pridwen is the name of Arthur's shield, which has the image of the Virgin Mary painted on its inner side.

Pseudo-Map Cycle See VULGATE CYCLE.

Questing Beast The name Questing Beast contains a pun: it is a creature that knights seek or quest for and a creature that has dogs barking, or 'questing', in one meaning of that term (cf. MED 'quest(e', 6b)) in its belly. The Questing Beast is also called the 'Glatysaunt Beest' or the 'Beste Glatissant' (from Old French *glatir*, to bark).

In *Perlesvaus*, the title character sees a snow-white beast which is smaller than a fox and which is terrified by the yelping of a pack of twelve dogs in her own belly. When the dogs burst forth, they attack the beast near a cross and tear her to pieces but do not eat her flesh. The beast is interpreted for *Perlesvaus by his uncle the Hermit King as signifying Christ, and the dogs as 'the Jews of the Old Law, whom God created and made in His image'.

In the Post-Vulgate *Queste del Saint Graal*, the Questing Beast is said to be a devil born to the daughter of King Hipomenes, who had intercourse with a devil after her brother, whom she loved, refused her advances. Intending to kill herself, she is stopped by the devil, who tells her how she can repay her brother for rejecting her by accusing him of rape. The brother, named Galahad like the knight whose coming will bring an end to the quest for the beast, is condemned to a death chosen by his sister—being thrown to hungry dogs. The brother predicts that she will give birth to a beast that will have within it dogs who will bark constantly in remembrance of the dogs by which he will be killed. At the time of the quest for the Grail, *Palamedes ultimately kills the beast in a lake, which boils ever after from the fire the dying beast shot forth.

In Malory's *Morte d'Arthur*, the Questing Beast is sought first by *Pellinore and later by Palamedes. Malory says that it had the head of a serpent, the body of a leopard, the buttocks of a lion, and the feet of a hart. T. H. White transforms Pellinore's pursuit of the Questing Beast into a comic incident in the first two books of *The Once and Future King* (1958). White's Pellinore is a bumbling knight who pursues the beast ineffectively but persistently. When Pellinore becomes love-sick because of his affection for the Queen of Flanders' daughter, called Piggy, his friends Grummore and Palomides create a Beast costume and parade inside it to distract the pining Pellinore. The humour of the scene is intensified when the real Questing Beast falls in love with the artificial one. In the poem 'The Coming of Palomides' (1938) by Charles Williams, the Questing Beast becomes a symbol of evil.

Ragnelle (Ragnel, Ragnell) In the fifteenth-century romance *The Wedding of Sir Gawain and Dame Ragnelle*, Ragnelle is a loathly lady who gives *Arthur the answer to a riddle that will save his life. In return, she demands that she be wed to *Gawain. Despite her extreme ugliness, Gawain consents to the marriage. On their wedding night, she becomes a beautiful woman, who tells Gawain that he must choose whether she will be fair at night when they are alone together or fair during the day when they are in public. Since he gives her the choice and thus control over her own fate, the spell cast upon her by her wicked stepmother is broken, and she remains beautiful all the time. Analogous tales of a loathly lady are told by John Gower and Geoffrey Chaucer and in the ballad 'The Marriage of Sir Gawain' (though without naming the Loathly Lady). Several modern authors have also retold the tale. In *Arthur Rex* (1978) by Thomas Berger, the spell on Lady Ragnell has been cast by *Morgan le Fay and is broken when Gawain refuses to treat her as his possession.

Red-Rose Knight See ARTHUR'S CHILDREN.

Renwein See ROWENA.

Rhongomyniad See RON.

Rich Fisherman See FISHER KING.

Rion (Royns, Ryence, Ryons) Rion is an enemy of *Arthur. He is sometimes depicted as a giant and sometimes said to be King of Ireland. His cloak is adorned with the beards of conquered kings, and he demands Arthur's beard as a sign of submission (this demand being the subject of the ballad 'King Ryence's Challenge' in Bishop Percy's *Reliques of Ancient English Poetry* (1765)). In some versions of the story, Rion is killed by Arthur in combat. Malory, however, says that *Balin and *Balan capture Royns and send him to Arthur.

Riothamus See ARTHUR.

Rivalin See TRISTAN'S PARENTS.

Roi Pescheor See FISHER KING.

Ron Geoffrey of Monmouth and Layamon say that Ron is the name of *Arthur's spear. In another passage (in which the spear is not named), Layamon says that Arthur's spear was forged in Carmarthen by a smith named Griffin and that it formerly belonged to *Uther. In *Culhwch and Olwen* (c.1100), Arthur's spear is called Rhongomyniad.

Rouland See TRISTAN'S PARENTS.

Round Table Wace first introduces the notion of the Round Table, which he says *Arthur had made so that all of the noble barons whom he attracted to his court would be equally placed and served and none could boast that he had a higher position at the table than the others. Layamon expands on this notion, describing a riot at which many nobles vie for place and precedence at Arthur's table. A skilled craftsman then offers to make Arthur a table that will seat more than 1,600 and at which high and low will be on an equal footing because the table is round. It is also constructed in such a way that it can be transported when Arthur travels. Béroul's *Tristran* (twelfth century) suggests that the Round Table revolves like the earth.

According to the prose rendition of Robert de Boron's *Merlin* and the thirteenth-century *Vulgate Cycle, *Uther Pendragon, instructed by *Merlin, established the Round Table to symbolize the table of the Last Supper and the *Grail Table established by *Joseph of Arimathea at the command of the Holy Spirit. Uther gives the Round Table to *Guinevere's father *Leodagan, who in turn gives it to Arthur when he weds Guinevere. Also according to John Hardyng's *Chronicle*, the Round Table is made in commemoration of the Grail Table. In the Vulgate *Queste del Saint Graal* (thirteenth century), the Round Table is said to represent the world, a significance supported by the fact that knights come to it from all countries where chivalry exists. Malory says similarly that Merlin made the table round to signify the roundness of the world.

Der Stricker suggests in his *Daniel* (between 1210 and 1225) that the Round Table refuses a seat to anyone who has ever been guilty of villainy and therefore is not worthy to become a comrade to King Arthur. The fourteenth-century Icelandic *Skikkju rímur* attempts to explain how the Round Table grants equality to Arthur's knights by suggesting that the king's throne is round and is placed in the centre of the floor with all the knights equidistant from it. The throne turns like the sun so that Arthur's back is not to any one knight longer than to another.

The Round Table has come to stand not only for the physical object at which Arthur and his knights sat but also for the order of knighthood and the code to which the knights committed themselves. The symbolic nature of the Round Table survives even into the youth groups of the late nineteenth and first half of the twentieth century. The founders of one of those clubs, the Knights of King Arthur, saw the roundness of Arthur's table and the equality it implied as representing 'democracy under leadership' and thus an ideal structure for a club for boys. (See also SIEGE PERILOUS.)

Rowena (Rowenna, Renwein) Rowena is the beautiful daughter of *Hengist. *Vortigern's lust for her causes him to give land to the Saxons. When the British nobles place *Vortimer on the throne, she poisons him, an act, Geoffrey writes, that was inspired by the devil. In John Thelwall's *The Fairy of the Lake* (1801), Rowenna poisons her husband Vortigern because of her love for *Arthur (who in this play is Vortigern's contemporary). A rare sympathetic portrait of Rowena is found in 'The Lady Rowena' in John Lesslie Hall's *Old English Idyls* (1899), which contains a series of poems told from the Saxon perspective.

Ryons See RION.

Sagremor (Sagremore, Sagramor) Sagremor is called by Malory 'le Desyrus', that is, the one desirous of or eager for battle. He makes a brief appearance in Chrétien's *Perceval*, where he tries unsuccessfully to bring *Perceval, who is contemplating drops of blood on the snow, back to Arthur's court. In the *Prose Tristan*, Sagremor is *Tristan's faithful friend. According to the Vulgate *Merlin*, Sagremor is the grandson and heir of Hadrian, Emperor of Constantinople. When he is 15 years old, he hears of *Arthur's fame and wants to be knighted by him. To that end, he goes to Britain and fights in the wars against the Saxons. Later, he is slain by *Mordred near the end of the final battle with Arthur. In the thirteenth-century English romance *Arthour and Merlin*, Sagremor is the son of the King of Hungary.

In Mark Twain's *Connecticut Yankee in King Arthur's Court* (1889), Sagramor takes offence at an innocent comment made by Hank *Morgan and challenges him to combat. Years later, when they actually fight, it is seen as a battle between two magicians, Hank and Merlin, who tries to give Sagramor invisibility and invulnerability. Hank unhorses Sagramor with a lasso; when Merlin steals the lasso, Hank must use his revolver to kill Sagramor. At the beginning of the novel, Sagramor's armour with a bullet hole in it, on exhibit in Warwick Castle, leads to Hank's telling his tale.

St Steven's Church See CAMELOT.

Saphir See PALAMEDES.

Sarras In the thirteenth-century Vulgate *Estoire del Saint Graal*, Sarras is said to be the city from which the first Saracens came. It is also the name of the kingdom ruled by *Evalach. In the *Queste* and in Malory's *Morte d'Arthur*, *Galahad, *Perceval, and *Bors travel in a ship with the *Grail to Sarras. Eventually, Galahad is made king of Sarras; but after a year he prays to leave the world, has a vision of the Grail, and dies, his soul borne to heaven by angels. At the same time, the Grail and *Longinus' spear are taken from Sarras to heaven. Perceval remains in Sarras until his death, at which time Bors buries him with his (Perceval's) sister and with Galahad and then returns to *Arthur's court.

According to the Victorian poem 'The Romaunt of Sir Floris' (1870) by John Payne, Sarras was located within the gates of Paradise before Adam and Eve fell. Sarras is also the subject of a poem by British poet Sally Purcell (in *The Holly Queen*, 1971), in which it is called an 'echoing shell | of the hermit's tranquil clarity'.

Sarrasinte See EVALACH.

Segwarydes (Segurades) Segwarydes is a knight with a beautiful wife loved by both *Mark and

*Tristan. When Sir Bleoberys rides off with Segwarydes' wife, Tristan does not try to rescue her because he believes it to be her husband's responsibility, a decision which causes the lady to forsake Tristan. The struggle for her affection is the beginning of tension and conflict between Tristan and Mark. Malory says that Segwarydes is the brother of *Palamedes and that he is one of those slain by *Lancelot and his allies in the rescue of *Guinevere from the stake.

Seraphe In the thirteenth-century Vulgate *Estoire del Saint Graal*, Seraphe is the brother-in-law of *Evalach. He performs great deeds of valour in Evalach's victory over the invader Tholomer. After being converted, he takes the baptismal name of Nascien. He is wounded as a divine punishment for drawing the sword of David on the ship of Solomon. Nascien's wife is named Flegetine, and his son is Celidoine.

Siege Perilous The Siege (from the French *siège*, seat) Perilous is the seat at *Arthur's *Round Table in which only the chosen knight can sit. In the prose rendition of Robert de Boron's *Merlin*, the empty seat is reminiscent of the seat that Judas vacated. There is also an empty seat at *Joseph of Arimathea's *Grail Table which destroys anyone unworthy of sitting there. In his Continuation to Chrétien's *Perceval*, Gerbert de Montreuil says that it was sent to Arthur by the fairy of Roche Menor. Six knights tried to sit in it and were swallowed by the earth before *Perceval sits in it and completes the adventure. When he does, the six are restored to Arthur's court. In a strange addendum to the episode, the six men, who have suffered torments, say that the fairy who sent the chair did so to reveal that the punishments of hell will be suffered by 'those wicked souls who prefer young men to girls'.

In the thirteenth-century *Vulgate Cycle, *Merlin instructs *Uther to build a table in commemoration of the Grail Table; at the table, there is an empty seat reserved for the Grail knight. In the *Queste del Saint Graal*, the Siege Perilous is said to parallel the seat of Christ at the Last Supper and the seat occupied by *Josephus at the Grail Table. Two brothers, jealous of Josephus, objected to his having a special place, and one of them sat in it only to be destroyed; so it came to be called the Feared Seat. *Galahad is the knight for whom the Siege Perilous at Arthur's table is destined. In the

Lancelot, a knight named Brumand, trying to perform an act that *Lancelot never dared to do, sits in it and is burned to a crisp. Malory says that Merlin made the Siege Perilous for the greatest Grail knight. (See also ROUND TABLE.)

Stonehenge The construction of the circle of stones known as Stonehenge and located on Salisbury Plain was begun about 2900 BC. According to Geoffrey of Monmouth, when *Aurelius Ambrosius wanted a monument to commemorate the British lords slaughtered by the Saxons, *Merlin suggested bringing the Giant's Dance from Mount Killaraus in Ireland, and *Uther leads an expedition to retrieve them. Merlin is able to transport the huge stones, originally brought by giants from Africa to Ireland, and erect the monument. Upon their deaths, Aurelius, Uther, and *Arthur's successor *Constantine are buried within the circle of stones.

Suibhne See MERLIN.

Sword Bridge See BADEMAGU.

Taliesin There is a historic sixth-century person named Taliesin, the bard of *Urien, who may have composed a number of the poems collected in the manuscript called the Book of Taliesin. There is also a legendary bard named Taliesin. In the Welsh tale *Taliesin*, Taliesin, whose name means 'radiant brow', is born when Ceridwen, in the form of a hen, swallows Gwion Bach, in the form of a piece of grain. Ceridwen has pursued Gwion Bach because he licked the drops that fell from her cauldron onto his fingers and gained knowledge of all things. She becomes pregnant from eating the grain and gives birth to a son, whom she wraps in a leather bag and tosses into the sea. Elphin finds the child in a weir and names him Taliesin. This story is also the basis for Thomas Love Peacock's satirical novel *The Misfortunes of Elphin* (London: Hookham, 1829). The legendary bard also becomes associated with Arthur. In *Culhwch and Olwen* (c.1100), Taliesin is said to be Arthur's chief bard.

In Charles Williams' Arthurian poems, Taliesin is, as C. S. Lewis has noted, 'the character through whom the poet (and therefore the readers) most often look at the world' (*Arthurian Torso* (London: Oxford University Press, 1948), 97). In the novel *The Last Harper* (London: Macrae, 1983) by Julian Atterton, a dying *Myrddin gives his harp and a new name, Taliesin, to a boy he has been training. Taliesin then becomes the bard of *Owain. And in Stephen Lawhead's novel *Taliesin* (1987), Taliesin is the father of Merlin.

Tanabos the Enchanter See CORBENIC.

Tarquyn (Tarquyne, Tarquin) According to Malory, Tarquyn is a knight hostile to *Lancelot, who slew his brother Carados of the Dolorous Tower. Because of his hatred for Lancelot, Tarquyn has killed a hundred good knights and maimed as many more. When Lancelot encounters him, he holds sixty-four knights imprisoned, including *Kay, Lancelot's relatives *Lionel and *Hector de Maris, and *Gawain's brother *Gaheris. In a long and fierce fight, Lancelot defeats and kills Tarquyn. Lancelot's battle with Tarquyn is depicted by N. C. Wyeth in an illustration for the 1917 edition of *The Boy's King Arthur*, the memory of which novelist Walker Percy said stayed with him from his youth and was influential in his writing of the novel *Lancelot* (1977).

Thirteen Treasures of Britain The Thirteen Treasures of Britain are a group of wondrous items referred to in numerous manuscripts of the fifteenth and sixteenth centuries. While only a couple of these treasures are specifically Arthurian—*Arthur's cloak of invisibility and the stone and ring of Eluned (Lunete)—others are related to themes and motifs that occur in Arthurian literature, such as the pot and dish of Rhygenydd the Cleric, which provides any food its owner wants; the cauldron of Diwrnach the Giant, which boils the food of a brave man but not a coward; the mantle of Tegau Efron, which tests a woman's chastity; and the drinking horn of Bran, which contains any drink a person desires. For a complete list and commentary on the treasures, see P. C. Bartrum's article 'Tri Thlws ar ddeg Ynys Brydain (Thirteen Treasures of the Island of Britain)', *Études celtiques*, 10 (1963), 434–77.

Tintagel According to Geoffrey of Monmouth, Malory, and numerous other authors, Tintagel is the impregnable castle where *Gorlois, Duke of Cornwall, secures his wife *Igraine from the advances of *Uther Pendragon. It is there that she conceives *Arthur when Uther, changed into Gorlois's form by the magic of *Merlin, enters the castle and impregnates her. In a number of *Tristan romances, Tintagel is *Mark's castle. In the twelfth-century *La Folie Tristan (Oxford)* Tintagel is called the Enchanted Castle because it vanishes twice a year, once in summer and once in winter. Tintagel is also the subject of an orchestral tone poem called *Tintagel* (1917–19) by Arnold Bax (1883–1953), which reflects both the literal turbulence of the coast of Cornwall and the emotional turbulence of the Tristan legend.

The castle whose ruins are still found at Tintagel was built in the twelfth century; but there is evidence that the site was occupied, perhaps by a nobleman, as early as the fifth century.

Tirry (Tirre) See ELAINE OF ASTOLAT.

Tom a Lincoln See ARTHUR'S CHILDREN.

Tom Thumb Tom Thumb is the diminutive hero of chapbooks and ballads. He is born to childless parents with the aid of *Merlin, to whom they had given hospitality. When they wish for a child, even if he were only as big as the father's thumb, Merlin grants their wish. Tom has a series of adventures, including being eaten by a cow, a giant, and a fish, the last of which makes its way to King *Arthur's table with Tom still inside. He becomes a courtier and delights both the ladies of the court and the king himself. Henry Fielding drew on the chapbook tradition of tales about Tom Thumb in two satiric plays, in which Tom is a slayer of giants and the object of desire of Arthur's queen, Dollalolla, and his daughter, Huncamunca.

Torre See PELLINORE.

Tristan (Tristran, Tristram, Tristrem, Tristano, Drystan) The character of Tristan is sometimes thought to be based on Drust, son of Tallorcan, an eighth-century Pictish king; but he is generally associated with southern England—with Cornwall and with *Lyones. And, if there is any connection between the character and the person named on the *Tristan Stone, he may originally have been a son and not a nephew to *Mark (the Cunomorus of the stone).

Tristan is one of the great tragic lovers of medieval romance. He is given the name Tristan, which incorporates the French word 'triste' ('sorrowful'), because of his sorrowful birth, which causes the death of his mother. The heir of the king of Lyones, Tristan is trained by *Governal, a faithful tutor and attendant. His first great deed of knighthood is to champion his uncle Mark against *Morholt, who represents the Irish claim to tribute. By defeating and killing Morholt, Tristan frees Cornwall but also earns the enmity of the king and people of the homeland of *Isolt. Wounded by Morholt's poisoned spear, Tristan must be cured in the land in which the poison originated. There he meets Isolt. Forced to leave when a chip that broke from his sword and lodged in the skull of Morholt is matched to his weapon, he later returns to ask that Isolt be given in marriage to Mark. As they sail to Cornwall, Tristan and Isolt drink a love potion (according to most versions of the story) intended for Isolt and Mark on their wedding night, and fall passionately and uncontrollably in love. In many versions, the potion is everlasting (though in Béroul's account its effects last for only three years). After Isolt marries Mark, the lovers meet whenever they have the opportunity. Various enemies—the wicked dwarf Frocin, Tristan's cousin *Andred, jealous barons—attempt to expose their affair. At one point, the lovers are forced to flee to a forest, where they live together until discovered. Mark accepts the return of his wife but banishes Tristan, who marries another woman named *Isolt (called Isolt of Brittany or Isolt of the White Hands) merely because of the similarity between her name and that of his beloved. Remembering his true love, however, he does not consummate the marriage. In many versions of the story, when Tristan is wounded by another poisoned weapon, he sends to Cornwall for Isolt. The ship that is to bring her will fly a white sail if she is aboard but a black sail if she is not. As the ship approaches, Isolt of Brittany, out of jealousy, says that the sail is black when it is actually white. Tristan despairs and dies before Isolt of Ireland can reach him. (In the prose tradition, which incorporates Tristan and his adventures more fully into the story of Arthur and the knights of the Round Table, Tristan is killed by Mark when he returns to see Isolt again; and there is no mention of the motif of the white and black sails.) The strength of the love between Tristan and Isolt is usually confirmed by the inextricable intertwining of the trees or plants that grow over their tombs.

In a number of late romances, Tristan and Yseut are said to have had children. In the French romance Ysaÿe le Triste, written in the late fourteenth or early fifteenth century, Ysaÿe is their son; and he in turn has a son named Marc. In the sixteenth-century Italian romance I due Tristani, which derives from the Spanish romance Don Tristan de Leonis (1534), the lovers have two children, a son and a daughter, whom they name after themselves.

Tennyson transforms the passionate love of Tristan and Isolt into a sordid affair in his idyll 'The Last Tournament' (1872). Edwin Arlington Robinson's poem Tristram (1927) removes the love potion as a cause of Tristan's love. Don Marquis's play Out of the Sea (1927), John Updike's novel Brazil (1994), and Jean Cocteau's screenplay for L'Éternel Retour (The Eternal Return, 1943) are but a few of many reworkings of Tristan's story in a modern setting.

Tristan's parents In the thirteenth-century Prose Tristan (which contains an extended account of the exploits of Meliadus) and in Malory's Morte d'Arthur, Meliadus or Melyodas is the King of *Lyones. He marries Elyabel/Elyzabeth, the sister of *Mark, and they have a son, *Tristan. When his wife dies in childbirth, he remarries. Because his new wife tries to poison Tristan, Meliadus condemns her; but Tristan intervenes and saves her life. In Tavola Ritonda (second quarter of the fourteenth century), Meliadus is said to be the brother of Marco (Mark). In The Enchanted Cup (1953) by Dorothy James Roberts, Meliodas shows little fatherly love and is happy to have Tristan out of his company.

In Sir Tristrem, Tristrem's father, the King of Ermonie, is named Rouland. He wins his wife Blaunchflour by being victorious in a tournament. Later, he is killed treasonously in a battle against the forces of his enemy Duke Morgan, and Tristan avenges the death. The slaying of Tristan's father and Tristan's vengeance are also treated in Hannah Closs's novel Tristan (1940).

In Eilhart's Tristrant (1170–90), Tristrant's father is called Rivalin, King of Lohenois. He wins Blankeflur as his bride by fighting for her brother Mark against his enemies. Gottfried also names Tristan's father Rivalin.

Tristan Stone See MARK.

Tristram (Tristrem) See TRISTAN.

Troynt See TWRCH TRWYTH.

twelve battles of Arthur In his Historia Brittonum (c.800), Nennius attributes to *Arthur twelve victories against the Saxons: the first was at the River Glein, the second to the fifth were above the River Dubglas; the sixth at the River Bassas; the seventh in the Forest of Celidon; the eighth at Castle Guinnion (the battle in which Arthur is said to have carried an image of the Virgin Mary); the ninth in the City of the Legion; the tenth on the banks of the River Tribruit; the eleventh on Mount Agned; and the twelfth and most decisive victory at Mount Badon, in which Arthur himself killed 960 of the enemy.

The battle of Mount Badon is mentioned by Gildas as a great victory by the British over the Saxon invaders. Gildas apparently dates the battle around 500, whereas the *Annales Cambriae* (*Welsh Annals*) suggest a date of 518 (given as 516 in most editions). Although a number of sites—Geoffrey of Monmouth, for example, equates Badon with Bath—have been suggested, one can say with confidence only that the battle was fought in southern Britain.

The twelve battles of Arthur are repeatedly referred to throughout literary history, even into the nineteenth and twentieth centuries. They are mentioned in Tennyson's *Idylls of the King*; and, as some of the few 'historical' facts to be associated with Arthur, they are used as the basis for numerous historical novels. Many of these novels are developed around or build up to Arthur's victory at Badon.

Twrch Trwyth One of the tasks given to Culhwch before he can marry the daughter of the giant Ysbadadden in *Culhwch and Olwen* (c.1100) is obtaining from between the ears of Twrch Trwyth, a giant boar, the comb and shears that Ysbadadden needs for grooming his hair for the wedding. Twrch Trwyth was once a king, but because of his sins God turned him into a boar. Arthur pursues the boar from Ireland into Wales and Cornwall before retrieving the comb and shears for Culhwch. Nennius tells of Arthur's hunting of a boar named Troynt with his dog *Cabal, which is almost certainly the equivalent of the hunting of Twrch Trwyth.

Ulfin (Ulfius) Ulfin is an ally of *Uther Pendragon. He advises Uther to seek *Merlin's help in satisfying his desire for *Igraine. When Uther is transformed into the shape of the Duke of Cornwall, Ulfin is transformed so that he appears to be Jordan, one of the duke's knights; in this shape, he accompanies Uther into *Tintagel.

Urien (Uriens) Urien is a sixth-century king who ruled the British kingdom of Rheged, one of whose principal cities was Carlisle. Urien and his son *Owain were praised in poems by the bard *Taliesin. Like his son, Urien is drawn into the world of Arthurian romance. Geoffrey says that Urien is the brother of *Lot. In the *Vulgate Cycle, Urien rules *Gorre and refuses to swear allegiance to *Uther. When Urien is captured, Uther threatens to hang him. To save Urien's life, *Bademagu, his nephew and the heir to Gorre, yields the land to Uther; but Urien later retakes the land and gives it to Bademagu. According to Malory, Uriens is one of the kings who rebel against *Arthur and who are defeated at the battle of Bedgrayne. He and Arthur are later reconciled. Uriens marries *Morgan le Fay, who attempts to kill him when she thinks her lover *Accolon has slain Arthur. Uriens is saved by the intervention of his son Uwaine.

Urre (Urry) In Malory's *Morte d'Arthur*, Urre is a Hungarian knight whose wounds can only be healed by the greatest knight in the world. Having travelled far seeking such a knight, Urre arrives at *Arthur's court. *Lancelot is the only knight able to cure him, a significant event since it occurs after the *Grail quest (but also after *Galahad has left the world). Urre is accompanied by his sister Felelolye, who subsequently marries *Lavaine, brother of *Elaine of Astolat. In *The Once and Future King* (1958), T. H. White adapts the incident of the healing from Malory. In White's tale, Lancelot's ability to work this miracle is a blessing that he thought had been taken from him when he lost his virginity by sleeping with Elaine and that he believed would never return because of his affair with Arthur's queen.

Utant See HUSDENT.

Uther (Uter) Pendragon Uther is the brother of *Aurelius Ambrosius and *Constans and the father of *Arthur. Geoffrey of Monmouth explains that Uther is called Uther Pendragon because of a comet in the shape of a dragon that appeared in the sky before a battle with the Saxons in which his brother Aurelius dies. The dragon is a sign of Aurelius' death and Uther's accession. Geoffrey also recounts Uther's passion for *Igraine. Merlin transforms Uther into the shape of Igraine's husband so he can satisfy his lust. He fathers Arthur and, later, a daughter named *Anna. The Saxons kill Uther by poisoning a well from which he drinks, and he is buried inside the Giant's Ring (*Stonehenge). Malory also tells the story of Merlin's transformation of Uther into the form of *Gorlois. Uther agrees to surrender the child conceived on that night to Merlin to be raised as he chooses. Gorlois is slain in battle three hours after Uther and Igraine conceive Arthur, and then Uther marries Igraine.

In Malory's Morte d'Arthur and in works based on his account, Uther is generally important only as the father of Arthur, but the events of the Middle English romance Sir Cleges are said to take place in the time of Uther Pendragon. Nor is Uther often a principal character in modern literature. He does, however, play a central role in Uther and Igraine (1902) by Warwick Deeping, a novel in which he is very different from the character of medieval chronicle and romance. Deeping's Uther is overly concerned with morality, a trait that almost causes him to lose Igraine. Uther also appears early in the film Excalibur (1981) as a warrior king who lacks the vision that his son will bring to Britain.

In his History of Britain, John Milton doubts the very existence of Uther, suggesting that Arthur was called Mab-Uther, meaning cruel son, and that later storytellers changed Uther to a proper name.

Uwaine (Uwayne) See YVAIN.

Vallet à la Cote Mautailliée See COTE MAL TAYLE, LA.

Vivien (Vivian, Nineve, Nyneve, Nenyve, Nimue, Niniane, Nimiane) Vivien is best known as the woman who seals *Merlin in a cave or a tree. Despite foreseeing his fate, Merlin is unable to prevent being captivated and captured by the woman that poet Richard Wilbur has called 'a creature to bewitch a sorcerer'. Nyneve (Vivien) is an ambiguous character in Malory's Morte d'Arthur. Even though Nyneve, who is a *Lady of the Lake, deprives *Arthur of Merlin's service, she rescues him twice, first by saving him from *Accolon who has been given *Excalibur to use against him by *Morgan le Fay, and then by preventing him from donning a destructive cloak sent to him by Morgan. Nyneve also uses her enchantments to punish *Ettarde for her mistreatment of *Pelleas, and in the end she and Pelleas 'lovede togedyrs duryng their lyfe'. By the end of the Morte d'Arthur, she is said to be the chief Lady of the Lake.

The character is ambiguous even in her earliest appearances. In the thirteenth-century French Vulgate Estoire de Merlin, Niniane loves Merlin and seals him in a beautiful tower, magically constructed, so that she can keep him always for herself. She visits him regularly and grants her love to him. In the continuation to the Vulgate Merlin, known as the Suite du Merlin, the relationship is quite different. When Merlin shows her a tomb of two lovers, magically sealed, Niniane enchants him and has him cast into the tomb on top of the two dead lovers, whereupon she reseals the tomb and Merlin dies a slow death. In the Vulgate Lancelot, Ninianne is the fairy who carries off *Lancelot and raises him.

Tennyson turns Vivien into the epitome of evil with none of the ambiguity of Malory's character. She lies and slanders good knights and is compared to a serpent. Using the charm that she tricks Merlin into revealing, she seals him forever in an oak tree, and thereafter does no service to Arthur or his kingdom. Influenced by Tennyson's character, Wilfred Campbell, in his play Mordred (1895), presents Vivien as the manipulator who plants in Mordred's mind the thought of causing Arthur's downfall and claiming the throne. In another play, Merlin (1907), Francis Coutts describes his character Nivian as a 'Saracen dancing-girl', whom Merlin forces to dance to draw gnomes from a cave so he can steal their gold to support Arthur's kingdom. Though borrowing much from Tennyson, Edwin Arlington Robinson, in the poem Merlin (1917), makes Merlin's 'captivity' voluntary, and his Vivian is less of an enchantress than an interesting woman whom Merlin truly loves. A number of modern poets, including Richard Wilbur and Thom Gunn, tell of Vivien's sealing Merlin in a tree or cave. Valerie Nieman describes the reunion and the reconciliation of the two in the twentieth century in her poem 'The Naming of the Lost' (1989).

Vivian is also the subject of the musical tone poem Viviane (1882) by Ernest Chausson and is the dominant figure in the well-known painting The Beguiling of Merlin, completed in 1877 by Edward Burne-Jones, in which she uses a spell to confine Merlin in a hawthorn tree.

Vortigern (Gwretheyrn) Gildas refers to a 'super-bus tyrannus' (proud ruler) who invites the Saxons into Britain. Bede names this figure Vortigern. Nennius tells of Vortigern's attempt to build a tower which will not stand. He is advised to sprinkle the site with the blood of a child with no father. The child—*Ambrosius in Nennius' account and *Merlin in the accounts of Geoffrey of Monmouth and others—saves himself by revealing the true cause of the tower's collapse: two dragons fighting beneath the foundation.

Geoffrey of Monmouth creates a picture of a wicked and foolish Vortigern whose ambition leads to the treacherous killing of a king and whose folly leads to inviting the Saxons into Britain. Geoffrey tells of Vortigern's persuading Constans, the brother of *Uther and *Aurelius, to leave a monastery and ascend to the throne. Thoroughly unsuited to rule, Constans gives all real power to Vortigern, who then engineers the assassination of Constans and has himself named king. Those protecting Constans' young brothers take them to Brittany to save them from a similar fate.

The Welsh Triad 51 names Gwretheyrn the Thin (Vortigern) as one of the 'Three Dishonoured Men' because he 'first gave land to the Saxons in this Island, and was the first to enter into an alliance with them'. According to a number of sources, his lust for *Hengist's daughter *Rowena causes him to give land to the Saxons. Merlin predicts Vortigern's death after revealing the fighting dragons beneath the tower. In the chronicles, Vortigern is virtually always presented as a treacherous, ambitious, and foolish king.

While much of what is written about Vortigern in the chronicles is standard, some authors of romances and novels introduce less traditional ideas about him. In Robert de Boron's Merlin, Vortigern is the seneschal to the British ruler Constans and his three sons. William Ireland's play Vortigern (written in 1795 and performed in 1796) recounts much of the traditional story, but Vortigern is spared when his daughter Flavia, whom Aurelius loves, pleads for his life. In Edison Marshall's novel The Pagan King (1959), Vortigern is the father of *Medraut and *Arthur, the latter being his son from an incestuous relationship with his own daughter *Anna. Vortigern's tragic story is a central symbol in Haydn Middleton's novel The Collapsing Castle (1990). One of the rare sympathetic depictions of Vortigern comes in

Parke Godwin's novel Firelord (1980), in which Arthur as narrator claims that although Vortigern had the soul of a tax collector, he had to invite the Saxons into Britain since the country was being overrun by invaders.

Vortimer Vortimer is *Vortigern's son. He is chosen by British nobles, who are angered by Vortigern's policies towards the Saxons, to rule in place of his father. Nennius says that Vortimer defeated the Saxons in four battles. In Geoffrey's account, Vortimer is poisoned by Renwein (*Rowena), and Vortigern rules again and recalls to Britain *Hengist and his followers, whom Vortimer had expelled.

Vulgate Cycle The Vulgate Cycle or the Lancelot–Grail Cycle is a sequence of prose romances written in France between about 1215 and 1235. The sequence has also been called the Pseudo-Map Cycle because of statements in two of the romances attributing them to a clerk at the court of Henry II, Walter Map (who died before these works were written). The cycle contains five romances: Estoire del Saint Graal (The History of the Holy Grail), Estoire de Merlin (The Story of Merlin), Lancelot, Queste del Saint Graal (The Quest for the Holy Grail), and Mort Artu (The Death of Arthur). These romances were translated into a number of languages and influenced much later literature, including Malory's Morte d'Arthur.

Walewein See GAWAIN.

Wasteland Many *Grail stories speak of a land laid waste, often because of a wound inflicted upon its king. The wound can only be healed—and thus the land restored—by the chosen Grail knight. In early Grail stories in which *Perceval is the Grail knight, the curing of the wound is usually dependent upon the asking of a question. In many Grail romances, the wounding of the king and the devastation of the land are caused by a *Dolorous Stroke. T. S. Eliot made the wasteland from the Grail stories a symbol of the sterility of modern society in his influential The Waste Land (1922), a poem that in turn influenced generations of modern writers, particularly novelists, to incorporate this symbol into their works.

Waynor See GUINEVERE.

Wigalois See FAIR UNKNOWN.

Winchester See CAMELOT.

Winchester manuscript In 1934, Walter F. Oakeshott (1903–1987), librarian at Winchester College, discovered a manuscript of Malory's *Morte d'Arthur*. Prior to this discovery, no manuscript of the *Morte* was known to exist, and all editions of the work had been based ultimately on Caxton's edition (1485). The manuscript was first edited by Eugène Vinaver in 1947 as *The Works of Sir Thomas Malory*. The Winchester MS (originally, Winchester College MS 13) of Malory's *Morte d'Arthur* is now in the British Library (where it is designated Additional MS 59678).

Wintwalite See GRINGALET.

Wynebgwrthucher Wynebgwrthucher is the name given to Arthur's shield in *Culhwch and Olwen* (c.1100).

Yder In Chrétien's *Erec* (c.1165), Yder is the knight whose dwarf insults Guinevere and who conducts the sparrowhawk tournament, in which Yder is defeated by Erec. In the early thirteenth-century romance *Yder*, Yder, the son of Nuc (or Nut), saves *Arthur's life; but the deed is soon forgotten by the king. As a result, Yder fights for a lord Arthur is besieging and is treacherously wounded by *Kay, whom he has fairly unhorsed several times. Later, when *Guinevere says that Yder, who saved her from a bear, is the one she would love if Arthur were killed, Arthur becomes jealous and desires his death, something Kay attempts to bring about by poisoning him. Yder's courage ultimately wins for him his beloved Guenloie. In the thirteenth-century *Vengeance Raguidel*, Yder is able to remove the rings from the fingers of the dead knight Raguidel, a feat which marks him as the knight who must assist *Gawain, who has removed the truncheon from the corpse, in avenging Raguidel.

Ygerne See IGRAIN.

Ygraine (Ygrane) See IGRAIN.

Ysolde See ISOLT.

Ysolt See ISOLT.

Yvain (Ywain, Iwein, Owain) Yvain is the cousin of *Gawain and the son of *Morgan le Fay and *Uriens. As Owain, he appears in the Welsh tale of *The Dream of Rhonabwy* and is the hero of the Welsh analogue to Chrétien de Troyes's *Yvain or the Knight of the Lion*. Owain is probably based on a historical person, Owain, son of Urien, who ruled the kingdom of Rheged near the end of the sixth century. Both Chrétien's tale and the Welsh *Owain* tell the story of Yvain's (or Owain's) adventures as he defeats a knight guarding a fountain and then takes over the protection of the realm in which it is located when he marries the slain knight's wife. Persuaded by Gawain, in the French version, he leaves his new realm and has a series of adventures, which include saving a lion from a serpent. The grateful beast befriends Yvain and helps him against some of his adversaries. Thus Yvain earns the designation 'The Knight of the Lion'. Chrétien's tale inspired the Middle High German *Iwein* by Hartmann von Aue and was translated into Old Norse as *Ívens saga*. It also influenced the English romance *Ywain and Gawain*, which is adapted from Chrétien's *Yvain* but is much less interested in courtly love. Yvain also figures in the Vulgate *Lancelot*, where Arthur assigns him to teach Lancelot how to behave as a knight, and in the *Mort Artu*. In Malory's *Morte d'Arthur*, when Arthur banishes Ywain from court because of Morgan le Fay's attempts on Arthur's life, Gawain rides off with him and they are joined by Marholt (*Morholt). The knights soon meet three ladies, who lead them to further adventures. In his retelling of Malory, John Steinbeck radically rewrites this section and has Ewain instructed in knightly combat by the lady with whom he rides.

Index